W9-CUZ-621

Jews, Germans, and Allies

Jews, Germans, and Allies

CLOSE ENCOUNTERS IN OCCUPIED GERMANY

Atina Grossmann

PRINCETON UNIVERSITY PRESS

PRINCETON AND OXFORD

Copyright © 2007 by Princeton University Press
Published by Princeton University Press, 41 William Street,
Princeton, New Jersey 08540
In the United Kingdom: Princeton University Press, 3 Market Place,
Woodstock, Oxfordshire OX20 1SY

Library of Congress Cataloging-in-Publication Data

Grossmann, Atina.
Jews, Germans, and Allies : close encounters in occupied Germany /
Atina Grossmann.
  p.   cm.
Includes bibliographical references and index.
ISBN 978-0-691-08971-3 (cloth : alk. paper)
1. Jews—Germany—History—1945–1990. 2. Holocaust survivors—
Germany—History—20th century. 3. Jews—Germany—Politics and
government—20th century. 4. Germany—Ethnic relations. I. Title.
DS134.26.G76 2007
940.53′1814—dc22   2007019952

British Library Cataloging-in-Publication Data is available

This book has been composed in Sabon

Printed on acid-free paper. ∞

press.princeton.edu

Printed in the United States of America

10 9 8 7 6 5 4 3 2

In memory of
Toni Bernhard Busse, 1884–1943?
Gertrud Dewitz Grossmann, 1873–1943?

Contents

Illustrations

Preface

Where Is Feldafing?

As the New York City–born child of German Jews, I grew up in a world of refugees where European Jewish life was deemed to have come to its catastrophic end in 1943. German Jews had fled throughout the globe. My parents had landed in New York after an adventurous decade in Iran and, for my father, wartime internment as a German enemy alien by the British in the Himalayas. Relatives and family friends sent photos and blue aerogrammes with exotic stamps from Israel, England, South Africa, Argentina, Denmark, France, and Japan (and eventually, after Stalin died, even from the Soviet Union) to our increasingly comfortable German-speaking enclave on the Upper West Side of Manhattan. Germany and Jews, I thought, had been irrevocably separated by a drastic and traumatic historical rupture since 1941, when the last emigration possibilities shut down, and 1943, when Goebbels promised a *judenfrei* Berlin and the deportation trains pulled out of the city toward the East.

I should have known better. The Jews, Germans, and (mainly American) Allies whose encounters are chronicled—and sometimes overlapping identities juxtaposed—in this book, all figure in my own family history. My maternal grandfather, part of whose story I tell here, spent the first postwar years in the Berlin he had never left. He had escaped into hiding in 1943, one of the remnant of German Jews who survived within Germany. His Berlin-born-and-raised nephew, by war's end an American GI, found him in July 1945 when the Americans took over their sector of the city. And, every summer of my childhood and adolescence, we traveled to Bad Homburg near Frankfurt to visit the family of my father's younger brother. He was a convert to Catholicism who had remained in Germany with his wife and five "half-Jewish" children until he was deported to Auschwitz in 1943. He, too, had survived, first as an inmate physician in the infirmary of the slave labor sub-camp Monowitz, and then as a prisoner in Mauthausen, where he was liberated by American troops. He died in the early 1950s, a belated victim of Nazi extermination. By then, however, he had had a sixth child, made it through the chaos and misery of German defeat to become the director of a German hospital, and—another story included in the book—joined my father in the struggle to reclaim some of their "aryanized" property in Berlin. So the blue aerogrammes that I found, many years later, in such abundance among my parents' yellowing file folders were filled with stories about Germans,

Americans—and Jews—in postwar Germany. But my grandfather had left Berlin for New York in 1947, and my cousins in Bad Homburg—the only close relatives I had who were remotely near my own age—weren't really Jewish.

It was only in 1971, when I was a college student traveling through Europe and Asia with my then-boyfriend Michael, that I first consciously encountered a Jewish history in postwar Germany quite separate from the refugee and émigré tales on which I had been raised. I knew virtually nothing about the strange historical circumstance that marked Michael's family stories: that by 1946/47, three years after Germany had been declared "*judenrein*," and within a year of the Third Reich's defeat, there were again a couple of hundred thousand Jews, mostly not German, living on—albeit defeated and occupied—"cursed German earth" (*verfluchte deutsche Erde*). The U.S. passport Michael carried listed his "place of birth" simply as "Germany." This was a source of great irritation to him, a kind of insult added to injury for someone who had been born in the displaced persons (DP) camp where his Romanian parents had finally found refuge after spending the war in various Nazi and Hungarian labor and concentration camps. Michael and I journeyed to Baie Mare, a medium-size Romanian town near the then-Soviet border where his Aunt Gittie and Uncle Shimon, fellow DPs who had returned to Romania, were awaiting their exit permits for Israel. On the train, I peered at the offending passport once again and finally asked him, "Michael, where actually were you born?" He responded with a name that I had heard frequently in conversation at his parents' house in the Bronx but had never thought to inquire about: "Feldafing." And where, I now wanted to know, was Feldafing? Michael paused for a moment, as if this was a question no one had ever needed to ask, and then said, quite definitively, "near Bremen."

And there the matter rested for over twenty-five years, until I began working on the topic of Germans and Jews in postwar Germany and discovered that Feldafing was nowhere near Bremen. Actually, it was quite at the other end of Germany, in Bavaria on the shores of the Starnberger See near Munich. Being the type who never quite lets go of old friends, I knew where to find Michael (at a newspaper editorial desk), called him up, and demanded to know why he had told me that Feldafing was near Bremen when it so clearly was not. We puzzled about this peculiar confusion for several minutes until we both realized what should have been obvious. When Michael, who had arrived in New York at the age of three, was growing up, he continually heard two place-names associated with Germany: Feldafing and Bremerhaven. Feldafing was the site of the displaced persons camp in which his family had lived, and Bremerhaven, the port from which his family had finally departed for the United States. So it made complete sense that, in his childish imagination, and preserved into his adult memory, Feldafing and Bremen merged into one contiguous area. As far as he could make out, no place in Germany existed or mattered other than an extraterritorial American- and UN-administered refugee camp filled with Jewish survivors and the city that signified separation from the "bloodsoaked soil" of Germany and Europe.

In fact, however, as Michael's mother Ita confirmed in an oral history interview in 2003 shortly before she died, the story of Jewish life in occupied Germany and indeed Michael's own family's experience were much more complicated. In her account, detailed in chapter 5, Ita talked with great verve about her relations with local Germans in and around Feldafing, revealing that the space occupied by "Germany" and "Germans" in Jewish DP life (and, conversely, by Jews in German life) was much more capacious and multifaceted than Michael's version or most historical accounts would suggest.

Abbreviations

DFD	Demokratischer Frauenbund Deutschlands (Democratic Women's League of Germany)
JDC, Joint	American (Jewish) Joint Distribution Committee (also abbreviated as AJDC)
KZ	Konzentrationslager (concentration camp)
MG	Military Government (U.S.)
OdF	Opfer des Faschismus (victim of fascism)
OFP	Oberfinanzpräsidium (National Socialist property and finance agency)
OMGUS	Office of Military Government, United States
SBZ	Sowjetische Besatzungszone (Soviet occupation zone)
SED	Sozialistische Einheits Partei (Socialist Unity Party)
SMA	Soviet Military Administration
UNRRA	United Nations Relief and Rehabilitation Administration

A Note on Abbreviations, Spellings, and Transliterations

Hebrew and Yiddish transliterations vary from source to source, and different historians have adopted different spellings. Names and abbreviations of organizations are also variously rendered in different sources. In both cases, I have attempted to use the simplest and most common version.

Jews, Germans, and Allies

Entangled Histories and Close Encounters

As WE REWRITE the history of the post-1945 years in the aftermath of the political upheavals of 1989, we are only now rediscovering what was amply obvious to contemporaries: that occupied Germany in the immediate postwar period was the unlikely, unloved, and reluctant host to hundreds of thousands of its former victims, housed both inside and outside refugee camps mainly in the American zone and in the American sector of Berlin. A significant number of the millions of people uprooted by war and persecution who remained on western Allied territory as "unrepatriable" displaced persons (DPs) were Jewish survivors of Nazi genocide and involuntary migration—precisely the people both the Allies and the Germans had least expected to have to deal with in the wake of National Socialism's exterminatory war.

In 1933, at the beginning of the National Socialist regime, Germany counted approximately 500,000 Jews. In 1946/47, some quarter of a million Jews were gathered in Germany, most of them in the American zone. Only about 15,000 of them were German Jews, of whom almost half were in Berlin. Some had endured in hiding or disguised as "Aryans." Others had survived forced labor as well as death and concentration camps (often elderly survivors from Theresienstadt). Most had managed a precarious aboveground existence in "privileged" mixed marriages or as Mischlinge ("partial" Jews). Still others were returned émigrés, many of them now in occupier uniform and serving as translators, interrogators, or civil affairs and cultural officers in all four Allied, and especially the American, armed forces. The majority, however, were Eastern European Jews, now classified by the victors as "displaced persons." Approximately 90,000 Jews had been liberated by the Allies on German soil, but many died within weeks, leaving about 60,000 or 70,000 survivors.

As the months passed, this remnant was augmented by tens of thousands of Jewish "infiltrees" who poured into the American zone from Eastern Europe. These predominantly Polish Jews constituted three distinct but sometimes overlapping groups. First were the survivors of concentration and labor camps and death marches, who had been freed in Germany but initially returned to their hometowns hoping, generally in vain, to find lost family members or repossess property. The second group encompassed Jews who had survived among the partisans, in hiding, or

"passing" as "Aryans." Finally, the largest, by a substantial margin—
and the least studied—cohort of European survivors of the Final Solution
comprised perhaps 200,000 Jews who had been repatriated to Poland
from their difficult but life-saving refuge in the Soviet Union and then
fled again, from postwar Polish antisemitism. All these Jewish survivors
became key elements in the "historic triangle" of Germans, Jews, and
Americans that defined postwar western Germany.[1] Moreover, the victors
also had overlapping and fluid identities. An essential and distinct group
among the American occupiers was composed of American Jews: chaplains, officers, and GIs or employees of Jewish relief agencies, notably the
American Joint Distribution Committee (JDC, the Joint). And some of
them, in turn, were themselves European, from Yiddish-speaking Eastern
European immigrant families or, in many cases, German and Austrian
Jewish refugees who had only recently emigrated and acquired U.S. citizenship through their military service.

This "historic triangle" existed everywhere in the American-occupied
zone, but it had a particular meaning in Berlin, the city with which the
book begins. Conquered by the Soviets in the chaotic weeks from April 24
to May 14, 1945, Berlin became in the summer of 1945, when first the
Americans and British and then the French officially moved in, a multinational polyglot city of border crossers (*Grenzgänger* in popular parlance).
Divided into four sectors, it served as a kind of laboratory of international
understanding, as U.S. Military Government officials initially preferred to
put it, in which the precarious relations among the victorious powers and
the management of the incoming refugee tide commanded virtually as
much, if not more, attention than the occupied Berliners themselves.[2]

The "greatest pile of rubble in the world" (*grösste[r] Trümmerhaufen
der Welt*), as both its residents and its occupiers sarcastically dubbed it,[3]
the vanquished Nazi capital was a city of women, refugees, and foreigners. Of a population of some 2,600,000 in May 1945, over 60 percent
was female. By August, when the first postwar census counted 2,800,000
residents, Berlin was crowded with returning soldiers and prisoners of
war, liberated slave laborers from across Europe, ethnic German expellees and refugees from the East, and repatriated political exiles (especially Communists returning to work with the Soviet Military Administration, SMA). There were Jews emerging from hiding, forced labor or
concentration camps, or fleeing renewed persecution in Eastern Europe,
and there were also Allied troops (including a highly visible group of
former German Jews). Huge numbers (by some estimates as many as half
a million) of displaced persons of multiple nationalities were streaming
into dozens of transit camps in Berlin.[4] Some 15,000 refugees, mostly
ethnic Germans (but also surviving Jews) from Soviet and Polish occupied territories in the East, poured into the city daily. At the same time,

Allied officials struggled to repatriate prisoners of war, concentration camp inmates, and freed foreign laborers—some of the 7.5 million who had been mobilized and coerced into the Nazi war economy before May 1945.[5] By the summer of 1945, the Allies also counted 6,000 to 7,000 Jews (or "partial" Jews) as residents of Berlin. Only a fraction of the 160,000 (out of a total of about 200,000) who had been registered as members of Germany's largest and most vibrant Jewish community in 1932, they were a significant proportion of the 15,000 German Jews who survived within the entire Reich. Their ranks were soon swelled by the "illegal infiltration" of Polish Jewish refugees for whom Berlin served as a transit station, with stays ranging from a few hours to several years, on their lengthy journey toward new homes outside Europe, principally in the United States and Palestine/Israel.[6]

During this liminal interregnum of four-power occupation and military government from 1945 to 1949,[7] and particularly in the turbulent first two years, defeated Germans, together with hundreds of thousands of their former enemies and victims, became literal border-crossers on the surreal stage of a broken country. This was especially evident in carved-up and bombed-out Berlin. Anti-Nazi journalist Ruth Andreas-Friedrich titled her diary of war's end *Schauplatz Berlin* (stage set), and Curt Riess, a Berlin Jew who had returned as an American correspondent, depicted his former hometown, with all its cinematic and operatic qualities and still carrying traces of its pre-Nazi Weimar cachet, as "hardly like a city anymore, more like a stage on which the backdrops are just standing around."[8] Hans Habe, another Jewish refugee in American uniform, wrote—surely reflecting also on his own bizarre position—"Life in general has a strange, unreal, make-believe quality."[9]

Throughout this period, in Berlin and in the western, particularly American, zones, defeated Germans and surviving Jews lived, as is often remarked, in different worlds on the same terrain, divided by memory and experience. But, regulated and observed by their occupiers, Jews and Germans also continually interacted. They negotiated daily life, and they contested issues of relative victimization, guilt, responsibility, commemoration, and reparations.[10] They debated a possible future for Jews in post-Nazi Germany as well as in Palestine and the rest of the world. Jews perceived their encounters and confrontations with Germans and occupiers, including those related to sex, pregnancy, and childbirth, as a means of resignifying their lives after the catastrophe of the Holocaust, indeed as a certain kind of revenge as well as "life reborn." By 1946/47, Jewish survivors residing among Germans were marrying and producing babies in record numbers. This difficult, tormented, but highly visible reconstruction of Jewish gendered identities and sexed bodies occurred in continual interaction, not only with the mostly American Allies who were their protectors and wardens, but also with the Germans who were their neighbors.

In this book I examine these complicated and yet commonplace "close encounters" in everyday life and political discourse in the years immediately after the war and Holocaust. I focus particularly on gendered experiences of the body, of sexuality and reproduction. Precisely because so many of these encounters have been shelved and forgotten, deemed insignificant and discomfiting, by both Jews and Germans, the stories told here are partial and fragmented. They signal how much rich material remains to be mined. Much more research remains to be done, by careful reading of the contemporary press, diaries, and memoirs and by digging in a wide variety of archives, on the local German and DP camp level as well as that of the Military Government and the nongovernmental international aid organizations.[11]

The existence of displaced persons and the "DP problem" in postwar Europe are not new topics for historians. Yet it has been particularly difficult for historians to chronicle or understand adequately the Eastern European and German Jewish experience in occupied Germany during the "DP years" from 1945 to 1949. For both scholars and survivors, these transitional years have generally been bracketed and overshadowed by the preceding tragic drama of war and Holocaust and the subsequent establishment of new communities and the state of Israel. Moreover, the history of the Jewish survivors, like that of any community that has suffered overwhelming losses and lived in transit, is not only their own, itself quite varied and hardly monolithic, but includes that of many other interested and more or less powerful parties. It involves Allied occupation policy and its trajectory from unconditional surrender and denazification to Cold War anticommunism and cooperative reconstruction in western Germany. It includes also British policy toward its mandate in Palestine, U.S. policy on immigration, American Jewish efforts to influence both American and British policies, and Zionist demands and actions for open entry of European survivors to Palestine and the establishment of a Jewish state. The politics of the Soviet Union and the newly Communist Eastern European nations from which many of the survivors came, and the emerging mandates of the United Nations and international relief organizations, played a role as well.

The problem then is certainly not one of meager sources. As with any "administered group" subject to large bureaucracies such as armies and relief organizations, DP life was methodically and voluminously documented. In a rich essay, Daniel Cohen notes that the DP experience, both Jewish and non-Jewish, crucially shaped the future of international refugee work as well as the development of a novel discourse about human rights. Indeed, many of the men and women directly involved in postwar relief and rehabilitation efforts published accounts documenting the crisis of the stateless and the displaced in a world of nation-states. But then, as the postwar moment faded, DP history was sidelined. Cohen speaks of the "absence of and the eviction of displaced persons from the 'frames of remembrance'"—to use Maurice Halbwachs' famous concept—"that have structured collective memories of World War Two and its aftermath" and their "appropriation" by national narratives, with their own political and emotional as well as intellectual agendas.[12] Since the mid-1990s there has finally been a proliferation of publications, conferences, films, and exhibitions on Jewish DPs, pushed in large part by the efforts of the baby boom "second generation" born in DP camps or communities.[13]

Yet, despite the truly overwhelming amount of historical, sociological, visual, and literary source material, as well as a substantial and ever growing secondary literature, we are just beginning to think about the social, rather than the political, history of Jewish DPs.[14] Historians are faced with a dizzying array of actors and agencies—sponsored by four Allied military occupations and a plethora of nongovernmental humanitarian aid groups—all dealing with a highly mobile, transient, stateless, and traumatized population, and operating on a territory that lacked central or universally legitimate authorities and record keepers. Statistical evidence is notoriously inaccurate, at times wildly so. And given the status of DPs as a stateless "client" population, their official record has been mostly constructed out of reports by those who managed them, rather than the substantial documentation that was created by the DPs themselves.

There has been very little reflection on the interactions, encounters, and confrontations among the different groups of surviving Jews and defeated Germans. If Jewish DPs, German Jews, and non-Jewish DPs all came with their own disparate wartime experiences inside and outside Nazi occupied Europe, the defeated German population was also diverse. It included returning soldiers, prisoners of war, and civilian refugees and expellees arriving from the East who were not considered DPs by the Allies. Furthermore, historians are only beginning to locate the experience of Jewish DPs in relation not only to Germans but also to the—at least initially— much more numerous other DP groups, notably Poles, Balts, and Ukrainians.[15] All these groups had their own gender, age, religious, political, regional, class, and war experience.

Most remarkably, researchers have barely addressed the momentous fact, discussed in chapter 4—and its significance for Jewish DP perceptions of their German surroundings and German perceptions of the Jewish DPs—that the majority of Jewish survivors in Germany actually spent a good part of the war years as refugees in the Soviet Union and not under Nazi occupation. Political and ideological factors, especially the pressures of the Cold War and the dominance of a Zionist-inspired narrative that subsumed all Jewish DPs under the rubric of the *She'erit Hapletah*, the surviving remnant of European Jewry, have shaped and distorted history and memory. An overarching and often undifferentiated story of "the" Holocaust, its victims and survivors, has effaced the role of the Soviet Union as the site where—with substantial financial support from American Jewish aid organizations—the great majority of Jewish DPs in fact survived the war. The subject of this book then is a fast-moving and bewildering target. Despite the increasing number of relevant publications, many of us researching DP history feel as though we are just beginning, virtually inventing and experimenting with a historiography that will surely be substantially expanded and revised in the next years.[16]

Many of the studies that do exist have come from the fields of Jewish history and Holocaust studies, and until recently some of the most significant have been available only in Hebrew or German. General postwar German history has mostly ignored the presence of living Jews; their story has been told as one of absence, tragic loss, and memorialization. Histories of Jewish survivors in Germany, on the other hand—and there are more and more, especially local studies—have generally treated them as an almost entirely self-enclosed collective, coexisting temporarily and quite separately from Germans, in a kind of extraterritorial enclave.[17] An extensive Israeli historiography has presented DPs and Jewish survivors as part of the contested history of Zionism and the role of Holocaust survivors in the founding of the state.[18]

Studies of American policies toward DPs have tended to focus on their many negative aspects. These were laid out early on in former Immigration Commissioner Earl G. Harrison's fiercely critical August 1945 report to President Truman on Military Government policy toward survivors, which denounced their continued detention behind barbed wire and famously (and hyperbolically) concluded that "we appear to be treating the Jews as the Nazis treated them except that we do not exterminate them." Harrison's account was preceded and reinforced by the horrified and furious reports American Jewish GIs sent home to their families and congregations. Often instigated by the passionate holiday sermons of army chaplains, their letters described the bedraggled survivors and their neglect by the U.S. military and (at least initially) American-Jewish aid organizations.[19] Understandably, historians have drawn attention both to American antisemitism and to U.S. Military Government tolerance for German hostility toward DPs, especially its apparent increase in the later years of the occupation.[20] These are all important approaches, but contemporary accounts and records, as well as memoirs and oral histories read "against the grain," can also present a rather different picture of close connections, and regular interactions, not only between Jews and Germans, but also between surviving Jews and their American keepers and protectors.

I come to this topic as a historian of modern Germany. My interest in Jewish survivors derived, at least at the outset, from my work on rape, abortion, and motherhood in Berlin at war's end and my efforts to understand how and why Germans were so convinced after the war that they were the primary victims.[21] The structure of the book, with its beginning focus on the German experience and how it was perceived by Allies and Jews, reflects that trajectory. Thus, this is neither an "inside history" of DP life nor is it the book on Germans as "victims" that I originally thought I might write.[22] Like many historians of modern Germany, I was perversely fascinated by what Jewish observers quickly identified as the postwar "enigma of irresponsibility."[23]

In "The Aftermath of Nazi Rule," a bitter 1950 report for the American Jewish journal *Commentary*, the political theorist Hannah Arendt identified this "escape from responsibility" with Germans' "escape" from the "reality" of defeat and ruins. Struck by the apparent "absence of mourning for the dead, or . . . the apathy with which they react, or rather fail to react, to the fate of refugees in their midst," she diagnosed "a deep-rooted, stubborn, and at times vicious refusal to face and come to terms with what really happened." Now a visitor from the United States, the land of the victors, Arendt decried the pervasive self-pity that allowed no reaction to her insistent revelation that she was a German Jewish refugee. Instead, they continually invoked the image of *armes Deutschland* (poor Germany), as the miserable and sacrificial victim—*Opfer* in its double sense—of history.[24] As Arendt pointed out, most Germans after 1945 understood themselves as victims and not as victimizers, even as they were unable to fully mourn their own considerable losses. To do so, Arendt surmised, would have forced them to confront more fully, beyond "apparent heartlessness" and "cheap sentimentality," their own responsibility for those losses.

In the early occupation period from 1945 to 1946, often described as the "zero hour" and the "hour of the women," processions past naked, emaciated corpses in liberated camps, denazification procedures, press reports and film images of "death mills," and the Nuremberg and other war crimes trials were intended by the Allies to assure that the immediate past of Nazi atrocities remained highly present. There was, in the immediate postwar period, a remarkable amount of discussion about precisely the issues of memory, commemoration, guilt, and complicity that continue to agitate historical and public debate in (and about) Germany. Yet, as so many reporters noted, despite the initial broad and graphic exposure and documentation in the occupier-licensed German press, the persecution of European Jews and the Final Solution seem absent or at best obscured in immediate postwar public and private discourse.[25] This putative "amnesia" became a truism for the "silent fifties" in West Germany, the years of nation building and economic miracle, supposedly broken only by the sea change of the 1960s.

Historians have increasingly and forcefully challenged this notion of postwar "silence." They have pointed to the selective nature of that silence and the vigor (if not depth) with which Germans bemoaned their losses. Robert Moeller, in his work on the "war stories" of German expellees (*Heimatvertriebene*) and prisoners of war, was one of the first to alert us that, by the 1950s, West Germans had constructed highly talkative "'communities of memory'" by "focusing on their own experiences, not on the trauma and suffering they had caused for others."[26] But even in the years from 1945 to 1949, "before the curtain" of the Cold War fell and Germany was officially divided, and even in the face of vivid images and documentation of Nazi crimes, for most Germans, the more powerful impressions—the stuff of which memories were made—derived from their own more direct experiences of war and defeat. The Berlin journalist Ursula von Kardorff, who had fled to Bavaria at the end of the war, reported in her diary that when German villagers were confronted in June 1945 with "horror photos of piles of corpses" taken just shortly before in nearby Dachau, they absolutely insisted that these were photos of bombing victims from Dresden.[27]

Such rapidly constructed and tenaciously remembered narratives of victimization worked, not only to block confrontation with recent Nazi crimes, but also to manage the chaos of the immediate postwar years, and eventually to authorize reconstruction of German nationhood and national identity. As Ernest Renan, in his famous 1882 disquisition "What Is a Nation" had already noted, "the essence of a nation is that all individuals have many things in common, and also that they have forgotten many things"[28] A postwar situation in which female bodies—raped, aborting, pregnant, mothering, fraternizing—were both public and private, and where neither public nor private was clearly defined or bordered, highlights, moreover, the (increasingly acknowledged) prominence of women's voices and memories in defining the early postwar period. Given the lack of a sovereign German state, and the lack of clarity about what it might mean to identify as German, it seems necessary to analyze such stories of victimization from a vantage point that is not exclusively "German." Germans confronted a ruined physical and political landscape. Suddenly, they had no legitimate national past, no clear national boundaries, or, for that matter, legitimated rulers, markets, or memories. For them, female experiences, such as rape, abortion, childbirth, caring for malnourished and sick children, and grief over dead children, as well as relations with occupiers, displaced persons, and returning German soldiers and prisoners of war, became especially powerful markers of victimization and defeat. They also signaled the need for healthy reconstruction.

The displaced remnant of European Jewry emerged from war and genocide demographically and socially decimated, with no viable claims to citizenship or homeland. For them, issues of sheer survival and reinvention of national and ethnic communities had such high political and cultural priority that they foregrounded reproduction—of children, families, and identity—both in public representation and in personal accounts. In this context, German and Jewish stories, taking place, after all, on the same territory, if not really in the same (nonexistent) nation, need to be juxtaposed and told together. Both Germans and Jews, I argue, turned, in different ways, to narratives and metaphors of fertility and maternity (in terms of both loss and possibility) to comprehend victimization and survival and to conceptualize and imagine future identities as nation or *Volk*. These stories in turn were given different public meanings by Germans, Allies, and Jews.

Particularly during the early years of military occupation from 1945 to 1949, when a legitimate "national" identity, history, or authority was not publicly available, German stories competed with, and were contested by, those of other protagonists who shared territory with defeated Germans: the Soviet, American, and British victors and the Jewish survivors.[29] The more I worked on these questions about the experience and memory of "poor Germany," the more I was convinced that they could not be adequately addressed in an exclusively German context or even as a story of occupiers and occupied. So much of postwar politics, as well as everyday life in defeated occupied Germany, was conceptualized and negotiated in terms of the contest over memories, definitions, and calibrations of victimization, over entitlement to victim status, and the material as well as moral consequences of that designation. Crucially, these debates and encounters occurred in the face not only of guilty memories—whether from the home or battlefront—but of provocatively present Jews, both DP and German, both part of the occupation and not. My tripartite focus on Germans, Jews, and occupiers forces me to wrestle with both the perils and what I see as the necessity of intertwining German and Jewish history and memory of World War II and the Holocaust. This project places into sharp relief the ongoing challenges of trying to tell in one book the stories of victimization and survival as perceived and expressed by all three groups. I discuss the ways in which Jews, Germans, and (especially American) occupiers variously claimed, contested, and negotiated their identities as victims, victors, or survivors, and understood—in quite different ways—their encounters with one another. At the same time, I aim to avoid the waiting traps of relativization or facile comparison of the incommensurate. Indeed, as the book developed, it became clear that despite my insistent focus on interaction, I am telling an asymmetrical story: although defeated Germans and Allied victors are essential actors, their actions and perceptions are often presented through Jewish eyes, that is, precisely through the eyes of those whose presence was—for all three groups— least expected.

Furthermore, Jewish survivors must be situated not only within defeated occupied Germany but also as part of the larger universe of postwar migration and displacement. Postwar historians have to balance these two perspectives. DPs must be analyzed as part of the broader context of the birth of a "refugee nation," a collective forged out of the resettlements and exterminations of the Second World War. Selected, categorized, administered, and observed by international organizations, DPs were grounded in the daily reality of standardized refugee camps. At the same time, however, they emerged out of this common institutionalized and extraterritorial universe as what they also were and primarily became: particular fragmented groups that were divided along ethnic and national lines—as had been the experiences that produced their displacement. While DP experience did produce a common institutional "refugee nation," especially in the eyes of international aid organizations (notably UNRRA, the new United Nations Relief and Rehabilitation Administration), it also heightened awareness of national and ethnic differences and encompassed interaction with the "local" German population. Jewish (as well as other) DPs themselves, as we shall see, rejected the transnational category that the Military Government and UNRRA initially tried to impose on them, and which the motley group of young aid workers sometimes claimed for themselves; the trauma of statelessness produced the drive for national and particular recognition and identity.[30]

The Jewish survivors, many of them the last remaining members of their large prewar families, were indeed a diverse and traumatized group. They spoke different languages, came from various nations, subscribed to different political beliefs and levels of religious observance, and had endured quite varied experiences during the war. In continual negotiation with Germans, occupiers, and relief organizations, Jewish DPs in occupied Germany, centered around the large camps near Munich and Frankfurt and in Berlin, generated between 1945 and 1949 a unique transitory society. DP life was simultaneously a final efflorescence of a destroyed East European Jewish culture, a preparation for an imagined future in *Eretz Israel* (land of Israel), and a "waiting room" in which new lives were indeed—against all odds—begun. From a ragged and exhausted group of displaced persons with very different backgrounds and wartime experiences there emerged over several years a new and self-conscious Jewish collectivity. They publicly identified as survivors of Nazi extermination plans, even if, as was the case for many of them, they had escaped because they had landed, either by choice or by force, in the Soviet Union. They appeared fiercely committed to Zionism and Jewish identity, even if, in many ways, this collective was only invented in the transitional protected and highly ideologized life of the DP camps. They named themselves the *She'erit Hapletah* (or in the Yiddish vernacular as the *sheyres hapleyte*), invoking biblical references to the saved (and left-over) remnant that has escaped destruction and "carries the promise of a future."[31] That this remnant of Jews gathered and constituted itself surrounded by, among, and in exchange with the Germans who had tried to exterminate them is the counterintuitive historical fact that this book only begins to address.

A Note on Method and Organization

German-Jewish history, heavily influenced by refugee historians, has not only been declared to have ended in 1943, at the latest, but has also been framed in terms of what has come to be called an "émigré synthesis," focusing on questions of degrees of assimilation, Jewish contributions to German culture, and this history's horrific end. Younger historians, seeking to move beyond this perspective and recognizing the complex interweaving of Germans and Jews, have increasingly begun to speak instead of "entangled histories." In this analysis, the history of Jews in Germany cannot be grasped in terms of either symbiosis during its flowering or negative symbiosis during its destruction. I hope in this book to move that perspective of "entangled" stories into the immediate postwar period.[32]

In order to capture some of those "entanglements," I interweave historical analysis, personal narratives (both from my own family and others), oral histories and written reports, published and unpublished texts such as letters, and citations from memoir, diary, and press accounts as well as novels and films, produced at the time or shortly thereafter. I have relied a good deal on contemporary accounts and testimonies, including correspondence and German restitution (*Wiedergutmachungs/Entschädigungsamt*) and expropriation (*Oberfinanzpräsidium*) files from my own family to which I have had privileged access. The use of such contemporary testimony, in addition to the archival sources to which historians always turn, seems to me particularly appropriate for this postwar period, when so many of the most committed and talented journalists and writers of the twentieth century were covering and studying the drama of Germany's defeat and the aftermath of the "Final Solution." Indeed, an astonishing number of those who were there, not only reporters, but relief workers, academics, members of the Military Government, GIs and chaplains, and the victims and survivors themselves—both Germans in bombed-out cities and Jews in Berlin and the DP camps—were acutely aware of their role in a critical historical moment and therefore kept diaries or quickly recorded their recollections.

The book focuses on two sites where the unexpected entanglement of German and Jewish history after the Second World War and the Holocaust as well as the triangular relationship among Jews, Germans, and occupiers are most evident: four-power occupied Berlin, and the large DP camps in Bavaria, in the heart of the American zone. I am aware that this triangular focus on "victors" as well as victims and survivors should really dictate attention to all four zones of occupied Germany and all four sectors of Berlin. Despite the clear relevance of British policy on Palestine to the fate of Jewish survivors, despite the fact that many camp survivors found on west German territory were liberated by the British, and despite the existence of one important (but relatively well studied) DP camp, Belsen-Hohne, in the British zone, I limit my discussion to the American zone of western Germany and the four sectors of Berlin, with particular attention to the dueling Soviets and Americans. I do this partly for practical reasons, because I have to contain an already massive topic. Mostly, however, I do it because, with the exception of the early occupation of Berlin in 1945, it was the American zone that received the overwhelming majority of Jewish DPs, and it was the Americans who served as their chief protectors and interlocutors in relation to Germans.

Chapter 1, on defeated Germans and the experience and perceptions of German victimization, pays particular (but not exclusive) attention to Berlin, hardly typical but exemplary for many of the issues addressed here. The defeated capital, a city of "border crossers," divided by the occupiers into four sectors with adjacent and competing denazification, democratization, and reconstruction projects, was a stage on which various actors contested in a cacophony of voices the questions central to the book: definitions of German identity, nation, or citizenship; and assessments of guilt, victimization, retribution, and survival. In this chapter, I present "poor Germany" and Germans' perceptions of themselves as victims through the eyes, in particular, of the victors—especially their American occupiers—and, to some degree, their Jewish victims. Chapter 2, on gendered defeat and the experience of both sexual violence and fraternization, considers the multiple ways in which defeat and occupation were quite directly inscribed on women's bodies. Chapter 3, the core of the book, bridges the treatment of German "victims" and Jewish "survivors" by focusing on Jews in Berlin. The defeated capital, with its significant numbers of both German and Eastern European survivors, offers an exemplary site for tracing intra-Jewish debates about identity, revenge, reconciliation, and possible futures for Jews in post-Nazi Germany as well as confrontations with Germans who perceived themselves as primary victims. In chapter 4, I shift attention further away from Germans and the center of defeat in Berlin to the constitution of the *She'erit Hapletah* in the DP communities and camps of the American zone, especially in

Bavaria. I stress both the heterogeneity of the Jewish DPs and the ways in which relief organizations, American Military Government, and the Zionist movement perceived the Jewish survivors and influenced the shaping of this new collective identity. In chapter 5, I directly engage the "entangled histories" of Germans and Jews in this toxic period of "fresh wounds" by returning to the analysis of gender, sexuality, and reproduction begun in chapter 2.[33] I consider fraught questions of co-existence, revenge, and everyday interactions in light of the Jewish DP "baby boom." In the concluding chapter 6, I move the discussion beyond the official end point of the occupation and DP period in 1948/49, when the establishment of the state of Israel and the two postwar German states, and the easing of American immigration policies, fundamentally reworked the triangular relationship among Germans, Americans, and Jews. This moment from 1948 to the early 1950s in turn set patterns that would persist at least through the fall of the Berlin Wall and the reunification of Germany in 1989/90. My hope is that this "entangled" approach can usefully complicate our understanding of gender as a historical category, "de-Germanize" a German history in which multiculturalism or heterogeneity is too often seen as an invention of the very recent past, and cut through the persistent division between German history and the history of Jews in Germany that still characterizes much of our work on modern and contemporary Germany.

Fig. 1.1. Berlin, May 1945.

CHAPTER ONE

"Poor Germany"

BERLIN AND THE OCCUPATION

> I have never read an adequate description of Berlin (and the American zone) in the early days of the Occupation; I think it would best be a subject for fiction.
>
> —Dewilda N. Harris[1]

> May 8: Germany has capitulated. It held out six years against a world of enemies, it will recover again [*wieder hochkommen*]. . . . Dear God—Berlin has had to endure so much, let this be over with.
> May 18: In the *Tägliche Rundschau* big reports about the death camp in Auschwitz. Even if only a small part is true, and I fear it is all true, then the rage of the entire world against the Nazis is understandable. Poor Germany! [*armes Deutschland*]
>
> —Anne-Marie Durant-Wever[2]

IN APRIL 1945, after almost six years of war, the Allied armies had battled their way through German territory. Many German towns and cities capitulated quickly, but no victory was as important and hard won, both symbolically and logistically, as the Soviet capture of Berlin. By April 21, a gruesome, costly battle on the Seelow Heights had brought the Soviets up to the city limits. The Nazi propaganda machine raged on, exhorting Berliners, "Our walls are cracking, but not our hearts." Contemporary reports estimated, however, that some ten thousand residents committed suicide as the Soviets entered, raping, looting, distributing bread, and assuring water supplies all at the same time.[3] Shocked and fascinated journalists (like future chroniclers) reveled in describing—or imagining, based on Soviet press reports—the spectacular last gasps of the "pounded corpse" that had been Nazi Berlin: "The world's fourth city, in its dying hours, was a monstrous thing of almost utter destruction. . . . Towers of fire surged into the pall of smoke and dust that overhung the dying city."[4] One American chronicler tried to render his impressions for the hometown audience by asking them to imagine the scene as if one were to knock down every building between 34th and 59th Streets and between Eighth and Park Avenues. Then reduce to a burned out shell seven of every ten homes and apartments between 60th and 86th Streets on the West Side, and in the same way that you might sprinkle salt on an egg sprinkle destruction on the remaining sections of just Manhattan.[5]

Within days, Berlin had finally become a battlefront (*Frontstadt*). There was no functioning transportation or communication system. By April 26, the telephones had stopped working and Berliners cowered in their cellars, cut off from news, awaiting the bitter end. The only thing that still seemed to flow was alcohol—successively liberated by the Berliners and the arriving Soviets—and the amphetamine *Pervitin*, which people had used to ward off sleep during the nightly bombing raids. Right before midnight on May 1, just as Stalin had envisioned, the red flag was hoisted atop the Reichstag. Some two hundred defenders hung on until May 2, when the SS, in a last-ditch effort to prevent the Soviet triumph, blew up a subway tunnel in which people had sought shelter. Horrific rumors of a "death chamber [*Todeskammer*] under the train tracks" and thousands of casualties (including foreign workers herded into the tunnels) circulated through the city.[6] Countless writers and filmmakers concluded that the city's fate could not be contained in sober, factual accounts, and have vividly depicted the savagery of war's end: the huge casualties as the Soviet armies, competing for Stalin's favor, fought their way into the city, the drunken brutality and sexual violence of the victors, and the determined sadism of the SS, which hanged deserters in the streets even as the flags of surrender were already flying a few streets over.[7]

Es Lebe Berlin: Out of the Rubble

Wolfgang Leonhard, a twenty-four-year-old political officer in the Red Army whose mother, the German Communist exile Susanne Leonhard, was imprisoned in the Gulag, remembered flying, with future East German leader Walter Ulbricht, into a smoldering, still battle-torn Berlin on May 2. Many residents were already wearing white or red armbands. The most prudent among them sported both. German soldiers were being marched out of the city into Soviet captivity. Many would not return for nearly a decade, if ever.

At the same time, the Soviets, fueled by alcohol and embittered by the stubborn German refusal to capitulate, were obsessed with finding and delivering the Führer's body to Stalin. The Soviet newspaper *Pravda* promised, "Whether he escaped to hell, to the devil's paws, or to the arms of fascist protectors, still he is no more. We shall find out what really happened to him. And if he escaped, we shall find him, no matter where he is."[8] Finally, on May 8, a day after an earlier ceremony with Eisenhower at Rheims, the Germans signed an unconditional surrender in a small villa in the Berlin suburb of Karlshorst, which had become the Soviet headquarters.

Reducing Berlin to the "greatest pile of rubble in the world"[9] was not, however, the Soviets' ultimate goal. Berlin was a trophy, not only to be conquered, destroyed, and sexually ravaged, but also to be molded, reconstructed, and displayed. The Red Army and its political advisers were prepared not only for relentless battle but for political and cultural propaganda and civic reconstruction. Already by April 28, the Soviet commander Marshall Berzarin had begun taking charge of the city and ordered it to come to life. Berliners were handed shovels and commanded to remove dead people and animals from the streets and to begin clearing rubble. Long lines of women appeared at the water pumps, and within an astonishingly few days basic order had been restored. Even as fighting still raged in the city center, municipal services lumbered into motion. While initial impressions impelled many observers to draw comparisons to ancient Pompeii—and John Dos Passos recorded that, "The ruin of the city was so immense it took on the grandeur of a natural phenomenon like the Garden of the Gods or the Painted Desert"[10]—Berlin's infrastructure was surprisingly intact, ready for both reconstruction and exploitation. Although the Potsdamer Platz, the lively center of Weimar and Nazi Berlin, had become a "steppe," both the western and eastern suburbs were eerily unscathed.[11] The original material damage, in fact, had been less severe than it appeared to be on camera and in the dramatic reports by both awed and triumphant occupiers or shell-shocked Berliners. Restaurants and cabarets were instructed to open for business. Radio Berlin returned to the air on May 4, and by May 14 the Berlin subway (*Ubahn*) was sputtering back into service.

As Berliners emerged from the cellars in which they had tried to escape the battle, so did, as is detailed in chapter 3, several thousand of their former neighbors, Jews and "partial" Jews who had survived in the "underground" of hiding and disguise, or in mixed marriages. Already on May 8, the first marriage in liberated Berlin was celebrated between two people who had not been allowed to marry under the Nuremberg racial laws. On May 12, the first Jewish religious service was reported in the reopened synagogue in the Lotringer Strasse. And on May 11 or perhaps 12 (the sources differ), another Jewish religious ceremony, also claimed as the first, was presided over by a Soviet army chaplain, in the Jewish Hospital.[12]

On May 18, the first concert played in the *Funkhaus*, with Marshall Berzarin seated proudly and reassuringly in the front row. The first public soccer game, on May 20, attracted ten thousand spectators. The first Soviet film was screened on May 22. On May 27, 1945, the Renaissance

Theater reopened—bizarrely, the Soviets licensed a premiere performance of *Rape of the Sabines*.[13] Berzarin, the relatively popular Soviet *Stadtkommandant* (soon to be killed in a motorcycle accident), and the new Soviet-dominated *Magistrat* (municipal government) declared "ES LEBE BERLIN!" (Long Live Berlin). Schools reopened and meals for children were organized. In early June, less than a month after war's end, the municipal swimming pools were filled and the telephones were working again. By the end of June, the city library had opened, three major banks (Commerz, Dresden, and Deutsche) were back in business, and four daily newspapers had been licensed.[14] For a while it seemed like everything merited a "first": the first school day, the first wedding, the first concert, the first day at the public beach on Lake Wannsee—even if such activities had been suspended only for a relatively brief time. Newspapers cheered the reopening of the much-worried-about Berlin zoo. Susi, the ape, had made it through everything "in good shape," Berliners were reassured (with accompanying photo) in some of the first editions.[15]

With the war barely over, the Soviets moved to shift away from the angry calls for vengeance issued by Red Army propagandists, such as the Russian-Jewish writer Ilya Ehrenburg, to Stalin's new line of "The Hitlers come and go, the German Volk remains." While Red Army soldiers continued to rape and plunder, other troops were handing out bread and working to rapidly restore municipal and cultural services. "Coal, food, and clothing" were the immediate issues, and "from the beginning food was used as a lever to make people work."[16] Soviet efforts at control also took more symbolic and fantastic forms; for example, in June the Soviet Military Administration (SMA) placed Berlin on Moscow time, leaving the already disoriented city brightly lit at midnight and dark at 7:00 A.M.[17] In some instances, the sense of insanity generated by the contradictions of Soviet occupation policy became entirely real, when, in some districts, "the Red Army took the job of liberation too literally and opened up not only the prisons and the concentration camps but the lunatic asylums as well."[18] Much to the consternation of the SMA and their German communist allies, a released patient named Spalinger declared himself *Kommandant* of a Berlin Soviet (workers and soldiers council). He plastered the city with notices calling for the immediate arrest of all Nazi Party members, to be followed by activation of electric, gas, and water supplies, and a complete street cleaning. In May 1945, only the insane, it seemed, could still want to set up a Soviet republic (as imagined by Rosa Luxemburg and Karl Liebknecht after World War I) or, for that matter, demand the full bringing to justice of all Nazis and members of Nazi organizations.[19]

The Soviets were the only Allied power on the ground in Berlin from late April until early July. The terms of unconditional surrender, however, called for dividing Germany into British, American, French, and Soviet zones, with Berlin to be split into four sectors overseen by a joint *Kommandatura* (military government). The Americans and Soviets would become the dominant and rival occupiers, but initially their approach to Berlin was quite different. For the Red Army, its generals competing fiercely for Stalin's favor, the Nazi capital was the prize that had to be conquered at all cost. To the Americans, hemmed in by Roosevelt's negotiations with Stalin and the various Allied agreements hammered out at Teheran and Yalta, it was not at all clear that Berlin, ugly and ruined, would be worth a conflict with the Soviet Union, not to mention the many casualties its capture would require. Eisenhower, it was widely assumed, was not unhappy to leave the Battle of Berlin to the Russians. Afterward he reportedly concluded that "it is quite likely, in my opinion, that there will never be any attempt to rebuild Berlin."[20] The U.S. diplomat Robert Murphy, who years later decided that American disdain for the Berlin trophy was a monumental error, recorded his impressions when the Americans moved into the city in July 1945:

> Two months after their surrender, Berliners still were moving about in a dazed condition. They had endured not only thousand-plane raids for years, but also weeks of Russian close-range artillery fire. In addition to three million Germans in Berlin, thousands of displaced persons were roaming around the shattered city.[21]

After accusing his Soviet allies of having created in Berlin "another Nanking, with Russians instead of Japanese doing the raping, murdering, and looting," Colonel Frank Howley, the American commander, remembered in 1950:

> Berlin in late July was still a shambles from the effects of Allied bombing, especially incendiary raids, and of Russian street fighting, but the Russians already had put large squads of German women to work clearing the rubble in various parts of the city. As the women wearily passed the fallen bricks from hand to hand, in a long human chain, they presumably were spurred on to heroic efforts by the great posters the Russians had erected to assure the Germans that they had not been conquered but "liberated" by the Communists from their Fascist oppressors.

When the Americans, practically sneaking past uncooperative Soviet sentries, finally made their way through—"On July 1, 1945, the road to Berlin was the highroad to Bedlam"—they found, somewhat to their displeasure, that everything crucial to the running of the city had already been organized by the SMA.[22] Berlin was divided into twenty administrative districts, each with its own mayor and council. As the Communist leader Ulbricht insisted, "Communists too must learn to become good bureaucrats."[23] He stated his plans for organizing the city in no uncertain terms: "It must look democratic but we must control everything."[24] Adhering to Ulbricht's plan, reliable cadres hovered in less visible second-ranking positions while the SMA installed Popular Front figureheads—such as the renowned surgeon Ferdinand Sauerbruch, who obediently served through all twentieth-century German regimes, or Catholic Center Party politician Andreas Hermes—in the newly constituted Magistrat. Deputy Mayor Kurt Maron, a tough Communist who was the real power behind the fellow-traveling Lord Mayor Werner, appealed in melodramatic tones, and with liberal repetition of its name, to the city's still extant local patriotism: "Get to work Berlin! Berlin must not and will not go under. . . . Berlin, our lovely Berlin has sunk in debris and rubble. Berliners, let's get rid of the filth in our streets and squares!" Evoking the physical destruction of the city as a reflection of Nazi rule, he admonished Berliners to "get rid also of all the filth in our hearts and minds." Indeed, by the time the Americans and British moved in, "the Russians had been in the city for nine weeks; a single Communist-controlled union, four political parties, a police force, and a municipal government were already established; and 80% of the factories that had survived the war had been dismantled."[25]

The Americans officially occupied McNair Barracks on July 4, and quickly discovered that they faced more outright opposition from their Soviet allies than from the thoroughly "whipped" Berliners.[26] The confrontation with the Nazi death camps had provoked deep anger at the Germans and uneasy compassion for their victims among the U.S. liberators, but the shock of witnessing what seemed to be a thoroughly destroyed capital, with its pathetic-looking, hungry, and exhausted population, also produced sympathy for the defeated Germans among top American officials. When Secretary of State James Byrnes—who a year later would articulate a new, more conciliatory stance toward Germany in the context of Cold War conflicts—toured the city with President Truman on the eve of the Potsdam Conference, he noted, "Despite all we had read of the destruction there, the extent of the devastation shocked us. It brought home the suffering that total war visits upon old folks, women, and children, besides the men in uniform."[27] Other observers were less charitable. "The city was like a vast archeological excavation where only foundations could be traced, with an occasional bit of wall," the American Jewish writer Meyer Levin noted with some satisfaction.[28] Berlin certainly was "all it was cracked up to be," an American Jewish GI wrote home sarcastically (and a bit jubilantly) on letter paper confiscated from Hitler's destroyed Chancellery.[29]

"The Germans" in the ruined city, a U.S. Military Government official noted, "were completely licked." The Russians "had beaten any thought of resistance" out of them, and they now had "no other interest in life than merely to stay alive." The Americans' "problem" proved to be their Russian allies, "a baffling combination of childishness, hard realism, irresponsibility, churlishness, amiability, slovenliness, and callousness," prone to reckless drunken firefights with their allies. Kommandatura sessions were often "stormy," and the Soviets never quite relinquished the notion that, as the victors of the bloody Battle of Berlin, they were the ones really in charge, while the others were their guests, there on sufferance (and ability to share enormous quantities of vodka).[30] Eventually, this officer remarked, "It became a continuing problem to remind myself that the Russians, who were giving us trouble, were our friends, and the Germans, who were giving us cooperation, were our enemies."[31]

FRAGILE REVIVAL: COMPETING VICTORS AND JEWISH TRACES

Since essential services had been rapidly restored by the Soviets and the Allies faced virtually no threats of resistance, culture and political education developed as key areas of competition among especially the Soviet and American victors. Under the direction of the powerful cultural commissar, Colonel Sergei Tulpanov, an afficionado of German culture, and his corps of German-speaking (and often Jewish) officers, the SMA had insisted on immediately reopening the shuttered theaters and schools and, very importantly, gaining control of radio transmissions. Russians focused on those they identified as the intelligentsia, partly out of their own sense of the importance of culture—Stalin was determined to win over these "engineers of the soul"—and partly as a kind of bread and circuses policy that aimed to deflect criticism of Red Army transgressions and distract Berliners from their misery. By mid-May, actors, writers, and musicians, attracted surely by the higher-level ration cards offered to "intellectual and cultural workers," had already found their way to the old *Reichstheaterkammer* in the Schlüterstrasse, now retooled as the Soviet-style *Kammer der Kunstschaffenden* (cultural workers chamber), a name redolent of course of the Nazi *Reichskulturkammer*. Returning émigrés, some in Allied uniform, others drawn by Soviet promises of a new democratic antifascist Germany, soon joined them.[32]

Almost overnight, it seemed, Berlin's cultural institutions were coming back to life, even if only as a truncated shadow of what had existed in the Weimar years. As Wolfgang Schivelbusch has noted in his marvelous evocation of culture in postwar Berlin "before the curtain" of the Cold War descended, "The time before 1933 belonged indisputably to a past world, yet at the same time it also represented, as the last stop before the descent into barbarism, the only possible orientation for rebuilding."[33]

Theater critic Friedrich Luft remembered those heady early days, when despite the hunger, the ruins, and the uncertainty, "We were so happy, so optimistic . . . we still thought that we could suddenly start over where we had had to stop in 1933."[34] On a gorgeous spring afternoon, Berliners, still without transportation, streamed in on foot to hear, along with pieces by Mozart and Tchaikovsky, the Midsummer Night's Dream Overture by the "Jewish" Mendelssohn-Bartholdy, whom the Nazis had banned. This first Philharmonic concert on May 27 in the Titania Palast was conducted by Leo Borchardt, who had, together with his journalist lover Ruth Andreas-Friedrich, helped coordinate a rescue network for Jews in Nazi Berlin (and would be killed by accidental American fire in an incident on August 23, 1945).[35]

"Berlin Is Coming Back" (*Berlin kommt wieder*) was the hit song in the summer of 1945. "*Berlin lebt auf!*" (revives), the *Berliner Zeitung* already proclaimed on Monday, May 21, 1945. Other headlines announced, "*Berlin ist wieder da*" (is back), suggesting naively that reconstructing Berlin could be a bit, in Schivelbusch's term, "like opening a time capsule left untouched" since 1933.[36] However, the vaunted "literature in the drawer" that many hoped would emerge from the cultural ice age of the Third Reich never materialized. Berlin's distinctive Weimar culture had emigrated or been silenced, and as Hannah Arendt commented in her biting 1950 assessment of German reconstruction, "The authors of the few really important books written in Germany since 1933 or published since 1945 were already famous twenty and twenty-five years ago." Five years after war's end, she saw only a "younger generation [that] seems to be petrified, inarticulate, incapable of consistent thought."[37]

Yet in the immediate chaotic aftermath of defeat and liberation, the resurrected memory of Weimar, a fascination with banned modernism, the return of some of the exiled, obeisance to Soviet cultural policy calling for peace and progress, and general dependence on Allied (first Soviet and then four-power) licenses produced a manic plethora of cultural events. Programs were printed in a babel of languages and included long explanations for the culturally starved audiences—the intensity of the theater experience only heightened by the surreal theatricality of the surroundings. Cold and hungry actors presented forty-six plays in the first postwar season, 1945/46, in freezing halls to ecstatic audiences "huddled in overcoats and rugs, oblivious of everything except the show," which ranged from "Shakespeare to Wilder, from Hebbel to Brecht, from Gorki to Weisenborn, from Offenbach to Weill."[38] Berliners hungrily consumed culture from the outside world, identifying with the Thornton Wilder characters who had also survived "by the skin of our teeth." Banned stars returned to the stage. Elisabeth Bergner's return was treated as front-page news. It was so cold that cultural officers even suggested opening schools in theaters; it would be easier to heat large halls than individual schools, and in the evening the audience would benefit from the heat that had been generated during the day. "That may sound fantastic," one officer noted, but "we are in Berlin."[39]

On September 7, 1945—ironically it was Rosh Hashanah—the first major theater production premiered in Berlin. Lessing's classic play *Nathan the Wise*, with Paul Wegener in the title role and directed by Fritz Wisten, had been rescued, as a Berlin critic put it, from "the stage silence to which racial fanaticism had damned it."[40] In his autobiography, the literary critic Marcel Reich-Ranicki, who had returned to Berlin in Polish uniform and in the service of the Polish Communist secret police after surviving (and escaping) the Warsaw Ghetto, described his first theater outing. He went expectantly, eager to observe how a German audience would now react to the long-banned play about a Jew "whose wife and seven sons had been burned." But he was disappointed, for the audience was not German at all. The theater was filled rather with officers of the four occupying powers, most of them, he noted, "Jews who spoke amazingly good German"—not surprisingly of course, because many of them were, or at least had been, German: "they were the exiles and refugees who now gathered together in a Berlin theater, not far from the ruins of the Reichstag and the Reichs Chancellery, under the sign of Lessing."[41] Friedrich Wolf's drama *Professor Mamlock*, about the vicious persecution of a Jewish academic, written in 1933 and first performed in Zurich, was also finally staged at the Hebbel Theater, with Wolf, a Communist-Jewish physician and playwright returned from Moscow exile, in the audience.[42]

This attempted resurrection of Weimar culture depended in important ways on the return to public view—and indeed the showcasing—of Jewish journalists, actors, and theater directors, with their links to Weimar (and exile Soviet or American) culture. Indeed, the small but significant presence of German Jews, both those few who had remained and those who returned (often only temporarily and in Allied uniform), was crucial, both to the tentative but remarkably swift restoration of orderly civil society, first by the SMA and then by the other three victors, and to the city's aura of rapid revival. Surviving Jews were often deployed as instant bureaucrats or public safety officials, and Jewish references, such as the command performances of *Nathan the Wise* and what one slightly cynical cultural officer called the "unavoidable" Mendelssohn compositions, were virtually de rigueur for early Allied-licensed cultural activities.[43] Along with Elisabeth Bergner, Jewish actors Ida Ehre, Lilli Palmer, Curt Bois, and Ernst Deutsch returned to the stage. As historian Frank Stern notes, shortly after the collapse of the Third Reich, "Almost all directors at Berlin theaters were of Jewish origin, about ten Jewish actresses returned to East Germany."[44] A young Hans Rosenthal, freed from his hideout in a Berlin garden colony (*Schrebergarten*) was recruited into the local *anti-fa*(scist) committee even as fighting still raged in the center of the city. Rapidly disillusioned with the Soviets he had initially served so eagerly, he then garnered a job with Allied-licensed radio and almost immediately became the host of the popular broadcast *Pulsschlag* (Heartbeat) *Berlin*, foreshadowing his later career as West Germany's most prominent television talk master. Despite the murder of his parents and his younger brother, Rosenthal, like many (especially young) survivors, felt the exhilaration of survival (*Überlebensgefühl*) and a passionate zest for life and desire to catch up on his lost youth.[45]

Berlin's strangely photogenic and cinematic rubble also offered a perfect feature film backdrop, and the Soviets lost no time in reactivating the old UFA studios in Babelsberg near Potsdam. By October 1945, a revamped (and renamed) DEFA was operating out of two studios and providing a major source of employment.[46] Carrying the all too appropriate title *The Murderers Are among Us*, the first licensed film, shot on location in the ruins, mixed antifascist, anticapitalist, and antimilitarist messages—including references to massacres committed by the *Wehrmacht* on the eastern front—with discreet (but entirely comprehensible) allusions to antisemitism. The story line exposes the murderous army service of a returned factory owner now masquerading as a democrat, but clearly hews to the new Soviet and Communist line of rejecting revenge for past Nazi crimes in favor of postwar antifascist reconstruction. The argument against revenge and for redemptive forgiveness is left to a beautiful young female victim of the Nazis. Played by Hildegard Knef, this ethnically unidentified concentration camp survivor turned improbably attractive *Trümmerfrau* (woman of the rubble) recognizes that Germans too have been victimized and that the past must be suppressed in order to build a new German future. Millions of people in the Soviet zone saw the film.[47]

The foregrounding of the remnants of German-Jewish culture was certainly encouraged by an open secret of the occupation: that many, if not most, of the cultural officers in the four occupying armies were themselves former German Jews.[48] At the Soviet club *Die Möve* (Seagull) in the Neue Wilhelmstrasse, Allied cultural officers and German intelligentsia, many of them just returned from exile, reunited with old friends and feasted on cheap borscht, sausage, beer, and of course vodka.[49] The Americans, keenly aware of the Soviets' energetic cultural policy and trying hard to play catch-up, also tried to mobilize cinema for denazification purposes. They appointed Henry C. Alter, a Viennese Jew, to take charge of their film-licensing operations and recruited Billy Wilder to return from Hollywood as an American film officer. "He who controls cinema controls Germany," Jack Warner supposedly said, but Wilder's project for propaganda through lighter entertainment would not be achieved until *A Foreign*

Affair was completed in 1948. Cultural officers fretted that documentaries about the Tennessee Valley Authority or U.S. Flying Fortresses in the Pacific war could not compete with sophisticated Soviet offerings.[50] In 1946 the Americans belatedly established RIAS (Radio in the American Sector) as a rival to the Soviet *Berliner Rundfunk*.

CONQUERORS AND LIBERATORS, NOT OPPRESSORS: THE PERKS OF OCCUPATION

The Americans had come, in General Eisenhower's notable words, as "conquerors" but not "oppressors." The battered Red Army, on the other hand, whose arrival had so terrorized Germans in the East, moved into Berlin promising liberation and "without the allures of a conqueror."[51] In fact, of course, conquest had its privileges. For the Soviets this meant not only access to the defeated city's women, liquor, and other still abundantly available consumer goods but also control over a cultural policy—frequently dominated by Jewish officers—that was much more liberal, and living arrangements more comfortable, than any they could have maintained at home in Stalin's war-torn Russia.[52]

The other occupiers also enjoyed the comforts of their victory, their daily lives a stark contrast to those of the shell-shocked Berliners. The British, drawing on long imperial experience, were inclined to create a central European Raj and "settled into the ruins as if they were in the White Highlands of Kenya."[53] They treated the Germans, one officer recalled, "as if they were a specially intelligent tribe of Bedouins."[54] The French, who joined the Kommandatura belatedly in August, came with much more modest resources and generally concentrated their (only minimally successful) efforts on educational reform. They appear, at least in German, American, and British accounts, to have been the least visible. Americans, who loomed the largest physically as well as (in the West) politically, "harked back" to images of the "frontier."

> They went about with pistols slung cowboy-style round their thighs. Like the railroad barons of the Old West, their generals kept lavish private railroad trains fully staffed and under steam twenty-four hours a day. . . . They drove around in supercharged Mercedes requisitioned from Nazi owners . . . [with a] predilection for living in castles and baronial villas.[55]

Although they had been removed from the center of Berlin, with the East and center controlled by the Soviets and the old West with its Ku'damm shopping boulevard by the British, the Americans compensated by claiming the grandest quarters in the affluent undamaged outskirts of suburban

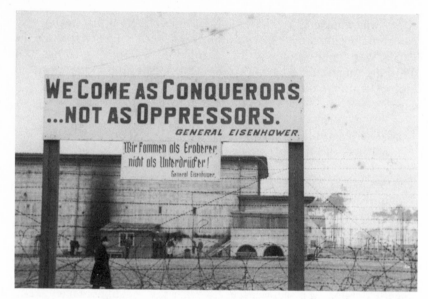

Fig. 1.2. General Eisenhower's message in English and German on a sign in front of a U.S. military installation, Berlin, 1945.

Zehlendorf. Top brass took over magnificent lakefront villas on the Wannsee, some of them confiscated from Nazis who had earlier "aryanized" them from their Jewish owners. Secretary of State James Byrnes recorded his mild discomfort at the quick takeover of the Reich's luxuries while on a fact-finding tour in the Führer's private train: "Hitler's suite consisted of two rooms and a large lavender-tiled bathroom. Mrs. Byrnes and I felt a little strange in these rooms formerly occupied by Hitler and Eva Braun."[56]

Berlin's black market also provided ordinary GIs with absurdly cheap luxury goods that would never have been available to them back home. Their success at such trade crucially shaped their encounters with members of other Allied forces, defeated Germans, and the many displaced foreigners gathered in the city. Occupiers and Germans alike suspected that the "crowds of furtive people with bundles under their arms scattered in groups over a wide area that looked like an American city dump," which John Dos Passos found "[a]t the further end of the Tiergarten [park]," consisted mainly of liberated slave laborers and Polish Jewish "dee pees," as the GIs called them, who had illegally jumped borders to escape renewed persecution in Poland.[57] For the most part, however, it was Allied personnel who hauled in the grand booty of Leica cameras, Zeiss binoculars, Meissen and Rosenthal china, French perfume, luxury furs, and antique jewelry. Jewish property confiscated or obtained at auction during the Nazi years, and valuables belonging to newly impoverished German bombing victims or refugees from the Soviet-occupied East, fed this flourishing—and desperate—commerce.[58] "The whole of Europe has become one vast black market," American photojournalist Margaret Bourke-White reported, its Berlin headquarters the Tiergarten and the Femina nightclub, where occupation officers and Germans lucky and disreputable enough to gain entrance traded women, rumors, and cigarettes.[59] Especially "during the first months of the four-power occupation," before the army "pulled the plug" in November, U.S. troops "sent home more money than they were paid." In the "great raid on the U.S. Treasury provoked by the cigarette economy," Americans could sell a carton of Lucky Strikes for up to RM 2,000, convert the cash at a rate of RM 10 to $1, and gleefully send the dollar proceeds home by the APO.[60] One lucky soldier, the story went, actually bought a whole movie theater with his proceeds.[61] An American "Mickey Mouse watch was worth more than a jewel-studded trinket from Cartier,"[62] and GIs collected large sums of dollars in exchange for the occupation marks shelled out by Russian peasant soldiers hoping to send home a timepiece so "his wife could barter it for a cow."[63] When the first modern art gallery opened in August 1945, on the Kurfürstendamm, the main commercial street in British-controlled Charlottenburg, occupier art-lovers could acquire a Chagall, Kokoschka, Kollwitz, Nolde, or Schmit-Rottluff, "degenerate" works that had been stowed in private collections, with their cigarette rations.[64] Antique stores, detective agencies, fortune-tellers, and the occult thrived in a chaotic world with no hard currency and few hard facts. Many could no longer discern what was real and what was surreal, or what had happened to their world as they searched for the lost and missing.

At a time when most Berliners bemoaned their losses and miserable living conditions, occupiers welcomed comfortable housing, black market profits, and easily available sex. For some, however, especially officers' dependents who began arriving, in part, to inhibit fraternization with German women, occupation life was simply boring, a kind of Main Street in Kalamazoo transposed onto the Kurfürstendamm, as reporters disparagingly noted.[65] Higher-ranking military personnel and civilian employees of the Military Government traveled in first-class trains and sleepers. They resided in quickly constructed American colonies "with many amenities of life back home—a commissary, a post exchange (PX) for shopping, a pharmacy, beauty parlor and barbershop, schools for the dependents' children, movies."[66] Their routine included drinks at the club, shopping for American-brand goods and alcohol at the commissary, miniature golf and bridge parties, and an occasional vacation at the American enclaves in Bavarian Garmisch or Berchtesgaden. They enjoyed their favorite programs beamed out of American Forces Network radio, excellent cheap housing complete with "exceedingly polite and outwardly respectful" servants (any servants being a novelty for most Americans), and access to the Sears Roebuck catalogue. This carefully produced familiar comfort led one young woman to complain that she had hoped to escape Cedar Rapids, and Berlin turned out to be Cedar Rapids![67]

The remarkable number of breathless memoirs, diaries, novels, and films produced by occupiers, relief workers, and journalists testify, however, to the great sense of mission and adventure that many found in postwar Berlin. At least until the Nuremberg trials began in the fall of 1945, the ravaged capital was the place to be for foreign correspondents. The *New York Times* had only two reporters in Paris but four in Berlin.[68] But like the Fräuleins, whose pert exterior was widely assumed to cover traumatic memories of rape and violation, Berlin, and certainly its culture and nightlife, was only a pale imitation of its celebrated pre-Nazi self. The Femina, famously depicted in any number of rubble (*Trümmer*) films, notably Wilder's *Foreign Affair*, was packed with military police and required to close at 9:30 P.M.[69] Dos Passos, for one, was not impressed: "We walked out with a feeling of disgust and pity stiffening our throats and drove out to the American Press Club, where there were comfortable chairs and it was warm and people still looked like human beings."[70] If the Russians celebrated with vodka and caviar, the other Allies and their cohort of journalists soon introduced a whole new repertoire of alcoholic delights to each other and some intrigued Germans: Manhattans, martinis, Cognac, whiskey, and crème de menthe were consumed in astonishing quantities at interminable parties and club gatherings. Despite their own considerable capacities, however, the Americans had a hard time matching the Russians' prodigious alcohol consumption, and many were the nights when Americans struggled in the early morning hours to hold their own with Russians who "liked to drink and give long speeches."[71] Eisenhower, it was said, tried to avoid Berlin because he couldn't tolerate the vodka-laden banquets that the Soviets liked to lay on, and Colonel Howley grumbled about the devious Russian habit of starting meetings late, after they had slept off the night's excesses: "By four o'clock in the afternoon we would be so ravenous that we were inclined to agree to anything—just to get something to eat."[72]

In some ways, despite—or perhaps because of—the tense and competitive proximity of Soviets and western Allies, the Cold War was slower to take hold in Berlin. The Allies had to collaborate in ruling the city, and Howley's suspicions notwithstanding, "at the top, at the vodka and banquet level," among the émigré officers (and on the black market), there was relatively lively contact among the four armies.[73] All kinds of borders could be crossed in early postwar Berlin. Years later, Markus Wolf, the son of Communist-Jewish exile playwright Friedrich Wolf (and later the East German spymaster) who had himself returned with the Red Army,

Fig. 1.3. American and Soviet soldiers in front of Stalin portrait, Unter den Linden, Berlin, 1945.

recalled the reunion in postwar Berlin of three young friends who had shared a Communist childhood in Moscow. One was his brother, the partly Jewish German Konrad Wolf, in Red Army uniform; another was now in the U.S. Army; and the third was a demobilized German veteran.[74] Despite all the tensions, despite the shooting incidents between nervous Americans and drunken Russians, despite the spy and kidnapping dramas of an emerging Cold War, the Allies were committed to uneasy cooperation. Each side practiced its anticommunism or its Stalinism in a milder form in Berlin than at home. There were those in the U.S. Military Government who insisted that, all things considered, the pre-1948 occupation of Berlin represented "a record of successful international adjustments and sympathetic understanding."[75]

THE POLITICS OF MISERY AND SELF-PITY: CONTESTED VICTIMIZATION

The occupiers' wild ride notwithstanding, and despite the efforts, by both occupiers and Germans, to revive the fabled *Berliner Luft* (Berlin aura) of the Golden Twenties, Berlin also presented a picture of relentless misery. Municipal officials, who had quickly been installed in the Magistrat and

then in the various districts of the four Allied sectors, frequently emphasized the city's continuing despair, in part to pressure the victors for higher
rations or fewer requisitions of the remaining intact housing. Native Berliners and refugees from the East who were billeted with them, the majority of them women, bickered over space, kitchen privileges, use of scarce
gas and electricity, and disrupted social and sexual relations. They coped
with grief over those killed in battle or on the home front and anxiety
about men who remained in captivity. Children and the elderly, lacking
proper coats and shoes, spent much of the winter—and the second winter
of 1946/47 was especially bitter—bundled under blankets in bed. The
conditions of total defeat, even the disorientation of a demolished street
grid and the difficulty of finding goods or establishing credit with shopkeepers in unfamiliar neighborhoods, made family survival at least as precarious as when the bombs were falling, and the Nazis, ever mindful of
morale and discipline, had kept the city running at almost full speed.

The misery (*Not*) of women and children in particular, more fully discussed in the next chapter, came in many ways to represent the situation
of the struggling city. The women's (*Frauenleben*) page of the *Tagesspiegel*, the liberal anticommunist paper finally licensed by the Americans in
September after much hand-wringing about the Soviet advantage on the
cultural and press front, conveyed this pervasive despair: "We have already broken the habit of the proverbial glance into the baby carriage,
which supposedly no woman would deny herself, because what we see
there so often makes us so sad."[76] Issac Deutscher, returning to the Berlin
he had covered as a correspondent for British newspapers, tried to make
sense of the bizarre contrasts between ruin and continued solidity that
characterized so much of Germany: "Strangely, people are very well
dressed, or maybe it is only their finery that survived. Other than the
refugees, the Berliners themselves seem to be astonishingly well dressed.
But if one looked beyond their clothing, their yellowed complexions and
thin bodies told a different story." He too was especially struck by the
"deathly pale faces in the baby carriages."[77] Indeed, images of baby carriages were central to the iconography of victimization and survival in
postwar Germany: those proudly pushed by Jewish survivor parents
through the streets of German towns and displaced persons camps or
stationed at the front of demonstrations demanding free emigration to
Palestine, and the buggies pushed by Germans, loaded to the brim, often,
with everything except their intended contents. As Margaret Bourke-
White noted about her famous photo of a woman wearing a gas mask
pushing a pram, "The babycart was becoming the universal carryall of
Germany"; it could "carry a good load" and needed no gasoline.[78]

Food supplies were a particular flash point, not only because of the
necessary sustenance they provided, but because of their clear political

symbolism. In a period of extreme scarcity, defeated Germans and their victims—Jews, former forced laborers, other displaced persons under UNRRA jurisdiction—all competed against each other and among themselves for basic necessities. "'Calories' became a kind of magical concept" as occupiers initially set ration allotments according to judgments of guilt as well as need and capacity for reconstruction work.[79] At the same time, there was no clear standard for such decisions, which often doubly disadvantaged women. Nazi affiliations, either by marriage or by membership in party organizations, mandated exhausting labor as *Trümmerfrauen*, but women were also most likely to be labeled "unproductive" housewives, eligible only for the lowest-level five ration card, dubbed the "ticket to heaven" card (*Himmelsfahrtkarte*) because it could not provide a life-sustaining diet.

By December 1945, American officials felt that they had the food situation in Berlin under control, with the black market increasingly policed and rations averaging 1,600 calories daily.[80] As the harsher winter of 1946/47 approached, German officials and newspapers complained that Berliners and up to 65 percent of their children were in danger of starvation. U.S. commander Howley dismissed their worries as "bushwah," part of the persistent sullen whining and "aggressive self-pity" that defined the postsurrender mood.[81] From the perspective of the "conquerors," German demands for more food unreasonably reflected the enormous quantities they had been accustomed to consuming before, and even during, the war. Rations of up to 3,000 calories a day had included alcohol, ample bread and potatoes, and—always the marker of a satisfactory diet—an astonishing 106 grams of fat. In an indication of American ambivalence about whether hunger and disease in Berlin constituted a potential humanitarian crisis or a defensible punitive deprivation, by the beginning of 1947 the Military Government had warned officers not to attribute deaths to starvation or freezing, for fear of causing "undue alarm among the civilian population."[82]

The relative misery of the defeated Germans, therefore, was a highly contested issue. Indeed, the post-1989 relegitimation of putatively tabooized memories of German suffering has not only obfuscated the vast extent to which that suffering was expressed but also—and perhaps even more fully—sidelined the degree to which those stories were both heard *and* vigorously challenged at the time.[83] The level of comfort the Third Reich had managed, despite everything, to bestow on its citizens almost until, and in some cases through, the very end of the war outraged many Allied observers, particularly those who had witnessed the liberation of the camps. Margaret Bourke-White determinedly punctured the prevailing picture of German "catastrophe": "All along the line we were amazed at the lavish food stores which we found in German cellars and at the excellent wardrobes hanging in the closets of the homes we requisitioned." Especially the Fräuleins, the object of so much controversy about fraternization, were in "good shape, their teeth are the giveaway. Much better than in any German occupied country."[84] Attractive young women and "plump Hausfrauen" contradicted the wartime image of the barbaric German but also belied the continuous litany of affliction intoned by Germans.[85] Despite the obvious hardships of life in the destroyed cities and the hair-raising tales of Soviet terror related by German refugees from the East, most American reporters were more inclined to be cynical (and incredulous) than sympathetic. While officers in Berlin did worry about the sheer survival of its residents, other observers throughout the American zone were more impressed by how many Germans had "plenty of cash, the results of years of high war earnings and few expenditures," as well as generous welfare provisions and pensions for civilians and military dependents. Nor did it escape notice that "the soldiers sent home a great deal of loot" now usefully available for barter and the black market.[86] Particularly in early American reportage, Germans appeared not only as "war damaged" victims or guilty aggressors but also (and even more) as comparatively privileged survivors, a baffling mix of abject self-pity and resentful entitlement. The extreme discordance in descriptions of German conditions, not only between victors and defeated, but among various occupiers, is striking.[87] These differences reflected both the differing prejudices of the reporters and changes over time and within regions. It may well be that initially the distress in a Berlin that had been heavily bombed and then partly sacked by the Soviets seemed especially dramatic. But it is certainly the case that the apparent and unexpected well-being of many Germans, as well as their obstinate rejection of guilt, figured in the bitter reactions of Soviet troops and Jewish survivors and Allied personnel as well as many Americans.

Denazification and Its Discontents: Conquered and Liberated

Confronted with a thoroughly crushed foe that was "unable or unwilling to believe what had happened," as Time magazine put it just before the war ended,[88] the Allies scrambled to combat Germans' weary political apathy and cynicism—which, to some surprise, turned out to be much more prevalent than enthusiasm for either Nazism or communism. American plans and proposals for the occupation ranged from severe purges and forced contrition—a kind of "mental hari-kari"—to rapid reinstatement of former Nazis to aid in economic reconstruction and the emerging common front against communism.[89] Most U.S. occupiers were not at all sanguine about the impact of denazification, as the Military Government struggled with conflicting goals of punishment and reeducation on the one hand and economic recovery and political stability on the other.[90] Indeed, this general pessimism can hardly be overestimated. Depending on their political attachments, the Americans feared that policies perceived as either too gentle and conciliatory or, conversely, as too draconian and vindictive could foment a resurgence of fascism. Germans and occupiers on both sides of this argument worried that communism would be more successful in harnessing postwar desires for peace. Furthermore, many occupiers, especially but certainly not only the émigrés among them, despaired of ever coercing or cajoling Germans into taking responsibility for the disaster they had caused and which they were now themselves experiencing. Quite in contrast to the many later tales of solidarity in suffering—a kind of postwar extension of the *Volksgemeinschaft* that had functioned throughout most of the war—critical observers were struck above all, as Arendt would be in 1950, by Germans' "selfishness and apathy" toward each other and their "surly" attitude toward the occupiers. At the same time, as Arendt also observed, the early "pointed finger" approach to reeducation not only failed to impress its targets but "quickly came into conflict with American plans for the reconstruction and re-education of Germany."[91]

American denazification regulations had initially required a ban on all "fraternization" with the enemy, proscribing all nonessential contact, from a handshake or casual conversation to sex and romance. The reality of German hardship, the need for German participation and expertise in rebuilding, the unwavering "whining" of the defeated, and fears that humiliated Germans might seek a new savior in communism, as well as the obvious attractions of the Fräuleins, all combined to assure that neither a nonfraternization policy nor a seriously tough denazifcation line could be long sustained. Journalists as well as former émigrés in the Military Government—who carried their own ambivalences toward the home that had expelled them—worried that denazification was just a "big swindle" and that soon Germany would once again appear to be a nation "more sinned against than sinning."[92]

The occupation eased, and the obviously unenforceable fraternization ban was quickly rescinded. But Germans never ceased to protest the "victors' justice," which, many claimed, relied heavily on a denunciation practice entirely reminiscent of the regime it was supposedly dismantling. They also interpreted Allied policies as a continuation of inhumane bombing strategies, which had seemed to follow the motto "War against the huts, peace for the palaces."[93] The clever Berlin cabaret *Conférenciers*, who had been forced into silence by the Nazis, found their voice again, but now they satirized occupation foibles, easily skipping over the recent past. "You are mistaken," one anti-Nazi pastor predicted to the Americans, "if you think that any honest person in Germany will feel personally responsible for things like Dachau, Belsen and Buchenwald. He will feel only that he was misled into believing in a regime that was led by criminals and murderers."[94] And such predictions seemed thoroughly confirmed. Many Military Government officials worried that restricted food rations, housing confiscations, and accusations of collective guilt would only reinforce the defeated in their injured innocence and perhaps push them toward communism.

The result of this rapid retreat from the politics of guilt was a political culture that acknowledged total defeat but allowed Germans to highlight their own victimization. The shift to a more politically palatable understanding took account of the stark fact that the vast majority of defeated Germans saw themselves as victims of the lost war, indeed of the Führer they had followed and who had betrayed them. Both the Soviets and the western Allies soon began to adjust their wartime image of Germans as barbaric Nazis. For the Soviets and their German Communist allies, what mattered was not so much what one had or had not done under the Nazis but how willing one was to accept the postwar antifascist line; Germans needed to be reeducated into democratic socialist antifascism, rather than punished for past fascism. In the Soviet zone, denazification served primarily as a means of political control, directed at the "weakening of the industrialists and the smashing of the large landowners and the bureaucracy as entrenched political forces." Unlike the more cautious Americans, the Soviets were actually eager to open up party-political life.[95] By June 15, 1945, a newly relegalized Social Democratic Party (SPD) in Berlin and the Soviet zone was calling on citizens to own their role as carriers of evil fascism but also embracing them as a cruelly misled and betrayed Volk in "unimaginable need [Not]," forced to pay the price for fascist "imposters" whose "dishonorable gamblers and power-mad politicians" had shamed their name throughout the world.[96]

Anne-Marie Durand-Wever, a middle-aged anti-Nazi physician who had been active in the Weimar women's and sex reform movement, was neither shocked nor disbelieving when she read the early reports about German atrocities in the Soviet-licensed press. She could well imagine and did not try to deny the horrors of which the Nazis were capable. Yet her response was to sigh for "poor Germany," whose sins had led it to total defeat and international condemnation, and to look forward to the day when Germany, and especially her beloved Berlin, would be delivered from its misery.[97] Socialist politicians also exhorted their constituents not to "despair." If even Stalin insisted that the "Hitlers come and go but the German Volk remains," then surely it would once again gather its strength, pull itself together, and "live on." Despite what was explicitly defined as their road of sacrifice and victimization (Opfergang), Germans would "recover" and regain their place in the world among "peace and freedom loving peoples" and never again become "victims of unscrupulous political adventurers."[98]

The Christian Democratic Party, a reworking of the moderate Weimar Center Party and other conservative groups, outdid the SPD's homage to German suffering with its rendition of how opportunistic Nazis had misled the German people "with hypocritical nationalist phrases and empty promises of peace." They had scandalously abused the idealism of its youth and left the Volk with—in a very common turn of phrase—"an awful legacy" (*furchtbare Erbschaft*) of moral and material ruin.[99] When the socialist-oriented *Volkshochschule* (people's college) in Berlin-Schöneberg reopened its doors, it offered courses on foreign affairs, the history of the workers' movement, and advice on hygiene and pregnancy, but never mentioned National Socialism.[100] To a surprising extent, the Soviets had modeled this muting of the guilt question. In its very first edition on May 21, the SMA's official organ, *Berliner Zeitung*, had already promised that the occupation's main goal was to "revive the normal life of the city." Such efforts, the paper admitted, with a rhetoric that managed simultaneously to decouple Germans from Hitler's crimes and attest to the magnanimity of the Red occupiers, were "much more than we could have expected and because of Hitler had any right to expect."[101]

The quick turnaround after May 8—which, as we have seen, left it to escaped madmen to demand the arrest of all Nazis and their followers—was unquestionably hard for many committed antifascists to follow, and their ambivalence is reflected in many of their early pronouncements. Communists who had returned from prisons and camps or exile were shocked not only by the rapacious behavior of the Soviet troops but also by the alacrity with which their leaders were willing to recognize Germans as victims. They noted, not unreasonably, that Hitler alone was not to blame for Nazi villainy, but also the ten million Germans who had cast their ballots for him in free elections in 1932. Skipping over the later interlude of the Nazi-Soviet Pact, these veteran antifascists recalled that in 1932 they had warned that a vote for Hitler was a vote for war.[102]

All four occupying powers and their German allies—in Berlin and throughout the former Reich—faced the same basic problem of balancing punishment and reeducation with the practical exigencies of governance and reconstruction. Captain John Maginnis of the U.S. Military Government succinctly stated the dilemma that bedeviled the Soviets as much as the Americans: "almost every capable administrator had some Nazi affiliations, and non-Nazis with experience were hard to find because they had been out of office for ten years or in concentration camps."[103] American, especially émigré, occupiers muttered that untainted Germans were likely to be dead or in exile, and, at least initially, they privileged antifascist over professional credentials, seeking out those who had been persecuted as leftists or non-"Aryans" for official positions such as *Bürgermeister* (mayor).

Quickly, however, competition between the Soviets and the western Allies decisively influenced occupation policies. Denazification and rationing policies were increasingly likely to be set with reference not only to the recent Nazi past but also to the Cold War present. The Americans (and British) were caught between their desire to impose punitive measures on the Germans, assuring for example that their diet should not exceed the low standard of postwar Great Britain, and their fear of being outdone in the propaganda and material comforts realm by their ever more troublesome new antagonists in the Communist East. Local officials adeptly played on American fears that, despite the Red Army's fearsome record, the U.S. insistence on having entered Germany, "not as a liberator, but as a victor" would drive Germans toward the Soviets who tended to overlook past transgressions if present loyalties were assured.[104] Referring to the anxiety-producing proximity of alternative models of denazification, Berliners could warn that "since the democratic sun shines on us, we become more brown every day, but before one turns brown, one becomes red."[105] *Life* photographer Margaret Bourke-White captured a scarily Aryan-looking female "Professor Koch" (cook) into whose mouth she put the lines that Americans imagined all Germans to be perfecting: "America must supply food, or Stalin will have an easy time."[106] Others warned in rhyme, "enough food we must get, or Hitler we cannot forget" (*Geben Sie uns genug zu essen, sonst können wir Hitler nicht vergessen*).[107]

In notable contrast to the views of most Jews involved with the U.S. or British occupation, one of the more unexpected advocates for the "whining" Germans was the British-Jewish publisher Victor Gollancz. Gollancz joined the chorus of those who worried that harsh treatment of the defeated Germans, no matter how severe their crimes, would dehumanize the victors and lead to possible renazification. "[A] visit to the camp at Belsen, where I saw the tattoo marks on the arms of the Jewish survivors," assured that he was "never likely to forget the unspeakable wickedness of which the Nazis were guilty." Later, however, he became more concerned with "the miserable 'shoes' of boys and girls in the schools" who would "come to their lessons without even a dry piece of bread for breakfast." When he went "down into a one-roomed cellar" where a mother was "struggling and struggling very bravely, to do her best for a husband and four or five children" he thought, "not of Germans, but of men and women," whose resentment might mean that "we have all but lost the peace."[108]

The transition to accepting Germans' self-perception as victims was, however, certainly not seamless. Colonel Howley groused, "Where the Russians parceled out extra bits of food in return for services rendered and for general political loyalty, I distributed food to the Germans to keep them from starving on our hands. I was not, however, in favor of giving them American sirloin steaks every night." By 1950, when he published his memoir, Howley had become a rabid anticommunist, but during his tour of duty Germans reviled him as the "beast of Berlin." With some irony, he noted, "Perhaps I had been unnecessarily blunt in saying so, but I had come to Berlin with the idea that the Germans were our enemies. Even though it was becoming more evident every day that it was the Russians who really were our enemies, I still was not prepared to embrace the Germans as allies."[109]

German Innocence and Guilt, Jewish Contempt

The evolving view of Germans as victims certainly corresponded to German self-perceptions. In myriad diaries, memoirs, and press accounts Berliners were represented, and represented themselves, as hapless "disillusioned and bewildered" victims of Nazi betrayal, Anglo-American bombings, and Soviet depredations. Only occasionally did they appear as now rightfully subjugated beneficiaries, or against-all-odds Jewish or anti-Nazi survivors, of a criminal regime.[110] The almost complete lack of active resistance to the occupation after the unconditional surrender was signed only confirmed these perceptions. Contrary to expectation, the Allies had encountered no underground "*Werewolves*," no fanatic endfighters. Referring to the rumors of Nazi resistance, one U.S. officer noted in his diary, "Nothing could have been further from the truth."[111] By the time the Allies arrived, most Germans, wearied by the heavy bombing, were more preoccupied with the misery caused by the lost war than with the regime they had once cheered. If the defense of Berlin against the Red Army had been fanatical and more prolonged than expected, the collapse of the Reich was also faster and more thorough than expected. As evidenced by the countless cynical jokes about how hard it was to find a Nazi anywhere in Germany, barely anyone admitted to having been a supporter of the regime. Even Hitler, it was said, had been found dead in a Munich street, holding a scrap of paper that read, "I was never a Nazi."[112]

Allied officials and journalists, especially but certainly not only Jews or leftists, recorded their impressions in virtually identical terms: no one, it seemed, had known anything about the atrocities that had been committed in the name of the Volk. Critical observers were particularly angered and sometimes mystified by this determined insistence on innocence of everyday complicity as well as Nazi atrocities—the "enigma of German irresponsibility," aptly named by U.S. Military Government official Moses Moskowitz. "The Germans have talked themselves into innocence. We cannot, therefore, expect them to atone for a sin they do not admit to having committed," he concluded with bitter resignation. They "complain[ed]" that they were the victims who had been "deceived and betrayed" (belogen und betrogen) and, even when directly confronted with evidence of German crimes, chose to blame the Nazis that none of them had ever been.[113] Beneath the Germans' defensiveness there lurked also, Jews sensed, some inchoate shame that led to a deep resentment of Jewish survivors, whose memories were a constant affront and reminder of German crimes and losses. "The Germans," Jews joked among themselves, "will never forgive us for what they did to us."[114]

Again and again, the single most common adjective used to describe the Germans was "sullen." The cover of Newsweek for April 9, 1945 posed a menacing Wehrmacht soldier with the title "Nazis in Defeat: Sullen, Vengeful, Treacherous." On the same day, Time, not to be outdone, described the almost beaten enemy as "unheroic, impenitent, apathetic, sullen, unable or unwilling to believe what had happened."[115] Two weeks later, with the war in Europe virtually over, correspondent Percy Knauth saw Germans as alternating between the "extremes of sullen impenitence and dumb docility."[116] "Morbidly obsessed with their own misery," they "allowed themselves to believe that they were the chief victims of the war." Reporters and occupiers were essentially unanimous in concluding that the German population just didn't get it; as State Department envoy Byron Price wrote in his December 1945 report to President Truman, "Notwithstanding the punishments Germans now suffer, and those still before them, there is no apparent realization of collective guilt for the unspeakable crimes committed by the German nation or for the unforgivable anguish and suffering spread by Germany throughout the world."[117] Bourke-White, in her now classic 1946 work Dear Fatherland, Rest Quietly: A Report on the Collapse of Hitler's "Thousand Years," pithily quoted an American major: "The Germans act as though the Nazis were a strange race of Eskimos who came down from the North Pole and somehow invaded Germany."[118] Delbert Clark, for a time head of the New York Times office in Berlin and in equal parts outraged by German irresponsibility and Allied indifference to serious denazification, wrote passionately about "the blind unregeneracy of the German adult."[119]

To the exasperation, especially, of Jewish survivors and occupiers, most Germans denied having been antisemitic as vociferously, if not more so, than they disclaimed their Nazi allegiances. A sarcastic Julius Posener, a German-Jewish refugee who had returned to Germany with the British forces, remarked, "If 'Judenverfolgung' means to have endorsed the 'Final Solution' in Poland or even to have actively participated in it, then indeed the overwhelming majority of the population is entitled to say that they were against it."[120] The Soviet-licensed Berliner Zeitung bitingly remarked about the Nuremberg trials:

Having now heard the testimony of more than half of the defendants, one could get the impression from their words that the inmates of the concentration camp had themselves carried out the selections for the gas chambers, ordered themselves to march into the chambers, themselves turned on the gas and obediently choked to death, or had in Belsen beaten and bestially mistreated themselves, . . . and shot themselves. All these villainous organizers of mass extermination claim to not have been there at all, in fact they were practically benefactors of the inmates.[121]

As Friedrich Wolf, just returned from his Moscow exile, supposedly remarked, the Germans in Berlin were "messed up, self-righteous and incorrigible."[122]

If the Nazis were held accountable, it was generally for losing and leaving the poor Germans to the dubious ministrations of the Allies. German POWs repeatedly tried to convince their astonished interrogators that they had been fighting the wrong enemy, and Berliners seemed genuinely insulted that the Americans were unwilling to join forces with them against the Soviets who had ravaged their city.[123] Intelligence reports clearly indicated that all propaganda efforts to instill a sense of collective German guilt had fallen flat, Byron Price's report to the president unambiguously concluded in December 1945.[124]

"Poor Germany": Discourses of Victimization

The discourse of victimization—the language of sacrifice and injury (*Opfer*)—pervaded and ranged across the political spectrum. It encompassed—in different ways—persecuted anti-Nazis, resisters, and Jews officially registered as "victims of fascism" as well as ordinary Germans.[125] In Berlin, celebrations of a resuscitated city alternated with images of destruction and also, it should be recognized, evidence of Nazi horrors, including clear references to, and eyewitness accounts of, the "bestial extermination" of six million Jews. Photographs of the "death mills" taken in the liberated camps appeared in the early editions of the *Neue Berliner Illustrierte*, and with the beginning of the Nuremberg tribunal and the Auschwitz/Belsen trials conducted by the British Military Government, in fall 1945, the daily papers in all four sectors prominently reported Nazi atrocities on their front pages.[126] Memorialization also proceeded apace, although on a separate track from the everyday life of either the western occupiers or the defeated Germans and generally sponsored by communist dominated organizations of "victims of fascism." These commemorations culminated in a mass demonstration on—and not until—September

22, 1946, in the Lustgarten off Unter den Linden, under the banner of "Honoring the Dead, Calling the Living to Duty."

At the same time, Germans collectively understood themselves as victims—first of the Nazi regime that had lured them into war, and then of the bombings, expulsions, harsh denazification, and ruined society that were the results of defeat. All accounts of Berlin in the immediate postwar period lay out some version of these dualistic narratives of victimization, survival, and guilt. In one variant, the city was thoroughly defeated, hungry, cold, sick, demoralized, and in the grip of what seemed to be a mass clinical depression. In another, Berliners were plucky survivors, recovering from a life "of bowed heads—looking for cigarette butts" (as the American military paper *Stars and Stripes* unkindly put it).[127] These competing but also complementary renditions of defeat's reality continually played out in the Berlin press and in official pronouncements, which, depending on the occasion, reinforced both stories. The *Neue Berliner Illustrierte* adorned its early issues in fall 1945 with exhortations to revival— "Despite everything. The will to life and to work"—as well as dramatic photographs of ruins, captioned as "the legacy with which we must begin again."[128] Accounts of Germany's fate that seemed to champion Berliners' will to survive simultaneously reinforced the pervasive mood of self-pity, which allowed for little insight into, or even memory about, Germany's very recent past. Just as the city landscape itself was marked by theatrical contrasts between the utterly destroyed and the eerily intact, the story of "Berlin is coming back" and the swift restoration of municipal services, civic order and, cultural life—often told by city authorities, occupiers, and reemerging elites—contrasted sharply with powerful popular perceptions of ruin, misery, disorder, and degradation of moral and social life.

Depending on their assigned tasks and political orientation, American occupiers also presented sharply divergent interpretations of the German mood. Official reports by occupiers and German authorities stressed the indomitable spirit and never quite extirpated sarcastic humor of the metropolis—its struggling but spirited theater, cinema, press, cabarets, and of course its black market. The sometimes still irrepressible Berliner *Schnauze* (cynical wit) lamented, with ironic reference to the discredited national anthem, "Germany, Germany, without everything [*ohne alles*], without butter, without fat, and the little bit of marmalade is eaten up by the occupiers."[129] Other accounts—often by women whose housecleaning efforts as *Trümmerfrauen* were key to that process of revival—related bitter experiences of rape, lack of fuel and food, suicide, and disease, such as dysentery, typhus, typhoid, and diphtheria, which particularly claimed children as its victims.[130] The antifascist Italian film director Roberto Rossellini was so struck by the sight of Berliners plodding through the ruins and cutting up dead horses on the street for meat that his planned documentary on Hitler's vanquished capital morphed into his celebrated meditation on the grim plight of Berliners defeated by the murderous and self-destructive degradation of the Third Reich. In *Germania Anno Zero*, a thirteen-year-old boy, as old as the Reich, falls prey to the degenerate seductions of youth gangs, black market dealings, and older homosexuals. In a desperate amoral act, signaling his inability to imagine a future beyond the ruins, he poisons his invalid father and then jumps from a jagged roof in an apparent suicide.[131]

Despite such contrasting depictions of postwar Germans' plight, virtually all occupiers would have agreed with diplomat Price's judgment about Germans' apparent immunity to any sentiments of collective guilt.[132] They differed, however, in their evaluation of how damaging these attitudes were to the efficacy of the occupation. Intelligence and psychological warfare officers dedicated to denazification, including many émigrés (attached to the OSS, Office of Strategic Services, and OWI, Office of Wartime Information), tended to focus on the stubborn unregeneracy of the defeated Germans. Postwar Military Government officials (and Price himself), however, aimed to circumvent the stringent regulations of JCS (Joint Chiefs of Staff) directive 1067, originally formulated in 1944 in the context of Treasury Secretary Morgenthau's "Program to Prevent Germany from Starting a World War III" and his "policy of anti-German revenge and an acceptance of an assumption of German collective guilt."[133] The latter group, many of them practical-minded engineers or businessmen, were determined to get the country moving again and above all assure that Germany would not long be dependent on the Allies to fund necessities, such as food imports.[134]

Sullen, dazed, and depressed, Berliners showed little enthusiasm for their occupiers but also engaged in no active resistance. Feeding the image of Germans as victims was their remarkable acquiescence to defeat. Americans were surprised to find themselves facing a docile population, in what appeared to be, especially outside the devastated urban centers, a "nice, clean, pretty country, with well-built homes and decent bathrooms."[135] In confusing counterpoint to their fierce reputation, Germans seemed a more well-ordered species of American, less alien, for example, than the French, who, the GIs griped, smelled of garlic and whose more recalcitrant women had hairy legs. Certainly, the defeated Germans were more appealing than the traumatized, unruly, and still displaced Jewish survivors. During the war, this German passion for order had been explained as a symptom of aggression and paranoia. In his pop psychoanalysis of the enemy, *Is Germany Incurable?* the psychiatrist Richard Brickner (working with, among others, Margaret Mead) had diagnosed women's "intense pride in dust-free curtains, vast stores of neatly stacked bed-linen, gleaming silverware and an almost surgical cleanliness of pot and pan" as "no mere matter of the crumbless table and the well-polished floor, but rather a moral duty, a furious insatiable pursuit of a culprit, personified as Disorder, carried out with fanatical energy."[136] After the war, this compulsive orderliness was a source of much sarcastic amusement for American journalists who opined:

> Discipline seems to be something with which German babies are born. If OMGUS issued an order that German babies were not to cry between the hours of 5 P.M. and 8 A.M., German babies would probably stop crying between those hours. And if some of them did not, it is more than likely that their mothers would bring them to the American authorities as offenders.[137]

Careful observers were suspicious of this superficial acquiescence. "It would be a great mistake to assume that German people love us, or are inclined to turn to American ways," cautioned Price's report to President Truman.[138] Even GIs, who, expecting to find Nazi monsters, were pleasantly surprised by the friendly attentions of the Fräuleins, were—at least at first—vaguely disgusted by German obsequiousness: "Now these same civilians," who would have beaten him had he been captured weeks earlier, one soldier told *Newsweek* as the war ended, "are very meek and humble. They give us the story that they don't like Hitler—never did—and are glad that we have come. Yet they raise a hell of a howl when we take over their houses."[139]

Indeed, it is hard to overstress the degree of frustration, contempt, and pessimism expressed by most antifascist Allied observers about Germans' willingness to confront the past or build a democratic future. These observers' frustration and anxiety was only exacerbated, as Arendt had noted, by the recognition that Germans had suffered genuine losses, albeit a suffering that would neither acknowledge its source nor the suffering of others. A major symptom of this "whipped" and "beaten" state, as the next chapter details, was the inability or unwillingness to bear children—as reflected in high abortion numbers and low birthrates. Berliners were described as listless and apathetic; they were dully, sullenly, willing to clean up and rebuild, to "look forward," but neither insightful into the root causes of their misery nor remorseful about their own agency or responsibility.[140]

Reporters had trouble sorting out their confused impressions; the barbarian warriors were suddenly replaced by sullen civilians or smiling Fräuleins. Moonscapes of urban destruction with people living "like troglodytes in cellars" coexisted with the still calm and bucolic towns and villages. A *Time* reporter told his readers that "correspondents at last inside Germany were flabbergasted by the kaleidoscope of contrasts: war and peace, ruin and feudal pomp, a fantastic blend of the modern and the medieval. Where the tide of war engulfed it, the German state was disintegrating into chaos. Elsewhere it was incredibly stable."[141]

Notwithstanding such early perceptions and later warnings, however, this very perception of Germans as orderly and obedient also made them attractive and unthreatening. This was especially true of course of the omnipresent Fräuleins who managed—even in Berlin, where the havoc of defeat had been more extreme than in the western zones occupied by the United States—to appear simultaneously needy and relatively unravaged, a combination that was apparently irresistible to their occupiers.[142] Some Americans in Military Government may have been unmoved by German "whining," but, in the face of a destroyed city populated mostly by women and refugees from the Red Army's advance in the East, they found it difficult to maintain their stern stance. As the thoughtful Captain Maginnis confessed in his *Military Government Journal*:

> I could sit in my office and say with conviction that these Germans, who had caused so much harm and destruction in the world, had some suffering coming to them but out here in the Grunewald, talking with people individually, I was saddened by their plight. It was the difference between generalizing on the faceless crowd and looking into one human face.[143]

Berlin's lively press, regardless of sector or political orientation, consistently shaped and reflected the focus on German victimization as well as questions about its legitimacy. "Too much or too little, should the newspapers cover this?" the *Berliner Zeitung* asked its readers in June 1945 about news of concentration camps and Nazi crimes.[144] There certainly had been wide coverage, with numerous photos published of the death camps and the documentary *Death Mills* playing in Berlin cinemas. But, just weeks after the collapse of the Third Reich, a major daily in the Soviet zone published (among others) responses that invoked "poor Germany":

> We have taken on a difficult legacy and must make good again what these criminals [the Nazis] have done. For that, however, we must look forward; only then we can rebuild, and not, if we look back on ugly past times.

In a rhetoric more commonly associated with the 1980s and 90s, readers called for a "*Schlussstrich*" (concluding line) to discussion of the Nazi era.[145] Despite all his sympathy, Captain Maginnis observed critically in his diary in 1945:

> The Germans in Berlin . . . were on very short rations, had only what shelter they could find . . . and looked beaten physically and in spirit. But what they were going through as they toiled, clearing up bricks and

rubble, did not compare with the hell of Belsen and Buchenwald. Still, I doubted that they knew that.[146]

By late February 1946, Maginnis's tone had changed somewhat. Throughout his assignment, he had worried that "Berlin was creaking in every joint—and each creak threatened to be the last." But as he prepared to leave Berlin, he proudly listed the occupation's formidable accomplishments on his watch: an adequate and unpolluted water supply; the limited but reliable five million kilowatts of electricity available daily; gas production at 75 percent capacity; waterproofing and repair on some thirty thousand housing units; the inoculation of the entire population against typhoid and all children against diphtheria; a functioning if not generous rationing system; the reopening of newspapers, magazines, opera, symphony, theaters, and cinemas; the purging of "died in the wool" Nazis from important positions; and, finally, a fourteen thousand-strong police force, recently armed and able to maintain order.[147] Berlin was regaining some of its traditional spirit; women in fur coats paraded on the Ku'damm, and he even dared to hope that the intensifying split of the city into East and West might provoke a beneficial competition to treat the city well. His task, he felt, was done.[148]

There were, however, plenty of anxious critics who feared that American eagerness to get the job done and bring the troops home endangered the denazification project and left Germany open both to fascist revival and Communist takeover. Those bitter over the retreat from denazification darkly predicted that the United States had created a "Frankenstein's monster" by encouraging the revival of German industry and allowing "friends of Hitler" to remain in power. Once the occupation ended, they warned, East and West would reunite, and "Tanks and guns will sprout behind every blank factory wall, and once more an army, mysteriously trained and equipped, will be ready to follow the new Führer when he appears."[149] Many were despondent about the possibility of creating a nonaggressive democratic Germany, convinced that the chances for serious denazification had been bungled by incompetence, laziness, false sympathy for the whining Germans, and overeagerness to spare the American taxpayer by reconstructing a self-sufficient German economy. Above all, doubters bemoaned a peculiarly American combination of anticommunism and isolationist unwillingness to pay the costs and spend the time required for true democratization. "It was," complained one journalist, "as if we had opened a huge school for incorrigibles and then withdrawn the teachers." The Americans, British intelligence officer Noel Annan lamented, were so eager to go home that "they did not give a damn which Germans were elected to govern, so long as they were not notorious Nazis"[150] The Military Government treated the occupation as they would a "great flood on the Mississippi," a technical problem to be solved by engineering, not politics, a disillusioned policy adviser wrote. Already by late 1945, some Americans were proclaiming "Our Failure in Germany" and criticizing the rapid turn away from the JCS 1067 program of denazi-fication, decartelization, and demilitarization, and toward an "accelerat-ing process of MG's self-liquidation." By the middle of November, Ger-mans had gained authority on local city and county levels; Jews, German antifascists, and Jewish and leftist anti-Nazis in Military Government watched apprehensively as homesick Americans "pile[d] aboard the homeward-bound planes at Tempelhof or Frankfurt."[151]

Soldiers collected their service points and headed home or, less fortu-nately, were reassigned to the Pacific. The low salaries in Military Govern-ment made it difficult to attract competent experts, especially to a per-ceived hardship station like Berlin. Even Eisenhower himself preferred to stay at headquarters in Frankfurt, where he did not have to deal with the Russians. *New York Times* correspondent Drew Middleton—who would change his tune considerably in 1948—remembered "Berlin as it was in the winter of 1945–46: a combination of garrison town, wide-open min-ing camp, espionage center sprawled across acre after acre of dark and frozen desolation. The soldiers of four nations brawled in the streets. Shots sounded in the night. Dives catering to raw sex, and for those so inclined, every perversion flourished."[152]

Others, less focused on denazification than stabilization, were more optimistic. Reflecting the triumph of an occupation policy in which the commitment to Cold War reconstruction and stability trumped the search for justice and retribution, special adviser Murphy concluded:

> Despite all the handicaps imposed upon OMGUS, Americans never-theless managed in a short time to bring order out of chaos in our zone. This is all the more remarkable when it is recalled that not one of our top-ranking American officers could speak German. . . . But the docility of the Germans and their eagerness to get back to work were a great help to us, and so was the comparatively dispassionate attitude of our people toward their recent enemies. Geography had saved the United States from such Nazi atrocities as the massacres in Russia, the aerial bombardments in Britain, and the imposition of forced labor upon French men and women. Americans had relatively few bitter memories and so could approach the reconstruction of our zone in a businesslike manner.[153]

In fact, Military Government officers who could speak German were often émigrés and precisely those considered most unlikely to be "dispas-sionate" or purely "businesslike." By the summer of 1946, most of them had returned to their new homes in the United States or had been edged out.[154]

American journalists Andy Rooney and Bud Hutton, self-styled intrepid reporters, determinedly resisted the military brass's plea not to focus on "the superficial picture of the pregnant Fräulein, venereal disease and scandal." They presented the gloomier picture of the American "investment" in Germany: "It is a naked Fräulein sprawled dead on a GI blanket, and it is a black market dollar in Berlin. . . . It is a homeless Jew and a homeless Pole thrusting knives into each other's guts in a dark German street after the American patrol has passed." Yet even they recognized the benefits of stable occupation: "It is food in hungry bellies. It is, after a fashion, peace."[155]

Fig. 2.1. Cover of American novel *The Big Rape*, published 1951.

CHAPTER TWO

Gendered Defeat

RAPE, MOTHERHOOD, AND FRATERNIZATION

> Until that time I had lived so happily with my husband and
> the children. I had four children, the youngest I had to bury
> on May 18, it was 4 months old. Now I am in a desperate
> condition and do not want to have this child under any
> circumstances.
>
> —Request to District Health office, Berlin Neukölln,
> December 1945[1]

> It might under ordinary conditions be called rape, but this
> case comes under the heading of justice.
>
> —Bill Downs, *Newsweek* correspondent, on rape of
> German girl by Soviet POW, April 1945[2]

"ENJOY THE WAR, because the peace will be terrible," the mordant Berlin
wags had warned even as the Red Army drew nearer and the bombings
and casualties, both civilian and military, mounted. Allies and liberated
victims of the Nazis may have approached the "whining" of the vanquished with jaundiced skepticism, but for many Germans the uneasy
peace that relatively quickly emerged was haunted by the chaos, fear, and
violence produced, not by the regime that had catapulted them into war,
but its defeat. Both that *Zusammenbruch* (collapse) and the moves toward reconstruction that would bring "after a fashion, peace" were experienced in gendered terms. On the home front of unconditional surrender,
the effects were inscribed directly and publicly on the bodies of women,
whether they figured as victims of mass rape (most visibly in the Soviet
zone and Berlin), as willing or pragmatic fraternizers (most visibly with
American troops), or as mothers struggling to feed and keep alive their
children (in all zones and sectors).

GERMANS AS VICTIMS: RAPE IN BERLIN

The defeated Reich that the victors encountered in spring 1945 wore a
predominantly female face. German men had been killed, wounded, or

taken prisoner, leaving women to clean the ruins, scrounge for food, and serve the occupiers, often as sexual partners and victims. One Berlin district counted 1,873 women to 1,000 men in August 1945, and the city ratio was 169 to 100.[3] As the Red Army fought its way westward, the retreating Wehrmacht put up an embittered defense, forcing exhausted and in part disbelieving Soviet commanders to continue hard fighting right into the center of destroyed Berlin. By February, the Red Army was only thirty-five miles east of Berlin, and still the Germans would not surrender as they tried to carve out escape routes for themselves to the west and north. Fortified by huge caches of alcohol conveniently left behind by the retreating Germans, reinforced by brutalized Soviet prisoners of war liberated along the way, and enraged by the street-to-street, house-to-house German defense loyally carried out by young boys and old men as well as regular soldiers, the Red Army pushed through East Prussia toward Berlin in what the military historian John Erickson has called "a veritable passion of destructiveness."[4] In a remarkably infelicitous sentence, Erickson concluded: "The fighting drained both sides, though Russian lustiness won through."[5]

After years of remarkable inattention since the 1950s, Red Army rapes became in the early 1990s (provoked in part by the sexual violence associated with the conflicts in former Yugoslavia) the subject of vigorous scholarly and feminist debates on German women's role in the Third Reich. The sixtieth anniversary of war's end—with its new emphasis on public recognition of German suffering, combined with a growing global awareness of rape as a war crime in civil and ethnic conflicts—brought renewed public attention, albeit in a less carefully contextualized manner, to the story of German women's victimization.[6] The numbers reported for these rapes vary wildly, from as few as 20,000 to almost 1 million or even 2 million altogether, as the Red Army pounded westward. A conservative estimate might be about 110,000 women raped, many more than once, of whom up to 10,000 died in the aftermath; others suggest that perhaps one out of every three of about 1.5 million women in Berlin fell victim to Soviet rapes.[7]

Whatever the figures, it is unquestionably the case that mass rapes of civilian German women signaled the end of the war and the defeat of Nazi Germany. Sexual violence was an integral part of the final bitter battle for Berlin from April 24 to May 8, 1945. Norman Naimark concludes in his careful study of the Soviet zone that although "it is highly unlikely that historians will ever know how many German women were raped by Soviet soldiers in the months before and years after the capitulation," there is no doubt that "the taking of Berlin was accompanied by an unrestrained explosion of sexual violence by Soviet soldiers," and that "rape became a part of the social history of the Soviet zone in ways unknown to the Western zones." Moreover, "incidents of rape continued to plague the lives of German women in the Soviet zone at least until the beginning of 1947."[8]

Sexual assaults on German women by Red Army troops had been massively prefigured in Nazi propaganda. Terrifying images of invading Mongol barbarians raping German women were a vital part of the Nazi war machine's feverish (and successful) efforts to bolster morale on the eastern front and keep the home front intact. Nazi propaganda had been relentless in characterizing the Russians as subhuman and animalistic. The threat of a surging Asian flood and marauding "Red Beast" tearing through what was supposedly still a pacific and ordinary German land was used to incite desperate resistance even long after it was clear that the war was fundamentally lost. By the end of the war, most German women had already seen graphic newsreel footage of the bodies of "violated women, battered old people and murdered children." Indeed, the very last newsreel released in 1945 showed a white fence with the desperate message scrawled on it, "Protect our women and children from the Red Beast."[9] Moreover, Germans knew enough of Wehrmacht and SS crimes in the East to have reason to believe that vengeful Russians would commit atrocities and to make plausible the oft-repeated (and explicitly denied) account of Soviet Jewish writer Ilya Ehrenburg's infamous call for Soviet soldiers to seek retribution by raping "flaxen-haired" German women—"they are your prey."[10] Whatever the level of ordinary Germans' detailed knowledge of the systematic extermination of European Jewry, it was no secret that Wehrmacht actions on the eastern (in contrast to the western) front went well beyond the standards of ordinary brutal warfare. German soldiers had been explicitly commanded to liquidate all putative "Bolsheviks," and during their "scorched earth" retreat they laid waste as a matter of policy (not of indiscipline) huge territories of civilian population and massacred entire villages. Again and again in German recollections about what Russian occupiers told them, the vengeful memory the victors summoned was not a parallel violation, that of Germans raping Russian women, but a horror on a different order; it was the image of a German soldier swinging a baby, torn from its mother's arms, against a wall—the mother screams, the baby's brains splatter against the wall, the soldier laughs.[11]

Soviet rapes secured a particularly potent place in postwar memories of victimization because they represented the one instance in which Goebbels's spectacular anti-Bolshevik propaganda turned out to be substantially correct. Millions of Germans were trekking westward in flight from the Red Army, and millions of German soldiers were marched eastward as POWs, but as Berliners—primarily women, children, and elderly—emerged from their cellars during the piercingly beautiful spring of 1945, the Soviets did not kill everyone on sight, deport them to Siberia, or burn down the city.

The musician Karla Höcker reported with genuine surprise, in one of the many diaries composed by women at war's end, that "the Russians, who must hate and fear us, leave the majority of the German civilian population entirely alone—that they don't transport us off in droves!"[12]

In fact, as we have seen, the SMA moved quickly and efficiently to organize municipal government, restore basic services, and nurture a lively political and cultural life. In regard to violence against women, however, the Nazi "horror stories" (Greuelgeschichten) were largely confirmed. Yet official Soviet policy obstinately refused to acknowledge that soldiers who had sworn to be "honorable, brave, disciplined, and alert" and to defend the "motherland manfully, ably, with dignity and honor," would engage in atrocities on anything more than the level of "isolated excesses."[13] Ilya Ehrenburg, having quickly assimilated Stalin's new, more conciliatory line toward compliant Germans, insisted that "the Soviet soldier will not molest a German woman. . . . It is not for booty, not for loot, not for women that he has come to Germany."[14] "Russian soldiers not rape! German swine rape!" a Soviet interrogator bellowed at the actress Hildegard Knef when she was captured after having disguised herself as a soldier in an effort to escape the fate of the female defeated.[15] Clearly, however, that new message did not impress the troops engaged in a costly final battle who had been told that "every farm on the road to Berlin was the den of a fascist beast."[16] Shocked at the continuing affluence of the society they had so determinedly defeated, and at Germany's contrast to their own decimated country, Russian soldiers told their victims, "Russia—my home. Germany—my paradise."[17]

For women huddled in "cellar tribes" as the Battle of Berlin raged around them during the notorious days of mass rape from April 24 to May 8, Goebbels's fevered prophecies about the threat from the Asiatic hordes seemed to be fulfilled. When soldiers with heavy boots, unfamiliar faces (invariably coded as Mongol), and shining flashlights entered a darkened basement shelter, searched for weapons and watches, and then, revolver in hand, commanded the proverbial "Frau Komm," many women felt that they were reenacting a scene in a film they had already seen. Mass rapes therefore confirmed the self-identity of Germans—both the women who were attacked and the men (beaten, dead, wounded, maimed, or in prisoner of war camps) who were unable and/or unwilling to protect them—as both superior to their barbarian vanquishers from the East and as victims of Missbrauch (abuse). The term was ubiquitous when used by women to circumscribe their experience but was also deployed more generally to suggest all the ways in which the German Volk had been woefully abused—by corrupt Nazis, by Hitler, who had reneged on his promises of national renewal and led them into a war that could not be won, by the losses on the front and the Allied bombing raids, and then by defeat, occupation, and a denazification that was generally perceived as arbitrary and unfair.[18]

For German women in 1945—certainly in Berlin and to its east—rape was experienced as a collective event in a situation of general crisis, part of the apocalyptic days of Berlin's fall. Rape confirmed their expectations and reinforcing preexisting convictions of cultural superiority; it came as just one more (sometimes the worst, but sometimes not) in a series of horrible deprivations and humiliations of war and defeat: hunger, homelessness, expulsion and displacement, plunder and dismantling of factories, the harsh treatment of German prisoners of war in the Soviet Union, the death or maiming of menfolk, watching one's children die or sicken of disease and malnutrition. The story of rape was told as part of the narrative of survival in ruined Germany. "Rape had," many noted, "become routine."[19] A certain matter-of-factness (*Sachlichkeit*), in some ways still reminiscent of the pre-Nazi Weimar "new woman," pervades many of these Berlin accounts. Margaret Boveri, a journalist who had continued working throughout the Nazi years, was laconic about the Soviet "liberators" in her "Survival Diary" for May 6–8, 1945:

> Rode [on her bicycle] a ways with a nice bedraggled girl . . . imprisoned by Russians for 14 days, had been raped but well fed." . . . May 8, 1945. "The usual rapes—a neighbor who resisted was shot. . . . Mrs Krauss was not raped. She insists that Russians don't touch women who wear glasses. Like to know if that is true . . . the troops were pretty drunk but did distinguish between old and young which is already progress.[20]

Others accepted their fate as an inevitable, to-be-expected consequence of defeat, almost like a natural disaster that could not be changed and must simply be survived: "In those days I endured the Russians as I would a thunderstorm."[21]

Anne-Marie Durand-Wever, the physician who feared the revenge that would descend on "poor Germany" as its crimes were uncovered, also kept her diary notes on rape stoic and pragmatic. After "gruesome" nights in her cellar she returned to work in a first aid station; she hastened to test women and girls for venereal disease and to ferret out gynecological instruments, since "I guess we'll have to do abortions." Durand-Wever was sure that "our" soldiers had comported themselves no differently, but on May 23 she made a sad note about her own daughter: "This afternoon Annemie was here with her child. Four Russians. Swab inconclusive. In any case, sulfa medication (Albucid). For this one tends one's child!" Still in February 1946, she portrayed a "loathsome" situation of continuing rapes, venereal disease, unwanted pregnancies, and mass abortions.[22]

SURVIVING AND NARRATING RAPE

During these "dark times" of conquest and occupation, women, so often seen by both Germans and occupiers as innocent victims (of rape and war in general) or villains (as manipulative fraternizers), also presented themselves as resourceful agents. Some unknown but not insignificant number committed suicide to escape, or in reaction to, such violations. Many more, now "standing alone," as historian Elizabeth Heineman has described them, prioritized survival and their role as caretakers and providers. They scrounged and bartered for food and shelter, and negotiated protection for their children and themselves with occupation soldiers.[23] In diaries composed at the time as well as in reworked diaries, memoirs, and oral histories recorded years later, women reported extremely diverse experiences of what they variously named as rape, coercion, violation, prostitution, or abuse. Some women and young girls were brutally gang-raped in public with a line of soldiers waiting for their turn. In some cases, women's bodies were slit open from stomach to anus, or they were killed afterward. Others were forced to have sex alone in a room with a lonely young soldier for whom they occasionally even developed ambivalent feelings of hate, pity, and warmth. Some consciously offered themselves in exchange for protecting a daughter or made deliberate decisions to take up with an occupier—preferably an officer with power—to shield themselves from others and to garner privileges. And of course there were also moments of genuine affection and desire. Women recorded brutality but also, at times, their own sense of confusion about the fine lines between rape, prostitution, and consensual (albeit generally instrumental) sex.

Indeed, the more one looks at the diaries, memoirs, and novels of the postwar years, rape stories are omnipresent, told matter-of-factly, told as tragedy, told with ironic humor and flourish. In a recurring trope, women are gathered at water pumps in bombed-out streets, exchanging "war stories" with a certain bravado. Almost gleefully they reveal their stratagems to trick Russians as gullible as they were brutal: masquerading as men or ugly old women disguised by layers of clothing or faces smeared with dirt and ash, pretending to have typhus or venereal disease. But they also marvel at soldiers' apparently indiscriminate "taste" in women, the fact that they seemed to prefer fat ladies, or their astounding sexual prowess even when utterly inebriated. In both official affidavits and more private accounts, women mobilized a wide range of direct and indirect vocabulary—*Schändung* (violation), *Vergewaltigung* (rape), *Übergriff* (encroachment), *Überfall* (attack)—to denote the "it" (*es*) that had been endured.[24] Sometimes they recounted stories of surprising escape or reprieve; often they resorted to generalities and passive voice (the awful scenes went on all night, we all had to submit), or referred specifically to the ghastly experiences of neighbors, mothers, and sisters that they themselves had supposedly been spared. "But many fewer escaped than was later claimed," journalist Curt Riess asserted a few years later.[25]

In a compelling diary edited and published by a popular German writer in the 1950s, an anonymous "woman in Berlin"—recently identified as Marta Hillers, another young journalist who had continued to work in the Third Reich, occasionally composing minor propaganda texts for the Nazis—explained her reaction after a series of brutal rapes during the first chaotic week of April–May 1945:

> Then I say loudly damn it! and make a decision. It is perfectly clear. I need a wolf here who will keep the wolves away from me. An officer, as high as possible, Kommandant, General, whatever I can get. For what do I have my spirit and my little knowledge of foreign languages? As soon as I could walk again I took my pail and crept onto the street. Wandered up and down . . . practiced the sentences with which I could approach an officer; wondered if I didn't look too green and wretched to be attractive. Felt physically better again now that I was doing something, planning and wanting, no longer just dumb booty.[26]

Such unsentimental directness in reporting and dealing with sexual assaults or efforts to elude them was quite typical. Riess, a Berlin Jew who had come back with deeply "mixed feelings" was both horrified and cynical: "But it was strange, when the horrific had happened five or six times, it was no longer so horrific. That which one had thought one could not survive, was survived by many twenty—or thirty times."[27] Another younger Berlin Jew, who had returned from Auschwitz, recorded with bittersweet amusement an exchange between two women in the familiar rough (and quite untranslatable) Berlin dialect that, almost despite himself, he was happy to hear again. Justifying her usurpation of a space on the impossibly overcrowded train they were riding into the city, one loudly announced, "We Berliners had to let the bombs whip around our heads. I sat in a bunker for almost two weeks, was bombed out four times, and the Russians didn't exactly treat me with kid gloves either; in fact they raped me three times if you really want to know." Which pronouncement provoked her equally loudmouthed competitor to an often-reported retort: "She actually seems to be proud that at her age the Russians would still take her."[28]

In a peculiar way, women's apparent *sangfroid* in the face of mass sexual assault became part of the story (and myth) of "Berlin *kommt wieder,*" of the city's irrepressible irreverent spirit. Their self-preserving sexual cynicism can be attributed, at least in part, both to the modernist *Sachlichkeit* of Weimar culture and to the loosened mores of the Nazis' war, including

women's experience of fraternization with foreign laborers either recruited or forced into the war economy. Ironically, as Heineman has observed, a "regime obsessed with racial purity had become the catalyst of
an unprecedented number of relationships between Germans and foreigners."[29] Even more broadly, the fraying of bourgeois morality that had
alarmed cultural conservatives at least since World War I and the Weimar
Republic clearly continued into the Third Reich and the Second World
War, albeit in complex and selective ways—a process recently delineated
by Dagmar Herzog in her provocative study of sexuality during and "after
fascism." The Nazis' war had inevitably and paradoxically led to a loos-
ening of domestic bonds and an eroticization of public life, unevenly pros-
ecuted, sometimes denounced and sometimes accepted by the populace.
Indeed, as Annemarie Tröger already argued in an important 1986 essay,
the dissasociative endurance with which women survived rape as well as
their instrumental fraternizing affairs bore an uncanny resemblance to the
sachliche encounters in the Weimar "new woman" novels of an Irmgard
Keun or Marieluise Fleisser. German women, Tröger contended, had been
trained into a sexual cynicism "freed from love," which served them well
during the war and its aftermath.[30] In the postwar novel Westend, the
main character narrates her rape with precisely the cool, distant tone associated with "new woman" writers: "he carried out the act which he perhaps saw as a kind of self-imposed duty coldly and without interest. She
felt sorry for the man on top of her."[31]

The Russe, whose arrival had been so desperately anticipated by victims
and opponents of Nazism and so dreaded by most Germans, became, in
Berlin, an object not only of terror but of intense fascination and bewilderment for fellow occupiers and occupied alike. In keeping with the images
provided by Nazi propaganda, there was the drunken, primitive "Mongol" who descended on Germany like a vengeful "hungry locust" in an
"orgy of revenge." This slanty-eyed ravager from the Far Eastern steppes
demanded watches, bicycles, and women, had no clue that a flush toilet
was not a sink or a refrigerator, and was astounded that the wurst he
had stored in the tank disappeared when a handle was pulled. He loaded
expensive precision instruments or optical equipment like potato sacks
for transfer to the Soviet Union, only to have them rust on blocked roads
or train tracks.[32] He was accompanied, however, by the cultivated officer
who spoke German, recited Dostoyevsky and Tolstoy, deplored the excesses of his comrades, and could be relied on for protection even as he
eloquently described German war crimes. Germans frequently coun-
terposed these "cultivated" Soviets from European Russia to the equally
if differently fascinating American occupiers, who—in keeping with the
images of American POWs in Nazi newsreels—were categorized as vulgar,
gum-chewing primitives. GI conquests, however, came primarily via ny-

lons and chocolate, rather than rape. "The difference," Berliners quipped, "is that the American and the British ask the girls to dinner and then go to bed with them, while the Russians do it the other way round."[33] Both victors and Germans circulated macabre jokes about the consequences of total war: "About many raped women, it is said, actually they should be grateful to the Russians. Without them they never would have gotten a man anymore."[34]

The Soviets baffled their conquests with their seemingly strange behavior. They assaulted women but were tender and protective toward children and babies. They would brazenly rip a watch off someone's arm or grab a bicycle and then offer a big bear hug, two kisses on the cheeks, and a friendly farewell. Women reported that their attackers could be distracted or even cowed, like a child or puppy, by firm commands, or seemed genuinely convinced that looting was not a crime but proper restitution, and that rape too was merely part of their due. Allies and Germans were especially intrigued by the Soviets' capacity for drink, debauchery, and eye-popping portions of caviar. "We went to Berlin in 1945, thinking only of the Russians as big, jolly, balalaika-playing fellows, who drank prodigious quantities of vodka and liked to wrestle in the drawing room," Commander Frank Howley recalled. The Russians had arrived not only with tanks and deafening cannons (the *Stalinorgel* that figures in so many memoirs) but with horse- and even camel-drawn vehicles; they quaffed gasoline and 4711 cologne in their endless search for alcohol. A Jewish youth remembered his first glimpses of his liberators, both mesmerizing and frightening: "They were dressed in olive-brown, high collar blouses and had rope belts around their waists. Their pants were stuffed into their boots. I had never seen anything like them. If they hadn't been so terrifying, they might have been funny."[35] These contradictory impressions reflected the generally schizoid quality of the Soviet occupation: "By day they put the Germans, both men and women, to work in dismantling commandos, clearing up rubble, removing tank barricades; and by night they terrorized the city," even as some of their own officers were moved to shoot offending soldiers on the spot.[36]

In the end, perhaps, such negative but also confused interpretations of the Russians helped women to distance the horror of their own experience. The narrative of the Russian primitive or exotic curiously absolved him of guilt, as it also absolved women themselves. Such uncivilized, animal-like creatures could not be expected to control themselves, especially when tanked up with alcohol. Nor could women be expected to defend themselves against an elemental force, backed up of course in most cases by rifle or revolver. As one woman remembered, after the initial panic about a fate worse than death, "It became clear to me that a rape, as awful as it might be, had nothing to do with loss of honor."[37] Not a few women favorably compared Russian officers to contemptible, defeated German men who either abetted the women's humiliation or sought to punish them for it, sometimes to the point of killing victims to preserve that honor. Pathetic parodies of the manly Teutonic genus valorized by the SS, they were preoccupied with saving their own skin and not above pressuring women to submit, in order not to endanger themselves—rape, after all, was a less devastating fate than Siberia or getting shot. The narrator of *A Woman in Berlin* says of the Soviet officer she has finally cornered into her bed, hoping that he will fend off rivals:

> On the other hand, I do like the Major, I like him the more as a person, the less he wants from me as a man. And he won't want a lot, I can feel that. His face is pale, his wounded knee gives him trouble. Probably he is searching for human, womanly companionship more than the purely sexual. And that I give him freely, even gladly. Because among all the male creatures of the last several days he is the most tolerable man and human being.[38]

In American war correspondent James W. Burke's 1951 potboiler *The Big Rape*, his heroine Lilo is determined not to have "painstakingly preserved her life thus far to foolishly lay it down at the altar of such a spurious and pretentious virtue." She characterizes her (temporary) protector, Captain Pavel Ivanov, in terms remarkably similar to those used by the diarist in *A Woman in Berlin*: he "was all that she had bargained for. He was kind, he was considerate, he was gallant. And he safeguarded her from wanton attack."[39] In a later interview, a woman remembered, "we never could quite make sense of the Russians, sometimes they were mild-mannered, sometimes sadistic."[40]

The turn-of-the-millennium explosion of memory (and memory politics) about German suffering during and after the war relies in part on the nagging sense that this victimization was never adequately expressed or recognized, and always overshadowed in both West and East Germany by the demand for a recognition of collective guilt for Germany's crimes. This insistence on what historians have called "the silence that never was" certainly applies to popular perceptions that German women's massive and collective experience of sexual assault was quickly and profoundly silenced or tabooized. It is indeed the case that the ubiquitous stories of rape were—not denied—but rather downplayed or "normalized" by virtually everyone, including, as we have seen, the victims themselves. Depending on who was talking, rapes were presented as the inevitable by-product of a vicious war, or, in the "antifascist" narrative, as understandable retribution or exaggerated anticommunist propaganda.[41] In no way, however, did these framings mean that rape stories were denied or silenced.

MANAGING RAPE: MEDICAL AND POLITICAL RESPONSES

On the contrary, in the direct aftermath of the war, there was no lack of speech or documentation about rape. If anything, we find a plethora of talk in many different voices and venues, although it is indeed difficult to measure those expressions against our current expectations of treating and "working through" trauma (an issue that will trouble us in the discussion of Jewish survivors as well). Evidence of rape appears in detailed police and medical reports, statements by Communist Party, SMA, and then U.S. authorities, and in diaries and memoirs, as well as in the affidavits women presented to district health offices that authorized terminations of pregnancies resulting from rape. Most concretely, the communist and Soviet-dominated Magistrat quickly recognized the situation and particularly its public health consequences by authorizing a moratorium on the long-standing and controversial antiabortion paragraph 218 of the penal code (as well as by instituting stringent venereal disease surveillance and treatment). Already on May 23, 1945, Ferdinand Sauerbruch, the famed surgeon installed as head of the Berlin Health Department (after the Soviet offer of a bottle of vodka had persuaded the suspicious and politically compromised doctor to accept the position), summoned public health doctors (*Amtsärzte*) to a meeting discussing the provision of abortions. The recorded minutes are more abbreviated than the obviously contentious discussion in which "the opinions of the doctors present were very polarized," but the result of several sessions that summer was the introduction of a medical indication for abortion that clearly included "social" and "ethical" (the shorthand for rape) considerations. In September, abortion was still the first item on the agenda of Health Department meetings.[42] The quick turn to discussions of abortion conveniently shifted the crisis of mass rape from one of violent sexual assault by a "liberating" army into a public social and health problem. Yet it was in the context of this medicalized response that women were able to document their experience as well as receive safe abortions and treatment for venereal disease—and, moreover, that much of the clearest historical record was produced. Local Berlin health officials initiated the liberalized abortion policy despite some grumbling on the part of doctors and explicit but irrelevant protest from Walter Ulbricht, the new KPD (Communist Party) leader. Rehearsing the party's pre-Nazi position, veteran German communists argued that given the drastic circumstances Berlin's working women were "owed the right to abortion." To the shock of the resurfacing comrades who nonetheless reluctantly accepted party discipline, Ulbricht not only remained unmoved by pleas for a crackdown on Red Army depredations but refused even to consider allowing termination of resulting pregnancies: "The gentlemen doctors should be reminded to exercise a bit of restraint in this matter," he tersely remarked. But the very statement shows how widespread the practice already was.[43]

Physicians' ad hoc decision to suspend paragraph 218 and perform abortions on raped women was quickly institutionalized by a highly organized medical and social hygiene system that had never really broken down, at least in the cities. Indeed, despite the strict restrictions on voluntary abortions, secret wartime Nazi directives had permitted—or coerced—abortions on female foreign workers and women defined as prostitutes and non-"Aryans," as well as on the growing number of German women who became pregnant, via consensual sex or rape, by foreign workers or prisoners of war. Ministry of Interior plans already in place for the establishment "in large cities [of] special wards for the care of such women" and for the elimination of their unwanted Mongol or Slav offspring were in fact sanctioned by all the occupiers after the German defeat. In the summer of 1945 a young Wehrmacht surgeon just released from an American POW camp in France and ordered to work for no pay in a Berlin hospital noted in his diary:

> There is much medical work on the gynecological ward. On orders of the British and American authorities all pregnancies which can be proven to have resulted from rape (mostly by Russians) are to be terminated. There are also many illegal abortions by quacks which are then admitted infected into the hospital.[44]

Drawing on a mixed legacy of Weimar and National Socialist maternalist population policy, as well as Nazi racial discourses and the legal protection of occupation policy, women by the thousands related their rape stories in very specific terms to medical commissions attached to district health offices, which then sanctioned abortions right up to the very last months of pregnancy.[45] Matter-of-factly and pragmatically they asserted their right to terminate pregnancies that were not socially, economically, or medically viable—in the name of saving the family or themselves and because, as another woman later recalled, "It was irresponsible that in this terrible time of need I would put another child into the world."[46] Invoking this Weimar-inflected discourse of social (not moral or racial) emergency, one woman wrote to the Neukölln district health office, "I am pregnant due to rape by a Russian on April 27, 1945. I request removal of the fetus since I already have an illegitimate child and live with my parents who themselves still have small children." A woman who had been robbed of her bicycle and raped wrote on November 9, 1945, "Since I am single, my mother dead for 15 years, my father a half-Jew from whom I have had no sign of life for six years, it is impossible for me to set a child into the world under these conditions." Another affidavit, submitted on August 6, 1945, simply stated, "I have three children aged five to eleven years. My husband as a former soldier is not yet back. I have been bombed out twice, fled here in January from West Prussia and now request most cordially that I be helped in preventing this latest disaster for me and my family."

Along with the conviction of social necessity, women also deployed the vocabulary of Nazi racial hygiene, so ingrained into public discourse over the past twelve years. They frequently identified perpetrators among the western victors as Negro if American or North African if French. And since the vast majority of accusations in Berlin were directed against Soviets, women availed themselves of the rich store of Nazi racial imagery of the barbarian from the East, especially the Mongol associated with the cruel frenzy of Genghis Khan. In a typical petition from July 24, 1945, a woman wrote, "I hereby certify that at the end of April this year during the Russian march into Berlin I was raped in a loathsome way by two Red Army soldiers of Mongol/Asiatic type." Even the young German-Jewish fugitive Inge Deutschkron, who had initially been so happy to greet the Soviets, described her first "Russian" as small, with crooked legs and "a typical mongolian face with almond eyes and high cheekbones, clad in a dirty uniform with his cap perched lopsided on his head."[47]

Many petitions freely mixed the social-necessity discourse (familiar from Weimar debates over abortion reform) and the racial stereotypes (popularized by the Nazis) with threats of suicide or descriptions of serious physical ailments that might have legitimated a medical indication under any regime. A letter from August 20, 1945:

On the way to work on the second Easter holiday I was raped by a Mongol. The abuse can be seen on my body. Despite strong resistance, my strength failed me and I had to let everything evil come over me. Now I am pregnant by this person, can only think about this with disgust and ask that I be helped. Since I would not even consider carrying this child to term, both my children would lose their mother. With kind greetings.[48]

The frequent references to the need to care for existing children testify to the linking of sex, sexual violence, and motherhood in stories of victimization and survival. In sociologist Hilde Thurnwald's detailed 1946 survey of family life in immediate postwar Berlin, all the women in her core sample of two hundred families insisted that this was not the moment to bear children, although five women in the group were (unhappily) pregnant. This maternal pessimism was, Thurnwald stressed, quite a turnaround, even from the war years under National Socialism, when men on the home front earned well and women whose husbands were at the front received generous allowances and were exempted from wage labor.[49] Victor Gollancz, the maverick British-Jewish publisher so sympathetic to Germans' plight, spoke for many when he foregrounded the reluctance to reproduce as a symptom of the misery in *Darkest Germany*: "The wish to have a child is waning. Instead of desiring a new child, many women are now succumbing to a new despondency, thus the diagnosis of a new pregnancy often arouses fits of despair."[50] The general postwar panic about motherhood among Germans stood in dramatic contrast to the simultaneous "baby boom" among Jewish survivors that we will encounter in further chapters.

The desire to avoid childbirth, regardless of whether pregnancy had resulted from rape, reflected the shocked confusion and depression that gripped many Germans after a defeat that they knew was coming and yet had still not fully expected. It was also part of women's efforts, during a period of extreme shock and privation, to save the children they already had, even at the price of submitting to sexual violation and exploitation: "My heart was pounding but I believe my soul was dead. He ripped open the door, placed the revolver on the night table, and lay down beside me in bed. The anxiety about my sleeping child let me endure everything."[51] Women reported offering themselves in order to protect their young daughters: "They wanted to take my then 10 year old girl. What mother would have done such a thing? So I could only sacrifice (*opfer*) myself instead."[52] Such tales clearly expressed the double meaning of the term *Opfer*, so pervasive a reference in German wartime and postwar rhetoric, by claiming the negative connotation of "victim" but also a more positive, redeeming, and even heroic sense of sacrifice. In another oft-repeated but somewhat different scenario, women recounted trying to take advantage of the Soviet troops' kindness to children by clutching a young child to their body, or taking children along wherever they went. In one version, a mother remembered that she pinched her baby in the behind to make him cry piteously, said the child was very ill, and the soldiers let her go.[53]

Rape as Revenge and Result

At the same time, German women expressed their inchoate anxiety about retribution for Nazi crimes in the East when they explicitly interpreted rape as vengeance, or at least as an unsurprising result of defeat. The Russians, women recollected, called, "*Dawai, Dawai* [Get going]. Your man wanted war, then German women want what we want."[54] Jewish Red Army soldiers in particular spoke about the German invasion and how Nazis had brutalized the Russian people, raping Russian women and killing hundreds of thousands of men: "Their homeland had been invaded, raped and looted by Germans and they were wild for revenge."[55]

Germans feared, and complained about, rapes and pillage by DPs as well as Soviet troops, but the culprits were generally identified as non-Jewish Eastern European former slave laborers. Significantly, there is very little record of this form of bodily revenge by Jewish survivors or soldiers. Despite the widespread acknowledgment among occupiers and occupied alike that for conquerors the spoils of war generally included access to women's bodies, Meyer Levin, an American Jewish war correspondent, was among the very few reporters to reflect seriously on the meaning of rape in wartime and defeat. He detected feelings of lust and revenge that overcame not only Soviet but also Jewish soldiers in all Allied armies when they saw the surreal comfort in which especially nonurban Germans were still living: "Why, the standard of comfort in a German village seemed beyond that in an American town. Why, any house you burst into had closets crammed with linen and good clothes, the loot of Europe and gadgets, electric blankets, excellent radios, heaters, irons, eiderdowns, silverware, all the comforts. . . . They had plenty, they had a good life." Partly, this rage was exorcised by looting, he mused, but there was something more: "Like all men, we wondered about ourselves—how far would we go, in war? of what were we capable?" He sensed something more primordial: "the taking of the enemy into and upon oneself, the devouring of the enemy so that one might have his strength and the symbolic way of devouring the enemy was through his fetish—carrying his weapons, wearing his scalp, taking his women. All this was a way of obliterating the enemy and at the same time absorbing his power, his strength." In his account of his journey across devastated liberated Europe, Levin admitted to tormented fantasies about raping "blond German" women, fantasies, however, that wilted in the face of the women's abject surrender. He and a buddy steered their U.S. Army jeep, imagining their revenge: "the only thing to do was to throw them down, tear them apart," on "a wooded stretch of road" with "little traffic, and a lone girl on foot or on a bicycle." But when they finally encountered the perfect victim, alone on a bike "young, good looking and sullen . . . her presence . . . a definitive challenge," they realized that while her fear was "exciting. . . . It wasn't in us."[56]

In the early Yiddish edition of his memoir *Night*, Elie Wiesel referred to early nights of rape and plunder by liberated Buchenwald survivors: "Early the next day Jewish boys ran off to Weimar to steal clothing and potatoes. And to rape German girls" (*un tsu fargvaldikn daytshe shikses*). But the passage is not central to his account and is revised and then expurgated in later editions.[57] Israeli novelist Hanoch Bartov's autobiographical novel about his service in the British Army's Jewish Brigade from Palestine contains a riveting description of his unit's efforts to contain and come to terms with the rapacious actions of some of their comrades while also insisting on understanding and protecting the violators. For him too, "even the "unwritten law of the Red Army," granting a twenty-four-hour free zone for acts of vengeance, could not "help my sick heart. I could not shed innocent blood, I would never know peace."[58]

There was little sympathy to be found among Jewish survivors for the women victimized by the Red Army, but also little appetite for joining in. Larry (Lothar) Orbach recalled with bitter satisfaction his trip home to Berlin from Auschwitz and Buchenwald after a three-week quarantine for typhus:

> I wore the dark blue Eisenhower jacket the Americans had given me on which I had sewn my number, B.9761, and my yellow prison triangle on the lapel pocket so that any Nazis I might meet could appreciate the dramatic reversal in our relationship. The other travelers tried to avert their eyes from me, but they could not. Beyond the trauma, they were now compelled to confront the living reminder of the monstrous horror they had so long ignored, or from which they had at least managed to blind themselves. . . . As the train chugged on under the night sky, a drunken Russian soldier raped a young German girl in full view of everyone. No one raised a hand to help her; there was no sound but her screams. So much for the Master Race, who, in Auschwitz, I had watched slam the head of a Jewish baby into the wall of a shower room. The baby had died instantly, his brain protruding and his blood spurting; they had laughed, full of triumph and swagger. Now they were too meek even to protect one of their own children. Nor did I intervene; these were people who had set me apart, told me I could not be one of them.[59]

Such perceptions of standing a world apart from German victims did not, however, prevent attacks on Jews and antifascists who had eagerly awaited the liberating Red Army. Gabriele Vallentin, the sister of the executed Jewish communist Judith Auer, wrote bitterly, "What became of Goebbels' 'horror-stories?' Reality! . . . Many committed communists turned their back on the party. They were not prepared for this random vindictiveness."[60] Henny Brenner, a "half" Jewish girl who had survived in Dresden as a forced laborer, was initially unconcerned about the Soviet rampage, convinced that after all the years of "humiliation and fear" the Germans had brought, "it serves them right." But then she grasped that no one was exempt: "We couldn't have dreamed that first of all we had to hide from our liberators."[61] In the chaos of war's end, Jewish women found themselves threatened by (sometimes literally) the same soldiers who also freed and protected them, sometimes with extraordinary kindness. Inge Deutschkron, hidden in Berlin with her mother, remembered her growing joy and relief as she heard the rumble of approaching Russian tanks. But one of the soldiers she greeted with a happy smile grabbed at her clothes muttering the already classic phrase, "*komm, Frau, komm.*" At first uncomprehending, she ran to her mother, who sighed, "So it is true after all," and added hopefully, "we must show them our Jewish identity cards"—they had been hidden in the goat shed for just this occasion—"they will understand." But, Deutschkron adds, "they understood nothing. They couldn't even read the identity cards." Another kind of chase began—flight and hiding not from deportation to the death camps but from sexual violation. Eventually the shooting was over, the Nazis gone, and a semblance of order restored; yet Deutschkron "could no longer be really happy."[62]

In a somewhat different register, disappointment and disillusionment with the liberators' behavior were surprisingly explicit in the laments of German communist activists. One unhappy comrade wrote:

> Men and women from the working population say to us over and over again: We had so hoped that it would finally become better, we were so happy that the Red Army was coming, and now, they are behaving just like the SS and the NSDAP always told us they would. We cannot understand this. The hope that things will get better, which we have promised people over and over again; most of them no longer have that hope.

Antifascist activists, many of them recently released from Nazi prisons and camps, despaired of their potentially promising political work:

> The mood in the population has become very bad due to these incidents. . . . One woman on the street said to me today, while telling me how the Red Army had again been at their home at night, raping women, "In that regard we had it better with the SS, at least in that respect they left us women alone."[63]

The Soviets' liberator image was dismantled as rapidly as the goods and infrastructure the SMA requisitioned for "reparations" to the Soviet Union:

> For us, who fought against fascism for twelve long years, the concentration camps were no sanitoria and when we now have to watch, the workers are more and more disappointed, we too could despair . . . if we did not have our strong faith in the party leadership of the KPD.[64]

Rank-and-file communists pleaded with their leaders that "even the Red Army soldiers, now that the war is already over for 8 weeks, absolutely must discipline themselves."[65] These cadres presented themselves, however, as motivated less by outrage at the soldiers' crimes than by angry frustration about the problems it posed for their political reeducation projects. When the Berlin Philharmonic played its first, much-heralded concert on May 27, 1945, women in the audience were seen fleeing when soldiers arrived to take their seats.[66] One group of comrades helpfully suggested that the army set up brothels staffed with "bourgeois" and Nazi women to satisfy the liberators' seemingly boundless lust.[67] The memory and fear of rape engendered concrete material as well as ideological problems. Urgently required agricultural production was endangered, not only by the plunder of farm animals and equipment, but because women were afraid to work in the fields. Female activists even boldly countered SMA criticism of women's inadequate political involvement by protesting that women did not attend meetings because they were simply afraid to walk the streets after dark.[68]

Given the realities of mass rape, German communists and SMA authorities could not, certainly not in the immediate postwar years 1945 till 1947, impose a total silence around Red Army actions. They sought instead to find ways of talking about and containing the massive incidence of rapes. They denied, minimized, justified, and shifted responsibility. They freely admitted violations, excesses, abuses, and unfortunate incidents and vowed to get them under control (or to demand that the Soviet army do so). But they also trivialized rape as an inevitable part of normal brutal warfare, as comparable to Allied violations, and as understandable if not entirely excusable in view of the atrocities perpetrated on the Russians by the Germans. In the words of a KPD newsletter, "We cannot and will not try to provide justifications, even if we do have explanations and could answer the question by referring to all the havoc that Hitler wreaked in the Soviet Union."[69]

In a common pattern of simultaneous acknowledgment and denial, party memos and press reports referred frequently and openly to (purportedly unjustified) rumors of rape by Red Army soldiers, thereby reproducing and disseminating stories that, their coding as rumors or pernicious anti-Soviet propaganda notwithstanding, everyone presumably knew to be true. The *Berliner Zeitung*, which often resorted to cartoon characters speaking in Berlin dialect to explain unpopular positions (such as unwillingness to take responsibility for having profited from "aryanized" Jewish property), even ran a cartoon strip satirizing women's fears while encouraging their labor as *Trümmerfrauen*. Under the headline "Mongols in Berlin, the Latest Rumor," the sensible Frau Piesepampel informs her hysterical neighbor Frau Schwabbel that she has "no time for such nonsense" and no intention of worrying about "Mongols" now that the war is finally over. There is cleanup work to be done, and she will not be distracted.[70] Thus, the official Soviet-licensed press, while formally denying stories of rape or passing the blame to "bandits," may have actually contributed to circulating and confirming them.[71]

This attempted strategy was clearly visible in the extensive front-page daily press coverage—competing for space with the Nuremberg trials—given to the highly publicized 1946 Eberswalde trial of several German "bandits." During their spree of plunder, murder, and rape, they had dressed in Soviet uniforms, announced themselves with Russian phrases, and in general mimicked what they thought the local population would expect from Russians.[72] A sympathetic 1947 account published in Britain summarized the official line:

> What is the truth about the most widely circulated allegations of all the stories of crimes committed by Soviet army men against the German population? It is impossible to check up on all the reports, but two facts emerge. First, the Soviet authorities took and are taking the most ruthless measures against any of their own people convicted of criminal acts, and they are not afraid to discuss the problem with the Germans. . . . Second fact: criminal elements both among the Germans and the large number of foreign nationals constantly posed as Russians.

The Soviets claimed, "It is only necessary for a bandit to put on a fur hat and speak broken German for the word to go round that there has been a crime committed by the Russians." Finally, there was the resort to undermining women's stories: "Girls who want to explain an awkward pregnancy always find it easy to blame a Russian."[73] For the Soviet Military Government, which instigated and presided over the Eberswalde trial, it was an important propaganda moment; the proceedings were widely publicized and carefully performed in the town's largest theater. The public was urged to attend and apparently did so in great numbers. The two death sentences and long terms of forced labor imposed on these German "bandits" both confirmed that the crime of rape was being taken seriously and punished, *and* denied that it was primarily Russian occupiers who were responsible. Moreover, the term "bandit" rhetorically linked rape with the fear spread by supposedly lawless roving bands of liberated prisoners and slave laborers and other displaced persons, as well with the crimes of the other German bandits, the "Hitlerites."[74]

Despite all efforts at containment, rapes figured prominently as public relations and political control problems. They provoked anti-Soviet sentiment, especially among women, youth, and dedicated anti-Nazis, precisely those groups considered most likely to support a new socialist and democratic peace-loving Germany. All protestations notwithstanding, it was generally if not explicitly acknowledged that the communist-dominated Socialist Unity (SED) Party's embarrassing loss to the Social Democrats (SPD) in Berlin's first open elections in October 1946 was due in no small part to a heavily female electorate remembering and responding to the actions of the Soviet "friends" (*Freunde*).[75] The Soviets had worked hard to present themselves as liberators, organizing city services, licensing newspapers and political parties, and promoting cultural revival, but in many ways their efforts came too late; the damage of the first few weeks could not be undone. In his report to the London paper *The Observer*, Issac Deutscher had predicted that "next Sunday the women of Berlin will take their revenge against the humiliations that were forced upon them during the first weeks of occupation." The election results indicated that he was right.[76]

For their part, German communist leaders and the SMA continually griped that discussions of guilt, complicity, and responsibility or calls for *Wiedergutmachung* (referring to reparations to the Soviet Union) were met with "icy silence."[77] Germans, they clearly implied, should be grateful to have gotten off as easily as they did. Even in regard to rape, both Soviet occupiers and German communists contended that women would have had more of a right to protest if only, rather than senselessly battling the Red Army to the bitter end, right into the center of Berlin, the German working class had fought fascism for even a day or two, thereby preserving some German honor and credibility vis-à-vis the Soviets. One communist intellectual petulantly remarked that those who had supported the war and the attack on the Soviet Union could not later cry "*Pfui*"; war was not, after all, "a socializing tool."[78] But there was little popular sympathy for Ulbricht's perhaps irrefutable logic in an early leaflet promising swift punishment for "excesses." Had the Soviets "exacted revenge eye for an eye (*gleiches mit gleichem*)," he asked, "German Volk, what would have happened to you?"[79] And while Soviet officers did sometimes exact summary punishment by shooting soldiers accused of rape, few worried as did the dissident Lev Kopelev in his memoirs of life as a political officer in the Red Army: "Why did so many of our soldiers turn out to be common bandits, raping women and girls one after another [*rudelweise*] on the side of the road, in the snow, in doorways? How did this all become possible?" His "bourgeois human[ist]" compunctions led to his arrest for being pro-German.[80]

Even three years later, in 1948, when two overflowing meetings were held in the *Haus der Kultur der Sowjet Union* to discuss the ever sensitive subject "about the Russians and about us," the subject most on the predominantly female audience's mind was Soviet soldiers' violations. The SED argued that the memory of rape was whipped up and kept alive by Western propaganda. In frustration, party ideologue Wolfgang Harich demanded from the podium:

> Why in all the world is there only one kind of trauma? Why not the bomb nights when American and British bombs hailed down on women and children. Why does one speak only of the trauma of the encounter with the Russian soldiers?

Harich insisted that the Soviet rapes were mere "natural" expressions of "hotblooded" victors' excess as compared to German crimes, which were "coldblooded actions of master-race consciousness."[81] The topic was abandoned after two crowded, four-hour meetings threatened to get out of control. After the rubble had been cleaned up, the men returned home, the pregnancies aborted (at least 90 percent apparently were, especially in Berlin), and the venereal disease treated, the initial explosion of speech about the rapes was muted. Discussion of the topic could be publicly restrained but not, however, closed.

Rape continued to figure in German narratives of victimization for many years. Public conversation, however, so common in the immediate postwar months and even years despite all communist and SMA efforts to block the discussion, was indeed curtailed in both East and West once conditions had somewhat normalized. With the return of prisoners of war and the "remasculinization"[82] of German society, the topic was suppressed as too humiliating for German men and too risky for women who feared—with much justification, given the reports of estrangement and even murder—the reactions of their menfolk. But rape stories continued to circulate and indeed were repeatedly invoked or alluded to by contemporary chroniclers, both German and occupier. In immediate reports and in later memoirs, women reported over and over that the cry "*Frau komm*" still rang in their ears.[83] Moreover, the importance of Berlin as the conquered capital and the millions of refugees from the East who poured into western Germany assured the centrality of rape stories in memories of defeat even in areas where there had never been a Red Army soldier.

RAPE AND AMERICAN CONQUERORS

The continuing prominence of rape in German narratives of victimization in the period 1945–1949 was not, however, as suggested by the SED, due to propaganda by the western Allies. When Colonel Howley, who had served as the first U.S. commander in Berlin, published his virulently anticommunist memoirs in 1950, he wrote at length about the horrors of the Soviet regime of rape, murder, and looting. With the Cold War in full swing, he asserted that "two hundred and thirty German girls were treated at the same Berlin hospital in a single day—all victims of Russian lust and brutality" and recalled that one of his own secretaries had to be "wheeled in a baby carriage several blocks down her street to a hospital" after she and her mother had been gang-raped by seven Russian soldiers."[84] But, in his earlier official military reports from Berlin, he had downplayed German anxieties about crime, disorder, and hunger.

With a touch of sarcasm, he noted that the per capita crime rate in 1945/46 Berlin was lower than that of most cities in the United States, especially New York![85]

Even among the Americans, therefore, where such tales might have served as useful anticommunist propaganda, the discussion was restrained. In the early occupation years, U.S. officials were far from seizing on rape stories to discredit their Soviet allies and competitors, whom they viewed as "hard bargaining, hard playing, hard drinking, hard bodied, and hard headed."[86] Russians might be barbarian rapists, but they were also tough fighters and exotic celebrators who could drink, eat, and copulate prodigiously—often to the admiring frustration of U.S. colleagues unable to match their levels of consumption.[87] Nor were Americans necessarily unsympathetic to Soviet "excesses." Shortly before the war ended, a *Newsweek* reporter had no trouble explaining as an act of "justice," a rape "behind the barn" by a liberated Soviet POW. He had been "badly treated, particularly by the farmer's daughter who was a Hitler Maiden and took delight in trying to prove the Russians were second class human beings."[88] Over ten years later, in his lurid 1956 novel *fräulein*, the American writer James McGovern sneered, "Poor Frau Graubach. When she had voted *ja*, she had not bargained for this."[89]

On September 6, 1945, Military Government officer John Maginnis noted, "We had another incident tonight. . . . The MPs were called in by the German police on an attempted rape by two Russians which ended in a shooting contest. Captain Bond went along the see the fun [*sic*] and almost got himself killed. The Russians were subdued but one of the MPs was shot in the thigh. I gave Captain Bond a good dressing down for getting mixed up in such a brawl; he should have known better."[90] This generally lighthearted tone of American reporting about Soviet abuses surely had something to do with the fact that the U.S. forces had their own problems, not only with fraternization and prostitution, but also with sexual violence. Observing that "our army has done a little on occasion," William Shirer coolly remarked in his *End of a Berlin Diary* that

> taking into account that the Soviet troops had been in the field constantly fighting for two to three years and that capturing Berlin was a costly operation and that some of the Russian divisions were made up of very inferior material, not to mention a weird assortment of Asiatic troops, then the amount of raping by Russian troops here apparently was not above the average to be expected.[91]

When William Griffith took over as a denazification officer for the Military Government in Bavaria, where there were many more American troops than in divided Berlin, he discovered that an important military police task was "largely to parade weeping German rape victims past their suspected GI assailants for identification." Luckily for the GIs, "the poor girls, I regret to say, never identified any of our soldiers."[92] As reporters Hutton and Rooney smirked about Soviet rapes, "The great novelty for the United States Army was, however, that for the first time in the history of living man someone was behaving worse than the American soldier."[93]

If German Communists worried about the effects of Red Army behavior on support for the occupation and for the Socialist Unity Party they had established in April 1946, American officials and journalists certainly also debated the negative and corrupting effects—on both occupier and occupied—of servicemen's looting, brawling, raping, and general "sexual antics."[94] Defeat and military occupation, with their enormous pressures to engage in instrumental sex, make it in many cases difficult to disentangle coercive, pragmatic, and what might be called genuinely consensual sex. Kay Boyle captured this ambiguous state well when, in one of her "Military Occupation Group" short stories, an American occupier declares, "Let me tell you that Berlin's the territory for the man who's got a flair. They're still pretty hungry there, so they come to terms without too much of an argument."[95] As we have seen, such blurring of lines was by no means limited to sexual encounters with western Allies. Voluntary (or equally instrumental) sexual liaisons between German women and Soviet troops, especially officers who had something to offer and troops who were billeted in local households, clearly did develop, especially in the early period of occupation before soldiers were confined to quarters. The military tolerated such "campaign wives" and Russenflittchen, but, worried by a high rate of desertion, the SMA was quick to send soldiers home if serious romances developed, sometimes leaving women behind with a Russenkind.[96] Still, despite many complaints about Americans' boorish and violent behavior, the lack of precise figures, and the unmistakable evidence that Soviets were also active fraternizers, there was a general consensus among the Allies and the press that the level of American sexual violence, while certainly higher than generally acknowledged, at no point compared to the mass rapes perpetrated by the Red Army. Many liaisons between Americans and German women were voluntary, and American assaults fell more into the (admittedly problematic) category of "normal" wartime and occupation sexual violence than of mass rape.[97]

Certainly, the many American fictionalizations of postwar Berlin—a genre in itself, often written by men who served there—stressed the unique advantages of the GIs' sexual bonanza: what a historian of the U.S. occupation summarized as the "general willingness on the part of German women," and Meyer Levin, more bitterly, as "the lustful eagerness of the German girls to fulfill their roles as conquered women."[98] In McGovern's fräulein, the jaded women survivors of the Battle of Berlin hopefully await the American conquerors: "The Americans had not suffered in the war.

Their homes had not been bombed, their women raped, their industries razed. Their casualties in Europe had been smaller than those of the Wehrmacht at Stalingrad alone. They would be free from the spirit of revenge for which the French, British and Russians could hardly be blamed." Cynically, the women repeat the dominant American view: "Rape? They don't have to rape. All those women who swarm outside their barracks would rape them for a carton of cigarettes or a chocolate bar." American privilege also assured a more benign general level of exploitation and looting: "The Russians steal power plants and cranes and whole factories, while the Amis are content to ship Meissen china, Zeiss cameras, and family heirloom jewels through their Army Post Office."[99]

FRATERNIZATION: SEXUAL, POLITICAL, AND RACIAL BORDER CROSSING

The other side of the rape story was indeed sexual fraternization. The bans imposed with all serious intent by the Americans (and British) very quickly showed themselves to be utterly and hopelessly unenforceable, "an immense and sordid joke." In one of the many apparently autobiographical novels published in the years right after the war, an officer, marveling at the sudden bounty of "guns, wine, silver, paintings, women, and various combinations thereof" that greeted the Americans, tells his men: "In this outfit we stand on Patton's unofficial ruling that it is not fraternization if you don't stay for breakfast. Sleep with 'em but don't shake hands."[100] With everyone agreeing that "surely it is necessary to go back to Prohibition to find a law so flagrantly violated and so rarely enforced," General Eisenhower eased the ban on July 7 just as the Americans were taking up their positions in Berlin. He then essentially lifted it on July 15, 1945, by officially permitting public conversations between Germans and Americans.

Technicalities notwithstanding, any political fraternization suggested by a handshake was clearly not the major issue; as an American observer bluntly put it in 1946, "Fraternization is strictly a matter of sex. An American with a German woman is with her because she is a woman, not because she is a German."[101] Furthermore, "No court-martial system could possibly try the thousands who refused to follow the non-fraternization orders" or chose to interpret them in idiosyncratic and self-consciously cynical ways, such as disguising a "furline" as an Allied national DP in order to circumvent the restrictions on contact with German civilians. Indeed, there is no shortage of quotable commentary on GI/Fräulein relations produced by journalists, writer, filmmakers, diarists, and letter writers, both German and American. The American Jewish intelligence officer Saul Padover noted the obvious when he wrote, "The dictionary" may have "define[d] fraternization as 'bringing into brotherly love,'" but the relations between Americans and Germans did not belong in that category," and the term quickly "came to have the exclusive signification of fornication." It was no accident that the ever creative German joke makers nicknamed the Military Government "government by mistresses."[102]

In the early months after April 1945, handshakes were, however, a major issue, especially for anti-Nazis who had expected the Americans to act as liberators rather than conquerors. They were outraged that fraternization guidelines did not permit Americans to shake hands with a decent German who had been in the opposition, or even with a liberated German Jew, while the rules against contact with German women were openly flouted. As many irritated Germans pointed out, this only made it even less likely that Americans would connect with any upright Germans, since they were the only ones who might take the ban seriously. Indeed, even as the prohibitions were eased, perhaps the only Berliners hesitant about fraternization were those more conservative anti-Nazis such as Durand-Wever who, drawing surely on Weimar-era ambivalence about "Americanism," now thought it undignified to grovel before the occupiers.[103] Journalist Ursula von Kardorff grumbled in her end-of-war diary about the "primitive" American who misunderstood her offer of German lessons in exchange for English instruction: "But he only wanted to know what 'love' was in German and only spoke about 'fraternization' . . . and since I didn't want either his cigarettes or his chocolate, he never showed up for the second lesson."[104]

In many ways, the ban's stunningly obvious unenforceability reflected and confirmed the difficulties of maintaining any of the harsh denazification directives that had originally been imposed. Joint Chief of Staff Order 1067 limited contact with and reconstruction aid for Germans, and Occupation Law No. 9 ordered purges that would have removed Nazis from all but the most menial of occupations. Both had to be quickly adjusted to the realities of a broken society in which virtually all professionals and technical experts had been nazified.[105] Americans were dependent not only on the cooperation of German professionals, clergy, and recycled Weimar politicians but also, to a very large degree, on the services of German women, who constituted the great majority of the available younger civilian population. Not all contact with German women was sexual or flirtatious. Women served in multiple ways as social navigators and interpreters for their male occupiers, and the victors depended on them as housekeepers, translators, and secretaries. Desperate expellee women from the East were most likely to be stigmatized as *Amiliebchen* or *Russenflittchen*, while educated middle-class women with some English-language skills were able to acquire legitimate employment (which might or might not include sex) with the occupiers.[106] As Petra Goedde has pointed out, the recognition by summer 1945 that the fraternization ban could not be sustained may well have been the first clear sign that, for Military Government on the ground, the stringent denazification "policy of quarantine and revenge," as ordered by Roosevelt and reaffirmed by Truman in JCS1067, was both "unenforceable and unwise."[107]

Fraternization of course brought its inevitable corollary, venereal disease, which both Soviet and western-zone authorities ordered treated with severe measures such as police raids and compulsory medical examinations.[108] As mocking reporters pointed out, "the final hypocrisy" of the fraternization ban and one "not lost to the Germans—was the appearance in large communities and at all headquarters of neat Prophylaxis Station signs at a time when intercourse of any sort was banned."[109] Fraternization also led to other embarrassments, such as the obvious presence of German women in even high-ranking officers' quarters or, as recorded in Captain Maginnis's Berlin diary, the distressing incident of an officer's court-martial for fatally shooting a woman he had brought into his room.[110] The 1947 DEFA (Soviet zone) film *Strassenbekanntschaften* (street encounters) vividly depicted this corrupt world of parties, bars, and cafés, of crime and sexually transmitted disease, as well as the frantic black market for penicillin among Germans resentful that the effective new drug was primarily reserved for occupiers. The film's idealistic young journalist hero, in an attempt to rescue a young woman from vice and return her to a "clean and decent" life, invokes the social hygiene and sex reform language of the 1920s that was still commonplace after the war, especially in the East. However, neither such public health efforts, nor the hand-wringing among American reporters and politicians about the corrupting liberties of the occupation, nor even Don Sheppard's famous cartoons in *Stars and Stripes* warning GIs against the devious, sexy "Veronica Dankeschön" (VD) and the fat, slatternly "Hausfrau Hilda" had much effect on what was "surely the most ignored rule ever published by an American administration."[111] By fall of 1945, the ban on all forms of fraternization was all but lifted, leaving in place only the prohibition (also widely ignored) on overnight stays and marriages.[112]

As *Newsweek*'s Berlin bureau chief reported in June 1947, it had "now, for all intents and purposes, [become] legally possible to do everything with the German girl except marry her."[113] Marriages could not take place in Germany, but by Christmas 1946 German war brides were allowed into the United States after a supposed political screening. The first bride was a poster girl for reconciliation with the former enemy: twenty-three-year-old Anna Maria Christina Heinke, a ballet dancer from Dessau, wanted to marry Robert J. Lauenstein of St. Louis, Missouri. Of course she came from an antifascist family; her father had died after sixteen months in a concentration camp while Anna had been drafted into war work at an aircraft plant.[114] This sugarcoated story would later be caricatured in the 1950 Hollywood film *The Big Lift*, whose hero, a gullible young GI stationed in Berlin during the airlift, falls for a girl whose virtually identical story turns out to be a pernicious lie. *The Big Lift* conveyed a lingering sentiment among many Americans, both at home and abroad, that despite its pervasiveness, fraternization with German women embodied all that was corrupt and somehow wrong about the occupation. Superior officers eyed skeptically the many marriage petitions, such as the one handed in by Danny, the film's eager (and deluded) GI hero. They were inclined to see only sex where their men might feel love. As the officer in charge remarks in the film, most GIs who come at eight thirty in the morning to request permission for marriage change their mind by five in the afternoon.[115]

Countless commentators, especially journalists and congressional delegations, fulminated over the shamelessness of American liaisons with German women. Officers fraternized as eagerly as enlisted men. Even the chief of political affairs in Military Government, Dr. Shepard Stone, married a German "girl." No matter how high-minded Frl. Anna had been, many feared that the Military Government was getting a very bad name because of "dishonesty, alcoholism, sexual exploits and the like," and because, as another young Berlin fraternizer saucily points out to her GI boyfriend in *The Big Lift*, the democratizing reeducators were themselves so blatantly engaging in all the privileges of hierarchy.[116]

On the most basic level, the harsh measures of denazification and reeducation programs simply could not withstand the day-to-day American experience with postwar Germans. The fact that so many of the demonized enemy civilians first encountered by American GIs were female—needy, attractive, and eager to please—left American soldiers with a "feminized image of German society that contrasted sharply with the aggressive masculine wartime image of the Third Reich,"[117] and reinforced the otherwise often cynically received German self-presentation as victims. Very quickly, GIs concluded that if there had not been and "weren't so many men in Germany it would not be a bad country."[118] Fraternizing relationships between male occupiers and German women— who functioned as interpreters and secretaries as well as sex partners and girlfriends—went a long way toward transforming the perception of Germans from ruthless aggressors to sympathetic victims, a mediating process that worked well in tandem with the changing allegiances of the Cold War.[119] The nation of storm troopers and ruthless killers had morphed into a country of neat landscapes and clean, acquiescent women.

Over and over again, using virtually identical phrases, reporters highlighted occupied Germany's ubiquitous *Fräuleinwunder*. "There is nothing like it this side of Tahiti," they marveled about the accessibility of young German women. When a young officer inquired about bringing his wife to his Berlin posting, he was greeted with incredulity: "Wife? You must be nuts!" said the general. "You're bringing a sandwich to a banquet."[120] Or as one decidedly not amused female American reporter sniffed about German women who treated "all American women with contempt and all American men as gods": "If there was any rape, it certainly wasn't necessary."[121] Particularly titillating was the picture of German women quickly shedding all the baggage of racial indoctrination, at least in matters sexual or romantic. Especially initial reports highlighted fraternization with both Jewish and African-American soldiers as ironic racial transgressions: "the Negro troops are doing particularly well with the Fräuleins. . . . It is also true that Jewish boys are having a field-day."[122]

Field day or not, the politics of fraternization was particularly fraught for Jewish Allied soldiers. In a report on a "ride through Berlin," posted to the refugee weekly *Aufbau* in July 1945, a German-Jewish master sergeant reflected on how hard it was to resist the temptations of well-dressed, well-fed, and appealing Fräuleins. He described his own painful discipline of staring into their eyes and visualizing Buchenwald and Dachau.[123] For Jewish occupation official Moses Moskowitz, the fact that "German women have been known to be on intimate terms with Jewish men who only a year ago were behind concentration camp gates" was one of the most difficult and inexplicable aspects of the German "enigma of irresponsibility."[124] Kurt Hirsch, the Czech-Jewish American GI whom the actress Hildegard Knef married, was excruciatingly explicit about the clash of memories and identities. On their first date in bombed-out Berlin, he took her to the movies in the Russian sector to watch the Soviet newsreel about the liberation of Auschwitz. "I lost sixteen relatives," he told her on the way home.[125]

The combustible mix of race and sex played out in different but even more tense ways for African-American troops serving in a still segregated military. William Gardner Smith, a reporter for the African-American newspaper *Pittsburgh Courier*, echoed black GIs' own highly ambivalent feelings about fraternization in his semiautobiographical 1948 novel *Last of the Conquerors*. Drinking with "sultry-looking" German women, one of the soldiers remarks, "Two years ago I'd a shot the son of a bitch that said I'd ever be sittin' in a club drinking a toast with Hitler's children. . . . The same people we're sittin' with tonight is the ones that burned people in them camps and punched the Jews in the nose." One of the girls retorts angrily, "'How can you talk? What about the white Americans? In your country you may not walk down the street with a white woman.'" Musing on his initially carefree love affair with a "white girl" named Ilse, the narrator notes "bitter[ly]" how "Odd, it seemed to me, that here, in the

land of hate, I should find this one all-important phase of democracy."
He remembers the pleasures of postwar Berlin, border crossing through
the sectors, strolling along the Wannsee in the summer, or going to the
opera in the East with his girlfriend even as they "could still smell the
bodies of the dead buried beneath the rubble as we walked." Not wanting
to face the reality that Ilse's dream of marriage could never be fulfilled in
Jim Crow America, he has no ready response to the buddy who blurts
out, "I like this goddamn country, you know that? . . . It's the first place
I was ever treated like a goddamn man. . . . You know what the hell I
learned? That a nigger ain't no different from nobody else. . . . I hadda
come over here and let the Nazis teach me that."[126]

Women had their own reasons for making themselves sexually available, as the sharp-eyed sociologist Hilde Thurnwald surmised in her report on family life in postwar Berlin. Aside from the bare necessities provided by American foodstuffs and supplies, the Fräuleins were lured less
by sexual interest than by a general postwar "yearning for life's pleasures"
(*Lebenshunger*). If soldiers' rations could ease "the hunger which had
replaced the bombs in making life into hell," as Curt Riess put it, then
Berlin's women were also seeking a bit of warmth, a bar of chocolate, an
ice cream from the American club, some untroubled hours. The *Amis*,
they said in a reference to the Weimar enthusiasm for American efficiency
and rationalization, were "so streamlined." And indeed the crack Eighty-
second Airborne, which had marched into Berlin in July, was well fed,
well groomed, and fragrant, as many recalled, with aftershave lotion—
quite a contrast to the ragged German men returning from the front or
POW camps—and, in most cases, the feared Russians.[127]

Married women and mothers also sought the multiple benefits of fraternization. Housewives, many of them with absent husbands, were assigned
the lowest "ticket to heaven" (*Himmelfahrt*) ration level, as "unproductive" workers. Exhausted and overworked, they were busy trading their
(sometimes still considerable) goods on the black market, quite simply
the only viable economy available and, as Thurnwald declared, a "necessary evil." They foraged for fresh food in the countryside and struggled
to maintain the precarious household economy. They sewed scraps, fixed
worn clothes and shoes, searched for food and fuel, and tried to establish
orderly and clean homes in overcrowded apartments, with bickering
neighbors and erratic heat and electricity. They struggled to keep control
of children and teenagers in a city where boys frolicked in the ruins and
girls quickly learned that a relationship with an occupier was the best
way to support their mothers. Marriages, strained by war and absence,
fragmented and split, unable to withstand the shock of reunion between
veterans brutalized by war and imprisonment and women toughened by
responsibilities on the home front. In 1946, 25,000 divorces were regis-

tered in Berlin; until December 1947 there were about 1,700 to 2,000 a month, a trend that, as we shall see, was radically different from that of the Jewish survivors we will meet in the next chapters.[128]

MEMORIES OF WAR

Fraternization and the shadow of rape tainted those reunions. As Elizabeth Heineman has pointed out, "Despite the popular contrast between rape in the Soviet zone and fraternization in the Western zones, upheavals in women's sexual lives transcended zonal boundaries." Women carried with them not only remnants of Weimar's open sexual culture but also the experience of "marital infidelity and premarital sex" which "had increased during the war."[129] In Berlin, the very experience of rape may have made embittered women less resistant to the casual prostitution that also characterized fraternization. Much has been written about the postwar estrangement and sexual misery of the men who returned from the front and prisoner of war camps and the women who received them.[130] In World War I, the phenomenon of "homecoming divorces" and the "indescribable gulf of experience" between men and women caused immense anxiety. But now, brutalized, angry, and weary veterans and returning POWs confronted women who had endured a home front that had been, at least in urban areas, at times more dangerous than the battlefront. Women in Berlin had lived through the sexual violence of the Soviet victory and the fleeting pleasures of fraternization, not only with the victors but sometimes also with the many foreign workers mobilized into the Nazi war economy.

Returning German servicemen, sullen and filled with "maudlin self pity," coined such nasty ditties as "He fell for the Fatherland, she for cigarettes." The German soldier, it was often said, had fought for five years while his woman did not fight for even five minutes. Beyond the threat of rape from the victors, German women "faced a [less well-known] significant threat of violence from [their own] men, especially returning Wehrmacht soldiers, who were attempting to hinder [the women's] relationships" with the occupiers. There were cases of men murdering women to spare them from rape or as punishment for having succumbed; they also sometimes attacked—whether by haircutting or worse—women seen as fraternizers and therefore besmirchers of whatever honor was left to Germans. Jewish survivors, embittered by the cozy relationships developing between Americans and Germans, often suspected that GIs specifically harassed them in order to impress their German girlfriends, but it was certainly also the case that those same couples risked facing violence from embittered German men.[131]

In response to this postwar estrangement, magazines offered sympathy and tips on how to reintegrate homecoming husbands and fathers into families unaccustomed to their presence. As the *Neue Berliner Illustrierte*, pushing an official line, gently caricatured in 1945 (under a cover celebrating the reopening of Berlin schools), "Is your husband also sometimes so strange since he came back? Now he suddenly trashes all the bookshelves because he says that he is sick and tired of anything to do with standing neatly in a row."[132] The process by which a "strange man would become 'Pappi'" was supposed to gently resocialize soldiers into peaceful citizens and loving fathers: "In my dream I still slide through that land full of the sounds of butchery, cannons, dead horses. But always Katrinchen's small warm child's hand leads me quickly away from death and fire, on the way back to becoming a human being again."[133] Acutely aware of the postwar "surplus women" crisis and women's supposedly desperate "hunt for a man," advice columns and counseling centers tried to mediate the many gender and sexual conflicts generated by wartime and postwar conditions. Husbands resented wives who had had other—coerced or voluntary—sexual encounters while they were at war; wives discovered that they had been replaced by so-called "fried potatoes brides" who had provided, domestically and sexually, for their husbands while women and children had been evacuated to the countryside to escape bombings. Both sexes carried their own bitter and guilty memories.[134]

Such postwar gender tensions were well captured in the film *Strassenbekanntschaften*. In one scene, a hardworking streetcar conductor wife confronts the suspicions of her demobilized spouse: "How we women lived here at home is something none of you know today; early morning to the factory, coming home late at night, hungry, cold rooms, air-raid alarms, fears, helplessness. Is it so hard to understand that sometimes one wanted to numb oneself?" The wife presents herself as a victim of war, seeking some comfort and pleasure, rather than an immoral villain. She holds her husband to account for Wehrmacht fraternization in occupied territories: "those gentlemen in Paris, Warsaw, Copenhagen. Why did the women submit to you? For bread, for their children, because they were hungry." "Everyone sees the world with their own eyes," she adds, implying that in this postwar moment of gradual remasculinization, male and female eyes are quite different, even antagonistic. He, the traumatized veteran, can only say, "I simply don't know how to go on" (*Ich weiss einfach nicht mehr weiter*). He does not know that he has infected her with the venereal disease that will probably destroy their chance to have the children and the "normal" family life that she—despite everything—still craves. She assures him that he was always her only love even as she resolutely puts on her uniform and leaves for work.[135] Numerous films presented versions of this postwar social and psychic crisis, from the young boy vulnerable to homosexual advances in Rossellini's *Germania Anno Zero* to another 1947 DEFA production, *Irgendwo in Berlin* (Somewhere in Berlin), which dramatized the plight of traumatized returning German soldiers and POWs. In the latter, one young veteran is still sleepwalking the war, saluting as he stands rigid on a balcony in the ruins, and another returns barely recognizable to his own family. A young boy playing in the rubble falls to his death, leading his shocked friends to grasp that little boys can be killed by war even if they are only playing soldier and the battles have ceased. If the motto in *Strassenbekanntschaften* is the introduction of a "clean" socialist morality that recognizes some form of equality between men and women, in *Irgendwo* the restoration of male identity and the family comes through the acceptance of returning to productive labor and family life.[136]

Memories of rape, motherhood, and the sexual bargaining of fraternization, marginalized in official histories but retold and alluded to in multiple public and private forms, did much to shape women's sense of both endurance under duress (*durchhalten*) and victimization. Particular traumatic images were repeated over and over again in women's recollections: soldiers ordering "*Frau komm*" in Berlin; the mother on the dreadful trek westward who would not relinquish the frozen infant in her arms. In their postwar stories, women recounted last-minute escapes, from attack in the cities or onto the "last" train or boat westward. Often they insisted that they had been rescued only by some kind of miracle or "guardian angel."[137] "Flight is women's business just as the war was men's work," Ilse Langner noted in her postwar novel, *Flucht Ohne Ziel* (Flight without Destination).[138]

Certainly, young Berlin women reported excitedly on their encounters with well-fed fraternizing GIs, and reporters were quick to remark on how good the defeated Fräuleins still looked. But as Curt Riess caustically observed, even they "were only ruins of their former selves, just like the houses in which they now lived out their days."[139] If young, single women found some adventure and perhaps romance, older women's stories were more likely to highlight hunger and rape, or the terrible hardships of motherhood at war's end: nursing a child through typhoid or diphtheria, the harrowing experiences of mothers and children separated while fleeing the Soviets, on the road, or in the packed refugee trains. The virulent dysentery epidemic of the first winter reportedly killed sixty-five of every one hundred newborns in Berlin,[140] and Gabrielle Vallentin's 1955 account poignantly recalled streetcars where "one saw many such sad pictures; mothers who sat silent and rigid [*stumm und starr*], on their lap, a cardboard box, in which they had picked up their dead child from the hospital."[141] For many, the "dark times" began only with "liberation." In a classic testimony about the horrors of defeat by the Soviets, one woman wrote in a 1975 memoir, "The bombs in winter 1944/45 were bad, but the days that came now, were almost impossible to bear."[142]

German women, especially in the East and among refugees from the East in the West, were left with un-worked-through memories that had no easy public place even as they were repeatedly invoked or alluded to. There were no rituals of guilt and expiation as there were in commemorations of "the victims of fascism," no structures of compensation and memory such as those provided by veterans' organizations and benefits.[143] In their privatized but pervasive discourse, women remembered and passed on to their daughters their experiences: of bombing raids, flight from the advancing Red Army, rapes and fear of rape. But they also transmitted memories of sturdy *Trümmerfrauen* tidying up the ruins of the bombed-out cities. In an analogue to their heroic and pathetic brothers, fathers, husbands, lovers, and sons on the eastern front—who also expressed no shame or guilt, because they perceived themselves as having had no choice—women too invented themselves as both victims and heroines. They expressed little shame or guilt about either sexual violence or fraternization, even though many of their menfolk expected it of them—a circumstance that left its depressing traces in postwar gender relations.[144] The memories remained raw, distorted, and repressed but hardly completely silenced. They can be found abundantly in postwar literature, film, and government documentation.[145] Women's stories were combined with men's more openly validated tribulations on the eastern front and as prisoners of war to construct a new national community of suffering that served not only to avoid confrontation with Nazi crimes but also as a strategy for reauthorizing and reestablishing the unity of the Volk, providing the basis for a "sick" Germany to "recover" once again—a metaphor much used by postwar women's groups from all political camps.

This sense of victimization as well as women's pained pride in carrying on—often with children, and without men, at their side—entailed, as Hilde Thurnwald's detailed study documented, a considerable amount of nostalgia for the order and material comfort of life in the Third Reich, even under the bombs. Even if hardly anyone would admit to having been a bona fide Nazi, expressions such as "If Adolf were here now, things would get straightened out fast" (*käme bald Ordnung in die Bude*), or "things were better with Adolf" (*Bei Adolf hatten wir es besser*), were entirely common and hardly taboo. Mothers, overburdened by managing a household in the ruins and now deprived of a male breadwinner and the rather ample allowance that had been paid to wives of Wehrmacht soldiers, missed the disciplining influence of Hitler Youth activities on their increasingly wayward children; indeed the language of "wilding" (*verwildert*) applied to youth is identical to that used to mark the aftermath of defeat in World War I. Their children mourned the loss of

Fig. 2.2. German civilian women and children sit on steps of a bombed-out building.

camaraderie, the singing, the hikes, the sense of belonging to a larger cause. Occupation officers who tried to recruit young people into baseball games and democracy seminars discovered that a generation of young Germans was not ready to replace their lost cause with a new one. They turned instead, it was often bemoaned, to cynicism and the trivial entertainment of movies and light literature. Moreover, they were particularly unreceptive to accusations of collective guilt, often refusing to acknowledge responsibility, at least as vehemently as their parents. "One pulls at us from too many different directions; often I say things that I don't even really mean," one young female student told Thurnwald, suggesting that she was holding onto Nazi ideals out of sheer resentment and defiance.

German women were criticized—in much quoted terms—for having surrendered to the "enemy" much more quickly than the soldiers. But some German women, more angry at having their "ideals" betrayed than horrified at what Germany had done, asserted that it was dishonorable to turn tail too quickly and fraternize with the victors. Using the well-worn language of "honor" (*Ehre*), they asserted that to acknowledge guilt and responsibility would have been dishonorable: "One can lose a war, one can be humiliated, but one doesn't have to besmirch one's own honor." A former Nazi League of German Girls (BdM) leader reflected in 1946: "It slowly became clear to my comrades and myself that a collapse [*Zusammenbruch*] could come. Like many other young people however, we felt it would be cowardly to now betray our cause, and believed, despite quite a few doubts, that we had to hold fast. We had hardly a clue about the inhumane treatment in the KZs, the murder of the Jews, the incompetence and brutality [*Bestialitäten*] of leading figures, and much else that has now become known."[146]

WOMEN, VICTIMIZATION, AND THE GUILT QUESTION

If German women at war's end viewed themselves as largely innocent, albeit sturdy, victims, Americans seemed to be of two minds about them. On the one hand, they appeared as sexually appealing, politically harmless victims; on the other hand, as villainous or certainly complicit seducers and Hausfrauen. American journalist Julian Bach presented a pithy justification for putting women to work in the ruins: "It is not generally realized that the supreme German leadership, especially Hitler, Himmler, Bormann and Sauckel, were against putting women into uniform or even employing them in war plants. This was actually the chief reason why the Germans imported millions of foreign men and women to work as slaves, thereby enabling German women to remain at their sinks."[147] Indeed, in most immediate postwar sources, the *Trümmerfrauen* are hardly heroines. They appear as resentful and reluctant conscript labor—"human conveyor belts,"[148]—former Nazis or Nazi wives, or hungry mothers desperate to escape the "ticket to heaven" category 5 ration cards. In competing versions, they appear as sullen but strong and stoic, wielding shovels and clad in trousers and kerchiefs determinedly clearing away the rubble of dictatorship and war, or as salacious fraternizing "furlines," driven by material need and moral degeneration. Only in the last several years have these portrayals been complemented by stories of German women as victims of mass rape.[149]

Soviets and German communists also struggled to coordinate their presentation of German women as victims—without of course directly referring to their actual experience as victims of the Red Army rather than of National Socialism and war. In the SBZ, National Socialism, militarism, and war were all bundled together as equivalent and connected evils. Women, now constructed as the natural carriers of pacifism, could therefore exorcise past political sins by proper behavior—support for peace and unity in Germany—in the postwar present. And even their sins could be construed as part of their gendered victimization; according to the Communists, it was women's inadequate political education and their entrapment in the domestic sphere that had left them vulnerable to the false appeal of the Nazis. In the last twelve years, women were told, they had endured only the "duty to work, the duty to reproduce, and the duty to silently endure their torment" (Qual). It was precisely their lack of political maturity that had turned millions of German women into voters, supporters, and victims of the Nazis. If only German women had been politically conscious and able to act, the Soviet-licensed press argued, then "Hitler would have never been able to shoot away her husband, son, and the roof over her head." The solution—and women's atonement—was to enter the labor force (where they were now desperately needed) and become active socialists.[150] At the same time, however, new women's magazines that catered precisely to women's supposed concern for the frivolous and domestic were launched in both western and eastern zones. The openly communist Frau von Heute (Today's Woman), first published in February 1946, promised its readers features on "What interests women most? Fashion and cooking." However, most of its tips were of the makeshift variety appropriate to a rubble society, such as how to make nice clothes out of remnants and how to live well without furniture.[151]

Arguments about the particular relationship of women to National Socialism are therefore clearly not just a product of 1970s feminist requestioning or the 1980s Historikerinnenstreit.[152] Despite the experiences and quickly formed memories of female victimization, and precisely because of German women's visibility as victims of sexualized and gendered defeat as well as fraternizers and accomplices of the victors, debates about women's relative complicity or innocence began immediately after war's end. They attained an early peak with the intense and sensationalist press coverage of the Belsen trial and its star defendant, concentration camp guard Irma Grese. If Nuremberg was, in the words of liberal feminist journalist Ursula von Kardorff, "a trial of men" where the only women to be seen were on the prosecution and press bench or defendants' wives,[153] the proceedings in Lüneberg (British zone) in October 1945 dramatically introduced the female face of evil. Journalists, intellectuals, and feminist leaders (many of them Weimar veterans suddenly reemerging into public life) also confronted the role of female nurses and physicians in the "euthanasia" program in the Hadamar Asylum trial and debated the continued public role of Gertrud Bäumer, the leader of the Weimar Federation of German Women's Associations, who had remained partly active and fully unscathed in the Third Reich.[154]

Faced with the undeniable misery of defeat, especially of mothers and children, on the one hand, and the stark presence of female war criminals in the dock at various trials on the other, women journalists and activists were forced to consider how women's active role in Nazi crimes challenged conventional notions of the womanly and maternal. Grese's British defense lawyers relied on an argument that would be examined years later by German feminist scholars. Grese, who had done duty in both Auschwitz and Belsen, was not, they claimed, as she was pictured by the press and prosecution, "the beast, but the scapegoat of Belsen." They suggested that it was precisely the shock of her being female and openly sexual that caused her to be singled out as particularly demonic and inhumane (literally inhuman).[155]

Two sides of the same gender-stereotypical coin were invoked to blame women for involvement in atrocities or more generally for not blocking the rise of Nazism and the catastrophe of war. Christian conservatives and some mainstream feminists accused women of not having been "womanly" enough; they had allowed their essentially female qualities of nurturance and peaceableness to be overpowered by male-identified militarism and destructiveness, and therefore had not adequately asserted female (speak maternalist) values. Communists, socialists, and liberal feminists, on the other hand, tended to accuse women of having been too "womanly"; they had succumbed to their essentially female trait of submission to male dominance and lack of interest in the public and political, and had followed men into violent catastrophe.[156] Particularly in the East, communist activists used this latter argument as a bludgeon for organizing women into antifascist women's councils, and then in 1947 into the Democratic Women's League of Germany (DFD), a SED front organization. In both cases, the "problem" of insufficient resistance was derived from the condition of being a "woman." At the same time, of course, assertions of women's innocence or distance from the evils of National Socialism relied on assumptions about their feminine and maternal qualities. Women were constructed in depressingly familiar terms as both victim and villain; the same reasoning was used to exonerate and condemn.

All these exchanges about guilt and gender had a particular charge in Berlin, where the tangled politics of fraternization between the victors and the former enemy's women were widely considered to have played out differently than in the western zones. This was, as we have seen, in part because the city remained an important media and cultural capital, still identified with its pre-Nazi status as home to the sophisticated and emancipated "new woman," in part because of the competing denazification projects provided in adjacent sectors by four different occupiers, and especially because the background of mass rape continually insinuated itself into the debates about relative German and Soviet barbarism. It was no secret in postwar Berlin that a politics of guilt, revenge, and punishment had been recently enacted on the bodies of German women. The "furlines" and Veronicas, as depicted in the politically and physically infected cartoon character in *Stars and Stripes*, as well as the stolid cleaner-uppers and self-sacrificing mothers designated as *Trümmerfrauen*, were both desirable and dangerous. They were freighted with the shame and horror of rape and the guilt of Nazism as well as emblematic of the victims that war produces.

McGovern's 1956 novel professed to capture this mood: "The cook had lost one son at Orel, another at Kasserine pass, her husband and small apartment in a Liberator raid on Prenzlauer Berg, her modest life savings in the black market chaos, had narrowly escaped being raped by a Russian, and she stubbornly muttered that if she were going to feel guilty, or sorry for anybody, it would be for herself."[157] Berlin's women appeared, however, not only as victims and villains but also as determined, unsentimental, do-whatever-it-takes survivors. James Burke's Lilo personified this tougher, younger version: in July 1945, having made it through the initial Soviet occupation, she walked into the U.S Military Government Press Office to offer her services. She had, after all, worked for the Nazi press. The Americans needed people with skills and experience; they could denazify her "later." Her motto was "Survival! Above all things she must survive. . . . She had survived the rape of Berlin. Surely she could manage from here on."[158]

The 1950 American film *The Big Lift* offered a different critical view of German self-pity and "irresponsibility," which also focused on gender and sexuality. Produced in the context of the new German-American relationship developed during the Berlin airlift, it reflected, in many ways, an antifascist suspicion of German claims to victimization more characteristic of the immediate postwar period. The film features Montgomery Clift

as Danny, the naïve GI supplying the besieged city during the Soviet blockade, who has to learn the hard way that the Germans to trust are the ones
willing to stay and fight for democracy and anticommunism, and not
those who simply want to cozy up to the Americans. The key is re-
ceptiveness to reeducation: "to find out what is right is not so easy," says
Gertie, the cheeky Berliner girlfriend of Danny's more watchful buddy,
gruff and honest Private Kowalski. Danny's devious lover is masquerading as an anti-Nazi in order to persuade him to spirit her to America as
his fiancée, where she can reunite with her German POW husband; Gertie
by contrast is a bona fide antifascist who cleverly uses the American rhetoric of democratization to challenge her GI boyfriend on his patriarchal
attitudes.

By the end of the film, all have learned the proper lesson. Kowalski
concedes, rather melodramatically, that in his male chauvinist behavior
he has "been acting like a storm trooper," and Gertie decides, "I stay here.
I want to see the right kind of Germany." In the meantime, the idealistic
but lovelorn Danny has realized that he has been conned and seduced by
the false anti-Nazi. For this Hollywood production, the older narrative of
the whining, duplicitous German embodied by the amoral, opportunistic
Fräulein (and victim; she is, after all, a *Trümmerfrau*) still had power. The
two American buddies are finally free to go home, having learned a few
lessons about democracy and left behind their foreign women, whether
virtuous or not. In fact, the debate between Danny and Kowalski about
the character of the two Fräuleins with whom they fraternize articulated
the tension in America's relationship to postwar Germany. Kowalski, the
Polish-American (and in some ways, one suspects, a stand-in for a Jewish)
protagonist, is less susceptible to the allures of sham alliances and, even
in the face of the communist threat, less forgetful of the very recent Nazi
past. Like Captain Maginnis, who reflected in his *Military Government
Journal* on Berliners' blinding preoccupation with their own suffering,
Kowalski concludes about the Germans he was protecting from the Soviets: "They can't remember Dachau, Lidice, Buchenwald, Rotterdam, Warsaw. That they can't remember, but that they couldn't get meat last week,
that they remember."[159] With that ending, the film—produced in Hollywood for an American audience but shot on location in Berlin with active-
duty U.S. military personnel as actors—voiced the fears and bitterness of
the Jews who had remained in, or gathered after 1945 in, what had once
been so much their city.

Fig. 3.1.
Jewish Community of Berlin, certification as someone of the "mosaic" faith, who had worn the "yellow star" and survived as an "illegal."

Fig. 3.2.
Magistrat of the City of Berlin, certification as a "victim of fascism."

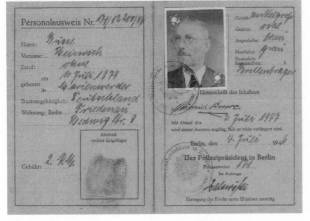

Fig. 3.3.
Berlin police commissioner, certification as resident.

CHAPTER THREE

"The survivors were few and the dead were many"[1]

JEWS IN OCCUPIED BERLIN

> Unfortunately I have heard nothing more from my beloved
> wife, the beloved parents and the rest of the beloved relatives,
> and so I must unfortunately assume, as sad as it is, that
> unfortunately they have all perished.
>
> —Erich Nelhans, November 25, 1946[2]

> The defeated Germany, forced to its knees, fascinated me
> more than any other land on earth.
>
> —Marcel Reich-Ranicki[3]

No SOONER had the Soviets battled their way into the bombed-out capital than Jews began to surface. By the summer of 1945, the Allies counted between 6,000 and 7,000 Jews as residents of Berlin, a surprising and complicated presence in the immediate postwar period. Jews had endured in precarious niches. They had survived "underground," as "illegals" or "submarines" (*U-Boote*), with false papers, hidden in factory lofts, apartments, and the shacks of Berlin's many garden plots (*Schrebergärten*), on the grounds of the Weissensee Jewish cemetery, and both officially and secretly in the strange, ambiguous world of the Jewish Hospital right under the eyes of the Gestapo. Others, categorized as "mixed race" (*Mischlinge*) or partners in "privileged" mixed marriages, had existed aboveground as forced laborers. Two-thirds of those identified as Jewish survivors in Berlin shortly after the war were intermarried or the children of mixed marriages; of the 5,000 to 7,000 Jews who had actually gone underground, perhaps 1,400 made it to liberation.[4] Each of these German Jews, targeted by Nazi racial terror, had an improbable, against-all-odds story of survival. Each one had somehow escaped not only the intense bombing raids, the fire of the antiaircraft flak, and the final battle for the city endured by all Berliners, but also the lack of rations and housing, the constant danger of denunciation or betrayal, and the nerve-racking fear of capture and deportation specific to the Jewish experience.[5]

SURFACING: IDENTIFYING AS JEWISH

As city districts were liberated by the Red Army, Jews returned to public view. German memoirs speak of Jews disappearing but then suddenly, unexpectedly, reappearing in the spring of 1945. In Jewish memoirs, the same stories are told over and over again: the anxious wait as the Soviet tanks rolled closer; the struggle to convince disbelieving Red Army soldiers, some of them "wild for revenge," that not all *Ivrey* were *kaputt*, that the carefully preserved yellow stars or documents marked with a *J* were genuine and not an SS disguise; and, for women, the unanticipated threat of rape. Invariably, the stories continue with the miraculous deus ex machina appearance of a Yiddish-speaking Red Army officer who announced, "*Brider, ihr sayt frei,*" but sometimes not until after the *Sh'ma* prayer had been recited as proof.[6] Gad Beck, a member of the Zionist youth resistance group *Chug Chaluzi* (Pioneer Circle) had barely escaped from his bunker in the Jewish Hospital when he was briefly installed by the Soviets as a "representative for Jewish questions."[7]

Already on May 9, 1945, one day after Germany's unconditional surrender, the apparent presence of so many Jews—the formerly hidden and the newly arrived—so soon after the end of the regime that had been determined to make Germany *judenfrei* unnerved the journalist Margaret Boveri, who had more coolly recorded the horrors of Soviet rapes. She was nonplussed and a bit irritated by her encounter with a young "Rabbi" on a bicycle. Having "successfully hidden himself under a false name" and now armed with two prized possessions, he was riding a bike through the ruins of Berlin carrying a radio:

> So it is no wonder that important positions are crawling [*wimmelt*] with Jews, they have simply crawled out of obscurity. Reinforcements are also supposedly coming from East Europe, especially from Poland—those who are smuggling themselves in with the refugee treks.[8]

By June 6, the Soviets had reinstated police registration. Jews obtained ID cards from an official *Gemeinde* (Jewish community) that Marshall Berzarin of the SMA had quickly ordered reopened and eventually "victims of fascism" (*Opfer des Faschismus, OdF*) insignia from the Magistrat. Martin Riesenburger, who had served as an unordained rabbi at Weissensee cemetery throughout the war, advertised on radio and on remaining building walls for Jewish children to "contact him so that he could organize the first classes in Jewish religion in the city after liberation."[9] The first Bar Mitzvah was celebrated at Weissensee cemetery, presided over by Riesenburger and Edmund Lehmann, a former cantor at the Oranienburger Strasse temple; both men had survived with the help of their "Aryan" (if converted) wives.[10] On June 14, the first postal delivery—crucial for tracking down the lost—arrived in civilian homes and the first, mostly elderly, returnees from Theresienstadt concentration camp were asked to register with the Gemeinde. In July, some two hundred people gathered for a memorial service in the "eerie setting" of the cleaned-up stone ruins of a synagogue in Charlottenburg in the British sector. The young GI Kieve (Akiva) Skiddel described to his wife a service "impressive in the extreme" during which everyone "wept" and "one of the men switched on the Eternal Light which had been out since I don't know when." The ceremony, a conscious reassertion of German-Jewish liberal religious identity, began, heartbreakingly, with a familiar recitation of the *Shehechiyanu*, the Hebrew prayer thanking God for having allowed one to survive unto the present day. It proceeded, however, to a sermon appealing to the values of the Enlightenment and was accompanied by Lewandowski's German-Jewish liturgic organ music, which incorporated in its melody, to the GI's dismay, what he heard as "Arioso" by Handel. Both moved and disconcerted, Skiddel, raised in an East European tradition, commented that it "had the character of a reform service," but "there wasn't a trace of that chill."[11]

Shortly after the Americans entered the city in July, *New Yorker* writer Joel Sayre, in his "Letter from Berlin," also described an encounter in the midst of the rubble:

> Next we got to talking with a pale youth who was carrying a portfolio. He told us he was a Jew and showed us his card to prove it. Jews and half-Jews in Berlin have identification cards issued by the Russians. Each card has the bearer's photograph, declares that he is a victim of National Socialism, and asks that he be given special consideration.[12]

In a dizzying reversal, designations that only days, certainly weeks, earlier would have meant deportation and almost certain death now had concrete, if very limited, benefits; once the "entry card to hell," they "now became a ticket to freedom."[13] During the Third Reich, categories such as degrees of "Jewishness" or marriage to "Aryans" had determined survival possibilities; now new meanings attached to questions about who was Jewish and why. In a time of tumult and extreme scarcity, when goods and services were doled out according to calibrations of victimization or guilt, such assigned identities carried great material weight. They determined access to the protection of the Gemeinde, positions with the occupiers, food rations, housing, and claims to property, or became simply a means of clarifying identity after loss and negotiating bitter and conflicted memories.

The story of my maternal grandfather Heinrich Busse, detailed in fragments of letters and documents, illuminates these drastic shifts of identity. On May 21, 1943, he smuggled a letter to relatives in Switzerland. Several months earlier, after his wife, my grandmother, had been deported to Auschwitz from her forced labor job at Siemens-Schuckert during the infamous Factory Action in late February, Busse, along with several thousand other Berlin Jews, had slipped underground: "My situation is desperate and not to be endured for very long. I am of course homeless and much of the time I have no roof over my head. Everything else you can imagine. . . . I fear, my dear ones, that this is the last sign of life that I can give you." They probably could not imagine, and most traces of his underground existence have disappeared. But, in fact, he did survive, defying Goebbels's promise that the deportation of the "fully" Jewish slave laborers would finally make Berlin *judenfrei*. A March 1945 lodging house receipt under a false name marked him as a still-hunted illegal. On July 28, 1945, three weeks after the Americans had entered Berlin, he filled out the questionnaire on war experiences and current situation issued by the reconstituted Gemeinde in the Oranienburger Strasse, next to the damaged central synagogue in the Soviet sector. In response to the query about when he had been released and from which concentration camp, he reported that he had fled from Gestapo agents when they came for him in the early morning hours at his "Jews' house" in the Berlin suburb of Schlachtensee. Asked about what losses he had suffered, he answered simply, "Everything" (*Alles*), underlining the word, and then elaborated, "house, business, money and property, family." And to a question about whether he had been a member of the Jewish community, he, an avowed secularist, noted defiantly "all my life," something that, as we shall see, was often not true of many of the surviving Jews.[14] He received a modest typed certificate from the Gemeinde, dated August 13, 1945, which certified that Heinrich Busse was a "full" Jew who had worn a star and then lived in hiding. On August 16, 1945, Busse registered with his local Berlin police precinct in quiet intact Friedenau; he was now living as a subtenant in the Fregestrasse, several buildings down from the small villa he had bought and lovingly renovated in 1925, only to see it "aryanized" in 1938. A year later, on July 15, 1946, the Gemeinde issued him identity card number 2584, which confirmed that he was of the mosaic faith, had worn a star, had not been part of a "mixed" or "privileged mixed" marriage, and had lived as an "illegal." His signature attested to the "veracity" of the data, and the back of the card recorded provision of a pullover, socks, shirt, and food. On August 30, 1946, the Magistrat's Office for Victims of Fascism finally issued him a proper identity card with photograph, certifying in German and Russian that he was a full-fledged OdF. He was now stamped as both a Jew and a victim of fascism, identifications filled with painful memories as well as useful for coping with everyday existence in defeated Berlin.

The definition of, and access to, status as either Jewish and/or "victim of fascism" was, however, elastic, unstable, and much contested. The label Jewish denoted first of all those—their ratio of affiliation still measured by various Nazi-imposed standards of blood and marriage—who had survived either under- or aboveground in the Nazi capital. But, as Boveri had already intuited on May 9, 1945, and as the first chapter of this book has indicated, defeated Berlin quickly reverted—albeit under drastically different circumstances—to its prewar role as a magnet for Jews from elsewhere. Jews came to Berlin with the victors. Emigrated German Jews now among the Allied victors, many of them new Americans but also members of the British (including the Jewish Brigade from Palestine), French, and Soviet military, returned to their home city. All four armies also had East European Jewish soldiers—often Yiddish speaking and hailing from the same towns and villages in Russia and Poland—and the Red Army included partisans who had joined up as the war progressed.

Within a short time, other former Berliners slipped back. They hoped to find friends and relatives, reclaim property, or participate in the reconstruction of a new democratic Germany. The latter group included some 3,500 to 4,000 communist exiles identified as Jewish or of "Jewish ancestry" who had returned from Moscow, London, Mexico, and elsewhere.[15] Jews trickled back from the death camps (especially Auschwitz) and were repatriated from Theresienstadt; in 1947, several hundred came from Shanghai.[16] Berlin was unusual in occupied Germany, because of the significant remnant of German Jews who had survived in the capital and also because of the highly visible presence of Jews, in and out of Allied uniform, returning from the camps, slave labor, or exile. But Berlin also sheltered many displaced persons (DPs). By late 1945 and escalating after the vicious massacres in and around Kielce, Poland, on July 4, 1946, in which a charge of ritual killing led to the murder of dozens of Jews, a flood of "infiltrees," as the occupiers called them, was streaming into Berlin. Survivors of the camps, ghettos, hiding, and partisan movements, and in many cases Polish Jews repatriated from the Soviet Union, were now fleeing renewed persecution in Poland. Berlin became a transit stop—sometimes for days and sometimes years—for those seeking safety and possible emigration to Palestine by way of DP camps in the American zone.

Because of these numbers of Jews and their diversity, because the largest group among the small remnant of surviving German Jews was gathered there, and because of the city's emblematic status in both German and Jewish history, Berlin remained a unique, if utterly truncated, center for a continuing German-Jewish community. Inevitably, it also became a center of anguished and sometimes bitter controversy about the larger meaning of Jewish identity and memory in the aftermath of the "Final Solution." Survivors and those who sought to aid them argued about how (and whether) a German-Jewish future could or should be constituted and conceptualized. There were divisions among those who had survived underground, those who had been liberated from the camps, the émigrés who had returned from exile, and the Eastern European Jews who came to Berlin as DPs. There were endless cogitations about whether it was better to stay or to leave, whether the task at hand was simply to administer a fading ghost community (*Liquidationsgemeinde*) or attempt to build a new German-Jewish life. Among those who wanted to leave, there were disagreements between those hoping to head to Palestine and those with other destinations, especially after the U.S. consulate reopened on April 1, 1946. There were disputes between those who were fully Jewish and those who were not; between those with non-Jewish partners and those who did not want to include non-Jews in the fragile reconstituted community; about whether the Jewish remnants should define themselves as German Jews or Jews in Germany; and over who counted as Jewish at all. The latter was an especially wrenching question because of the prominence in the community of those who were partly Jewish or who had non-Jewish spouses to whom they were often especially indebted. Moreover, the meanings ascribed to the term "victims of fascism" were equally fraught and confusing. Who even qualified as a Jew, and how did their fates under National Socialism compare to the suffering of other Jews, "Aryan" antifascists, and ordinary Germans? Were Jews "racially persecuted" victims—a less honorable designation in Soviet-occupied Berlin than the "victims" (OdF), valorized by the communists, who had also been resistance "fighters?[17] Or did they deserve an entirely separate category acknowledging their unique experience of persecution—a recognition that was eventually granted by the American victors?

Just days after the Americans entered Berlin, Gemeinde representatives sent out a distress call to the American Jewish Joint Distribution Committee (JDC or "the Joint"), the major relief organization supporting Jews in Poland and the Soviet Union, which had not yet managed to set up its operations in Germany. All men, some were survivors of concentration camps, but most had survived aboveground or in hiding, often because they were married to non-Jews. They expressed their frustration with the Soviet-appointed authorities' reluctance to recognize all these different categories of Jews—by now they counted some eight thousand—as proper "OdF." Already they felt worn down by the effort to explain and differentiate their fate from that of all war victims, and to mold their experiences into a broad antifascist discourse acceptable to both the Soviet and the American occupiers. The tension was palpable even in their awkward English: "We Jews are just the first victims of every form of Fascism: during 12 years we have been persecuted and our relatives have been killed in the Terror Camps of Maidaneck, Auschwitz, Sachsen-hausen, and all others. If, with a few thousands of Jews, we succeeded to escape, the new German Representation could have considered it an honor, to help us."[18] Carefully testing the new postwar situation, the improvised Jewish leadership tried simultaneously to appease and to remonstrate with the major occupiers. Another letter thanked "most sincerely the heroic troops of the United Nations, especially those of Red Army, for having liberated us few, still surviving Jews from the Nazi villains, and for having saved us from the death by gas chamber and shooting which was planned for us." Pushing the point, they then added, "We who for twelve long years suffered grievous injury to body and soul, who risked our lives to listen to foreign radio broadcasts, heard with great enthusiasm the proclamations, especially from the unforgettable late President Roosevelt, which promised compensation (*Wiedergutmachung*) to us as the racially and religiously persecuted, and now, contrary to our justified expectations, we are disadvantaged."[19]

"We are hungry," the delegates wrote to the Joint, as hungry as the "Aryans," who however had not suffered the previous long years of persecution and privation, and in many cases could still rely on stores of goods and property—some undoubtedly acquired from deported Jews—which they could consume or barter on the black market.[20] Indeed, when the Theresienstadt survivors returned in August 1945, the Gemeinde received poignant letters carefully listing precious last belongings lost or stolen in the confusion of arrival: two little stitched colored tablecloths, two blue and two black skirts, a woolen blouse, silk stockings, nightgowns, and leather gloves. Such were the ironies of life in ruined Berlin that ordinary goods, painstakingly conserved from a pre-Nazi life and brought back from a concentration camp, were then stolen as valuable items to be sold on the black market.[21]

Jewish pleas did not fall on entirely deaf ears; Allied authorities recognized the injustice of expecting Jewish survivors, many of them elderly, infirm, or ill, and unable to work, to subsist on the minimal rations granted to "nonproductive" Germans. On August 3, 1945, the senior British military chaplain argued compellingly (if, unfortunately, not entirely accurately) to his commander, "I am certain that the democratic world would be appalled were it to learn that the Jews, who were the first victims of the Nazis, are deprived of any privileges of suffering."[22] The Magistrat offered 400 marks and privileged rations to concentration camp returnees and their families. On September 29, the joint four-power Kommandatura decreed that Jews were entitled to one ration class higher than the equivalent non-Jewish Berliners, a still inadequate amount for people weakened by years of ever tightening restrictions, slave labor, and persecution, and without legal access to vegetables, fruit, butter, and meat since 1940.[23]

Struggles over money, property, and restitution therefore commenced immediately after May 8, and the Gemeinde quickly began to tussle with the new Magistrat for access to confiscated property and frozen bank accounts. Jews who had been forced out of their homes and into "Jews' houses" (*Judenhäuser*) during the war found themselves essentially homeless. In a war-torn city with extremely limited intact housing, even former "PG" (Nazi Party member) apartments preferentially assigned to "victims of fascism" were liable to requisition by the occupiers or reclamation by denazified tenants, while Jews still struggled to repossess their own "aryanized" homes.[24] Many survivors were in no shape to work, and there were very few Jewish businesses available to employ those who were (with the exception of the relatively few who could reenter professions like law or medicine, where "untainted" personnel were at a premium). For the most part, therefore, Jews in Berlin who were unable to use their own (former) property or money depended on relief supplies and positions with the Allies or the Gemeinde for their livelihood and social contacts.[25]

In March 1946, in its first issue, *Der Weg*, the Gemeinde's semiofficial newspaper, took grim statistical inventory. According to a February census, most of the 7,768 members were single survivors and lived, as the paper perceived, "in infinite loneliness." Only seventy *Glaubensjuden* (of the Jewish faith) were under six years of age, and the largest component was over sixty. The relatively large numbers of elderly, professionals, and those who had identified themselves as "businessmen" were completely atypical for survivors, as was—in sharp contrast to the DP figures—the slight preponderance of women.[26] This unique, mostly elderly, and dependent population reflected the fact that most remaining German Jews in Berlin had not been deported but had survived in hiding, in mixed marriages, or in exile. The Gemeinde therefore functioned not only as a social service and community center but also as a crucial employer; by April 1946 it supported a remarkably large staff of 540.[27] The October 9, 1945, curriculum vitae of Lucie Levy, a social worker at the Jewish Hospital, is probably typical of the Jews who found work within the small community. After a stint as a forced laborer in a Berlin factory, she was deported with her husband to Theresienstadt in January 1943. He was taken to Auschwitz in October 1944, her brother shot "while attempting to escape" from Mauthausen, her parents "deported to the East" in 1942, her sister with her husband and their two children in 1943. Now, half a year after liberation, she was "the only survivor of a large healthy family."[28]

CONTESTED IDENTITIES: DECIDING WHO IS JEWISH AND WHY

Questions of identity assumed even more urgency because of the very real if limited material benefits and possible future compensation now attached to classification as a Jew. Indeed, the files reveal that even as all aspects of past and future were subject to intense argument, much of Gemeinde business was about the banal, about money and bills, about who is entitled and who is not, who is legitimate and who is not. Newly instated officials argued with military, municipal, and JDC representatives, and with each other, about matters such as whether the postwar community should be liable for the cemetery upkeep bills of the Nazi-controlled Central Association of Jews (*Reichsvereinigung*), which was no longer in charge but, with some of its functionaries still in the leadership, not entirely discredited either. Seemingly petty matters loomed large, not only because more or less substantial sums were potentially at stake, but also because they were fraught with memories of pain and guilt, as well as ambivalence about past and future relations with both other Jews and Germans.

The community's exit and reentry records document these confusions of identity and purpose, and the contradictions of attempting to administer in semi-"normal" bureaucratic terms a traumatized community that had been declared exterminated three years earlier.[29] By June 1946, the Berlin Gemeinde had registered some 2,500 petitions for entry and reentry and had to "create a special commission to cope with this phenomenon."[30] Reentry requests came from Jews who had at some point either before or after 1933 quit the Gemeinde, often when they married non-Jews, and who now found membership morally or materially beneficial. Others came from non-Jews. Some applicants had married into the religion but had tried to reverse their conversion to Judaism during the Nazi years and now wanted to reclaim it; others were new converts, carriers of the weird philosemitism of the immediate postwar years who sought repentance or rehabilitation by identifying with Jewish victims.[31] Some of the most poignant pleas came from Jews who had proclaimed their exit very late, during the war, in a desperate effort to protect non-Jewish spouses or partly Jewish children. In bizarre counterpoint to Nazi efforts to categorize Jews and "Aryans," an extraordinary amount of pained energy was now devoted to determining who was Jewish and who was not, whose defection had occurred under sufficient duress to be forgiven, and who was judged undeserving of the modest but all-important relief services and packets offered by the Magistrat, the Jewish community, and Jewish aid organizations.

In the early days right after the war ended, documents certifying Jew-ishness, stamped with a star of David and signed by—as he was called—"Preacher" Riesenburger, were handed out quite liberally to Jews hoping for protection from Soviet soldiers, and looking for food and shelter.[32] With the establishment of a central Gemeinde in the Oranienburger Strasse, the recovery of records, and pressure from the JDC, which had finally set up shop in November 1945, however, the situation quickly changed. All kinds of confusing and contentious decisions had to be made. In the absence of an established religious authority—on occasion, imported rabbis adjudicated queries—American Jewish relief officials ended up setting the standards of Jewish affiliation in the strange situation of postwar Berlin, where so many Jews had only a tenuous connection to their religion. Constrained by limited resources and the need to serve the multiple needs of as many as four hundred clients daily, the JDC insisted that, among survivors living *outside* DP camps, it would support only those who identified as "confessionally" Jewish (*Glaubensjuden*) and were associated with the Gemeinde. Despite the misgivings of Gemeinde members, the main private aid provider to European Jews thereby explic-itly excluded both "non-Aryans" who were not of the Jewish faith and all non-Jewish spouses who had shared their family's fate and often been key to saving their lives.[33] The significance of such a policy becomes appar-ent when one considers that of the circa 8,000 Gemeinde members in mid-1946, 5,500 had non-Jewish partners![34] Those "non-Aryan" Christians, estimated at some 2,500 Protestants, 1,500 Catholics, plus 1,500 without confession, who had been constructed as Jews only by Nazi regulations, had to turn for aid to the less well-supplied offices for the victims of the Nuremberg laws, run by the Magistrat, or Protestant and Catholic confes-sional organizations; in some ways, they were the most isolated.[35]

In a perverse twist, the "Aryan" partners whose continued survival had been so crucial to their families—if they died, the spouse and unbaptized children would immediately lose their protected status and face deporta-tion—now lost, in addition to the Joint relief they had already been de-nied, their right to Gemeinde privileges when their Jewish partner died. As one bereft widow protested, "Were all the years of humiliation and endurance for nothing?" Women who had sustained their husbands with "love and loyalty" should not be denied the few extra food rations granted to Jews, just because their spouses, ailing and exhausted after years of slave labor, had succumbed soon after liberation, "especially since every-one knows it is virtually impossible to live within the legal limit." Care-fully blaming the Joint for such decisions, the Gemeinde replied regret-fully: "There is absolutely no doubt that you shared the miseries of the past years with your spouse, and we would be—if we were only in a posi-tion to do so—most willing to keep on helping you."[36] And in what was perceived as a final indignity, non-Jewish spouses who had stood by their partners while alive were not allowed to be buried at their side in the Jewish cemetery at Weissensee.

In another spooky reversal, the Gemeinde, critical of the Joint's religiously defined limits on aid but desperate to manage its welfare rolls and dependent on the American Jewish organization for relief supplies, actually turned to local police precincts for information on whether applicants for membership or aid had been registered as Jews prior to May 1945. This practice, defensively explained as interest simply in religious affiliation and not "racial" origin, was apparently common enough for the Gemeinde to submit mimeographed typed forms.[37] So the pernicious categories concocted by the Nazi racial laws continued to do their bewildering and divisive work after liberation.

The relevance of these classifications for everyday life, especially for food and housing but also social support, prompted some of those affected to write anguished letters explaining their exit from the Jewish community, and why their return was now a matter of conviction rather than opportunism. The letters addressed to the reentry commission offer glimpses of the dramatic survival stratagems and agonizing dilemmas of Jews—however defined—who had remained in Berlin. Interestingly, in contrast to the public accounts, which have almost always focused on the statistically more numerous Jewish husbands of "Aryan" women, these pleas for reentry into the community came mainly from Jewish women, often wives of non-Jewish men.[38] One woman explained that her fearful "Aryan" husband had pressured her to resign from the Gemeinde. Her mother and three siblings had been deported and murdered, and she had endured years of forced labor for Siemens and constant fear of deportation. With the collusion of a local pastor she had managed to baptize her infant born in 1942 as a Protestant, but now that "we Jews are once again free, I have the urgent wish to see in my child a carrier of a Jewish generation." She therefore beseeched the Gemeinde to "grant as quickly as possible my urgent request for acceptance" so that she, once again a Jewish mother, could then also enroll her child. Other pleas for reinstatement came from "Aryan" women who had converted long before the Nazis came to power, lived as Jewish wives, and then left the Gemeinde in an effort to save themselves and protect their spouse and children. All the petitioners highlight the irony of being denied their Jewish identity now that being Jewish could mean life rather than death.

Making a distinction more plausible in societies with state-regulated religion, many argued that they might have left the Gemeinde, an official organization, but never the religion; they had never abandoned Judaism. Almost all the writers insisted that Jewish officials themselves living under duress in Nazi Berlin had been far more sympathetic to their choices than their postwar counterparts. Another woman explained that when her "Aryan" husband had been very sick and she feared that she would lose his protective presence, she had been comforted by a Gemeinde official who assured her that if she left, she could always immediately rejoin once the terrible years ended. "Internally I always remained a Jew," she wrote, even offering to supply witnesses attesting that she had fasted on every Yom Kippur. A Jewish man married to a partly Jewish woman recounted that when in his frantic confusion he had consulted Leo Baeck, the leader of the Gemeinde until his deportation to Theresienstadt, the rabbi had assured him that he could return to the faith: "We should think of ourselves as *Marranos*, who will, when the right time comes, again publicly affirm our Jewish (mosaic) faith." Over and over, petitioners swore that "in my heart I have always remained a loyal Jew, have always held on to my loyalties internally." It is true, to be sure, that those who had survived often did so precisely because they had only a partial or distanced relationship to the Jewish community. Yet reading their statements, it is hard to believe that these "marginal" or "decimal" Jews—*Paketjuden* (package Jews), as they were sometimes derisively called—wanted to rejoin only because of the puny material benefits; they needed, as a lonely widow wrote, to "know again where I belong and have some support."[39]

The Gemeinde itself acknowledged the delicate complexities of judging not only Jewishness but proper behavior in the aftermath of National Socialism by setting up, in similar form to those organized in the DP camps, its own honor courts (*Ehrengerichte*), to mete out internal discipline on matters judged better left internal. In a situation where survival had depended on secrecy, deception, and lawlessness, and had sometimes been bought by a spectrum of actions ranging from sexual favors to denunciation of others, and where current material claims were also at stake, it was excruciatingly difficult to establish standards of justice and forgiveness for both past and present. In a recognition of the continuing reality of intermarriage, the Gemeinde Assembly found it necessary in 1947 to decree that any of its own officials who married former National Socialist Party members or opted for church weddings could be excluded; even such an apparently obvious ruling was so touchy that it included a provision for appeal to the honor court.[40] The community courts also had to order, for example, that Jews who had helped drag other Jews out of their homes for deportation should be stripped of OdF status.[41]

Sometimes the very ruses required for survival in hiding caused trouble later on, as documented in the elaborate case of a woman who had converted to Judaism upon her marriage in 1921. Hoping to rescue herself and her ("racially") "half-Jewish" child, she had, on the recommendation of her sympathetic—and secretly communist—block warden (*Blockwart*), aggressively collected money for the National Socialist welfare organization, on the theory that an enthusiastic member of the Nazi women's movement would not be suspect. Afterward, one of her neighbors accused her of collaboration with the Nazis. In a mirror image of previous years' charges, the woman countered that in fact her accuser had been the vicious Nazi and was now denouncing her because she coveted her apartment. As actively as she had tried to hide her Judaism, she now tried to prove its authenticity. The supportive affidavits submitted by other residents of the building in working-class Kreuzberg revealed a good deal about social relations in Berlin neighborhoods during and after the war. Indeed, in new variants on the denunciatory practices of Berlin landladies or tenants, letters now arrived at the Gemeinde seeking to expose undesirable neighbors—who were, for example, too loud or likely to fight with each other—as having been especially evil to Jews. Perhaps, one cannot resist thinking, these were the same people who had once denounced their troublesome Jewish neighbors, and perhaps for the same reason: "We finally want to have some peace and quiet."[42]

In the Kreuzberg case, another neighbor reported that "I always felt sorry about" the accuser's merciless harassment of the woman's "half-Jewish" daughter, and had "asked Frau Proske to stop, after all the kid couldn't do anything about it." That neighbor's daughter, also called as a witness, testified that she had continued to play with little Jutta despite Frau Proske's admonitions not to associate "with that Jewish kid." The Jewish convert mother who had pretended to be a Nazi argued that she should not be blamed for actions undertaken "only to save my child and to maintain her and my existence." If she were now to be excluded from the Gemeinde "after all that I have suffered for my husband and for Judaism," it would be an "enormous injustice . . . also toward my child whom," in keeping with a promise made to her late husband, "I have raised and continue to raise in the Jewish faith." In an extraordinary move to seal her case, she even offered to divorce her second (non-Jewish) husband, if that was what it would take get her daughter recognized as Jewish. Pressing the sincerity of her case and doubtless also aware that, at various points, the Gemeinde had made the provision of aid, including ration supplements and emergency cash grants from the JDC, contingent on children's attendance at Jewish religious instruction, she pointed out that little Jutta was currently doing very well in her Hebrew school classes.[43]

TRYING TO EXPLAIN: THE EARLY REPORTS

The first letters posted from occupied Berlin to relatives and friends abroad also provided hints of what Jewish life had been like in Nazi Berlin and how the survivors were coping. Generally they brought devastating news, often in remarkably similar language, as if the Gemeinde had handed out cue cards, but more likely simply a reflection of a common experience and the paucity of vocabulary suitable for narrating unprecedented catastrophe. Erich Nelhans, who had emerged from hiding and immediately immersed himself in his work as a community leader, did not send messages until June 25, 1946. Then, using virtually the same phrases as my grandfather did in his letters, he wrote: "My dear ones, To my deepest regret, I have to tell you that of our entire family only Trude Moses and I are still alive. Deep down, I still have some hope that one or the other will still surface, but after this length of time, it seems pretty impossible." In November he confirmed, "Unfortunately I have heard nothing more from my beloved wife, my beloved parents and all the other beloved relatives, and so, as sad as it is, I have to assume that they have all perished." About himself he was closemouthed, noting only "that I'm doing as well as can be expected under the circumstances." And finally, in April 1947, again relying heavily on the word "unfortunately" (leider), he reiterated that "as hard as it is, we will have to come to terms with the fact that whoever has not yet reported in, is unfortunately no longer alive."

To a young woman who had escaped to London, perhaps as a domestic or with a Kindertransport, and was now inquiring about the fate of her parents with whom he had shared a "Jews' house," he revealed a bit more: "When they came to pick up your parents, I managed to vanish through the back door and up a flight of stairs." Like others who had survived underground, he felt obliged to justify himself, insisting that he tried all that was in his power to help them, but since they were unwilling to venture anything illegal, "They too, like all the others, were taken to Auschwitz and I never heard from them again." He added, knowing surely that it could be no consolation, that he too was now a sole survivor: "All my relatives met the same fate as your parents. I lived illegally for 1 1/2 years and thank God I made it."[44] In a telling omission, which speaks volumes about how painfully difficult it was to convey the complexity of survival, these early letters give no hint of a story told many years later by Gad Beck, the young "half" Jewish Zionist resister whom Nelhans had befriended. According to Beck's perhaps embellished version, it was his comrade in the underground, an "absolutely fearless" former aristocrat turned Scheunenviertel (the old Berlin red-light district that was also home to many East European Jewish immigrants) prostitute named Fräulein Schmidt, who cared for Nelhans in "the storage basement" of a carton factory and later sheltered him in her own apartment in the same building. When Beck met him again in 1946, Nelhans referred to Fräulein Schmidt as his wife, and she "remained Erich Nelhans's partner even after he became the first chairman of the Berlin Jewish community after the war."[45]

Heinrich Busse, my grandfather, also felt compelled to explain his own survival in the first letter that he was able to post to his family in England on December 12, 1945. Recounting his escape in riveting (and occasionally sardonic) detail, he immediately addressed the most important question head-on, unsparingly, and with evident pain: "You will all be wondering, above all, how it is that I am saved and our dear mother was not able to escape the rabble. Well in brief. . . ." His wife, my grandmother, had been deported from Siemens during the Factory Action after he had failed to convince her to attempt a last-ditch flight into Switzerland. Early the next morning, Busse managed to outwit and outrun the three SS men who had come for him, with a "now or never" leap out the window and dash for the nearby Grunewald forest and into hiding. Perhaps still bewildered by his own survival, he reflected, "This was definitely an achievement, it required willpower and determination, as well as quick thinking, but I also cultivated a lot of dumb luck. . . . Well you see I made it."

Busse too took on the grim task of reporting, to those who had escaped abroad, the scope of the horror. To his son-in-law in London (whom he had never met) he sent a "devastating document," the final letter from his mother before her deportation, and warned, "It seems senseless to speak about any further hopes." People were loath to accept what Heinrich Busse, using the same stark formula, had already written to still hopeful relatives abroad in December 1945:

> I am very much afraid that we will all have to accept the awful fact that there is no more hope. Whoever hasn't returned by now, will hardly have, as the Gemeinde tells me, the possibility of reporting or to suddenly surface with the countless refugees who are crisscrossing the country. All the search actions are only a tranquillizer, because how are we to find anyone in the midst of these millions upon millions, especially given the lack of lists and documentation.[46]

Return and Fragile Reconstruction

Those few Berlin Jews who did return from the camps, or safer havens, met a reception both celebratory and anguished. When 295 Berlin Jews were repatriated from Shanghai in 1947, the media presented an upbeat picture of lost natives coming home. Seventy-one-year-old Martin Hamburg, the former London correspondent of the *Berliner Tageblatt*, brought back the same faithful dog that had accompanied him to exile in 1939. A much reprinted photograph showed the actor Martin Rosen, liberated from Auschwitz, at the Görlitzer train station as he embraced

Fig. 3.4. Jewish man in concentration camp uniform makes application for clothing, Berlin.

his eight-and-a-half-year-old daughter Eva, whom he had sent to safety in China when she was only five months old (a mother was not mentioned).[47] The returnees were first taken to Reinickendorf DP camp where, unlike the regular East European residents, they were "lavishly entertained."[48]

The Berlin press also greeted with considerable fanfare the miraculous survival, and return to Berlin and his mother, of one seven-year-old child. Peter Dattel, according to newspaper reports, the youngest child survivor of Auschwitz, was the only one of 8,000 deported Berlin children to return; of the adults, barely one hundred came back. Thanks to the heroic efforts of other inmates, determined to rescue at least one child, mother and child had somehow managed to stay together in the medical experimentation block. But liberation found the mother in another camp, searching frantically for her son. The child, who barely remembered his pre-Auschwitz life, had been taken in by foster parents in Czechoslovakia; Jewish and Czech authorities cooperated to assure a reunion with his mother, who had pursued her search back to Berlin. The Gemeinde marked Peter Dattel's singular homecoming with a festive event attended by members of the occupying powers, the local antifascist committees, the Magistrat, and the Czech military attachés. Fellow Auschwitz survivor Julius Meyer, representing the Gemeinde and the OdF, used the occasion for public antifascist ritual, articulating the survivors' pledge to look forward with hope rather than backward with agony:

> We survivors of this murderous system want to deploy all our efforts to assure that Peter Dattel will become a happy child [*Menschenkind*] whose life will not be destroyed by enmity and persecution.

Such brave rhetoric notwithstanding, Peter's story, like that of most rescued children reunited with parents from whom they had been traumatically separated, was clearly not unproblematic. Mother and son, it was noted, no longer spoke the same language—and not only in a linguistic sense. Indeed, in a scene sadly familiar to UNRRA child welfare workers mandated to reunite long separated families, the child was so terrified of leaving his foster family that he had to be forced into the car taking him home to Berlin. Peter's mother's name or presence at the ceremony was not mentioned.[49] As the first anniversary of liberation approached, *Der Weg* spoke for its readers: "Rescue has come, but we still await salvation."[50]

Such ambivalent stories of loss and haunted new beginnings were central to Berlin's Jewish life. The advertisement and announcement pages of *Der Weg* were filled with notices pleading for any word of lost loved ones, alongside a beginning trickle of wedding, birth, and Bar Mitzvah announcements. The first Bar Mitzvah and engagement notices appeared on August 23, 1946; between July 1, 1945, and March 31, 1946, the Gemeinde counted eleven circumcisions, seven Bar Mitzvahs, and twenty-two weddings.[51] Scattered family members placed death notices for relatives without graves: "In anguished memory of our beloved mother, mother-in-law and grandmother, born 22.12.76, perished in Birkenau," signed by her children in South Africa, Palestine, Shanghai, and Berlin.[52] Another family simultaneously announced its emergence from illegality, the reunion with their mother who had returned from Theresienstadt, and the death of the father in Theresienstadt.[53] Brave new bulletins bordered the unspeakably tragic. In October, community leader Julius Meyer and his wife announced the birth of their daughter Renate. Meyer, who had made it through Auschwitz and the death marches west, had lost eighty-three family members in the camps, including his first wife and child.[54] On the same page as his seemingly miraculous announcement, "A desperate wife and mother" was "searching for her husband and five children" (including twins born in 1927). In postcatastrophe Europe, where so much survivor energy was bound up in trying to locate, or at least to find traces of, the dead and missing, people pleaded that they would be grateful for "any, even the tiniest information."[55]

Advertisements for magicians and seers fed on hopes that perhaps the occult could make the lost visible again. When Hans Winterfeldt finally reunited with his parents in Berlin, he discovered that his parents, with whom he had been deported to Auschwitz after a "Jew catcher" had betrayed their hiding place, had, despite never having been in the least superstitious, spent many hours with a woman who laid cards and sustained them with predictions of his safe return.[56]

While many items declared departures for new homelands—the first train carrying the postwar Jewish refugees from Berlin left from Wannsee station for Bremerhaven and the ships across the Atlantic in May 1946[57]—others publicized the services of re- or newly established Jewish doctors, dentists, lawyers, hoteliers, storekeepers, and stamp and antique dealers or the opening of a kosher butcher shop on July 1, 1946. A Berlin orthopedist simply announced a reopened practice, "Back from Auschwitz"[58]

The Joint's establishment of a tracing office as well as *Der Weg*, with its personal announcements and testimonies, ads for goods and services, and heartfelt polemics, crucially facilitated Jews' tormented efforts to document their past, organize a difficult present, and make sense of a continually contested future. Assisted by five German-Jewish helpers, twenty-one-year-old director Larry Lubetsky, a quickly Americanized young KZ survivor, made it his mission to uncover as much information as possible about the crimes of the Nazis and what had happened to their victims. Lubetsky himself seems to have been a colorful and beloved figure; famous for having "bluffed his way through the gates" of Dachau disguised as an SS officer, he then joined up with U.S. troops and fought with them long enough to receive two honorary bronze stars. He then became a zealous CIC (Central Intelligence Corps) investigator skilled at identifying SS men among German POWs. By 1946, his office in Berlin had processed some fifteen thousand cases, and, in a major coup, he had unearthed an index of deported Berlin Jews, the first actual record of what had happened to the community.[59] The JDC also ran an informal mail service via the U.S. Army Post Office (APO) that provided vital links to family and friends scattered throughout the globe and facilitated emigration plans.

In its first issue on March 1, 1946, *Der Weg* had posed key questions about the future: defining Jews as "co-citizens" (*jüdische Mitbürger*)—a term denoting something less than full integration that, strangely, remains current in today's Germany—the editors adopted a wait and see attitude toward emigration or participation in the reconstruction of Europe and Germany. Germans, they seemed to insist, needed to prove themselves worthy of the Jews' staying or returning; equally obvious was the intense hope—soon dashed—that a reconstructed postwar Germany would be welcoming. As the lead article stated, in a rather astonishing expression of undaunted German-Jewish Enlightenment tenets, the journal wished to "contribute to eliminating totally the rift between Jews and non-Jews that has been ripped open by a twelve-year uninhibited hate campaign against Jewish people." It proceeded to note gravely, as if any readers in 1946 were in need of reminding, that "despite all efforts the anti-Semitic poison that Hitler infused into the German Volk, and not only since his coup d'état, has not yet been everywhere totally eliminated."[60] With each further issue, the journal documented the increasing (rather than diminishing) anger and anxiety about continued antisemitism and lack of remorse among Germans. If, as the former Berliner and British occupation officer Julius Posener reported back to Palestine, "In the summer of 1945, it was considered good form to say that something should be done for the Jews," that sentiment quickly faded, turning to German resentment over perceived privileges and a familiar conviction that "since they were Jews, they would probably do just fine (after all, Jews always know how to get along)."[61]

Views on the proper future for Jews in Germany inevitably reflected wartime experiences. Those who had survived underground, whose voices were more numerous and powerful in Berlin than elsewhere in Germany, tended to have both the most positive and the most narrow perspective. Often they were the most hopeful about the possibilities of reconciliation and cooperation for building a new democratic Germany. During the worst of the Nazi years, isolated in their hiding places, they had encountered primarily the best of the Germans. They generally owed their survival not just to one individual but to entire networks of people, albeit mostly unorganized, willing to help or at least tolerate others who did.[62] Hans Rosenthal, who became a leader of the "reconciliationist" faction in the community even as he developed his radio (and later television) career as one of Germany's best-known talk show hosts, put this into perhaps extreme form in his memoirs. It was, he wrote, the memory of three elderly women who had protected and mothered him in a working-class Berlin garden colony that sustained him in his identification with post-Nazi Germany. They had made it possible, "after this for us Jews so terrible time, to live freely (without reservation) in Germany, for me to feel as a German, to be without hatred, a citizen of this country."[63] Others urged a differentiated attitude, arguing that while "The population was indifferent" and "[a] large majority just didn't care about the fate of the Jews, another [smaller] group helped the Jews and supported them." They added that "in part, however, this help was provided only in return for significant compensation. Still, it cannot be denied that a part of the population did provide selfless help."[64]

Reflecting the shell-shocked mood of its readers, *Der Weg* often seemed burdened by a split personality. At points its invocation of the Jewish contribution to German *Kultur*, as if in a surreal time warp, read like a revived, if reduced, version of a pre-Nazi perspective represented by the Central Union of Germans of Jewish Faith (*Central Verein*, the mainstream self-defense organization). Articles about the early nineteenth century Jewish *salonières* Henriette Herz and Dorothea Schlegel and other German-Jewish luminaries honored the destroyed German-Jewish symbiosis, as if insisting on that history could somehow lead to its resurrection. At the same time, virtually all had to agree that "the few exceptions only proved the rule that in general the crimes against the Jews were tolerated and approved." Moreover, the courageous solidarity of the few did not cancel out the guilty responsibility that Jews assigned to (and did not see accepted by) the great majority: even if those "brave people who supported us will not be forgotten in the judgments of collective guilt and bear witness for the German Volk, they will never be able to wipe out that collective guilt."[65] The "illegals" who had survived in Berlin found themselves on the defensive, prodded into protesting that they too had suffered, albeit in different ways than those who had actually been in the camps. And yet, even for those who had come back from the death camps, there was, as Hans Winterfeldt recalled, a peculiar, bittersweet sense of having returned to a place that was, despite everything, still familiar. This was especially the case for those, like the then-nineteen-year-old Winterfeldt, who had lived underground and were caught relatively late. Despite himself, when he returned, he "still felt somehow at home." The Berlin dialect sounded the same, and "despite the ravages of the bombs and fighting, I knew exactly how I had to get places."[66]

Right after liberation, Jewish observers like the GI Kieve Skiddel were convinced that what Berlin's Jews wanted was "1) food and 2) a chance to get out of Germany."[67] But in reality, the mood was more hesitant and conflicted. A year later, those who wanted to reclaim German citizenship defended themselves, insisting that they were not "bad Jews . . . because we want to stay and work there where we, thanks to our birth and language, our worldly culture and lifestyle, belong."[68] German Jews also struggled with their ambivalent feelings about contributing to the recovery of the German nation and economy. This was a tension less keenly felt by the East European DPs, who carried no obligation whatsoever to German reconstruction, or (at least initially) by the Jewish communists, who had returned from (mostly western, in London and Mexico) exile explicitly committed to building a new democratic Germany in the Soviet zone.

Far-flung German-Jewish refugees followed these debates and anxiously perused lists of survivors in the pages of the *Aufbau*, the New York–based German-Jewish weekly established in 1935 as the flight from Nazi

Germany was just beginning. The *Aufbau* paid intensive attention to the volatile situation in the former center of German-Jewish life. An anonymous but "Authentic Report on the Conditions of the Jews in Berlin" in the September 21, 1945, issue described the varied fates of the Jews who had survived in Berlin, under- and aboveground, as "star-wearers" or as privileged mixed-marriage partners. More ominously, the report already accused Germans of wanting to forget their recent crimes and expecting the Jews to forget them as well. At best, as the *Aufbau* sarcastically put it, the situation was "reminiscent of the old story of the man who slaps another in the face, and then generously remarks, 'for the sake of peace, let's just consider the matter settled.' Or to put it another way, the Jews are now given the right to continue to live peacefully as if nothing had happened." The refugee paper recognized that while unconditional surrender had curbed the open expression of antisemitism, it had certainly not changed "the hate and the hate propaganda that had been injected into the German Volk by all possible means for twelve years."[69] At the same time, however, it defended its brethren remaining in Germany from the distrust and indeed condemnation expressed by international Jewry. *Aufbau* sharply criticized, for example, an open letter to the *New York Times* from Louis Finkelstein, the president of the Jewish Theological Seminary of America—in which he alleged that "a considerable number of German Jews, although victims of the most cruel persecution, still feel that, in this war, Germany was right"—as an outrageous attack not only on "surviving German Jews" but also the "murdered ones."[70]

In fact, Jews' presence in Germany sometimes provided for a measure of justice and revenge. In a crowded city where victims and perpetrators could and did encounter each other face-to-face, Jewish survivors played important roles in the sighting, identification, and (at least initial) bringing to justice of Nazi criminals. One family enjoying a boxing match encountered the "Gestapo man Müller" and immediately called Soviet authorities, who arrested him. A week later, an Auschwitz survivor out for a night at the Metropol theater recognized a female Auschwitz guard; she too was handed over.[71] Such confrontations—and they seem to have been not infrequent—provide a lens on vexed questions about Jewish revenge (or the lack thereof), which are further addressed in chapter 5. They also suggest at least one powerful reason to stay in the land of the murderers after liberation: the drive to expose and punish the guilty. At least at the beginning, it seems, Jewish survivors counted on Allied support and gratitude, especially from the Soviets and Americans, for these acts of vigilante justice. Most important in some ways was settling accounts with Jewish collaborators, particularly the dreaded "Jew catchers," who had, toward the war's end, become one of the greatest dangers for Jewish illegals in Berlin. *Der Weg* noted the capture of the notorious Stella Kübler with satisfaction; she had been "rendered harmless."[72]

Everyday life in occupied Berlin offered multiple opportunities for various forms of revenge. Winterfeldt, the young survivor who slowly made his way home from Auschwitz, stubbornly refused to give up his seat in the S-Bahn for elderly Germans, even as he abashedly took pleasure in hearing once again the familiar rough, sarcastic Berlin dialect.[73] Lothar Orbach, who had also spent most of the war hidden in Berlin, registered similarly complicated feelings. Not unlike Gad Beck, who recorded with glee his homosexual as well as political adventures underground, Orbach had lived a nerve-racking life not without its pleasures. In his memoir, which reads like a heterosexual version of Beck's account, Orbach recalls the thrill of wartime Berlin, his love affairs, his contacts with communist resisters, his hideouts in seedy pool halls and brothels—"romance, friendship, delight, and adventure in the midst of murderous oppression"— with a certain degree of embarrassment and disbelief. But Orbach also spent "eight months in the hell of Auschwitz and Buchenwald," after nearly two years as an "illegal" in Nazi Berlin. When he returned to Berlin in 1945, his mourning for all that was lost and relief at finding his mother still alive mingled with intense feelings of triumph and revenge: "I wore the dark blue Eisenhower jacket the Americans had given me so that any Nazis I might meet could appreciate the dramatic reversal in our relationship." Hired by the U.S. Army as an interrogator, Orbach felt "grateful for the chance to be involved in a small way in the process of retribution," tasks that extended well beyond those officially sanctioned by his American employers. Immediately after his return, he went straight to the apartment of a Jew catcher, thoroughly beat him up, dragged him out, and turned him over to a Russian officer. It "was only a token gesture," Orbach conceded; the man was released shortly thereafter: "But the fact that it was a score settled, no matter how trivial in the larger scheme of things, relieved me of a burden, and helped me close the book on a long nightmare."[74] In gratitude to the Soviet communists who had liberated him, Marcel Reich-Ranicki returned to Berlin in the service of the Polish secret police: "In order to see Berlin again," he reflected, "who knows, maybe I would have even made a pact with the devil." The temptation had as much to do with revenge as nostalgia: "The defeated, the forced to its knees, Germany fascinated me more than any other land on earth."[75]

REVENGE AND COMPENSATION: EARLY CONFLICTS

The intensity of these early debates and confrontations was fueled by their attachment to concrete current questions of livelihood, money, and property, as well as bitter memories. The special office for the restitution of Jewish property, right off the Kurfürstendamm, opened in 1945, was undoubtedly one of the most important addresses for Berlin Jews. After

May 8, some residents appeared at the Gemeinde headquarters in the Oranienburger Strasse to drop off Jewish property that they had acquired at auctions or that had been entrusted to them by neighbors or friends for safekeeping. Others, such as a dentist eager to hang on to his new equipment, maintained that the items had been genuine gifts from "relocating" Jews. Women responded to the Gemeinde's call for hidden children or infants, raising heartbreaking dilemmas of whether Jewish children raised by Christian rescuers should be removed from their foster parents and sent to bare-bones orphanages run by the Jewish community.[76] Survivors returned home only to find that neighbors were not only claiming cherished objects left behind by their deported families but also constructing their own versions of what those possessions signified. One man encountered a friendly woman in his parents' apartment who was convinced that lighting candles on the family menorah, supposedly given to her on the eve of his parents' transport to the East, had protected her from the Allied bombs.[77] Stephen Spender, the British poet who worked for the British occupation, alluded to such stories when he reported that "now no one will admit guilt, but during the war as bombs hailed down, people said openly 'this is what we have asked for. This is how we acted toward the Jews and this is being visited against us.'"[78]

Nazi Finance Office (*Oberfinanzpräsidium, OFP*) records provide a meticulous accounting of the possessions auctioned off to Berliners after their Jewish neighbors had "disappeared." Complete with precise descriptions, prices paid, and names and addresses of the lucky bargain hunters, they give a sense of how many people must have helped themselves to such wares, certainly many more than those who appeared—for whatever motive—at the Gemeinde with their Jewish booty. My paternal grandmother Gertrud Grossmann's file, one example among many, catalogues the auction on December 12, 1942, of the paltry goods she had left behind when she fled a deportation order in June. Everything of value had apparently already been sold, a Gestapo agent noted with disapproval, but for 140 Reichsmarks a Frau Anna Fischer, Andreastrasse 15, garnered a suitcase containing a few vests and old down quilts, some bookshelves, a round little table with winged legs and a glass top, and two armchairs. Two tennis rackets went to Karl Stahl in the Woldenbergerstrasse, for 35 marks each; the list is several pages long.[79]

Many of those who did return goods surely were hoping for a *Persilschein*, the (in)famous certificate named for a detergent that did a particularly good job of whitewashing. These simple, typed documents generally required that someone identified as "non-Aryan" attest to good behavior toward Jews during the Nazi years.[80] Others wanted to guarantee or regain OdF status by having Jews certify their persecution as antifascists. Former Nazis turned to the "black market in grandmothers," approaching Jewish survivors and offering money or food for certification as partial "non-Aryans." Or, as rumor had it, they purchased their fraudulent *Persilschein* from enterprising DPs, or hired German-Jewish lawyers to defend them in their denazification proceedings. The Gemeinde censured such cynical (or sentimental) actions, warning of a common dilemma: even if Germans had been personally helpful in individual cases, such "subjective" judgments did not take into account that the same people might very well have sent others to their death.[81] American reporters, disgusted by this traffic in expiation, claimed that "some Germans after the war actually gave themselves a KZ tattoo."[82]

Insa Eschebach's study of rehabilitation petitions from former Nazi Party members offers a classic example of how Germans, now in the ironic position of hoping for a favor from those who had shortly before had no rights whatsoever, often equated the victimization of Jews—if they acknowledged it at all—with their own supposed victimization: "As a reference for my husband and myself, I would like to name the attorney Julius K . . . who has known us for over 30 years, and as a Jew, suffered just like us [*sic*] under the Nazi regime."[83] Hilde Thurnwald's remarkably open early postwar interviews recorded numerous examples of the dissociated and self-serving stories that Germans told themselves about what had happened to their Jewish neighbors, and how the interviewees had reacted. These recitals, rendered in the innocent passive voice that so exasperated occupiers and embittered Jews, were not about silence or not having "known" or "seen." They readily acknowledged persecution of Jews while simultaneously skirting the reality of the "Final Solution," deflecting any personal responsibility, and asserting German victimization. A twenty-three-year-old former Nazi student teacher told Thurnwald in 1946:

I can still remember the persecutions of the Jews pretty precisely. One had [*Man liess*] the stores plundered and the people who carried out these tasks enriched themselves with the goods and property of these people. When my father first talked about this at home, I did not want to believe it, but then several acquaintances spoke about it also and I was appalled by these things. Later the Jewish families were evicted from their homes and I felt sorry for those people, for they had surely not deserved such treatment. My father then got into trouble because he bought his cigarettes in a shop whose owner was a Jewish woman. We didn't care about that however, and my father continued his purchases there until the closing of the store.

So in a perverse linkage that circumvented—but somehow also took for granted—the fate of the Jews, the young woman's father was endangered because he had bought his cigarettes in a Jewish-owned store until it "closed."[84]

Thus, even as Jews struggled to have their basic needs met, their access to supplies and their positions with the Allies and the Jewish and UNRRA relief organizations provoked a familiar resentment. Defeated Germans now saw Jews as privileged, with more than their fair share of scarce material and political resources in a smashed city. Infuriated, pained, and sometimes shocked by this persistent antisemitism, Jews saw Nazis go unpunished or lightly punished and former party members peremptorily repossess property while the Jews had to wait for the inadequate compensation they quickly demanded. Following the May 26, 1945, SMA order that buildings obtained from Jews after January 31, 1933, be restituted to their (mostly dead or emigrated) owners, some Berlin districts actually tried to ask inhabitants about what they had acquired from Jews during the Third Reich. Despite promises of amnesty, of some 160,000 inhabitants in affluent Zehlendorf, only seven replied.[85] The Soviet-controlled *Berliner Zeitung* addressed this issue directly, albeit with a bit of affectionate humor, and in the voice of a Berliner speaking the distinctive (and untranslatable) local working-class dialect: "We were always against it. . . . Well, OK, that thing with the Jews' apartment and the furniture—if I hadn't taken it, someone else would have. With us, the stuff was in good hands, and if the folks come back—well, they're all supposed to be dead—then they will shake my hand in thanks. That's the way it is."[86]

Proposals for the inadequately named *Wiedergutmachung* (reparations program, literally "making good again") were immediately on the agenda (the *Aufbau* began running columns on the topic starting in 1945). In the absence of any possibility for appropriate revenge or really "making good again," the extraction of monetary compensation became a major means of trying to enforce memorialization of the dead and German responsibility for Jewish suffering. For Berlin's Jews, the sometimes manic exhilaration of survival was severely tempered, therefore, not only by the loss of (as Busse had put it) "everything," but also by the growing awareness of how inadequately Germans, and even Allied authorities, relief agencies, and other Jews recognized, much less understood, their ordeal. Germans resented the benefits granted their former neighbors by the Allies and muttered about Jewish "revenge" driving war crimes trials and denazification measures. Jews in turn were outraged that defeated Germans profited from "aryanized" homes and businesses while they had to struggle for minimal restitution.

Struggles over Restitution: The Hotel Astoria in the Fasanenstrasse

The dusty folders of my family's *Wiedergutmachung* files tell a story that, in its irreconcilable narratives of what had really happened in the Nazi period, is entirely typical of the bitter gulf of experience and memory that separated those who had once been fellow Berliners after 1945. One version—not my family's—can be found in a brochure published for tourists coming to Berlin in the millennium year 2000/2001. Celebrating "The Story of a Hotel" with "a special style and service like in the good old days," it announces that Paul Berghausen, the grandfather of the present owner, had "purchased the lot and building Fasanenstrasse 2" in 1938. After being "partially destroyed by the vicissitudes of the Second World War," the business was "confiscated" by the British occupiers of Charlottenburg from 1948 to 1950. But then "things started looking up." Reopened in time to catch West Berlin's postblockade "economic miracle," the Astoria "continued its prewar history. . . . In a house that had been constructed in 1887 according to old-fashioned artisan tradition, the charm and solidity of the past century could be preserved."

In fact, the Astoria's early postwar years were marked by a bitter battle between my father, whose parents had owned the building from 1913 to August 1938, and the Berghausens over that prewar history, the sordid events of "aryanization," and the forced sale of Jewish property in Nazi Berlin. In a twenty-one-page deposition, the Berghausens angrily rejected his claims, asserting with the righteous certitude of many Germans determined to protect their economic gains that at issue was not National Socialist expropriation but "a completely apolitical and economically justified contract in which no coercion or pressure of any kind had been applied." Indeed, the Berghausens' lawyer argued, in the unmistakably and quite unselfconscious antisemitic language that was still normal in the late 1940s and early 1950s, the remarkably low sale price was entirely appropriate. Far from praising the "charm and solidity" of their 1938 acquisition, the Berghausens described a "failed speculation" that had produced no profit from its newly renovated luxury apartments, leading the "businessman" Grossmann to lose his "zest" (*Lust*) for further investments after World War I. Moreover, when his widow took over the building in 1931, she "maintained the venal commercial principles of her late husband, avoiding extra expenses and letting the building fall into disrepair." The "aryanizers'" attorneys did not mince words: "Under no circumstances can one hold the buyer responsible for any injustices perpetrated by others in the context of Nazi ideology that the seller *might* have experienced."

Gertrud Grossmann managed to elude her first deportation order for almost a year and a half, but in 1943, on the thirty-ninth *Osttransport*, she was deported to Auschwitz, where she was murdered.[87] Gertrud's three sons survived. One was liberated at Mauthausen after having made it through two years in Auschwitz. Another settled as a doctor in Hartford, Connecticut, and the third, my father, spent the war as an enemy alien interned by His Majesty's government in British India. Now the two physicians were counting on their brother, the former Berlin lawyer, to use the reparations edict forced on Berlin by the Allied Kommandatura on July 26, 1949 (Article 23 REO, Restitution of Identifiable Property to Victims of Nazi Oppression), to rescue what he could. My father's memories of the 1938 transactions, transcribed in the court papers, were furiously different from the Berghausens' innocuous version:

> Herr Berghausen had repeatedly boasted of his good connections to the party . . . and that if my mother did not sell him the house on his terms, he would find ways and means to acquire it in any case. Considering the general lack of basic rights for Jews in Germany, and Mr. Berghausen's barely concealed threats, my mother and I decided it was only prudent to accede to his threats.

On September 14, 1953, after a lengthy and bitter legal battle, the *Berlin Wiedergutmachungskammer* (Restitution Court) finally ordered the hotelier Paul Berghausen to pay the heirs of Gertrud Grossmann the modest (and today, of course, absurdly small for a property in the heart of Berlin) sum of DM 20,000.[88] Like so many ordinary Germans who had profited by buying the property of desperate German Jews at extreme bargain prices, and had managed to preserve their new possessions through the war and defeat, the Berghausens were then free to pursue the economic success that was, in their perception, completely honorable and well earned. In 2002, they received an award, personally handed over by Mayor Klaus Wowereit in a City Hall ceremony, for the "friendliest small hotel in Berlin." They never again had to confront or publicly acknowledge the unfriendly history of their family and of the hotel they proudly celebrate.[89]

Jews and Allies

That any early restitution occurred, and that a skeleton of German-Jewish life quickly revived, had a great deal to do with the presence of the Allied and especially American victors. The German-Jewish return was relatively tiny and in many cases temporary, even as the city, a traditional crossroads of Eastern and Western European Jewish life, became—also with the collaboration of the Americans—a key destination for fleeing Eastern European survivors.[90] In the liminal early postwar years from 1945 to 1947, however, the Jewish presence was highly visible and much commented on—in a manner quite disproportionate to the number of surviving German Jews who remained or had returned. That presence was even more noticeable because it appeared so often in occupier uniform. Berliners found themselves surprised by some occupiers' flawless German or, as actress Hildegard Knef remembered, a German that somehow became better and better with each sentence.[91] One of young Polish officer Marcel Reich-Ranicki's first excursions in Berlin took him to the apartment of Reinhold Klink, a beloved teacher from the traditionally liberal (mostly Jewish) high school he had attended in the 1930s. "Quite by the way," Klink "remarked that he received visitors often now. The guests usually wore American or English uniforms. They were his former Jewish pupils"[92] For these Jews in victors' garb, it was a strange "*Heimkehr in die Fremde*" (homecoming to the foreign), a peculiar, poignant, in-between position. They could no longer see themselves as German but were also not yet fully Americanized, and were distrusted to some extent by both their new and their old compatriots. As the playwright Carl Zuckmayer, a non-Jewish exile, remembered, "I did not belong to the victors, but also not to the vanquished. Only now after the return had I become really homeless and did not know how I would ever find a *Heimat* again." But he acknowledged that he might have felt less ambivalent if, like many of the Jewish émigrés, "my mother had been murdered."[93]

Such returnees, whether permanent or temporary, also faced the resentment of Berliners who had stayed behind. Even antifascists imagined that somehow the Jews who had been able to flee the Nazis were lucky to have been forced into exile instead of having to remain in Germany and endure the war. The physician Anne-Marie Durand-Wever also articulated such sentiments, in terms remarkably uninformed about the possibilities for emigration: "Back then, if they were smart enough and were warned in time, the persecuted Jews and dissidents still had the possibility to go abroad; in the early days they could even take part of their fortunes; the whole world stood open to them."[94] In the postwar competition of victims, as Hannah Arendt caustically noted, Jews were often treated to recitations of how many family members a German had lost.[95]

Jews, with their OdF and Gemeinde ID cards, did benefit from their access to the victors and the various relief agencies, especially UNRRA, which was responsible for DPs; the British Relief Unit, which cared for German Jews; and the Joint, which dealt with both groups. Yet these "privileges," which included, as Germans pointedly noted, supplies that could be profitably traded on the black market, were hardly straightforward or trouble-free, and always subject to negotiations among four often quarreling occupying powers. As in western Germany's American zone, military chaplains quickly assumed a leading role in organizing relief and rehabilitation efforts. In the first months of the U.S. occupation, when the JDC did not yet have access to the defeated capital, it was literally the cast-off rations of American Jewish GIs and their packages from home that supplied survivors' basic needs. Yiddish-speaking American and former German-Jewish GIs and officers stationed in Berlin became a first lifeline; some five thousand Red Cross packages intended for GIs were distributed to the survivors. Soldiers collected the memorabilia of destroyed European Jewish life; a Purim *megillah* that a camp survivor had somehow managed to preserve, the surgical knife that had been used to perform the first ritual circumcision in liberated Berlin, books on Jewish religion and history.[96] Jewish soldiers subverted American and British antifraternization regulations to contact survivors—both those for whom they were searching and those whom they simply encountered on the street—and quickly provided them with food, the opportunity to send and receive messages, and sometimes jobs. Lothar Orbach's three older brothers who had managed to emigrate all worked for U.S. Army Intelligence and helped him find work as an army investigator and interrogator.[97]

Jewish Allied military personnel, Berlin Jews, and DPs all gathered at the American officers' club, Harnack Haus, in the intact suburb of Dahlem for religious services; many attended their first High Holiday services there in fall 1945. The American Chaplains Center, in a comfortable Dahlem villa requisitioned from a Nazi family and still filled with an "abundance of Nazi literature, pins, emblems, and paraphernalia," became a gathering place for Jewish soldiers from all four armies and the British Army's Jewish Brigade. The center functioned as a social and political first aid station for the many different groups of Jews in Berlin and as an effective intermediary between the Gemeinde and the JDC, between German Jews and DPs, between Americans and other Allies, and among the JDC, UNRRA, and U.S. Military Government.[98] By the summer of 1946, the Berlin Jewish Club, supervised by U.S. Army chaplain Herbert Friedman, was serving about 450 Jewish Allied soldiers and civilians, and had become another important site for cross-national Allied encounters. Especially the squabbling Americans and Soviets (whose officers often knew German) found that "if one of the Americans happened to be a Jewish boy who spoke German-Yiddish, the Russian and the American found some common ground there where they could understand each other's words."[99] In the Chaplains Center, a Soviet captain and a Jewish officer could be found shaking hands; in a GI photo album the photo caption read, "Solidifying international friendship."[100] Kieve Skiddel had already noticed in July 1945 that "the proportion of Jews among the higher ranking Russian officers is uncommonly high. I haven't enough to go by naturally, but I did actually talk with as many as three majors, 1 captain and 2 senior lieutenants."[101]

In April 1946, an enormous public Passover Seder for over two thousand soldiers from the four armies, and including local Jews, was held in the Schöneberger Rathaus (City Hall), which would later become famous as the site of John F. Kennedy's "I am a jelly-doughnut" speech honoring

Fig. 3.5. Passover Seder for Allied soldiers and Berlin Jews and Jewish DPs, presided over by U.S. Army chaplain Rabbi Herbert Friedman, Rathaus Schöneberg, April 1946.

the citizens of West Berlin. It was led by Chaplain Herbert Friedman, who was, as we shall see, precariously balancing his duties as U.S. military rabbi and an operative for the Zionist *Bricha* (flight) movement working to smuggle Polish Jews into the American zone. Heinrich Busse, the still malnourished, assimilated Berlin-Jewish *U-Boot*, offered his daughters in London a rather pragmatic "Berliner *Schnauze* [wit]" rendition of the celebrated event: "there was a very good meal for free, but in exchange one had to listen for hours to an English-Hebrew service, which not a soul understood."[102]

For American Jews, the encounter with the remnants of European Jewry and the remarkable power granted by their uniform to offer aid and comfort—often at the expense of Germans—made a profound and lasting impression. GI Saul Loeb recalled the "unforgettable moment" in 1945 when, after he had driven the elderly cantor Gollani to the Oranienburger Strasse temple in his jeep, Gollani "cried as he walked through the rubble" and "began to chant a prayer in his old, wavering voice." Photos preserved in Loeb's album depict a variety of Berlin-Jewish scenes in the first half year after liberation: a Sabbath service at Harnack Haus, attended by somber young men in hats and women with dark hair and curls among the uniforms; a meeting with a sergeant from the Jewish

Brigade and a Polish Army captain at the Chaplains Center; a visit to the Jewish Orphans Home; a November 1945 Hanukkah party marked (surely erroneously, as were so many formerly banned events in postwar Berlin) as the first one since 1932. At the end of the holiday service, a photo of a large star of David marked with the word "*Jude*" was "brought out and later torn to bits!" to cheers from the audience of over two thousand. Very quickly, a kind of family life developed at the Chaplains Center, with a Polish Jewish boy who had been adopted as a kind of live-in mascot, children's parties, jazz and swing bands improvised by the DPs, and the all-important wedding celebrations.[103]

By February 1946, in a coup that gave great pleasure to the JDC and the U.S. Army accomplices who helped engineer it, the Sarotti baking plant, reopened under the supervision of a Jewish family that had been "baking matzoh for five generations" and had survived in hiding, was already preparing *matzos* for the first postliberation Passover. Assuring that such holiday landmarks could be properly celebrated became a consuming interest for both relief workers and survivors, necessitating complicated (and often illegal) but satisfying escapades in production, transport, and distribution. Dairy products and kosher meat from Denmark and Palestinian wine and raisins arrived just in the nick of time, and *Mashgeachs* (food supervisors) recruited from the DP camps certified that everything was indeed properly kosher for the festivities.[104]

Transit Station Berlin: DPs, German Jews, and Amis

While Germans and Allies treated the return of Berlin's native Jews with ambivalence at a minimum and sometimes even satisfaction, the daily arrival of several hundred non-Berliner Jewish survivors in the officially closed city caused what one U.S. officer termed a "red-hot" crisis. Squabbles about the "Polish Jewish problem held center stage" at a surprising number of Allied Kommandatura sessions.[105] The major challenges, as was the case throughout occupied Germany, were "food, coal, motor fuel, and transport," but even seemingly minor problems were always on the verge of becoming international incidents. The British and the Soviets, anxious to stop the flood of refugees, vigorously opposed, for example, U.S. efforts to sanction Yiddish as an approved language for postal service into and out of Berlin.[106] By the end of 1945, almost fourteen thousand Polish Jews had come through Berlin's transit camps, with many more arriving in 1946, especially after the shock of the July pogrom in Kielce. These troublesome Polish-Jewish "infiltrees," who were now fleeing the nations to which they had been repatriated or to which, according to citizenship protocols, they belonged, thoroughly flummoxed U.S. authorities:

Something drastic had to be done. At one time, we considered throwing a barricade around the city, but that would only have caused camps to spring up on our doorstep. . . . The only thing we really could do was to maintain control over the refugees passing through, giving them one meal at night and shipping them out the next morning.[107]

The Americans tried hard—but unsuccessfully—to transfer new arrivals, especially pregnant women and mothers with young children, quickly to larger and ostensibly better-equipped UNRRA camps in western Germany. Hoping to stem the flow, U.S. Military Government initially resisted establishing anything more than transit centers, arguing that "the Jewish population resident in Berlin in the main did not desire to have a camp created for them, stating that they had seen enough of camps."[108] Yet the numbers of refugees—mostly funneled into the city by the "open secret" of the underground Zionist *Bricha* network, which planned to use the DP camps in Berlin as a way station to the American zone and eventual illegal emigration (*Mossad Le-Aliyah Bet*) to Palestine—continued to grow.[109] U.S. officials, under pressure from American Jewish organizations and constrained, as we shall see, by the August 1945 Harrison Report's call for better treatment of surviving Jews, could not as easily, guiltlessly, and unilaterally ban all Jewish DPs from their sector as the British and French, and certainly the Soviets, did. The British, determined to stop illegal immigration to Palestine, flatly said no. Jewish refugees, they insisted, were to be treated no differently from other repatriable displaced nationals. The French, with only one DP camp (Wittenau), over which they exercised very little control, in their sector, while sympathetic, pleaded poverty and lack of resources. The Soviet general, with "a puckish smile on his face," took a "hands off" attitude, rather gleefully noting that the refugees all snuck into the West anyway. In fact, by the end of December, the Soviets succeeded in ridding themselves of the remaining 2,500 Jewish DPs in their sector, including some 200 pregnant or postpartum women, by threatening to move them to camps near the Polish border. Predictably, this prospect provoked them to flee west immediately. The U.S. Military Government officer responsible recalled, "Everyone was irked by the way we were being browbeaten into assuming responsibility for all of the Polish Jews, regardless of what sector of Berlin they were in."[110] Local German authorities, for their part, had no compunctions about categorizing East European Jewish "infiltrees" as unwelcome and threatening foreigners who threw their supposedly considerable money and goods into the flourishing black market. Already in December 1945, the Magistrat demanded that the Allies deal with the problem, preferably by a rapid deportation (*Abtransport* [sic]).[111]

By November 1946, Berlin was housing a total of 7,845 Jewish DPs—including some 1,000 infants and children—in DP camps under UNRRA management. The best known was a former Soviet POW camp in Zehlendorf known to the Americans as Düppel Center and to the DPs, referring to the nearby S-Bahn station, simply as Schlachtensee.[112] About 200 people a day "arrived and left, all put through delousing, medical checks, and cleaned up; none were allowed to leave unless they were free of disease and [had] proper clothing." As if surprised, an American officer noted: "We had a large number of stateless persons. The Germans certainly had mixed up a lot of people in Europe." The camps were quickly pulled into "shape, spic and span, spacious and well-organized," and the Americans, turning necessity into virtue, boasted that they had become a "showplace for visitors interested in seeing how comfortable DPs could be made and how sensibly they could be cared for."[113] Unsurprisingly, many of them did not leave as quickly as the Americans had hoped. When Joseph Berger's family fled Poland via Stettin right after the Kielce massacre, they rode a truck to Berlin and then took the U-Bahn to Schlachtensee, where they were greeted with their "own room in Block 11. . . . We had four olive-green American army cots, four olive-green blankets, four olive-green sheets, and four olive-green pillows. I began thinking of this room as my home," wrote his mother.[114]

The steady influx from the East, while often spontaneously driven by Jewish desperation to escape Poland and not always (as many Allies suspected) conspiratorially organized, certainly had much to do with the combined efforts of *Bricha* agents from Palestine and some American Jewish military personnel. American Jewish soldiers and chaplains became deeply involved in the Zionists' "cloak and dagger" activities. American cigarettes, coffee, and chocolate, "liberated" from army supplies or sent in packages from home by parents and wives from the States to Jewish GIs, eased the border crossings. A young Reform rabbi named Herbert Friedman, who had presided over the giant Passover seder at the Rathaus Schöneberg, was recruited by Zionist operatives in Paris to help transfer Jewish refugees from Poland into Berlin. Friedman, who had been attached to Patton's Third Army and was working with survivors in Bavaria, finagled a transfer to Berlin, and, in a remarkable feat of wearing multiple hats, served both as chaplain to Jewish servicemen and facilitator of a huge human smuggling operation. Years later, in a 1992 interview, he recounted his exploits, with undiminished pride, to an interviewer at the United States Holocaust Memorial Museum. A ready supply of three hundred cartons of cigarettes per trip, initially donated by Jewish GIs—who forfeited the Leica or many "occupation marks" they could acquire with these cartons, which cost them only $7.00 at the PX—and by his father's congregation back home in New Haven (and then eventually by

Fig. 3.6. Two young friends on motorcycle, Schlachtensee DP camp, Berlin.

the JDC, which shipped them from Antwerp to Bremerhaven and then to Berlin), placated border guards and fueled the mission. Six "liberated" army trucks, each manned by two "Palestinians" (one driving, the other riding shotgun) and filled with siphoned gas, would leave Berlin at dusk and reach Stettin, 150 miles away in the Soviet zone, at around midnight. *Bricha* agents had people lined up on the Polish side of the border; some three hundred Jews, fifty to a truck, were quickly loaded. Leaving Stettin at midnight, they rolled into Wittenau at dawn and then moved on into the American sector. It was a tough and adventurous operation, filled with romance for the Americans and the Jewish agents from Palestine, and much anxiety and uncertainty for the determined refugees. As Friedman remembered, if there were too many people and not enough space on the trucks, the baggage was simply thrown overboard. Even people's last, most precious possessions and mementos were cast off, "the poor crumbling pieces, suitcase, a valise, that mostly had in it things like photographs, diaries . . . it was "kind of ruthless."

Crucial to the success of these semiclandestine border crossings was the "one eye closed" tolerance of sympathetic non-Jewish superior officers and buddies: "The key was to get to know the supply sergeant." Army postal inspectors were not oblivious to the increased flow of packages to Berlin but disinclined to interfere, once initiated into the goals of the operation.[115] Friedman insisted that he also always made sure to cover his back by keeping the "top echelon" informed. He assured the army brass, including General McNarney, who had replaced Eisenhower as supreme commander in Germany, that a controlled flow of refugees with some American knowledge and supervision was preferable to the chaos that might otherwise ensue.[116]

As commissioned officers, chaplains were able to take advantage of the double privileges of the "cloth" and the "conqueror" in order to support those Jewish DPs who settled into the Berlin camps. Mayer Mayerowitz, who also worked the *Bricha* route, proudly produced "more than 3,000 copies of seven Hebrew language textbooks" for the DP camp schools. Dressed up in his most impressive uniform and armed with "A dozen bags of coal and twenty tons of cigarettes," as well as "hundreds of tons of bond paper, hundreds of file folders and a few gallons of mimeo," secured with the help of the indispensable supply sergeant, he quickly convinced a German printer to do the job.[117]

Again and again, the JDC and American Jewish military officials explained to skeptical U.S. authorities that the Jewish refugees were fleeing real persecution in Poland, rather than simply seeking better economic opportunities in the West. Young, apparently healthy, and carrying whatever goods they had been able to scrounge in Poland, they did not necessarily look as desperate as they were. But even months before a day of murderous antisemitic violence in Poland on July 4, 1946, had left forty-two Jews dead in Kielce and perhaps twice as many killed on trains and in neighboring towns, Jews arriving in Berlin were telling stories of fear and panic. They were "insulted in the streets . . . [with] calls of Jid . . . pushed off public conveyances; attempts were made to break into their homes at night." Many refugees still carried the typed notices posted to Jews who tried to reclaim lives and property, giving them ten days to pay an "indemnity" of 10,000 or 20,000 *zloty* to their local social welfare offices or face execution, "for harassing the Polish population and enriching themselves with their fortunes."[118]

As was so often the case, private antisemitic sentiments ultimately did not prevent Jewish organizations from getting the services they were demanding from the American occupiers.[119] Despite the fact that JDC workers labeled Commander Howley "a subtle anti-semite of the 'my best friends are Jews' school," by mid-1946 they were pleased with their cooperative relations with the U.S. Military Government and the American consulate as well as—perhaps even more unexpectedly—with UNRRA. UNRRA officials, hardly uncritical toward their charges, even conceded that "it was generally agreed that there is no alarming or sensational 'Black Market' activities at the Düppel Center."[120] The JDC too, always alert to image control, allowed that, perhaps because of the anomalous situation in the divided city, "All things considered . . . the problem on this score has not been a really serious one."[121] In fall 1946, in one of the many brilliant public relations moves orchestrated between the Americans and the DPs, General Lucius Clay participated, with tears in his eyes, at a *Yizkor* memorial service in the synagogue at Schlachtensee's Düppel Center.[122]

The Soviets forced the *Bricha* to curtail its "flight and rescue" missions in fall 1946, but still, tens of thousands of mostly Polish Jews would pass through Berlin from November 1945 through January 1947. Several thousand of the estimated 90,000–100,000 people who took that route remained, at least temporarily, in Berlin.[123] By 1947, the DP camps housed anywhere between 6,000 and 10,000 people, including over 1,000 infants and children.[124] The DP camps in Berlin, while certainly not entirely isolated from the Gemeinde, developed a lively existence of their own. Three schools and two summer camps opened. In fall 1946, the Herzl Public Hebrew School had 400 students; altogether almost 1,000 children attended school. Zionist youth organizations of all stripes, from the right-wing *Betar* to the socialist *Hashomer Hatzair*, flourished. A JDC mobile film unit toured the camps, showing Yiddish and Hollywood films. Legal aid teams worked to straighten out the status of the many "infiltrees." In fall 1947, Yehudi Menuhin came to play the violin and was greeted with an icy boycott for having had, in the name of peace and reconciliation, agreed to a joint appearance at the Berlin Philharmonic with the recently denazified conductor Wilhelm Furtwängler.[125] Eli Rock, the JDC representative in Berlin, described Schlachtensee as a kind of "luxury camp" compared to Feldafing, near Munich, where he had previously worked. It was more spacious, and above all it was in Berlin, with its urban cultural and entertainment opportunities, including of course the black market.[126] Some seventy Jewish DP students registered at Berlin universities. A young mother who had come from Poland after having survived in the Soviet

Union remembered: "Some days, I would head to downtown Berlin, to the Kurfürstendamm. A few shops had survived the bombing and there were dressmakers who were willing to sew stylish dresses for little money." Street photographers on the Ku'damm stood ready to take pictures of young people eager to reconstruct their shattered lives.[127]

The city's attractions notwithstanding, the one point on which everyone—the local Gemeinde, the Americans, the other occupiers, the Germans, and the DPs themselves—could agree was that there should be no future for East European Jewish DPs in Berlin, or in fact anywhere in Germany (or probably in Europe). Indeed, it was directly in response to the presence of (still relatively few) Jewish DPs that, in December 1945, the liberal U.S.-licensed *Tagesspiegel* editorialized:

> So one may hope that the millions of sacrifices [*Opfer*] by the Jews have not been in vain, but that rather after hundreds of years of effort it will finally be possible today to solve the Jewish problem in its totality [*das jüdische Problem in seiner Gesamtheit zu lösen* (*sic*!)]; namely, on the one hand, through emigration of the homeless Jews and, on the other hand, through the complete assimilation of those Jews who wish to remain in Europe.[128]

Most of the DPs, of course, themselves viewed the camps as way stations. They wanted nothing more than to escape the "cursed soil" of Germany. German Jews in Berlin, who were much more divided in their sentiments about remaining in Germany, shared German and Allied anxieties about the East European survivors in their midst, but by no means as crassly or censoriously as is often assumed. *Der Weg*, the voice of the German-Jewish community, judged the DPs "aliens in Germany who also want to remain that way."[129] Hans Habe, the rémigré journalist, complained that "these survivors of mass murder were not necessarily the best elements among the Jews," while simultaneously expressing his outrage that "not a single attempt has been made to call the German Jews back; the ones who returned were in for bitter disappointments."[130] Yet *Der Weg* also pointed out the logical error characterizing all the uproar about DP black marketeering and petty crime; it was, after all, not the DPs who were responsible for antisemitism but antisemitism that was responsible for the plight of the DPs. In contrast to Rock's rosy picture, the paper published photographs of DP children playing behind barbed wire, without sufficient space, clothes, and care; it also presented the story of a representative Jewish refugee: a young man who had fled from the Nazis to Russia. His wife and child did not survive their exile, and when he returned to Poland grieving and alone, none of his possessions remained: "Every corner in his birthplace reminded him of his wife and child—the attitude of the population was anything but friendly." So he fled west and landed in a DP camp in Berlin.[131] Some Gemeinde officials, notably Erich Nelhans, even encouraged the flight of East European Jews and helped to smuggle deserting Jewish Red Army soldiers into the West, disguised as Jewish DPs headed for the UNRRA camps. These efforts aroused SMA suspicions and anxious debate within the Gemeinde about the consequences of abusing their privilege of issuing Jewish identity cards to transiting refugees. In Nelhans's case, it is likely that this activity led him from a relatively privileged relationship with the SMA to his sudden arrest by Soviet agents in March 1948.[132]

The two Jewish worlds were not, therefore, as tightly separated as many accounts assume. In November 1946 some 1,000 children from the DP camps and the Gemeinde enjoyed a joint excursion to a performance of *Robinson Crusoe* at the Neue Scala theater. On OdF Day they marched together in the commemorative parades.[133] Gemeinde and DP children, along with some American military dependents, also went together to the Circus Blumenfeld, just reopened by a KZ returnee. The gala publicity show sold out, the U.S. Army and UNRRA brought in candy, peanuts, popcorn, and chocolate, and the Coca-Cola company contributed seventy-five cases of Coke. The Joint delightedly reported that the children were treated to "dancing horses, dancing bears, zebras, elephants, trapeze artists, juggling acts, and to the delight of the American boys and girls but to the complete bewilderment of the others, a tribe of American Mohawk Indians. After a few short minutes, however, the European-born Jewish youngsters were giving war-whoops that rivaled the combined efforts of the Mohawks and the American children."[134] Despite the expected jibes from Polish Jews about "the questionable Jewish character of the Gemeinde members," and Gemeinde sniping about "the high degree of black marketing practices among the Polish Jews," Berlin's exceptional situation seems to have mediated even the generally strained relations between German and East European Jews.

At the same time, however, the JDC engaged in painful and wearying disputes—petty but potent—with those German Jews who did not see Berlin as a mere way station out of Europe. The dislike was in many cases mutual, with JDC workers repeatedly expressing their exasperation with the poor and sometimes corrupt quality of the Jewish leadership available in post-Nazi Berlin and Jewish survivors venting much of their sadness and fury on the American Jewish aid officials on whom they depended. The stories are tedious and quite ugly, but offer perhaps a fuller picture of the "banality" of daily life as a survivor in occupied Germany. A Gemeinde "steeped in tradition" and once possessed of "great wealth" and wielding "important influence" had been reduced to a rump of some seven thousand, "with almost no leadership of any stature." As we have discussed, from the moment of liberation—and especially given the realities of who had been able to survive in Berlin—conflicts arose over who could and should legitimately represent the survivors and reconstitute a Jewish community.

JDC official Philip Skorneck, reporting from his Paris office on February 21, 1946, about his work with both Military Government and UNRRA teams in Berlin, characterized Auschwitz survivor Julius Meyer, an early leader of the Gemeinde who was associated with the Soviets and communists, as someone who "returned from the concentration camp without a mark and is now a very wealthy man." Meyer's colleagues were also seen as less than honest or forceful, but as a kind of necessary evil in the absence of sufficient American staff or a truly legitimate Jewish leadership. As Skorneck ruefully but honestly concluded, rehearsing the classifications that had been coerced by the Nazis, "The Jewish community itself is a complex and confusing one. There are full Jews, half Jews, and quarter Jews and there are Jewish Protestants, Jewish Catholics and there are Jews married to non-Jews without children and there are Jews married to non-Jews with children who are either Jewish or non-Jewish and each of these categories had a different status under Hitler."[135] This community was, the JDC noted with some understatement, "a far cry from the Gemeinde of fifteen years ago," and likely to "decrease even more in importance and in quality as the Berlin Jews emigrate abroad."[136]

The JDC was understandably dubious that the remaining Jews, many of whom had been only marginally connected to Jewish life, should be the proper inheritors and guardians of "some of the finest Jewish literature and some of the finest cultural objects in all of Europe." Jewish aid workers quickly decided that it would be better to entrust these surviving treasures, which included a potential 13,785,676 Reichsmarks of confiscated (and not yet returned) assets, to an international Jewish institution, along the lines of what would later become the Claims Conference.[137]

Still, it fell to the "complex and confusing"—and confused—tiny German-Jewish remnant in Berlin to begin not only the battles over restitution and legitimate representation but also the endlessly controversial debates about commemoration and memorialization (including, interestingly, its architectural manifestations). At Yom Kippur Kol Nidre services in Weissensee cemetery in 1946, worshippers laid the cornerstone for a future memorial. In April 1947, sculptor Carl Cramer published a blueprint for a menorah-like memorial inscribed with the letters KZ. Despite what appears to have been considerable discussion, no resolution or consensus was found, and the proper precise shape and form were left open to further arguments.[138] Shortly before Rosh Hashanah 1946, two thousand Berlin Jews, including children from the community's orphanage and DPs from the various camps, joined communist marchers in the first Day of Remembrance for the "victims of fascism." They gathered at the Lustgarten, the old parade ground off Unter den Linden, to declare "honor for the dead, obligation for the living."[139]

"THE GESTAPO FORGOT ME": AMALIE'S STORY

If all the "few" survivors agreed in principle on the imperative of honoring the "many" dead, there was clearly no such consensus on how to fulfill their "obligation for the living." Virtually all DPs assumed that Berlin, no matter how temporarily enticing, would never again become a home for Jews (even if some would remain). Most German Jews were agonizingly undecided, even if, as we shall see, their hopes for reconstructing a Jewish community in Berlin became increasingly forlorn. They were, however, convinced that a minimal but indispensable part of their "obligation" was to provide for those Jews who had resurfaced and were—for whatever reason—still there.

The powerful shadow of the immediate past, and the importance of the community for the present, were painfully summarized in one account, sent to the Gemeinde in 1948 by a fifty-two-year-old Berlin woman. She was living, bereft of friends or family, in a mental hospital, trying desperately to get the care she knew she required, while struggling to negotiate life between sad reality and the haunting voices of memory. Amalie had grown up in Kreuzberg, where her family owned a cigar store. They tried to emigrate to England, but just when they had tickets and visa in hand, the war trapped them in Berlin. She and her sisters were assigned, like so many other Jewish women, to forced labor at Siemens, and when her health gave out she was ordered to work as a cleaning woman in a Jewish hostel. Amalie slipped into underground life, staying away from the hostel on deportation days and returning when the raids seemed to have ended. In a story of split-second decisions and narrow escapes, echoed in other survivor accounts, "the Gestapo"—the shorthand for all that made Jews' lives hell—"seemed to have forgotten me." When the constant anxiety about whether and when the Gestapo would actually appear, and the even more unsettling realization that Jewish "catchers" were lurking in wait wherever Jewish illegals were known to gather, became too nerve-racking, Amalie decided simply to "let fate take its course." After her sisters received their deportation orders during the Factory Action, she was ready to join them. But when the massive Allied air raid that hit Berlin on

March 1, 1943, prevented her from finding her sisters before they were deported, Amalie was again "fated" to be left behind, consigned to a tense and dangerous existence.

In brief passages composed in pencil on notebook paper, Amalie tried to communicate the horrors of an illegal daily life in which she "had neither ration nor identity card. How often did I, without regard for poor health, carry coals or do other hard labor for a lunch packet." In the meantime, she observed bitterly, Germans, even under threat of bombs in an increasingly ruined Berlin, continued to live a fairly normal life: "while the Aryans went to work, took trips, ate and dressed well, I had to hide and disguise myself, and live in constant dread of the Gestapo." Her nerves finally snapped when she was caught in—and made it through—a control and began to see the "nightmarish ghost" of the Gestapo everywhere. It was these visions, delusional in the psychiatric terms of the hospital in which she was now writing her story but only too realistic, given her situation, that plagued her after the war. Excruciatingly aware that she had to find a language able to limn the incomprehensible, she struggled to tell her story in a way that could articulate to both Jews and Germans the differentials of suffering in wartime Berlin: "I have tried," she wrote from her ward,

> to describe my time of suffering in sober matter-of-fact form. What kind of fear and psychological torment stands behind the word Gestapo can only be understood by a Jew, because while Aryans might have been picked up once on a violation, we Jews had to endure this psychic burden for months, yes, even years. A forbidden onion, lemon, some meat, etc. in the house . . . was enough to deliver us into the hands of the Gestapo.

She expressed the deep disappointment (and indeed incredulity), common to survivors after liberation, that after all they had endured, Jews were only grudgingly recognized as "victims of fascism" and certainly not granted full recognition as honored antifascists. Adding insult to injury, so many people, including Jews who had returned from the camps, now believed that those who had remained in Berlin, even underground but spared deportation and gas chambers, had been, by grotesque comparison, privileged. "I think," she mused, "that one has a false picture of us 'illegals.' It may be that some of us had an identity card and could even buy some food, but most of us will have had it just as hard as I did." Now, in 1948, all that was left for her was to beg to be freed from the German sanatorium that could not heal the terrifying voices in her head and be transferred to the Jewish Hospital, where even though most of the patients were "Aryans"—as Jews persisted in calling Germans—the personnel was 80 percent Jewish and survivors were offered priority admission. Amalie hoped that there, perhaps, she could be safe among her own people.[140]

Between 1945 and 1948/49, while the fragile and mostly elderly German-Jewish community in Berlin struggled with these anguished memories, with the pressures of daily existence, and with an uncertain future, a new, quite different, and entirely unexpected Jewish world would be temporarily constructed among the DPs, to a limited degree in the Berlin camps but mostly in the American zone in western Germany.

Fig. 4.1. "We are here": Young DPs on bench at Wannsee S Bahn Station, Berlin.

CHAPTER FOUR

The Saved and Saving Remnant

JEWISH DISPLACED PERSONS IN THE AMERICAN ZONE

> I can tell you one thing, with a lot of luck, we . . . stayed
> alive. I was in Auschwitz-Buchenwald etc. Main thing is one
> is alive.
>
> —Teenage Auschwitz survivor[1]

> When I raised my right hand and took the oath as an officer, I
> never dreamed that there were jobs of this sort.
>
> —Col. Irving Heymont, U.S. commander,
> Landsberg DP camp[2]

EVOKING THE CONSTANT STREAM of refugees trying to enter the city, *Life* photographer Margaret Bourke-White named a chapter in her sarcastically titled *Dear Fatherland, Rest Quietly,* "Berlin: A River of Wanderers."[3] In the spring and summer of 1945, all of war-torn Europe became such a moving stream of humanity. Around 20 million people clogged the roads, straggling from east to west and west to east. Millions, including ethnic Germans who had fled the Red Army or been expelled from Eastern Europe, as well as former soldiers and prisoners of war, forced laborers, and survivors of death and work camps, were on the move. The available statistics, both those cited by historians and those collected at the time, are highly variable and surely inaccurate, their unreliability itself a sign of the chaos that accompanied peace and the speed with which conditions changed.

Astonishingly, between May and September 1945, the Allied victors, in what can only be called "a near miracle in logistics,"[4] managed to repatriate about 6 million of the 7 million persons defined as "displaced" and eligible for return to their homelands (DPs whom the Allies had initially faced in the occupied areas). During the initial period of "organized chaos," the United Nations Relief and Rehabilitation Administration (UNRRA) and the occupation Military Government successfully organized mass repatriations, avoided widespread disease and hunger, and quickly set up assembly centers that provided basic shelter, food, and family-tracing services.[5] Foreign workers—mostly forced and some volunteer labor—who had come to constitute almost 30 percent of the Reich industrial and 20 percent of the entire workforce by 1944, trooped home.[6] The 12 million ethnic German expellees, while bedraggled and not exactly welcome, were nonetheless recognized as German nationals and integrated into the makeshift postwar society; so too were the slowly returning German POWs.

By January 1946, a group of about 1 million unrepatriables remained in western territory. These DPs were concentrated in the American and British zones. Some 20 percent were children, many of them, in the euphemistic language of postwar relief, "unaccompanied," abandoned, lost, and orphaned.[7] About half (400,000–500,000) were non-Jewish Poles and Polish Ukrainians, and 175,000–200,000 were Balts (from Estonia, Latvia, and Lithuania) unwilling to return to sovietized lands. There were also Hungarians and Yugoslavs, collections of Greeks, Bulgarians, Czechs, Slovaks, and even Iranians and Turks. The rest, between 10 and 20 percent, were, for the most part, Jews.[8] Survivors of the Final Solution and forced exile in the Soviet Union, they were indeed an unexpected presence (and problem) for both the Allies and the Germans.

Mir Zaynen Do ("We Are Here")

As difficult as it was to comprehend that European Jewry had been subjected to systematic extermination, in the postwar chaos it was at times almost more difficult to grasp that there were in fact survivors who required recognition and care. American officer Saul Padover's early description of the "veritable *Völkerwanderung*" (mass migration) of refugees is telling in its assumption that the Jews had all been murdered:

> Thousands, tens of thousands, finally millions of liberated slaves were coming out of the farms and the factories and the mines and pouring onto the highways. . . . They were all there, all except the Jews. The Jews, six million of them, the children and the women and the old men, were ashes in the incinerators and bones in the charnel houses.[9]

But, in fact, not all European Jews had turned to ashes. Between 1945 and 1948, the U.S. and British zones of occupied Germany became a temporary home for an approximately quarter of a million Jews—altogether perhaps some 300,000 in occupied Austria, Italy, and Germany. These survivors constituted themselves into what they came to call the *She'erit Hapletah*, the saved remnant of European Jewry who had been "left over."[10] The small number of remaining and returning German Jews, so visible in Berlin, was augmented by the mostly East European death march and camp survivors who had been liberated by the Allies on German soil. Jews from Western Europe, and generally from Hungary and Czechoslovakia as well, were rapidly repatriated. Those who remained alive as DPs in occupied Germany were soon joined, however, by tens of thousands of "infiltrees" pouring in from Eastern Europe, into Berlin and most significantly into the large DP camps in American-controlled Bavaria. Mostly Polish Jews, they had survived the war in hiding, with the partisans, or in the Soviet Union.[11]

The Allied victors were not entirely unprepared; they had expected to face millions of victims of Nazi displacement and persecution. Haunted by memories of the devastating post–World War I flu epidemic and fearing that the flow of refugees would disrupt military operations, cause general disorder, and spread disease, they had established UNRRA in 1943 precisely to handle the anticipated crisis. A November 1944 agreement between UNRRA and SHAEF (Supreme Headquarters Allied Expeditionary Command) stipulated that relief and rehabilitation operations would be carried out in accordance with military "standstill" or "stand in place" requirements.[12] As victory drew close, the number of DPs corralled into assembly centers grew exponentially, even as additional millions of German expellees and refugees for whom the United Nations were not responsible crossed into western Germany. German barracks and housing were requisitioned, and small—fewer than planned or needed—UNRRA teams were rushed in "spearhead formation" into occupied territory.[13]

By war's end in May 1945, five hundred assembly centers had already been set up in the U.S. and British zones, and almost a million people sent home. Already during the war, before the scope of the Final Solution was fully understood, Jewish officials had warned UNRRA that "great numbers of people," of whom the "overwhelming majority would be the Jews," who had been "deported or expelled to foreign countries and also many of those displaced within their own country would be unable or unwilling to be repatriated." They knew full well that "when the War of the Tyrants will be over, the War of Survival will still continue to be waged."[14] For the most part, however, the Allies did not specifically focus on Jews, assuming that they would be few in number. At a conference on "U.N.R.R.A.'s work for displaced persons in Germany," held in London on October 9, 1945, the most that could be said about the fate of surviving Jews was the rather helpless observation that "there are obviously some cases which need special treatment." Noting the "complex" problem of "finding a home for the remnant of Europe's Jews," a spokesman said, "I will only say that, if mercy is not extinct, the world must very quickly find a place for these survivors of an unspeakable crime."[15]

UNRRA's mandate, as defined in 1943, was the four "Rs" of rescue, relief, rehabilitation, and reconstruction. One year after liberation, there was an expectation that at least the first two Rs should have been accomplished and "a place" found. But in May 1946, there were still 715,625 displaced persons in the three western zones, most of them Jews or Balts for whom, for quite different reasons, repatriation was not, as Jewish relief workers had predicted and as UNRRA and the Military Government both reluctantly realized, a realistic option.[16] Even those Jews who had returned to their former homes in Eastern Europe "laboriously retraced their steps back to the camps in the Western parts of Germany whence they had come—or if they found a survivor of their family, they took him along."[17] Survivors' very first instinct had been to return home and search for loved ones: "Really we all only had one thought," Ignatz Bubis remembered of his liberation from a labor camp by the Red Army: "maybe someone from the family is still alive?"[18] But they found that Eastern Europe had become, as was repeatedly noted in just these words, one vast Jewish graveyard. Jewish relief officials understood that

> return to the home country had been a pseudo-repatriation. It had lacked the necessary ingredients of a bona-fide homecoming. It was rather the final visit of a mourner to his family burial plot—the refugee's last look at his native land to which his forefathers had been attached for generations, but which he had to leave forever. His homage paid to dear ones, his last glimpse taken, he then set out on a new exodus in the hope of eventually reaching more hospitable soil.[19]

Jews' resistance to repatriation, their insistence on gathering in separate, homogeneous camps, and their determination to leave the blood-soaked soil of Europe raised in a dramatic way issues of their own religious, ethnic, or national identity. Months after liberation, there remained in the American zone tens of thousands of survivors for whom there had to be found not just "relief" but a new life—what was still called "a final solution"—outside Europe.[20] As numerous contemporary observers as well as historians noted, "It belonged to the ironies of history that Germany, of all places, became under the occupation of the Allied powers a sheltering haven for several hundred thousand Jews."[21] At the same time, the refugee camps became the incubator of dreams for a "separate, distinct, Jewish ethnological nationality."[22]

For defeated Germans and Allied victors, the irony of the Jewish presence on ostensibly *judenrein* territory was underscored by the visible presence of Jews among the occupiers as well as among the war's victims. Ursula von Kardorff, herself a refugee from the Soviet takeover of Berlin, was struck by the rapid reversal of power relations when a military caravan including cars displaying a "Zionstar"—apparently "a Jewish division"—passed on the Bavarian Autobahn. In what she perceived as a "demonstration of divine justice," while these soldiers "wearing the uniform of the victors drove on one side of the road, open trucks with German prisoners of war sped by on the other." Kardorff, no Nazi but a dedicated journalist who had continued her career in the Third Reich, flashed back to scenes only a few years earlier on the Kurfürstendamm in Berlin, where decorated young German officers had strutted past humiliated Jews wearing the very star now proudly displayed by the victors.[23] Jewish survivors and American Jewish victors took satisfaction in the taunting slogans and Star of David insignia on the British Army's Jewish Brigade trucks rolling north into Germany from Italy. "*Kein Volk! Kein Reich! Kein Führer! Achtung! Die Juden Kommen,*" the Brigade announced, "invariably" striking "terror," as an American-Jewish officer reported, or at least shock, "into the hearts of the German population."[24] Local residents, suddenly confronted with tattered and emaciated KZniks (camp inmates) and then with a further influx from Eastern Europe, approached their new neighbors with "a mixture of fear, contempt, and bewilderment."[25]

A former Nazi academy (*Napola*) in Feldafing, a bucolic town "in beautiful rolling country" on the shores of the Starnberger Lake, about twenty miles outside Munich, became the first all-Jewish DP camp in the American zone. Feldafing's barracks and elegant villas were confiscated and converted into "a town of hospitals, dreary and off-limits." The Americans' and Germans' shock at encountering the ghostlike survivors, and the survivors' own sense of disorientation, were only exacerbated by the incongruous setting. The bomb-damaged Bavarian capital, "a ballet of brooms, ladders, bricks," with locals already "complaining of the pillaging D.Ps," was surrounded by the stunning, peaceful landscape of the Bavarian Alps and the lakes at its foothills.[26] It was in those outskirts that the three major DP camps for Jews in American-occupied Bavaria, Feldafing, Landsberg, and Föhrenwald, were established.[27]

Feldafing's core inhabitants were Jews rescued from the bomb-strafed cattle cars that were trying to carry KZ inmates away from General Patton's ever advancing Third Army. Those stalled trains, whose SS guards had finally fled, held, as it turned out, many of the men who would comprise the postwar DP leadership in the American zone. A group of mostly Lithuanian prisoners, who had already worked together in Dachau's Kaufering labor camp, quickly managed to connect with shocked American troops, who distributed "chocolates, canned good, and repeatedly cigarettes." These few survivors negotiated for food and shelter with Swiss Red Cross representatives, ordered newly powerless Wehrmacht soldiers to bring them supplies, and joined up with the American officers who took charge of them. Their liberation, made possible by American victory but engineered by the KZniks themselves, foreshadowed the energy and organizational talent they would bring to the DPs in Bavaria. Their actions quickly became the stuff of Jewish legend, complete with an "American Negro" who "wept as he embraced the people," as the "angel of redemption," and a Yiddish-speaking American officer from New York as the guarantor of liberation. Dr. Zalman Grinberg, a radiologist from Kovno, one of the Kaufering survivors, quickly became legendary himself. Grinberg was already revered for having hidden his young son in a barrel in the ghetto with the "tubes of his stethoscope to funnel air" until the child could be smuggled out to a "Christian friend for safekeeping" in a credenza (or, depending on the version, in a potato sack). Now he convinced the director of a Wehrmacht infirmary in a monastery in nearby St. Ottilien that he was a representative of the International Red Cross sent by the Americans, and then worked with a U.S. Army captain to commandeer the facilities as a first aid station and hospital for the liberated Jews.[28]

On April 29, Lieutenant Irving J. Smith, an American-Jewish officer, entered the nearby town of Tutzing and found more death march survivors, over one thousand "starving, almost raving maniacs, half paralyzed with hunger and fear."[29] The Americans, joined by an UNRRA team, quickly took over the former Nazi school in Feldafing, drafted dozens of German doctors and nurses, turned a former hotel into a hospital, requisitioned the services of the *Napola* cook, and began to organize daily life. The initial Jewish DP camp population, mostly composed of direct death camp and forced labor camp survivors, most of them in much worse shape than the Kaufering men, rapidly grew to about four thousand.

Feldafing became a center of Jewish DP life, run by Lieutenant Smith and his unpopular Danish UNRRA adjutant (and presumably mistress) Ethel Otto.[30] By the end of May, U.S. Army chaplains presided over the first survivor wedding. On May 27, 1945, the Jewish survivors, already forming a self-conscious collective, organized their first cultural event. The remnants of the Kovno Ghetto orchestra, dramatically dressed in their striped KZ pajamas, played a concert for the patients who had been gathered in the St. Ottilien monastery by Dr. Grinberg. On June 20, Feldafing survivors met in the former German Freimann-Barracks to form the Central Committee of Liberated Jews in the U.S. zone in Bavaria. Kaufering survivors Samuel Gringauz and Dr. Zalman Grinberg took over as president and chairman. At their side was a very young American chaplain, Rabbi Abraham Klausner, whose life had been turned upside down by his experience of the liberation of Dachau. He had basically gone AWOL, becoming "A strange kind of an army officer, without a unit, without a commanding officer, even without an official army billet." He had cast his fate with a new congregation of East European survivors, for whom the soldiers of the Jewish Brigade from Palestine and American-Jewish troops constituted the first lines of recognition and relief.[31] Recognizing that "their material needs [were] only secondary in importance to the urgency of their desire to come in contact with any of their remaining kin" and to find "some link on earth,"[32] Klausner immediately began the signature project of the *She'erit Hapletah*. With the assistance of the U.S. Army, he collected names of survivors in volumes of the same name; the first list was published on June 20. Jews were desperate for news of their loved ones, and—in contrast to liberator Saul Padover's stunned sense that "I never knew what to say to these people. What sense did words make?"—survivors of the unimaginable needed listeners for their "torrent" of talk.[33] When American relief worker Katie Louchheim arrived in Feldafing, she was faced with such an urgent "carousel of unbelievable stories" that she concluded, "I wish I were a typewriter."[34]

She'erit Hapletah: Recognition and Politics

Like the ragged German-Jewish Gemeinde in Berlin, Jewish DPs also moved quickly to constitute themselves as a separate political entity with claims on German money and space as well the conscience of world Jewry and the Allies. But for the *She'erith Hapletah*, composed of Jews from Eastern Europe, relief and rehabilitation encompassed demands not only for aid, justice, and restitution but also for emigration to Palestine. On July 1 at a meeting in Feldafing, also attended by representatives from the U.S. military and the Jewish Brigade, the committed Zionists from Dachau-Kaufering marginalized smaller groups of Bundists and communists still hoping for a return to a Soviet-liberated Eastern Europe and again proclaimed themselves the Central Committee of Liberated Jews in Bavaria. Taking seriously their witnessing obligation and their independent status as representatives of the saved remnant, they prepared to send representatives to the upcoming war crimes tribunals.[35] A day later, on July 2, the Central Committee occupied its new headquarters in the damaged Deutsches Museum in Munich, the former "capital" of the Nazi movement. On July 25, a larger conference was held at St. Ottilien, the requisitioned monastery that had become Dr. Grinberg's hospital. Ninety-four delegates from all over western-occupied Germany, representing over forty thousand Jews from almost fifty camps and assembly centers, voted to confirm the Central Committee leadership. The next evening, fully aware of the dramatic symbolism of their actions, delegates drove down to Munich to demonstrate to the surprised Germans and Americans that *mir zaynen do* (we are here).[36] Against a backdrop of torn Torah rolls, in the beer hall famous as the launching site for Hitler's attempted coup in November 1923, they read a proclamation demanding entry to Palestine.

In August this politicization, and the DPs' alliance with American-Jewish chaplains and soldiers who sent home shocked and outraged letters describing the horrific condition of the survivors, bore momentous fruit. Earl G. Harrison, a Philadelphia lawyer and President Roosevelt's former commissioner of immigration and naturalization, who had just been appointed dean of the University of Pennsylvania Law School, was asked by President Truman to lead an official mission "To inquire into the condition and needs of those among the displaced persons with particular reference to the Jewish refugees who may be stateless or non-repatriable." As soon as Harrison arrived in Munich, Chaplain Klausner convinced the envoy to join him on a tour of former concentration camps and DP assembly centers in the U.S. zones of Germany and Austria. The report Harrison submitted to President Truman at the end of August 1945, just as the Nuremberg war crimes tribunal was getting under way, proved to be a political "bombshell."[37]

This unlikely advocate, who had been responsible among other things for wartime alien registration and the internment of Japanese-Americans, now gave voice to the bitterness and frustration of survivors three months after liberation and validated the Zionist goal of resettlement in Palestine: "The civilized world owes it to this handful of survivors to provide them with a home where they can again settle down and begin to live as human beings." Most dramatically, he declared:

> As matters now stand, we appear to be treating the Jews as the Nazis treated them except that we do not exterminate them. They are in concentration camps in large numbers under military guard, instead of the S.S. troops. One is led to wonder whether the German people, seeing this, are not supposing that we are following or at least condoning Nazi policy.

The passionate outrage of this highly publicized report—the full text appeared in the *New York Times* on September 30, 1945—was in parts hyperbolic and unfair to the substantial relief efforts that had been made by the U.S. military. It did, however, cause the sensation that DPs and their supporters had hoped for, and is worth quoting at some length. Harrison expressed Jewish bitterness at American ignorance of the Jews' particular wartime experience and the ingrained antisemitism of some commanders and troops. He powerfully channeled DPs' anger at the contrast between their trapped living conditions and the relative freedom, comfort, and conviction of victimized innocence they saw in the Germans who surrounded them:

If it be true, as seems to be widely conceded, that the German people at large do not have any sense of guilt with respect to the war and its causes and results, and if the policy is to be "To convince the German people that they have suffered a total military defeat and that they cannot escape responsibility for what they brought upon themselves," then it is difficult to understand why so many displaced persons, particularly those who have so long been persecuted and whose repatriation or resettlement is likely to be delayed, should be compelled to live in crude, over-crowded camps while the German people, in rural areas, continue undisturbed in their homes.[38]

The fact that the large DP camps in the U.S. zone were located outside the devastated cities, where civilian suffering was most visible (even in Berlin the camps were in suburban locations), reinforced this perception of German well-being. The contrast between the daily lives of Germans and their victims was most crass in relatively undamaged rural areas. Notwithstanding the recent massive influx of desperate German refugees from the Soviet-occupied East, rural dwellers had "escaped most of the personal discomforts of war" and were, as Americans reported, less likely to act properly "licked."[39]

A Jewish relief team also noted the relatively good condition of the defeated Germans in late 1945. Germans were still seen strutting about in boots and uniforms without apparent fear or shame, and Nazi tracts were still available in the back rooms of bookstores, as were films made in the Third Reich. "The country," the representatives of the Jewish children's aid organization O.S.E. observed, "almost everywhere is intact, the herds of horses, of cows, of sheep, are well fed, the barnyards are well, even very well stocked." There were a surprising number of private cars on the roads; unlike the DPs, Germans had freedom of movement. In cities like Berlin, the aid workers acknowledged, "No doubt the children loitering in railway stations or wandering on the roads, suffer cruelly at the approach of winter from a total lack of food and clothing," but elsewhere "poor Germany" still had "swarms of fat, gay, turbulent children. . . . Probably not a town, not a village in the rest of ravaged Europe can show so many children in such good condition."[40] In a similar tone, a German-Jewish GI from Berlin described for his Richmond, Virginia, hometown paper sickening scenes of decaying bodies, "shrunk, only bones and skin," being dug out of mass graves by the local German population, even as, he bitterly observed, "six kilometers away were people living in a town as good as you can imagine, a bit rationed but not suffering, in nice houses, with dogs and cats that had to be fed and with good clothes to wear."[41] "I don't wish to be depressing darling," a Jewish officer wrote to his wife in December 1945, but the stark fact was that SS and

Wehrmacht prisoners and German civilians received "more calories per day than the people who really suffered under the Nazis."[42]

Specifically referring to the unsettling presence of "'Gretchens' so alluring in their innocence," the Jewish relief workers echoed Harrison's worries about setting a bad example to the local population and provided an even more stinging indictment of U.S. occupation practices:

> If one can understand, though deplore the fact, that the American soldiers prefer the company of German men and women, clean, healthy, well dressed, to that of the D.P., dirty, destitute, in frayed garments, and torn shoes, we must, however, infer that the attitude of the responsible officers, benevolent and sometimes even, —horribile dictu—obsequious towards the Germans, but impatient, severe, incomprehensive, intolerant and often hostile towards the religious and political victims of these last—is due to the anti-democratic and pro-fascist mentality of many responsible commanders and their subordinates.[43]

Controversially, and in defiance of State Department preferences (but presumably in accordance with the U.S. desire to limit its own immigration opportunities), the Harrison Report expressed clear support for the provision, urgently demanded by the DPs, of 100,000 entry permits to Palestine. In the short term and less controversially, the report reinforced the most significant development for the *She'erit Hapletah* in the American zone: the establishment of separate camps for Jews that could serve as transitional communities as well as staging areas for further emigration. This stance was stoutly resisted by the British, who, determined to prevent large-scale European Jewish immigration into their Palestinian mandate, rather disingenuously insisted that acceding to Jewish demands for separate treatment would represent a reinstatement of Nazi racial policies. Harrison minced no words in dispatching that argument: "The first and plainest need for these people is a recognition of their actual status, and by this I mean their status as Jews." He insisted that "while admittedly it is not normally desirable to set aside particular racial or religious groups from their nationality categories, the plain truth is that this was done for so long by the Nazis that a group has been created which has special needs." Unlike most Germans and many of the occupiers, Harrison grasped the historical situation of the surviving European Jews:

> Jews as Jews (not as members of their nationality groups) have been more severely victimized than the non-Jewish members of the same or other nationalities. Refusal to recognize the Jews as such has the effect, in this situation, of closing one's eyes to their former and more barbaric persecution, which has already made them a separate group with greater needs.

To deny them separate and special recognition now was not to continue a discriminatory practice but to begin undoing it. This was not favoritism but a form of justice.[44]

Harrison was diplomatic in pressing his case, even as he was, in effect (as Dan Diner has argued), making the radical move of defining Jews as a "national collective that should also be treated as such."[45] He praised the "phenomenal performance" of American troops in managing a huge repatriation and argued for admission to Palestine in as careful terms as possible: "Now that the worst of the pressure of mass repatriation is over, it is not unreasonable to suggest that in the next and perhaps more difficult period those who have suffered the most and longest be given first and not last attention." Neither the Harrison Report nor the recommendation a year later by a jointly appointed Anglo-American Committee of Inquiry to grant the 100,000 emigration permits could compel the British to open up Palestine to large-scale immigration. But, reinforced by American press reports and American Jewish organizations, Harrison's statement did push the American military authorities and especially commander in chief General Eisenhower to appoint a special adviser on Jewish affairs and meet Jewish demands for separate camps with improved conditions and rations and some internal autonomy. This support for separate Jewish DP camps guaranteed by Military Government after the Harrison Report meant that the American zones in Austria, Italy, and especially Germany became, by late 1945, magnets for Jewish survivors fleeing renewed persecution in the homelands to which they had briefly returned, as well as for Zionist organizers seeking to prepare them for aliyah to Palestine.[46]

In October, President Truman issued a "Yom Kippur" statement, which, while calling for compromise, seemed to favor the Zionist plan for partition in Palestine over the British proposal for provincial autonomy.[47] On December 22, 1945, a presidential directive offered limited immigration preference to displaced persons, and Jewish DPs began to register for U.S. visas. Had the doors to the United States been opened earlier, many have speculated, the pressure for large-scale emigration to Palestine might have eased significantly.[48] So many obstacles remained, however, that relatively few Jewish survivors were admitted to the United States before the immigration reforms of 1948 and 1950. This situation assured that the number of Jews demanding entry to Palestine kept growing, especially as more and more Jews fled Eastern Europe into the American zone. In the event, the Zionist project of emigration to Palestine and the U.S. interest in limiting immigration meshed quite well. As Harrison pithily declared, blithely ignoring British concerns, "The evacuation of the Jews of Germany and Austria to Palestine will solve the problems of the individuals involved and will also remove a problem from the military authorities who have had to deal with it."[49]

"TAKING THINGS INTO OUR OWN HANDS": AMERICAN JEWISH MESSAGES AND PERCEPTIONS

The Americans, in cooperation with UNRRA , had indeed made the commitment, as they did in Berlin, that "reasonable care be taken of these unfortunate people."[50] In retrospect, and in contrast to critical contemporary reports and equally critical recent evaluations of American mistreatment, incomprehension, and outright antisemitism, the U.S. military for the most part managed the unprecedented situation with remarkable competence and no little empathy. The occupiers were pressured by Jewish organizations, American Jewish officers and chaplains and, after the Harrison Report, specially appointed Jewish affairs advisers, and dispatches in the American press. Advocates assured that journalists, congressional delegations, and army officials directly confronted the DPs themselves in their barren, overcrowded quarters. Soldiers, however, are neither trained for, nor inclined to, humanitarian work. Certainly, as American reporters noticed, the lower ranks did not inquire into the history of the scruffy, unruly refugees they had to control. For many GIs, as reporters Hutton and Rooney observed, "A DP in soldier slang was the lowest form of human life."[51] Even those troops who had penetrated into what Meyer Levin, recalling his entry into Ohrdruf concentration camp with the U.S. liberators, famously called the "black" and "vicious heart" of the Nazi system often took on the task of caring for the surviving remnant of European Jewry with reluctance, resentment, and as Colonel Heymont confessed, a good deal of befuddlement.[52]

Some of the most dramatic reports, about both the miserable circumstances and astonishing energy of the DPs, came from American Jewish military personnel who shuttled between the DP camps with their Eastern European survivors and German towns where they found the few remaining German Jews. U.S. chaplains, some of them American-born and quite unprepared for what they found after their wartime duties were over, others themselves from Eastern Europe and Yiddish speaking, became indispensable mediators and advocates in the encounter with survivors. Relying, as they did in Berlin, in most cases on the one-eye-closed tolerance of their superior officers, many "virtually forgot that they were U.S. Army chaplains."[53] They abetted the infiltration into the American zone of Jews from Eastern Europe, cooperated with the Zionist *Bricha* network, cared for the social as well as spiritual needs of the survivors, and, perhaps most important, urged Jewish servicemen to do the same.

For many of these young men (and later, as JDC workers, women), the confrontation with the "surviving remnant" was the great adventure of their lives, recounted in numerous letters, diaries, and memoirs. They used their status as victors to intimidate German civilians into providing supplies and space and used their mail and travel privileges to locate and carry messages to survivors. They "liberated" army fuel and vehicles to transport Jews into the relative safety of the U.S. zone, handed over their rations and packages from home, provided everything from jobs with the occupation to items for religious services, and assured that the survivors' calls for help would be heard in the Jewish communities of the United States. Twenty-seven-year-old Irving Heymont was careful to identify himself only as a "professional soldier in the US Army" when he took over as commander of Landsberg DP camp. He feared being overwhelmed by the needs of those who might count him a fellow Jew, a status to which he never officially admitted during his army service. Later he recalled that "there is no doubt in my mind that the few months I spent at Landsberg had a greater impact on my outlook on life than any other experience in my career, including infantry combat in both World War II and the Korean War. Landsberg made me a conscious Jew again."[54]

The letters that arrived at Jewish homes throughout the United States in the spring and summer of 1945 vividly document the swirl of shock and anger that gripped American Jewish soldiers as they confronted the reality of what had happened to their European brethren. We know about the shock of even battle-hardened soldiers who liberated the concentration and labor camps, but less well known, perhaps is the reaction of the American Jewish troops when they encountered the survivors. In a letter home from Frankfurt in June 1945, a Jewish soldier described a quickly organized Friday night service for about 140 remaining German Jews, "not one of them . . . what you and I would recognize as full Jews," and his encounters with young DPs, "homeless, naked, hungry, and no one to do anything for them." GIs were aware of the inadequacy and perhaps unbelievability of this reporting: "All the stories you read about atrocities are only half truths compared to what these youngsters tell." There were eight-year-olds "about the 3 year-old size at home" and "Women who have lost entire families—one whose family of 23 members were gassed." The survivors' prayers were "filled with bloodshed and broken families," and "when the Army boys called a name" on a search list, worshippers might cry out "*farbrent*" (burnt) or "my brother, where is he?" in tormented scenes that seem to have moved these soldiers more than anything they had braved during the war itself.[55]

By the summer of 1945, throughout the American zones of Germany and Austria, the "Jewish boys of the Army" were, as one of them declared, "taking things into our hands."[56] "I got busy and got all of them jobs," another one named Dave explained; soldiers adopted orphans as mascots, and proudly served as honorary *Tatte* (father) at the first Bar Mitzvahs and weddings. Dave knew that these efforts were crucial but nowhere near what was required: "I tell you, my *Kinderlech* keep me busy day and night. I wish the HIAS or Joint Distribution Committee would get into Germany and assemble these youngsters and send them where they can live again. I am not," he acknowledged, "big enough to solve all their problems."[57] Chaplain Max B. Wall, assigned to the Ninth Infantry Division, echoed Dave in a letter to his mother on August 19, 1945: "Up to present time all of our fancy organizations at home like the Joint Distribution Committee, the B'nai Brith, etc haven't done a thing for these poor souls." Since "there is no one, absolutely no one who is trying to help—you can believe me they do need help, and need it as soon as possible," he gave precise orders for supplying the DPs who were gathering around Munich: "14,000 Jewish people who have somehow lived through the past 10 year . . . hell." His mother was to recruit aunts Hanna, Belka, and Ann, and "as many other people as you can get," to "get a regulation box" and start packing "new (not old) pants, stockings, toothbrushes and paste, face soap, small siddur, tallis, tiffilin, german american dictionary," as well as "some razor blades and combs."[58]

Unlike later critics, GIs were more likely to criticize the slow response of Jewish organizations, especially the JDC, than the military itself. As battle-hardened soldiers, they argued: "The Army has its job. The American Jews must do theirs." Despite what army lingo commonly described as the "SNAFU" (situation *n*ormal, *a*ll *f*ouled *u*p) conditions of war and occupation, it is probably the case that, as Albert Hutler, an American officer in charge of DP affairs, decided:

> No voluntary social welfare agency—the Joint Distribution Committee or United Nations Relief and Rehabilitation Committee—could have conceivably met the needs of the survivors of concentration and slave-labor camps as did the Army of the United States in those early days. It required a massive backup of men and material that could only be found in the Army.[59]

Soldiers who had fought their way into Germany and in many cases participated in the liberation of camps or found survivors on the crowded roads, in abandoned railroad cars, or in the rubble of cities were, however, unlikely to be impressed by such rational arguments. Nor were they persuaded by the JDC's nervous assurance that the organization, a bureaucracy in its own right that was necessarily subject to the further restrictive regulations of the U.S. military, was "Doing the utmost, but the obstacles are overwhelming."[60] When the JDC explained to concerned constituents and donors back home that it had taken "longer than we had hoped" to get into the refugee camps, that they lacked trucks and jeeps, and that their relief efforts could only be "supplementary" to those of the army and UNRRA, it further outraged the chaplains and GIs who preferred to bulldoze, charm, or manipulate their way through such obstacles.

Especially mavericks like Klausner and, as we have seen, Chaplains Friedman and Mayerowitz in Berlin delighted in circumventing army regulations or "liberating" its supplies and equipment. They were supported by the sometimes even two-eyes-closed connivance of superior officers like the commander in charge of DPs, whose orders were limited to warning Klausner to "go easy on the gasoline."[61] Klausner was brilliant at exploiting soldiers' outrage, much to the admiration and exasperation of JDC workers, who were bound to respect the occupiers' rules lest they jeopardize what would become a huge operation.[62] Klausner modeled the rhetoric of outrage in his own letters, writing to his teacher at Hebrew Union College in Cincinnati about his unexpected rabbinical duties:

I have a great congregation. 14,000 Jews. Graduates from death. They live in the hospitals and the camps we have built. We have received no aid from the outside world. Much can be written of the failure of the great Jewish world, but it would serve little purpose. Tomorrow morning we shall . . . try to release a Jew from prison because he stole a cucumber. Tomorrow we shall cry for beds because our people are still sleeping on cement floors. Thank God for the cement.

And signaling the first wave of refugees from the East, he announced, "Tomorrow we shall receive hundreds who will have fled from Poland where the banner reads—A Democratic Poland—Without Jews."[63]

Clearly, different interests and perspectives were involved. Most of the chaplains and GIs wanted immediate action to deal with an extreme and unprecedented emergency. To those already working with the survivors, the JDC seemed to be almost criminally negligent in its adherence to procedures, spending "more money on surveys than on food or clothing," and "more time in organizing offices than in getting direct help to the Jews in Europe."[64] The venerable JDC, on the other hand, which had been founded in 1914 to assist European Jews in the wake of the outbreak of World War I, worried that its large-scale relief project would be jeopardized by the insubordination, no matter how well intentioned, of individuals. American Jewish commanders in charge of DPs had to balance their duties as U.S. officers against the demands of the DPs themselves and their army supporters. At a 1995 Munich conference on the history of DPs in Bavaria, Colonel Heymont still remembered with some vehemence that Klausner's flouting of all military regulations had so infuriated him that he had threatened to punch him out.[65] The irrepressible and flamboyant Klausner was so committed to the DPs that the Central Committee of

Liberated Jews even authorized him to act as an official representative. He was apparently one of the few Americans who succeeded in gaining their trust—at the price, however, of losing it with the U.S. military and the JDC. Klausner was, one of his admiring DP assistants recalled, a "captivating personality," unusually capable of galvanizing people usually not easily motivated, whether they were exhausted and mistrustful Jewish survivors or sullen Germans, such as the printers whom he goaded to typeset two thousand copies of a Jewish DP literary magazine by simply buying out an army PX's entire supply of cookies and candy for their children.[66] When the army finally forced this enfant terrible of chaplains out of Germany in July 1946, the Central Committee protested vociferously: "The whole *Shearith Haplitah* is deeply insulted by this action for Klausner was since liberation the highest symbol of a helping brother from the outside world."[67] Ironically, it may be that, of all his insubordinate acts, the young rabbi was ultimately brought down by that most common of U.S. military failings. As a slightly bemused JDC worker reported back, "While this Chaplain did much good, he also lost much respect in the eyes of the survivors by locating himself a German Fräulein for a girl friend." When he stuck "a Mogen Dovid on her gown . . . everyone began to find a source of delight in calling her Rebitzin. Her naive wonderment at the Epithet has made the rounds of all the cities in Bavaria and its survivor camps, and even now the legends surrounding the Rebitzin continue to amuse the cynics."[68]

His hijinks notwithstanding, in what must have been a "sensational sermon" delivered under admittedly extraordinary circumstances, Chaplain Klausner virtually singlehandedly mobilized hundreds of Jewish soldiers attending Rosh Hashanah services in September 1945, at—of all places—the Munich Opera House, to launch a letter-writing campaign in defense of the survivors. The letters, many of them collected by the JDC, which received copies from horrified American Jews, are strikingly similar in tone and language, warning that "immediate help must come from you if these newly liberated victims of Nazism are to survive this coming winter." Like the messages that had already been dispatched by Sergeant Dave and Chaplain Wall, they followed a prescribed and urgent formula, apparently intoned by Klausner from the bimah and repeated in makeshift leaflets, about the inadequacies of JDC as well as International Red Cross and UNRRA relief, and about the injustices of American policy that confined DPs in camps behind barbed wire while their German tormentors remained free in their own country, or that, in an oft-repeated story, allowed the arrest of a DP for stealing a fresh cucumber to liven his drab diet. Soldiers instructed their family and friends to use pre-Christmas package allowances to send supplies and to enlist local rabbis and Jewish groups to join in the emergency effort. Leaflets for a "Fellow Soldier" demanded immediate aid for the "stateless Jews—all of whom thus far have miraculously lived through the tyranny of Europe's gas chambers and concentration camp."[69]

Deploying an indignant turn of phrase that became notorious when Earl Harrison used a similar one in his report to President Truman, GIs wrote home that "despite the many relief agencies and the money donated in the States, Jewish DPs live a life hardly better than the life they were used to under the Nazis."[70] A Rosh Hashanah service worshipper described why a survivor "still living a camp life" might be moved to steal a fresh cucumber: "Soup and black bread three times a day everyday; sleeping on wooden double-decker beds with straw mattresses and no linens; crowded conditions; eating from tin cups in their own dark rooms; wearing the same tattered clothing that they had managed to bring with them from Dachau, Buchenwald, etc.—no one has offered them other clothes that would remove the horrible reminder of their miseries from their backs."[71] Another starkly depicted the "Polish Jew fresh out of Dachau" he met in the men's room during the Munich services who "was crying like a child. I didn't have to ask him why he cried; the answers are all the same anyway, and go like this: Parents tortured to death; wife gassed to death and children starved to death, or any combination of such three."[72] Having just emerged victorious from the war against the Nazis, an officer remarked, "I really felt today as if I had something to atone for the first time in my life. We have really sinned and are sinning each moment we procrastinate. This is one helluva letter to write you upon joining my new outfit, but I've thought about nothing else since the sermon. The sermon was not propaganda, but truth. I could go on like this for pages but I'm sleepy and tired so I'll stop." He concluded with the simple plea, "Please do something about it."[73] The only war that Hitler had won, it seemed to these young men, was "his war to destroy the Jews."[74]

These impassioned letters home underscored Earl Harrison's accusation that the Jewish DPs, while not being systematically exterminated, were nonetheless being treated in much the same way as they had been by the Nazis. The image of the trapped refugee was carved early: "So they sit and wait. Most of them are undergoing the further mental anguish of hoping against hope that they may still find somewhere a wife, a child, a mother." Yet the tracing services were inadequate: "How long must they wait, and hope and suffer?"[75] Indeed, the term "waiting" became a kind of incantatory chorus of accusation. Publicity and fund-raising films produced by the DPs and American Jewish aid organizations showed men and women restlessly walking up and down the streets of the DP camps, exchanging rumors, devouring newspapers, making shady deals, and everywhere pushing baby carriages, holding toddlers by the hand, "waiting, waiting, waiting" for the world to take notice.

"Living Corpses": "We were so much human debris"

The spontaneous outrage of Jewish Allied troops at the early treatment of the survivors was accompanied by shock at their condition.[76] Indeed, Jewish DPs were often characterized by a vocabulary similar to that defining the Berliners, whom their occupiers had quickly judged "shocked and apathetic . . . concerned almost exclusively with problems of food and shelter."[77] Echoing his Military Government colleagues' gloss on the defeated Germans in the former capital, Irving Heymont portrayed his Landsberg charges: "With a few exceptions, the people of the camp themselves appear demoralized beyond hope of rehabilitation. They appear to be beaten both spiritually and physically with no hopes or incentives for the future."[78]

Given our own late-twentieth-century and turn-of-the-millennium romance with the language and theory of trauma and memory, with its valorization, even sacralization, of Holocaust survivors, it is salutary to recall how very unromantic, unappealing, and alien the DP survivors appeared even to those who meant to aid them.[79] The survivors seemed, "truly like creatures from another world."[80] In his autobiographical novel, Hanoch Bartov recalled the reaction of the tough Jewish Brigade soldiers from Palestine who entered Germany determined to "Hate the butchers of your people—unto all generations!" and fulfill their mission of "The rescue of the Jews, immigration to a free homeland," with "dedication, loyalty and love for the remnants of the sword and the camps." Despite these "Commandments for a Hebrew soldier on German soil," the narrator and other Brigade men were not prepared for what they found once they actually encountered the remnants they had pledged to avenge and rescue: "I kept telling myself that these were the people we had spoken of for so many years—But I was so far removed from them that electric wire might have separated us."[81] The Israeli historian Idith Zertal has characterized the painful, shocking encounter "between the Jews of Europe and the 'reborn Israel' " as a kind of "return of the repressed" that provoked the fear and anxiety Freud diagnosed when something that has once been "*heimlich*," familiar and homelike, becomes "*unheimlich*," frightening and inexplicable.[82] American occupiers, international relief workers, Germans, Zionists, and Jewish observers alike shared a perception of survivors as "human debris," an "unattractive lot," as I. F. Stone, the American Jewish leftist journalist covering the underground route to Palestine, noted about his first impression.[83] At best, they could be rehabilitated and resocialized into good citizens (and soldiers) of a future Jewish state, at worst marked as "asocial" and hopelessly traumatized. As one survivor ruefully stated, "the concentration camp experience is nothing that endears you to people."[84]

Both sympathetic and hostile witnesses regularly and graphically bemoaned the "uncivilized" state of the survivors. Either apathetic or bounding with hostile aggression, they seemed oblivious to the most elementary rules of hygiene and the proper use of latrines, "obsessed" with food, and uninhibited in regard to the opposite sex. Some, suspicious of German soaps because of rumors that the name of one common brand, RJF, suggested that it might be composed of "pure Jewish fat" (*reines jüdisches Fett*), refused to bathe. New arrivals horrified officials by smearing excreta on the walls of toilets and vandalizing DP camp facilities. When General George S. Patton, after inspecting Feldafing DP camp in fall 1945, concluded in a particularly egregious outburst that "others ('Harrison and his ilk') believe that the DP is a human being, which he is not, and this applies particularly to the Jews, who are lower than animals," he may have been dismissed by Eisenhower, already embarrassed by the Harrison Report, as unsuitable to be the first American military governor for Bavaria, but he was certainly not alone in his disgust. As Helen (Zippi) Tichauer, an Auschwitz veteran married to the head of the Feldafing DP police sadly recalled, "The toilets were clean but in the halls, there they made their business." Survivors "didn't know what a toilet was, they knew what was a latrine."[85]

Military Government and local German officials as well as overwhelmed and horrified American Jewish and UNRRA relief workers in the camps, Zionist emissaries from Palestine, and DP teachers and leaders themselves often saw the DPs as apathetic and listless, afflicted with "inertia" and "an air of resignation," unsuited to any kind of normal life. At the same time, survivors were labeled "jittery, excitable, anxiety prone."[86] They were on edge, unable to "tolerate any contradiction," susceptible to rumors and quick to panic, and allergic to authority or change. Disturbances erupted quickly and unpredictably. DPs had to be constantly scrutinized, administered, and managed. Susan Pettiss, the sympathetic UNRRA child welfare worker who helped set up the Assembly Center at the Deutsches Museum in Munich, described the Jews as

> terribly difficult to help. They have been demanding, arrogant, have played upon their concentration camp experience to obtain ends. I saw rooms in our camp after they left—filthy, dirty, furniture broken, such a mess as no other group ever left. They are divided into factions among themselves. One of our camps has to have six synagogues to keep the peace. They refuse to do any work, have had to be forced by gun to go out and cut wood to heat their own camps. American soldiers have developed bitter attitudes in many cases.[87]

On a superficial level, however, the urgent and immediate labor of "relief" was quickly done, especially for the first wave of camp survivors. U.S Army Signal Corps films present DPs being briskly sprayed with DDT guns, poked and prodded in medical examinations, loaded on and off trucks, in sometimes eerie echoes of other resettlement and vermin extermination measures. As the many film images deliberately demonstrated, public health measures were extensive and effective. Immunization against typhus, typhoid fever, diphtheria, and smallpox as well as delousing, the use of sulfa and even penicillin, the establishment of TB sanatoria, and the quick provision of adequate sewage systems, food, and shelter assured that immediate physical needs were met with extraordinary dispatch and efficiency. By fall 1945, aid teams were pleased with the results: "It is difficult to believe that they are the same beings who are shown in photographs taken only a few months ago, almost reduced to skeletons and dragging themselves about with difficulty."[88]

Observers were consistently surprised by what appeared to be the "amazingly good" health of the survivors, concluding that "those who had been anything less than the fittest of the fit physically had long since joined the six million Jewish dead lying in Nazi graves."[89] But the DPs' astonishingly robust exteriors, their "unnaturally fat" recovering bodies masked hidden dangers, both physical and psychological, and became themselves a cause for concern. There was something creepy, "unnatural," about their outward good health. Tuberculosis lurked undiagnosed because of the shortage of proper radiological equipment. Many DPs had lost their teeth to malnutrition and disease or to SS blows, and venereal disease and suicide were seen as constant threats.[90] Seemingly sturdy survivors suddenly collapsed and succumbed to disease, depression, and sometimes suicide, weeks or months after liberation. Such deaths often came when the loss of loved ones whose possibility of survival had sustained hope and strength was finally confirmed but also, aid workers thought, when survivors grasped the apparent indifference to their plight by the Allies and even by international Jewry.[91]

Curiously, JDC psychiatric surveys uncovered relatively few diagnosable problems; fewer than one hundred certifiable psychotic cases in the U.S. zone. Yet relief workers were as perplexed about the DPs' disconcertingly inappropriate affect as they were about their physical resiliency. Children and young people with "tales to tell" that made "the spine crawl" were hardened and independent way beyond their years, tightly knit into a supportive peer culture that permitted little adult intervention. Susan Pettiss "fretted" that "I missed seeing what I thought of as normal children's behavior—shouting and laughter, spontaneous games and songs. . . . These kids were serious, focused, even militant; marching in formation to meals and special activities, eating in silence."[92] Yet, even when gathered together in Zionist youth groups (kibbutzim), they were still somehow vulnerable and traumatized children who tended to be "emotional at the wrong moments" and "preternaturally calm" when one would expect them "to be shaken," dry-eyed during recitations of prayers for the dead, but quick to fly into a rage at slight provocation. They described the most horrific experiences, such as the murder of parents and siblings, with complete indifference but "storm[ed] over some trifling incident: having to wait a week before having their hair cut again, or a Red Cross parcel without a pot of honey in it."[93]

Aid workers struggled with how to cope with clients whose life experiences defied comprehension and language (that is, what would later be seen as the essence of "trauma"). The JDC social worker Miriam Warburg was shocked when a group of wild teenage boys who had somehow survived together and now clung to each other for support refused to cancel a planned party after the death of one of their close comrades from appendicitis (in part because of their insistence on sneaking him forbidden food). "Why," they asked, "because one of us died? But what does one dead boy mean? We have been so many, many dying." They gave their comrade a full dress burial, with no tears shed, and "later on," Warburg reported, the staff "discussed whether we should try to change this strange attitude of the young people towards life and death—or whether life might not be easier to bear for them, if they kept it up."[94]

Babies and young children were likely to be watched over and carefully nourished. It was, doctors and social workers realized, the surviving adolescents—tough, "sober, determined, as though they had skipped childhood and grown up overnight," but also enormously lonely and vulnerable—who required the most attention.[95] They were eerily laconic, probably aware they lacked the cultural, social, as well as linguistic vocabulary to convey their experiences. Sometimes, however, they also exploded in a "torrent of talk." As a teenager who had come into the camps at age twelve and was liberated at fourteen wrote in broken German from a Paris orphanage to his only surviving relative, the Gemeinde leader Erich Nelhans in Berlin, "I have so much in my heart, but I cannot it write. . . . I can tell you one thing, with a lot of luck, we all stayed alive. I was in Auschwitz-Buchenwald etc. Main thing is one is alive."[96]

All these symptoms of course—both the agitation and the lethargy, as well as the incapacity of language and narrative—are now clearly associated with "post-traumatic stress disorder." Indeed, already in 1946, social workers and psychiatrists were defining pathologies that the psychiatrist William Niederland, himself a refugee from Nazi Germany, would later explain as a particular "survivor syndrome."[97] Most doctors serving with the relief organizations, however, were not trained psychiatrists. Expecting "normal" and obvious wartime damage and confounded by the symptoms they were seeing, they applied their notions of survival of the fittest to the psyche as well as the body. They expected that if the "people who broke down were allowed to die of starvation or sent to the gas chambers," it followed that "those who were left alive" should be not only "physically but also psychologically" healthy. But the suffering of the survivors was not definable by available terms. It was rather a "generalized emotional disturbance which does not fall into any specific diagnostic categories," and manifested as "a general distrust and suspicion of everyone and of each other" as well as a listless lack of initiative. For their part, the DPs argued with a certain undeniable logic that "we have worked enough, let the Germans do the work," and were unwilling, even within the confines of their own camp, to do anything in the way of improvements that might "[hint] at a permanent or prolonged residence in Germany."[98]

If anything, their most obvious—and to a military administration, most frustrating—symptom, was an intense "dislike of authority." DPs, with no good memories of uniforms and arrests, often reacted with panic or belligerence to the routine checks or movements demanded by an occupying force or the intrusive processing by UNRRA workers. Their critically important survival technique, "the habit of defying authority, of using any subterfuge to violate the express desires and the public decrees of authority," also of course made it very easy to irritate those in charge and end up in legal trouble and even jail.[99] The supposedly more intact refugees from Poland brought with them their own horrific stories of escape, of fearful "passing" as "Aryans," or of hiding in dark caves and forests. Those who had survived in the Soviet Union had endured famine, disease, and forced labor. Precisely because they often came in families, with women and small children, they were in some ways more needy. All had suffered the loss of most other kin and extended families.[100]

Social workers, trained to focus on relief and rehabilitation and schooled in a psychology that focused on early childhood development, were generally loath to attribute behavioral problems "just" to the horrors of war, genocide, and displacement. JDC officials thought that survivors' background experiences in "Eastern Europe, where they lived poorly, without amenities, with primitive sanitation, and in an atmosphere of insecurity among peoples who were strange and antagonistic to them," in a community and state to which they "did not feel obliged to offer loyalty," were as formative as the "tragic experiences of the war years and the equally [sic] tragic time that followed in Germany in the postwar years." The enforced idleness in the camps, the dependence on, and the protection offered by, the voluntary organizations, and the uncertainty of their future only reinforced "their sluggishness and lack of initiative, their attitude toward the voluntary agencies in general and to the health agencies in particular and their poor cooperation in regard to sanitation." JDC doctors conceded that "it is perhaps unjust to generalize in this way," but nonetheless saw DPs as obsessed with how many "Joint packages and cigarettes are we entitled to?" Survivors, they insisted, needed to "regain their self-respect" and be trained in self-sufficiency and initiative.[101] In one of many instances of paradoxical expectations and interpretations attached to the DPs, relief workers expected them to act "normal" but not inappropriately "dry-eyed." They were expected to mourn at the appropriate moments but otherwise "order[ed] their lives with eyes on the future."[102]

Even their most sympathetic keepers, including Jewish Military Government and JDC workers, felt that survivors should be handled gently but firmly, cared for but not coddled. Influenced by prevailing therapeutic wisdom, which believed in the virtues of forgetfulness, a JDC physician proposed in 1945 that "the least we can do for these people, without pampering them, would be to relieve them of the undue burdens of adjustment to life, and to give them a chance to forget the horrors of the past, and to enjoy a sense of well being."[103] In 1946, UNRRA was already of the opinion that "the Jewish question has been a 'cause célèbre' long enough. The more is said about it, the more oppressed the Jews will feel and then more people will become conscious that there is a Jewish question. To eliminate this, treat these people justly and firmly but equitable with other persecutees. Do not single them out."[104] Frederic Morgan, UNRRA's irrascible British director who, like Patton, was eventually forced out, at least in part because of his impolitic antisemitic remarks, surely spoke for many of his colleagues when he carped that "they have an excellent case, but in my view they are hard at work spoiling it by protesting too much." Having spent, as he confided to his diary, an unpleasant afternoon in a DP camp listening to the complaints of "miserable creatures [who] rehearsed all the usual Jewish grievances and were determined to radiate gloom," he was able to cheer himself only by dashing off with "great relief" to Munich "in time for a quick change, a delicious snack," and a rush to the Bavarian State Opera "where we sat in Hitler's box to hear 'Fidelio'" followed by a "delicious late dinner in company with a gang of visiting women."[105]

"Joint" and UNRRA: Ambiguities of Relief

In spite of these sometimes egregious—and even at the time widely publicized—inadequacies in relief efforts by the JDC, as well as the army and UNRRA, it is important to stress the complicated, intense, and in many ways productive relationship that developed among the U.S. military,

American Jewish organizations, and Jewish survivors. UNRRA, established by and directly responsible to the Allies, had started its work even
before the war ended. The JDC had, as we have seen, taken what appeared
to be an excruciatingly long time to negotiate proper entry permits for
Jewish relief teams, refusing to take advantage of the general chaos and
cross borders illegally, as the DPs themselves were constantly doing and
rather expected their helpers to do also. But, as happened in Berlin, once
the "Joint" was able to set up operations in the late summer and fall
of 1945, it immediately became the single most important organization
serving Jewish survivors throughout the American zone, as it already was
in Eastern Europe and the Soviet Union. An initial staff of about fifty
grew to seven hundred, funded by a total budget of over $200 million
raised mostly from American Jews.[106]

The JDC's role as mediator among Military Government, UNRRA, and
the DPs themselves, and as supplier of precious "supplemental" resources
specifically to Jewish survivors, inevitably provoked tensions and resentment on all sides. DPs and their advocates criticized the mostly American
aid workers as insufficiently Zionist, overly deferential to the military,
and hopelessly bureaucratic. DPs felt insulted by the worn, used clothing
that arrived in aid packages from the United States—its main benefit apparently the loose dollar bills and change that sometimes fell out of the
pockets.[107] Almost sixty years later, Chaplain Klausner still fumed that
the activities of the late-arriving JDC were "a patronizing affront to the
liberated" and accused it of "treat[ing] people as wards, incapable of determining their own future."[108] German Jews complained that the JDC
favored the DPs. DPs were convinced that the American Jewish aid workers, some of whom could not speak Yiddish, were more sympathetic to
the German Jews. Germans, already embittered by what they saw as Jewish DPs' privileged relations to the occupiers, resented the packages from
America, filled with goods valued on the black market. Military Government and local German authorities, in turn, were frustrated by the JDC's
vigorous defense of DPs who were accused of trading those goods on the
black market.

UNRRA officials often suspected that the JDC workers' loyalties lay
more with their religious compatriots than with the emerging bureaucracy
of international aid organizations. When General Morgan, overtaxed by
the same stream of refugees from Poland that was so disturbing the Americans in Berlin, asserted that "well dressed, well fed, healthy" Jews were
infiltrating into Germany "with rosy cheeks and pockets full of money
aided by a well-organized underground railroad," American Jews protested his antisemitism with a full-page ad in the *New York Times* headlined by entertainer Eddie Cantor. The comment eventually helped cost
Morgan his job in 1947.[109] As a new international organization with a

multinational staff, largely financed by and under ultimate control of the U.S. Military Government, UNRRA found itself in an ambiguous position. At times DPs complained to the Americans about UNRRA. At other points UNRRA workers, who were themselves often depicted by Jewish DPs as unsympathetic, complained about the insensitivity of U.S. Military Government, which was "in many instances obstructive in favor of the German population to the detriment of the displaced persons, especially Jewish displaced persons."[110] Survivors' daily existence, as well as their personal and political future, were indeed subject to the shifting agendas of international politics and humanitarian bureaucracies. The latter's poorly trained aid workers, themselves subordinate to military control and exigencies and facing novel challenges, became the pioneers of what developed into a global fraternity of aid workers. A quite remarkable corps of men and (and many) women, they, as Katie Louchheim put it, "no longer consider[ed] themselves as nationals of their homeland but as internationals responsible for the saving of the lost and abandoned."[111]

Susan Pettiss, who had left genteel Alabama and a failed marriage for occupied Germany, eloquently recalled the double world of the young female UNRRA workers. They were confronted with a completely unprecedented situation, dealing with people whose experiences, languages, and culture they did not understand. Most were remarkably clueless about the forces and groups that were driving so many Polish Jews into their care even after UNRRA's initial immediate postwar task had been completed. At the same time, they were also having a fabulous time, drinking and playing and romancing, enjoying all the benefits of domination and affluence in a defeated nation. UNRRA's necessarily inexperienced personnel had to learn quickly how "to remain sufficiently vulnerable to other people's sufferings whilst remaining tough enough not to break oneself."[112] In December 1945, Pettiss saw the Deutsches Museum, in a Munich with only limited electricity, as a place of "gloom, bleakness and depression. . . . the most depressing thing, however, was the creepy feeling caused by the implication of all sorts of underground maneuvering. The place is filled now with Jews and stateless people who will not go back to their own countries. They have learned to live by their wits, have learned all the answers so that we find it difficult to know who is a DP and who is not." At the same time, as Morgan's diary indicated in much more extreme form and with sentiments that Pettiss learned to abhor, "social life with its dates, parties, dancing continued unabated," and she took great pleasure in steering a scrounged BMW through the German countryside.[113]

UNRRA frequently clashed with both the Military Government and the JDC over the proper treatment of Jewish DPs. After Patton was removed and replaced by General Lucian Truscott in September 1945, Jewish observers mostly agreed that, prodded by Eisenhower, who in turn was pressured by President Truman, commanding officers were generally sympathetic. However, the orders for improved treatment of Jews often did not translate down to field officers and enlisted men; in some cases they even backfired or were deliberately misinterpreted or flouted.[114] UNRRA's outspoken Morgan was surely correct when, irritated by attacks on UNRRA and British policy, he noted "the wide gulf that exists between promises given in Washington and performance by the military authorities in Germany."[115]

JDC workers, for their part, were indeed able and willing to unleash the authority and economic power of the U.S. occupation, which included a grand supply of cigarettes, Mickey Mouse watches, and occupation marks, in order to "organize" what they needed. When Lucy Dawidowicz, the future Holocaust historian, arrived in Munich in fall 1946 as a Joint employee, sporting the "blue-and-white chevrons, with the letters AJDC" on her uniform, she was entitled to the "privileges and priorities" of an army major. Pleased to lord it over the Germans she hated, she nevertheless felt a bit uneasy in "the most polarized society I had ever known," summoning up for her "the image of the Raj, the British reign in India." Echoing the reports of Americans who enjoyed but were also disturbed by the potentially corrupting hierarchies of occupation, she was both discomfited and pleased to be living in "a militarily secure and materially comfortable society for the 150,000 Americans working in the army, military government, and Allied voluntary agencies." Army scrip (money), and the "tissues, peanuts, cigarettes, and whisky" from the PX, were all useful tools for her "distasteful" but also satisfying negotiations with defeated Germans. Even DPs employed by the JDC in lower-status Class II staff positions still gained priceless access to American personnel and merchandise. Moreover, the steady supply of coveted American goods like cigarettes and chocolate bars opened many doors for the JDC and its employees, allowing for the requisite bribes to obtain whatever was necessary, whether printing matrices (astonishingly, Dawidowicz found that some companies still had Yiddish font), paper, film, fuel, border permits, or just fresh food. When JDC officials had to negotiate with army personnel for supplies or permissions, they were likely to encounter not only uncomprehending Americans but also U.S. officers who were surprisingly helpful and proficient in German or Yiddish. Not a few of them were German-Jewish refugees.[116] This crosscurrent of identities was absolutely crucial to Jewish life in postwar Germany.

DPs certainly suffered from harassment and were arrested, with some frequency, for black market activities and petty offenses, including the proverbial sentence of thirty days in jail for the stolen cucumber. Jews, however, also had quick access to skilled legal help from the Theater

Judge Advocate's Office. American Jewish chaplains, soldiers, and the offices of the special advisers were indispensable mediators, interpreting the DPs to the Americans and vice versa. Abraham Hyman, who served with the Military Government as Assistant Theater Judge Advocate, fondly recollected how his intervention saved General McNarney from opening his Hanukkah greetings to a group of formerly hidden children with a cheery "Merry Christmas" and instead led him into a stirring hora dance with the orphans.[117] Chaplain Mayer Abramowitz recalled a revealing anecdote about the sometimes amusingly well-meaning and sometimes infuriating cluelessness of the American soldiers who had to manage these alien and obstreperous refugees: Called into a drab camp to mediate a brawl between two sets of DPs, a group of young men eager to play soccer and a Hasid "leading a demonstration" against desecrating the Sabbath, he found the MP trying to restore order: " 'Look, Pop,' he said to the bearded Jew, 'let them finish the game, you can play next.' "[118] And in another example of the enormous—and literally untranslatable—gulf between even the most well-meaning helpers and their clients, the American Jewish writer Marie Syrkin described the cruel absurdities of trying to recruit young survivors for college Hillel scholarships by administering American-style entrance examinations in early 1947 to young people who had gained their education in camps, hiding, or on the run. Their curricula vitae were hard to score: "My parents and brother were killed by the Nazis and I don't have mood to go back to a land where I was managed in such a way," wrote one. Another boy, describing his cold and lonely life as a student in Munich, tried to explain, "I should like to hope that I am not quite abundant in this world," leaving Ms. Syrkin to figure out that he was translating from a German word for superfluous (*überflüssig*).[119]

Distraught at the lack of attention and understanding of their situation, DPs faced, as one of their leaders succinctly stated in November 1945, "The bitter yesterday, the bad to-day and the hopeless to-morrow."[120] Far from being silent about their experiences, they stood out—and not in positive ways—because of "the abundance and minute details of their stories; most of them repeat the account tirelessly, on all possible occasions, with a prodigiality of detail."[121] Most observers concluded that the uprooted were "not fit now to take their places in a normal, law-abiding society" and required at best a long period of disciplining and resocialization.[122]

DP leaders themselves saw the issue of "survival of the fittest" differently. They agreed that those who had survived had been the strongest, but saw themselves as now bearing a taint, as well as an obligation to bear witness and create a better future. As Dr. Zalman Grinberg explained to JDC officials in 1946, "People say that we who stayed alive are the selection of our people. But we know that many of us have been demoralized by the sufferings, though it has been worse with other peoples. In the concentration camps we experienced people who ate the flesh of their brethren."[123] Survivors understood that "worse than the visible scars and injuries they bear are the hurts which they carry on the inside."[124] At the same time, DP leaders were painfully aware of the image the DPs presented to relief workers and the many delegations that toured the camps. They were anxious to make a good impression, in both appearance and behavior, and resocialization became a crucial part of the rehabilitation project.

Dr. Henri Heitan, the JDC's chief medical officer in Feldafing, decided, for example, to use a consfiscated castlelike former hotel and Wehrmacht hospital in the foothills of the Bavarian Alps as a sanatorium and vacation retreat. Despite fears that the brutalized and ragged DPs would ravage the well-tended alpine Schloss Elmau, as they had the villas and barracks to which they were assigned in Feldafing, they seemed transformed in this magical and restful world. The food in the elegant dining hall was appetizing to the eye as well as to the stomach. People could gather in a library, play chess and bridge, listen to an orchestra practice and a jazz band play, and gather at a table set with porcelain and linen napkins. In one of the many incongruities that marked Jewish life in occupied Germany, the requisitioned Schloss Elmau, now directed by a camp survivor, became itself a rehabilitation measure, a refuge where DPs would learn "good behavior and contact with human beings."[125]

For the DP leadership, "moral rehabilitation" required not only immediate relief but a future-oriented Zionist political perspective. Camp committees continually admonished camp residents about their obligations as representatives of the Jewish people.[126] Violations by any individuals, whether conspicuous blackmarketeering, sexual liaisons with German women, or filthy quarters, would reflect badly on the entire *She'erit Hapletah* and jeopardize the Zionist project, because, as leaflets pointed out, Jews were always "lumped together according to the old [antisemitic] recipes." Emigration to Palestine as well as elsewhere depended not on sympathy for their suffering but on their ability to appear productive and nontraumatized: "The eyes of the whole world are set on the heroic struggle for Palestine and nothing must undermine the sanctity of that struggle."[127]

Zionists, both the emissaries sent from Palestine and the young leaders of kibbutz groups, were determined to look ahead rather than dwell on the effects of trauma. *Yishuv* (Jewish community in Palestine) leader David Ben-Gurion was unabashed about the survivors' significance for the future of Zionism when he visited the DPs in fall of 1945: "You are not only needy persons; you are a political force. . . . At this moment—

the most crucial in the past two thousand years of our history—strange as it may sound, you can accomplish a great deal. You, the direct emissaries of the suffering of our people, are the driving force."[128] The Jewish Agency, the umbrella organization for all Zionist groups in Palestine, stressed the political rather than humanitarian aspects of the moral rehabilitation project. Contrasting itself to the JDC, it insisted that "in all contacts with displaced persons we are at pains to avoid treating them as objects of philanthropy and patronage. It is our endeavor to restore their self-respect by fostering initiative and self-government, encouraging the realization that their present predicament notwithstanding, it is up to them once more to assume responsibility for their lives."[129]

JDC professionals, however, were often skeptical about the value of militant Zionism to youth who had lost their homes and families. Although it gave meaning to disrupted lives, these professionals mistrusted the indoctrination of damaged minds in political kibbutzim, where children bonded with leaders (*Madrichim*) not much older then themselves, filled with partisan zeal but not attuned to the psychological (or educational) needs of their charges. They worried that the single-mindedness of the Zionist message limited the range of material taught. They feared that youngsters who had already lost so much might be set up for further cruel disappointment if the goal was not achieved, or not in the manner so enticingly laid out. Indeed, JDC social workers complained, Zionist passions, verging on the "totalitarian" imposition of "disciplined unity," disrupted family reunification programs and harshly penalized children who wanted to leave the youth groups and camp life to join relatives abroad or who simply did not want to join the Zionist future for which they were being trained.[130] A teacher in a Berlin DP camp responded with a by now much quoted reflection about the priority of hope over realism for Jews in postwar Germany. He acknowledged that "indoctrination may not be good for normal children in normal surroundings. But what is normal here? How can you make the same demands of us in the DP camps . . . as you do of your colleagues in a free American high school? A crooked foot needs a crooked shoe. (*Auf a krumme fuss passt a krumme shuh.*)"[131]

"THEY THOUGHT WE HAD DIED AND WOULD NEVER RETURN": THE EASTERN EUROPEAN "INFILTREES"

Already by the end of 1945, the DP camps were becoming more a world of refugees than of direct survivors. Jews escaping renewed, murderous antisemitism in postwar Poland poured into the American zone, causing frantic confusion among the American and UNRRA officials in charge of the DP camps. From her post at the Deutsches Museum, which served as headquarters for both UNRRA and the Central Committee of Liberated Jews, Pettiss noted: "Groups pouring in from all directions. . . . Population is going up and up." It is important to keep in mind that although some of the Polish Jews moving into the American zone had survived in hiding or with the partisans, most of the East European refugees she was trying to identify and manage had been repatriated to Poland from the Soviet Union. They had survived the Nazi Final Solution because they had fled, or been deported, to the Soviet Union. It is yet another irony of history that Stalinist Russia, which was engaged in its own purges and persecution of Russian Jews, also proved to be a crucial if difficult haven for Polish and Lithuanian Jews. Some had fled the advancing Wehrmacht into Russia and western Ukraine in 1939 and had been pushed farther east into Siberia as forced labor. The German invasion in June 1941 prompted their release and a rush south to the central Asian republics based "on [distorted] rumors of warm climates and abundance of fruits and other food products." Others had been deported as "capitalists" from parts of (then) Poland occupied by the Soviets as a result of the Nazi-Soviet Pact in 1939 and then also evacuated farther into the Soviet interior with the onset of war.[132]

During the war, Jewish aid groups credited the Soviet Union with having "not only admitted those refugees, but sought to help them by providing them with food and sending many of them as workers to the interior of the country." That "work" in the interior—as "wood cutters in the taiga forests; as laborers at coal and timber-loading stations of trains and ships; or as miners in lead and coal mines"—generally took place under catastrophic conditions, but it also provided the main chance for East European Jewry's survival.[133] As one young survivor recalled when thinking about her uncle who had managed to escape the Soviets and remain in Vilna, it would have been "Better to have been deported with [her and the others] as a capitalist and enemy of the people than to fall into the hands of the Nazis as a Jew." In the end, "we were alive. Our exile had saved our lives. Now we felt ourselves supremely lucky to have been deported to Siberia. Hunger, cold, and misery were nothing; life had been granted us."[134]

Here, too, statistics are vague and problematic. While some sources have estimated that in 1942 the JDC was supporting 500,000–600,000 refugee Jews in remote communities in Siberia and central Asia, most agree that somewhere around 200,000 Jews returned to Poland after the war, of whom many quickly fled again. When about 175,000 to 200,000 of these Jews came into the DP camps from late 1945 onward after having been repatriated to Poland, they brought with them a different spirit and demographic profile. Many arrived in family groups. Eventually—

and with apparent speed—they were integrated into DP society, now dominated by a common Zionist dream. At the time, however, the differences were clear, not only to the American and UNRRA officials confronted by "infiltrees" who did not strictly meet the eligibility criteria for "DPs," but also to the DP camp leaders and Jewish officials. Joseph Schwartz, JDC director in Paris, noted in November 1946: "They did not spend the war years in concentration camps and most of them had to perform some kind of work during their stay in Russia. . . . These people, therefore, complain less about their accommodations because they did not expect as much from their liberators as did the group that was found in Germany. In fact, they are grateful that they have been admitted into the safety of the American zone."[135] Moreover, these "Asiatics," as they were called, were perhaps better prepared for DP life. They had managed to maintain a certain level of Jewish community during their Soviet exile, especially after Jews were released from labor camps in 1941 and many moved south to Kazakhstan. The Yiddish culture of theater and newspapers they had set up, supported by JDC funds, was not all that different from the culture the refugees would find and help to nurture in the DP camps. Moreover, as one refugee remarked, "Russia had given us an elementary education in trading and deal making." Only at war's end did the Jews who had survived (and unknown numbers of them did not) in the Soviet Union realize how relatively lucky they had been: "As harsh as our own lives in Russia had been, the stories we were told about Auschwitz and other camps made us shudder, not only because they were so inconceivable in their brutality but because we had to face what our own kin had suffered."[136]

In an unpublished memoir, a New Jersey pediatrician named Regina Kesler described her first hopeful and then painful return to Poland after the war. No sooner had Germany surrendered than her family started planning their repatriation from the Soviet Union, hoping to reclaim belongings and find the relatives they had left behind. When permits arrived from the NKVD (People's Commissariat of Internal Affairs), UNRRA and the Joint "gave us ample supplies for the long trip back: powdered milk, salami, canned foods, and other provisions." Kesler recalled both the excitement and the confusion these unfamiliar American goods caused, suggesting also the sense of abundance and energy that immediately caused resentment when Jews, thus provisioned, arrived back in a hostile, war-torn Poland. Poles greeted their former neighbors with embarrassment and surprise at best, murderous hostility at worst, usually with resentful surprise: "They thought we had died and would never return." Eventually, "after some negotiation," the new occupants of the family's home in Suwalki "yielded two rooms in the apartment for our use and moved into the remaining parts." The artifacts of

Regina's comfortable childhood were all still there, the furniture and her toys "practically untouched," having been taken over by some German generals whose "orderlies had kept the house clean and in good condition." Only the people had disappeared, all taken to Treblinka and gassed. The few survivors told the now familiar, yet still incredible horrific stories about what the refugees in the Soviet Union had escaped: "They snatched the children from the arms of my crying aunt; she never saw the children again. . . . My poor aunt went nearly insane from grief; she stopped eating, drinking, and even talking."

Regina moved on to Lodz, which for a brief period after liberation by the Red Army in 1944 and the postwar repatriation from the Soviet Union became a center of Jewish life, culture, and business. Young people started university, met in nightclubs, went to movies and concerts, trying to catch up on the youth they had missed. They were "filled with hope and the desire to live, to produce, and to achieve." Others were "determined to make money; they speculated with jewelry, furs, and American currency, and in a short time, became quite wealthy." Most Jews, whether they had survived under the Nazis or in the Soviet Union, did not want "to talk about their war experiences" because "What happened during the war was so unbelievable, so psychotic, that we had to suppress the events in order to maintain our sanity, in order to start a normal life again."

Soon, however, and certainly after the pogrom in Kielce, Poland, on July 4, 1946, this tentative new beginning crumbled. Despite the hopes of some Jews and Poles for a joint antifascist democratic reconstruction, Jews scrambled to escape once again. They fled from a complicated concatenation of dangers: traditional Polish antisemitism overlaid with murderous Nazi antisemitism learned during the German occupation, and finally topped off with resentment at Jewish efforts to reclaim property, supposed support for the communist-dominated new governments and privileged access to American relief supplies.[137] Regina did not want to be transplanted yet again, but her parents no longer trusted the old world and wanted to get as far away as possible as fast as possible.[138]

Defeated Germans, Displaced Jews, American "Protectors, and Jailers"

This flight of Eastern European Jews began just as the great majority of the millions of postwar displaced had returned home. Germans, especially in areas of Bavaria, Hesse, and Württemberg, where Jewish DPs were concentrated, complained loudly and bitterly about the insistent and unexpected Jewish presence in their midst. The Harrison Report had pushed Eisenhower to authorize seizures of German homes. German residents

Fig. 4.2. General Eisenhower touring Feldafing DP camp with DP police chief and UNRRA security officer Erwin Tichauer.

were shocked to learn that they would be forced out of their homes, sometimes within hours of receiving notice. Without being able to take their possessions, and with few prospects for decent alternative housing, they were also fearful of violent revenge by their former victims. A year or more later, freed of their initial anxieties about serious retribution, Germans were all the more aggrieved that the American zone had become a haven for Jews. Incredulous that they would be displaced for scruffy refugees from Eastern Europe, they faced the confiscation of their homes and belongings and the perceived favoring of the Jews by the occupiers with sullen resentment and occasional outbursts of rage.[139]

American support for these confiscations, even if sometimes resisted by lower-ranking officers in the field, was signaled by General Eisenhower's visit to the Bismarck Strasse housing block in Stuttgart and to Feldafing on the same day in September 1945. Shortly after the release of the Harrison Report, Eisenhower, together with other top brass (including a reluctant General Patton), inspected the camp and attended Yom Kippur services in Feldafing. Judah Nadich, Eisenhower's special adviser on Jewish affairs, remembered that "His sudden unannounced appearance at the Yom Kippur service at Feldafing, at which several thousand people were present, electrified the large congregation." Not coincidentally, the visit gave the

American commander an opportunity to beseech the DPs to "be patient until the day comes—and it will come—when you will leave here for the places you wish to go." "The American Army," he admonished his charges, "is here to help you. The part you must play is to maintain good and friendly relations with your appointed authorities. I know how much you have suffered and I believe that a sunnier day will soon be yours."[140]

To this day, Feldafingers remember General Eisenhower, moved both by his own inspection of Nazi death camps and by pressure from President Truman, strolling through their picturesque lakeside town, pointing out villas for confiscation. They recount their outrage at the DPs' less than gentle treatment of still elegant and well-stocked furnishings, gardens, and houses. In his Feldafing memoir, survivor Simon Schochet described, with both "bitter remorse" and satisfaction, the dismantling and plunging down the villa stairs of a "glorious Bechstein" grand piano to make room for beds and lockers.[141] For DPs, however, these villas—all in all there were about forty, with fanciful names such as "Waldberta"—were "anything but luxurious." Bert Lewyn, who found himself in Feldafing after having journeyed to Lodz from Berlin in search of family, recalled sharing "one 'large' room, approximately 16' × 24'," packed with a "pair of bunkbeds, two other single beds, a small table and four chairs," with his aunt and a young couple who had nothing but a "thin curtain" for privacy—an estimated "60 square feet per person."[142]

As the stream of Jews fleeing Eastern Europe intensified, Germans now faced, as Jewish observers saw it, "another kind of fear, fear lest the few tens of thousands of Jews remain where they are. The Germans and Austrians are afraid that their countries, made *Judenrein* by the Nazis, may again be 'flooded' by Jews from the East."[143] As Michael Brenner has pointed out, "one has to realize that in Bavaria and other parts of southern Germany there have never been as many Jews as there were one year after the destruction of European Jewry. Ironically, some places that the Nazis never had to make *judenrein* because Jews had never lived there were eventually populated by several hundreds, if not thousands, of Jews."[144] It often seemed, therefore, to both Germans and the American Military Government, that Jews in post-Nazi Germany were more present than ever before, increasing in numbers and demands daily, populating the black market bazaars, demonstrating loudly and sometimes violently for emigration permits, even outnumbering Germans in small towns in Bavaria or Hesse.[145] Sullen (hands down the term most frequently used by the American victors to describe their former enemies), resentful, and self-pitying in defeat, Germans viewed the DP camps that sprang up in and around former Wehrmacht barracks, Nazi schools, or confiscated housing blocks as a kind of *Schlaraffenland* (magic kingdom) of "sugar and spam, margarine and jam, plus cigarettes and vitamized chocolate bars." They saw the refugee camps as centers of black market activity fed by easy access to the cigarette and food supplies of the occupiers and Jewish relief organizations, especially the "Joint."[146]

To some extent, to be sure, DPs competed for scarce housing, both in towns and in barracks, with German refugees from eastern territories and with the Military Government, which requisitioned housing for its own members. Most DPs, however, were housed in camp barracks, and it seems that those evictions that did take place were publicized and remembered quite out of proportion to their actual occurrence.[147] But these German memories of victimization by Jews and Americans reflect a common attitude. As battlefield troops collected their service points and returned home, and a Cold War emphasis on German reconstruction supplanted denazification, both victors and defeated came to see the victims of Nazism, still displaced and unruly, as inconvenient and disreputable disturbers of the peace. Germans, meanwhile—with their "clean German homes and pretty, accommodating German girls"—styled themselves, and were increasingly recognized as, victims.[148]

Zorach Wahrhaftig, an emissary from the orthodox Jewish aid organization Mizrachi, who authored many reports on the DPs' situation, worriedly observed "the hostile and gloomy looks of the Germans" and "the whispering campaign against the Jewish DPs conducted by the soldiers' German girl friends." Six months after liberation, he informed the American and World Jewish Congress, "The Jewish DPs are looked upon as intruders, the Germans as the autochthonic population suffering from the plague of DPs."[149] Eighteen months after liberation, an even more depressed Wahrhaftig reported: "the war is not yet over for European Jewry. They are impossible to repatriate and almost as difficult to resettle. No one wants them now just as no one wanted them before and during the war."[150]

Survivors who had expected the occupiers to treat them as allies vociferously protested the injustice of their plight. Their German victimizers were free in what remained, even under occupation, their own country, while Jews were confined in refugee camps waiting to depart "bloodied cursed" German soil. As much as the Germans resented the perceived special treatment accorded to the displaced Jews, the Jewish survivors resented their handling by the Americans who served as both "protectors and jailers," subjecting them to arbitrary and "inexplicable" rules and regulations and a steady "flow" of "complicated and frequently misinterpreted army directives . . . all the way from apparently compulsory repatriation down to a reduction in the quantity of milk allowed to [a man's] pregnant wife."[151] DPs tartly observed that "it is better to be a conquered German than a liberated Jew."[152]

Yet, in spite of the often tense relationship with GIs, and despite rapidly improving U.S. relations with the former enemy, Jewish DPs did have a privileged relationship with the *Amis*. Right after liberation, Jewish Brigade soldiers attached to the British Army provided crucial aid and hope, and Zionist emissaries from Palestine continued to play a key role in influencing relief work in the camps and the policies of the Central Committee. But for most Jewish survivors, the key interlocutors were Americans within Germany—both Jewish and not, both military and civilian relief—and also in the public sphere of U.S. policy making agencies and the media. Jewish DPs "were on exhibit to visitors," including journalists, congressional delegations, and American Jewish groups "from the moment of their liberation." Their leaders knew very well how to stage these events and manipulate them into calls for better treatment and entry to Palestine. It was not an accident that the only department of the Central Committee of Liberated Jews with an English, not Yiddish, name was "public relations."[153]

DP leaders relished the presence of high-ranking U.S. military officers at their conferences and services, promoting these visits as a way of garnering sympathy and legitimizing their community. High-ranking officers popped up not only at the famous Feldafing Yom Kippur service, attended by both Eisenhower and Patton, but at all kinds of Jewish ceremonies, from Passover Seders to Hanukkah parties. Simultaneously moved and uncomfortable in their exotic surroundings, some of them were less uncomfortable than they might have claimed. Numerous DP camp commanders were Jewish, such as Lieutenant Irving Smith at Feldafing, "a young American Jew from South Bend, Indiana," and Colonel Irving Heymont at Landsberg (although, as we have seen, not all of them would admit it).[154] Even some American generals, such as General Bedell Smith, who informed surprised DP advocates that his mother was Jewish, and General Mark Clark, were known to be at least partly Jewish, although certainly not as many as the German rumor mill complaining about "jew infested Military Government" suggested.[155] DPs were favored with high-level inspection tours by journalists, politicians, military officials, and American Jewish representatives, who treated them, as it seemed to UNRRA worker Kathryn Hulme, an adventurous young American wartime welder turned UNRRA worker, with "kid gloves."[156] Eleanor Roosevelt dramatized her efforts to draft a Universal Declaration of Human Rights with her 1945 tour of the Zeilsheim camp near Frankfurt. Kathryn Hulme explained that while Jews comprised less than one-fifth of the U.S. zone's DP population, "they were such an articulate minority that if you only read the newspapers to learn about occupation affairs, you gained the impression that they were the whole of the DP problem." She conceded, however, that while the Jews were treated as and "sounded like the prima donnas of the DP world, . . . I thought that perhaps they deserved the rating."[157] Germans openly resented this supposed "kid gloves" treatment, driven by the impression, in General Lucius Clay's words, that "if we sent an MP in to arrest them, why it would be in every headline in the United States—'US soldiers Invading Jewish Camp,' and so forth, just as if the Nazis were back at work, and so on."[158] Jewish survivors, on the other hand, would have not only underscored the second half of Hulme's statement that "perhaps they deserved the rating" but pointed to the painful inadequacies and ironies of their situation as homeless refugees or disowned former citizens in the "bloodsoaked" land of their tormentors.[159]

Unquestionably, Jews, having gained their own separate camps and a significant degree of internal self-governance, received high levels of both assistance and scrutiny. On September 7, 1946, in an impressive ceremony held in the War Room of U.S. headquarters in the IG Farben Building in Frankfurt, Eisenhower's successor, General McNarney, recognized the Central Committee of Liberated Jews as official representatives of all Jewish displaced persons on matters of social welfare and self-governance. In the spirit of reeducation, American Forces Radio excitedly broadcast the recognition of this "little democracy of 160,000 people liberated in the heart of Germany."[160] As an American major responsible for DPs noted in an AFN (American Forces Network) newscast attempting to educate U.S. troops about the situation of Jewish survivors, "It has always been a source of pride to Americans that they never have turned a deaf ear to the cries of people who are distressed and in dire need. It is a fact that the bulk of these infiltrees are at present of the Jewish race [sic]. No one who really understands the suffering of the Jews in Europe would want our country to deny help to these people." And, he added, in clear reference to narrow U.S. immigration policies, "We are taking care of them in UNRRA centers and we will continue to do so until such time as either the American government or the American people change their attitude." About the ongoing movement of Jews into the American zone, he said: "There is absolutely no way we can really be sure in advance how many persons we will handle. Human misery cannot always be measured at the same level. But it is our effort always to use the same measurement: the yardstick of humanity and justice."[161] Only a day earlier, however— an indication of the simultaneous American sympathy for, and distancing from, Jewish DPs—Secretary of State James Byrnes's conciliatory speech in Stuttgart on September 6 had signaled U.S. support for German reconstruction and the Cold War turn away from denazification. It also marked the upcoming end of the brief (relatively) "golden age" of special DP access to American power, protection, and rations that had been inaugurated by the Harrison Report.[162]

IMAGINED HOMELAND

Unlike other DPs in occupied Germany who relied on American protection, Jewish DPs, at least in their official voice, both sought an alliance
with the victors and insisted they had another homeland to go to, albeit
one hardly any of them had ever seen. In a sense, the sanctioning of separate Jewish DP camps by the Americans signaled the final demise of the
cosmopolitan identity that Jews had embodied in prewar Europe. For
most surviving European Jews, Zionism—as utopian ideal, if not real destination—represented finally the only ideological as well as psychologically affirming alternative. Displaced persons had lost their national attachments by virtue of having been deprived of citizenship, home, and
life. Paradoxically, however, this very catastrophe and their statelessness
resulted in an elaboration and intensification of a new Jewish national
and ethnic identity.[163]

The Central Committee of Liberated Jews strove to enhance that identity both by its actions within the DP camps and by its relentless public
relations campaigns. On Sunday, January 12, 1946, it convened its first
major conference, its opening ceremonies pointedly held in the ornate
halls of the Munich City Hall. One hundred and twelve representatives
of the She'erit Hapletah came together with a remarkable array of guests,
including journalists who had taken time off from covering the trials in
Nuremberg, Military Government officers, the mayor of Munich, the
minister president of Bavaria, the newly appointed state commissioner for
victims of fascism, and David Ben-Gurion representing the Jewish community (Yishuv) in Palestine. Mindful of the conference's political significance, the Central Committee captured it in a film called *These Are the
People*. The film is narrated by an anonymous young American lieutenant
in uniform—in fact it is Chaplain Klausner, who, in defiance of army
regulations, was the film's main instigator, producer, and director.[164]
The documentary clips are framed by an accusatory chorus repeating
"These are the People. Our People. Waiting. Waiting. Waiting." As the
camera pans the faces of Jews trapped in Landsberg DP camp, the town
in which Adolf Hitler composed his "bible of tyranny, *Mein Kampf*," the
film asks, "How long will tyranny hold fast the hopes and aspirations of
a broken people? How long will homelessness pack the dreams of the
suffering children of Israel and fill their hearts with despair?" Other clips
show the somber opening of the conference as men (interestingly, with
their heads apparently uncovered) chant the Hebrew prayer in memory
of the dead, *El Mole Rachamin*. The first speaker, the well-known "young
courageous Dr. Zalman Grinberg," challenges his audience of survivors

and dignitaries with an angry and passionate *j'accuse*. In clipped, perfect German and using terms frequently invoked by DP leaders pressing for emigration to Palestine, he caustically announces the brutal death of any European-Jewish synthesis. The Europe to which Jews have contributed monotheism, poets, writers, doctors, lawyers, professors, and Nobel Prize winners has returned the favor with gas chambers and crematoria. As the camera flashes to the listening Ben-Gurion, Grinberg links the world's refusal to hinder the extermination of its Jews to the current resistance to opening the gates of Palestine: "These last nine months, we have discovered the great secret of why . . . they could not prevent the death marches; we have understood this secret. We now know that the will to give us a free, secure life, which is missing now, is the same will that was not there then to rip us away from death."

Fierce and intense, dressed in a dark suit and tie, he virtually screams at the applauding assemblage. The world is certainly accustomed, he notes, to brutality and horrors, but this level of human devastation could only have occurred because the victims were Jews. Nine months after the liberation, Jews remain packed into camps, stateless and homeless, dependent on the studies of committees and commissions, "a bitter lump in the throat of international politics." His voice at fever pitch, Grinberg, the radiologist from Kovno who survived ghettos, forced labor, and death camps, calls out that now is the chance "for the great leaders of the great empires" to solve the momentous historical injustice that has cost six million lives. It is time to give the Jews a homeland and a state: "And give us back *Eretz Israel*."

After this powerful opening, the remaining speakers, however, provide a jolting reminder of the bizarre realities of Jewish DP life in occupied Germany: not only are the survivors still far from *Eretz*, busy with internal squabbles and dependent on the United States, UNRRA, and international politics, but they also reside in the midst of a defeated Germany negotiating its own precarious path toward sovereignty. Next on the podium, his presence as fitting and incongruous as the setting—the Munich Rathaus draped in Zionist flags and overseen by the American military—is Dr. Wilhelm Hoegner, the minister president of Bavaria. A Social Democrat and antifascist who returned from exile in Switzerland, Hoegner gives what seems in retrospect a remarkably inappropriate speech. It is, however, entirely in keeping with the difficult politics of the early postwar years and Hoegner's need to satisfy his own electoral constituency as well as the American occupiers. Acknowledging that "the extermination of a great part of the Jewish people by the National Socialists was one of the most terrible events in the history of a humanity already rich in horrors," Hoegner now greets "the liberated Jews in a Bavaria liberated from the tyranny of the National Socialists." As did many Bavarians, he insists on the "Free State's" provincial separatism and bemoans its betrayal by a defeated Prussian militarism. He reminds the gathering that the Germans too have suffered in the war and proceeds to insist that for the Nazi "criminals" the persecution of the Jews was only a "means to incite and control their own Volk." Speaking to an audience that has just heard an angry cry about the world's indifference to the suffering of the Jews, he manages to present the genocide of the Jews as another facet of the great betrayal perpetrated on the German Volk by the Nazis.

Hoegner is followed by David Ben-Gurion, the leader of "Palestinian Jewry," who calls for the fulfillment of promises for "a free and democratic Jewish commonwealth in Palestine." He is followed in turn by an envoy from the World Jewish Congress (the only woman on the podium), and a representative of the U.S. Third Army, as well as Simon Rifkind, the current adviser on Jewish affairs to the U.S. Military Government. With the symbol of the *She'erit Hapletah*, a "stump of a tree . . . felled at the base, . . . " out of which springs a new shoot, alive and firm," as backdrop,[165] the conference concludes with the stirring singing of "Hatikvah," the Zionist anthem of hope. In the film, the narrator vows, "We despair not, though our road stretches through an endless history. In the classroom with print and thought, in the workshop with hammer and lathe, on the field with sweat and brawn, and in the evening with song and dance, our march to peace and freedom is begun." The film moves on to images of Jews and their "waiting" life in the peculiar refuge of American-occupied Germany: working the land on communal farms in Bavaria, men drinking coffee under a portrait of Theodore Herzl while studying maps of Palestine, women feeding chickens and milking cows, their arms marked by KZ tattoos and their fingers bearing new wedding rings. This was the picture of productivity and regeneration while "waiting, waiting, waiting" that the Central Committee and Jewish relief agencies wanted to present to the Jewish funders and international commissions that would determine the future of the *She'erit Hapletah*.[166]

Jewish leaders who sought international attention and support through events such as the Munich conference and films such as *These Are the People* had to orchestrate relations with the American occupiers, American Jewish agencies, the representatives of the Yishuv, and the DPs themselves. They also had to worry about the DPs' relationship (and that of the occupiers and the relief agencies) to the Germans on whose land they were camped. The Central Committee urged leniency for DPs and severity toward German antisemitic offenses, while at the same time admonishing Jews toward self-discipline and restraint, even in the despised German "waiting room." Jewish leaders pressed the latter injunction with an impatience that strikes the present-day reader as highly unrealistic, some-

Fig. 4.3. Major Irving Heymont (*left center*) converses with David Ben-Gurion (*right center*) during his visit to the Landsberg DP camp, October 1945. *Far left*: U.S. Army chaplain Abraham Klausner; *far right*: Abraham Glassgold, UNRRA camp director.

times fretting, as if surprised, that Jews "were still not completely rehabilitated, even though two years have passed since their liberation from the concentration camps and prisons."[167] American Jewish legal officers attached to Military Government staunchly defended survivors against the often uncomprehending sanctions of both German and occupation authorities. They clearly felt that the "disorganized, demoralized, and undisciplined" DPs, "fearful and resentful of authority," were hardly "blameless," particularly in their disinclination to respect the niceties of German property rights. They also recognized, however, that even with the not always understanding protection of the Americans, the DPs hardly felt, as the title of a recent book—not entirely ironically—would have it, "safe among the Germans."[168]

Indeed, the survivors' very obvious presence—their astonishingly rapid (at least superficial) physical recovery, their takeover of housing requisitioned by the Americans, and their entrepeneurship in black market commerce—produced resentment and competition for Allied favors. It also fed doubt about denazification program claims that the Germans had murdered millions of Jews. Such sentiments could be summarized as "if there had really been so many death camps, then why are there so many Jews around, and why do they look so healthy and well dressed and have so many children?" The fact that, within a year of war's end, Jewish DP camps were crowded with "infiltrees" from newly communist Poland, who could be labeled as victims of communism and Polish antisemitism rather than Nazism, only strengthened these perceptions and made Germans even less likely than they already were to express sympathy or accept responsibility. Jewish officials insisted that "evidence of the irresistible factors which drive the Jews from Poland to Berlin to Munich" abounded and that "every refugee [carried] horrific stories." Even if the new communist rulers would be able to establish a safe environment for Jews, which they clearly were not, there were good reasons to flee: Jews had no desire to live in a vast graveyard, "in a land where they once lived and worked and laughed with their families and friends—now all dead. Clearly their backgrounds of heartache and physical suffering leave them in no mood for the social and physical hardships of life in Poland today."[169] And even if, as some JDC workers reported, "They say life in Poland is not too difficult—relatively good food situation, a friendly govt. Helping them recover their business, etc.," the reality remained that "they are simply not safe with their lives—pure, brutal terrorization and persecution at the hands of the Polish people which is simply unbearable."[170] But the fact that these Jewish refugees from the East were not, or at least no longer looked the part of, emaciated death camp survivors did not increase their credibility as victims. They had tried to flee with those possessions they had managed to rescue or acquire during their time in Poland. Much was again lost or stolen along the way, but these Jewish "infiltrees" still appeared well clothed and quite healthy, particularly in comparison to the misery evident on the streets of German cities such as Berlin or Munich.

END OF THE "GOLDEN AGE" AND THE "EMOTIONAL ECONOMY" OF OCCUPATION

Protected by the American occupiers from any serious revival of Nazi-style persecution, DPs were nonetheless acutely aware, as our discussion of Berlin has shown, of a "new" antisemitism, building on the old but also feeding off Germans' resentful sense that they were victims of both the victorious Allies and the alien Eastern European refugees the Americans had allowed to enter their defeated land. Debates about how to evaluate this "new" antisemitism, elaborated when the other genocidal variety had only just been defeated, raged among Jews. Sometimes, but certainly not always, as we have seen in the case of Berlin, these debates divided German Jews who still hoped to rebuild lives in a denazified Germany from Eastern European Jews. Sensing an echo, not only of Nazism but of the persecution they had fled in Poland, the DPs were determined to leave Europe and embrace Zionism.

A highly controversial 1946 text and Munich radio broadcast by Ernst Landau, a German-Jewish camp survivor, both identified this renovated antisemitism and revealed the sharp disagreements about who was to blame and how to respond. Germans, restrained by the occupiers and their own genuine revulsion from endorsing the extremes of Nazi exterminatory antisemitism, now labeled Jews as "foreigners" (*Ausländer*) and then blamed those foreigners for "everything bad." Turning a pervasive German protest on its head, Landau pointedly noted that if Germans resented being held collectively responsible for all crimes committed by Germans, then it could hardly be proper to blame all Jews for black market activities and other crimes, especially given that—in another frequently made point—Jews constituted the smallest percentage of foreigners engaging in lawless behavior. At the same time, Landau's rejection of all notions of collective guilt and his suggestion that Jews "had the duty to maintain the principle of humanity" (*Begriff der Menschlichkeit*) and model a sense of ethics rather than cause commotion and unrest drew furiously sarcastic responses from his East European fellow survivors. They fulminated about German Jews' "typical assimilatory attitude," which had weathered the horrors of recent years much as a "preserved" bedbug endures severe frost, only to "crawl out of her crack alive and active" as soon as the seasons turned. DPs mercilessly mocked Landau's call for teaching humanism to the Germans: "We are loaded with so many obligations toward the poor defenseless Germans! We must prove that we are 'decent' carriers of humanism. We, the victims of Nazi barbarism, still are obligated to prove [something] to the people who conceived this barbarism, nurtured and sated themselves with it." The Allies perhaps had such an "obligation" for denazification, but they were the victors with "armed divisions," while the Jews had "armies of unemployed and homeless people, who have been uprooted by the horrible German [the typescript has "Nazi" crossed out and replaced] deeds. They have zones and we also have zones! Their zones embrace all of Germany and our zones are called: Camp Landsberg, Camp Feldafing, Camp Ulm."[171]

As in Berlin, by 1947, both German and DP Jews in the American zone sensed a new openness about German prejudice and resentment. Philipp Auerbach, the outspoken German-Jewish survivor who had been appointed to a curious and novel position, Bavarian "commissioner for the racially, religiously, and politically persecuted," bemoaned Germans' conviction that "what the Allies were doing to the German Volk today was much worse than everything that had been done in Auschwitz." He saw around him the merchants who refused to sell to Jews, the barkeepers who wouldn't serve the Jewish players after a soccer match, the citizens who once again felt free to abuse Jews on urban trams and trains, the jokes about gassing told in the reviving cabarets, the Nazis who hung on in important positions, and, particularly galling to Auerbach, who campaigned relentlessly for financial compensation, restitution (*Wiedergutmachung*) office officials who had only recently worked for the finance (OFP) agencies that expropriated the property of deported Jews.[172]

Secretary of State Byrnes's Stuttgart address had both confirmed and foreshadowed what was becoming more and more obvious. Initial U.S. policy toward Germany, as manifested in the measures of JCS (Joint Chiefs of Staff) Order 1067, signed by Truman in May 1945 was harsh, and had already been intensely contested in the Roosevelt administration. By the fall of 1946, however, it was clear that this controversial program of revenge and quarantine, of thorough deindustrialization, demilitarization, and denazification, would not be enforced. It was no secret that those opposed to the punitive stance embodied by the rejected Morgenthau Plan were inclined to blame a revenge-seeking "clique" of American Jews and European-Jewish émigrés in Military Government for unrealistic policies hindering German reconstruction. By mid-1946, much of the responsibility for the unwieldy denazification process had been handed over to local German authorities, who, unsurprisingly, were much more lenient. Germans disposed quickly of the enormous backlog of millions of denazification cases. In August 1946, anyone born after January 1, 1919, with the exception of high-ranking Hitler Youth leaders—who, others complained, might have been just the idealistic and politically interested young people most in need of reeducation—was amnestied; by Christmas those of all ages with low incomes, little property, or disabilities were added to this protected category.[173] In 1947, the Military Government under General Lucius Clay began to enforce a State Department rule that stipulated that naturalized U.S. citizens could not serve in Military Government in their country of origin until they had been U.S. citizens for at least ten years. The rule was clearly designed to reduce the influence of European refugees from fascism, many of them Jews who were seen as "vengeful" supporters of stringent denazification and resistant to the newer policies of reconstruction and reconciliation.[174] In July 1947, the already weakened hard-line JCS Order 1067 was replaced by JCS directive 1779, confirming what was already obvious to the Military Government: that "an orderly and prosperous Europe requires the economic contributions of a stable and productive Germany as well as the necessary restraints to insure that Germany is not allowed to revive its destructive militarism." By the end of the year, in a significant signal to the Jewish survivors, the Military Government had eliminated its policy of assigning higher food rations to the victims of Nazism.[175]

In 1943 already, the anthropologist Margaret Mead warned American policy makers planning the future of a defeated Nazi Germany about the importance of rationing for establishing control over an occupied population. "Whenever a people feels that its food supply is in the hands of an authority," she reminded them, "it tends to regard that authority as to some degree parental." Moreover, she added, "probably no other operation, even the provision of hospitalization and emergency care, is so effective in proving to an anxious and disturbed people that the powers that be are good and have their welfare at heart." As she had predicted, in the aftermath of unconditional surrender in 1945 and the flight of millions of refugees into the western occupation zones, differential access to food supplies or to goods that could be exchanged for food became a key gauge of the occupiers' favor, an issue that became particularly acute after mass repatriation had been accomplished and Jews were among the significant remaining groups of refugees under UNRRA and U.S. jurisdiction. Defeated Germans and surviving Jews competed for the favors of the "good parent," embodied by the American occupiers and the relief organizations. For Jewish survivors, for whom food supplies were generally—at least after the early period of chaos—adequate, the problem became, just as Mead had sensed, one of quality rather than quantity. How the food was prepared, she had cautioned, was often more important than what was served, "a sign of the sympathy and understanding emanating from the occupying power."[176] Constant hassles ensued; in the early period, Jewish aid officials begged Military Government to release to the DPs Red Cross packages that had been destined for U.S. prisoners of war who thankfully no longer needed them, while DPs themselves were none too thrilled with their contents. For UNRRA and Military Government authorities responsible for feeding the DPs, food was indeed a political issue, but one primarily expressed in terms of grams and calories. UNRRA files are filled with careful charts on the caloric value of foods, more meticulously broken down than in any diet book, and ranging from beef carcasses (544 cal/lb) to sweets and candies (1,680/lb).[177] DPs were continually subjected to nutritional studies and mass weighings by public health workers. Jews insisted—to the point of engaging in protest hunger strikes—that now it was the turn of Germans to provide for them and the occupiers' task to enforce that responsibility: "They, who are guilty of our sufferings and tortures, they who robbed us of our fortunes, they must be forced to feed us during the time we are compelled to stay in this country in order to make it possible for us to regain our health."[178]

Food, as the DPs repeatedly pointed out, was not merely a matter of calories and physical survival. Clearly, it was defined according to an emotional and political as well as a physical economy. The apparent disparity in calories and rations for Germans and Jewish DPs masked the fact that most Germans in the towns and villages near the DP camps did not rely on those rations but on their connections with local farmers. DPs who maneuvered to supplement their (somewhat more ample) rations were, however, condemned and often arrested for their black market dealings. In the most notorious and tragic incident, in March 1946, some two hundred German police officers, resonantly accompanied by dogs and bullhorns, and a handful of U.S. military police, raided a DP camp in Stuttgart. In the ensuing upheaval—the DPs resisted the searches—German police shot and killed Schmul Dancyger, a survivor of Auschwitz and Mauthausen, who had just the night before been reunited with his wife and children. The raid succeeded in recovering several illegally held chickens.[179] Jewish Military Government and relief officials were constantly at pains to point out to their disapproving colleagues that when it came to black market activities, Jews were only participating in what had become a virtually universal and necessary practice—as pervasive and impossible to ban as fraternization—and were in fact rare among the large-scale operators, "small fish" among mostly German "whales and sharks."[180] As targets for charges of black marketeering, Jews were doubly vulnerable. On the one hand, as camp survivors or "infiltrees" from the East, they looked "shabby" compared to the docile and well-scrubbed if sullen Germans. On the other hand, sometimes they actually looked better, fattened up by carbohydrate-laden rations, quick to dress in stylish clothes stitched by master tailors in the camps, clinging to the possessions they had managed, as in Regina Kesler's and many others' stories, to acquire, scrounge, trade, or sometimes steal during their brief return to Poland.

The black market is of course key to any account of postwar food politics, but, in contrast to the experience of either Germans or occupiers, black marketeering for most Jews had little to do with either bare survival or the accumulation of large-scale luxuries for major trade enterprises. The desire for more appetizing and nurturing food, rather than, as most critics insisted, the drive for profit or even the search for necessities, pushed people toward the black market, where they could acquire the fresh meat, fruits, and vegetables that Germans were able to take off the land or that occupiers and aid officials took for granted.[181] People complained—obsessively it was said—about the quality of clothing and housing and especially about both the quantity and the taste of food; it was never enough and never good enough. American white bread and the hated UNRRA green peas could not satisfy.

Food desires, relief workers concluded, were not rational. While conceding that "the realistic component of these complaints is unquestionably large and these complaints are in most instances justified," aid workers also reported that "we have all seen instances where these complaints continue even though, from an objective standpoint, the complaints are excessive in relation to the reality of the situation."[182] They noticed that there were fewer complaints about the UNRRA rations among those DPs living outside the camps. Perhaps, they figured, food just tasted better in a non-mass-institutional setting, and these so-called "free livers" were better able to supplement their military-style rations with familiar items such as sauerkraut, garlic, and onions. Survivors suffered from a hunger that could not be satiated by calories and vitamins, a deep and ultimately insatiable longing for care and dignity that no amount of institutional improvements or calories would be able to assuage.[183] As one frustrated but understanding UNRRA pediatrician reminded her calorie-counting superiors, "people do not eat calories, but food," and that food had to be appealing.[184] "How are we going to live—on calories?" one DP bitterly asked an American visitor who, like many observers, realized that "calories in the DP camps had ceased to be a heat or food unit but had become the symbol of the drab, squalid existence" of the refugees.[185]

Food provision, such as receipt of American CARE (Cooperative of American Remittances) packages (for Germans), UNRRA rations (for DPs), or JDC supplements (for Jews), served therefore as important terms through which questions of guilt, victimization, and entitlement were conceptualized—and enforced—in the early postwar years. UNRRA's definition of "relief and rehabilitation" tended to separate psychological needs, which were recognized to a limited degree, from the more immediate, urgent requirements for food, medical care, and shelter. The two kinds of needs were in fact inextricably linked. Immediate needs were met relatively quickly and with remarkable efficiency. But food remained a key issue well after the initial problems of severe hunger and malnutrition had long been solved, indeed until currency reform and the emigration of most displaced persons in 1948. Not only the numbers of calories but also the kinds and quality of food available to Germans and Jews often came to stand in for the highly contested recognition of relative suffering and the entitlement to human rights and dignity.

The squabbles between Germans and Jews over food were intricately tied to each group's sense of its own victimization. Ironically, the victims, classified as stateless refugees dependent on "handouts," were inevitably cast in the position of "nudging" mercenary complaints or as "privileged" when they received or demanded the puny benefits they had been granted in recognition of their past suffering. Germans, for their part, increasingly expected to be rewarded for their good (that is, docile) behavior in the present rather than punished for possible crimes in the past. This enabled them to contrast their own position as citizens simply demanding their rights to the satisfaction of basic needs with the undeserved "special pleading" and "privileging" of their victims. The vulnerable and often begrudged status of surviving Jews as needy supplicants led them to a growing recognition that the key to the granting of human rights (seen as just and universal) rather than benefits and privileges (seen as unjust and inherently particular) was the claim to nationhood and national identity, a position that the *She'erit Hapletah* quite successfully articulated in their embrace of Zionism and the demand for a Jewish national homeland.

THERAPEUTIC ZIONISM

Paradoxically, then, the flip side to the stigmatization of Jewish DPs as both incorrigible and pathetic was a kind of romantic vision, heavily influenced by the Zionist ethos that dominated DP life, of the tough survivor who had emerged like a phoenix from unimaginable devastation. When it came to the Jewish DPs, disgust and fear were mingled with, and sometimes outweighed by, admiration and sheer awe at the fact of their survival. UNRRA worker Kathryn Hulme described her reaction to the Jewish DPs assigned to her camp. They were hardly the "ashes of a people" announced by so many reporters; on the contrary, they were indeed survivors, "charged with the intensest life force I had ever experienced." They—or at least their toughened leaders—were entirely unlike either the docile, well-behaved, defeated Germans or the "professional" non-Jewish Polish and Baltic DPs with whom she had previously worked. The Jews were "contrary, critical, and demanding," so well versed at "organizing" that they had even managed to acquire their own cache of that most precious commodity, penicillin. Resorting to nonetheless admiring stereotypes, she described "their wiry bodies . . . smoldering eyes . . . voices unmusical and hoarse . . . their hands moved continuously." In fact, she concluded, "They didn't seem like DPs at all."[186]

For young people who had lost their entire families, the Zionist peer culture, in all its passionate intensity, offered self-affirmation and community, and perhaps the utopian vision that sustained survival or at least hope, as it had already in ghettos, partisan groups, and camps. As one impressed American Jewish GI noted, "the recuperative powers of the average human being, physical and mental, are remarkable, provided only that there is something to recuperate for."[187] Even UNRRA officials concerned about the role of "undesirable" outside agitators in the camps recognized that, for the displaced, the "magnet of Palestine" was the single best antidote to "lethargy and hopelessness."[188] For many, Palestine surely was, as one U.S. reporter astutely observed, "a kind of magic word . . . which means not so much Palestine as some never-never Utopia of which they dream. It might be anywhere they could live freely," the dream of a home where they would be peaceful, safe, and above all among themselves.[189] For most DPs, Zionism was not a deeply held ideological or religious belief but rather, as various Israeli scholars have suggested, a "catastrophic Zionism," born of the conviction that there could be no viable future in a blood-soaked Europe. It was a "functional" Zionism that provided a coherence to their lives and some sense of future possibility, both individual and collective.[190]

Recent critical, especially Israeli, historiography has decried the cynical instrumentalization of Jewish survivors (the "seventh million" in Tom Segev's terms) by the Yishuv. Historians have critiqued the contempt its leaders felt, more or less openly, for the traumatized survivors, the manipulation of media and officials to create the impression that every Jew was desperate to go to Palestine, and the harsh determination with which the "reservoir" of "human material" in the DP camps was recruited to populate the land and man its military.[191] At the time, however, virtually everyone, including skeptical American JDC workers and DPs who hatched individual plans for emigration to the United States and elsewhere, agreed on the political importance of demanding a Jewish homeland in Palestine. The JDC officially supported the integrity of individual decisions and possibilities in regard to emigration destinations. As we have seen in the Berlin case, however, the JDC and individual UNRRA workers like Susan Pettiss increasingly "abandoned hope of restoring Jewish life in Eastern Europe" and turned their hopes toward Palestine.[192]

Early JDC estimates suggested that of the DPs in one representative (Landsberg) camp, as of October 1, 1945, 62.6 percent (3,112) wanted to go to Palestine and 17.8 percent (884) to the United States.[193] Over time, however, as emigration to the United States remained restricted and the Americans ceded more and more self-government to local German authorities unwilling to connect their DP "problem" to Nazi crimes, Zionism became more and more appealing. It worked as a kind of therapeutic ideology that could offer a sense of collective identity, hope, and future to those who had lost both family and home. A year after that initial JDC survey, an UNRRA "census" in 1946 revealed to receptive members of the Anglo-American Committee of Inquiry on Palestine that of 19,311 adults (over the age of fourteen) who stated a preference, 18,072 said Palestine was their first choice, with 95 opting for other European destinations, 393 for the United States, and 13 listing Germany. To add (highly effective) drama, up to 1,000 announced that their only second choice would be the "crematorium."[194] The numbers may have been inflated, but the fact that many survivors were willing to fudge their responses indicates that even when individuals dreamt of going to the United States or elsewhere

Fig. 4.4. Main dining hall, Landsberg DP camp, December 6, 1945.

in the Diaspora—to unite with family, to seek an easier life—they nevertheless firmly believed that the collective future of Jews lay with the state of Israel. What to some post-Zionist critics now looks like misrepresentation and coercion was probably more an honest reflection of personal and political complexities.[195] Even those who disapproved of the harsh, monolithic pressure for emigration to Palestine, such as many JDC officials, had to admit that even if "a great deal of this Zionist sentiment was no doubt the product of organized propaganda and even to some degree subtle terrorization," it was also the case that "the propaganda fell on heedful ears. . . . The Zionists were the only ones that had a program that seemed to make sense after this catastrophe."[196]

DPs considered it their moral and political obligation to proclaim their absolute determination to go to Palestine, and saw no contradiction in announcing this to questioners even if they knew that individually they might opt to go elsewhere. American adviser Abraham Hyman, clear-eyed and unsentimental as ever, commented that Jewish DPs were no different from the "countless Zionists in the Diaspora who year in and year out recite the prayer *Leshanah Haba'ah Yerushalayim* (Next year in Jersualem). Next year, but not this."[197] In his personal notebook, JDC representative Leo W. Schwarz preserved a cartoon referring sarcastically to Jews' penchant for commerce rather than pioneering. It depicted a Jew with beard and suitcase asking at a travel information counter about the location of the New World's equivalent to Munich's bustling center of Jewish life and trade: "Excuse me, my friend, where can I find the Möhlstrasse in America?"[198] For many, the United States was still a kind of *goldene Medina*, a dream destination if they could only get there. Numerous American Jews who worked with the DPs suspected that large numbers would have been happy to go to the United States if only the doors were open: "Their longings" were "expressed in names they give to streets—Independence Square, Pennsylvania Avenue and Franklin Roosevelt."[199] It was no accident that the dusty streets in Föhrenwald DP camp were named New York, Michigan, or Wisconsin Avenue. Amazingly, a Jewish envoy argued in 1946, with no irony and no apparent awareness of the language's resonance, that "what the displaced Jews are most interested in are not the problems of relief but those of their final solution."[200] For virtually all the survivors, this meant leaving Germany, whether they headed for Palestine or joined relatives in the United States or elsewhere. Indeed, where people ended up was to some degree the result of accident, of timing, of when visas came through, of what relative had ended up where.

In the meantime, however, and regardless of their destination, Jewish survivors in the American zone settled into the "waiting life." In spite of its "anything but luxurious," cramped quarters, a Feldafinger remembered, the camp, which at its height housed some five thousand to six thousand mostly Polish and Lithuanian Jews, was "warm, safe and Nazi-free." It offered "some semblance of normality."[201] Between 1945 and 1949, Jewish DP life in occupied Germany, centered on the large camps near Munich and Frankfurt, had generated a unique transitory society. DP camps were functioning communities with schools, hospitals, political parties, elections, police and postal services, and disciplinary courts. The dream of *Eretz* provided what Israeli historian Hagit Lavsky has called a "functional Zionism," offering pride and hope for the future, if not necessarily a viable real destination.[202] Despite the overcrowding, the unappetizing rations, the lack of privacy, the smells, the sheer hopelessness of idle waiting, the sometimes humiliating and uncomprehending treatment by military and relief workers who "looked down on us . . . as if we were some kind of vermin or pests,"[203] the DP camps and the new families they housed provided a makeshift therapeutic community for survivors who had "been liberated from death" but not yet "been freed for life."[204] Magda Denes, who had survived in hiding with her mother in Czechoslovakia, evoked in her memoir, published half a century later, her reaction to the chaotic, depressing DP camp, where "being processed was a protocol to which we were subjected again and again." She asked a friend: "'Do you think we live in a madhouse?' She looked at me sadly. 'No, my dear,' she said. 'You have never been in a concentration camp. This is normalcy. This is practically heaven.'"[205] Carrying with them a catastrophic past, the DPs looked forward to the establishment of new homes and new families, all the while engaging with their unlikely and unloved German environment.

Fig. 5.1. Five new mothers in maternity ward of Feldafing's Elisabeth Hospital, July 1948.

CHAPTER FIVE

Mir Zaynen Do

SEX, WORK, AND THE DP BABY BOOM

I was lonely; she was lonely. Perhaps together we will be half as lonely.

—Young male survivor, 1946[1]

All I wanted right away was a baby. This was the only hope for me.

—Young female survivor[2]

Even the biggest hater cannot live in total loneliness if he is compelled to continue to live at the sites of his tortures (*Orte der Qual*).

—Julius Posener, 1946[3]

IN 1946, occupied Germany, far from being *judenrein*, counted a Jewish birthrate estimated to be "higher than that of any other country or any other population" in the world.[4] Only a year after liberation, at the same time that Germans bemoaned the high incidence of suicides, infant and child mortality, and abortion, and German women were desperately seeking to keep alive the children they already had, Jewish DPs were marrying and producing babies in record numbers. "In the midst of the depressed desert life" of the DP camps (the recurring exodus metaphors were not accidental), one male survivor wrote in a memoir titled *Risen from the Ashes*, "a noticeable change occurred: people who had survived singly in all age groups were struck with a strong desire to be married." In a "steady rush of weddings,"[5] DPs married, sometimes within days, neighbors in the next barrack or distant kin or acquaintances from what had once been home. Many of the newlyweds barely knew each other; there were "so many marriages, sometimes really strange marriages that never would have happened before the war."[6]

Gathered in refugee camps, the young survivors were both unprepared for, and prevented from creating, the "normal" family and domestic life for which most of them yearned. As teenagers on the run or in Nazi camps, they had been given no time to grow up. Their parents were generally dead, often killed or selected for death before their eyes. In immediate postwar accounts, so many told their interviewers, "The hardest moment was when they took my mama away."[7] Some older survivors had had children before the war—now lost and murdered. In June 1945, a shocked U.S. Army rabbi reported back to Jewish agencies in New York:

> Almost without exception each is the last remaining member of his entire family. . . . Their stories are like terrible nightmares which make one's brain reel and one's heart bleed.[8]

Photographs of daily life in Feldafing DP camp, preserved in the United States Holocaust Memorial Museum, vividly evoke those stories of mass death and new life. Of five new mothers portrayed in the maternity ward of Feldafing's Elisabeth Hospital, one told her all-too-common story. Zlata Distel (Malcmacher) had been born in Vilna in 1926. Forced into the ghetto, she was sent with her family in 1943 to a factory camp near the ghetto, producing fur garments for the Germans. In March 1944 her younger sister was taken to Ponary and shot. In May 1944 the work camp was liquidated, and the remaining family was sent to Kaiserwald KZ in Riga and then to Stutthof death camp near Gdansk. After a few days in Stutthof, the young Zlata was separated from her family and sent to Mühldorf labor camp in Bavaria, the forced labor assignment that gave her and other young women without children a chance for survival. She was liberated in Bavaria in May 1945, and in June she came to Feldafing, where she learned that her father had drowned during evacuation from Stutthof and that her mother and remaining sister had "died of typhus shortly before liberation." In August 1946 she married Issac Malcmacher, a survivor of the Radom ghetto and three concentration camps, and in 1948 she delivered a daughter, Rascha Riwka. Zlata was nineteen when she was liberated and twenty-three when she gave birth.[9]

As Meyer Levin recognized, survivors' primary need was "to seek some link on earth. . . . This came before food and shelter." But he also reflected bitterly on the sentimentalization of the desperate search for lost children, as if miracle rescues like that of Zalman Grinberg's son from the Kovno ghetto could redeem or ease the catastrophe confronted by the remnant:

> There were heartbreaking stories of children seeking their mothers; in a few cases they found them, and these cases were so endlessly overplayed in the radio dramas of American Jewish organizations for the next few years that Europe and its DP camps must have seem [sic] to the mind of the American Jew to be one large happy reunion center where every half-hour another distracted mama called out a long-forgotten childish pet name, whereupon a curly haired five-year-old who had disguised her dark eyes for blue eyes in order to survive as a Polish

child under the name of Wanda, rushed to the call of *Bubaleh* into mama's arms.

His own vision was different. Remarking on a young woman he encountered as he drove through devastated Europe in his U.S. Army jeep, he wrote:

> She hadn't been able to save her child, nobody had been able to save the child in this place. And somehow her tragedy seemed more terrible than that of the mothers who went into the gas chambers with their babies clutched to their breasts.[10]

SEX AND MARRIAGE

In this overwhelming, unprecedented, and confusing context, perceptions of the Jewish drive for marriage and children, by both DPs and those who dealt with them, were at least as multilayered, strongly felt, and paradoxical as those of Jewish DP life in general. Contemporary psychoanalytically oriented psychiatrists and social workers often diagnosed the baby boom as a "manic defense" against catastrophic experience and overwhelming loss.[11] They noted with a certain astonishment, both impressed and appalled, two separate but related phenomena: "[T]he appearance of numbers of new-born babies" as "a novel feature of the Jewish DP camps"[12] and a kind of desperate "hypersexuality." In the immediate aftermath of liberation, many young girls and women, Jewish relief workers reported, "give themselves up to debauch without restraint." Left all alone in the world, they were acting out "an irresistible desire for affection and forgetfulness, which they seek to satisfy with the means at their disposal."[13]

The rabbis who observed this hectic activity and blessed the many "marriages of desperation" that followed liberation struggled with their own ambivalent responses. As U.S. chaplain George Vida, who had himself fled Eastern Europe only a few years earlier, reflected, "Especially the young parents who lost their children were driven by a sense of urgency. . . . You lost the most valuable years of your life, make up time for that which you lost." Some, he realized, were feverishly seeking entertainment: "eat, drink and be merry because it is later than you think." Others were equally feverishly trying to rebuild families. Having lost almost everything, their homes, their families, their place in the world, they exhibited, in his eyes, the urge not only "To bring children into the world to take the place of those children who were killed" but also "to love and be loved. To be accepted, to be respected far more than normally needed by every human being."[14] Dumbfounded "Jointniks," as the JDC workers called themselves, scrambled to import wedding canopies, build Jewish ritual baths for brides, and to supply plain gold wedding rings and wigs for Orthodox wives as well as layettes and baby food.[15] Rabbis and camp authorities encouraged these early marriages partly as a way of channeling what they saw as rampant sexual acting out. They also struggled with the frequent dilemma of proposed marriages among people who could not definitively establish the death of previous spouses, and indeed such quick unions were sometimes disrupted by the sudden and unexpected appearance of someone who had been presumed dead.[16] Most sympathetic observers recognized that "after the years of repression, gloom, terror and want," frenetic sexual activity was an attempt to satisfy the "pent-up desire to live."[17]

In a 1951 report to the World Jewish Congress that carefully charted the astoundingly high birthrates, German-Jewish refugee (and refugee expert) Kurt R. Grossmann retrospectively reflected on the "Irrepressible urge of the Jewish DPs to reconstitute family life and to replace the children who had perished at the hands of the Germans."[18] Abraham S. Hyman, the legal affairs officer attached to the U.S. Jewish Adviser's Office, characterized this impulse somewhat differently, as an "overpowering desire to end the loneliness," or at least to be "half as lonely." At the same time, however, Hyman—again, like virtually everyone who came into contact with the Jewish DPs—was moved and impressed by their "amazing recuperative powers" and apparently irrepressible "zest for life."[19] They were young and finally freed from constant fear; they wanted to live, to taste the pleasures of youth long denied: "our young bodies and souls yearned to live."[20] Folded within the files of the Central Committee of Liberated Jews is a poem suggesting an instinctive incorporation of prescriptions devised later by trauma specialists for creating new memories that could not supplant, but perhaps promise a future beyond, the current nightmarish ones:

> We only met each other a couple of months ago.
> And already, dear, I find I love you so!
> And what do you know, she smiled at me
> In my dreams last night,
> My dreams are getting better all the time![21]

Romantic and sexual longing mixed with a painful sense of inexperience, of having missed out on some crucial youthful socialization and pleasures. The quick marriages—"Hitler married us," DPs wryly noted[22]—promised some sense of comfort and stability to people who possessed neither, but often they also caused more anxiety and insecurity. Young men who had known only sex-segregated labor and death camps were tough way beyond their years but also painfully aware of their own sexual and social inexperience. Helen (Zippi) Tichauer, an

Auschwitz survivor who distributed food rations for pregnant women in Feldafing, recalled that blushing young men arrived to collect food for their newly pregnant brides. The women themselves, who were so often proudly posed with their infants, were too embarrassed by their unfamiliar state even to appear.[23] Women survivors carried with them memories of rape and sexual violation, not only by Germans, local fascists, and Soviet liberators, but also in forest encampments, ghettos, and hiding, where women were subject to sexual coercion by partisans, rescuers, and fellow victims. Many had endured the sheer bodily terror and humiliation imposed by Nazi roundups and concentration camp processing, when they were ordered to undress or their pubic hair was shaved along with the hair on their head.[24] Women especially had buried within them complicated, uncommunicable stories about prostitution and rape, about instrumental sex, or even about genuine love affairs—and all the "gray zone" situations in which sex functioned as a crucial currency of survival.[25] Because of those experiences and precisely because "after liberation, when chaos reigned . . . all women were considered fair game by Soviet liberators," the experience of liberation (and the prospect of future heterosexual relations) may have been profoundly different for women and men.[26]

BABY BOOM

Nonetheless, in response to, and in defiance of, these experiences, over and over again, relief workers and interviewers heard the same message from women: "All I wanted right away was a baby. This was the only hope for me."[27] Early in 1946, there were still barely any children under five to be found among the Jews who had survived Nazism's murderous selections. These numbers changed dramatically by the second half of the year. A JDC survey recorded 750 babies born every month just in the official U.S. zone DP camps. Perhaps even more astonishing, "nearly one third of the Jewish women in the zone between 18 and 45 were either expectant mothers or had new-born babies," and the number of Jewish infants under one year had reached eight thousand.[28] In just one month, from July 6 to August 5, 1947, the Religious Department of the Feldafing camp administration recorded eight weddings and thirty-five ritual circumcisions.[29]

As with the shifting and unreliable statistics about the total numbers of Jewish DPs, the birthrate figures were neither consistent nor precise. Yet they all told of an "unprecedented rise in Jewish birthrate," which was immediately attributed by Central Committee and JDC record keepers to "the overwhelming desire of Jewish DPs, most of them sole survivors of destroyed families as a result of Nazi persecutions and horror, to propagate and perpetuate their kin" as well as to the survivors' rapid physical

Fig. 5.2. Double wedding of two brothers and their brides, Feldafing, August 27, 1946.

recovery, their unusually youthful age cohort, the high level of food rations (up to 2,500 calories a day), good medical care, guaranteed (if primitive) housing provided to DPs, and, finally, a general trend to increased fertility after periods of "suppression."[30]

Whatever the surely highly variable nature of individual experiences, there is no doubt that for the DPs themselves—and for those who managed and observed them—the rash of marriages, pregnancies, and babies collectively represented a conscious affirmation of Jewish life as well as definitive material evidence of survival. This was true for both men and women. But women especially were determined to claim domestic reproductive roles that they had once been promised in some long ago and now fantastic past. Women survivors of the death camps, sometimes of medical experiments, were anxious to reassure themselves of their fertility as well as prove male potency (which, it was widely rumored, had been subjected to emasculating potions and experiments in the camps). Pregnancy and childbirth defied the fears of many survivors "that well over the majority of Jews alive—certainly 90% of those the Nazis could get at, will not have children."[31] Jacob Biber poignantly described the birth of his son, the first baby born in Föhrenwald. Chaim Shalom Dov was named in honor of Biber's first child, who had been murdered in his father's arms as the family fled to the forest in the Ukraine, and in celebration of life and peace. In hiding, after the death of their son, Biber and his wife had "lived like brother and sister," not daring to risk pregnancy, and now "this pleasant surprise was a sign of the continuity of life."[32]

The rapid appearance of babies and baby carriages in the dusty streets of DP camps throughout the American (and British) zones thus served as a purposeful (and as we shall see highly ideologized) reminder—to the occupiers, to the Germans, and to the DPs themselves—that *"mir zaynen do."*[33] In fact, this perceived flood of Jewish babies reflected not only a post-1945 boom in births but also the influx of Jews from Eastern Europe who had survived in the Soviet Union in relatively intact families. It was impossible to know whether the 9,098 infants the JDC reported caring for in 1947 had been conceived in the DP camps or conceived and/or born on the trek west from Poland, or even while still in the Soviet Union.[34] Nonetheless, the extraordinary demographic phenomenon suggested by these birth statistics requires careful attention, beyond the reflexive use— on current book covers and exhibit posters—of photos of women and babies and prams.[35]

The "wave of Jewish births immediately after the second World War" was certainly part of a "baby boom in all the developed countries" (albeit delayed, as we have seen, in Germany by war casualties and the slow return of prisoners of war). Yet this process was, as demographers of European Jewry have confirmed, particularly "conspicuous among Holocaust survivors who sought to reconstitute truncated families" and compensate for the "drastic reduction of Jewish births" that would have otherwise been expected to occur by "natural increase" during the years that had been lost to war and genocide. The spike in births was not just a normalizing continuation of prewar rates, which had already begun to drop rather precipitously even in prewar Poland.[36] Moreover, the birthrate outstripped even that of countries such as the United States or Sweden, which were less affected by war and in the midst of their own baby booms, or France, which managed a relatively high birthrate after the war and occupation ended.[37] By 1948, as prospects for emigration improved with the establishment of the state of Israel and the easing of U.S. regulations, the Jewish population showed a slightly slowing but still whopping annual birthrate of (depending on the source) 31.9 to 35.8 per 1,000 population. This was less, JDC statisticians noted, than that of Chile, Russia, or Egypt, but still higher than that of the United States, Sweden, or Switzerland, and certainly remarkable compared not only to the low German rate but also to the prewar Eastern European Jewish birthrate. There were no "precise statistical records" for the earlier years, but the current figures were definitely "much higher." Some estimated the 1947 rate at an incredible 50.2 per 1,000.[38] These exceptional rates did not persist; they yielded relatively quickly to the continued overall twentieth-century tendency toward fertility declines in the West. The DP baby boom must be understood, therefore, as a specific and direct response to the catastrophic losses of the Holocaust. The JDC expressed its pride as well as amazement by decorating its statistical chart with a cute line drawing of an infant in a cradle with a Jewish star at the back and a heart-shaped opening at the front. Other illustrations depicted an infant at a woman's breast and a happy mother stretching out her arms to a toddler riding a cloud.[39] In February 1948, the illustrated DP journal *Yiddische Bilder* even sponsored a contest for "The Most Beautiful She'erit Hapletah Baby," asking readers to send in glossy photos of children aged eight months to five years. A jury composed of Joint officials, representatives of the DP medical and cultural agencies, and the editorial board chose several winners, whose pictures were prominently displayed in the August issue. The first prize, presumably funded by the JDC, promised a very generous RM 1,000, a box of candy, two Yiddish books, and a subscription to the journal.[40]

Such documentations and celebrations of birth obscured another inevitable and controversial social reality, namely, the number and experience of Jewish women who considered, sought, and/or underwent abortions (at a time when they were widespread among German women). The topic arose publicly only in oblique ways—for example, when, in an effort to dramatize survivors' determination to emigrate to Palestine, DP representatives insisted to members of the Anglo-American investigative commission that "in many camps . . . Jewish women had deliberately suffered abortions rather than bear a child on German soil."[41] Clearly, there were women survivors who felt that after all they had endured they could not bring new children into the world. They feared the fate that might await those children, or that their own traumatic experiences might somehow infect their offspring. As one woman told her husband, "Let's not have children. I was afraid that my kids will not be normal. I was afraid what I went through I will give to the kids."[42] If, as later trauma researchers have argued, pregnancy, childbirth, and caring for a baby provided "alternative scenarios" and bodily sensations to counter nightmarish memories, they surely could also reactivate sensations of physical terror and helplessness, exacerbated perhaps by the fact that so often the childbirth attendants were German.

Unwanted pregnancy and subsequent abortion were especially visible problems immediately after liberation, when survivors paired off quickly and women were subject to rape as well as more welcome advances from liberators. Doctors "deplor[ed] the "high number of single women and girls in a condition of pregnancy" who sought abortions. Without access to birth control or sex education, they were "entirely alone, with nobody to advise them, and not a soul to whom they can confide their trouble. . . . Terrified, bowed-down, and impelled by despair, they can see no way out other than the suppression of their coming maternity."[43] One Jewish chaplain, horrified by the "fornication" he observed among the recently liberated, was convinced nonetheless that resulting pregnancies should be carried to term. He "recounted a wrenching debate about the ethics of abortion, conducted amongst the human wreckage of Belsen" survivors. A woman doctor challenged him:

> In Auschwitz I committed abortion under compulsion. I also saved many mothers from the gas chambers by taking from them the lives that were legitimately theirs to produce. Now the girls and women here are becoming pregnant; they come to the hospital and implore me to help them. I can do nothing—I have to turn them away. Rabbi, I learned my skill in a hard school; let me at least use it for the benefit of those poor creatures who in the first flush of freedom sought to prove to themselves that they were still women.[44]

On the whole, Jewish medical and religious officials condemned abortion and encouraged births as part of the surviving remnant's collective responsibility. They reminded the DPs that despite the "superhuman efforts" of parents who separated from their children in order to hide them or even committed suicide so that orphan status might offer their children better emigration chances, one million Jewish children had been murdered. Outside Russia, they estimated, only about 150,000 children had survived:

> One entire generation of Jewish children has been exterminated; today, they have left our hearts cruelly empty . . . Of all the irreparable losses which we have suffered, this is the gravest. . . . Thus, every Jewish child survivor, every Jewish child to be born, represents for us the most precious and inestimable treasure. We may not freely renounce any single one of them; on the contrary it is our sacred duty to develop all our energy and agree to no matter what effort in order to preserve them. So we must help these mothers in their task of giving life to the children, we must aid them to bring up their little ones to become good and useful members of the community.

Jewish doctors argued, as indeed did German physicians with German women, that "in most, if not all, cases the child whose coming had first of all presented all the appearances of a catastrophe and afterward those of a tiresome necessity would at last become the woman's main reason for living."[45]

Yet a 1947 Central Committee Health Department (*Gesundheitsamt*) reference to a five-doctor "commission" that could adjudicate abortion requests offers intriguing evidence (demanding further research) that abortions could at least sometimes be obtained legally throughout the

DP period and that their necessity was recognized. Remarkably, the DP leadership seemed to accept the medical and social indication model in force in the Soviet zone, at a time when such procedures were illegal for Germans in the West.[46] It is however safe to assume, as the JDC's Medical Department in Munich did in 1948, that the number of abortions was quite low, certainly in comparison to the very high birthrate.[47] Even as doctors worried about how to handle unwanted pregnancies, they also found themselves both scavenging for, and warning against, the overuse of hormone medications to restore fertility for women with amenorrhea or irregular periods and men who feared they had become "castrates."[48] Major Heymont noticed in Landsberg "that the use of contraceptives is highly frowned upon by the camp people. They believe it is everyone's duty to have as many children as possible in order to increase the numbers of the Jewish community."[49]

REDEEMING THE FUTURE

Most women and indeed men, it seems, shared the doctors' conviction that a baby "would give to their solitary, ravaged, and shaken existence a meaning and an object."[50] Far more common than the resort to abortion is the testimony of women for whom childbearing offered a path back to life. As Sara Horowitz, one of the most astute feminist analysts of the Holocaust has noted, it was often the intense memories of a mother's parting words that could "give the daughter permission to survive and to rebuild her life," which meant for most to marry and have children.[51] Gerda Weissmann Klein remembered years later how "in the slave labor factories, I constantly dreamed of some day having children, the ultimate horror being the sterilization programs that we knew were being carried out in other camps. I would rejoice every month that confirmed that I was still capable of bearing children, while others complained at still having their periods." She married the German-Jewish American soldier who had liberated her and moved with him to Buffalo, New York. Only then did she find "The greatest relief from the burdens of my past. . . . That was when death truly turned into life and the ultimate question was answered: Yes, I could have a healthy, normal child."[52] Linking the desire for children and the dream of *Eretz*, psychologist David Boder described a young woman who had lost her entire family. Now, "Recently married and visibly pregnant, she eagerly awaited her turn to emigrate to Palestine," and "was perhaps the most cheerful and open of the survivors."[53]

In this tense time, every Jewish child was a valuable resource for the Jewish people, potentially an object to be fought over as well as nurtured. Jewish organizations struggled to reclaim Jewish children who had been handed over for safekeeping to Christians. In some cases, children had been appropriated by "Aryan" rescuers who would not release them or, most painfully, the children themselves did not want to give up their new identities.[54] The fate of orphaned or still unclaimed "unaccompanied children," as well as those who had been informally adopted by other survivors, sparked hot debates. UNRRA and even JDC child welfare workers often tangled with DP and Zionist groups about the best interest of a child or adolescent and the balance between consideration of personal circumstances and the collective will to send Jewish children to the Jewish homeland. Relief personnel agonized over the disposition of children who had found stable homes with (generally non-Jewish) foster families or were awaited by more distant relatives in the United States, elsewhere in the world, or sometimes in Germany. Were children really better served by remaining, possibly for years, in youth and child assembly centers, hoping to depart for Palestine? Generally—and sometimes to the distress of relatives or (more rarely) a youngster anxious to escape camp life—the relief organizations trod lightly and allowed the children to join groups bound for Palestine. Obstacles to emigration in general and to any return to Eastern Europe in particular also drove this deference to Zionist goals over repatriation or distant family unification. UNRRA officials acknowledged that "in most instances, the National Governments have felt that, while they would be very willing to have Jewish children return to their own countries, they cannot urge it in view of the possibility of persecution and discrimination."[55] These issues became particularly urgent when thousands of "unaccompanied" children entered the American zone after 1945 as "infiltrees." Many of these "unaccompanied" children were not in fact orphans but had been sent ahead to Germany by parents in Poland hoping to speed their emigration to Palestine within organized youth groups. Such strategems created additional dilemmas for UNRRA child welfare workers, who had to walk "a thin line . . . coordinating the activities of the Jewish agencies in the U.S. zone while representing the UNRRA." Despite the reality that incorporation into a youth group or kibbutz might mean a prolonged stay in refugee camps in Germany or Cyprus rather than immediate emigration, many field workers, both Jewish and not, came to agree with UNRRA's Susan Pettiss, who later explained, "I had begun to feel that remaining in Germany was detrimental to the well-being of the children and there seemed no other answer than Palestine."[56] Children had become simultaneously political icons for the Jewish collective and a tangible (as well as anticipatory) expression of normality for individuals.

For Jewish survivors, fertility and maternity provided a means both of claiming personal agency and an intact individual body, and of constructing a viable new community—after extraordinary trauma and even in transit. Let me be clear: despite the frequent invocation of the term "replace" by contemporary observers, and the clear conviction that new babies were intended to assure a future for the Jewish people, the baby boom among the *She'erit Hapletah* could not offer any redemptive meaning to the catastrophe (*Churban*) that had been experienced.[57] But it did, perhaps, offer a means to "redeem the future" or at least to begin the regenerative work of making and imagining one.[58] For people without a permanent home or even a clear destination who had just faced extinction, children seemed to promise a "guarantee of a future" and, as we shall discuss in more detail later in the chapter, a measure of what was, however problematically, identified as revenge.[59] The significance of children for populations traumatized by exile, flight, and genocide—the case of the Holocaust is both extreme and exemplary—underscores Dominick LaCapra's insistence that those studying trauma "be attentive as well to the efforts of victims to rebuild a life and to make use of counterforces that enable them to be other than victims, that is, to survive and to engage in social and political practices related to the renewal of interest in life (for example, having children)."[60]

As the anthropologist John Borneman has noted in his article "Reconciliation after Ethnic Cleansing," in more recent contexts, "because most survivors cannot die," even if they feel that their survival is only a peculiar accident of fate, "they are continually confronted with the psychic, social, and political tasks of dealing with the ever-present loss of those who did die. They must, in some way, attempt to recuperate or redeem this loss" even in full awareness that the loss is so monumental, so irreparable, as to be "never fully recoupable." Borneman identifies "two common attempts to recuperate loss" as "physical reproduction and revenge." Both elements are part of the story I tell in this chapter about Jewish survivors in occupied Germany, their babies, reconstructed families, and interactions with Germans. For the DPs, while the presence of a new child certainly did "not end the despair," it did provide, as we shall see, for a kind of normalization and productive forgetting and—improbably—a link to the Germans among whom they lived.[61]

Having babies, the most normal of human activities under normal circumstances, was indeed precisely what would have been expected by East European Jewish religious and social tradition. Now it became both miraculous and an entry into "normal" humanity, even if it often seemed to offer only a kind of make-believe normality, a "parallel life" to the memories of the preceding trauma. New babies and families provided a means of bridging the "radical discontinuity" of life cycle that the survivors had endured. If, as many psychologists and psychiatrists have now argued, Holocaust survivors' loss of "basic trust" had fundamentally and permanently damaged their faith in themselves and the outside world, caring for an infant could perhaps initially offer the most direct and primal means of reaffirming the self. It could help create what trauma experts call necessary "alternative scenarios."[62] For Gerda Weissmann Klein, "Being a mother yielded other benefits. It allowed me to enter the mainstream of the life around me, put me on an equal footing with my contemporaries, closing that chasm that had existed between us. The routine of caring for babies became the great equalizer."[63]

In another sense, the quick construction of new families could also be interpreted as a kind of genealogical and biological revenge in a situation where the possibilities (and indeed the motivation) for direct vengeance were extremely limited. Jewish infants, born on territory that had been declared *judenrein* to women who had been slated for extermination, were literally dubbed *Maschiachskinder* ("children of the Messiah"), a "biological miracle."[64] Dr. Joseph Schwartz, the JDC's European director, informed his board in 1947 that "children have become a kind of religion here . . . a symbol of the continuity of a people."[65] Marriage, pregnancy, and childbirth clearly represented a possible reconstruction of collective or national, as well as individual, identity for the Jewish DPs. As Rhoda Ann Kanaaneh, another anthropologist analyzing reproductive "strategies" during and after situations of collective trauma, notes for the case of Palestinian women in Israel, while "nationalist framings of reproduction are only one component" in a "web of longings," it is always the case that individual "reproductive decisions play on a shifting combination of socially constructed emotional and material desires."[66] Jews—certainly in the published record and in political representations—looked to pregnancy and maternity as emblems of survival, as signs that they were more than just "victims," and precisely did not dwell obsessively on the traumatic recent past. As a kind of utopian step, the baby boom was the counterpart—indeed was closely linked, although in ambivalent ways (since, in reality, pregnancy and young children were likely to delay emigration)—to the passionate, political Zionism that gripped, in one form or another, virtually all survivors. It offered a means of establishing a new order and a symbolic sense of "home," even and especially in the refugee camps. It offered a concrete means of both starting anew and honoring the past.[67]

REVENGE AND MEMORY

DP culture did place a premium on collecting personal histories, on bearing witness for the future. Almost immediately after liberation, the first memorials were raised and a day of remembrance was proposed; the latter was set for the anniversary of liberation as a deliberate link between mourning the catastrophe and building hope for renewal. DPs quickly set up their own Central Historical Commission, headquartered in Munich, and charged it with collecting eyewitness accounts of persecution as well as any cultural artifacts such as art and songs that could be recuperated from camp, ghetto, and partisan life. The commission's fifty branches gathered about 3,500 testimonies and over 1,000 photographs, some of them published in the short-lived memorial journal *Fun letstn Churbn*.[68] Theater, music, cabaret, and the press in the refugee camps directly addressed the horrors of the war years, so much so that Jewish relief workers were both shocked by the matter-of-fact treatment of extreme horror in DP culture and irritated by what they deemed obsessive remembering. The DP orchestra in the U.S. zone performed its premiere in striped pajamas, with a piece of "barbed wire fence" marking the stage.[69] Many well-meaning relief officials, already disturbed by the militant influence of the teenage youth group leaders (*Madrichim*) on their even younger charges, discouraged this kind of "emotional reliving of the past," firmly believing that "rehabilitation to normal childhood should emphasize obliteration of these memories." Koppel S. Pinson, the educational director of the Joint in Germany, complained: "The DP is preoccupied almost to a point of morbidity with his past. . . . He is always ready to account in minutest detail the events of his past or the past of his relatives.[70]

But in its preoccupation with the mundane everydayness of camp life and political association, with all its intense political factionalism and bickering, daily life in the DP camps also fostered a kind of productive forgetting. Young militant Zionists were too intent on planning their future to spend time recording a painful past; others were consumed with the burdens of daily life. As Israel Kaplan, the Riga historian on the Historical Commission, noted with some chagrin, "In such a period of instability and living out of suitcases, and given the background of dramatic events, it is possible to make history, but not to write history."[71] In another example of the paradoxical expectations and images—as victims, villains, and survivors—attached to Jewish survivors, they were simultaneously berated for remembering too much and not enough.

Indeed, it is useful to note at this point in our discussion how much current public and scholarly attention to memorializing is a product of our own "postmodern" preoccupations. It is perhaps our own panic about the loss of individual and collective memory that shapes our conviction that memory is crucial for recovery and reconstruction.[72] Directly after the war, both survivors and those who worked with them did not (albeit in different ways) necessarily consider remembering to be the optimal way to deal with trauma. Indeed, the need to be with someone who required no explanation or rehearsal of the traumatic recent past was surely one of the most powerful forces driving the quick endogamous DP marriages. Survivors turned to each other for partners who recognized the many references that were invoked, and who understood, at least on some level, the lack of words, or the inadequacy of available words, to bridge the tension between "the imperative to tell" and "the impossibility of telling."[73] Those survivors who were determined to collect the voices of the murdered and to remember their lives and deaths also understood, better than anyone else, what the American psychologist David Boder declared when he titled his 1949 volume of survivor accounts *I Did Not Interview the Dead.*[74] At the same time, it is clear that the conventional impression of "silence" or "speechless terror," constituting the very essence of trauma as formulated by current psychoanalytic and literary theory, has to be revised. Memorialization and commemoration commenced, as we have seen, virtually immediately. Survivors quickly started not only to talk but also to write. Their testimonials were published in the lively DP press and in memorial volumes, such as the pages of *Fun letstn Churbn.*[75] "Every DP is a private document center," JDC educational director Koppel Pinson said with some impatience.[76]

There were certainly those, especially in UNRRA and also among American Jewish social workers in the JDC, who saw the marriage and baby boom as well as militant Zionism and the determination to bear witness as a kind of manic "acting out."[77] Already on his first tour of the DP camps in fall 1945, Ben-Gurion had indeed explicitly argued that the establishment and defense of a Jewish state in Palestine was dependent on a rapid population increase, which could be achieved only via large-scale immigration from the DP camps and remaining East European Jewish communities (and also from the rest of the Middle East). Skeptics, at the time and later, mistrusted, in both political and therapeutic terms, the displacement of grief onto militarist Zionist culture and/or "compulsive reproduction" and marriage. Others spoke with awe of the survivors' resilience. Both interpretations did not perhaps adequately honor the more straightforward desires of young people—both men and women, in different ways—to claim their right to whatever degree of "normality" could still be wrested from the cataclysmic disruption of their individual and collective lives. Today we might argue differently, and less romantically or censoriously. The baby boom and DP culture were in many ways expressions of a parallel life, a living on, when one had in a sense, as the philosopher Susan Brison has put it, outlived oneself. *Leben aufs neu* (new life) did not replace or displace the horrors that had been experienced but existed alongside them, in a highly vibrant form.[78]

DP experience suggests important questions about the intersection of the personal and the political, and about definitions of mourning, trauma, and revenge. It poses questions about the place of sexuality, pregnancy, childbirth, and motherhood in defining survival and victimization as well as furnishing possible reconstructions of ethnic or national identity in the aftermath of murderous violence and displacement. Precisely because, as legal scholar Fionnuala Ní Aoláin has pointed out, during the Holocaust, "established conventions of motherhood [were] deliberately ravaged and assaulted," the emphasis in DP culture and politics on "life reborn" raises "stubborn" issues about how to recognize the centrality of maternity without reproducing in our analysis conventional gender assignments. How, in Denise Riley's words, can we "assert a category without becoming trapped within it"?[79]

The most powerful metaphor for "life reborn" was the dream of a new Jewish state, physically and emotionally cut off from the traumatic history of European Jewry. In the DP film *Lang ist der Weg* (Long Is the Road), filmed in Munich and Landsberg, the young heroine tries to tell her handsome partisan veteran lover about how damaged she is; he cuts her off, telling her that he doesn't want to know, she must not remember. He pledges to spirit her away to *Eretz Israel* because she will not be able to forget as long as she remains on bloodied and cursed German, indeed European, soil. In dramatic vignettes, the survivors' love affair plays out against the background of the overcrowded camp. The hero's marriage proposal is framed by Ben-Gurion's address to the Congress of Liberated Jews in January 1946 and the stirring tones of "Hatikvah." In the final scene, the young couple are well on the "long road" to escaping their past. While they have not yet reached Palestine, and the plow working the land is surrounded by the German Alps rather than the Middle Eastern desert, they are lounging on the grass of a kibbutz (*Hachschara*, agricultural settlement) in Bavaria, preparing for their aliyah, and playing with a newborn child—the most eloquent statement of survival and ability to start anew.[80]

In many ways, Zionism represented for the survivors a kind of "nullification of time and space," a turning away from the recent history of catastrophe and a refusal of the geographical reality in which they were confined. "We are not in Bavaria. . . . We are nowhere," DPs insisted, deciding instead to focus on a future defined by the imagined homeland in *Eretz* and the generation of new families.[81] DPs were left, as Simon Schochet noted when trying to explain the survivors' attraction to photographs that could capture the moment, "with a great sense of unreality and fantasy concerning our past. It is as if we were truly displaced—that is, without a previous history and lacking a physical relationship to the present. And so we are like newborns and must start recording the events of life anew."[82]

On another level, bearing children also worked to mediate the continuous tension between remembering and forgetting. Babies, in their names and in their features, bore the traces of the past, of those who were dead and lost. Indeed, in some significant ways, the generation of new life was not only a signal of survival and hope but also an acknowledgment of loss. Since the Jewish religion (in Ashkenazi practice) prohibits naming children after the living, survivors recognized in their naming practices the death of loved ones, whom they had, for the most part, not been able to bury or even to confirm as dead. Certainly, however, symbolically and in their ever present, quite concrete demandingness, children also represented the future. As the first issue of the DP newsletter *undzer hoffenung* stated, employing the language of health and hygiene that remained dominant after the war: "We must turn to today and prepare a better tomorrow, a beautiful and a healthy tomorrow."[83]

BABIES, BABY CARRIAGES, AND THE OBLIGATION TO HEALTH

Jewish women survivors, living in a kind of extraterritoriality on both German and Allied soil, were prefiguring on their pregnant bodies a kind of imaginary nation that they hoped—at least this was the public message—to realize in Palestine/*Eretz Yisroel*. Their babies had "red hot" political valence, not only for the Allies but also for the Zionists who dominated political and cultural life in the DP camps. Women pushing prams and strollers led demonstrations and marches demanding open emigration to Palestine. The DP press as well as films and photos produced for fund-raising and publicity purposes invariably foregrounded images of mothers with babies and baby carriages, of men celebrating a circumcision, or of toddlers playing in kindergartens.[84] These repetitive (and quite realistic) representations of women as mothers reflect the fact that women did not fill important public positions in the DP camps and were not part of the DP leadership. Indeed, when David Ben-Gurion attended the first Congress of Jewish DPs in January 1946, he asked with some bewilderment and genuine "censure" why there were no women delegates. Contrasting this glaring absence with women's often prominent roles in the anti-Nazi resistance and the celebration of resistance heroines in Palestine, he demanded (according to at least one observer):

> Don't the women . . . who endured so much and showed so much courage have anything to say here? In Palestine I met women who fought in the ghettos. They are our greatest pride. Isn't it sad enough that you lack children? Must you in addition artificially eliminate the women and create a population of men only?[85]

Ben-Gurion's early admonition about the lack of children contained of course at least part of the answer to his own question about women's apparent nonparticipation in the active and often rancorous political life

Fig. 5.3. UNRRA camp director Harold Fishbein and an unidentified colleague pose with three babies in carriages at Schlachtensee DP Camp, Berlin.

of the DP camps; very soon most women survivors would be busy with the bearing and raising of new families.[86] In the aftermath of a Nazi Final Solution that had specifically targeted pregnant women and women with young children for immediate and automatic extermination, childbearing was desperately overdetermined. Problematizing, and not merely noting—as do the many posters and book covers depicting DP mothers proudly pushing their baby carriages—the privileged place of motherhood in DP women's lives on the one hand, and in DP politics in general on the other, is all the more crucial because for Jewish women during the Holocaust motherhood became, in historian Judith Baumel's words, literally "lethal."[87] Confronted with a racial system in which biology was indeed destiny, "Jewish women were," as Holocaust scholar Joan Ringelheim has put it, to be killed "not simply as Jews" but as "women who may carry and give birth to the next generation of Jews."[88] Afterward, so many felt—as memoirs attest—"an eagerness to get our lives under way . . . to create new families and bring Jewish children into the world."[89]

Jewish postwar babies were precious, and they were carefully monitored. DP leaders, camp administrators, and relief workers mobilized all the principles of modern social and preventive medicine—from immunization and cleanliness campaigns to home visits by nurses and hygiene lectures in clinics and schools—to assure not only the survival but the good health of the next generation. No effort was spared, from referrals to German specialists to negotiations for limited supplies of penicillin or even, when required, transport to Switzerland or the United States for specialized treatment.[90] Jewish survivors had, it was clear, the collective obligation to be strong and healthy and, above all, to produce healthy babies. Yiddish posters and pamphlets urged mothers to visit the clinic or camp nurses regularly and to be conscientious about pre- and postnatal care. For DPs, the availability of health services, especially prenatal and infant health care, implied a requirement to take advantage of them; their "right to health" became in many ways synonymous with, and dependent on, "an obligation toward health."[91]

Despite this pervasive rhetoric of duty and obligation, multiple complaints by social workers, nurses, and doctors demonstrate that, in keeping with a traditional pattern of suspicion among women and the working class of the medicalizing social hygiene efforts of twentieth-century reformers, women sometimes resisted such helpful disciplining efforts. Both the Jewish relief agencies and the internal DP camp administrations worked hard to convince women to avail themselves of expert medical care and not rely on the "old wives' tales" advice of neighbors and friends, which led women, for example, to refuse to bring in their infants for checkups when the weather was cold. Like all helping professionals dealing with a client population, JDC and UNRRA nurses complained about noncompliance with their well-meant advice about matters such as breast-feeding and nutrition. At the same time, women's reliance on nonmedical resources and counsel may have been the result not only of their recalcitrance but of the fact that expert medical care was not as easily available as the pamphlets and official reports claimed. The written record and DP memories sometimes offer rather different versions of the extent of medical care. JDC and camp files delineate a comprehensive and effective medical system. Zippi Tichauer, the survivor who distributed rations to pregnant women in Feldafing, insists, however, that there was no clinic inside the camp and that the busy maternity ward in nearby Elisabeth Hospital was supervised by a dedicated DP physician with no obstetrical training. Such discrepancies of evidence notwithstanding, there can be no question that, in whatever form—expert intervention or, as Tichauer observes, more simply the regular supply of good rations and careful attention—pediatric care was a top priority and generally of high quality.

Recognizing that no matter how careful or devoted these new mothers were, they often felt "helpless," nurses—both Jewish and German—visited the new mothers in their rooms. They checked that doctors' orders were followed and urged that babies be brought back to the nurses or doctors at the first sign of problems. The health departments of the JDC and the Central Committee of Liberated Jews wanted women to be examined once a month in the first half of pregnancy and every two weeks in the second; children from birth to six months could be checked as often as once a week, and even one- to three-year-olds were expected to come in once a month. Immunizations, height and weight, and TB status were carefully checked, in keeping with the general interwar faith in mass screening and measurement of health.[92] Whether or not these schedules were actually followed, medical officers held out the promise of rapid emigration to encourage women to take care of themselves and their babies. They admonished them not to complain if they had not availed themselves of health services and then found themselves rejected for emigration or aliyah for medical reasons. If the incentives did not produce the desired response, camp health authorities and JDC nurses had no problem resorting to more immediate threats, including the possibly counterproductive sanction of withdrawing rations.[93]

Clearly related to the emphasis on good health was the preoccupation with hygiene and cleanliness. Jewish leaders pressured UNRRA and American Military Government to provide decent accommodations, but great demands were also placed on the weary camp inhabitants themselves. Camp administrations established so-called "sanitation *Kommandos*" (or sanitary police), which, in a style highly reminiscent of social medicine campaigns of the 1920s and 1930s and still tellingly inflected by the vocabulary of Nazi camps and forced labor, tried both to entice (with promises of extra rations and cigarette allotments) and coerce (with threats of prosecution by camp honor courts) DPs into keeping their overcrowded camps clean and orderly. The "sanitary police" patrolled the housing blocks and villas in Feldafing and other camps, doing detailed inspections and dispensing warnings to residents and barracks leaders (*Blockälteste*) about unpenned chickens and clogged toilets (or toilets used for laundering). Often they hired German plumbers to clean and repair them. Occasionally the sanitary police moved to arrest egregious loiterers. Leaflets called on camp residents to be healthy through cleanliness (*Gezund Durch Zojberkajt*) and warned that slovenliness would make a bad impression on outside delegations, thereby potentially imperiling emigration opportunities and the entire Zionist project. In spring

1947, an exasperated Feldafing Sanitation Department complained that the melting snow had revealed a sea of "dirt, cans, bottles, and garbage of all sorts," and insisted that overcrowded conditions were no excuse for the "apathy" toward cleanliness that brought the threat of disease and demoralization, and jeopardized public relations.

Feldafing camp authorities appealed to residents to "combine the practical with the useful." If they volunteered for four consecutive days of picking up dirt, paper, and rags during the "cleanliness week" of a spring "cleaning action" (*Säuberungsaktion*), they would be compensated with ten cigarettes a day—an excellent black market resource. Trying to incite a competitive spirit, the camp Health Commission urged sloppy inhabitants to prove that the accusations were unfair and that "our camp will not be outdone in cleanliness."[94] One response to this pressure for order and cleanliness, as we shall see, was to turn the tables and petition the camp officials for German employees to help maintain the rather unrealistic standards DP administrations were trying to enforce. Even UNRRA pointed out that "to expect sanitary conditions in displaced persons camps to equal military standards is naïve"[95] These demands for healthy reproduction and family life and the eagerness to exhibit the results for political as well as rehabilitative purposes were connected, in turn—as they were in different ways for defeated Germans—to the urgent need for the rebuilding of properly gendered bodies and roles.

BODIES ON DISPLAY

All contemporary evidence makes strikingly clear the obvious but still underanalyzed point that lives and identities, both individual and collective, were reconstructed—and that reconstruction was represented—in gendered and embodied ways. Just as the persecution and murder of all Jews had been differentiated by age and gender, so too was their return to life. Precisely because gendered roles and sexed bodies had been so catastrophically unsettled by a Nazi Final Solution that aimed to produce desexed *Musselmen* and that prioritized the annihilation of mothers, children, and the "unfit," life was reborn and identity remade through the reconstruction of gendered roles and sexed healthy bodies. As a collective, the *She'erit Hapletah* conceived and represented renewal and rehabilitation in terms of the body, which was after all easier to cure and to exhibit than the psychic wounds, most of which did not lend themselves to display for political purposes, or did not manifest themselves until many years later.

In the many images of the DPs preserved in films, newsreels, and photos, and in the stories told in memoirs and contemporary reports, we find the story of Jewish bodies. The visual trajectory moves from images of rotting corpses to those of emaciated bodies, both female and male, being examined, poked, and measured, their scars exposed for the cameras, and then being treated, disinfected, and slowly patched together. The story concludes with new pictures of healthy, strong, and well-fed bodies. Women appear as young mothers in the ubiquitous and by now iconic processions pushing baby carriages, cradling newborns, holding chubby toddlers by the hand, hanging laundry, and caring for children in DP camp kindergartens. Men appear muscled and bare-chested in sleeveless T-shirts, playing soccer, boxing, or running track during the many sports competitions that were such an important part of DP life, or even more powerfully (and eerily perhaps) strutting in the marching formations of the DP police.[96] At times, the gender divisions are complicated by generational factors; young fathers are seen bouncing babies on their laps, or both boys and girls are presented in their Zionist youth groups, marching, singing, doing calisthenics, and wearing paramilitary-style uniforms.[97] Inevitably, these images obfuscate as well as make visible; they show health and vigor but efface the pain and the scars also carried by tough bodies and smiling young parents.

But the DPs were not only filmed and photographed for others; they also photographed themselves. "We are obsessed with the need to have ourselves photographed, and to possess photos of our friends," Simon Schochet remembered about Feldafing. For people who often retained no photos of their lost loved ones or of themselves as children, "To have a pictorial image of yourself which you can critically look at, laugh at, or admire, is to us the final unmistakable proof that we are really living creatures." Staring back at themselves they saw the strong, healthy people that so surprised observers: "we can confront ourselves vis-a-vis from a glossy paper print and be reassured that we truly resemble in face, body, and dress all the other men and women with whom we share this great planet." In ways similar, perhaps, to how babies bearing the marks of dead relatives or themselves when young offered survivors a sense of normality and continuity, photographs served to negotiate the distance between a traumatic past and a quotidian if still temporary present. Photography became another means of normalization, even if it sometimes required a certain amount of embellishment. Schochet remembered the popularity of Zoltan, the Feldafing camp photographer, who lent his clients an array of props for their portraits, from a silver fox jacket for women to "empty American whiskey and scotch bottles whose labels have been carefully kept intact" or, for even greater effect, a jeep as background for outdoor photo sessions. If necessary a lab assistant added a bit of retouching to worn faces and bodies.[98] If these photos and films tended to make invisible or remediate scars and painful memories, they

Fig. 5.4. A couple take their daughter for a walk, Ansbach DP camp, 1948.

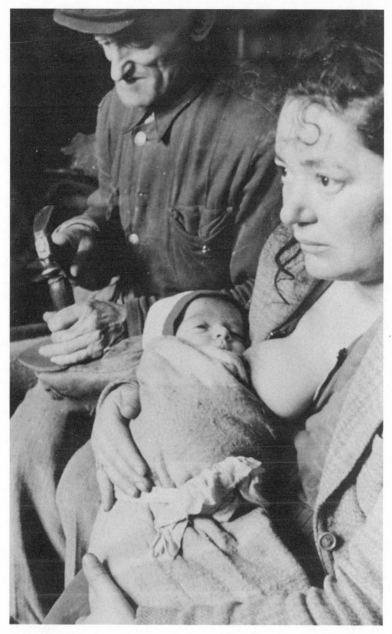

Fig. 5.5. Mother nurses her baby while her elderly father fixes a pair of shoes, Feldafing.

also did not show a crucial and ongoing aspect of everyday life for Jewish DPs: the interactions, both ordinary and fraught, between Jewish survivors and defeated Germans, in part produced and made necessary by the baby boom. It is imperative at this point to turn again to the encounters with the Germans, who were always part of the picture if not actually in it.

Jewish Mothers and German Nannies

The explosion in births and marriages, and indeed Jewish life in general, did not simply go on behind the in any case porous gates of the DP camps, unnoticed by Germans. Nor were Jewish encounters with Germans limited to the oft-cited arenas of black (or gray) marketeering or management of bars and cafes catering to GIs and their Fräuleins (and prostitutes), although all those arenas were certainly important.[99] Jews gave birth in German hospitals, where they were attended by German physicians and nurses.[100] Jewish marriages and births were registered in the German town halls. Sleepy Bavarian registry offices (*Einwohnermeldeämter*) were staggered by the stream of Jewish DPs—as many as fifteen daily—who suddenly appeared, offering their rations of American cigarettes in exchange for official certificates registering marriages and births. Every day, DP mothers crisscrossed the streets of German towns with their baby carriages; they veritably "paraded their babies," Meyer Levin reported.[101] And Jews hired German women as cleaners and nannies.

DP camp medical records indicate that virtually all young Jewish mothers—exhausted, inexperienced, and bereft of the support traditionally provided by mothers, sisters, and other relatives—were assigned a German baby "nurse" or maid from the surrounding towns and villages. These women were listed as camp employees, vetted and paid by UNRRA and the camp administration. In some cases camp residents, either individually or in small groups, also used their own resources to hire local women. Applications for such assistance invariably included a formal certificate of medical necessity from a (nearly always German) physician, composed with a peculiar combination of medicalized terminology, sympathy, and (if one reads between the lines) touch of contempt for young mothers apparently unable or unwilling to care for their own children. Doctors sometimes hedged their diagnoses of severe postpartum complications with a dubious "she claims." Or they seemed to deem poor housekeeping an indication of pathology, noting, for example, "an extreme state of nervous exhaustion that makes it impossible for the patient to do her housework in addition to caring for her child. She urgently requires a baby nurse."[102]

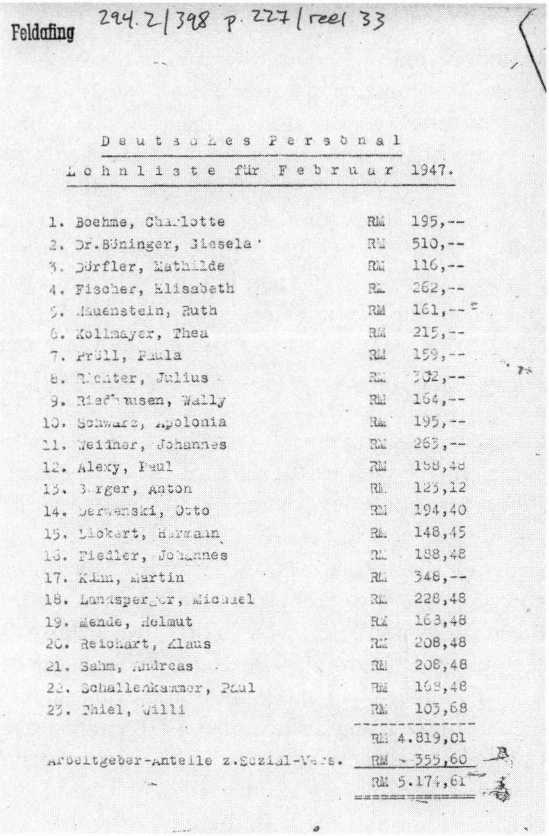

Feldafing 294.2/398 p. 227/reel 33

Deutsches Personal

Lohnliste für Februar 1947.

1.	Boehme, Charlotte	RM	195,--
2.	Dr. Böninger, Giesela	RM	510,--
3.	Dörfler, Mathilde	RM	116,--
4.	Fischer, Elisabeth	RM	262,--
5.	Hauenstein, Ruth	RM	161,--
6.	Kollmayer, Thea	RM	215,--
7.	Prüll, Paula	RM	159,--
8.	Richter, Julius	RM	302,--
9.	Riedhausen, Wally	RM	164,--
10.	Schwarz, Apolonia	RM	195,--
11.	Weißner, Johannes	RM	263,--
12.	Alexy, Paul	RM	158,48
13.	Burger, Anton	RM	123,12
14.	Derwenski, Otto	RM	194,40
15.	Eickert, Hermann	RM	148,45
16.	Fiedler, Johannes	RM	188,48
17.	Kihn, Martin	RM	348,--
18.	Landsperger, Michael	RM	228,48
19.	Mende, Helmut	RM	163,48
20.	Reichart, Klaus	RM	208,48
21.	Sahm, Andreas	RM	208,48
22.	Schallenkammer, Paul	RM	163,48
23.	Thiel, Willi	RM	103,68
		RM	4.819,01
	Arbeitgeber-Anteile z. Sozial-Vers.	RM	355,60
		RM	5.174,61

Fig. 5.6. List of German personnel and their salaries, Feldafing, February 1947.

The applications from the Jewish DPs themselves, both women and men, express a quite different complicated jumble of need, anxiety, and entitlement. A typical request to the Feldafing camp administration Health Department on May 6, 1947, reads (in German): "I ask for a permit for a nurse for the care of my five-month-old child. Since my wife is still sick, as can be seen from the enclosed affidavit, and cannot take care of the child, I ask most sincerely that my request be granted, especially since the infant is also very weak."[103] A day later, another Feldafinger sought "permission to engage a German maid. My reason is that I have a child of 11 months and also work as custodian of the Villa Andrea. I also intend to employ the German (*die Deutsche*) for cleanup duties in the kitchen of the villa."[104] The requests, by young mothers, or sometimes by husbands whose wives were either ill or themselves employed, were painfully honest about how unprepared for parenthood and desperately alone many men and women felt, even in the middle of a crowded camp: "As you surely know, I am busy all day as a building manager so that my wife is totally alone and since she has not a clue (*keine Ahnung*) about child care, I need ... help."[105] Particularly among the young KZ survivors, very few women had been mothers, "and virtually none of those who had been mothers had children who survived the war."[106] One mother underlined her request to keep employing the German woman who had already helped her for two months and was in possession of the all-important camp entry permit (*Lagerausweis*) by stressing her isolation: "Since I, as well as my child, are in a very poor state of health, and since I have no relatives here who can take care of my child while I am in the hospital, I ask most politely that you grant my request and renew the assignment."[107]

These applications, as well as the accompanying medical certificates, therefore document not only Jewish claims on German labor and service but also the very real exhaustion and ill health of the survivors, which belied their generally healthy appearance. Some requests were scrawled on scraps of paper; others were slotted into pretyped forms suggesting frequent and repeated use. They were written in Yiddish, occasionally in Polish, but mostly in German, sometimes broken but often perfect, suggesting that DPs might have had help in preparing them. The records also reveal the shifting demographics of the DP camp population after 1946. The initial group of new mothers had been young survivors who quickly married and became pregnant with a first child (or a new one after their other children had been murdered). After 1946, many of the DPs asking for assistance were families who had arrived from the Soviet Union with young children and then had another child in Germany. In numerous cases, the intervals between children were quite short, indicating probably both a lack of easy access to, and a lack of desire for, birth control. Although these later refugees were supposedly more stable than those who had emerged from the camps or hiding, their years of exile, harsh living conditions, and hard labor had left them with their own set of grave health problems. Many women had suffered miscarriages and the death of infants and small children during their multiple escapes and displacements.[108]

The Feldafing Health Department records collected in the files of the Central Committee of Liberated Jews present a depressing litany of physical and psychological complaints and injuries requiring care and assistance. The stream of images, in DP films and periodicals, of pregnant bellies carefully patted and measured by professionals in white coats and of well-tended new mothers cradling healthy infants do not tell the parts of the "life reborn" story contained in these requests and medical certifi-

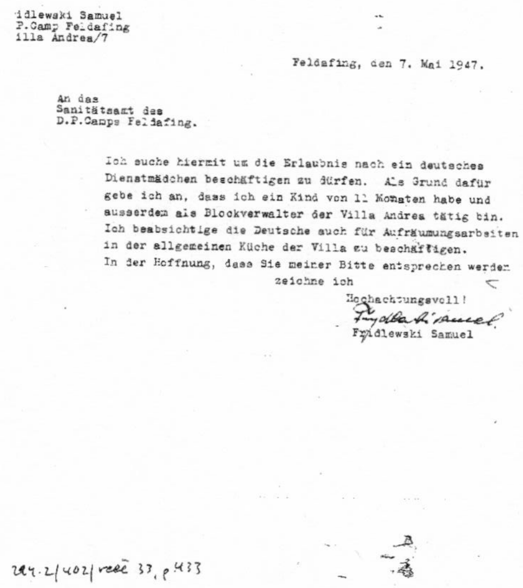

idlewski Samuel
P.Camp Feldafing
illa Andrea/7

Feldafing, den 7. Mai 1947.

An das
Sanitätsamt des
D.P.Camps Feldafing.

Ich suche hiermit um die Erlaubnis nach ein deutsches Dienstmädchen beschäftigen zu dürfen. Als Grund dafür gebe ich an, dass ich ein Kind von 11 Monaten habe und ausserdem als Blockverwalter der Villa Andrea tätig bin. Ich beabsichtige die Deutsche auch für Aufräumungsarbeiten in der allgemeinen Küche der Villa zu beschäftigen.
In der Hoffnung, dass Sie meiner Bitte entsprechen werden zeichne ich

Hochachtungsvoll!
Frydlewski Samuel
Frydlewski Samuel

294.2/402/reel 33, p.433

Fig. 5.7. The "*Blockverwalter*" of Villa Andrea requests permission for a German domestic servant to help care for his 11-month-old child and to help with general cleaning, May 7, 1947.

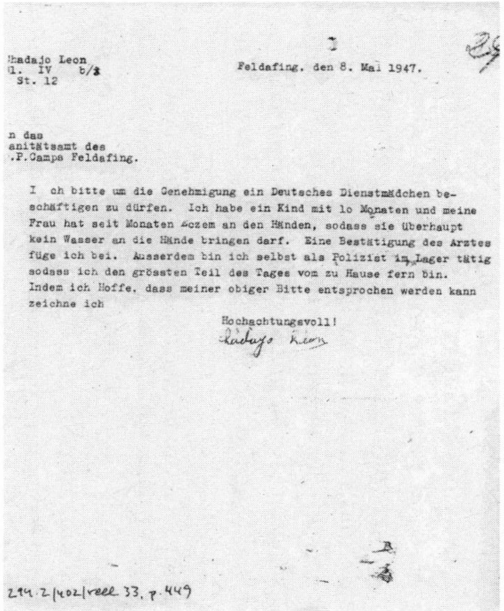

hadajo Leon
l. IV b/3
St. 12

Feldafing, den 8. Mai 1947.

n das
anitätsamt des
.P.Camps Feldafing.

Ich bitte um die Genehmigung ein Deutsches Dienstmädchen beschäftigen zu dürfen. Ich habe ein Kind mit 10 Monaten und meine Frau hat seit Monaten Eczem an den Händen, sodass sie überhaupt kein Wasser an die Hände bringen darf. Eine Bestätigung des Arztes füge ich bei. Ausserdem bin ich selbst als Polizist im Lager tätig sodass ich den grössten Teil des Tages vom zu Hause fern bin.
Indem ich Hoffe, dass meiner obiger Bitte entsprochen werden kann zeichne ich

Hochachtungsvoll!
Chadajo Leon

294.2/402/reel 33, p.449

Fig. 5.8. Request for a German household helper, Feldafing, May 8, 1947.

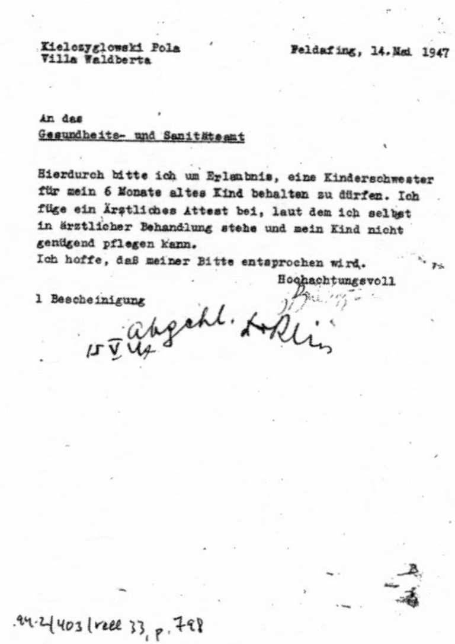

Kieloszyglowski Pola
Villa Waldberta

Feldafing, 14. Mai 1947

An das
Gesundheits- und Sanitätsamt

Hierdurch bitte ich um Erlaubnis, eine Kinderschwester für mein 6 Monate altes Kind behalten zu dürfen. Ich füge ein ärztliches Attest bei, laut dem ich selbst in ärztlicher Behandlung stehe und mein Kind nicht genügend pflegen kann.
Ich hoffe, daß meiner Bitte entsprochen wird.

Hochachtungsvoll

1 Bescheinigung

abgehl. 15 V 47

294.2/403/reel 33, p.798

Fig. 5.9. Request for a nurse for 6-month-old infant, with attached medical affidavit, Feldafing, May 14, 1947.

cates. The records reflect both the treatment ambitions of a still (and again) well-functioning German health and welfare system, and Jewish expectations of service from relief agencies and German physicians. They detail the numerous childbirth complications, such as cesarean sections, anemia, heart disorders, tears from forceps, and injuries from previous births or abortions, that afflicted DP mothers. Many observers (and women themselves) were quick to assume that women's capacity for pregnancy and childbearing facilitated an easier recovery into (apparent) normality. Men, who had been socialized into a male breadwinner norm, were assumed to be more disoriented and endangered by the enforced idleness of the DP camps, as they had perhaps been more devastated by their loss of status under the Nazis. While not entirely wrong, this perspective did not take into account women's struggles with broken bodies and "catastrophic anxiety."[109] A not atypical petition from Maria Abramawicz, dated May 9, 1947, describes her life in a single room with thirteen people, nine of them in one family; three were bedridden and one woman partly paralyzed. Three of the children were hers—eight months, three years, and four years old—and she was in such ill health that "I cannot help myself" (kann mir selbst nicht helfen). So this recently arrived "infiltree" was granted the services of a German housekeeper/nurse.[110]

Jews, for whom survival during the war had so often depended on their ability to work (Arbeitsfähigkeit), could now use their very lack of that ability as a lever for gaining German assistance and labor power. DPs demanded that Germans be hired to help them perform their daily chores and meet the incessant demands by camp administrators for levels of hygiene and cleanliness set unreasonably high for a refugee population housed in overcrowded and temporary quarters. If you want us to be so tidy, the message often seemed to be, send us some Germans—the generally acknowledged cleanliness mavens—to clean up after us. The head of the Feldafing tailor shop coolly informed the camp Sanitation Department that since his workshop had been deemed too messy, he had engaged an elderly German woman, so "she should keep it clean."[111] In a complicated multivocal (and medicalized) transaction, Jews, legitimated and regulated by their own camp authorities, and certified by mostly German physicians, constructed themselves as needy victims in order to gain the benefits of service from Germans who in turn, as we have seen in previous chapters, thought of themselves as victims and often saw Jews as privileged employers who enjoyed the protection of the occupiers and the bounty of the "Joint." As disgruntled JDC officials noted, Jewish survivors were often of the opinion that "we have worked so much for the Germans, it is about time the Germans now worked for us."[112] A German Pflegerin or Bedienerin (caregiver or servant) was one of the odd privileges of survivor status in postwar Germany.

Indeed, DPs often assumed that the services of German professionals as well as more menial laborers such as cleaners, plumbers, and cooks constituted an element of restitution. These expectations extended to the most lowly jobs, including, in another complicated reworking of conditions endured under the Nazis, literally cleaning up Jews' excrement. The widow of the Feldafing DP police chief who accompanied Generals Patton and Eisenhower on their highly publicized tour of the camp on Yom Kippur in October 1945 is convinced, for example, that Patton's notorious comment that "others ('Harrison and his ilk') believe that the DP is a human being, which he is not, and this applies particularly to the Jews, who are lower than animals," was influenced by his disgust at viewing DP quarters where new arrivals were relieving themselves in the hallways. The German men who came in daily to hose down the barracks had unfortunately not yet arrived when the inspection tour passed by.[113] Such assumptions of entitlement clearly shocked some of the German providers, as expressed in a nonplussed letter to the Feldafing camp administration from a physician unsuccessfully trying to collect his fee: "I had untold difficulties and much work with Mr. Benschowski, and he behaved toward me in a manner that I have never experienced in my entire life."[114]

German women, for their part, often themselves raising children alone because their husbands had been killed or were still prisoners of war, were pleased to garner a job with a salary and health benefits. Especially at a time when UNRRA guidelines stipulated that DP expectant and nursing mothers were entitled to 2,968 food calories daily, such employment also offered coveted access to black market goods and trade.[115] At the same time the Germans were acutely aware that Jews, firmly under the protection of the Americans, "could now play the masters." As the German woman who registered DP births at the Feldafing town office reminisced, Jewish women were simultaneously pleased to be able to demonstrate that they could afford such services and eager for competent and experienced help with their precarious "new life" (*Leben aufs neu*)."

Both groups carried unspoken memories of different, disrupted prewar relations, now being reworked in a radically revised context. German women remembered that some of the Feldafing villas confiscated for DP housing had once belonged to affluent Munich Jews for whom the local Germans had worked. Jews remembered that gentile servants or nannies were also not unusual in Eastern Europe.[116] Many applications pleaded for a *Deutsche* to help with housework since mother or child (and often both) were in weak health, implying, perhaps, that given their limited strength, mothers wanted to pass housework off to Germans so that they could care for their babies. But numerous other requests, both from men and women, quite explicitly asked for "infant" or "child care nurses" (*Säuglings/Kinderschwester*). In any case, given the very tight quarters in which DPs were housed, and the fact that housework and child care are impossible to separate in any mother's life, the distinction between asking for a nurse, a "maid" (*Bedienstete*) or simply the proverbial "*deutsche*" or "*deutsche Frau,*" probably meant little in the reality of everyday life.[117]

The reliance on German doctors and nurses, on the other hand, certainly created tensions. Relief officials were frustrated by DP mistrust of German personnel even if they were caring and competent (which was not necessarily the case). Ita Muskal, a DP from Romania, remembered with gratitude the kindness of the German doctors and nurses at the Elisabeth Hospital, where she gave birth to her son Michael. She was charmed when the local public health nurse who came by regularly to check up on how she was managing quite unselfconsciously referred to her dark-haired infant as the "little Gypsy." But she also recalled that when her sister-in-law's premature baby had to be rushed to an incubator available only at the university hospital in Munich, a Jewish nurse was recruited to ride in the ambulance with the aunt and the fragile newborn while the recovering new mother remained behind in Feldafing. For such an important mission, "They didn't trust the German nurses."[118]

Yet, determined to keep their babies alive, Jewish survivors had little compunction about hiring the most proficient help or insisting that a sick baby be seen by the best *Herr Dr. Professor* at the University of Munich or Frankfurt, his record during the war and an inevitable "deep-rooted antipathy" (which, for example, led one mother to tell her daughter that the doctor who delivered her was still wearing his SS boots) notwithstanding.[119] Opinions about the dependence on German medical personnel were sharply divided. JDC and UNRRA workers alternately complained about Jewish insistence on using German services or supposedly exaggerated claims of mistreatment. UNRRA rejected repeated efforts to establish a big central Jewish facility at Bogenhausen Hospital in Munich, where Jews from the entire American zone could gain medical training as well as be treated, as ultimately "not feasible"; there were barely enough qualified German doctors available, much less Jewish ones.[120] But there were also German doctors, such as the Feldafing couple named Struppler, who appealed to clearly ambivalent camp administrators for permission to treat their Jewish patients within the camp grounds. Citing their anti-Nazi credentials, they argued that "since we are particularly well known among our Jewish patients for our political convictions, we do not understand why we should now shut our doors to our Jewish patients who come to us urgently requesting a house call." The Strupplers phrased their request for maximum effect, asking how they should "react to the complaints of patients that they are after all no longer in a KZ, but liberated Jews, and can now finally choose the physician they want, just like any other free citizen."[121]

On both sides, it seems, the immediate larger past was silenced in favor of an explicitly temporary but mutually advantageous interaction.[122] These complicated but ubiquitous—and highly pragmatic—connections, which developed between Germans and Jews so quickly and often quite harmoniously after liberation and the defeat of Nazi Germany, have received virtually no attention from scholars. Relations between women, especially in regard to something as intimate as infant care, have been particularly invisible. They may be accessible only via oral history—with Germans *and* Jews—with all the difficulties (and pressures of passing time) inherent in that approach. Trying to make initial sense of these everyday experiences, I found myself frustrated, both with historians who have completely ignored these relationships, mentioned them only in passing, or at best professed not to understand them, as well as with the emphasis on memory and literary narrative and concomitant lack of attention to the seemingly mundane (i.e., "nontraumatic") in the trauma analysis that has been so important in Holocaust studies. I discovered the most useful hints in comparative anthropological studies.[123] The elements of physical reproduction and revenge that John Borneman postulated as key to healing efforts "after traumatic violent loss" were also key—and in surprising ways—to structuring postwar relations between Germans and Jewish DPs.[124]

Not only was the Jewish birthrate extremely high in comparison to German figures; the infant mortality rate of this battered and displaced refugee population was "phenomenon[ly] low," even lower than that of New Zealand, which boasted the world's lowest.[125] In Bavaria, where there had "never been as many Jews as there were one year after the destruction of European Jewry,"[126] the 1946 Jewish birthrate was 29 per 1,000 versus 7.35 per 1,000 for Germans. In 1947, as we have seen, the Jewish rate throughout Germany was announced as 50.2 per 1,000 compared with 7.6 per 1,000 for Germans. Whatever the variability of the numbers, the key point is the trend and the drastic contrast. Almost one-tenth of all live births in Bavaria in 1946 were to "foreign displaced persons," and the fertility rate for foreign (*Ausländer*) women was two and a half times that of German women.[127] The general death rate for the predominantly youthful population of Jews was also much lower: 1.6 versus 8.55. At a rate of 27.7 versus 2.8, there were also many more Jewish weddings.[128]

The radically different reproductive and sexual patterns of Germans and Jews—unsurprising as they may have been in light of their divergent social histories and circumstances, and difficult as they are to compare accurately—were saturated with, and represented as carrying, highly charged political meaning. For Jews and Jewish organizations, the rocketing birthrate denoted determined survival and also the pressing need for a secure, welcoming homeland far away from a resentful Germany. For Germans, with many men of marriageable age lost in battle or still held in prisoner of war camps, these demographic differences constituted another aspect of the perceived privileged status of DPs. German officials bemoaned "the horrific bloodletting that the German Volk has suffered during the last war" and noted with concern and clear envy "the unusually great marriage and birth willingess of foreigners living in Germany."[129] Jewish medical aid groups praised the "special care given by Jewish mothers to their infants" as a major factor assuring the high birth and low infant mortality rates, but given what the files reveal about the reliance on German baby nurses, perhaps those nannies also deserve some of the credit.[130]

Sara Tuvel Bernstein, who had come to Feldafing after the death camps and recovery from typhus in St. Ottilien Hospital, found herself alone "in a country that did not want me." Ironically, her urge for both connection and independence brought her not only into a quick marriage with a fellow survivor but also into close contact with the Germans whom she loathed and feared. Despite her anxiety about "boarding with someone who surely still regarded me as the enemy," she "had had enough of living in camp situations" and was "desperate to leave communal life" and assuage her loneliness. So, "At the beginning of October, less than two months after we met, five months after I entered the hospital at St. Ottilien . . . Meyer and I were married." Her wedding in Feldafing was typically rushed and "strange." With a feast acquired on the black market, her veil splattered by mud in the pouring rain and barely covered by the chuppah, she was haunted by the hopeless wish that her mother would be there to see her wed. Afterward, she felt, "Now that I was married, now that I had someone with whom I could build a new life, I wanted only one more thing—to be able to leave Germany," the land where, "If I or any other Jew entered one end of a train car, the German civilians on board rushed to get off the car at the other end." Instead, while attending a Jewish Organization for Rehabilitation and Training (ORT) trade school in a nearby village, she and her new husband were billeted in the home of a German widow who studiously and, as it turned out, fearfully, avoided her. Bitter and alienated, Sara competed for food with the local German housewives, seething as the grocer ostentatiously doled out butter and meat rations to his familiar customers, leaving nothing for the young Jewish refugee. Eventually, however, the close quarters impelled negotiation as well as icy distance. Sara confronted the German woman with whom she shared a kitchen and mutual suspicion. They began to talk "politely," and soon, in an arrangement that benefited both of them, the widow volunteered to take Sara's precious food coupons to the nasty shopkeepers.

An excellent cook who had been in service to a baron, the German land-lady made it her business to teach the young Jewish Romanian bride how to cook hearty German dishes.

Even though she "was not so sure of [her] feelings, of bringing a child into the midst of a people who would regard him or her as one of the enemy," Sara soon became pregnant. When she gave birth to a premature infant, Anna, the lonely German widow who had initially locked her doors against the alien refugee in her house, "rocked" the little boy "to sleep" when Sara was at work or when the young parents went to the cinema. Sara even reported that her child's first word was not Mama but Anna. In keeping with the strange dance of distance and intimacy that defined the relationship between Jewish mothers and the German women who cared for their babies, Anna was heartbroken when the family's visas for Canada finally came through. Sara and Meyer, however, left as fast as they could and never looked back.[131]

Sara and Meyer's experience was certainly not unusual. Reflecting on daily life in Feldafing, Simon Schochet stressed the "transient aspect of our lives" and insisted that "when we do strike up an acquaintance with a German, we do so safe in the knowledge that he [sic] is but a temporary acquaintance who in time will be separated from us, much to the relief of both parties involved."[132] In John Borneman's view, and indeed that of many contemporary observers, the leap into "compulsive reproduction" after traumatic events such as ethnic cleansing or genocide—usually, as was the case with the Jewish DPs, in endogamous marriages born of deep suspicion of outsiders—not only denies the time necessary for losses to be "relentlessly mourned" but carries the danger that children born of despair will carry on the trauma of loss and possibly perpetuate the cycle of violence. But he also suggests that a possible "departure from violence" does not require common long-term visions but simply the sharing of "a present, a present that is nonrepetitive." Borneman goes on to argue, moreover, that such a trucelike, transient present also requires "new rela-tions of affinity marked not by cyclical violence but by trust and care." The Jewish baby boom in occupied Germany certainly fits in many ways his negative criteria for "compulsive reproduction" and for the instru-mentalization of women as mothers in the wake of ethnic catastrophe, especially for nationalist or militarist purposes. Yet it also created pre-cisely those relationships between Germans and Jews, notably between mothers and their nannies, which required a certain amount of the "trust and care" Borneman imagines as necessary, if not for reconciliation, at least for a "departure from violence" and active hatred, even, or espe-cially, within a limited time frame.[133]

Among the Germans: Varieties of Coexistence

Thus, DP life provided, and frequently necessitated, numerous opportunities for other encounters and interactions between Jew and Germans, among women, among men, and between women and men. Like so many former DPs, Bert Lewyn insisted that, in Feldafing, "My world was divided into two parts, those who had lived outside the camp and those who lived inside. Outside the camp were enemies."[134] But in reality, the "enemies"—the people of "Amalek," referring to the biblical king who had tried to exterminate the Jews—were part of everyday life, within as well as outside the camps. DPs and Germans mixed in the village cafés, bars, and cheap dance halls run by Jewish DPs, such as the Varieté Gong, where "all of Feldafing" went to dance for RM 5 every Thursday and Sunday afternoon. Local youth snuck into the DP camps to watch American movies not yet available to Germans. Village bands played at the many weddings celebrated in the DP camps. Survivor Jack Eisner's touring DP band, the Happy Boys, could not be everywhere. Despite the disapproval of DP sports officials, Jewish soccer teams sometimes included German players, trainers, and referees, and in Feldafing, the town clerk recalled, occasionally a particularly good Jewish player would be recruited for the village team. The journals of the Bavarian DP camps were produced by the same printer in Starnberg as the skeptical local paper, *Land und Seebote*.[135]

The thriving Yiddish-language press, which managed to produce some eighty journals and newsletters as well as publish some three hundred books in occupied Germany from 1945 through the early 1950s, relied on the equipment, facilities, and skills of German printers. Tamar Lewinsky, one of the very few researchers to have examined DP daily life via Yiddish literary and journalistic sources, relates a revealing story about the gap between the public presentation of tense and separate life in "*goles daytschland*," as the DPs called the "cursed earth" (*farflukhte erd*) of their Diaspora (*Galuth* in Hebrew) domicile, and the realities of everyday cooperation and confrontation. In a short story published in a collection called *goles bayern*, the Yiddish writer Hershl Vaynroykh described the collision of two incompatible postwar German worlds. A Jew suddenly puts on tefillin while on a train heading through the beautiful countryside from Feldafing to Munich. Germans watch "silent and fascinated," and, fixated on the strange sight, they are suddenly unable to appreciate the beauty outside the train window. In another bitter short story, a "*bafraytn*" (liberated) survivor coerces a reluctant Munich landlady to rent him a room, only to discover when he returns the next day to claim his space that she had removed all the good furniture, leaving only a broken bed and a ragged spread. For a German, he concludes, a *Yid* is not a human being, just a *"katsetler, a heftling, a rasn-farfolgter* (A KZnik, a prisoner, racially persecuted)." Between the two groups there could be only bitterness and silence. Lewinsky tells us, however, about an author's note, added in 1982, that casts a somewhat different light on these uniformly negative depictions of German-Jewish relations. In his postscript to the manuscript, preserved in Jerusalem's National Library, Vaynroykh explained the context that had been invisible in his stories. In fact, the stories were published—albeit with many errors—only because he had found a "German gentile typesetter who owned a full set of Hebrew letters" and who not only "agreed to prepare the typesetting" but also mastered the rudiments of the alphabet "within two days."[136]

Germans and Jews also encountered each other within the borders of DP camps, which were officially off-limits to Germans. Germans with permits (*Lagerausweise*) entered daily to perform a wide variety of menial, skilled, and professional labor. They worked not only as baby nurses but also as cleaning women and men, drivers, mechanics, plumbers, locksmiths, photographers, teachers, and doctors. DP camp functionaries employed German secretaries, virtually a necessity at a time when all official communiqués had to be in German (and often translated into English as well for Military Government). Camp administrators were clearly ambivalent about this border crossing. They approved and referred German personnel, but at the same time they sought to control contacts, reminding residents that Germans they employed had to be cleared for entrance and observe a (surely transgressed) 6:00 P.M. curfew.[137] One artifact, both poignant and bizarre, of the regular contact between Jewish camp residents and German employees was the formal but, it would seem, heartfelt New Year's greeting sent by the German staff in Feldafing for Rosh Hashanah 1947: "We as your more distant coworkers nonetheless know very well what sorrows and burdens rest on your shoulders. We partake of your fate and want to stress again our openness to further productive cooperation."[138] For its part, the Jewish "Camp Council" had earlier expressed its appreciation for the "harmonious cooperation between Camp [*Lager*] and community" and extended best wishes for a happy Christmas holiday to the mayor of Feldafing.[139]

While such amicable encounters were to some extent an inevitable result of close working relationships, they may also have been facilitated by several particular historical circumstances. By 1947, in keeping with the focus on the Zionist future, much of official Jewish wrath had been transferred from the Germans to the British, who were refusing to open the gates of Palestine. If Hitler had been the stand-in for Haman at the first Purim celebrations, the hard-line British Labour Party minister, Ernest Bevin, was now burned in effigy and excoriated as a "hangman" on

Zionist banners. Moreover, many of the "infiltrees" from Eastern Europe had more direct or at least more recent memories of mistreatment by Poles and Soviets than by Germans. Finally, there was the peculiar fact that many Bavarians—blithely ignoring their "Free State's" status as incubator and center of the National Socialist movement—insisted on their regional rather than German identity. They emphasized, as Minister President Hoegner had in his address to the January 1946 DP Congress, that the evil brought upon the world by Germany had been perpetrated by "Prussians."[140]

Over 20 percent of all Jewish DPs, the so-called "free livers," chose, like Sara Bernstein, to leave the protective (and restrictive) confines of the camps. They lived in German towns and cities, freed of UNRRA controls but still supported by the Joint. Further and hopelessly confusing all population statistics, many of them also remained registered in the camps, not only to qualify for rations (and swell the camp allotments) but also to assure a safe haven in case of trouble. Despite resistance from locals and strict German trade laws, determined Jewish DPs, able to rely on support from the U.S. Military Government and, in Bavaria, the State Commission for the Persecuted, led by survivor Philipp Auerbach, managed to pass craft exams and set up businesses. Jews who lived in German towns and cities certainly hired German employees, housekeepers, and nannies. In an indication of how difficult it can be to trace this mostly unwritten history, another survivor (and colleague) responded incredulously when I said that I was studying encounters between Germans and Jewish DPs. That didn't happen, she insisted; we had nothing to do with them. But when I pressed her about the German nannies, she said, "Oh, well of course, we had a German housekeeper and chauffeur, but that didn't count." Such hierarchical interactions, often cushioned by businesslike transactions, were indeed rarely conceptualized as "relationships." Yet they were undeniably interactions, hence my use of the terms "close encounters" and "confrontations."[141]

Over five hundred young DPs attended German universities, especially in technical fields such as medicine, dentistry, or engineering. With their tuition paid for by German state restitution funds and their food rations provided by the DP camps, these young men and women were happy to finally pursue their education and use their student IDs for cheap entry to Munich's, Frankfurt's, or Berlin's cultural attractions. While they generally kept to themselves in Jewish student groups, they also maintained a (mostly) friendly coexistence—in classrooms, study sessions, and beer gardens—with fellow students, some of whom they knew to have served in the army or even in the SS. Arnold Kerr, a young survivor who went on to study engineering at the Technical University of Munich, took three free meals a day in the cafeteria at Eschwege DP camp. Thus nourished, he financed his preparatory sessions with a private tutor in Kassel by supplying him with an ample weekly portion of UNRRA ration Quaker Oats, a popular object of trade (if not of consumption). That his teacher, a former high school professor (*Gymnasialrat*), had a photo of himself in Wehrmacht uniform prominently displayed did not bother either student or teacher. "I couldn't care less," Kerr remembered. "I wanted to get an education, even if I was going to get it from the devil." He was not about to "waste [his] time" discussing their recent polarized pasts. For many students, it seemed only proper that the Germans who had destroyed their youth and family should now at least fund their training for a future they planned to pursue outside Germany.[142]

TRADE, TRUST, AND HOSTILITY

Germans for their part continually professed themselves shortchanged by the DPs' easy access to Allied commodities and command of the black market. At the same time, they participated with gusto in the many exchanges of goods and services—even including, as Kerr's story shows, preparation for admission to a German university—made possible by the DPs' stream of supplies. Germans too benefited from the black or gray markets operated by DPs, which could provide otherwise unavailable goods in the seemingly exotic bazaars of the Möhlstrasse in Munich, or Schlachtensee and Hermannplatz in Berlin. In certain distinct parts of Germany, Jewish DPs were an integral part of the social and commercial landscape. German farmers sold their products to Jewish DPs, getting good prices from kibbutzim and *Hachscharot* for their cows (in a reversal of the traditional arrangement in which the cattle dealers had been German Jews), and, after the initial conflicts around confiscated housing, landlords were generally pleased with the rents paid by DP "free livers."[143] Indeed, new research indicates that over 20 percent of *Hachscharot* had German managers; many employed German farmhands and sometimes even agricultural instructors.[144] Trolley Car Nr. 12, which traveled through Munich Bogenhausen, was dubbed the "Palestine Express" as it headed toward the Jewish agency offices in the Siebert Strasse or shops on Möhlstrasse, "filled," as Meyer Levin reported, "with wanderers from all over Europe, on their confused searches . . . a veritable marketplace," where Jews hawked "everything from bread to cameras."[145]

Surrounded by Germans and other DPs, Jews out and about in German cities and towns developed their own jargon, a successor to KZ language, by which they could identify each other. "*Amkho?*" (are you of the people?) they asked, or ironically referred to their KZ stays by querying what "pension" (small hotel) they had stayed in. On Fridays, in Feldafing and in other small towns in the American zone, Jewish women would take over the local bakery, exchanging their strange white-flour rations (*Amerikanerbrot*) for the use of ovens to prepare *challah* for the Sabbath. Feldafing prided itself on its "haute couture," more elegant than anything the German women had seen in years, and for any number of goods and services DPs traded the chic jackets that the skilled tailors in camp workshops produced.[146] Jews sought, as we have seen, escape from their institutionalized and dependent existence by creating an autonomous cultural and political life within the DP camps. But they also ventured farther afield, trading for fresh food and small luxuries on the black market, studying in German schools, and moving away from, or back and forth between, the camps and the world outside. And that pursuit of the ordinary pleasures of everyday life—whether food, education, entertainment, or even sex—brought them into both conflict and contact with their German neighbors.

BECOMING A "BUSINESSLADY" IN FELDAFING

As the following oral history illustrates, trade in food provided not only an occasion for resentment and conflicts over entitlements but also a crucial site for negotiations among Jews and Germans: about revenge, guilt, and benefits, and about how to coexist in the post-Nazi present. Ita Muskal, for example, recalled with some pride how at age eighteen, as a young refugee from Romania, she became a "businesslady" and a bit of a "big shot" as a Feldafing DP camp black marketeer.[147] Working in the camp kitchen with Hans, the chef with a "heart" who, she believed, had been taken over from the elite Nazi *Napola* school that had previously occupied the camp premises,[148] she was able to turn her paycheck of cigarettes, chocolates, and sardine cans into the beginnings of a trading career. On a walk one beautiful May morning, she stumbled upon a rich garden filled with fruits, vegetables, and flowers. Thinking of the upcoming *Shavuot* harvest holiday, she asked the owner if she could buy some flowers. The woman initially said, "We sell nothing, go to Munich," but then seemed to think better of it and asked Ita where she lived. When Ita explained that she was from the nearby DP camp, the women offered the flowers in exchange for a big loaf of army rations bread. A mutually satisfying if limited relationship was established. The two women never exchanged private greetings, never even knew each other's names, and never acknowledged their German or Jewish identities. But, Ita said, Yiddish and Bavarian worked well for communication, and the villager was honest and straightforward. She would give Ita a precious tomato or cucumber as a gift when they concluded their business.

Ita could go to her "best provider" in the lovely garden, loaded with her cigarette wages and her treasures from the camp kitchen—margarine, peanut butter, and dried and canned goods such as the ever useful Quaker Oats, peas, sardines, and tuna fish, which the Germans prized and the DPs disdained. "I'll show you" what I've got, she would say, and the woman would respond, "This is good, this I don't want." Ita collected marks and goods, which she could take to the nearby villages or into the bourse—the main black market exchange on Möhlstrasse—in Munich for serious trading. Decades later, she still vividly remembered the deep satisfaction of walking the two and half miles to a nearby village café with her cash and ordering a German pastry, just like the "businesslady" she was, or the defiant pleasure of going to the German grocer, ordering bread, salami, and buttermilk, and insisting on real Swiss cheese. The grocer, like those who ignored Sara Bernstein, wanted to sell her a lesser, smelly soft cheese, but Ita would have none of it. "Too expensive," he told her, but Ita said, no, "I have money and ration cards. I want the cheese with the holes." And then she treated herself to the short train ride home, munching her cheese on the way. Ita sometimes took her wares all the way to Munich, where she pocketed real dollars from the storekeepers. Hard currency bought her further luxuries such as a dress or a $10.00 pair of shoes crafted by expert DP cobblers and tailors. Armed with a picture from an illustrated magazine, she could take her dollars to the shoemaker and get the shoes she wanted, just like those pictured in the German paper. And sometimes she traveled into Munich with her husband Sam and played the "big shot." They went out, to the theater or circus, even to a real restaurant to eat the liverwurst that she loved.

CLOSE ENCOUNTERS AND CONFRONTATIONS

This chapter has been arguing—against conventional wisdom, most historiography, and much received memory—that Jews and Germans did not live in entirely separate worlds and, moreover, that their encounters were also often mutually useful and relatively harmonious. I have stressed this point precisely because it is so rarely made. But the degree of mutual suspicion and resentment, portrayed in *goles bayern*, must not be underestimated. Both groups were competing for scarce resources and the favor of the occupiers. Both groups felt aggrieved and unfairly treated. Jews were infuriated, and sometimes just astounded, by German self-pity and unwillingness to acknowledge responsibility for their crimes—the much discussed "enigma of German irresponsibility." Germans increasingly saw Jews not as victims but as privileged "foreigners" unwilling either to work in the reconstructing German economy or to emigrate elsewhere.

Fig. 5.10. Wedding portrait of Ita and Sam Muskal, Feldafing, November 3, 1946.

When Jews worked for the Americans, the relief organizations, and within the camps, or participated in the black market, they reinforced prejudices, both familiar and refurbished, that saw Jews as "parasites" living off American favor or international "welfare." At the same time, when Jews did seek employment or training by Germans, they were often not welcomed.[149]

Moreover—and this was a particularly sore point for Germans—once Jews entered the confines of the DP camps, they were subject to internal and occupation control. They seemed frustratingly beyond the reach of local law and police, protected, many Germans believed, by fellow Jews in Military Government. As Ruth Kluger later insisted, "We were hated, parasites of Jew-infested (*verjudeten*) Military Government."[150] DPs in the meantime protested the support given by American MPs to German police prone to reviving cruel memories by their use of dogs, bullhorns, and occasionally, as we have seen, guns. There were violent and occasionally deadly confrontations between Jews and Germans or between Jews and the U.S. military, and later even between Jews and Jewish aid workers. Shortly after the March 1946 murder of Schmul Dancyger in the Stuttgart raid, UNRRA officials were so fearful that Jewish anger was producing both a desperate turning to the "mass psychosis" of Zionism and the potential for clashes with a resentful German population that they urged: "Concentrate all Jews into as few localities as possible."[151]

Even after the trigger-happy German police had been reined in after the Stuttgart incident, there was a major riot near Landsberg camp. Its circumstances reflected the difficult proximity of Germans and Jews with their very different sets of recent memories and experiences. On the evening of Saturday, April 27, 1946, as the Nuremberg trials were in full session, a number of Germans were celebrating the return of some local POWs "with beer and song." Some ten miles away, Jewish DPs were marking the third anniversary of the Warsaw Ghetto uprising. Moved by this toxic "concatenation [sic] of events," DPs were quick to respond to a rumor that two young guards at a Jewish kibbutz near the German party had been "kidnapped." It turned out that the youngsters had actually taken off on their own in response to another rumor that some lost relatives had turned up nearby. But by the time this rather common scenario of quick chases after news of loved ones was sorted out, chaos had broken out in Landsberg. According to several—all somewhat different—versions, a bus had been burned, rocks thrown, MPs assaulted, and maybe even warning shots fired by German police as frantic military police, UNRRA officials, and JDC workers tried to restore order. Twenty young men, all of them camp survivors with horrific stories of murdered families, were detained and sentenced to considerable jail time by an American military court. May brought further confrontations in nearby Föhrenwald camp, where another DP, a twenty-year-old camp survivor with a pregnant wife, was killed by German police.[152] Jewish chaplains and members of the U.S. Theater Judge Advocate staff mounted a major defense effort for the Landsberg prisoners, which eventually led to the commutation or substantial shortening of their jail times. Depending on whether the point of view was German, American, or DP, this outcome confirmed either the privileged position of unruly Jews among the tolerant Americans, the efficacy of American Jewish intervention, or the outrageous lack of justice in American treatment of survivors who should never have been jailed in the first place. In any case, there was no doubt that, as one of the Americans assigned to defend them recognized, "The people also felt that their past suffering had more than paid for minor violations and indiscretions which they might commit and resented punishment which might be given them for illegal acts."[153]

Safeguarded by the Americans and the fundamental reality of unconditional surrender from any real threat of revived Nazi persecution, Jews were nonetheless increasingly on edge, vulnerable to rumors and panics. They were, as we have seen in our discussion of postwar Berlin, acutely conscious of the "new antisemitism" responding to the influx of East European Jewish refugees. Jews got into fights with GIs whose Fräuleins, they believed, poisoned young soldiers' minds and egged them on into "striking Jews for the amusement of their German girlfriends."[154] It did not escape aggrieved Jews that even as Jewish DPs were accused of exploiting Germans on the black market, GIs were busy bestowing the bounty of their rations on Fräuleins and their families, and officers were taking German women into their quarters.

Most observers and DPs themselves nonetheless insisted that Jews' "bitterness . . . rarely led to active conflict with Germans." Moreover, they claimed that even though "individually" Jews "carry on business relations, sex relations and there are even some cases of intermarriage," they still had "as little to do with Germans as possible, carrying on whatever relations may be necessary in a purely formal and business-like manner."[155] Yet this rather forced insistence on distant and instrumental relations did not capture the everyday reality that it was precisely in the "individual" basic and intimate arenas of food, reproduction, and sexuality that relations were both most fraught and most close.

The much photographed parades of baby carriages proudly steered by DP parents in German cities and towns were intended as displays of self-assertion, for the DPs themselves and also for others. So, in a different way, were the use of German labor and even the liaisons between Jewish men and German women. They clearly communicated the politics of "we are here" to politicians debating Palestine and immigration policy, to relief organizers adjudicating rations and housing, or to German citizens confronted with their discomfiting former victims. Jewish survivors in Germany, it should be stressed, did not see their presence on that "cursed soil" only, as we tend to do today, as a perverse historical "irony" but also as a form of justice and "payback," even "revenge." The Germans, Jews contended, owed them their space, their former barracks and estates, their rations, and their services.

There was a kind of in-your-face quality to Jewish mothers brandishing their babies, just as there was to the Zionist banners flying from former German official buildings or the posters carried in processions and parades through German towns. There was pleasure in rousing a village baker and insisting that he bake challah for *Shabbes*, or ordering a grocer to supply pounds of herring for a holiday feast.[156] Jews strolled through the streets of German spas and towns such as Bad Gastein, whose hotels and personnel had been commandeered for treatment and rehabilitation of survivors.[157] At the idyllic Schloss Elmau in the mountains above Garmisch, which served as a sanatorium and hotel for survivors, the manager was a former KZnik turned "master of a Bavarian castle," and children donned Hitler costumes to play Haman in the first postwar *Purimspiele*.[158] More dramatically, as a DP bluntly recalled, "Revenge did not mean only killing Germans. We had revenge when we saw the Germans acting as

Fig. 5.11. Soccer team, Zeilsheim DP camp.

hewers of wood and drawers of water . . . when we saw them cleaning
Jewish houses, the Jewish school I attended, buying cigarettes and paying
for them in gold—gold that had undoubtedly been taken from Jews. We
sold them bread and coffee and they gave everything they had. . . . Revenge also meant living with German women."[159]

INTIMATE ENCOUNTERS

Jews did have sex and sometimes live with German women, and even (in
a stigmatized minority of cases) married them. By 1950, over one thousand such marriages had been registered. Surely there were many more
relationships, both fleeting and more permanent. They were driven in part
by the surplus of Jewish men resulting from the approximately 60/40
skewed sex ratio among survivors, and the easy access afforded by German women's employment as nurses or domestic servants. The tensions
aroused by these connections are evident in DP literature, in the records of
bitter debates within the camps, and even in prosecutions by DP tribunals
(*Ehrengerichte*), leading to, in particularly nasty cases, banishment from
the camps.[160] An early debate among young survivors in Kibbutz Buchenwald indicated the seriousness of the issue:

No. Comrades, don't misunderstand me. I don't call for blood revenge on German civilians. I am only saying that simple human self respect must prevent us from having relations with German women. Yes, it is true that we were shut up for years in camp, without the sight of a woman, and now, coming out of prison into a glowing world of free-dom, our blood is warmed and we want to live a bit. This is quite natural. But friends, I ask you to remember one thing: When our be-loved Jewish girls burned in the crematoria, their clothes were brought to Germany, and these very girls might be wearing their dresses, their rings. It seems to me there is no more to say on this subject. After all, comrades, we are people who can, when necessary, control our instincts.[161]

The anxious and angry appeals not to dishonor the memory of mur-dered Jewish wives, mothers, and girls by relations with German women were emotionally powerful but not always effective. Not only were young Jews ready to "live a bit," but there were Germans more than willing to engage sexually with Jews. Some even tried to convert so that they could marry them. Rabbis, realizing that "unfortunately, in our abnormal con-ditions proselytes are an abnormal occurrence and unexpected for us," worried that "our young people, after all their tribulations and sufferings have not learned a lesson from the past." They were irritated and non-plussed by Germans who "want to be converted to Judaism!" and "Jewish young men who wanted to marry German girls." They were especially surprised by the (considerably fewer) "Gentile men who want to marry Jewish women," who "come to the Rabbinate every day" asking to be converted, "although they have to face an operation."[162]

This disapproval also extended to gentile liberators who fell in love with their charges. Such survivor/liberator matches were of course more likely to involve Jewish women and gentile men, and "girls who would have been ashamed to associate with Germans were proud to be seen with the Allied soldiers."[163] American or British Jewish liberators did not arouse the same suspicions, and those matches, though also apparently few in number, seem to have been more likely to be recounted in "love story" mode.[164] It may have been that "the ardours of the time overcame restraint," but it was also true that, for lonely female survivors as well as German women, "The soldiers had a great deal to offer."[165] As a young Hungarian survivor remembered her stint as a secretary for the Americans in Heidelberg, "Life and youth surge happily in us. We get acquainted. Those of us who speak English are the first to be approached."[166]

On a larger scale, relations between Jewish men and German women remained a troubling and contentious issue for survivors long after the immediate postliberation furor had calmed and the Allied military had given up on trying to enforce antifraternization regulations. For Jews, the problem had two distinct aspects. On the one hand, as the chapter on Berlin has shown, many of the remaining German Jews owed their survival to "Aryan" spouses, and reemergent Jewish congregations had to negotiate their policies in regard to the participation of non-Jewish partners. On the other hand, there were the generally illicit relationships between DPs and German women. The latter became more visible and proportionally greater in number after 1948, when the easing of U.S. immigration regulations and the establishment of the state of Israel finally sped up survivors' exit from Germany. It then became clear that some Jews had decided to remain in Germany not only because they were too exhausted and sick to move on but because they had established businesses and/or settled down with German women. Those relationships and marriages between Germans and the small group of Jews who remained in Germany are, however, easier to document than the sexual or romantic encounters that were, not unlike the black market, an integral if sub-rosa part of transient Jewish DP life in the immediate postwar years.

For young male survivors who "didn't know anything about women," except anguished memories of their murdered mothers and sisters, German women, often themselves refugees, lonely, and eager to "have some fun," provided an easy and relatively carefree introduction to sex, unburdened by the obligations and associations attached to Jewish women. One then-seventeen-year-old survivor of the Vilna Ghetto, forced labor, Auschwitz, and Stutthof recalled of his time at Schlachtensee DP camp in Berlin: "The Kurfürstendamm was a good place to start having sex." While others were busy on the black market, he was "interested in meeting women." A friend organized three German girls for his buddies in a hotel on West Berlin's main commercial street, the young men brought some vodka, and otherwise "it was all free." He didn't really know what he was doing, he confessed, but still it was fun (in retrospect he wondered why "protection" had not been an issue). And there was perhaps some added satisfaction in the knowledge that they were engaging in a bit of "*Rassenschande*," that "Hitler would not have agreed with it; he had other things in mind for me."[167]

In a manner not dissimilar to the transactions between Jewish mothers and the German women who cared for their babies, these encounters, while always shadowed by the recent past, were fleeting, pragmatic, and generally able to satisfy mutual (if different) needs. When, not wanting to offend, I carefully asked one of my interview partners, an Auschwitz survivor and Feldafinger, to tell me what she remembered about Jewish men "going out" with German women, she looked at me indignantly and burst out, "Jewish men did not *go out* with German women, they *slept* with them!" Opportunities presented themselves easily, she recalled

230 • Chapter Five

matter-of-factly. German women came to clean the DP quarters, and in the daytime there were plenty of available beds; "it was very easy to go to bed."[168]

One male DP explained in retrospect, "It is hard to believe—and even harder to understand—how that happened . . . many German women were attractive and knew how to handle their love affairs." He meant perhaps that, toughened and scarred by war, they were not only savvy about sex and birth control but also knew not to make too many unrealistic demands on men highly unlikely to remain with them.[169] Zippi Tichauer, wife of the head of the DP police in Feldafing, saw these encounters more darkly. For Jewish men, she sensed, "a German woman was dirt," easy to exploit and easy also to leave behind with an illegitimate child. She is still haunted by one painful episode when a Jewish DP, whose wife had been unable to bear a child, simply appropriated his half-German offspring. With his wife's blessing and over the mother's objections, he passed it off as their own, and they took the boy with them to the United States. Asked whether this might be an exceptional story, she snorted, "If there was one, there were more." Most of these half-Jewish illegitimate children, however, remained with their mothers. Unlike the "mixed breed" offspring of African-American GIs and German women, in a postwar situation where single mothers were entirely common, with a "Jewish baby, nobody knew" (and the facts are correspondingly impossible to verify). Moreover, Jewish DP men were surprisingly desirable fraternizers; they had a "rich" store of goods like cigarettes and chocolates to offer, were generally present for a longer period of time than occupation soldiers, and did not require any knowledge of English. Unlike the GIs, they often knew German, and in any case Yiddish was close enough.[170] As another male survivor ruefully recalled, even though German women had "gained a reputation for easy virtue" and were "held in contempt by the group," they were "as a whole . . . more physically attractive than the refugee women, if only for the reason that they did not live under such bestial conditions." He acknowledged that while most such relationships were motivated by "a mixture of revenge and the desire to taste the forbidden fruit," there were also "singular cases" of "deep reciprocal feelings" in which "the answer would simply have to be that a man and woman met and fell in love."[171]

LIVING WITH THE "ENEMY"

The use of the term "revenge"—and the word does come up a lot—in the context of sexuality is noteworthy. Historians have had little problem recognizing as "symbolic revenge" public actions such as staging Zionist rallies in former Nazi strongholds such as Munich's Bürgerbräukeller, or treating "visitors" to the kibbutz on the former estate of the notorious Bavarian gauleiter "to the experience of seeing the dogs on the farm respond to Hebrew names that the trainees had taught them, as their salute to Streicher."[172] They have not problematized social interactions such as those involving labor, trade, childbearing, or sexuality in such terms, situating them rather as "personal" responses, naturally linked to the effort to restore a sort of normality to traumatized, disrupted lives or simply as necessary for daily survival.[173] Attention to the histories and memories of everyday life, however, clearly indicates that, for Jews, these "personal" experiences—and the interactions with Germans they provoked—were also part of the fraught and defiant resignifying implied by the obligation, often repeated, to "find revenge in existence." Their (normal/abnormal) everyday lives demonstrated that while they did insist on documenting and memorializing the catastrophe, they were more than just "victims" and precisely did not dwell obsessively on the traumatic past.

Despite some dramatic incidents and plans, such as assassinations of SS men, the aborted well-poisoning scheme linked to Vilna partisan hero and poet Abba Kovner, and an only minimally successful plan to taint the bread supply of an American POW camp near Nuremberg in 1946, which resulted in the (nonlethal) sickening of some two hundred SS and Gestapo prisoners, there were few real efforts at large-scale revenge (*Nakam*). While observers professed astonishment at Jews' "incredible self-restraint," simultaneously impressed, relieved, and suspicious that they did not "tear" Germans "limb from limb," the survivors were painfully aware that in the face of genocide there could be no adequate retribution.[174]

The evidence is actually quite varied and contradictory. On the one hand, Jews, exhausted and bitter, insisted that they lived in a separate extraterritorial universe, not even wanting to engage with Germans enough to violate them. In her book on the aftermath of a brutal sexual assault, Susan Brison has suggested that survivors of trauma may not want to risk anger because to do so requires a certain level of engagement and "proximity" with one's violator.[175] Using a word that was ubiquitous in Jews' characterization of their attitudes toward Germans, a German-Jewish camp survivor said of her liberation and her success at identifying SS guards for British war crimes trials, "I felt no joy—only hatred and contempt." Helping the Allies was an obligation, but above all, "I wanted to forget, to get away, to leave Germany forever and put the Germans out of mind."[176] On the other hand, there were violent confrontations, and Military Government officials groused that Jewish DPs "love getting into fights with Germans."[177] This was definitely a population with a "chip on its shoulder." Finally (in the third, least examined case), there were countless everyday instances of matter-of-fact, even friendly, interaction, fixed in the present moment, apparently heedless of the recent past and denying that there would be any mutual future.

For the most part, revenge took symbolic but nonetheless highly visible forms. One of the most striking features of the DPs' presence was the calculated appropriation of former Nazi "shrines" and German space for their own practical and symbolic purposes. Representatives from the first conference of liberated Jews at St. Ottilien in July 1945 traveled to Munich to press their demands for open emigration to Palestine in the Munich Beerhall, from which Adolf Hitler had once launched his attempted putsch in 1923.[178] In August 1945, a German-Jewish private in the British Army's Jewish Brigade described being greeted by an American sentry at Berchtesgaden, "the holiest [shrine] of German National Socialism," with a hearty *"scholem Aleichem."* Adolf Hitler, he concluded, must have "turned over in his grave or scratched his head somewhere in Argentina."[179] American Jewish soldiers took particular pleasure in the reversal of fate they witnessed at Hitler's mountain nest. Eisenhower's special adviser on Jewish affairs, Judah Nadich, was pleased to discover Hebrew graffiti left behind by the Jewish Brigade; of all the "strange episode[s]" involving the postwar Jewish presence in occupied Germany, "none could be more topsy-turvy, none more satisfying, than this sign of the visit of Jewish soldiers in Jewish uniforms to the heart of what had been Hitler's stronghold, his fortress and pride."[180]

When Lucy Dawidowicz arrived in Munich in fall 1946 as a Joint worker in U.S. uniform, she found that the famous beer hall "had been converted into a Red Cross center where you could get hot dogs, ice cream sodas, and other American fare."[181] Others praised the "excellent beer."[182] And when the Central Committee of Liberated Jews of Bavaria moved into a "bombed out floor" of the Deutsches Museum in Munich, U.S. Military Government lawyer Abraham Hyman pointed out with a certain amount of glee that "Hitler once prophesied that the time would come when a person would have to go to a museum to find a Jew."[183] "The nice part," a woman survivor who worked there as a social worker noted, was "that one does not hear much, if any, German being spoken."[184] Munich's Möhl and Siebert Streets, where ORT, the JDC, the Jewish Agency, and the Central Committee of Jewish DPs were all located, "somewhat resembl[ed] a wartime division headquarters, consisting of a series of requisitioned residences now turned into combination offices and living quarters for various organizations," surrounded by the lively street life of a Yiddish-speaking East European Jewish community.[185] When the Congress of the Central Committee of Liberated Jews met in January 1946 in the Munich City Hall, center of the former unofficial Nazi capital, it was festooned for the occasion with a banner that read, "So long as a Jewish heart beats in the world, it beats for the Land of Israel." Examples of such resignifying abound; perhaps the most famous was the Streicherhof, a socialist Zionist kibbutz on the former estate of the notorious Bavarian Gauleiter. It had been renamed Kibbutz Nili by its young occupiers, the Hebrew expression for "The Strength of Israel will not be denied," and "became a prime attraction for journalists and others."[186]

Buffeted between their assigned roles as fonts of moral authority, bearers of new life, and asocial self-pitying wrecks, survivors were keenly aware of their role as guardians of memory and eyewitnesses to the indescribable, as well as of the obligation, often repeated, to "find revenge in existence." In a sermon on September 17, 1945, that noteworthy first Yom Kippur after liberation, DP leader Samuel Gringauz admitted that "we, the elders live with the memories of the dead, day and night. We who saw daily the best of our people murdered feel closer to the dead than to the living." He acknowledged the fundamental dilemma of any efforts at revenge, for "Not even Satan has created a revenge fitting for the spilled blood of a little child." Instead he exhorted especially the young survivors—"the carriers of our revenge"—that "you, the youth may not and dare not live with the memories of our dead and with lamentations. . . . You must show the world that we live. You must create and build, dance and sing, be happy and live, live and work."[187]

"Revenge" is a necessary term for the historian because of its frequent contemporary use. Yet, for our purposes, it is surely an insufficiently pliant term to convey Jewish DPs' excruciatingly complicated mix of grief from overwhelming loss, satisfaction at surviving against all odds, urgent desire to reclaim "normality," and finally, determination to demonstrate—to Germans, Allies, and other Jews—that "we are here," albeit (and this is a critical point) "on the road" to someplace else, away from Germany and Europe. On an immediate level, revenge as well as recovery also encompassed the careful calibration and negotiation of pragmatic contact with, and distance from, Germans, always, to be sure, in the context of a perhaps disapproving but nevertheless protective Allied presence and the conviction that the sojourn in Germany was merely temporary.

Jews had contempt—perhaps the second most ubiquitous word next to sullen—for the oblivious self-pity of defeated Germans. They were especially disgusted by what they repeatedly described as the Germans' creepily obsequious, groveling demeanor. Richard Sonnenfeldt, a twenty-two-year-old German-Jewish private in the U.S. Army who became the chief interpreter for the Nuremberg Tribunal, remembers having had only contempt for the mediocre "bootlickers" (Speichellecker) he saw before him in the holding cells and on the stand.[188] Amongst themselves Jews repeated Churchill's nasty diagnosis that the Hun either leaps at your throat or falls at your feet.[189] At the same time, Jews also had to confront the reality that, as one survivor told a German researcher, "But on an individual basis it was very hard to hate them once you knew a person and faced them and you lived with them in the same apartment. It was so much easier to hate the child or other teenager that I saw on the streetcar that I didn't know. It was different when you knew someone."[190]

Writing in both the Yiddish *Landsberger Lager Cajtung* and in the German-language DP paper *Die jüdische Rundschau*, Gringauz, the president of the Central Committee of Liberated Jews in the American zone, bitterly formulated—in, for today's ears, perhaps shockingly strong terms—his farewell to Western Enlightenment culture:

> We do not believe in progress . . . we do not believe in the 2,000-year-old Christian culture of the West, the culture that, *for them*, created the Statue of Liberty in New York and Westminster Abbey on the Thames, the wonder gardens of Versailles and the Uffizi and Pitti palaces in Florence, the Strasbourg *Münster* and the Cologne cathedral; but *for us*, the slaughters of the Crusades, the Spanish Inquisition, the bloodbath of Khmielniki, the pogroms of Russia, the gas chambers of Auschwitz and the massacres of entire Europe.[191]

The ideology of the *She'erit Hapletah* turned away from Germany and from the Europe that had betrayed the faith invested in it by modern Jewry. But in fact, in the years right after the war, Germans and Jews did know each other and come face to face in daily life. As a German-Jewish British officer reported back to friends in Palestine in 1946:

> "I hate the Germans" is a common expression. "I can't stand to look at them, I could kill them all in cold blood." But when the conversation continues, it becomes evident that one is speaking about "my friend Schmidt" and "our dear neighbors, the Müllers," because, after all, even the biggest hater cannot live in total loneliness if he is compelled to continue to live at the sites of his tortures.[192]

"How can I stay, Kurt?" Gerda Weismann asked the German-Jewish GI fiancé she was desperate to join in the United States after she discovered that her presence was protecting her kind, but completely compromised, landlord from denazification penalties. "What am I to say to people who treated me civilly, no matter what their motives might be?" she agonized, acknowledging that "I can hate Germany and all things German with a passion, but I can't hate individuals."[193] Indeed the desire to escape Germany may have had to do not only with fear or revulsion at living in the land of the murderers but also with an entirely realistic fear that duration and proximity would breed more contacts and perhaps even—against all memory and judgment—personal and economic attachments.

For the Jewish DPs, the personal and the political of survival were linked: in the birthing of babies, in the social glue of the fervent Zionism that dominated the fractious political life in the DP camps, and in the pursuit of everyday life. The birth of children and creation of families, as well as daily life in occupied Germany, inevitably produced not only a sense of historical irony, of memory and revenge, of desire for compensation and satisfaction at wresting goods or privileges or money from Germans but also a kind of quotidian normalization and commitment to building new lives.[194] That this *Leben aufs neu* should develop on German territory surrounded by, and in interaction with, defeated and occupied Germans was seen by the DP survivors not only as a great irony, a cruel joke played by history, but somehow also as just and appropriate.

Fig. 6.1. Two young DPs pose in front of the destroyed Kaiser Wilhelm Memorial Church on the Kurfürstendamm, Berlin, 1947.

CHAPTER SIX

Conclusion

THE "INTERREGNUM" ENDS

> There is no issue from their dreary tales even though we say happy ending in Israel.
>
> —Meyer Levin[1]

> Of all those now homeless in this foreign land, the Jews are the cheeriest. . . . Their . . . faces . . . turned . . . toward Israel.
>
> —Janet Flanner in the *New Yorker*, 1948[2]

> What they claim not to have known yesterday they wish to forget again today!
>
> —Report on trip to Germany, April 1950[3]

BY LATE 1947, the chaos and flux—but also the sense of openness about Germany's future—that marked the immediate postwar period was over. Political conditions and everyday life were changing for everyone: defeated Germans, American victors, and both German and DP Jewish survivors. U.S. Military Government's turn away from policies of denazification, justice, and restitution—and toward cooperation with the former enemy, in the service of intensifying Cold War conflicts, the push for German economic reconstruction, and greater political autonomy—became ever more pronounced. General Lucius Clay's April 1947 directive to remove from Military Government service anyone who had been naturalized after 1933 clearly signaled the declining influence of anti-Nazi émigrés, whether Jewish, leftist, or both. The era that Samuel Gringauz retrospectively saw as a "golden age" for the DPs, from the fall of 1945 until the summer of 1947, was coming to an end. Germans were chafing for more control over their own affairs. Americans and Germans were growing ever more impatient with the dependent Jewish refugee population, especially given the social and economic pressures involved in integrating some eight million ethnic German expellees from Soviet-dominated territories.

Jewish DPs themselves were becoming more impatient and frustrated with their "waiting" life. Their volatile mood was in many ways exacerbated by the uproar over the fate of the refugee ship *Exodus* in summer 1947, and the United Nations vote approving partition of Palestine in November.[4] In 1948, DP Central Committee leader Samuel Gringauz took stock of the situation and sourly declared in the American Jewish journal *Commentary* that "Jewish survivors in German DP camps are an obstacle to Cold War reconciliation with Germany. . . . They are still in acute conflict with the nation which Allied occupation policy wants to make into an ally."[5] At the same time, the Yishuv in Palestine, struggling for statehood and foreseeing the heightening of conflict with the Arabs once the British pulled out, was increasing pressure for young and able Jews to emigrate and populate and defend what would become a new Jewish state. And most Jewish DPs were increasingly anxious to leave a more and more assertive Germany. Nineteen forty-eight, therefore, would prove to be the crucial transition year, bringing the preparations for the establishment of the German Federal Republic in 1949 and the switch from Military Government to civilian "supervision" by a High Command for Germany (HICOG), the easing of U.S. immigration regulations, the declaration of the state of Israel, and the escalation of the Cold War in the flash point city of Berlin.

Changing Enemies: Berlin

Once again, events in Berlin marked a momentous political shift. As Berlin had been the center of defeat in 1945, it was the June 1948 Allied decision to extend the newly stabilized deutschmark currency to the western sectors of Berlin, the ensuing Soviet blockade of Berlin, and the Anglo-American airlift to overcome the blockade in 1948/49 that most clearly symbolized the changed status of western Germany from World War II enemy to Cold War ally.[6] The recognition of a new enemy in the Soviet Union and its East Bloc was now irreversible and nonnegotiable, a process that would have consequences also for the Jews remaining in Germany. Reconciliation with the defeated Germans, already well on its way since Secretary of State Byrnes's speech in Stuttgart in spring 1946, entered a new stage with the blockade. The Soviets' attempt to cut Berlin off from the western zones of Germany allowed Berliners finally to achieve what they had wanted—and been convinced they deserved—since the summer of 1945 when the western Allies joined the Soviets as occupiers of the ravaged former capital: at least in West Berlin, the Americans victors became allies rather than conquerors. Once more struggling for survival, Berliners were both victims and heroes, but certainly not Nazi villains. They now lived, not in the capital of a hated and besieged Third Reich, but on a "heroic peninsula," serviced by the Americans and British who had relentlessly bombed them just a few years earlier. In what has to be one of the more remarkable reversals in modern history, Operation Vittles supplied 13,000 tons of food daily to the population of the former enemy in the former capital of the enemy. Some fifty-seven thousand people carried off a feat of logistics, technology, and political will, bringing in 200,000 flights by 380 British and American planes transporting 1,500,000 tons of goods, including 950,000 tons of coal and 438,000 tons of food.[7]

The fear of communism united victor and defeated, and the threat from the East, rather than the faltering and divisive efforts at denazification, became the guarantor of West German democratization.[8] In fact, the fears on both sides of the debate—those who perceived the occupation as too lenient and feared a revival of fascism, and those who perceived the occupation as too harsh and feared the triumph of communism—proved to be unfounded. West Germany, much to the surprise of many who were there shortly after the war, did develop, gradually, in fits and starts, into a democratic, peaceable, and nonthreatening European nation. Just as the expected fanatical *Werewolves* had failed to appear, neither did any kind of Nazi revival. Contrary to virtually all expectations, and for whatever reasons—German obedience, the lure of postwar consumer culture, anxious anticommunism—the democratizing experiment in Germany succeeded, taking as its price the fact that the urge for order and stability trumped hopes for revenge and justice.[9]

Currency reform, blockade, and airlift sealed the division of Berlin and fundamentally changed its status from vanquished Nazi capital to plucky Cold War ally. A level of tense stability was established. By the end of 1947, morbidity and mortality rates had been relatively normalized, epidemics brought under control, many prisoners of war returned, refugees moved out, and the worst of the rubble cleared away. The year 1948/49 marked a renewed cycle of crisis and recovery, but with a valence very different from that of the period right after war's end. In the early years, the Anglo-American occupiers had resisted Germans' "whining" and preoccupation with their own victimization. They had insisted (in often ironic contrast to the Soviets) that they had come as conquerors and not as liberating friends. The Soviet blockade and the forceful response of the western Allies, however, reconfigured Allied airpower as missions of mercy rather than destruction, and allowed Berliners to place especially the Americans in the generous liberator role that many had wanted to force on them all along. In 1948, during a spring as lovely as that of 1945 but in an entirely different kind of crisis, the *Amis* finally accepted the position. But this time of course they came as liberators from the communists and not from the Nazis. The irritation at German "whining" transformed into wholehearted admiration for Berliners' heroic endurance. Once again, Berlin's children were being sent away to the countryside, out of harm's way, but now it was British and American planes, not Nazi women's organizations, transporting them to the West German countryside for a bit of *Luft, Licht, Sonne* (air, light, and sun).[10] The Americans were rightfully worried about the stamina of the Berliners, who in turn were intensely distrustful of what had been, after all, an initially reluctant commitment to maintain a western stake in the ruined capital. As American correspondent Drew Middleton noted, the recent "memories of Russian occupation, looting, rape, and murder still painfully vivid after three years" had left inhabitants "psychologically . . . unprepared for any test of will." Using language that is worth pondering, he explained that given "the suddenness of complete defeat, coming so soon after the '*Sieg Heil*' years, the fury and duration of the Allied bombing, the well-remembered holocaust [*sic*] of the Soviet siege and its terrible aftermath," the city needed to be convinced that it would not be deserted by the West.[11] Once the airlift was in full, impressive operation, however, the compact with West Berlin was essentially sealed. At its height, "The airlift was running like clockwork," and on "record days" in April 1949 "the millionth ton of supplies" was flown into Berlin, with a plane landing "every 63 seconds." At that point, Colonel Howley reported in his fiercely anticommunist account, even those "spineless" Berliners who early in the blockade had registered in the East to assure food rations were allowed to change their minds, and about 100,000 reregistered in the West.[12] In reality, the airlift, dramatic as it was, could not fully support the city, and Berliners would not have survived without foraging for supplemental supplies in the surrounding countryside and East Berlin.[13]

Still, the city's stoic endurance, the "unexpected [political] courage shown by the friendly Germans in Berlin,"[14] convinced even the skeptical Middleton: "My opinion of West Berliners began to change on September 9, 1948." In response to the giant anticommunist rally of 250,000–300,000 people in front of the scarred Reichstag, he wrote: "I have seen and been moved by many crowds. But none, not even the people of London bidding goodbye to Winston Churchill has moved me as much as that vast throng."[15] A *Newsweek* reporter who observed the determined but at times violent crowd was less impressed: "If the fate of Berlin was to be decided in the streets, the West still seemed to have the bigger and tougher mobs." Moreover, he reminded his readers, Berliners were still preoccupied with their own suffering. "A 12-year-old German boy marched off with a ten-foot section of the flagpole," explaining, "'I'm taking it to my uncle . . . We need fuel for the stove.'"[16] Even as the Cold War alliance was cemented, German self-government was installed, and the great majority of remaining Jews were exiting Germany, conflicts about victimization and entitlement continued to shape Germans' relations with Jews and American occupiers.

Interestingly, in this moment of crisis, women, who had figured in the direct aftermath of the war as seductive fraternizers, pitiable victims, and stoic managers of everyday life, emerged as particularly compelling symbols of anticommunist resistance. The matronly mayor, Louise Schroeder, rallied her fellow citizens at a time when electricity was available only two hours a day and the future was uncertain. Jeanette Wolff, a Jewish survivor and Social Democratic city councillor, deployed her unassailable antifascist credentials when she compared, and called for opposition to, both Nazi and Communist totalitarianism. A Jew who had lost two daughters to Nazi murder and endured numerous concentration camps, she was beaten up when Communist protestors invaded the newly constituted West Berlin municipal assembly.[17] Indeed, as our discussion of the film *The Big Lift* suggests, images of women and children were key to the debates about "changing enemies" and the success of the airlift. When a grateful German mother showed Colonel Howley her healthy "blue-eyed" baby, sustained by airlifted formula after the milk supply from Soviet-sector cows was halted, he was persuaded that the occupation had been a success. Howley, who had been so unmoved by German "whining" right after war's end, was finally at peace with his anticommunist inclinations: "The German mother's tribute was as high a reward as I will ever merit. I treasure it."[18] The airlift's protection of women and children solidified the privileged status of the Americans as the primary occupiers—protectors as well as fraternizers—in the West. At the same time it ingrained them as the primary enemy in the East, where the Cold War—and then, starting in 1950, the Korean conflict—offered communist women's organizations ample opportunity to attack the Americans as warmongers willing to bomb innocent women and children all over the world.[19]

The *Rosinenbomber* (raisin bombers), which dropped food and candy rather than bombs, held particular resonance for women and children who had endured the wartime "home front." The Soviets' blockade of the city raised specters of hunger and violation that built particularly on women's memories of war's end. In Howley's apocalyptic terms, women feared that "the soldiers who had sacked the city with all the Asiatic savagery of Genghis Khan's hordes, were coming back. . . . Remembering the evil excesses of the early days, terror filled the hearts of the German women who had survived the first Mongol invasion."[20] Yet women themselves averred, at least in the narrative now presented to the West German and American public, "So it is bad. . . . But better than to have electricity *and* the Russians."[21] If, in 1945, some women had still imagined, "Better a Russian on my belly than an *Ami* in the air," they now acknowledged, in reference to the tasteless American mashed potato mix that came with airlifted packages, "But better POM than *Frau komm.*"[22]

A more critical view of the mutual German-American embrace solidified by the airlift—and again clearly drawn in terms of gender relations—was expressed, as we have already seen, in the 1950 American film *The Big Lift*. In a scene reminiscent of the masses who had not so long before gathered to cheer Adolf Hitler, the film opens with documentary footage of the giant rally in West Berlin in the square before the bombed-out Reichstag. It concludes with the anxious ambivalence that marked the end of formal American military occupation and the establishment of "supervised" German self-government. Hollywood clearly showed the German determination to resist communism, but its references to willful amnesia about the war and genocide and its invocation of "Dachau, Lidice, Buchenwald, Rotterdam, Warsaw" signaled the anxieties that were besetting Jews in a reconstructed Germany. In the film, with the success of the airlift and the lifting of the blockade, the two well-meaning GIs who serviced the besieged Berliners during the crisis are free—in a wonderful act of American male bonding—to go home. They leave behind the Fräuleins, both honest and devious, with whom they fraternized and a nation of hopefully (but clearly not entirely) democratized West Germans.[23]

No Longer "Home": Jews in Berlin

By the time the movie was released, the Americans had also taken with them, in empty airlift planes returning to the Rhine-Main Airport base, almost all the remaining Jewish DPs in Berlin. But the uneasy debates about a Jewish future in Germany crossed the 1948 dividing line, especially among the truncated community of German Jews. By 1947, the Berlin Gemeinde's mood and tone had changed. The tentative hopes and occasional euphoria of the immediate postwar period had faded. German Jews now expressed more pessimism about German penitence and willingness to engage the past than they had shortly after the war ended. Fewer notices about searches for missing relatives, and more statements confirming deaths, appeared in *Der Weg*. More and more ads said farewell "before our departure for the USA."[24] In the hard winter of 1946/47, community leader Hans-Erich Fabian confessed that Germany had only now become fully *"unheimlich"* (both eerie and no longer home) to him: "we see that antisemitism in Germany today is becoming stronger by the day, that wide circles of people have learned nothing on this score and [worst of all] don't want to learn anything."[25]

In March 1947, one anonymous Jewish returnee (*Heimkehrer*) to Berlin diagnosed "unprecedented depression."[26] Jews living in occupied Germany were acutely aware that it was not the dead six million—already the established figure—whom resentful Germans noticed but the handful who were present. Having been visible in Allied uniform, as denazification and cultural officers, as interrogators, translators, and prosecutors, and maintaining their connections to the victors, Jews were perceived once again as much more numerous and powerful than they actually were. Familiar antisemitic stereotypes and resentments were openly voiced; Germans grumbled about the disproportionate number of Jewish lawyers and the unfair advantage they enjoyed over "Aryan" colleagues (temporarily) disqualified by their Nazi past. The Jews hanging on in Berlin yearned for more understanding of their choice to remain (at least for the moment), but they were entirely sympathetic to the many who wanted to leave or refused to return. They were outraged at the temerity of those, like the Social Democratic politician (and KZ veteran) Kurt Schumacher, who, in the name of antifascist solidarity, chastised Jews for their manifest disinterest in returning to rebuild the land that had expelled them. Jews were painfully cognizant of their isolation. "The best of us have fallen victim to the persecutions," Fabian wrote, and those who remained had only very limited psychic and physical energy.[27] The Berlin Jewish world was narrowing.

One who chose to leave was my grandfather Heinrich Busse. By July 1947 he had finally reacquired his German civil identity—a real Berlin identity card, signed not by occupation or Gemeinde authorities but by the Berlin police chief, listing his citizenship as "German" and omitting any mention of religion. But at the same time he had also obtained a much more valuable document. Printed in French and English, a *Titre de Voyage*, or "Travel Document in lieu of a national passport," issued on June 27, allowed him to enter Folkesstone, England, on October 20, 1947, and rejoin two daughters who had fled to England as domestics in early 1939.

Busse had at times briskly described his life in the underground as just another challenge to a hardened German gymnast, for whom "there was no such thing as bad weather, just inappropriate clothing."[28] For such a very German Jew, the real recognition of the irrevocable loss of his *Heimat* (homeland) came only after the war had ended. He realized that, despite the hopeful excitement of liberation, which had made him feel as if "newborn," there would always be, as he put it in a birthday letter to his thirty-six-year-old married daughter in London on June 18, 1946, "a sediment of mourning in the cup of your and all of our joy in life and ability to experience pleasure."[29] But only in 1947, over two years after his liberation, when Busse had left Berlin behind forever, did he fully articulate the enormity of the German-Jewish catastrophe and the persistence of antisemitism. Busse had, he acknowledged to a former rescuer, "always, as you may know, considered myself more as a German than as a Jew, and rejected the stupid and pernicious artificially constructed division between people who have lived in one land for many hundreds of years." Safely arrived in London, his perspective shifted: "Due to the very sharp and general condemnation of Germany—not only here [in England] but everywhere abroad, I have myself become more self-critical and perhaps more clearsighted."[30] Ironically (and tellingly) Busse was most bitter not about the mass of Germans, whom he had long since written off, but about the minority of good Germans. They had helped him survive, and he had maintained faith in them throughout the darkest days, even after his wife had been deported to her death, even after the rest of his family had either emigrated or been murdered. During the war, the "illegals" and those living in mixed marriages or as *Mischlinge* had relied on the help and cooperation of "Aryans." Even at their most desperate, those in hiding or in touch with resistance news felt somehow vindicated in thinking that they were dealing with a "real" if minority Germany, with which they might join in reconstructing a better *Heimat* after the Nazis were defeated. After liberation, Jews were shocked and aggrieved by the sentiments revealed among even the "decent" minority. Their rescuers complained about ungrateful Jews who received special favors from the occupiers or were quick to emigrate, leaving their helpers behind hungry, cold, and self-pitying in a devastated city, or who (in Allied uniform) treated them insensitively in denazification procedures. Confronted with Germans preoccupied with their own misery and indifferent to, or in denial about, what had happened to their Jewish compatriots—the much observed "enigma of German irresponsibility"[31]—surviving German Jews felt the force of antisemitism even more painfully than when hiding in a friendly *Schrebergarten*.[32] Indeed, as American Jewish officials observed, "The fact that the German people feel no compulsion to make amends for the crimes of Nazism is the most important reason why a substantial part of the few remaining German Jews have decided to emigrate."[33]

Busse was infuriated by hectoring letters from an old business acquaintance, the furniture maker Hermann Paul. Paul had sheltered him during the war's chaotic final months (at great personal risk, but not without hope of advantage after Germany's inevitable defeat). Smarting from the miserably cold winter of 1947, when the "mood was [also] below zero," Paul complained that Busse, now safe in England—"We are pleased that you are doing so well," he cuttingly noted—was ungrateful, greedy with his CARE packages, and moreover, had tried, right before his departure, to sell him a radio at inflated black market prices. Suddenly, it seemed to Busse, he was no longer the fellow Berliner who had needed help and been rescued but just another Jewish speculator and war profiteer, seen as cheating the poor Germans with "Jewish brazenness" (*jüdischer Frechheit*). He responded fiercely:

I was dumbfounded. . . . Even you seem to be accepting this silly as well as pernicious "antisemitism." . . . I am not indifferent to what you think of me. Not in the least do I want to minimize or deny that I owe you much thanks. You behaved decently and with courage, quite unlike the overwhelming majority of Germans, toward a criminal, treacherous, and in every way deeply contemptible regime. I have expressed this to you repeatedly. But I must tell you one thing in regard to your current attitude and your outrageous version of events. As much as I value your help and your previous rejection of National Socialism— your brother Erwin had himself at the time not been shy about declaring that under the existing circumstances [late in the war] the dangers of taking me were not so great, the benefits of helping someone persecuted possibly greater. I completely understood that, and would never have thought about even mentioning this. Now however, it is necessary. Because it might at least make you—I have no such hopes anymore about your brother Erwin—more thoughtful.[34]

In another letter from London, Busse responded passionately to the laments of a young woman who had supported him (and perhaps more) during his years as an *U-Boot*. She was, he insisted, so immersed in her own experience as a victim of war, defeat, and victors' justice that she had lost all sense of moral and historical proportion:

You have no idea how provocative it feels to those whom it affects when you now ask, when will the liberators finally have satisfied their bloodthirstiness against us. When you as a German accuse them of horrendous tortures, after the entire world is still stunned with horror over the exposed and still not really admitted, somehow excused or trivialized, atrocities of the Germans, of which no one wants to be guilty or even involved. When you, despite all that has happened, literally write, "and after all, our hearts and hands are pure and with them [the victors] the blood is flowing out of their collars," and other stuff like that, you refer personally to yourself and yours, but you can't possibly assume that the same would hold for the Germans as a whole and that one can expect the world simply to forget the horrors of Hitler, with which after all the broad masses generally identified.

He did not want to live in a city where he had to explain, even to his friends and rescuers, "the not in the remotest way comparable difference between the conditions in Berlin or Germany now and those in Auschwitz, Belsen, etc."[35] On December 21, 1948, Heinrich Busse crossed his last border. The United States Immigration and Naturalization Service admitted the seventy-four-year-old to New York City, where he became an enthusiastic resident of Morningside Heights, all the while still battling in the Berlin courts to reclaim—finally, in 1954, successfully—his house in Friedenau from the man who had acquired it shortly after *Kristallnacht* in December 1938. His auctioned-off belongings were irretrievable.[36]

There were, to be sure, also other resolutions, other ways, to situate the conflict of being a German Jew in post-Nazi Germany. The debates about whether to stay or go, to stay away or return, were played out in countless conversations and letters that moved back and forth between Germany and the far-flung German-Jewish refugee community. Most remaining Berlin Jews were horrified at the naïveté of enquiries from refugees thinking about returning, which came most frequently from the more difficult and unlikely exile destinations such as India, Africa, or Latin America. Erich Nelhans hastened to inform a relative who had landed in British India that a return "would be the most weird thing imaginable; here we are all trying as hard as we can to leave this land that sent millions of our brothers and sisters to their death."[37]

Some Berlin Jews however, a tiny minority of surviving German Jewry but significant in public life, did not want to leave the city they once again found enticing. Siegmund Weltlinger, who was appointed by the Magistrat as the first "commissioner for Jewish affairs" after he and his wife emerged from hiding, and later served as a conservative Christian Democratic (CDU) deputy in the Berlin Assembly, insisted that he again felt at home. In the hard years 1946/47, like so many Berliners, he and his wife went to the theater, heard Wilhelm Fürtwängler conduct a violin concert by Yehudi Menuhin, admired Gustav Gründgens and many other great actors and actresses on the reopened, if unheated, stages. He was a minor big shot, with good contacts to the Allies, enjoying the many receptions and parties with German and occupation officials. His letters, however, were marked by silences, ruptures, and inconsistencies. On September 9, 1946, he carefully chronicled the lost and murdered, listing the names of the missing, "unfortunately gassed" [*leider vergast*] . . . actually most of our old friends—one mustn't think about it." Yet he and his wife stayed on even as their children made new lives abroad. "We have found a new and stimulating circle which makes a lot of music. We hear good operas and concerts. Berlin is right up to par," he contended in 1951.

But Weltlinger was unusual. Hans-Erich Fabian, the Gemeinde official who had expressed the dominant sense of unease in his lead article in *Der Weg* on January 31, 1947, struggled with the common and tellingly named notion that Jewish life in Germany could proceed only in the context of a *Liquidationsgemeinde* (a self-liquidating community) for those too old and disabled to leave. He finally resorted, as did others including Weltlinger, to the minimalist (and, as it turned out, prescient) argument that some Jews must remain in Berlin, if only to help the many refugees from the East who would continue to pour through.[38] Fabian understood clearly all the reasons why Jewish life in Berlin should end, but still he lingered. East European Jewry had provided the basis for Jewish religion and ritual, but, he mused, German Jewry had offered an important road out of the ghetto into the civilization offered by the West. To finally close the door on that legacy would be, he lamented, "a hard to endure loss."[39] Nonetheless, he too departed (more unhappily than most) for New York.

The official separation of Berlin into East and West in spring 1949 also shifted the already transient and unclear nature of Jewish life in Berlin. It basically eliminated the Jewish DP "problem." Almost all of the approximately 6,500 Jewish DPs in Berlin—who had originally been kept in Berlin as another sign of American commitment—were flown out into the western U.S. zone in empty airlift planes returning to their base at Rhine-Main, another step toward the normalization of divided Berlin. Berlin had been a crucial entry point, the "first frontier for this Jewish migration from East-Central Europe," but the center of Jewish DP life in occupied Germany had, as we have seen, shifted to large camps near Munich and Frankfurt.[40]

The borders, through which tens of thousands of East European Jews had slipped on their way to the American zone and eventually new homes outside Germany, were closing. Jewish aid organizations curtailed their programs in Berlin, even as East Bloc countries barred any official activity by the JDC and other groups. Cold War tensions increasingly separated Jews in the West and East, both in Berlin and throughout central Europe. In 1948, in a sign of the fracturing anti-Nazi coalition, Jeannette Wolff and other Jews resigned from the umbrella organization Victims of the Nazi Regime (*Vereinigung der Verfolgten des Naziregimes*, VVN), now seen as a Communist front group.[41] If Jews decided to stay on in the Cold War outpost, then that would be their "affair."[42] When Heinz Galinski, the Auschwitz survivor who would become the longtime head of the Jewish community in West Berlin, reported in 1949 to the World Jewish Congress that most of the remaining Jews in Berlin intended to make their lives there, the response was unambiguous: "One spoke clearly, in fundamental terms, and very aggressively, against Jews remaining in Germany."[43] The burden was placed on the small numbers of Jews, both native German or Eastern European, who remained in the land of the murderers.

END OF THE DP ERA

Similar issues were played out in different ways among the Jews in the American zone proper. By 1947 Jewish DPs, notwithstanding their early bitterness about the "sardonic postscript to their tragedy" on German land, were already remembering with a certain nostalgia "the days when Eisenhower's troops had liberated them and GIs had showered the starvelings of Buchenwald and Dachau with sympathy, chocolate, and ciga-rettes." Then, the U.S. military had been their "unwilling" but "clear" protector and "guardian."[44] Unlike the British, the Americans, together with UNRRA and then UNRRA's successor, the IRO (International Refu-gee Organization), had been willing to accept and help provide for not only the liberated Jews but also the "infiltrees" from the East. After April 21, 1947, however, in a signal of impatience, Military Government no longer recognized "infiltrees" as United Nations displaced persons; this meant that while the IRO was still in charge of maintaining the DP camps and the borders remained essentially open, funding of refugee services devolved onto Jewish aid organizations, especially the Joint.

The DP story was becoming ever more complicated. It had become clear that, despite all the reported respect for the DPs' Zionist dream and the Yishuv's success in building a refuge in Palestine, the promise of the Harrison Report and the subsequent recommendation of the Anglo-American Committee of Inquiry for the immediate provision of 100,000 entry permits for Palestine would not be fulfilled. Jewish DPs were trapped by the stated British refusal to consider withdrawing from Pales-tine unless the Jews renounced all violent resistance to English control and by the United States' reluctance to admit them as immigrants.[45] In the event, the unwillingness of both Allies, in different ways and for different reasons, to accept the Jewish refugees reinforced the *She'erit Hapletah*'s public voice of militant Zionism. The prolonged stay in refugee camps and/or as "sojourners" on German territory had only further encouraged the development of a new Jewish nationalism that could counter the hu-miliations and despair of statelessness and exile.[46] The hope expressed in the Joint Committee of Inquiry report that Palestine would become "nei-ther a Jewish nor an Arab state, but must ultimately become a state that affords all the inhabitants the fullest measure of self-government" would not be fulfilled. Those Jews who did finally make it to *Eretz* would get off the boats and face yet another war, one that many of them, angry at the British, Poles, and Germans but only dimly aware of the realities in the Middle East, did not really understand or expect.[47]

The Harrison Report's warning that American treatment of Jewish sur-vivors offered Germans an object lesson in reeducation and denazification had helped assure them a protective haven in the American zone. As U.S. priorities shifted toward reconciliation with the defeated Germans, that commitment became increasingly problematic, and the pressures for ei-ther emigration or integration of remaining DP Jews mounted. At the same time, it is important to remember that the American policy of lim-iting the Jewish presence in Germany and restricting—often with clear antisemitic grounding—Jewish emigration to the United States was en-tirely compatible with, indeed inextricably linked, to the two prime goals of Jewish survivors: supporting Jewish DP life in Germany and ultimately emigrating to a newly established state of Israel. In that sense, and in stark contrast to the situation in the British zone, American and Jewish desires, while not always reconcilable in the immediate situation, were ultimately mutually supportive. In retrospect, it is not so surprising that the man who had overseen alien registration and internment during the war would also vigorously support the Zionist demand, and indeed the public demand of the Central Committee of Liberated Jews in the name of the entire *She'erit Hapletah*, for rapid emigration to Palestine.

Despite the Americans' and UNRRA/IRO's considerable efforts to organize repatriation or resettlement, however, Janet Flanner, the *New Yorker*'s correspondent in Europe, reported in 1948 about the mass of both Jewish and non-Jewish DPs that "after more than three years of peace, three-quarters of a million uprooted European human beings" were "still living in the American zone of Germany, all of them willing to go anywhere on earth except home." They were living side by side with the Germans "who guiltily hate[d] them." Yet, as "Genêt" (Flanner's nom de plume) pointed out, with a copious dose of romanticization, the Jewish story was distinct. Unlike non-Jewish Polish or Baltic DPs whose lands had turned communist and who therefore now constituted themselves as "nations in exile," necessarily uprooted, Jewish DPs imagined an end to exile and insisted that they did have a national home, which they only needed to reach. Improbably, "Of all those now homeless in this foreign land, the Jews" were "the cheeriest," because "their faces" were "turned . . . toward Israel."[48]

The situation in the DP camps did shift drastically after the acceptance of partition in Palestine by the United Nations General Assembly in November 1947, the subsequent onset of Arab protests and riots, and the declaration of the state of Israel in May 1948. The doors to the new state not only opened but demanded. Ita Muskal remembered trucks with loudspeakers that cruised the Feldafing camp grounds, calling for young DPs to sign up for the *Haganah* defense forces, blaring, "We got a country. C'mon. Get on a truck." And in an indication of the tensions between the Jewish drive to rebuild lives and families (also often framed, at least theoretically, in Zionist terms) and the practical exigencies of Zionist determination to build a state in Palestine, she replied, "I can't. I have a husband."[49] From late 1947 onward, Zionist leaflets in Hebrew and Yiddish (and, in Berlin, even in German) featured photos of Jewish soldiers, both women and men, with rifles, proclaiming that every new settlement in Palestine (and then Israel) was a "fortress that is defended with great sacrifices, because every step of Jewish soil is also a piece of the battlefield on which the fate of the Jewish people is being decided." The pioneers were fighting against swamp, desert, rock, and neglect. Farming, for which DP youth had prepared in the *Hachscharot*, was a battle task for the Yishuv. The more Jewish territory was cultivated, the stronger the military situation and the safer the Jews. The Jewish Agency stated bluntly, "Possession of property is the main weapon for defending the land."[50] But the land needed to be taken and defended. In yet another unprecedented manifestation of the strange new nationalism born in the DP camps and out of the cataclysm of the Holocaust, the *Haganah*, first as the Yishuv's underground army and then as a fledgling Israeli defense force, undertook a draft for a nation that did not yet exist or had just been founded, in order to conscript soldiers who had never seen the land for which they would be fighting.

While Jewish survivors often imagined *Eretz* as a peaceful land where they could finally live at rest and among themselves, the new state's propaganda was determinedly militarist. Recruitment for the *Haganah*, unashamedly called a draft (*giyus*), was determined and sometimes coercive. Historians have bitterly debated the nature and impact of this remarkable conscription campaign, but there is no doubt that soon after the state was declared on May 14, 1948, young DPs, mostly (but not exclusively) men from the Zionist youth movements, and between seventeen and thirty-three and childless, left for the front lines in the Middle East. They were given big farewell parties, presented as examples of reformed men who were ready to give up the "golden calf" of the black market and the "fleshpots" of Germany to go and defend the young Jewish state. Certainly there was "moral pressure" to enlist, and possible sanctions included dismissal from public posts and denial of immigration permits to Palestine, as well as threats of, or actual, physical reprisals. At the same time, even though the great majority of DPs did not join the fighting force, they supported the struggle for the new state by contributing to a kind of national tax, publicized and collected among all DPs. Some 7,800 DPs did take off for combat duty. Although many arrived too late to bear the brunt of the fighting, they nonetheless formed a significant part of the Israeli defense forces, which numbered only 88,033 in 1948. It has now been clearly demonstrated, after much contentious argument among Israeli historians, that, in large part because of the timing of their arrival, the conscripted DPs did not serve as "cannonfodder" and their casualties were relatively low. Yet it remains a dramatic fact that young people who had survived camps, partisan warfare, hiding, or the harsh exile of the Soviet Union exited from the DP camps into a new war, where they often could not even understand orders that were shouted at them in Hebrew. As Hanna Yablonka points out in her study of Holocaust survivors in Israel, the Israeli army had a provision for the exemption of only sons, but this humanitarian provision could not be enforced among the *She'erit*

Hapletah recruits, because so many were sole survivors. There simply would have been no army for the new state.[51]

The Zionism of the DPs had been inclusive, demanding entry to Palestine for all the surviving remnant, including the babies that were their pride. With the outbreak of hostilities, however, there was a return to the more elitist selectivity of the prewar years, and emigration priority was given to the young, healthy, and unencumbered. Before the proclamation of the state of Israel in May 1948, only 69,000 Jews had already arrived, legally or illegally. Despite the collective insistence on the necessity of a Jewish state and the near universal acceptance of Zionism as the best political hope for European Jews after the Holocaust, many individual DPs continued to dream about crossing the ocean to the United States. Particularly for those with family already there, that other "promised land," whose geography—organized by states—was enshrined in the street names in Föhrenwald, still beckoned. The long-awaited June 1948 U.S. DP Act, however, with its 30 percent quota for agricultural workers, was much more welcoming to ethnic Germans and non-Jewish Eastern Europeans, especially from the Baltic states, than Jewish DPs, as was repeatedly noted by Jewish relief officials (and subsequent historians). Moreover, the initial provision that DPs had to have entered what was defined as American-occupied Germany, Austria, or Italy between September 1, 1939, and December 22, 1945, essentially made ineligible the great majority of Jewish DPs who had arrived in the American zone as "infiltrees" from Eastern Europe starting in 1946. The immigration bill did contain sufficient loopholes, some actually encouraged by a somewhat embarrassed President Truman, to allow entry to thousands of Jews between 1948 to 1950; the rest would arrive after the amended, more liberal DP Act of 1950.

The June 16, 1950, DP Act extended the cutoff date for entry to the U.S. zone to a more realistic January 1, 1949. Many DPs rushed to get U.S. visas, scrambling for sponsors and trying to balance the economic benefits of staying to try and organize reparations money—which initially required residence in Germany—with the urge to catch the boat out at Bremerhaven. The U.S. Citizens Committee on Displaced Persons, which had been formed in fall 1946 and was led by Earl Harrison, Eleanor Roosevelt, Marshall Field, and labor leaders A. Philip Randolph and David Dubinsky, dispatched garment workers' union (ILGWU) organizer Dubinsky to Germany to recruit skilled workers. His promise of visas for tailors finally offered a way out from Feldafing via Bremerhaven to the Bronx for Ita Muskal, her husband Sam, and their young son.[52] All in all, from 1945 to 1952, about 400,000–450,000 DPs, of whom some 72,000–100,000 were Jews (about 20 percent to one-third of all Jewish DPs), entered the United States.[53] They came as displaced persons, became "New Americans," and only in the last few decades of the international Holocaust memory boom did they morph, for the general public and the Jewish community, into "survivors"—to be honored, interviewed, and memorialized.

So finally, in 1950, the reformed U.S. immigration provisions and the promulgation of the Law of Return by Israel opened more doors for those waiting to emigrate, including several hundred TB patients still trapped in Gauting sanitorium whom only Israel was willing to accept.[54] Of circa 250,000 Jewish DPs, somewhere between 100,000–120,000 and 142,000 settled in Palestine and Israel. The numbers, as usual, are far from precise, not to mention ideologically freighted. Canada took in 16,000–20,000; Belgium 8,000; France 2,000; Australia 5,000; and various other countries, including South Africa and Latin American nations, another 5,000.[55] In April 1948, there were perhaps 165,000 Jewish DPs left in Germany; by September their numbers had dwindled to 30,000.[56] In 1951, when the Federal Republic of Germany formally assumed control over the DP camps from the IRO, about 12 percent of all Jews worldwide lived in Israel as compared to about 3 percent in Palestine prior to the Holocaust. In a major demographic and cultural shift, about half of all Jews resided in the United States compared to about a third before the Second World War. The once "flourishing" communities of central and Eastern Europe had been decimated, with only some concentrations left in the Soviet Union, Romania, Hungary, France, and England. By 1950, the great majority of Jewish survivors had in fact left blood-soaked Germany behind.[57]

Jewish DPs who had not left with the emigration wave that followed Israeli independence or emigrated elsewhere faced the establishment of another state, that of the Federal Republic of Germany, in 1949. The Americans were relieved to hand over responsibility for the remaining DPs to the IRO and Jewish aid organizations and then, in 1951, officially to the West Germans. The DPs, however, regretted the loss of the Americans' reluctant, ambivalent, but ultimately benevolent authority as military occupation ended and shifted to civilian "supervision" led by the State Department.[58] Moreover, it was no secret that the vaunted currency reform that would bring good fortune to West Germans was, at least initially, bad news for the DP economy. A stabilized currency along with the reduction of American forces from an initial high of 400,000 to about 75,000 reduced both the supply and the need for the DPs' black market goods. As American Jewish envoy William Haber delicately put it, "The reform will, obviously, also affect the economic position of the DPs who depend upon the black market. . . . With reform will come also substantially more access to imported consumer goods, so that items of barter such as foreign cigarettes will lose their value."[59] It became imperative to participate in the official West German economy in order to reap its benefits. These new possibilities, in turn, became an incentive for some DPs to stay. Indeed, as a somewhat cynical relief worker observed, currency reform provided a potential novel benefit to the baby boom. Every resident was entitled to an initial lump sum payment of forty freshly printed deutschmarks; with that rather princely amount, new babies had material value.[60]

Although some Jews stood to benefit from the developing West German welfare state and economic miracle, the birth of a stable anticommunist Germany and the essential end of an already steadily reduced denazification program dashed remaining hopes that a recognition of collective responsibility for Nazi crimes could lead to serious reparations. Compensation had been, as we have seen, a major issue since the end of the war, and not only for German Jews. Despite the many obstacles, determined surviving or returning German Jews were able to take advantage, in ways not open to DPs, of Military Government Law 59 issued by General McNarney on November 10, 1947, which assured restitution of property in the American zone to persons "who were wrongfully deprived of it between January 30, 1933 and March 8, 1945, for reasons of race, religion, nationality, ideology or political opposition to National Socialism." But Jews from Eastern Europe who had been displaced by the Nazis' war also demanded recompense. They aimed to finance rehabilitation, relief, and resettlement, as well as decrease dependence on the JDC, which had, by summer 1947, taken over the economic burden of caring for the "infiltrees." All these considerations, by both German and DP Jews, demanded a new political engagement with the still ambiguous (not occupied but "supervised") entity of the Federal Republic of Germany.[61]

DEBATES ABOUT A JEWISH FUTURE IN GERMANY

In July 1949, just as the Federal Republic was being established, a remarkable conference was convened in Heidelberg by Harry Greenstein, the last adviser on Jewish affairs to the U.S. Military Government. Representatives of both DP and German Jews, international Jewish organizations, the "other Germany" of anti-Nazi resistance, and the American occupiers gathered to take the measure of Jewish life in the new semisovereign Germany. They argued over the future of the greatly diminished but stabilizing number of Jews, their proper relationship with Germans, and the disposition of Jewish property and claims. They debated whether there was any justification for Jews to remain in Germany, and about the nature of those justifications. Were they purely instrumental—that as long as Jews were there for whatever reason they must not be abandoned, and that Jews fleeing "from behind the iron curtain" were likely to continue to need a welcoming outpost in the West? Or were they existential and symbolic—that for all Jews to leave would be to grant Hitler a final victory? In a discussion that encompassed both the practical and the symbolic, delegates argued vigorously about the always pressing financial questions. Should the extensive cultural and monetary assets of the pre-Nazi German-Jewish community—both those already recovered and the considerable ones still to be compensated—devolve onto the tiny rump postwar Gemeinden, composed for the most part of people who had been only marginally Jewish? Or should they also be distributed to the much larger majority of German Jews who had become refugees throughout the world? Greenstein tried to play the honest broker, but his very presence suggested an openness, unusual among American Jews, to the idea that there might be room for a Jewish future in Germany. "There are honest differences of opinion on the question of whether Jews should or should not remain in Germany," he noted, with some understatement. Not surprisingly, the representatives of the DP Central Committee were unalterably convinced that there was "no place for Jews in Germany" and that it would be "suicidal" to remain. Others, especially among the German Jews, believed equally strongly that "the extinction of the Jewish community in Germany would be tragic, and constitute a very dangerous precedent."[62]

By 1950, the numbers themselves told a sobering tale. With the Jewish DP population in the U.S. zone rapidly declining—in 1948 the rolls had dropped from about 165,000 to 30,000 in a matter of months—local communities (Gemeinden outside of DP camps) counted only 3,650 members, with an additional 3,382 in the British zone and some 7,044 in four-power-controlled Berlin. In contrast to the demographic profile of the DP camps, these German-Jewish communities were elderly, with few children and very high rates of intermarriage. In Berlin, the official intermarriage rate was 52 percent, and only 10 percent of the gentile partners had converted. In Darmstadt, however, where, in keeping with a more frequent—but also frequently contested—practice in numerous West German cities whereby DPs had joined the existing Gemeinde, only 1 percent of the members were intermarried. At the same time, it was clear that most Jews eager to go to Israel had already gone; indeed some had gone and come back. Emigration to Israel had "slowed down to a mere trickle," as disillusioned returnees and depressing letters from emigrants told of disappointment, war, and hardship in the young Jewish nation.[63]

Ironically, it was left to the American high commissioner John McCloy, who had succeeded Military Government commander Lucius Clay when the Americans instituted civilian oversight of an independent Federal Republic, to make the most impassioned case for a Jewish future in Germany. Even if only some 30,000 remained, of the over 500,000 who had lived in Germany before 1933 and the several hundred thousand who had passed through after the war, that remnant, he insisted, had a symbolic significance. But McCloy fell back on essentially the same argument that had earned Ernst Landau such scorn from his fellow survivors when he made it in 1946: he asked the Jews to take on a moral obligation to the land of their murderers. The continued presence of Jews, he claimed, served as a kind of barometer of and guarantee for the moral rehabilitation of the Germans. They were a living reproach to the pervasive desire for normalization and closure of the guilt question (*Schlussstrich*), of those who wanted only to "forget the Auschwitzes and the Dachaus and the other concentration camps and think in terms of the new Germany we are trying to rebuild."

"To end Jewish life in Germany would be almost an acknowledgment of failure," McCloy argued. Like so many hoping for reconciliation, however, he placed the onus for taking the initiative on the victims. Resorting to his own well-meaning stereotypes and with none too subtle reference to Jews' reputation for shady business activities, McCloy suggested that "with the tenacity, persistence, courage and vigor of the race [*sic*] and with the habit of honest and fair dealing, the Jew in Germany will be restored to a position which he occupied in the past in this community and will reach even higher levels." He acknowledged, however, that "I do not know how long that will take." Presenting what would become his signature remark on the importance of the Jewish presence as a test of post-Nazi West German political maturity, McCloy stated: "What this community will be, how it forms itself, how it becomes a part and how it merges with the new Germany, will, I believe, be watched very closely and very carefully by the entire world. It will, in my judgment, be one of the real touchstones and the test of Germany's progress." Moreover, it would be the task of the Jews themselves to do the work of assimilation and integration, precisely a mission that the remaining DPs were utterly uninterested in undertaking. "The success of those that remain," the high commissioner insisted, "will to a large extent depend upon the extent to which that community becomes less of a community in itself and merges with the general community." To his credit, McCloy fleetingly took notice of how off-base his comments must have seemed to much of his audience: "It is a little difficult for me to choose the right words to express my sympathy and my interest in the reestablishment of the Jews in Germany . . . and I realize that however sympathetic one may be, you have feelings whose depth no one can plumb."[64]

Representing a liberal, antifascist "other Germany," Dr. Eugen Kogon, a non-Jewish Buchenwald survivor and editor of the journal *Frankfurter Hefte*, took a somewhat different and more credible tack to lobby for the same conclusion that Jews should not desert Germany. He expressed his deep disappointment with Germans' preoccupation with their own victimization. Not only had there been "no horrified outcry" about the atrocities they had perpetrated, but the very presence of the survivors had given rise to a new antisemitism, driven by resentment of Jews as the visible but unwanted reminders of German crimes, demanding some restitution. Yet he too still pleaded for some measure of reconciliation. His position was forcefully challenged by the energetic and controversial Philipp Auerbach, a Hamburg Jew who had survived Nazi concentration camps and had, in an unusual move, been appointed Bavarian state commissioner for racial, religious, and political persecutees in 1946. The campaign for financial restitution, Auerbach contended, was not, as so many even ostensibly friendly critics suggested, "an unwarranted fixation with compensation,"[65] or an incitement to antisemitism. It was rather the only means left by which to force responsibility on a "German people" who had "no sense of guilt and are not held culpable by others." Where Germans saw corruption and special favor as well as confirmation of old stereotypes about moneygrubbing Jews, Jews pressed the demand for minimal justice.

A broad range of opinions were represented in this open and sophisticated debate. Representatives of the scattered emigrated German Jews insisted in no uncertain terms that it would be a "travesty" if "Whatever has been built up by and for 550,000 people in the course of many hundreds of years of history and designed for the needs of such a great number of people, can be claimed by 20,000 to 25,000 people," many of them with only the most tenuous relationship to the Jewish religion. There were, after all, over 200,000 surviving German Jews elsewhere in the world whose claims were being pressed by newly established organizations: the JRSO (Jewish Restitution Successor Organization, 1948) for the American zone, and the Jewish Trust Corporation in the British (1949) and French (1950) zones.[66] While the issues were not resolved, and indeed they continued to be contested for many years to come, the Heidelberg conference did establish an umbrella organization of Jewish communities in the new Germany. It quickly developed into the Central Council (*Zentralrat*) of Jews in Germany, an organization that, recognizing both the diversity of its membership and the ruptures of recent history, tellingly did not refer to "German Jews" in its name.[67] A year and a half later, on Sunday, December 17, 1950, the Central Committee of Liberated Jews held its last meeting in the Deutsches Museum. The Jewish DP era was officially closed, even as control of the remaining two camps passed into the hands of German authorities and more DPs were joining local German-Jewish Gemeinden.

By 1950, Jewish visitors were noting with palpable regret and concern "the almost complete normality" that had been restored to a rapidly prospering West Germany, while Jews were still displaced and austerity continued in European victor nations, notably Great Britain. Jews continued to bemoan the perceived failures of denazification, such as the restoration of former party members to public office and the infuriating general absence of "public conscience." Ironically, it often seemed that those who were least "guilty," such as Kogon, were most willing to accept responsibility, while the great majority of Germans remained awash in self-pitying "moral obstinacy." They obdurately remembered their own victimization but, as an embittered Jewish envoy reported in 1950, forgot the crimes they claimed not to have noticed while they were happening.[68] In one biting satire, a DP leader suggested that it was so hard to find Nazis in Germany that perhaps the ever helpful Joint could be called on to provide some![69]

NEW ANTISEMITISM

The putative absence of Nazis notwithstanding, Jewish officials in the Federal Republic were kept busy protesting the ever more obvious "neo" antisemitism. They had already begun to identify this tendency shortly after the defeat of the Nazis' racial state, but once the mass of Jewish DPs had departed, it seemed to intensify. Germans were even more likely to perceive those still there not as victims of persecution but as "asocial" and "homeless" foreigners, "parasites" on West Germany's developing economy and efforts to integrate millions of ethnic German refugees.[70] In 1946, Jewish relief officials suspected that traumatized DPs were inclined to "frequently see anti-semitism where it may not exist."[71] After 1948, however, most were forced to agree with the ever outspoken Auerbach when he remarked, "The antisemitism in Germany hardly needs to be exaggerated because it is sufficiently present."[72]

As sympathy and memory faded (to the degree that it had ever existed), familiar stereotypes about financial and real estate speculation, endangerment of youth and women in bars owned or managed by DPs, prostitution and black market dealing, and filth and disorder became more common and acceptable. The first year of the Federal Republic saw a wave of cemetery desecrations. The now fully empowered German police, determined to safeguard the new currency reform, routinely raided locales where Jewish black marketeers were thought to congregate. German officials, partly freed from American disciplinary control, were now more apt simply to deny any charges of antisemitism resulting from such actions, insisting that they were merely enforcing law and order. In a particularly blatant statement, preserved in DP files, and using vocabulary that would have been entirely familiar to anyone who had lived through the Third Reich, local officials in Bamberg in southern Germany, anxious to prevent any settlement of Jewish DPs near ethnic German refugees, preemptively declared in 1950, "We know that in certain circles our position against the DPs is seen as reviving antisemitism." Absolutely not, they self-righteously contended: "None of us are plagued by such thoughts, but the population is justifiably defending itself against people who feel comfortable in dirt and vermin and therefore constitute a dangerous site of infection."[73] Since it was in fact not quite proper to attack Jews as Jews, they were instead criticized as "foreigners" or as "certain circles." They were labeled as outsiders in a kind of extraterritoriality that the DPs—and for that matter virtually all Jews living in Germany— would, in different but quite functional ways, also claim. Indeed, there should be no doubt that the philosemitism or shamed silence that tabooized anti-Jewish acts or utterances—attitudes often attributed to postwar Germany—not only coexisted with, but were often overwhelmed by, a strong and entirely acceptable antisemitism. Even if it was clothed as resentment of, and outrage over, all manner of perceived shady dealings and social irresponsibility by especially East European Jews, and even if the explicit references to "race" had shifted to groups defined by skin color, especially African-Americans, antisemitism was still clearly legible in a language of Volk, hygiene, and xenophobia that drew from both pre-Nazi and Nazi terminology and practice.[74]

DPs and Jewish organizations were, however, quick to react to such egregious incidents, as indeed were some German politicians and civic groups. At the same time, the JDC especially, which remained the major Jewish group responsible for DP welfare, fretted about how simultaneously to counter such prejudices and (with the departure of many leaders, young people, and families) the increasingly disorganized everyday reality of DP life that seemed sometimes to confirm them. In August 1949, shortly after the Heidelberg conference, Munich's liberal *Süddeutsche Zeitung* printed an article quoting approvingly McCloy's statement that "the gauge of the democratic regeneration of Germany would be the development of a new attitude on the part of the Germans toward the Jews." A week later, four letters to the editor, three of them supportive, were published, without any editorial comment. The fourth, filled with antisemitic vitriol, was signed Adolf Bleibtreu (Adolf stay faithful). With an address listed as Palestina Street, it stated, "I am employed by the *Amis* and many of them have already said that they forgive us everything except for one thing and that is that we did not gas them all, for now America is blessed with them." When the paper appeared, a crowd of, depending on the source, several hundred or thousand DPs, taking the

Fig. 6.2. Over 1,000 Jews demonstrate against antisemitic violence and German police action, Munich, 1949.

letter as a kind of editorial opinion, decided to march on the newspaper office. Interestingly, a second spontaneous protest of DPs targeted the JDC offices. In response to these demonstrations, German police on horseback charged the crowd, which fought back with sticks and stones and set a German police bus on fire. This riotous behavior provoked the arrival of more police reinforcements, swinging their clubs and reportedly shooting into the air. JDC officials and a U.S. Army chaplain managed to calm the crowd, but order was finally restored only when American MPs—still exercising authority—ordered the Munich police officers to leave the scene.[75]

As the uproar at the JDC office indicated, much survivor anger was directed not toward Germans but against the Jewish relief agencies that supported and tried to control them. When JDC officials attempted to mediate between angry DPs and aggressive German police, they were sometimes rewarded with "pitched battles" and unruly sit-ins at their offices by their fellow Jews. Perhaps Jewish officials provided a safer but also more intimate target for venting the bitterness and frustration of those who still had no home, no clear future, and no possible adequate compensation for their staggering losses. The belligerence of the Jewish crowd suggests a sort of delayed gratification; under the protective if exasperated eye of the American military and international Jewry, survivors

were able to engage in assertive resistance without fear of severe consequence.[76] These confrontations were intensely embarrassing, of course,
for the JDC, which had to invest a good deal of public relations energy
in explaining incidents to their donors back in the United States while
also pressuring German authorities not to overreact with more violence.
The early years of the Federal Republic thus set the postwar pattern for
Jewish institutions; they would spend much of their time on managing
a volatile constituency and on documenting and protesting antisemitic
incidents, rather than on building community or religious identity.

THE "HARD CORE"

By late 1948, about 30,000 Jewish DPs remained in Germany; by 1953
perhaps half that number. Some 2,500–3,000 had emigrated but then returned, mostly from Israel between 1949 and 1953.[77] This so-called "hard
core," which so agitated both German and Jewish authorities, stubbornly
resisted either resettlement outside Germany or integration within. Some
were successfully pursuing economic opportunities that had first been
opened via the black or gray market; many were simply too sick or exhausted to move out of the protective DP camp confines. In June 1950,
only four camps with 9,000 residents—the sick, the recalcitrant, and,
most uncomfortably, returnees from Israel—were still operating. Landsberg closed on October 15, 1950; Feldafing on May 31, 1951. Many of
Feldafing's remaining 1,585 residents moved to Föhrenwald in Wolfratshausen near Munich, the very last haven for the "hard core." The IRO,
which had taken over from UNRRA in 1947, was replaced by the
UNHCR, the United Nations High Commissioner for Refugees, and formal authority for the DPs in Germany, including those living in Föhrenwald, was passed to the Federal German government. These Jews, no
longer DPs but rather "homeless foreigners," were now officially the responsibility of the Germans and not the international community. The
Bavarian state government moved to restore the Feldafing villas to their
German owners; the fairy-tale Elmau castle in the Bavarian Alps was returned to its eccentric, denazified owner.[78]

Many American Jewish supporters probably agreed with Abraham
Hyman, who had so energetically defended the Landsberg rioters, when
he reflected: "No group of Dps had suffered as much as the Jewish survivors. On the other hand, no group of post–World War II refugees had as
much attention and devotion lavished on them as the Jewish Dps."[79] Joint
workers worried that they had created a population on "welfare" that
did not want to leave the dubious but real comfort and safety of the
camps. These survivors were unwilling and/or unable to face the economic and psychological rigors either of emigration or integration into

an emerging West German society, which made no secret of its desire to rid itself of the newly imposed obligation of caring for Jewish refugees in addition to the millions of German expellees and returned prisoners of war who required assistance.

The JDC files are filled with dramatic stories of angry, sometimes even violent, confrontations with headstrong DPs. JDC officials continually worried about how best to deal with entrenched, supposedly corrupt, DP camp committees, especially in Föhrenwald, and camp residents who obstinately refused to leave. Those who had not left by 1949 were the ones least likely to leave, either because they could not or because they would not. Further complicating matters, very few were willing explicitly to forswear emigration plans, creating the often cited postwar Jewish population always perched on "packed suitcases," and most comfortable in the air somewhere between New York, Tel Aviv, and Frankfurt.[80] Irritated JDC officials complained that "the DPs have no notion of reality." Even their offers to pay all transport costs and to waive the already generous baggage allowances could not dislodge the "hard core." One man, heedless of how difficult it was to garner an immigration visa, even announced that he had not yet decided whether to grace the United States with his presence: "I'm not making any other plans until I see whether Stevenson is elected."[81] Some claimed they still needed to make money and buy up more furniture and supplies in Germany before decamping for a harsher life in Israel; some shelved plans to emigrate at the last minute when German reparations plans, which needed to be pursued on-site, were announced; some still hoped for a visa to the United States that had been denied them because of ill health or a criminal record. In some cases, women with babies wanted time to raise children in familiar and easier conditions, and young people wanted to complete studies or apprenticeships. Others were simply too exhausted to contemplate another move. And, the JDC acknowledged, quite a few, especially single men, were attached to German women and the "easy" life in Germany and feared a harder life abroad.[82]

Sex and money, the two temptations of postwar German life, figured prominently in the difficult discussions about the "hard core." By 1954, the JDC reported, "approximately one-third of all married women" in Föhrenwald DP camp, the last of the camps, which held the most intractable of the DPs, were non-Jewish. This number did not even include those German women who had already converted or those living illegally in Föhrenwald as domestic workers or "camp followers." Adding to the ill will toward the returnees from Israel was the fact that these men were deemed the most likely to have taken up with German women.[83] By the early 1950s, therefore, numerous factors had coalesced to hold some Jews in Germany. The disruptions of the currency reform had eased, and the economic miracle was taking hold in West Germany. The promise of financial compensation beckoned as the German parliament, prodded by Konrad Adenauer, passed reparations (*Wiedergutmachung*) legislation in 1952. By then, some 2,000 Jews had returned to Germany from Israel. Despite the formal prohibition on travel to Germany, Israel had no interest in preventing the departure of troublemakers and apostates who preferred life in a semisovereign West Germany, where, still subject to U.S. and JDC support and surveillance, they could rely on the reluctant but assured aid and protection of Jewish agencies and the young West German government. Of these "returnees," 690 had settled in Föhrenwald. The JDC was left to tear its hair out over how to deal with the "baffling" problem of both the DPs who refused to leave in the first place and those who, most ironically and embarrassingly, illegally slipped back in from Israel.[84]

JDC and other relief workers had worried from the outset about the development of an inevitably corrupting refugee subculture dependent on the creative manipulation of both welfare aid and the German black and gray markets. Those Jewish DPs who remained in or returned to Germany after the state of Israel opened its doors to all refugee Jews found little sympathy from the same Jewish relief groups that had supported them in the early postwar years. In 1952, when U.S. chaplain George Vida returned to Munich, the DP world was, he felt, a very different, sadder, and more pathetic place than it had been when he left in 1946. Now it was marked by the awkward presence of returnees, renewed antisemitism, and scandals around the administration of restitution funds. The Möhlstrasse, the former vibrant, volatile, and "proud" center of DP life, headquarters of HIAS (Hebrew Immigrant Aid Society), the JDC, and the Central Committee of Liberated Jews, was now the "sad and shabby" refuge of the hard-core remainders. Vida described his visit to the Munich city jail, where some one hundred Jewish men, illegal returnees from Israel, were detained. It was all sordid and depressing: the Jews who fled back to the land of the murderers, resorting to illegal entry to circumvent the rules of their own state, which had stamped their Israeli passports invalid for entry to Germany; the German authorities who dutifully locked them up; the Protestant orphanage that (in an eerie reminder of the fate of some "hidden children" during the Holocaust) benevolently took in their children.[85]

RESENTMENTS AND REPARATIONS: THE AUERBACH CASE
   AND THE JEWISH PRESENCE

The resentment of Germans and the frustration of relief officials hardened with time. Remaining Jews, supposedly privileged by JDC "supplements," served as an unwelcome reminder of Nazi crimes and occupation authority. Germans became increasingly and unapologetically vocal about the "asocial" and criminal character of the remaining "hard core." Defeated Germans seemed to have regained their former arrogance without losing their sense of entitlement as victims. At the same time JDC workers, who had become more sympathetic to the Zionist aspirations of their charges, made no secret of their frustration with the endless demands and apparently undisciplined behavior of those Jewish DPs who did not act on those aspirations. The DPs who remained were perceived as either gangsters and opportunists or demoralized victims, incapable of or unwilling to adjust to the normal life that was now expected. The JDC clashed with the Central Committee and its successor groups in the Gemeinden (especially in Berlin), which it reluctantly continued to support quite generously. Representatives of Jews living in Germany wanted more control and autonomy in their internal affairs without relinquishing the JDC's financial support. The JDC agreed that more self-sufficiency was a worthy and necessary goal, but it did not trust Jews still residing in Germany to handle their financial affairs and aid supplements properly. All these problems were exacerbated by the disdain of most of international Jewry for Jews living in Germany, on the one hand, and the resentment of Germans about the perceived material benefits and political protection that were accorded this "outsider" population on the other hand. Ironically, this dislike was often couched in unflattering comparisons between the "good" German Jews who seemed to have mysteriously vanished and the "bad" Eastern European Jews who had taken their place.[86]

By 1950, fellow Jews expected Jewish survivors to have left Germany. The World Jewish Congress expressed its view in no uncertain terms in a stark letter to all members of its Executive Committee reminding Jews that "the dictate of history is not to forget." The letter added:

Concerning everything connected with the question of helping Jews take root again in Germany, our answer must be completely negative. We reject as utterly irrelevant the argument that the World Jewish Congress cannot assume the role of a final judge and decide whether or not a Jew shall remain in Germany. We neither have nor seek any power of coercion. We merely say that if Jews in small or larger groups choose to continue to live among the people who are responsible for the slaughter of six millions of our brothers, that is their affair. The World Jewish Congress is no longer concerned with these Jews.

Unwilling to consider the possibility that "choose" might be a problematic concept in these cases, the majority of the international Jewish community, having contributed a good deal of energy and funds to the surviving remnant, now declared that they would in a sense excommunicate those who were unable or unwilling to leave the "cursed soil" of Germany. Those who stayed were unapologetically called "this vestige of the degredetion [*sic*] of the Jewish people" and had to pay the price: "If a Jew remains in Germany, he no longer has any portion in world Jewry."[87]

These early confrontations around antisemitism and intense debates about the future of Jews in Germany culminated in 1951 with the sensational prosecution in Munich of Bavaria's most prominent survivor, Philipp Auerbach. The brash German-Jewish survivor had, remarkably, become the powerful Bavarian state commissioner for the persecuted, making common cause with DPs and aggressively pursuing reparations and recognition for all Jews in Germany. Auerbach, dubbed the "Caesar of *Wiedergutmachung*" by the German press, was accused in a Munich court of corruption and fraud. Notorious for floating proposals such as the payment of DM 10 to every former KZ inmate for each day of incarceration, his both exposed and mediating position had become increasingly isolated and precarious. He was caught between the conflicting demands of German and East European Jews and between his advocacy for Jews and his employment by the German state. He was ensnared also by his position defending the claims of the Jews living in Germany against international Jewish organizations, such as the Joint and the JRSO, which wanted Jews out of Germany and saw no reason why the "hard-core" remnant of Jews in Germany should become heir to the financial and cultural legacy of a German Jewry now dispersed throughout the globe. One of the many jokes circulating among DPs referred to Auerbach's ambiguous and vulnerable position: Two Jews meet in the much coveted sleeper car of the express train from Munich to Paris and inquire of each other how they managed to secure seats. "Philipp Auerbach," says the German Jew, referring to the state commissioner's relentless efforts for restitution, but the Polish Jew has an even better rejoinder, "Philip Morris," alluding to the power of cigarettes as black market currency.[88]

Auerbach was convicted on lesser charges, including—ironically for a Germany always obsessed with honorifics—having illegitimately granted himself a *Doktor* title. In August 1952 he was sentenced to a fine and two and a half years in prison. Auerbach, who had, as numerous historians have pointed out, not always pursued his mission of political denazification and financial compensation "by the book," denounced the "terror sentence" of this new "Dreyfus case" and committed suicide. The story of his rise and fall remains one of the most dramatic and least well-researched moments in the early postwar history of Germans and Jews. Auerbach was given an impressive funeral in Munich's Jewish cemetery, and, after four years of investigation, a commission of the Bavarian parliament (*Landtag*) concluded that he should be "completely rehabilitated."[89] Journalist Hans Habe drew the bitter conclusion that "thus an unsympathetic and controversial but innocent man became the first victim of Nazi justice seven years after our victory over Hitler's Germany."[90]

Despite the official line and precisely because of the continuing dangers of antisemitism, the drive for reparations, and the undeniable existence of Jewish communities, the JDC did not desert the Jews who, for whatever reason, remained in this "poignant, painful and perplexing" situation.[91] Even after Auerbach's fall, DPs continued to benefit not only from the ongoing JDC supplements but from the relatively generous if grudging welfare provisions that were dispersed by the West German government as part of its general program for absorbing (mostly German) refugees from the East. These programs produced temptations, which only reinforced Jews' persistent and exaggerated reputation as masters of speculation and corruption. In late 1951, JDC officials told the tale of one Jewish businessman in Bavarian Regensburg who repeatedly took advantage of a government program that offered 5,000 marks incentive for the employment of refugees and allowed them to be fired only if another refugee was hired in their place, creating a pyramid scheme that apparently netted him the tidy sum of DM 200,000.[92]

JDC records document the American Jewish organization's growing exasperation and even desperation about such incidents among the "hard core." Joint officials in Munich faced riots and physical assaults on its workers. They saw themselves operating "literally in a state of siege" in the face of sit-ins at their headquarters in Munich, and what they finally concluded was "the almost insane atmosphere that has developed in Föhrenwald." Despite all their troubles, however, they were resigned to the fact that the Joint could and would never renege on its commitment to its annoying brethren. Jewish representatives continued to defend the (former) DPs to the federal German and Bavarian state governments, rescue from detention returnees who had entered Germany illegally from Israel, and provide welfare supplements. They continued to push emigration, while acknowledging that some Jews would remain regardless of all moral pressures or financial incentives. The DP holdouts in Germany were equally frustrated by their dependence on the Joint's grudging and, they felt, condescending charity. But they also took full advantage of that unhappy but steadfast assistance. Well aware of the Joint's dependence on American donors to fund its extensive international relief projects and perfectly willing to exploit both German and Jewish eagerness to close the camp, the "racketeering" camp committee successfully instigated bad publicity in the United States about the JDC's insensitivity to survivors. The Föhrenwalder representatives, whom the JDC had come to regard as not only entirely unreasonable but virtually criminal, essentially demanded a generous financial payout as an inducement to vacate a site that had been a Jewish community in the heart of Bavaria for over a decade.[93] When both the Germans and the Jewish Claims Conference refused demands to pay each resident several thousand DM as incentive (and compensation) for leaving the camp, more clashes with German police and JDC officials ensued. As Ron Zweig bluntly concluded in his history of the Jewish Claims Conference, Föhrenwald had become the symbol of "Everything that was problematic about these victims of Nazism."

An unapologetically hostile version of these events published in a local (*Heimat*) history of the *Judenlager Föhrenwald bei Wolfratshausen* as recently as 1982 confirms Zweig's assessment that, by the mid-1950s, the struggle over the fate of the last Jewish DP camp had led to "the worst stereotypes" being "confirmed for a large part of the German public who in any case believed that the reparations process had been an act of extortion."[94] From the perspective of local Germans, many of whom had, as we have seen, always perceived the Jewish camps as unjustly favored centers of crime and disorder, the DPs who had dug in at Föhrenwald were now acting like "state pensioners," entitled to generous welfare, including free room and board, from both the government and the JDC. As the local historian bitingly remarked, for people who insisted that they were victims unable to work, they were surprisingly energetic in pressing their compensation claims.[95] In fact, when the last Jews left on February 28, 1957, they had negotiated a settlement whereby the JDC contributed $650,000 toward emigration costs and the German government DM 3 million for resettlement—payable, however, only after the camp was truly vacated. In the end, two hundred apartments were rented in Munich for those unwilling or unable to leave Germany.[96]

In a telling example of the multiple continuities of personnel and attitude that crossed the "zero hour" divide, it was the Hamburg physician and population policy expert Hans Harmsen who quickly commissioned a study of the former Föhrenwalders. Like Friedrich Burgdörfer, who had produced the 1948 memorandum on the disturbingly high birthrate of these "foreigners" in postwar Bavaria, and so many other German officials in charge of health and social welfare (and indeed restitution) in the postwar years, Harmsen had successfully—and relatively seamlessly—pursued his practical and research interests in racial and social hygiene through three German regimes. A conservative sex reformer in the Weimar Republic, he was a sterilization advocate in the Third Reich, and then became a prominent demographer and "social hygienist" in the Federal Republic and eventual cofounder of German Planned Parenthood (*Pro Familia*).[97]

Indicating how much East European Jewish DPs had transmuted from identification as survivors to "homeless foreigners," the study, out "of consideration" for the subjects, did not ask questions about persecution. "KZ" experiences were elicited only if the interviewees brought them up; this reticence was perhaps also a reflection of the fact that many of these DPs had spent the war in the Soviet Union, an ambiguous and convoluted fate that many evidently found even harder to talk about (and seriously listen to) than direct persecution by the Nazis.[98] Almost despite themselves and their focus on the 1950s present, however, Harmsen's researchers collected testimonies about Jewish life during the war, including flight to the Soviet Union, service in the Red Army, and lengthy periods of hiding. Ironically, their interviews provide, in some ways, a more complex and differentiated picture of the Föhrenwald "hard core" than the impatient JDC reports. Many of those who remained were old and single. Most young families had left, and some families that had finally been permitted to emigrate to the United States had left behind members who were too ill to travel or had been denied entry because of tuberculosis infection.

Following prevalent postwar "liberal" wisdom, the "social hygiene research report," published under Harmsen's aegis in 1960, urged the West German government to do precisely what the separate Jewish DP camps had tried to avoid, namely, to "disperse" the refugees to prevent any kind of "ghetto formation" in so-called "foreigners districts." The study acknowledged that this "suddenly liberated slave Volk" would find Germany to be a "most unsuitable" place for integration. Yet it concluded, in carefully abstract but optimistic terms, that despite their "ineradicable (*unausrottbaren*) animosity toward the former oppressor," the Föhrenwalders' "existential fear" about living among a people whose government had persecuted them had been "overcome." Dire predictions about disorderly behavior and violent confrontations had not been fulfilled. From the perspective of these German professional observers, despite continuing antisemitic incidents such as cemetery desecrations, the pragmatic coexistence and interaction that had in fact characterized Jewish/German relations during the DP era continued. "The majority lives in peace with the Germans, albeit without much further contact or friendship," they noted, adding, however, that "it remains the mission of the German neighbors to try to live in peace and with personal tolerance with these people who have, it is true, other peculiarities than themselves." The Jews were praised, with no little surprise, for having tried to "overcome their prejudices against the Germans, and hav[ing] proven by their actions that, despite bad health and difficult conditions, they have succeeded in finding a place in the work and business world."[99] At the same time almost a third—perceived as too many by the German researchers but actually rather on the low side from the perspective of Jews abroad—still maintained their packed-suitcases stance and continued to plan for (or at least contemplate) eventual emigration.

The camps closed in the early 1950s—the last, Föhrenwald, in February 1957, just as the last German prisoners of war were returning from the Soviet Union and two years after the Federal Republic had attained full sovereignty. The Jewish DP era, which had been such a significant but, in most historical accounts, strangely invisible part of postwar German history, was over. But the small and fragile communities (Gemeinden), led by the *Zentralrat*, that took over Jewish life were substantially marked by the presence of those DPs who remained. Membership was divided between about 52 percent DP and 48 percent German Jews, although it was, as we would expect, very unevenly distributed according to place (in Berlin 71.4 percent were German, in Bavaria only 6.3 percent in 1949).[100] By the late 1950s, some 25,000 Jews lived in West Germany, but for the most part, still with the (by now often symbolic) packed suitcases close at hand and with many familial and emotional connections around the world, especially in Israel.[101] The sense of transience that had facilitated everyday encounters among Jewish survivors and defeated Germans during the DP period continued to shape the lives of the minority of Jews who stayed. They participated in German life while denying any real attachment.

Thus, the peculiar ambivalent, sometimes contradictory, orchestration of collective suspicion and individual contact, of suspicious distance and pragmatic coexistence, established at a point when there were several hundred thousand Jewish displaced persons in Germany, continued into the early years of the Federal Republic. The pattern was not so different for most German Jews, and indeed set the model for the next decades of postwar relations. The fall of the Berlin Wall in 1989, the collapse of the Soviet bloc, and the reunification of Germany in 1990 once again fundamentally changed the situation and initiated a new problematic and still evolving revival of Jewish life in a united Germany within the European community. Indeed, Siegmund Weltlinger's prediction that Berlin would once again become a center for Jews migrating from the East turned out to be correct. But despite the fast growth of the Jewish community in the Federal Republic, mostly driven by emigration from the former Soviet Union, and the astonishingly enduring preoccupation with the history of National Socialism, World War II, and the Holocaust, with Germans as victims and perpetrators and with Jews as victims and survivors, both Germans and Jews have persisted in assiduously forgetting their brief and intense common—both joint and separate—postwar history. In Landsberg, only the efforts of the former American-Jewish DP camp commander Irving Heymont forced the placement, in 1989, of a plaque marking the site of the DP camp; he initiated the marker, and he paid for it.[102] There is to this day, as far as I can tell, nothing in Feldafing that marks its history as the site of the first Jewish DP camp in Germany, arguably one of the birthplaces of the state of Israel and of the postwar Jewish community not only in Germany but also in the United States and other nations where European Jewish survivors of World War II and the Holocaust made new homes.

Abbreviations in Notes

AJDCA	American Jewish Joint Distribution Committee Archives, New York
AJHSA	American Jewish Historical Society Archives, New York
BAB (Sapmo)	Bundesarchiv Berlin, Stiftung Archiv der Parteien und Massenorganisationen der DDR
CJA	Stiftung "Neue Synagoge Berlin–Centrum Judaicum" Archive
DFD	Demokratischer Frauenbund Deutschlands (Democratic Women's League of Germany)
DPG	Displaced Persons Camps and Centers in Germany, Records 1945–1952, YIVO
JMB	Jewish Museum, Berlin
LAB	Landesarchiv Berlin
LAZ	Zeitgeschichtliche Sammlung (Contemporary History Collection), LAB
LBI	Leo Baeck Institute, New York
LWS	Leo W. Schwarz Collection, YIVO
NL	Nachlass (personal papers)
OFP	Oberfinanzpräsidium Brandenburg, Staatsarchiv Brandenburg, Potsdam
OMGUS	Office of Military Government (United States)
UNRRAA	United Nations Relief and Rehabilitation Administration Archives, New York
USHMM	United States Holocaust Memorial Museum, Washington, D.C.
YIVO	YIVO Institute for Jewish Research, New York

A Note on Citations

For the convenience of readers who want to look further into the historiography discussed in the introduction, the first citation of any work in the notes to the introduction includes the full publication details. Thereafter, throughout the remaining chapters, works that are listed in the bibliography receive only shortened citations in the notes.

Notes

INTRODUCTION
Entangled Histories and Close Encounters

1. Frank Stern, "The Historic Triangle: Occupiers, Germans, and Jews in Postwar Germany," *Tel Aviver Jahrbuch für deutsche Geschichte* 19 (1990): 47–76. Statistical data are inexact and bewildering, largely because of change over time, inconsistencies in categorizations among those collecting data, and the difficulties of counting a highly mobile and sometimes illegal population. See chapter 4, especially n. 11, for further discussion of numbers.

2. American Military Government officer John Maginnis referred on February 27, 1947, to "a record of successful international adjustments and sympathetic understanding." John J. Maginnis, *Military Government Journal: Normandy to Berlin*, ed. Robert A. Hart (Amherst: University of Massachusetts Press, 1971), 345. Julian Bach, *America's Germany: An Account of the Occupation* (New York: Random House, 1946), called Berlin a "great test tube of international cooperation," 5.

3. Senat Berlin, ed., *Berlin: Kampf um Freiheit und Selbstverwaltung 1945–1946* (Berlin: Heinz Spitzing Verlag, 1961), 10. Col. Frank Howley uses the same terms in his *Berlin Command* (New York: Putnam, 1950), 8. Indeed, the ubiquitousness and repetitiveness of certain phrases and expressions is striking.

4. Estimates of refugee numbers in the summer and fall of 1945 vary greatly, depending on who is counting whom how and when. In his *Military Government Journal*, Maginnis refers, pp. 278–279, to 15,000 daily. Eugene Davidson, in *The Death and Life of Germany: An Account of the American Occupation* (New York: Alfred A. Knopf, 1959), 77, counted 25,000–30,000 refugees daily. See also Landesarchiv Berlin (LAB) OMGUS 4/24–1/4 for discussions of efforts to keep refugees out of the beleaguered city. In August, the total population was counted at 2,784,112 (1,035,463 male, 1,748,649 female) vs. 4,332,000 in 1939. The male population was reduced by half, the female by a quarter. For every 100 men there were 169 women, vs. a ratio of 100 to 119 in 1939. Figures from *Berliner Zeitung* 1:91 (August 29, 1945), 1, citing the *Berliner Volks, Berufs und Arbeitsstättenzählung*, August 12, 1945.

5. By the end of the war, foreigners composed almost a quarter of the wage labor force in Germany. Mark Roseman, "World War II and Social Change in Germany," in *Total War and Social Change*, ed. Arthur Marwick (London: Macmillan, 1988), 63, 71. For a vivid picture of the immediate postwar period in Berlin, see the many microfilms in the Zeitgeschichtliche Sammlung (LAZ) of the Landesarchiv Berlin (LAB).

6. See chapter 3 on Berlin for discussion of these imprecise statistics.

7. For use of the term, see Leonard Krieger, "The Inter-Regnum in Germany: March–August 1945," *Political Science Quarterly* 64 (1949): 507–532. Many sources describe Berlin in 1945/46 as existing in an "in-between" time; for example, Karla Höcker speaks of a *Schwebezustand* (suspended time) in *Beschreibung eines Jahres: Berliner Notizen 1945* (Berlin: arani, 1984).

8. Ruth Andreas-Friedrich, *Schauplatz Berlin: Tagebuchaufzeichnungen 1945 bis 1948* (Frankfurt/Main: Suhrkamp, 1984); Curt Riess, *Berlin Berlin, 1945–1953* (Berlin: Non Stop Bücherei, 1953), 174. The notion of Berlin in ruins as a kind of surreal theatrical or operatic stage set was invoked by many observers—and filmmakers—at war's end; see discussion in chapter 1.

9. Hans Habe, *Aftermath*, trans. Richard F. Hansen (New York: Viking, 1947), 185.

10. See, for example, Frank Stern, "Antagonistic Memories: The Post-War Survival and Alienation of Jews and Germans," in *Memory and Totalitarianism, Volume I, International Yearbook of Oral History and Life Stories*, ed. Luisa Passerini (New York: Oxford University Press, 1992), 21–43. The term reparations cited here is both problematical and useful because it is used in so many various contexts. It specifically refers to nation-to-nation payments, associated for example with post–World War I arrangements; as a general term, however, it also denotes a nation's or people's effort to make amends or provide compensation for wrongs or injuries inflicted, as expressed in the problematically named *Weidergutmachung* (literally to "make good again") imposed by the Allies (in different ways) on defeated Germans and formally instituted by the Federal Republic of Germany, starting in 1952, as a program of material restitution and "compensation for individual suffering, loss of life, health, and liberty." In practice, historians and legal experts dealing with postwar Germany have used the term reparations rather broadly (and in relation to, sometimes interchangeably with, restitution, indemnification, and compensation). In this book, I have followed that general practice, endeavoring to use the term "reparations" (and also "compensation") in the general sense outlined above and to refer specifically to restitution in regard to issues of clear material compensation. For examples of usage, see Ron Zweig, *German Reparations and the Jewish World: A History of the Claims Conference*, 2nd ed. (London: Frank Cass, 1998); Menachem Z. Rosensaft and Joana D. Rosensaft, "A Measure of Justice: The Early History of German-Jewish Reparations," Leo Baeck Institute, New York, Occasional Paper #4. For the current Federal Republic definition, cited above, see for example the website of the German Information Services.

11. There are an overwhelming amount of possible sources including archival records of the American Military Government as well as those of the British, French, and Soviet zones; German local and provincial authorities; the Central Committee of Liberated Jews as well as individual DP camp administrative records; the local Jewish communities (*Gemeinden*); the United Nations Relief and Rehabilitation Administration (UNRRA); American Joint Distribution Committee (AJDC) and other Jewish and non-Jewish nongovernmental relief agencies. See the archives of UNRRA, AJDC, and YIVO Institute for Jewish Research in New York City, the United States Holocaust Memorial Museum in Washington, D.C. (especially its extensive oral history, photo, and film collections), and Yad

Vashem and the Central Zionist Archives in Jerusalem (to name just a few of the most prominent). Nonarchival sources include published and unpublished diaries and memoirs as well as extensive accounts in the German, American, and Jewish press. Especially important and mostly unmined are the Yiddish DP press, the local and national German press, and *Stars and Stripes*, the paper produced and read by U.S. troops. The archive of current historiography and memoir literature, films, and exhibits is growing so rapidly that I have surely only begun to exhaust possible sources.

12. See, for example, George Woodbridge, *UNRRA: The History of the United Nations Relief and Rehabilitation Administration*, prepared by a special staff under the direction of George Woodbridge, chief historian of UNRRA, in three volumes, vol. 3 (New York: Columbia University Press, 1950); Louise Holborn, *The International Refugee Organization: A Specialized Agency of the United Nations; Its History and Work, 1946–1952* (London: Oxford University Press, 1956); and Malcolm J. Proudfoot, *European Refugees, 1939–52: A Study in Forced Population Movement* (Evanston, Ill.: Northwestern University Press, 1956). As Daniel Cohen has pointed out, "the significance of DPs was amply obvious to migration scholars in the 1940s and 1950s," many of whom were former "field workers and international civil servants" who had themselves worked for UNRRA and its successor organization IRO (International Refugee Organizaion, 1947–1952). See Daniel Cohen, "Remembering Post-War Displaced Persons: From Omission to Resurrection," in *Enlarging European Memory: Migration Movements in Historical Perspective*, ed. Mareike König and Rainer Ohliger (Ostfildern: Thorbecke Verlag, 2006), 87–97, and idem, "Naissance d'une Nation: les personnes déplacées de l'après-guerre européen," *Genèses* 38 (March 2000): 56–78. See also Pieter Lagrou, *The Legacy of Occupation: Patriotic Memory and National Recovery in Western Europe, 1945–1965* (Cambridge: Cambridge University Press, 2000).

13. Popular and historical interest in the Jewish DP experience since the political and memory shifts after 1989 is reflected in several exhibitions, conferences, and publications. A conference in Munich in 1995, convened in part by scholars and writers who had been born or raised in Föhrenwald or other DP camps near Munich, launched the German exhibit "Ein Leben aufs neu—Jüdische 'Displaced Persons' auf deutschem Boden 1945–1948." See also "Rebirth after the Holocaust: The Bergen-Belsen Displaced Persons Camp, 1945–1950," exhibit at the B'nai B'rith Klutznick National Jewish Museum, Washington, D.C., 2000, and, on a larger scale, the exhibit catalogue *Life Reborn: Jewish Displaced Persons, 1945–1951; Conference Proceedings*, ed. Menachem Z. Rosensaft (Washington, D.C.: United States Holocaust Memorial Museum, 2000), and the museum's 2001 calendar with photographs and text from that exhibit, as well as the documentary film *The Long Journey Home* (Simon Wiesenthal Center, Los Angeles, 1997).

14. General histories of displaced persons in postwar Europe include Proudfoot, *European Refugees*; Jacques Vernant, *The Refugee in the Postwar World* (New Haven: Yale University Press, 1953); John George Stoessinger, *The Refugee and the World Community* (Minneapolis: University of Minnesota Press, 1956); and Mark Wyman, *DPs: Europe's Displaced Persons, 1945–1951* (Ithaca: Cornell University Press, 1998). Basic political histories of Jewish DPs include

Yehudah Bauer, *Out of the Ashes* (New York: Pergamon Press, 1989); Michael Marrus, *The Unwanted: European Refugees in the Twentieth Century* (New York: Oxford University Press, 1985); and Abram L. Sachar, *Redemption of the Unwanted* (New York: St. Martin's Press, 1983). For a detailed political history of Jewish DPs, see Zeev W. Mankowitz, *Life between Memory and Hope: The Survivors of the Holocaust in Occupied Germany* (Cambridge: Cambridge University Press, 2002).

15. See the important comparative work by Laura Hilton, "Prisoners of Peace: Rebuilding Community, Identity and Nationality in Displaced Persons Camps in Germany, 1945–52" (Ph.D. dissertation, Ohio State University, 2001). See also the local study by Anna Marta Holian, "Between National Socialism and Soviet Communism: The Politics of Self-Representation among Displaced Persons in Munich, 1945–1951" (Ph.D. dissertation, University of Chicago, 2005).

16. My thoughts on the "newness" of the field and how surprisingly much we still do not know, and how much of what we think we know needs to be revised, have been substantially influenced by the productive discussions at the July 2005 Scholars' Workshop on Jewish DPs at the United States Holocaust Memorial Museum, Washington, D.C., convened by Avi Patt and Michael Berkowitz, and also including Boaz Cohen, Laura Hilton, Laura Jockusch, Tamar Lewinsky, and David Weinberg.

17. There is a relatively new and constantly growing literature on Jewish survivors in Germany, almost all of it originally (or only) published in German. See Wolfgang Jacobmeyer's pioneering article, "Jüdische Überlebende als 'Displaced Persons': Untersuchungen zur Besatzungspolitik in den deutschen Westzonen und zur Zuwanderung osteuropäischer Juden 1945–1946," *Geschichte und Gesellschaft* 9 (1983): 421–452, and idem, *Vom Zwangsarbeiter zum Heimatlosen Ausländer: Die Displaced Persons in Westdeutschland, 1945–51* (Göttingen: Vandenhoeck & Ruprecht, 1985); Juliane Wetzel, *Jüdisches Leben in München, 1945–1951: Durchgangsstation oder Wiederaufbau?* (Munich: UNI-Druck, 1987); Angelika Königseder and Juliane Wetzel, *Waiting for Hope: Jewish Displaced Persons in Post–World War II Germany* (Evanston, Ill.: Northwestern University Press, 2001; German, 1994); Michael Brenner, *After the Holocaust: Rebuilding Jewish Lives in Postwar Germany* (Princeton: Princeton University Press, 1997; German, 1995); M. Paulus, E. Raim, and G. Zelger, eds., *Ein Ort wie jeder andere: Bilder einer deutschen Kleinstadt, Landsberg 1923–1958* (Reinbek bei Hamburg: Rowohlt, 1995); Susanne Dietrich and Julia Schulze-Wessel, *Zwischen Selbstorganisation und Stigmatisierung: Die Lebenswirklichkeit jüdischer Displaced Persons und die neue Gestalt des Antisemitismus in der deutschen Nachkriegsgesellschaft* (Stuttgart: Klett-Cotta, 1998); Angelika Eder, *Flüchtige Heimat: Jüdische Displaced Persons in Landsberg am Lech, 1945 bis 1950* (Munich: UNI-Druck, 1998); Angelika Königseder, *Flucht nach Berlin: Jüdische Displaced Persons 1945–1948* (Berlin: Metropol, 1998); Fritz Bauer Institut, ed., *Überlebt und Unterwegs: Jüdische Displaced Persons im Nachkriegsdeutschland, Jahrbuch 1997 zur Geschichte und Wirkung des Holocaust* (Frankfurt/M: Campus, 1997); Ruth Gay, *Safe Among the Germans: Liberated Jews After World War II* (New Haven: Yale University Press, 2002); and Eva Kolinsky, *After the Holocaust: Jewish Survivors in Germany after 1945* (London: Pimlico, 2004). On the British

zone, see also Hagit Lavsky, *New Beginnings: Holocaust Survivors in Bergen-Belsen and the British Zone in Germany* (Detroit: Wayne State University Press, 2002); Andreas Lembeck, *Befreit aber nicht in Freiheit: Displaced Persons in Emsland* (Bremen: Temmen, 1997); Patrick Wagner, *Displaced Persons in Hamburg: Stationen einer halbherzigen Integration, 1945 bis 1949* (Hamburg: Dölling und Galitz, 1997); Ursula Büttner, *Not Nach der Befreiung: Die Situation der deutschen Juden in der britischen Besatzungszone 1945 bis 1948* (Hamburg: Landeszentrale für politische Bildung, Hamburg, 1986). Two useful unpublished German theses are Nicholas Yantian, "Studien zum Selbstverständnis der jüdischen 'Displaced Persons' in Deutschland nach dem Zweiten Weltkrieg" (master's thesis, Technical University Berlin, 1994); and Jacqueline Dewell Giere, "Wir sind Unterwegs, Aber Nicht in der Wüste: Erziehung und Kultur in den Jüdischen Displaced Persons-Lagern der amerikanischen Zone im Nachkriegsdeutschland, 1945–1949" (Ph.D. dissertation, Goethe Universität, Frankfurt/M, 1993). A fine and diverse collection of articles can be found in Julius H. Schoeps, ed., *Leben im Land der Täter: Juden im Nachkriegsdeutschland (1945–1952)* (Berlin: Jüdische Verlagsanstalt, 2001). See, most recently, the excellent collection of articles by younger scholars, Susanne Schönborn, ed., *Zwischen Erinnerung und Neubeginn: Zur deutsch-jüdischen Geschichte nach 1945*, with foreword by Michael Brenner (Munich: Martin Meidenbauer, 2006).

18. The liveliest (and most controversial) discussions about Jewish DPs have been conducted in the context of Israeli debates about the treatment of Holocaust survivors in Palestine and Israel and the general revision of the Zionist historiographical narrative. Much of this material is only slowly being translated from Hebrew. See the review essay by Yfaat Weiss, "Die Wiederkehr des Verdrängten: Das jüdische Siedlungsgebiet in Palästina (Jischuw) und die Holocaustüberlebenden in der israelischen Historiographie," *Babylon: Beiträge zur jüdischen Gegenwart* 18 (1998):139–147; also Anita Shapira, "Politics and Collective Memory: The Debate over the 'New Historians' in Israel," *History and Memory* 7:1 (Spring/Summer 1995): 9–40. In translation, see Yosef Grodzinsky, *In the Shadow of the Holocaust: The Struggle Between Jews and Zionists in the Aftermath of World War II* (Common Courage Press: Monroe, Maine, 2005; original in Hebrew, *Human Material of Good Quality—Jews versus Zionists in the DP Camps, Germany, 1945–1951* [Tel Aviv: Hed Artzi, 1988]; Arieh J. Kochavi, *Post-Holocaust Politics: Britain, the United States, and Jewish Refugees, 1945–1948* (Chapel Hill: University of North Carolina Press, 2001; Hebrew, 1992); Lavsky, *New Beginnings*; Yisrael Gutman and Avital Saf, eds., *She'erit Hapletah, 1944–1948: Rehabilitation and Political Struggle; Proceedings of the 6th Yad Vashem International Historical Conference* (Jerusalem: Yad Vashem, 1990); Tom Segev, *The Seventh Million: Israel Confronts the Holocaust* (New York: Henry Holt, 2000; Hebrew, 1991); Shabtai Teveth, *Ben-Gurion and the Holocaust* (New York: Harcourt Brace, 1996); Idith Zertal, *From Catastrophe to Power: Holocaust Survivors and the Emergence of Israel* (Berkeley: University of California Press, 1998); Aviva Halamish, *The Exodus Affair: Holocaust Survivors and the Struggle for Palestine* (Syracuse, N.Y.: Syracuse University Press, 1998); and Hanna Yablonka, *Survivors of the Holocaust: Israel after the War* (New York: New York University Press 1999). See, most importantly, Mankowitz, *Life between Memory*

and Hope. In Hebrew, see also David Engel, *Between Liberation and Flight: Holocaust Survivors in Poland and the Struggle for Leadership, 1944–1946* (Tel Aviv, 1996); Irit Keynan, *Holocaust Survivors and the Emissaries from Eretz-Israel: Germany, 1945–1948* (Tel Aviv: Am Oved, 1996); and Tuvia Friling, *Arrows in the Dark: David Ben-Gurion, the Yishuv Leadership and Rescue Attempts during the Holocaust*, trans. Ora Cummings (Madison: University of Wisconsin Press, 2005).

19. For text of Harrison Report, see appendix to Leonard Dinnerstein, *America and the Survivors of the Holocaust* (New York: Columbia University Press, 1982). See chapter 4 for discussion of the extraordinary collection of letters to family, rabbis, and Jewish organizations sent in response to Rabbi Abraham Klausner's call at military High Holiday services in Munich, September 1945, American Jewish Joint Distribution Committee Archives (AJDCA), New York, files 399 and 399A.

20. This is true for both American and German publications. See notably Dinnerstein, *America and the Survivors*, and Königseder and Wetzel, *Waiting for Hope*. For a blistering critique, see Joseph W. Bendersky, *The "Jewish Threat": Anti-Semitic Politics of the U.S. Army* (New York: Basic Books, 2000), and the highly personal negative view in Robert L. Hilliard, *Surviving the Americans: The Continued Struggle of the Jews after Liberation* (New York: Seven Stories Press, 1997).

21. Atina Grossmann, "A Question of Silence: The Rape of German Women by Occupation Soldiers," *October* (Spring 1995): 43–63, slightly revised in *West Germany under Construction: Politics, Society, and Culture in the Adenauer Era*, ed. Robert G. Moeller (Ann Arbor: University of Michigan Press, 1997), 33–52, and idem, "Trauma, Memory, and Motherhood: Germans and Jewish Displaced Persons in Post-Nazi Germany, 1945–1949," in *Life after Death: Approaches to a Cultural and Social History of Europe during the 1940s and 1950s*, ed. Richard Bessel and Dirk Schumann (Cambridge: Cambridge University Press, 2003), 93–127; an earlier version was published in *Archiv für Sozialgeschichte* 38 (October 1998): 230–254. See also Grossmann, "Victims, Villains, and Survivors: Gendered Perceptions and Self-Perceptions of Jewish Survivors in Postwar Germany," *Journal of the History of Sexuality* 11:1–2 (January/April 2002): 291–318, reprinted in *Sexuality and German Fascism*, ed. Dagmar Herzog (New York: Berghahn, 2005), 291–318.

22. On German victimization, see especially Elizabeth Heineman, "The Hour of the Woman: Memories of Germany's 'Crisis Years' and West German National Identity," *American Historical Review* 101:2 (April 1996): 354–395; Robert G. Moeller, "War Stories: The Search for a Usable Past in the Federal Republic of Germany," *American Historical Review* 101:4 (October 1996): 1008–1048; and Robert G. Moeller, *War Stories: The Search for a Usable Past in the Federal Republic of Germany* (Berkeley: University of California Press, 2001). See also "Stunde Null: Kontinuitäten und Brüche," *Ariadne: Almanach des Archivs der deutschen Frauenbewegung* 27 (May 1995). See discussion in chapters 1 and 2.

23. Moses Moskowitz, "The Germans and the Jews: Postwar Report; The Enigma of German Irresponsibility," *Commentary* 2 (July–December 1946): 7–14.

24. Hannah Arendt, "The Aftermath of Nazi Rule: Report from Germany," *Commentary* 10 (October 1950): 342–343. Here Arendt obviously anticipates Alexander and Margarete Mitscherlich's famous discussion of the German "inability to mourn" in *Die Unfähigkeit zu Trauern* (Munich: Piper, 1967).

25. See for example the extensive coverage in the daily press during fall and winter 1945/46 of Allied war crimes trials, including the Belsen/Auschwitz and Ravensbrück trials in Lüneberg and Hamburg respectively in the British zone, the Dachau trial in the American zone, and the Hadamar Clinic "euthanasia" trial in Nuremberg, culminating in the headline-making Nuremberg trials beginning in November 1945. For Berlin and a representative sampling of reportage in both the Soviet and the American sectors, see especially *Tägliche Rundschau*, *Berliner Zeitung*, and *Der Tagesspiegel*. For a highly problematic analysis of divergent occupier and German interpretations of the war and its aftermath, highlighting German experiences of victimization, see Dagmar Barnouw, *Germany 1945: Views of War and Violence* (Bloomington: University of Indiana Press, 1996).

26. Moeller, *War Stories*, 12. On supposed German silence, see Wolfgang Benz, "Postwar Society and National Socialism: Remembrance, Amnesia, Rejection," *Tel Aviver Jahrbuch für deutsche Geschichte* 19 (1990): 1–12. For revisions of the 1950s "amnesia" argument, see among many others Michael Geyer and Miriam Hansen, "German-Jewish Memory and National Consciousness," in *Holocaust Remembrance: The Shapes of Memory*, ed. Geoffrey H. Hartman (Cambridge, Mass.: Blackwell, 1994), 175–190; Alf Lüdtke, "Coming to Terms with the Past: Illusions of Remembering, Ways of Forgetting Nazism in West Germany," *Journal of Modern History* 65 (September 1993): 542–572; Jeffrey Herf, *Divided Memory: The Nazi Past in the Two Germanys* (Cambridge, Mass.: Harvard University Press, 1997); and Jeffrey K. Olick, *In the House of the Hangman: The Agonies of German Defeat, 1943–1949* (Chicago: University of Chicago Press, 2005).

27. Ursula von Kardorff, *Berliner Aufzeichnungen aus den Jahren 1942 bis 1945*, revised ed. (Munich: Bilderstein, 1962), 287, entry for June 25, 1945.

28. Ernest Renan, "What Is a Nation," in *Becoming National: A Reader*, ed. Geoff Eley and Ronald Grigor Suny (New York: Oxford University Press, 1996), 45.

29. For a useful discussion of the ambiguities and vagueness of the term "nation," see Clifford Geertz, *Die Welt in Stücken: Kultur und Politik am Ende des 20. Jahrhunderts* (Vienna: Passagen Verlag, 1996), 37–67.

30. For the "refugee nation" analysis, see especially Cohen, "Remembering Post-War Displaced Persons." See also Hilton, "Prisoners of Peace," and Holian, "Between National Socialism and Soviet Communism," which discuss Jewish DPs along with other DP groups. These scholars are rethinking post-1945 European history in comparative and transnational terms and stress the role of international organizations established to deal with the DP problem in the shaping of contemporary asylum and emigration policies.

31. On the biblical references from Genesis, First Chronicles, Ezra, and Jeremiah driving the use of the term *She'erit Hapletah* (or its spoken Yiddish variant *sheyres haypleyte*) see, among many brief discussions, Mankowitz, *Life between Memory and Hope* 2–3. Yehudah Bauer cites the biblical term "The rest . . . that were escaped" from I Chronicles 5, 43, in "The Initial Organization of the Holo-

caust Survivors in Bavaria," *Yad Vashem Studies* 8 (1970): 127. Abraham J. Peck, "Jewish Survivors of the Holocaust in Germany: Revolutionary Vanguard or Remnants of a Destroyed People?" *Tel Aviver Jahrbuch für deutsche Geschichte* 19 (1990): 35, refers to the Jewish remnant that survived the Assyrans. See also David Rosenthal, "*She'erit ha-Pleytah*, The Remnant That Was Saved: Recalling the Liberation," *Midstream* 36:6 (1990): 25–28. For fuller explication, see Dan Michman, "On the Definition of the 'She'erit Hapletah,' " in *Holocaust Historiography: A Jewish Perspective; Conceptualizations, Terminology, Approaches and Fundamental Issues*, ed. idem (London: Parkes Wiener Series on Jewish Studies, Vallentine Mitchell, 2003), 329–332.

32. See, for example, Dan Diner's use of the term "entangled histories oder histoires croisées," in reference to European Jewish history, in *Gedächtniszeiten: Über Jüdische und Andere Geschichten* (Munich: Beck, 2003), 12. For an example of the term's usage in the new German-Jewish studies, see Todd Presner, "At the Cutting Edge: Rethinking German and Jewish Cultural and Intellectual History," paper delivered at conference, Schloss Elmau, July 12–14, 2005.

33. I borrow the term "fresh wounds" from Donald L. Niewyk, ed., *Fresh Wounds: Early Narratives of Holocaust Survival* (Chapel Hill: University of North Carolina Press, 1998).

CHAPTER ONE
"Poor Germany": Berlin and the Occupation

1. Dewilda N. Harris, "My Job in Germany, 1945–1954," in *America and the Shaping of German Society 1945–1955*, ed. Michael Ermarth (Providence: Berg, 1993), 177. Defeated and occupied Berlin has been the subject of an enormous amount of fiction (and film) in German and English, produced at the time and afterward; one could speak of a genre of occupation novels. A classic of the genre is Berger, *Crazy in Berlin*.

2. Anne-Marie Durand-Wever, "Als die Russen kamen: Tagebuch einer Berliner Ärztin," unpublished diary, with kind permission of Dr. Madeleine Durand-Noll, 36, 51.

3. Many accounts speak of an "epidemic" of suicides as the Thousand Year Reich crumpled. See, for example, Ernst Lemmer, *Manches war doch anders: Erinnerungen eines deutschen Demokraten* (Frankfurt/M: H. Scheffler, 1968), 227. The Battle of Berlin, as dramatic as it was (for the Germans) militarily hopeless, has attained mythic proportions in film and literature. Innumerable books have described the Armaggedon of April 25 to May 2, 1945. See, as a recent example, Beevor, *Fall of Berlin* (2002). Despite his use of Soviet archives opened since 1989, Beevor seems to follow very closely the story line of the contemporary Soviet newsreel *The Battle of Berlin*, which was shown in Berlin cinemas in 1945 and re-released in Germany in 1984 in a version (*Bomben auf Berlin*) directed by Irmgard von zur Mühlen. For minute-by-minute notes from Red Army officers on the conquest of Berlin, see V. Sevruk, ed., *How Wars End: Eyewitness Accounts of the Fall of Berlin* (Moscow: Progress Publishers, n.d).

4. *Time*, May 14, 1945, 20; May 7, 1945, 40.

5. Bach, *America's Germany*, 22.

6. See LAB LAZ Berlin, Rep. 280, film Nr. 1. Taken from memoirs published in *Heim und Welt*, February 24–March 30, 1952. It is unclear how many people, if any, actually perished. Beevor, *Fall of Berlin*, says no one died.

7. An extraordinary number of Allied occupiers and journalists published memoirs. See also Davidson, *Death and Life*, 75; Edward N. Peterson, *The American Occupation of Germany: Retreat to Victory* (Detroit: Wayne State University Press, 1977); Hans Speier, *From the Ashes of Disgrace: A Journal from Germany, 1945–1955* (Amherst: University of Massachusetts Press, 1981); James Stern, *The Hidden Damage* (New York: Harcourt Brace, 1947); Jean Edward Smith, *The Defense of Berlin* (Baltimore: Johns Hopkins Press, 1963), 67; Richard Brett-Smith, *Berlin '45: The Grey City* (London: Macmillan, 1966); Osmar White, *Conquerors' Road: An Eyewitness Report of Germany, 1945* (Cambridge: Cambridge University Press, 2003); W. L. White, *Report on the Germans* (New York: Harcourt Brace, 1947), 158ff; Zink (OMGUS adviser on political affairs), *American Military Government*. See, for example, the feature film *Downfall* (Untergang, 2004), directed by Oliver Hirschbiegel, depicting the last crazed days in Hitler's bunker during the Battle for Berlin.

8. Quoted in *Time*, May 14, 1945, 22. See also the account by Yelena Rzhevskaya, "Berlin, May 1945," in *How Wars End*, ed. Sevruk, 216, especially her shock at discovering the six poisoned Goebbels children.

9. *Berlin: Kampf um Freiheit*, ed. Senat Berlin, 10. Col. Frank Howley uses the same terms in his *Berlin Command*, 8. Indeed, the ubiquity and repetitiveness of certain phrases and expressions is striking.

10. Dos Passos, *Tour of Duty*, 319.

11. There are frequent references to Pompeii; see for example *Neue Berliner Illustrierte* 1:8 (December 1945). Most observers, however, agreed that the damage "seemed worse than it actually was." Amazingly, once the debris was cleared away, up to 80% of German industrial infrastructure had survived the bombing (agriculture was in worse shape due, among other factors, to the overreliance on slave labor and imports from occupied countries). Supplies of raw materials and fuel were more abundant than expected and the labor force, well fed and relieved of the worst work by slave labor, was in relatively good shape. Indeed, it was only defeat and early occupation that worsened living and working conditions. Zink, *American Military Government*, 252–253, 299. By 1946, one British observer noted that Berlin seemed in much better shape than Hamburg; see Brockway, *German Diary*, 60–70. Issac Deutscher also noted in his reports for British papers that Berlin was less destroyed than Kassel or Mannheim; see "Berlin—September 1945," *The Economist*, September 29, 1945, in idem, *Reportagen*, 114–118. For a review of the most recent debates about the impact of British and American bombing on the German civilian population, set off by Jörg Friedrich's *Der Brand: Deutschland im Bombenkrieg 1940–1945* (Munich: Propyläen Verlag, 2002), see *Ein Volk von Opfern? Die neue Debatte um den Bombenkrieg 1940–1945*, ed. Lothar Kettenacker (Berlin: Rowohlt, 2003).

12. *Berlin: Kampf um Freiheit*, ed. Senat Berlin, 54. Andreas Nachama, Julius H. Schoeps, and Hermann Simon, eds., *Jews in Berlin*, 250, place the first

Jewish service on May 6 and the second near the Weissensee Jewish cemetery on May 11.

13. Chamberlin, ed., *Kultur auf Trümmern*, 16.

14. See *Die Chronik Berlin* (Dortmund: Chronik Verlag, 1991), 427–443; Albert Norman, *Our German Policy: Propaganda and Culture* (New York: Vantage Press, 1951), 319, and Davidson, *Death and Life*, 74–75, among many sources.

15. For example, *Berliner Zeitung* 1:26 (June 15, 1945): 4 (with photo). Most of the animals had not been so lucky.

16. Gordon Schaffer, *The Russian Zone: A study of the conditions found in the Soviet-Occupied Zone of Germany during a stay of ten weeks* (London: George Allen & Unwin, 1947), 101, in a highly sympathetic account of the Soviet conquest and administration.

17. Davidson, *Death and Life*, 76.

18. Schaffer, *Russian Zone*, 16.

19. BAB Sapmo NL 182/246, pp. 5–8. See Wolfgang Leonhard, *Die Revolution entlässt ihre Kinder* (Cologne: Kiepenheuer and Witsch, 1955), 374–377, and Leonhard in *Das Jahr 1945*, ed. Krauss and Küchenmeister, 52–64.

20. Wyman, *DPs*, 16. British intelligence officer Noel Annan suggested in his memoirs, *Changing Enemies*, 125, that the Battle of Berlin would have been much less bloody if Eisenhower had pushed on. Some of the hundreds of thousands of casualties, including c. 200,000 among the Soviets, could have been avoided because resistance would not have been so desperate if the Germans had expected to fall into American rather than Soviet hands.

21. Murphy, *Diplomat*, 264. Former ambassador Murphy became political adviser to the U.S. Military Government in Germany.

22. Howley, *Berlin Command*, 65, 42.

23. LAB LAZ Nr. 2560, film Nr. 4. Statement by Walter Ulbricht, June 10, 1945.

24. Wolfgang Leonhard, "Als Mitglied der 'Gruppe Ulbricht,' " in *Besiegt, befreit . . . Zeitzeugen erinnern sich an das Kriegsende 1945*, ed. Werner Filmer and Heribert Schwan (Berlin: C. Bertelsmann, 1995), 193.

25. Davidson, *Death and Life*, 21, also 70.

26. Maginnis, *Military Government Journal*, June 26, 1945, 258.

27. Byrnes, *Speaking Frankly*, 68.

28. Levin, *In Search*, 384.

29. Kieve Skiddel, unpublished letter home to his wife in New York, July 3, 1945. I am grateful to Professor Arthur Goren, Columbia University, for giving me copies of these extraordinary letters. On Skiddel, see also Deborah Dash Moore, *GI Jews: How World War II Changed a Generation* (Cambridge, Mass.: Harvard University Press, 2004), 107–111.

30. Zink, *United States in Germany*, 340–345, makes this argument.

31. Maginnis, *Military Government Journal*, August 30, 1945, 291, also 242, 269.

32. Much more systematically than in western Germany, the Soviet zone cultivated the return of sympathetic émigrés, and quite a few did arrive, many, if not all of them, Jewish. For an excellent account, see Schivelbusch, *Cold Crater*. For an intimate (and poignant) account of exiled intellectuals' return and their

experiences in the Soviet sector, see Edith Anderson, *Love in Exile: An American Writer's Memoir of Life in Divided Berlin* (South Royalton, Vt: Steerforth Press, 1999).

33. Schivelbusch, *Cold Crater*, 14. The German edition of Schivelbusch's book uses "before the curtain" in the title *Vor dem Vorhang: Das geistige Berlin 1945–1948* (Frankfurt/M: Fischer, 1997).

34. Friedrich Luft in Höcker, *Beschreibung*, 68. Many observers lamented that "the so-called 'literature in the drawer' supposed to have been written and hidden away under Hitler's rule, failed to come forth after his fall." See Muhlen, *Return of Germany*, 219.

35. See Andreas-Friedrich, *Berlin Underground*, 312, originally published as *Der Schattenmann* (Frankfurt/M: Suhrkamp, 1947). Andreas-Friedrich wrote an afterword to her wartime account on August 24, 1945: "The stray bullet of an American patrol wounded him mortally. It was just after he had given his last concert for Allied troops. . . . Andrik Krassnow [her name for Borchardt] is dead. He was forty-six years old when he gave up his life. And he enjoyed living."

36. Schivelbusch, *Cold Crater*, 14.

37. Arendt, "Aftermath of Nazi Rule," 344. See also Hermann Glaser, "Der Weg nach innen. Kultur der Stunde Null, die keine war," in *Ende des Dritten Reiches-Ende des Zweiten Weltkriegs: Eine perspektivische Rückschau*, ed. Hans-Erich Volkmann (Munich: Piper, 1995), 771–794.

38. Schaffer, *Russian Zone*, 112. Programs in Walter Karsch, "Bekenntnis zum Theater. Rückblick auf die Berliner Spielzeit 1945/46," *Berliner Almanach 1946*, 60, 70.

39. Henry Alter in *Kultur auf Trümmern*, ed. Chamberlin, 16; also reports by officers Hogan, Bitter, and Joseph, 141. For a collection of short literary memoirs of Berlin life in the "zero hour," see Peter Kruse, ed., *Bomben, Trümmer, Lucky Strikes: Die Stunde Null in bisher unbekannten Manuskripten* (Berlin: Wolf Jobst Siedler, 2004).

40. Karsch, "Bekenntnis," 76.

41. Reich-Ranicki, *Mein Leben*, 319.

42. See *Berliner Zeitung* 2:8 (January 11, 1946), 3.

43. Davidson Taylor, "Report on Trip to Berlin," July 20, 1945, in *Kultur auf Trümmern*, ed. Chamberlin, 68. Émigré British officer Julius Posener also noted, "It was already a little bit embarrassing that at the beginning it was impossible to hear a concert, which didn't include at least one Mendelssohn." Posener, *In Deutschland*, 53. See also LAB LAZ Nr. 13898, film Nr. 4.

44. Frank Stern, "The Culture of Dissent: Jewish Writers and Filmmakers and the Re-casting of Germany," paper, German Studies Association, Atlanta, October 1999. See also Stern, "Facing the Past: Representations of the Holocaust in German Cinema since 1945," Joseph and Rebecca Meyerhoff Annual Lecture, June 14, 2000, USHMM.

45. Rosenthal, *Zwei Leben*, 117, 126.

46. Among many sources, Schaffer, *Russian Zone*, 117.

47. Not everyone was impressed by the film (*Die Mörder sind unter uns*, 1946, directed by Wolfang Staudte). The disillusioned American reporter Delbert Clark, in *Goose Step*, 224, judged it "a hopeless melange of wild melodrama and perni-

ciously confused political philosophy . . . distinguished mainly for its skillful camera work." See also Ulrike Weckel, "The *Mitläufer* in German Films: Representation and Critical Reception," *History and Memory* 15:2 (2003): 64–93.

48. See the reports in Chamberlin, ed., *Kultur auf Trümmern*. Elizabeth Janik, in " 'The Golden Hunger Years': Music and Superpower Rivalry in Occupied Berlin," *German History* 22:1 (2004): 86, points out that while the Soviets brought German refugees "back to Berlin to assume leadership positions as Germans, the United States naturalized its émigrés and made them American officers." See also idem, *Recomposing German Music: Politics and Musical Tradition in Cold War Berlin* (Leiden, Boston: Brill, 2005), 81–208.

49. See the lively descriptions in Zuckmayer (himself just back from exile on a farm in Vermont), *Als wär's ein Stück von mir*, 551–552.

50. Norman, *Our German Policy*, 284. See also report by officers Hogan, Bitter, and Joseph in Chamberlin, ed., *Kultur in Trümmern*. In general, on culture and competing cultural politics, see the excellent accounts in Schivelbusch, *Cold Crater*.

51. Lemmer, *Manches war doch anders*, 229. See Zink, *American Military Government*, on denazification and its problems, 198. See also Davis, *Came as a Conqueror* and W. L. White, *Report on the Germans* (New York: Harcourt Brace, 1947). For a comparison of Soviet and American policies, see also Krieger, "Inter-Regnum in Germany," 507–532.

52. Janik, " 'Golden Hunger Years,' " 78, notes that both the Americans and the Soviet cultural officers cultivated a more liberal atmosphere than would have been possible at home.

53. Botting, *In the Ruins*, 165.

54. Kurt Schumacher, the antifascist SPD politician, reportedly protested to the British that "we are not a *Neger Volk*," Annan, *Changing Enemies*, 157. For an angry critique of the British occupation style, see the report by British trade unionist Fenner Brockway in his *German Diary*, published by Victor Gollancz, a British Jew who was famously sympathetic to the plight of the defeated Germans. See also Frances Rosenfeld, "The Anglo-German Encounter in Occupied Hamburg, 1945–1950" (Ph.D. dissertation, Columbia University, 2006).

55. Botting, *In the Ruins*, 161.

56. Byrnes, *Speaking Frankly*, 183.

57. Dos Passos, *Tour of Duty*, 319.

58. See for example Syrkin, *State of the Jews*, 43. A careful viewing of early films, such as the 1947 DEFA (Deutsche Film Aktiengesellschaft) production *Strassenbekanntschaften*, will reveal black market scenes with characters who certainly "look" Jewish.

59. Bourke-White, *Fatherland*, 158.

60. Harris, "My Job in Germany," 177.

61. Bach, *America's Germany*, 64.

62. Howley, *Berlin Command*, 91.

63. Hutton and Rooney, *Conquerors' Peace*, 84. Also, Howley, *Berlin Command*, 91; Botting, *In the Ruins*, 187–188.

64. Höcker, *Beschreibung*, 92.

65. "Main Street" in Bach, *America's Germany*, 30; "Kalamazoo" in Clark, *Goose Step*, 161, see 160–180.

66. Description from Dawidowicz, *From That Place and Time*, 282.

67. Clark, *Goose Step*, 163. For a litany of complaints about the corruption and ignorance of U.S. occupation officials, see also among many other contemporary reports Bach, *America's Germany*; Hutton and Rooney, *Conquerors' Peace*; and Dos Passos, *Tour of Duty*. For a later statement, see Peterson, *American Occupation*. Standard works on the U.S. occupation of Germany include Ziemke, *U.S. Army*, and John Gimbel, *The American Occupation of Germany: Politics and the Military, 1945–49* (Palo Alto: Stanford University Press, 1961). See also Boehling, *Question of Priorities*.

68. See the dispatches collected in Settel, ed., *This Is Germany*. See also the sharp and beautiful short stories "Military Occupation Group 1942–1950" in Kay Boyle, *Fifty Stories* (New York: New Directions, 1992; orig. 1980), 379–574.

69. See Bach, *America's Germany*, 28–29. See in general Robert R. Shandley, *Rubble Films: German Cinema in the Shadow of the Third Reich* (Philadelphia: Temple University Press, 2001).

70. Dos Passos, *Tour of Duty*, 323.

71. Zink, *American Military Government*, 109.

72. Howley, *Berlin Command*, 63.

73. Marguerite Higgins, "Obituary of a Government—the Story of the East-West Breakup in Germany," in *This Is Germany*, ed. Settel, 311.

74. Markus Wolf, *Die Troika*. See also Konrad Wolf's 1968 semiautobiographical DEFA film *Ich War Neunzehn*, which chronicles a young refugee's return to Berlin in 1945 as a Red Army soldier.

75. Maginnis, *Military Government Journal*, February 27, 1946, 345. On shootings, see August 30, 1945, 291.

76. *Tagesspiegel* 29 (November 23, 1945), 3. For reports on physical and psychological damage to children, see LAB Rep. 210/840/91/1 Gesundheitsamt Zehlendorf.

77. Deutscher, "Berlin–September 1945," *The Economist*, September 29, 1945, in idem, *Reportagen*, 115.

78. Bourke-White, *Fatherland*, 168, and caption to photo before p. 167.

79. Hermann Glaser, *1945. Beginn einer Zukunft: Bericht und Dokumentation* (Frankfurt/M: Fischer, 2005), 127. See Margaret Mead's prescient discussion of this issue in "Food and Feeding." See also chapter 4 on the "emotional economy of food."

80. Maginnis, *Military Government Journal*, December 3, 1945, 319.

81. Howley, *Berlin Command*, 85. The references to German self-pity are legion; the term "aggressive" self-pity is from Irmela von der Lühe, "'The Big 52': Erika Manns Nürnberger Reportagen," in *"Bestien" und "Befehlsempfänger,"* ed. Weckel and Wolfram, 32.

82. Letter, February 13, 1947, from Adam J. Rapalski, Lt. Col. MG, Chief Public Health Branch, Office of Military Government to *Amtsärztin*, Gesundheitsamt Zehlendorf. LAB Rep. 210/840/89. See the comprehensive study by Jessica Reinisch, "Public Health in Germany under Soviet and Allied Occupation, 1943–1947" (Ph.D. dissertation, University of London, 2004).

83. The bibliography here is vast and ongoing. On perceptions of victimization among the German "war damaged" and their claims for compensation, see Hughes, "'Through No Fault of Our Own.'" Before Jörg Friedrich (re)discovered the trauma of the bombings for Germans on the home front in *Der Brand* (2002; English, *The Fire: The Bombing of Germany, 1940–1945*, trans. Alison Browne [New York: Columbia University Press, 2006]), W. G. Sebald had unleashed a debate on the topic in 1997 with a series of lectures titled "Air War and Literature," published as *On the Natural History of Destruction* (New York: Random House, 2003; German, 1999). See also Günther Grass, *Crabwalk* (Orlando: Harcourt, 2002; German, 2002), and Thomas W. Neumann, "Der Bombenkrieg: Zur ungeschriebenen Geschichte einer kollektiven Verletzung," in *Nachkrieg in Deutschland*, ed. Klaus Naumann (Hamburg: Hamburger Edition, 2001), 319–363. On the recent debates about German suffering during the war, see also the review articles by Robert G. Moeller, "Sinking Ships, the Lost *Heimat* and Broken Taboos: Günter Grass and the Politics of Memory in Contemporary Germany," *Contemporary European History* 12 (2003): 147–181, and "What Has 'Coming to Terms with the Past' Meant in Post–World War II Germany? From History to Memory to the 'History of Memory,'" *Central European History* 35:2 (2002): 223–256; also Mary Nolan, "Germans as Victims during the Second World War: Air War, Memory Wars," *Central European History* 38:1 (2005): 7–40. Recent years have brought, however, not only an intensified focus on German suffering but also a discussion about the legacy of Nazism in the second- and third-generation families of perpetrators, and how steadfast denial did, in a perverse way, transmit an inchoate awareness of guilt. See, for example Harald Welzer et al., *Opa War Kein Nazi: Nationalsozialismus und Holocaust im Familiengedächtnis* (Frankfurt/M: Fischer, 2002). For a fine résumé of the German victimization debates ignited by the approach of the sixtieth anniversary of war's end, see Robert G. Moeller, "Germans as Victims? Thoughts on a Post–Cold War History of World War II's Legacies," *History and Memory* 17:1/2 (Fall 2005): 147–194. For a sense of the new attention to the plight of German expellees from Soviet-occupied territory, see the exhibition catalogue *Flucht, Vertreibung, Integration*, ed. Stiftung Haus der Geschichte der BRD (Bielefeld: Kerber Verlag, 2006).

84. Bourke-White, *Fatherland*, 33, 61. For a highly negative analysis of this critical (and according to the author, self-righteous) view of suffering Germans (illustrated with multiple images of baby carriages), see Dagmar Barnouw, *Germany 1945: Views of War and Violence* (Bloomington: Indiana University Press, 1996).

85. One example among many is Hirschmann, *Embers Still Burn*, 99.

86. Lewis F. Gittler, "Everyday Life in Germany Today," *American Mercury* 61 (October 1945): 400–407. Götz Aly has recently picked up this theme, arguing in *Hitlers Volksstaat: Raub, Rassenkrieg und nationaler Sozialismus* (Frankfurt/M: S. Fischer, 2005) that ordinary Germans' capacity to profit from wartime occupation and expropriation was key, not only to support for the war, but also to their acquiescence to the Nazi's exterminatory project in Germany and occupied Europe.

87. Barnouw, *Germany 1945*, xvi, tries to argue that American reportage and photojournalism unfairly manipulated images to portray Germans solely as aggressors rather than as victims. See also Hughes, "'Through No Fault of Our Own.'"

88. *Time*, April 9, 1945, 38.

89. Bach, *America's Germany*, 300.

90. See, for example, John H. Herz, "The Fiasco of Denazification," *Political Science Quarterly* 63:4 (1948): 569–594, and Franz L. Neumann, "Re-Educating the Germans: The Dilemma of Reconstruction," *Commentary* 3 (1947): 517–525.

91. On "surly" Germans, see among many Gittler, "Everyday Life in Germany Today." See also Arendt, "Aftermath of Nazi Rule," 349. The official report, "Relations between the American Forces of Occupation and the German People: Report of Byron Price to the President," *US Department of State Bulletin* (December 2, 1945), also noted with surprise German disappointment that the American "conquerors" were not more friendly.

92. Habe, *Love Affair*, 27. Quote from *King Lear*, act 3, scene 2, cited in Posener, *In Deutschland*, 33.

93. See the report of British political officer Julius Posener, who had emigrated from Berlin to Palestine in 1935, *In Deutschland*, 10–11. See also Clark, *Goose Step*, 272.

94. Pastor Niemoller, quoted in *Time*, June 18, 1945, 29.

95. For one of many versions of this analysis, see Krieger, "Inter-Regnum in Germany," 531.

96. Aufruf der SPD, June 15, 1945, LAB LAZ, Rep. 280.

97. Durand-Wever, "Als die Russen Kamen."

98. Aufruf der SPD, June 15, 1945, LAB LAZ, Rep. 280.

99. Aufruf der CDU, June 26, 1945, LAB LAZ, Rep. 280.

100. Brochure advertising Volkshochschule courses, Berlin Schöneberg, LAB LAZ, Rep. 280.

101. *Berliner Zeitung* 1:1 (May 21, 1945), 1–2.

102. See, for example, correspondence in papers of Walter Ulbricht, BAB (Sapmo) NL 182.

103. Maginnis, *Military Government Journal*, April 20, 1945, 242.

104. Dale Clark, "Conflicts over Planning at Staff Headquarters," in *American Experiences in Military Government in World War II*, ed. Carl J. Friedrich and Associates (New York: Rinehart and Company, 1948), "Rules for Occupation Officers," 233.

105. Riess, *Berlin Berlin*, 33.

106. Bourke-White, *Fatherland*, caption on photo before p. 7.

107. Grigor McClelland, *Embers of War: Letters from a Quaker Relief Worker in War-Torn Germany* (London: British Academic Press, 1997), 145.

108. Gollancz, *Darkest Germany*, letter to the editor of *The Times*, Düsseldorf, November 12, 1946, 29–30; letter to the editor of *The News Chronicle*, Düsseldorf, November 8, 1946, 31.

109. Howley, *Berlin Command*, 85, 87.

110. See, for example, Emlyn Williams (*Christian Science Monitor* correspondent), "Tomorrow Is the New Moon," in *This Is Germany*, ed. Settel, 2.

111. Maginnis, *Military Government Journal*, July 9, 1945, 269.

112. Jack Raymond, "Der Kleine Mann," in *This Is Germany*, ed. Settel, 151. In one sociological study, of 200 families in immediate postwar Berlin, 71% of men and 73% of women claimed not to have been members of the National Socialist Party. See Thurnwald, *Gegenwartsprobleme*, 169.

113. Moskowitz, "The Germans and the Jews," 8, 10, 11. British Army interpreter William Peters headlined a diary entry for October 30, "This is a red letter day! Today I met the first German who admitted having voted for the Nazi party in 1932 and 1933." William Peters, *In Germany Now: The Diary of a Soldier, Impressions in Germany, August–December 1945* (London: Progress Publishing Company, 1946), 68. See entire diary for a vivid and mostly clear-eyed and balanced view of social, cultural, and political conditions in Berlin.

114. Muhlen, *Return of Germany*, 154–155.

115. *Newsweek* cover, April 9, 1945; *Time*, April 9, 1945, 38.

116. *Time*, April 23, 1945, 38. In another of many examples, Davidson, *Death and Life*, 48, uses the adjectives "sullen, dazed, [and] spiritless."

117. "Report of Byron Price to the President," 888. See also Hyman, *Undefeated*, 343.

118. Bourke-White, *Fatherland*, 5. Interestingly, many years later, Daniel Goldhagen in *Hitler's Willing Executioners: Ordinary Germans and the Holocaust* (New York: Knopf, 1996) seemed to take up that notion in all seriousness, imagining the Nazis as a kind of exotic tribe, far removed from any world his Western readers would recognize.

119. Clark, *Goose Step*, 272.

120. Posener, *In Deutschland*, 54.

121. *Berliner Zeitung* 1:141 (October 26, 1945). The correspondent was probably the twenty-year-old Markus Wolf.

122. Quoted in Fritz Kortner, *Aller Tage Abend* (Munich: Kindler, 1959), 51.

123. For example, Riess, *Berlin Berlin*, 33.

124. "Report of Byron Price to the President," 885–892, 888. On the problematic role of the churches in discussions about victimization and guilt, and their relations with the Allies, see for example Matthew Hockenos, *A Church Divided: German Protestants Confront the Nazi Past* (Bloomington: Indiana University Press, 2004); Mark Edward Ruff, *The Wayward Flock: Catholic Youth in Postwar West Germany, 1945–1965* (Chapel Hill: University of North Carolina Press, 2005); and, for a critical summary, Stern, *Whitewashing*, 302–310.

125. For a longer-term perspective on language of victimization, see Greg Eghigian, "The Politics of Victimization: Social Pensioners and the German Social State in the Inflation of 1914–1924," *Central European History* 26 (1993): 375–403.

126. For example, *Berliner Zeitung* 1:183 (December 15, 1945), 1, 3. The front-page headline read "Six Million Jews Murdered by Nazis." In a characteristic juxtaposition, it was placed just under a report announcing "Holiday Joys for the Population: Extra Rations for Christmas."

127. Botting, *In the Ruins*, 85. Joel Sayre wrote in his "Letter from Berlin," *The New Yorker*, July 28, 1945 (July 14 dispatch), "The butt collecting in Berlin,

I do not hesitate to say, is the most intensive on earth, and I am not forgetting the *Kippensammlung* on the Bowery and in the Middle East."

128. *Neue Berliner Illustrierte* 1 (October 1945), 2–5.

129. Quote is from LAB/Rep. 240. Acc. 2651/748. The ironic reference is of course to the national anthem, "Deutschland Über Alles." Irmgard Heidleberg had submitted her mother's diary. For discussion of politics of scarcity and the black market in Berlin, see Paul Steege, *Black Market, Cold War: Everyday Life in Berlin 1946–1949* (New York: Cambridge University Press, 2007) and Jörg Roesler, "The Black Market in Postwar Berlin and the Methods Used to Counteract it," *German History* 7:1 (1989): 92–107.

130. There were at least 15,000 deaths due to epidemic diseases from May to December 1945 (plus a very high venereal disease rate). Municipal and occupation officials were more likely to stress the rapidity and efficacy of public health measures such as mass immunizations, examinations, and disinfection. For a brief overview, see Dieter Hanauske, ed., *Die Sitzungsprotokolle des Magistrats der Stadt Berlin 1945/46* (Berlin: Berlin Verlag, 1995), 74.

131. According to one version, the two main actors were an eleven-year-old boy, a son of circus performers, and a retired Reichswehr general who was a *Warmer Bruder* (as homosexuals were called). Rossellini supposedly told the general "that all he had to do was corrupt the morals of a German orphan boy, whereupon he replied, 'Oh, if that is all, I am at your service.'" Clark, *Goose Step*, 225.

132. "Report of Byron Price to the President," 888.

133. Boehling, *Question of Priorities*, 15, 19.

134. "Report of Byron Price to the President," 888.

135. Bach, *America's Germany*, 261. It is important to remember that the U.S. forces included not only a significant number of German-Jewish refugees but also many non-Jewish German-Americans, with their own familial and historical ties to Germany. See Goedde, *GIs and Germans*, and Fehrenbach, *Race after Hitler*.

136. Richard M. Brickner, M.D., *Is Germany Incurable?* with Introductions by Margaret Mead, Ph.D., and Edward A. Strecker, M.D. (Philadelphia: J. B. Lippincott, 1943), 248.

137. Hutton and Rooney, *Conquerors' Peace*, 62.

138. "Report of Byron Price to the President," 886.

139. *Newsweek*, April 16, 1945, 10.

140. See, for example Maginnis, *Military Government Journal*, June 26, 1945, 258. This portrayal of whining self-pity is especially evident in reports by occupiers, and it only really changes to the spunky "Berlin ist wieder da" image with the blockade and the airlift. For an insightful analysis of this "depression," see Eric L. Santner, *Stranded Objects: Mourning, Memory, and Film in Postwar Germany* (Ithaca: Cornell University Press, 1990), esp. 1–56.

141. *Time*, April 16, 1945, 26.

142. Quote from Posener, *In Deutschland*, 18. The examples are legion, the descriptions almost identical. *Newsweek* 27:5 (4 February 1946): 58, reported that in an opinion poll of 1,700 GIs, 19% thought Germany somewhat justified

in going to war; 51% thought Hitler did some good for his country pre-1939; and 22% "believed the Nazis had 'good reasons' for persecuting Jews."

143. Maginnis, *Military Government Journal*, December 2, 1945, 319.

144. *Berliner Zeitung* 1:35 (June 24, 1945): 3.

145. *Berliner Zeitung* 1:39 (June 29, 1945): 3.

146. Maginnis, *Military Government Journal*, June 26, 1945, 258–259.

147. Maginnis, *Military Government Journal*, February 27, 1946, 345.

148. For example, Deutscher, "Zwischenbilanz nach einem Jahr Besatzung," *The Observer*, April 14, 1946, in idem, *Reportagen*, 181–184.

149. Clark, *Goose Step*, 18, IX, 295.

150. Annan, *Changing Enemies*, 145. By July 1946 the 2 million U.S. troops in Germany had been reduced to 342,000. By summer 1947 only 135,000 were left, and since they were concentrated in certain areas, many Germans no longer directly felt the force of the occupation and lived essentially under self-rule. By 1950 there were fewer than 75,000 American troops in West Germany. See Goedde, *GIs and Germans*, 23, 33.

151. See, for example William Harlan Hale, "Our Failure in Germany," *Harpers Magazine* 191 (October 1945): 515–523, 515–517. Hale was policy adviser to the U.S. Information Control Division.

152. Middleton, *Last July*, 148.

153. Murphy, *Diplomat*, 292.

154. Boehling, *Question of Priorities*, 33, notes that "only 5% of all US MG personnel in Germany knew enough Germans to function without an interpreter." Émigré officers were generally seen as too "emotional," vengeful, and overly influenced by their Jewish attachments. See, for example Peterson, *American Occupation*, 139–140.

155. Hutton and Rooney, *Conquerors' Peace*, 34, 10.

CHAPTER TWO
Gendered Defeat: Rape, Motherhood, and Fraternization

1. December 16, 1945, LAB Rep. 214/2814/221/2 (Gesundheitsamt Neukölln).

2. Bill Downs, CBS and *Newsweek* correspondent, *Newsweek*, April 16, 1945, 62.

3. In August, the total population was counted at 2,784,112 (1,035,463 male, 1,748,649 female) vs. 4,332,000 in 1939. The male population was only half of what it had been before the war, the female down by a quarter. The 100 men to 169 women ratio compared to 100 to 119 in 1939. *Berliner Volks, Berufs und Arbeitstättenzählung*, August 12, 1945, in *Berliner Zeitung* 1:91 (August 29, 1945): 1. On the meaning of the female "surplus" at war's end, see Heineman, *What Difference*, especially illustration, 10.

4. See (among many sources) John Erickson, *The Road to Berlin: Stalin's War with Germany*, vol. 2 (London: Weidenfeld and Nicolson, 1983), 512; also Omer Bartov, *The Eastern Front, 1941–45: German Troops and the Barbarisation of Warfare* (New York: St. Martin's Press, 1986); Richard Evans, *In Hitler's Shadow:*

West German Historians and the Attempt to Escape from the Nazi Past (New York: Pantheon, 1989), chapter 2.

5. Erickson, *Road to Berlin*, 603. In another, more recent version, Antony Beevor explains the Soviet rapes as the result of "a dark area of male sexuality which can emerge all too easily, especially in war, when there are no social and disciplinary restraints," and goes on to opine that "in war, undisciplined soldiers without fear of retribution can rapidly revert to a primitive male sexuality, perhaps even the sort which biologists ascribe to a compulsion on the part of the male of the species to spread his seed as widely as possible." Beevor, *Fall of Berlin*, 326.

6. See the broad reception in Germany, the United States, and Great Britain of the well-received and publicized but controversial publication of a revised and retranslated text about mass rapes in Berlin, Anonyma, *Eine Frau in Berlin: Tagebuchaufzeichnungen vom 20. April bis zum 22. Juni 1945* (Frankfurt/M: Eichborn, 2003); in English, Anonymous, *A Woman in Berlin*. This interest was preceded by the positive response to Beevor's discussion of rape in *Fall of Berlin*. See n. 24 below for further discussion of this "diary." Research published in the 1990s includes Naimark, *Russians in Germany*; Heimatmuseum Charlottenburg Ausstellung *Worüber kaum gesprochen wurde: Frauen und allierte Soldaten. 3. September bis 15. Oktober 1995* (Berlin: Bezirksamt Charlottenburg, Abt. Volksbildung, 1995); and the text accompanying Sander's film on the topic, Sander and Johr, eds., *BeFreier und Befreite*. For earlier feminist analyses, see Ingrid Schmidt-Harzbach, "Eine Woche im April. Berlin 1945. Vergewaltigung als Massenschicksal," *Feministische Studien* 5 (1984): 51–62; Erika M. Hoerning, "Frauen als Kriegsbeute. Der Zwei-Fronten Krieg. Beispiele aus Berlin," in *"Wir kriegen jetzt andere Zeiten." Auf der Suche nach der Erfahrung des Volkes in antifaschistischen Ländern. Lebensgeschichte und Sozialkultur im Ruhrgebiet 1930 bis 1960, Bd. 3*, ed. Lutz Niethammer and Alexander von Plato (Berlin: J.H.W. Dietz, 1985), 327–346; and Tröger, "Between Rape and Prostitution." For an even earlier feminist consideration of sexual violence in World War II, including attacks by Soviet liberators on German women, see Susan Brownmiller, *Against Our Will: Men, Women, and Rape* (New York: Simon and Schuster, 1975), 48–79. See also Norman M. Naimark's careful consideration in *Russians in Germany*, 69–140. On the thorny problems of historicizing rape at war's end and the controversy about Sander's film, see Grossmann, "A Question of Silence."

7. Barbara Johr, "Die Ereignissee in Zahlen," in *BeFreier und Befreite*, ed. Sander and Johr, 48, 54–55, 59. See also Erich Kuby, *Die Russen in Berlin 1945* (Bern/Munich: Scherz, 1965), 312–313, and especially Naimark, *Russians in Germany*, 69–90.

8. Naimark, *Russians in Germany*, 132–33, 79–80, 106–107, 86. Naimark suggests, 88, that the Red Army rapes continued "at least through 1947." Beevor's *Fall of Berlin* presents much of the same material.

9. *Deutsche Wochenschau* Nr. 755/10, 1945. Sander's film uses clips from this newsreel of a radio reporter interviewing German women about rapes committed by Soviet "bestial hordes." See also Nr. 754/9/1945 and Nr. 739/46/1944.

10. Ilya Ehrenburg, *The War: 1941–1945, Volume 5, Of Men, Years—Life*, trans. Tatiana Shenunina in collaboration with Yvonne Kapp (Cleveland: The

World Publishing Company, 1964), 32, explicitly denied long-standing accusations that he, a Soviet Jew in the Red Army, had been "urging the Asiatic peoples to drink the blood of German women. Ilya Ehrenburg insists that Asiatics should enjoy our women." See Brownmiller's discussion in *Against Our Will*, 70–71.

11. This terrifying image has a long lineage not limited to memories of World War Two. For a specific reference in this context, see Ingrid Strobl's response to Sander's film, "Wann begann das Grauen?" *Konkret* (September 1992), 55. There are no reliable comparative data on rapes committed by the Wehrmacht because, while rape by German soldiers on the western front was generally severely punished, "In the Soviet Union, however, we no longer hear of soldiers being tried, let alone executed, for acts of violence and plunder against Soviet citizens." See Omer Bartov, *Hitler's Army: Soldiers, Nazis, and War in the Third Reich* (New York: Oxford University Press, 1991), 70. The controversial exhibit "Crimes of the Wehrmacht," mounted by the Hamburg Institute for Social Research from 1993 to 1999, provoked a stream of publications dealing with German military conduct on the eastern front. New and ongoing research is revealing that assumptions about racial taboos having limited German sexual violations in the East cannot be sustained. See especially Birgit Beck, *Wehrmacht und sexuelle Gewalt. Sexualverbrechen vor deutschen Militärgerichten 1939–1945* (Paderborn: Ferdinand SchöninghVerlag, 2004), which does, however, confirm Bartov's assessment about differential handling of sexual violation on the eastern and western fronts, and idem, "Sexual Violence and Prosecution by Court Martials of the Wehrmacht," in *A World at Total War: Global Conflict and the Politics of Destruction, 1937–1945*, ed. Roger Chickering and Stig Förster (Cambridge: Cambridge University Press, 2006); idem, "Rape: The Military Trials of Sexual Crimes Committed by Soldiers in the Wehrmacht, 1939–1944," in *Home-Front: The Military, War and Gender in Twentieth-Century Germany*, ed. Karen Hagemann and Stefanie Schüler-Springorum (Oxford: Berg, 2002), 255–273; and Wendy Jo Gertjejanssen, "Victims, Heroines, Survivors: Sexual Violence on the Eastern Front during World War II" (Ph.D. dissertation, University of Minnesota, 2004).

12. Höcker, *Beschreibung*, 71, May 25, 1945, entry. For analysis of the outpouring of diary writing, see Susanne zur Nieden, *Alltag im Ausnahmezustand: Frauentagebücher im zerstörten Deutschland 1943–1945* (Berlin: Orlanda Frauenverlag, 1993). By 1968, even Christian Democratic politicians were acknowledging, "Despite the horrible things that happened, we should rather be amazed by the degree of discipline shown by most Red Army soldiers," Ernst Lemmer, *Manches war doch anders: Erinnerungen eines deutschen Demokraten* (Frankfurt/M: H. Schettler, 1968) 258. Interestingly—and typically—on the following page, he insists, "Our Wehrmacht does not need to be ashamed of its conduct in the war against the Soviet Union."

13. Harold J. Berman and Miroslav Kerner, *Soviet Military Law and Administration* (Cambridge, Mass.: Harvard University Press, 1955), 48.

14. Ehrenburg, *War*, 175. See also Hoerning, "Frauen als Kriegsbeute," 327–346.

15. Knef, *Gift Horse*, 95.

16. *The Economist*, October 27, 1945, in Deutscher, *Reportagen*, 130.

17. Gabrielle Vallentin, "Die Einnahme von Berlin Durch die Rote Armee vor Zehn Jahren. Wie ich Sie Selbst Erlebt Habe. Geschrieben 1955," 37, LAB Acc. 2421.

18. On rape as a generalizable symbol of German fate, see Heineman, "Hour of the Woman."

19. Michael Wieck, *Zeugnis vom Untergang Königsbergs. Ein "Geltungsjude" berichtet* (Heidelberg: Heidelberger Verlagsanstalt und Druckerei, 1990), 261.

20. Boveri, *Tage des Überlebens*, 126, 121–122.

21. Interview with G. C., conducted in early 1990s, quoted in Heimatmuseum Charlottenburg, "Worüber kaum gesprochen wurde," 22.

22. Anne-Marie Durand-Wever, "*Als die Russen kamen. Tagebuch einer Berliner Ärztin,*" unpublished diary.

23. Heineman, *What Difference*. See also Sibylle Meyer and Eva Schulze, eds., *Wie Wir das Alles Geschafft Haben: Alleinstehende Frauen berichten über ihr Leben nach 1945* (Munich: Beck, 1985).

24. See zur Nieden, *Alltag im Ausnahmezustand*, esp. 74, 95–96. This gamut of responses is well represented in Anonyma's diary; whatever its provenance (see n. 26 below), the text does not read very differently from many other reports or diaries (and for that matter novels) describing the situation in postwar Berlin. For reflections, see Hsu-Ming Teo, "The Continuum of Sexual Violence in Occupied Germany, 1945–49," *Women's History Review* 5:2 (1996): 191–218. For analysis of some interesting differences between women's contemporary diaries and memoirs and later interviews about their rape experiences, see Regina Mühlhauser, "Vergewaltigungen in Deutschland 1945: Nationaler Opferdiskurs und individuelles Erinnern betroffener Frauen," in *Nachkrieg in Deutschland*, ed. Klaus Naumann (Hamburg: Hamburger Edition, 2001), 384–408. See also Birgit Dahlke, "'Frau komm!' Vergewaltigungen 1945: Zur Geschichte eines Diskurses," in *LiteraturGesellschaft DDR: Kanonkämpfe und ihre Geschichte(n)*, ed. Birgit Dahlke, Martina Langermann, and Thomas Taterka (Stuttgart: JB Metzler Verlag, 2000), 275–311.

25. Riess, *Berlin Berlin*, 19.

26. My translation from Anonyma, *Eine Frau in Berlin*, 78. See also English version, *A Woman in Berlin*. See the republished version, Anonyma, *Eine Frau in Berlin* (2003), and the subsequent controversies about the legitimacy of "outing" Anonyma's name and identity as a kind of Nazi "new woman," as they played out on the feuilleton pages of major newspapers amongst male scholars and journalists. See especially Jens Bisky, *Süddeutsche Zeitung*, September 24, 2003, for Anonyma's "outing" as the journalist (*Kleinpropagandistin*) Marta Hillers, who had written propaganda texts for the NSDAP. For the enthusiastically received American edition, see Anonymous, *A Woman in Berlin*. See discussion of controversy about the German republication in Elizabeth Heineman, "Gender, Sexuality, and Coming to Terms with the Nazi Past," *Central European History* 38:1 (2005): 41–74, esp. 53–56.

27. Riess, *Berlin Berlin*, 23, 26, 19.

28. "*Die scheint ja och noch stolz druff ze sind, det se de Russen in ihrem Alter noch vorjenommen ham.*" Quoted in unpublished memoir by Hans Winterfeldt,

"Deutschland: Ein Zeitbild 1926–1945. Leidensweg eines deutschen Juden in den ersten 19 Jahren seines Lebens," 438, ME 690, LBI Archives.

29. Heineman, *What Difference*, 58.

30. Tröger, "Between Rape and Prostitution," 113. See also Birthe Kundrus, "Forbidden Company: Romantic Relationships between Germans and Foreigners, 1939 to 1945," *Journal of the History of Sexuality* (2002): 201–222, reprinted in Dagmar D. Herzog, ed., *Sexuality and German Fascism* (New York: Berghahn, 2005). On National Socialist incitement to "Aryan" sexuality and its aftershocks in the 1950s and 1960s, see Dagmar Herzog's nuanced analysis in *Sex after Fascism*.

31. Annemarie Weber, *Westend* (Munich: Desch, 1966), 104. For Curt Riess, Berlin's women had become "hart" and "sachlich" (the same terms that were used after World War I), *Berlin Berlin*, 44–45.

32. Deutscher, *The Observer*, October 7, 1945; *The Economist* October 27, 1945, in idem, *Reportagen*, 122–124, 129–130.

33. Anne-Marie Durand-Wever in *Proceedings of the International Congress on Population and World Resources in Relation to the Family, August 1948, Cheltenham England* (London: H. K. Lewis and Co., n.d.), 103.

34. Riess, *Berlin Berlin*, 22.

35. Lewyn and Lewyn, *On the Run*, 277.

36. Davidson, *Death and Life*, 74.

37. Gudrun Pausewang, in *NiemandsLand. Kindheitserinnerungen an die Jahre 1945 bis 1949*, ed. Heinrich Böll (Bronheim-Merten: Lavmuv Verlag, 1985), 62.

38. Anonyma, *Eine Frau in Berlin*, 138.

39. Burke, *Big Rape* (first printing December 1951, sixth November 1952), 145, 197. According to the (lurid) book jacket, Wakefield covered the war for *Esquire Magazine* and "served as a Public Relations Officer for Generals McNarney, Clay and Howley." The similarities between Lilo and the Anonyma of *A Woman in Berlin*, first published three years later, are striking and worth further study.

40. Dörr, "*Wer die Zeit nicht miterlebt hat . . .* ", vol. 2, 408. See the extensive interviews and commentary on women's occupation experiences, 375–586.

41. Consider the contentious discussions surrounding Helke Sander's film *Be-Freier und Befreite*, which explicitly claimed to "break the silence" around Soviet rapes of German women as well as the enthusiasm that greeted the post-2001 republication of Anonyma's *Woman in Berlin*. On the 1990s debates, see the special issue of *October* 72 (Spring 1995) titled "Berlin 1945: War and Rape, 'Liberators Take Liberties,'" particularly Grossmann, "A Question of Silence." On memories of rapes by French-Tunisian and Moroccan frontline troops and their consequences, including venereal disease, abortion, divorce, and suicide as well as the ongoing obstacles to telling the stories, see Ute Bechdolf, "Grenzerfahrungen von Frauen: Vergewaltigungen beim Einmarsch der französichen Besatzungstruppen in Südwestdeutschland," in *Kleiner Grenzverkehr/D'une rive à l'autre: Deutsch-französische Kulturanalysen*, ed. Utz Jeggle and Freddy Raphaël (Paris: Éditions de la Maison des sciences de l'homme Paris, 1997), 189–207.

42. Minutes in BAB (Sapmo), DFD BV (Bundesvorstand) 98, Sitzungen des Bundesvorstands des DFD. Meetings were held on May 23, July 26, and August 23, 1945; quote is from latter; Sauerbruch story from Hans Mahle, "Wie ich Prof. Dr. Sauerbruch und Dr. Hermes fand," in *Das Jahr 1945*, ed. Krauss and Küchenmeister, 65.

43. BAB (Sapmo), NL 182 (Walter Ulbricht)/246, Besprechung Gen. Ulbricht mit je 1 Genossen aus jedem Verwaltungsbezirk, Berlin, May 20, 1945, 47. See also LAB Rep. 12. Acc. 902/Nr. 5, Dienstbesprechungen der Amtsärzte 1945/6. For description of Ulbricht's meeting with KPD comrades, see Wolfgang Leonhard, "Mai 1945: Erinnerungen eines Mitglieds der 'Gruppe Ulbricht,'" in *Das Jahr 1945*, ed. Krauss and Küchenmeister, 61, and his memoir, *Die Revolution entlässt ihre Kinder*, 382–387; English version, *Child of the Revolution*.

44. Unpublished diary, Dr. Franz Vollnhals, by kind permission of Mrs. Itta Vollnhals. For discussion of the dubious legality but virtually full knowledge and tolerance by all relevant German and occupier authorities, including the Protestant (although not the Catholic) churches, see (Probst) Heinrich Grüber, *Erinnerungen nach sieben Jahrzehnten* (Cologne: Kiepenheuer and Witsch, 1971). Riess, in *Berlin Berlin*, also notes "a general permission" for abortion as of summer 1945, 33. Heide Fehrenbach points out in *Race after Hitler*, 59, that medical commissions to approve abortions were also set up in the American zone in Bavaria. The alacrity with which German and occupation officials turned to abortion as a remedy contrasts sharply to the French response to reports of rape by German soldiers in the First World War. See the excellent article by Ruth Harris, "The 'Child of the Barbarian': Rape, Race and Nationalism in France during the First World War," *Past and Present* 141 (November 1993): 170–206.

45. All depositions quoted from LAB Rep. 214/2814/220. See also Rep. 214/2814/221/1–2, 2740/156. For detailed discussion, including figures on timing of abortions, see Atina Grossmann, *Reforming Sex: The German Movement for Birth Control and Abortion Reform, 1920–1950* (New York: Oxford, 1995), 149–153 and 193–199; and idem, "A Question of Silence."

46. Report by H. Gnädig, LAB Rep. 240/2651/98.3. All quotes from Rep. 240/2651 are from an essay contest sponsored by the Berlin Senate in 1976, "Berlin 1945. Wie ich es erlebte"; 812 contributors, most of them women, described their experiences from May 1945 to the end of the blockade in June 1949.

47. Deutschkron, *Ich trug den gelben Stern*, 178. It is important to note that such stories about "plundering and murdering" Mongol-like Russians and "Russian-Asiatic destruction" also circulated about the "struggle on the eastern front" during World War I. See Elizabeth Harvey, *Women and the Nazi Far East: Agents and Witnesses of Germanization* (New Haven: Yale University Press, 2003), 203.

48. LAB Rep. 214/2814.

49. Thurnwald, *Gegenwartsprobleme*, 13.

50. Quoting a Hamburg gynecologist who also reports that "abortions are on the increase." Gollancz, *Darkest Germany*, letter to the ditor of *The Manchester Guardian*, December 4, 1946, 46–47.

51. Report by Gertrud Strubel, LAB 240/2651/131/1.

52. Report by Erna Köhnke, LAB 240/2651/655/1.

53. Report by Erna Beck, LAB 240/2641/83/1.

54. Report by Elli Fallner, LAB 240/2651/644/4.

55. Cited in Lewyn and Lewyn, *On the Run*, 277.

56. Levin, *In Search*, 276–277, 279–280. See longer discussion of "defiant and perverse" German women, 275–283.

57. See Naomi Seidman's careful study of Wiesel and the various versions of *Night*, "Elie Wiesel and the Scandal of Jewish Rage," *Jewish Social Studies* 3:1 (Fall 1996): 1–19, esp. 6. For a story of survivors' indirect "revenge" fulfilled by encouraging "three American soldiers who were known for their drunkenness and brutality" to violate German women, see Konrad Charmatz, *Nightmares: Memoirs of the Years of Horror under Nazi Rule in Europe, 1939–1945*, trans. Miriam Dashkin Beckerman, ed. Matthew Kudelka (Syracuse: Syracuse University Press, 2003), 239–240.

58. Bartov, *Brigade*, 117, 245; see also 46–47, 224–229.

59. Orbach and Orbach-Smith, *Soaring Underground*, 330–331.

60. Vallentin, "Die Einnahme von Berlin," 30.

61. Brenner, *"Das Lied ist aus,"* 99. The title of the chapter is "Befreit—und trotzdem voller Angst" (liberated and still full of fear).

62. Deutschkron, *Ich trug den gelben Stern*, 179–181. For discussion of Red Army rapes of women they had liberated from Ravensbrück concentration camp, see Jolande Withuis, "Die verlorene Unschuld des Gedächtnisses: Soziale Amnesie in Holland und sexuelle Gewalt im Zweiten Weltkrieg," in *Gedächtnis und Geschlecht: Deutungsmuster in Darstellungen des Nationalsozialistischen Genozids*, eds. Insa Eschebach, Sigrid Jacobeit, and Silke Wenk (Frankfurt/M: Campus, 2002), 96. For more on Jewish women's experiences, see chapter 5 below.

63. BAB (Sapmo), NL Ulbricht 182/853, 30.

64. BAB (Sapmo) NL 182/853, 97. See also report from Köpenick, 182/842, 132.

65. BAB (Sapmo) NL 182/852, 134. Report from the comrades in Köpenick.

66. LAB LAZ, Film 4, 13898.

67. BAB (Sapmo) NL 182/852, 132. To ZK from KPD Tegel-Süd, June 29, 1945. Naimark, *Russians in Germany*, 119, also cites this example.

68. See BAB (Sapmo), DFD, BV 1, Gründung des zentralen Frauenauschuss beim Magistrat der Stadt Berlin, 102; also protest by Käthe Kern, IV 2/17/80 ZK SED Abt Frauen. 1946, 71; and NL 182/853, 105. Also Naimark, *Russians in Germany*, 116–121.

69. BAB (Sapmo) NL 182/856, 27. *Der Funktionär*, KPD Bezirk Thüringen, October 1945.

70. *Berliner Zeitung* 1:10 (May 30, 1945): 2.

71. Berman and Kerner, *Soviet Military Law and Administration*, 48.

72. See, for example, "Prozess gegen Banditen in Eberswalde,"*Berliner Zeitung* 2:4 (January 6, 1946), front page, as well as regular coverage in *Tägliche Rundschau*.

73. Gordon Schaffer, *The Russian Zone* (London: George Allen & Unwin, 1947), 13. A British Army interpreter also downplayed women's "hysterical fear," quoting one victim who "even admitted that, had the soldier been American or British, she would have submitted with more grace and taken the whole thing as an incident to be expected from victorious armies." William Peters, *In Germany*

Now: The Diary of a Soldier, Impressions in Germany August—December 1945 (London: Progress Publishing Company, 1946), 69. American reporters were no different, satisfied that "terror tales from the Russian-held areas have dropped off sharply. No longer are bloodcurdling recitals of mass rape by U.S.S.R. soldiers gossiped about on the street corners of Berlin." Robert Haeger, "No More Conquerors," in *This Is Germany*, ed. Settel, 6.

74. *Berliner Zeitung* 2:4 (January 8, 1946), 3, for report on public attention and the verdicts.

75. According to the West Berlin women's magazine *sie* 45 (October 13, 1946), 3, women outnumbered male voters 16 to 10.

76. Deutscher, *The Observer*, October 13, 1946, in idem, *Reportagen*, 187. The results were devastating for the Communists and "extremely gratifying" for the western Allies: SPD got 48.7%, CDU 22%, LDP 9%, and the SED only 19.8%. See Zink, *United States in Germany*, 344. See in general, among many sources, Naimark, *Russians in Germany*, 119–121, and Donna Harsch, "Approach/Avoidance: Communists and Women in East Germany, 1945–9," *Social History* 25:2 (May 2000): 156–182.

77. BAB (Sapmo) NL 182/853, 39.

78. Wolfgang Harich, *Tägliche Rundschau* 291 (December 12, 1948): 3.

79. Aufruf der KPD, BAB (Sapmo) NL 182/853, 10.

80. Kopelev, *Aufbewahren für alle Zeit*, 19, 51, 137.

81. Wolfgang Harich, *Tägliche Rundschau* 291 (December 12, 1948), 3. I am indebted to Norman Naimark's work for steering me to this source. See also Naimark, *Russians in Germany*, 134–140.

82. I borrow the term "remasculinization" from Robert Moeller; he refers to Susan Jeffords, *The Remasculinization of America: Gender and the Vietnam War* (Bloomington: University of Inidiana Press, 1989).

83. See for example LAB Rep. 2651/2/184/1, report by Erna Kadzloch.

84. Howley, *Berlin Comand*, 65–66.

85. *6 Month Report* (4 January–3 July 1946), US Army Military Government, Report to the Commanding General US Headquarters Berlin District, 8. See the detailed Berlin police reports on rape, prostitution, drug addiction, and especially family suicides and murders in LAB Rep. 9/241, Polizeipräsident 1945–1948. New research shows that Berlin actually had the highest crime rate in the U.S. zone and that, despite the (understandable) focus on Soviet mass rape, after July 1945 a considerable number of sexual assaults were perpetrated by American soldiers. See Jennifer V. Evans, "Protection from the Protector: Court Martial Cases and the Lawlessness of Occupation in American-Controlled Berlin, 1945–48," in *GIs and Germans: The American Military Presence, 1945–1990*, ed. Detlef Junker and Thomas Maulucci (London/Washington: Cambridge University Press, forthcoming 2007). LAB Rep. 12. Acc. 902/Nr. 5, Dienstbesprechungen der Amtsärzte 1945/6, files demonstrate that crime, disorder, and the spread of infectious disease were also often blamed on refugees and displaced persons, leading to attempts to deny them entry to the city or at least limit the resources available to them.

86. *6 Month Report* (4 January–3 July 1946), US Army Military Government, Report to the Commanding General US Headquarters Berlin District), 8. By 1950,

with the Cold War in full swing, Frank Howley, who had been the American commander in Berlin, had changed his view of the Soviets: "We went to Berlin in 1945, thinking only of the Russians as big, jolly, balalaika-playing fellows, who drank prodigious quantities of vodka and liked to wrestle in the drawing room. We know now—or should know—that we were hopelessly naive." Howley, *Berlin Command*, 11.

87. Howley, *Berlin Command*; Maginnis, *Military Government Journal*; Murphy, *Diplomat*, among others, all make this point.

88. Bill Downs, *Newsweek*, April 16, 1945, 62.

89. McGovern, *fräulein*, 79. Here, too, similarities to Wakefield's *The Big Rape* and Anonyma's *Woman in Berlin* are worth investigating.

90. Maginnis, *Military Government Journal*, September 6, 1945, 294.

91. Shirer, *End of a Berlin Diary*, 148. See also Teo, "Continuum of Sexual Violence," 210–211. On the racial politics of rape accusations in the U.S. Army, see J. Robert Lilly and J. Michael Thompson, "Executing US Soldiers in England, World War II: Command Influence and Sexual Racism," *British Journal of Criminology* 37:2 (Spring 1997): 262–288. They count a total of 70 executions for rape in the European theater of operations during World War II (18 in England; of those 11 were African-American, and three others were of Latin or Mexican-American heritage, 267). See also J. Robert Lilly, "Dirty Details: Executing U.S. Soldiers during World War II," *Crime and Delinquency* 42:4 (October 1996): 491–516. African-Americans represented 83% of the soldiers executed for rape between 1942 and D–Day, 496. Lilly's book manuscript "Taken by Force: Rape and American Soldiers" has only been published in French: *La Face Cachée Des GI's: Les Viols commis par des soldats américains en France, en Angleterre et en Allemagne pendant la Seconde Guerre mondiale (1942–1945)* (Paris: Payot & Rivages, 2003). John Willoughby, *Remaking the Conquering Heroes: The Social and Geopolitical Impact of the Post-war American Occupation of Germany* (New York: Palgrve, 2001) notes 66, 69, that in 53.1% of rapes reported in 1946 the accused were African-American and that 55 of the 70 soldiers executed for crimes in the European theater were black.

92. William E. Griffith, "Denazification Revisited," in *America and the Shaping of German Society 1945–1955*, ed. Michael Ermarth (Providence: Berg, 1993), 155. See Fehrenbach, *Race after Hitler*, 54–55, for discussion of American sexual violence in Bavaria and the subsequent provision of abortions.

93. Hutton and Rooney, *Conquerors' Peace*, 67.

94. Zink, *United States in Germany*, 138. Among many contemporary sources on relations between American occupiers and German women (rape, fraternization, and venereal disease), see also Bach, *America's Germany*, esp. "GIs between the Sheets," 71–83; Hutton and Rooney, *Conquerors' Peace*; Ziemke, *U.S. Army*; and Habe, *Love Affair*.

95. Kay Boyle, "Summer Evening," in *Fifty Short Stories* (New York: New Directions, 1992), 405–406.

96. See for example Perry Biddiscombe, "Dangerous Liaisons: The Anti-Fraternization Movement in the U.S. Occupation Zones of Germany and Austria, 1945–1948," *Journal of Social History* 34:3 (Spring 2001): 611–647. For stories of

voluntary liaisons, see Heimatmuseum Charlottenburg, *Worüber kaum gesprochen wurde*. See also Beevor, *Fall of Berlin*, 27ff. According to reporter Robert Haeger, "No More Conquerors," in *This Is Germany*, 6, the Soviets cracked down on fraternization because of the large number of soldiers, some 20,000–30,000, stationed in Germany and Austria who deserted in 1946. For an astonishingly explicit record of multiple sexual encounters with both German women and women attached to the Red Army, as well as observations on (others') perceived excesses, see the recently compiled and translated diary by a Jewish–Ukranian Red Army officer, Wladimir Gelfand, *Deutschland Tagebuch. Aufzeichnungen eines Rotarmisten*, trans. Anja Lutter and Hartmut Schröder (Berlin: Aufbau Verlag, 2005).

97. According to Zink, *United States in Germany*, 138, "Sexual relations were prevalent, but rape was not frequent." In his official military history of the occupation, Ziemke, *U.S. Army*, 220–221, notes that "of the crimes committed by U.S. troops, the best—though by no means most accurately—documented was rape, and it showed a 'spiral increase' in the closing months of the war." Of 904 rape cases charged in the European theater between July 1942 and October 1945, 522 took place in Germany; 487 soldiers were tried for rapes allegedly committed in the months of March and April 1945. Zeimke adds, "By no means all the incidents were reported or, of those reported, brought to trial, and the conviction rate was relatively low. The legal requirement, a manifest lack of consent by the victim, was missing in so many cases that at last some courts began to hold that a man who enters a strange house, carrying a rifle in one hand, is not justified in believing he has accomplished a seduction." For further discussion of American sexual violence against German women and its racial coding in memory and prosecution, especially in southern Germany, see Fehrenbach, *Race after Hitler*, 46–73. Jennifer Evans's research, based on court-martial records for Berlin, exposes the darker side to American encounters with Germans in the divided city, rarely highlighted in the contemporary and ongoing focus on sexual liaisons: the violent assaults by U.S. soldiers on German women, in what Evans terms a "fraternization process gone wrong." Of 1,278 arrests of military personnel in 1947 in the American zone, 220 or 17% were for rape/sodomy; the number of arrests was obviously lower than the number of charges, which was in turn nowhere near the actual number of incidents. She notes a remarkable determination among Berlin women (perhaps influenced by their experience with the Red Army) to tell their story and see the perpetrators charged. See Evans, "Protection from the Protector."

98. Zink, *American Military Government*, 173; Levin, *In Search*, 179. Multiple novels and memoirs recount Americans' observations of rape and experiences of fraternization. Among many, see also Robert Peters, *For You, Lili Marlene: A Memoir of World War II* (Madison: University of Wisconsin Press, 1995).

99. McGovern, *fräulein*, 118. In 1958, Hollywood produced a sanitized film version, *Fräulein*, directed by Henry Koster. The German victim narrowly escapes rape and is eventually rescued (and presumably transported to America) by the American occupation officer whom her family had originally been kind to when he was shot down during the war, and who triumphs over her Nazi fiancé and her (false) registration as a prostitute in Berlin.

100. David Davidson, *The Steeper Cliff* (New York: Random House, 1947), 63, 33. Different sources give different dates. For discussion of shifts in U.S. fraternization policy, see Johannes Kleinschmidt, *Do Not Fraternize; die schwierigen Anfänge deutsch-amerikanischer Freundschaft 1944–49* (Trier: WVT Wissenschaftlicher Verlag, 1997).

101. Bach, *America's Germany*, 71–72, 75.

102. Saul K. Padover, "Why Americans Like German Women," *The American Mercury* 63: 273 (September 1946): 354–357.

103. On Americanism and anti-Americanism in Weimar, see Mary Nolan, *Visions of Modernity: American Business and the Modernization of Germnay* (New York: Oxford University Press, 1994). On continuing mixed feelings in the context of fraternization, see Heineman, *What Difference*, 97.

104. Kardorff, *Berliner Aufzeichnungen*, entries for July 9 and June 25, 1945, 289, 287 (the original diary was composed shortly after the war on the basis of letters, diary entries, and scrap notations).

105. Harris, "My Job in Germany, 1945–1954" in *America and the Shaping of German Society*, ed. Ermarth, 177. Among countless sources see Zink, *American Military Government*, 134; for a critique of American leniency see Tom Bower, *The Pledge Betrayed: America and Britain and the Denazification of Postwar Germany* (New York: Doubleday, 1982). For a recent account, see Michael Beschloss, *The Conquerors: Rooselvelt, Truman and the Destruction of Hitler's Germany, 1941–1945* (New York: Simon and Schuster, 2002).

106. See for example reports in Dörr, *"Wer die Zeit nicht miterlebt hat,"* esp. 430–432.

107. See Zink, *American Military Government*, 91–92. In general, see Goedde, *GIs and Germans*.

108. See for example LAB 210/840/91/2, for letters from occupation health officials regarding an "alarming" increase in prostitution near military bases and in bars in Berlin, July 9, 1947. The infection rate among U.S. troops reached a high of 19% in August 1945. See Goedde, *GIs and Germans*, 92. In early 1947, "over 9% of Berlin women aged nineteen to twenty and over 7% of those aged twenty-one to twenty-five were reported as infected," according to Heineman, *What Difference*, 103; on STD policies and rates, see also 99–105. Fraternization also, of course, brought pregnancies and offspring. An estimated 94,000 "occupation, babies" were born during the occupation 1945–1949. By June 1950, 14,175 German wives, 6 husbands, 750 children, and 1,862 fiancées of American forces had been permitted to enter the United States. See Petra Goedde, "From Villains to Victims: Fraternization and the Feminization of Germany, 1945–1947," *Diplomatic History* 23:1 (1999): 10–11. On the racial politics of fraternization and marriage policies, see Fehrenbach, *Race after Hitler*.

109. Bach, *America's Germany*, 75. *Newsweek* 28: 4 (July 22, 1946) 28 reported that by June 1946 the VD rate for troops in the European theater was 26% compared to only 7% on VE Day.

110. Maginnis, *Military Government Journal*, February 6, 1946, 337.

111. Produced by DEFA (Deutsche Film-Aktiengesellschaft), 1947, directed by Peter Pewas. On the limited availability of penicillin, see complaints in Gesund-

heitsamt Zehlendorf, December 30, 1946, LAB Rep. 210/840/91/1. Quote from Davidson, *Steeper Cliff*, 63, 33.

112. For further details of complicated regulations and how they shifted, See Goedde, *GIs and Germans*; Willoughby, *Remaking the Conquering Heroes*; Fehrenbach, *Race after Hitler*; and Raingard Esser, " 'Language No Obstacle': War Brides in the German Press, 1945–49," *Women's History Review* 12:4 (2003): 577–603. Heineman, *What Difference*, 98, cities U.S. Army reports that in 1946 an estimated "50–90% of U.S. troops 'fraternized' with German women; one in eight married men had entered a stable relationship in Germany."

113. "The GI Legacy in Germany," *Newsweek* 29 (June 16, 1947), 48–50, by James P. O'Donnell, Berlin bureau chief, 48.

114. Hutton and Rooney, *Conquerors' Peace*, 49, 50. See also Esser, "War Brides."

115. *The Big Lift*, 195, produced by William Perlberg, directed by George Seaton, with Montgomery Clift and Paul Douglas and active-duty military personnel. See Annette Brauerhoch, *Fräuleins und GIs: Geschichte und Filmgeschichte* (Frankfurt/M: Stroemfeld, 2006), for discussion of fraternization portrayals in postwar German and American films.

116. Zink, *United States in Germany*, 85.

117. Goedde, "From Villains to Victims," 2.

118. Padover, "Why Americans Like German Women," 357.

119. See Goedde, *GIs and Germans*. Semilurid novels like J.W. Burke's *The Big Rape* or William Gardner Smith's *Last of the Conquerors*, about African-American soldiers' adventures in Germany, and Thomas Berger's *Crazy in Berlin* tell much the same story. See also Höhn, *GIs and Fräuleins*, and Fehrenbach, *Race after Hitler*.

120. Middleton, *Last July*, 148.

121. Judy Barden, "Candy-Bar Romance—Women of Germany," in *This Is Germany*, ed. Settel, 164–165.

122. For example Cedric Belfrage, *Seeds of Destruction: The Truth about the US Occupation of Germany* (New York: Cameron & Kahn, 1954), 67–68. Belfrage had been a propaganda officer for SHAEF (Supreme Headquarters Allied Expeditionary Force); his report was written on a grant from the John Simon Guggenheim Foundation but then not published after he was accused of being a communist (and eventually deported to England after being called before Senator McCarthy's committee).

123. "Fahrt durch Berlin. Aus einem Brief von Master Sgt Charles Gregor," posted from Berlin on July 14, *Aufbau*, August 17, 1945, 32. Written on letterhead from the Führer's bunker, a favorite piece of stationery.

124. Moskowitz, "The Germans and the Jews," 7.

125. Knef, *Gift Horse*, 120–123. The marriage did not last. For a somewhat similar plot set in postwar Vienna, see the autobiographical film *Welcome in Vienna* (Austria, 1984/5), written by Georg Stefan Troller, directed by Axel Corti. Knef later starred in the German film *Hallo Fräulein*. See Esser, "War Brides," 593.

126. Smith, *Last of the Conquerors* 34, 35, 44, 57, 67–68. Smith also chronicles the antisemitism of some American officers, 105. For an excellent discussion

of Smith, his reporting for the *Pittsburgh Courier*, and the novel, see Fehrenbach, *Race after Hitler*, 35–39. See also Goedde's brief discussion in *GIs and Germans*, 109–112. All sources seem to pick up the same quotes. See also LeRoy S. Hodges, *Portrait of an Expatriate: William Gardner Smith, Writer* (Westport, Conn.: Greenwood Press, 1985). On race and U.S. occupation, see also Willoughby, *Remaking the Conquering Heroes*; Tim Schroer, "Race after the Master Race" (Ph.D. dissertation, University of Virginia, 2002); and Georg Schmundt-Thomas, "America's Germany: National Self and Cultural Other after World War II" (Ph.D. dissertation, Northwestern University, 1992).

127. Riess, *Berlin Berlin*, 60, 59. See also Thurnwald, *Gegenwartsprobleme*, 146.

128. Thurnwald, *Gegenwartsprobleme*, 77, 211. On women's "survival work," see also Annette Kuhn, "Power and Powerlessness: Women after 1945, or the Continuity of the Ideology of Femininity," *German History* 7:1 (1989): 35–46.

129. Heineman, *What Difference*, 95–96. On the impact of war on German sexual mores, see also Herzog, *Sex after Fascism*.

130. See Frank Biess, *Homecomings: Returning POWs and the Legacies of Defeat in Postwar Germany* (Princeton: Princeton University Press, 2006); "Survivors of Totalitarianism: Returning POWs and the Reconstruction of Masculine Citizenship in West Germany, 1945–1955," in *Miracle Years*, ed. Schissler; and "Men of Reconstruction—The Reconstruction of Men: Returning POWs in East and West Germany, 1945–1955," in *Home-Front*, ed. Hagemann and Schüler-Springorum, 335–358; also Robert G. Moeller, "The Last Soldiers of the 'Great War' and Tales of Family Reunions in the Federal Republic of Germany," *Signs* 24:1 (Autumn 1998): 126–146; and idem, *War Stories*.

131. Biddiscombe, "Dangerous Liaisons," says, n. 115, that "three U.S. soldiers were wholly or partially castrated by German assailants in 1946" while "during May and June 1946, there were five instances where young women were found dead in American barracks." Such incidents are particularly well documented in southern Germany, where there were so many U.S. soldiers (as well as Jewish DPs). On harassment of German women who fraternized, especially with occupiers of color, see Fehrenbach, *Race after Hitler*, 30–73. See also Perry Biddiscombe, "Sexual Behavior of American GIs during the Early Years of the Occupation in Germany," *Journal of Military History* 62 (January 1998): 155–174. For discussion of the 1950s, see Höhn, *GIs and Fräuleins*. For a critical view see Susanne zur Nieden, "Erotic Fraternization: The Legend of German Women's Quick Surrender," in *Home-Front*, ed. Hagemann and Schüler-Springorum, 207–307.

132. *Neue Berliner Illustrierte* 1:5 (November 1945), back page.

133. *Neue Berliner Illustrierte* 2:10 (November 1946), back page. On this transformation process, see Moeller, "Last Soldiers."

134. See Riess, *Berlin Berlin* (Jagd nach dem Mann), 76. See Franka Schneider, "'Einigkeit im Unglück'? Berliner Eheberatungsstellen zwischen Ehekrise und Wiederaufbau," in *Nachkrieg in Deutschland*, ed. Naumann, 206–226; and Annette Timm, "The Legacy of Bevölkerungspolitik: Venereal Disease and Marriage Counseling in Post World War II Berlin," *Canadian Journal of History* 18 (August 1998): 173–214.

135. See Heineman, *What Difference*, 100–104, on gender-specific politics of VD surveillance and treatment.

136. For excellent discussions of postwar marriage and family, see Heineman, *What Difference*, and Robert G. Moeller, *Protecting Motherhood: Women and the Family in the Politics of Postwar West Germany* (Berkeley: University of California Press, 1993). On perceptions and experiences of homosexuality in postwar Berlin, see Jennifer V. Evans, "Bahnhof Boys: Policing Male Prostitution in Post-Nazi Berlin," *Journal of the History of Sexuality* 12:4 (October 2003): 605–636.

137. Dörr, *"Wer die Zeit nicht miterlebt hat,"* 487.

138. Ilse Langner, *Flucht ohne Ziel: Tagebuch—Roman Frühjahr 1945* (Würzburg: Bergstadtverlag, 1984), 123. Interestingly, Langner also describes, 188, seeing liberated KZniks on the teeming roads and her sense that they were definitely not part of the same community of suffering. See also Heineman, "Hour of the Woman," and Moeller, *War Stories*.

139. Riess, *Berlin Berlin*, 47. This view contrasted with more cheerful portrayals of women in western Germany, and surely had to do with the experience of mass rape. For fraternization stories, see the interviews in Heimatmuseum Charlottenburg catalogue.

140. Maginnis, *Military Government Journal*, makes this point, 344. On the toll exacted by epidemics see *Berlin. Kampf um Freiheit* ed. Senat Berlin, 10.

141. Vallentin, "Die Einnahme von Berlin," 28.

142. Strobel, Nr. 131, 1, LAB, Rep. 240/2651.

143. Rape victims were not completely ignored by the Federal Republic. In the 1950s, some women in the West were minimally compensated, not for rapes, but in the form of support payments for any living children that had resulted. See BA (Koblenz) 189 (Federal Ministry for Family and Social Welfare) 6858 and especially 6863 for records of children of rape.

144. See Herzog, *Sex after Fascism*, and Heineman, *What Difference*, esp. 75–136.

145. See, among many sources, the massive documentation of Soviet crimes (prominently including rape) against Germans gathered in the 1950s by the West German Ministry for the Displaced and Refugees (Vertriebene und Flüchtlinge), *Ostdokumentation*, BArchK; and Cornelius Ryan, *The Last Battle* (London: Collins, 1966). For the GDR see Konrad Wolf's DEFA film *Ich war neunzehn*. Among more recent studies, see K. Erik Franzen, *Die Vertriebenen: Hitlers letzte Opfer* (Munich: Ullstein, 2001), and Pertti Ahonen, *After the Expulsion: West Germany and Eastern Europe, 1945–1990* (New York: Oxford University Press, 2003).

146. Thurnwald, *Gegenwartsprobleme*, 180. She is wonderfully clear-eyed in her description of this change of fortunes after defeat. For references to the "good life" under the Nazis, see also 31.

147. Bach, *America's Germany*, 236, 249.

148. Bourke-White, *Fatherland*, 147.

149. See synopsis of women's condition by the antifascist Annedore Leber, "Frauenprobleme," in *Bomben, Trümmer, Lucky Strikes: Die Stunde Null in bisher unbekannten Manuskripten*, ed. Peter Kruse (Berlin: Wolf Jobst Siedler, 2004), 180–186. For a summary (and good bibliography) of such dramatic versions, see Botting, *In the Ruins*.

150. *Berliner Zeitung* 1:44 (July 5, 1945), 1.

151. Berliner *Zeitung* 2:46 (February 24, 1946), 3, announcing new publication of *Die Frau von Heute*. See also Maria Höhn, "Frau im Haus und Girl im Spiegel: Discourse on Women in the Interregnum Period of 1945–49 and the Question of German Identity," *Central European History* 26 (1993): 57–90, and Jennifer V. Evans, "Constructing Borders: Image and Identity in Die Frau von Heute, 1946–1948," in *Conquering Women: Women and War in the German Cultural Imagination*, ed., Hilary Sy-Quia and Susanne Baackmann (Berkeley: University of California Press, 2000), 30–61.

152. See Atina Grossmann, "Feminist Debates about Women and National Socialism," *Gender and History* 3 (Autumn 1991): 350–358, and Adelheid von Saldern, "Victims or Perpetrators? Controversies about the Role of Women in the Nazi State," in *Nazism and German Society*, ed. David Crew (London: Routledge, 1994), 141–165. See also the special issue of *Ariadne: Almanach des Archivs der deutschen Frauenbewegung* 27 (May 1995) titled " 'Stunde Null': Kontinuitäten und Brüche."

153. *sie* 1:28 (August 25, 1946): 2.

154. See for example reports in *Berliner Zeitung* 1:77 (August 12, 1945), 4, on female doctors and nurses involved in "euthanasia"; and 1:25 (October 7, 1945), 1, on Irma Grese; 1:130 (October 13), 1, and 1:131 (October 14), 14, on Belsen trial; and 1:134 (October 18) on Hadamar Clinic trial in Nuremberg.

155. Quote from Bower, *Pledge Betrayed*, 182; see also 262, 354. Bower is, however, a rather tendentious source. In fact, their demonization notwithstanding, women defendants were, with some dramatic exceptions, treated more leniently. Serious research on women perpetrators (with an emphasis on representation of gender) has begun only in recent years. See Alexandra Przyrembel, "Transfixed by an Image: Ilse Koch the 'Kommandeuse' of Buchenwald," *German History* 19:3 (2001): 369–399; Weckel and Wolfram, eds., *"Bestien" und "Befehlsempfänger"*; and Gudrun Schwarz, *Die Frau an seiner Seite: Ehefrauen in der 'SS-Sippengemeinschaft'* (Hamburg: Hamburger Edition, 1997).

156. See for example discussions in *sie* (liberal feminist) and *Frau von Heute (SED)*; also Ilse Langner, *Flucht ohne Ziel*.

157. McGovern, *fräulein*, 129.

158. Burke, *The Big Rape*, 10, 259.

159. *The Big Lift*, filmed 1950. See also Hermann-Josef Rupieper, "Bringing Democracy to the Fräuleins: Frauen als Zielgruppe der amerikanischen Demokratisierungspolitik in Deutschland 1945–1952," *Geschichte und Gesellschaft* 17 (1991): 61–91.

CHAPTER THREE
"The survivors were few and the dead were many": Jews in Occupied Berlin

1. Boehm, *We Survived*, quote from original 1949 introduction, XVII.
2. Erich Nelhans papers, 5, CJA 5A1/36.
3. Reich-Ranicki, *Mein Leben*, 316.

4. It is crucial to note that the survival statistics for Berlin, as well as for Germany as a whole, are inconsistent, imprecise, and confusing; they depend heavily on when exactly the count was taken and by whom as well as on how "Jewish" and "end of war" is demarcated. The 6,000–7000 figure also included Jews, mostly East European survivors, who had arrived in the city after liberation. To the total of c. 15,000 Jews (of a pre-1933 Jewish population of about half a million) who survived within the Reich must be added perhaps 50,000 Jewish forced laborers who were liberated on German territory at the end of the war. See Stern, "Antagonistic Memories," 23. Andreas Nachama, "Nach der Befreiung: Jüdisches Leben in Berlin 1945–1953," in *Jüdische Geschichte in Berlin. Essays und Studien*, ed. Reinhard Rürup (Berlin: Hentrich, 1995), 268–269, estimates about 7,000 Jews in Berlin right after the war: 1,500 had survived the camps, 1,250 had been "U boats" in hiding, and c. 4,250 had been spared deportation because they lived in mixed-marriages with "Aryans"; of these 2,250 were so-called "star-wearers" while the rest who had children raised as Christians were "privileged" and not required to wear the star. Stern's corresponding figures are 1,155 camp survivors, 1,050 "illegals," 2,000 mixed marriage partners, and another 1,600 exempted from the star. Nachama also counts the pre-Nazi Jewish population of Berlin as about 200,000, which presumably includes those not officially registered as Jews. Michael Brenner notes that "More than 2/3 of the seven thousand members of the Berlin Jewish community of 1946 were intermarried or children of mixed marriages." See Brenner, "East European and German Jews in Postwar Germany, 1945–50," in *Jews, Germans, Memory*, ed. Bodemann, 52. Marion Kaplan in *Between Dignity and Despair*, while also noting, 232, the general figure of "approximately 15,000" surviving German Jews "within the pre-1938 borders," cites Konrad Kwiet and Helmut Eschwege in their *Selbstbehauptung und Widerstand: Deutsche Juden im Kampf um Existenz und Menschenwürde 1933–1945* (Hamburg: Christians, 1984) to state, 228, that "between 3,000 and 5,000 Jews came out of hiding in Germany. In Berlin, a city that once encompassed 160,000 Jewish Berliners, about 5,000 to 7,000 Jews hid, of whom only 1,400 survived." Here she counts those Jews who were hidden, and not those (included for example by Nachama, Stern, and Brenner) who had survived more or less aboveground in mixed marriages (or had themselves been "mixed"). For the figure of 1,400 underground survivors, see also Avraham Seligmann, "An Illegal Way of Life in Nazi Germany," *LBI Yearbook* 37 (1992): 327–361. The very latest figures, developed by a research project at the Institute for Research on Antisemitism at the Technical University, Berlin, suggest that perhaps 1,700 Jews who had gone underground survived. The interesting story here may not be the precise numbers but the variations of classification, and how they differ according to when and by whom the counting is done.

5. There is a relatively large literature—historical, memoir, diary, and fictional (and semifictional)—on Jews who survived in Berlin. See references in Atina Grossmann, "Versions of Home: German Jewish Refugee Papers Out of the Closet and Into the Archives," *New German Critique* (Fall 2005): 95–122. In general see Kaplan, *Between Dignity and Despair*, especially 145–228, and Wolfgang Benz, ed., *Überleben im Dritten Reich. Juden im Untergrund und ihre Helfer* (Munich: Beck, 2003). For the immediate postwar years, see also Gay, *Safe among the*

Germans, 144–201, and Atina Grossmann, "Home and Displacement in a City of Bordercrossers: Jews in Berlin, 1945–1948," in *Unlikely History: The Changing German-Jewish Symbiosis, 1945–2000*, ed., Leslie Morris and Jack Zipes (New York: Palgrave, 2002), 63–99. See also, besides the memoirs cited below, Leon Brandt, *Menschen ohne Schatten: Juden zwischen Untergang und Untergrund 1938 bis 1945* (Berlin: Oberbaum Verlag, 1984); Leonard Gross, *The Last Jews in Berlin* (New York: Simon and Schuster, 1982); Erika Fischer, *Aimée und Jaguar. Eine Liebesgeschichte, Berlin 1943* (Cologne: Kiepenheuer and Witsch, 1994); and Peter Wyden, *Stella: One Woman's True Tale of Evil, Betrayal, and Survival in the Holocaust* (New York: Simon and Schuster, 1992), the story of a notorious Jewish Jew catcher. For an account of imprisonment in the Gestapo prison located in part of the Jewish Hospital and a remarkable escape shortly before the fall of Berlin, see Lewyn and Lewyn, *On the Run*. According to Rivka Eklin, "The Survival of the Jewish Hospital in Berlin, 1938–1945," *LBI Yearbook* 38 (1993): 185, in February 1945 there were officially 162 "full" Jews in Berlin, including people who had been in hiding and caught by the Gestapo but not yet deported, some mental patients from neutral nations, a very few "protected" Jews, a few employed in deportation assembly centers (*Sammellager*) or as "catchers" and spies. Dr. Walter Lustig, the shadowy and compromised head of the hospital at war's end, who initially remained in the leadership of the remnant Jewish community, was arrested by the Soviet occupiers in late June 1945 and presumably executed. See Ulrike Offenberg, "Die Jüdische Gemeinde zu Berlin 1945–1953," in *Leben im Land der Täter*, ed. Schoeps, 133–156, esp. 133–136, and Charlotte Kahane, *Rescue and Abandonment: The Complex Fate of Jews in Nazi Germany* (Melbourne: Scribe, 1999), 61–72.

6. Among many examples, Lewyn and Lewyn, *On the Run*, 277–279. Also Barbara Lovenheim, *Überleben im Verborgenen: Sieben Juden in Berlin* (Berlin: Siedler, 2002), 21, 184–187; English version, *Survival in the Shadows: Seven Hidden Jews in Hitler's Berlin* (London: Peter Owen, 2002). On rape, see also Deutschkron, *Ich trug den gelben Stern*, 178–181.

7. Beck, *Underground Life*. On the remarkable Zionist youth resistance group Chug Chaluzi, see also Brandt, *Menschen ohne Schatten*.

8. Boveri, *Tage des Überlebens*, 127–128. On Boveri's career in the Third Reich, see Heike B. Görtemaker, *Ein deutsches Leben: Die Geschichte der Margret Boveri 1900–1975* (Munich: Beck, 2005).

9. Martin Riesenburger, *Das Licht verlöscht nicht. Ein Zeugnis aus der Nacht des Faschismus* (Berlin: Union Verlag, 1958, 1980), 54–59; also Stern, "Antagonistic Memories," 22.

10. "Erinnerungen von Roselotte Winterfeldt, geb. Lehmann, an ihre Schulzeit in Berlin 1938–1942," recollection of Edmund Lehmann's daughter, Yonkers, New York, January 2004, JMB archives.

11. Kieve Skiddel, unpublished letter, July 15, 1945. He also describes his amazement at discovering that there had been Germans who hid Jews, in particular, a worker in the Berlin subway system who had hidden a father and son for two and a half years. His own children "have gone to war and he knows nothing about them. He took in this family of three, though it would have meant his neck

if he had been discovered." Coincidentally, Marion Kaplan tells a later version of this family's story in *Between Dignity and Despair*, 217–220.

12. Joel Sayre, "Letter from Berlin," *The New Yorker*, July 28, 1945 (July 14 dispatch). One wonders whether Sayre fully meant the irony of the term "special treatment" (*Sonderbehandlung*).

13. Lovenheim, *Überleben im Verborgenen*, 187.

14. Fragebogen der Jüdischen Gemeinde zu Berlin, July 28, 1945, CJA, Berlin. I discovered Heinrich Busse's papers when I was clearing out my mother's Upper West Side apartment. See Grossmann, "Versions of Home."

15. The relatively small group of perhaps 2,000 Jewish Communists who returned to work in the Soviet zone have attracted a good deal of scholarly attention. Frank Stern, in a paper delivered at the German Studies Association conference, Atlanta, 1999, estimates 3,500–4,000, but he includes many who had claimed not the slightest identification with Judaism. See, for example, Jeff Peck and John Borneman, *Sojourners: The Return of German Jews and the Question of Identity (Texts and Contexts)* (Lincoln: University of Nebraska Press, 1995); also Herf, *Divided Memory*, and Jay Howard Geller, "Representing Jewry in East Germany, 1945–1953: Between Advocacy and Accommodation," *LBI Yearbook* 47 (2002): 195–214.

16. CJA 5A1/45, 14–19. Minutes, July 31, 1945, indicate that the Gemeinde was expecting about 900 returnees from Theresienstadt on August 12.

17. According to Ulrike Offenberg, initially the formal OdF designation was an honor, in contrast to the lesser recognition of victim status granted by the term "racially persecuted." By the end of September 1945, only 2,352 people had been recognized. See her "Die Jüdische Gemeinde zu Berlin 1945–1953," in *Leben im Land der Täter*, ed. Schoeps, 133–156, 145.

18. Report of the Jewish Community, Berlin, to the American Joint Distribution Committee, July 23, 1945, YIVO LWS 294.1/(folder)516/MK (microfilm) 488/R(eel)45. In 1946, all twenty-one members of the Gemeinde board were men. By 1948, a women's club under the leadership of camp survivor Jeanette Wolff, who had became a postwar social democratic city politician, had been established. Volunteers did social work, visiting the sick and lonely, including the otherwise excluded Aryan wives and widows. On women's role, see CJA 5A1/482–485. See also letter from Gemeinde to *Deutsche Volkszeitung* in 1945, filed in CJA 5A1/3, 127.

19. Letter addressed to occupiers, July 15, 1945, CJA 5A1/45, 43–44.

20. Report to AJDC, July 23, 1945, YIVO LWS 294.1/516/MK488/R45. For discussion of Jews under Soviet occupation, see Ulrike Offenberg, *Seid vorsichtig gegen die Machthaber: Die jüdischen Gemeinden in der SBZ und der DDR 1945 bis 1990* (Berlin: Aufbau, 1998), 9–77, and Geller, *Jews in Post-Holocaust Germany*, 90–122.

21. CJA 5A1/67. The file contains thirteen such letters (*Verlustanzeigen*).

22. Report to Major W. R. Holdsworth [British] Military Governor Berlin by the senior military chaplain on situation of Jewish community Berlin, August 3, 1945, CJA 5A1/45, 34–37.

23. On the situation of Jews, both under- and aboveground in wartime Berlin, see among many sources, Kaplan, *Dignity and Despair*, and Seligmann, "An Illegal Way of Life."

24. For discussion of varied Allied policies on, and struggles over, housing, see Clara Magdalena Oberle, "City in Transit: Ruins, Railways, and the Search for Order in Postwar Berlin (1945–1948)" (Ph.D. dissertation, Princeton University, 2006).

25. See for example discussions in Gemeinde Assembly in 1946, CJA 5A1/48.

26. *Der Weg* (Zeitschrift für Fragen des Judentums 1:1 (March 1, 1946). The Gemeinde census on April 1, 1946, in CJA 5A1/ 3, listing survivors by sector and categorized by gender, age, occupation, marital status, citizenship, and country of origin, registered 7,882 men, women, and children. The largest number (2,868) still lived in the Russian zone, followed closely by the British and American sectors (2,229 and 1,963), with the fewest in the French sector (762). Most (3,759) had been born in 1896 or earlier, and only a very small number (428) were seventeen and younger. Also quite atypically, the Berlin community listed 133 physicians, 53 lawyers, 105 artists, and 2,185 people who identified themselves as "businesspeople" (*Kaufleute*). Women were in a slight majority (4,017 to 3,905).

27. See the listing in CJA 5A1/3, 127. On this early period, see also Gay, *Safe among the Germans.*

28. Personnel file of Lucie Levy, Jewish Hospital Berlin, CJA 5A1/70. See Carola Sachse, ed., *Elisabeth Freund. Als Zwangsarbeiterin 1941 in Berlin: Die Aufzeichnungen der Volkswirtin Elisabeth Freund* (Berlin: Akademie Verlag, 1996), for a record of the year 1941 in Berlin, as experienced by a female Jewish slave laborer.

29. CJA 5A1/68. These *Eintritt* (entry) and *Austritt* (exit) records, still considered sensitive, are officially closed and available to the researcher only under very restricted conditions.

30. Brenner, "East European and German Jews," 58.

31. For one version of this quest for identification with the victims, see the postwar Berlin life of Lily Wust in Fischer, *Aimée und Jaguar*, 257–292. For figures on *Wiederaufnahme* (reentry), see CJA 5A1/3. On philosemitism, see Stern, *Whitewashing*. For an earlier analysis of this phenomenon, see Muhlen, *Return of Germany.*

32. See, for example CJA 5A1/65, 126. The certificate of return to Judaism for Dr. med. Konrad Fraenkel, born May 6, 1891, Berlin Weissensee, August 29, 1945, was signed by Martin Riesenburger, "Prediger der Jued. Gem. Berlin." Fraenkel attested that he had converted to Protestantism but had now left the Protestant faith. He had taken a prep course and declared his honest desire to return to Judaism and take the name David.

33. AJDCA file 446, Germany, Localities, Berlin, 1945–1946, Quarterly Report, Berlin Office, March 1–June 1, 1946; see also report by local director Eli Rock for June–July 1946. Assistance with other matters, such as family tracing services, package delivery, and emigration formalities, was granted more liberally.

34. Minutes of the Representative Assembly, March 6, 1946, CJA 5A1/48, 2. On the experience of intermarried Jews, see Beate Meyer, *"Jüdische Mischlinge." Rassenpolitik und Verfolgungserfahrung 1933–1945* (Hamburg: Dölling and Ga-

litz, 1999); Ursula Büttner, "The Persecution of Christian-Jewish Families in the Third Reich," *LBI Yearbook* 34 (1989): 267–289; and Kaplan, *Dignity and Despair*, 74–93. For background, see also Kerstin Meiring, *Die Christlich-Jüdische Mischehe in Deutschland 1840–1933* (Hamburg: Wallstein, 1998).

35. "Situation of the Jews in Greater Berlin," letter from Dr. Kurt Redlauer, director of the Evangelical Welfare Office, translated by U.S. Sgt. September 17, 1945, YIVO LWS 294.1/516/MK488/R45. The JDC itself estimated that an inclusive policy would have added at least 1,500 spouses to the rolls, and baptized Jews another 2,000. See "Quarterly Report, Berlin Office, March 1–June 1, 1946," AJDCA/446.

36. Letter to Rabbi Munk, September 9, 1947, and reply, CJA 5A1/190, 44–45.

37. CJA 5A1/46, 185.

38. In part because of the Rosenstrasse protest and Victor Klemperer's bestselling memoir, more attention has focused on "Aryan" wives. See Victor Klemperer, *I Will Bear Witness: A Diary of the Nazi Years, 1942–1945* (New York: Random House, 1999); Nathan Stolzfuss, *Resistance of the Heart: Intermarriage and the Rosenstrasse Protest in Nazi Germany* (New York: Norton, 1996); Wolf Gruner, "The Factory Action and the Events at the Rosenstrasse in Berlin: Facts and Fictions about 27 February 1943—Sixty Years Later," *Central European History* 36:2 (2003): 179–208; idem, *Widerstand in der Rosenstrasse: Die Fabrik-Aktion und die Verfolgung der "Mischehen" 1943* (Frankfurt/M: Suhrkamp, 2005); and the exchange between Stolzfuss and Gruner, *Central European History* 38:3 (2005): 450–464. See also the documentary by Michael Muschner, *Befreiung aus der Rosenstrasse* (1994), and the feature film *Rosenstrasse* (2003), directed by Margarete von Trotta.

39. From a widow who had converted to her husband's Christianity in 1935 and been forced underground when he died in 1944. All examples from CJA 5A1/221 and 218. My main sample is from *Wiederaufnahme* requests and approvals for last names starting with letters B–D.

40. Minutes of Representative Assembly, September 10, 1947, CJA 5A1/48, 32. In addition to those Jews who had already been intermarried during the Third Reich, memoirs suggest a significant number who married or formed liaisons with their rescuers. See, for example Beck, *Underground Life*. On *Ehrengerichte*, see also LAB Rep. 20, Nr. 4860–61), 332.

41. See for example CJA 5A1/50, 28.

42. CJA 5A1/189, 167; also 188, 323.

43. See complaints about children's religious school attendance as a condition for JDC assistance, including cash grants to help survivors reestablish businesses or professional practices, in CJA 5A1/45; also case documents in 5A1/453.

44. Erich Nelhans papers, 5 (June 25, 1946), 17 (November 25, 1946), 24 (May 30, 1947), 39 (April 18, 1947), and 196 (letter to Frl. Solomon, n.d.), CJA 5A1/36.

45. Beck, *Underground Life*, 33, 158–159.

46. Busse, letter, December 1945.

47. *Der Weg* 2:35 (August 29, 1947). The general Berlin press also covered the story.

48. Translation of "Odyssey of a Berlin Emigrant through Asia—Return of 295," *Der Telegraf*, August 22, 1947, LAB, Film Nr. 5, LAZ Nr. 2722, from OMGUS files 4/20–1/10. The article notes that 10,000 German Jews still remained in Shanghai. After the initial welcome, many Shanghai returnees reported a considerably less welcoming reception. For emigration to the United States from Shanghai under IRO (International Refugee Organization) auspices, see also Pettiss, *After the Shooting Stopped*, 225–227.

49. *Der Weg* 1:2 (February 7, 1946). The Hollywood movie *The Search* (1948) presents a similar story line, except that mother and son are non-Jewish Czechs. See chapter 5n10.

50. *Der Weg* 1:4 (March 22, 1946).

51. Ibid. See also "Die Lage der Jüdischen Gemeinde zu Berlin und ihrer Mitglieder, 1946." CJA 5A1/3, 241.

52. *Der Weg* 2:52 (December 25, 1947).

53. *Der Weg* 1:1 (March 1, 1946).

54. According to Meyer's curriculum vitae (*Lebenslauf*), CJA 5A1/25, 18.

55. *Der Weg* 1:33 (October 10, 1946).

56. Hans Winterfeldt, "Deutschland: Ein Zeitbild 1926–1945. Leidensweg eines deutschen Juden in den ersten 19 Jahren seines Lebens," 449, unpublished ME 690, LBI Archives.

57. *Der Weg* 1:10 (May 3, 1946).

58. *Der Weg* 1:26 (August 23, 1946).

59. Report by Eli Rock for June–July 1946, AJDCA/446.

60. *Der Weg* 1:1 (March 1, 1946).

61. Posener, *In Deutschland*, 139.

62. On such rescue networks, see Andreas-Friedrich, *Berlin Underground*; Beck, *Underground Life*; stories collected in Benz, ed., *Überleben*; Boehm, *We Survived*; Gross, *Last Jews*; and Kahane, *Rescue and Abandonment*.

63. Rosenthal, *Zwei Leben*, 80.

64. Report on conditions in the Gemeinde, CJA 5A1/3, 60–63. For a provocative analysis of how this division of the "Aryan" population into the largely indifferent and smaller groups of those actively helpful and those actively denunciatory worked in Nazi-occupied Warsaw, see Gunnar S. Paulsson, *Secret City: The Hidden Jews of Warsaw, 1940–1945* (New Haven: Yale University Press, 2002).

65. *Der Weg* 1:19 (July 5, 1946).

66. Winterfeldt, "Deutschland," 440.

67. Kieve Skiddel, letter, July 24, 1945.

68. *Der Weg* 1:6 (April 5, 1946).

69. *Aufbau*, September 21, 1945, 3. See also Ernst Günther Fontheim, "Bilanz eines Berliner Juden," *Aufbau*, August 24, 1945, 7.

70. *Aufbau*, September 14, 1945, 3. Finkelstein later withdrew the statement.

71. *Der Weg* 1:12 (May 17, 1946) and 1:13 (May 24, 1946).

72. *Der Weg* 1:3 (March 15, 1946), 3. See also Wyden, *Stella*. Some fifteen to twenty Jewish catchers operated in Berlin. See Kaplan, *Between Dignity and Despair*, 210. For an interesting analysis of discussions about revenge among German-Jewish survivors, see Jael Geis, *Übrig sein-Leben "danach"* (Berlin: Philo, 2000), 207–238.

73. Winterfeldt "Deutschland," 440–441.

74. Orbach and Orbach-Smith, *Soaring Underground*, 330–334. For another recent account of a young German-Jewish survivor's acts of revenge while serving as a U.S. Army investigator, see Matthew Brezinski, "The Secret: Giving Hitler Hell," *The Washington Post Magazine*, July 24, 2005: 8–17, 26. Such precious pieces of U.S. military clothing or other goods spontaneously offered by GIs to survivors were likely to eventually get Jews (especially DPs) into trouble for possessing "stolen" or otherwise illegally acquired military property.

75. Reich-Ranicki, *Mein Leben*, 316. The young Polish Jew became one of West Germany's leading literary critics.

76. See examples in CJA 5A1/76, file on children.

77. Letter from Loeb's widow, Saul M. Loeb collection, JMB Archive 2001/197/0.

78. Stephen Spender, *European Witness* (London: Hamish Hamilton, 1946), 215.

79. Gertrud Grossmann file, Oberfinanzpräsidium Brandenburg (OFP), Staatsarchiv Brandenburg, Potsdam.

80. CJA 5A1/45, 273–375, 413.

81. *Der Weg* 1:3 (March 15, 1946). Émigré British officer Julius Posener concludes his report from Germany, *In Deutschland*, 146, with the story of an elderly Theresienstadt survivor who, shortly after handing over to him the familiar letter to relatives reporting the death of all other family members who had not escaped, wrote another letter asking for clemency for a former Gestapo man with whom he was acquainted.

82. See Hutton and Rooney, *Conquerors' Peace*, 82. See also *Der Weg* 1:4 (March 22, 1946). Brenner also notes this phenomenon, "East European and German Jews," 58.

83. Insa Eschebach, " 'Wir möchten uns politisch bereinigen,' " in *Das Jahr 1945*, ed., Krauss and Küchenmeister, 206. Eschebach estimates that about 25% of the claimants whose files she studied mentioned some kind of support of Jews, 203.

84. Thurnwald, *Gegenwartsprobleme*, 149, 154, 158.

85. Reports from Zehlendorf, LAZ Rep. 280, Film Nr. 2. See also Bekanntmachung für den Verwaltungbezirk Tiergarten, 26 May 1945, LAB LAZ 13880.

86. *Berliner Zeitung* 1:7 (May 27, 1945), 4.

87. A thick OFP file documents the investigation into her escape and eventual capture. Upon receiving her deportation notice, Gertrud had decided to slip into hiding with her sister Erna, a remarkable step for two elderly ladies; almost all Jews who attempted to hide were under fifty. Gertrud and Erna apparently hid in a resort town in Brandenburg, probably protected by a faithful family maid, until they were denounced and caught in a complicated series of events that I am still trying to unravel.

88. Wiedergutmachungsamt files, 2WGA 1490/50 (Walter Grossmann) and 2WGA 3253/50 (Franz and Hans S. Grossmann). DM 20,000 was at the time less than $5,000; the Grossmanns had claimed a value of DM 110,000–125,000. For discussion of similar unsatisfactory legal struggles around "aryanized" property, using similar language, see Ronald Webster, "Jüdische Rückkehrer in der BRD

nach 1945: Ihre Motive, ihre Erfahrungen," *Aschkenas, Zeitschrift für Geschichte und Kultur der Juden* 5:1 (1995): 47–77. In fact, there were so many celebrations of 50-year business ownerships in 1988, a half century after the expropriation of Jewish property in Nazi Germany, that some localities embarrassedly asked their merchants to curtail their self-congratulatory advertising; it was a bit too obvious (*peinlich*), 72. As with so many issues concerning Jews in postwar occupied Germany, the situation in Berlin was unique in that a reparations edict had already been forced on Berlin by the Allied Kommandatura on July 26, 1949, well before the federal restitution program was approved by the Bundestag in 1956. Article 23 REO, "Restitution of Identifiable Property to Victims of Nazi Oppression from January 30, 1933 to May 8, 1945 on grounds of race, creed, nationality, or political beliefs" ordered "Where . . . the affected property has undergone fundamental changes which have substantially enhanced its value the Restitution Chamber may order the delivery of an adequate substitute in lieu of restitution. It shall consider the value of the property at the time of the unjust deprivation and the rights and interests of the parties."

89. When Paul Berghausen's grandson, the current owner of the Hotel Astoria, heard about my research via my brief article, "The Unfriendly History of one of the 'Friendliest Hotels' in Berlin," in *Aufbau* 13 (July 13, 2002), 13, he sent me a defensive and anxious (unsolicited) letter pointing out—just in case I should be harboring any notions about belated compensation—that for him the "the whole issue of the purchase" was long since "legally settled." He "protest[ed]" my "collective condemnation of the 'Berghausens,'" given that he after all "did not experience World War II (born in 1948) and thus can not be held responsible for the crimes of this era." Letter from Christian Berghausen, Berlin, 2002 (n.d). For a thoughtful meditation on "the claim to property" as "the site of a memory" see Cathy Caruth's analysis of Balzac's 1832 novel *Colonel Chabert*, about a Napoleonic Wars veteran for whom, 433, "The problem of property . . . represents an abyss of history that cannot be fully grasped by the legal Code" in "The Claims of the Dead: History, Haunted Property, and the Law," *Critical Inquiry* 28 (Winter 2002): 429–441. See also Dan Diner, "Restitution and Memory: The Holocaust in European Political Cultures," *New German Critique* 90 (2003): 36–44.

90. An estimated 46% of non-Jewish émigrés and only 4% of Jews returned. See Frank D. Hirschbach, "Heimkehr in die Fremde: Zur Remigration Deutscher Schriftsteller Nach 1945," in *Fremdheitserfahrung und Fremdheitsdarstellung in okzidentalen Kulturen*, ed. Bernd Lenz and Hans-Jürgen Lüsebrink (Passau: Wissenschaftsverlag Richard Rothe, 1999), 332.

91. Knef, *Gift Horse*, 110, 119.

92. Klink had taught at the Werner Siemens Realgymnasium. Reich-Ranicki, *Mein Leben*, 53. For a poignant evocation of a young Jewish U.S. Army soldier returning to his native Vienna, see the autobiographical film *Welcome in Vienna*, written by Georg Stefan Troller and directed by Axel Corti, 1986.

93. Hirschbach, "Heimkehr in die Fremde," 331–334. Zuckmayer quote, 334 from Zuckmayer, *Als wär's ein Stück von mir*, 559. Other writers who returned in occupier uniform, as either cultural officers or journalists, included Hans Habe, Albert Döblin, Stefan Heym, Hans Mayer, Klaus Mann, Golo Mann, and Erika

Mann. Zuckmayer resolved his conflict by returning neither to the Germany of his childhood nor the United States of his adult exile, but by moving to Switzerland.

94. Durand-Wever, "Als die Russen kamen. Tagebuch einer Berliner Ärztin," unpublished manuscript, 37 (February 1946). Especially younger refugees who were building new lives sometimes shared this sense of having been "lucky" in their misfortune. See, for example, Hans A. Schmitt *Lucky Victim: An Ordinary Life in Extraordinary Times, 1933–1946* (Baton Rouge: Louisiana State University Press, 1989).

95. Arendt, "Aftermath of Nazi Rule," 342, also notes the "deluge of stories about how Germans have suffered (true enough but beside the point)" and, at best, the resort to "draw up a balance between German suffering and the suffering of others." Curiously by 1950, she exempts Berliners from this indictment, claiming that Berlin is "so absolutely different from everything one sees and has to face in the rest of Germany, that Berlin is almost like another country." Indeed, "there is no embarrassment and no guilt-feeling, but frank and detailed recital of what happened to Berlin's Jews at the beginning of the war."

96. Loeb Collection, JMB.

97. Orbach and Orbach-Smith, *Soaring Underground*, 334.

98. Loeb collection, JMB.

99. Hutton and Rooney, *Conquerors' Peace*, 67.

100. Loeb collection, JMB.

101. Kieve Skiddel, letter, July 17, 1945.

102. Heinrich Busse, letter dated April 20, 1946. The Seder was conducted by U.S. chaplain Herbert Friedman and, in another odd twist, photographed by Gerhard Gronefeld (1911–2000), a German photographer who had worked for a Wehrmacht propaganda company on the eastern front. From 1935–36, he worked in the studio of Heinrich Hoffmann, official Nazi photographer, and also documented the Berlin Olympics. Fired by Hoffmann because he refused to join the Nazi Party, Gronefeld then worked as photojournalist for what was left of the *Berliner Illustrierte Zeitung*. He went on to work as a war photographer, posted first to Belgium and France, and then eastward to Poland, the Balkans, and the Soviet Union. As a *Sonderberichterstatter* (special correspondent), he photographed "military cleansing operations and reprisal actions." When he returned from the war, he made it his mission to document the revival of destroyed Berlin, and, through his (not entirely clear) connections with emigrated Jewish photojournalists, he received an assignment to photograph remaining Jewish life in the destroyed city. Encouraged by Gemeinde leader Julius Meyer, he produced a beautiful but also disturbingly decontextualized series of photos, "Die Juden von Berlin 1945/47," capturing certain "types" (somewhat in the style of August Sander) and "exemplary" life stories. Under the rubric "Liberated from the KZ and now back in their old occupations" (Aus dem KZ befreit, nun wieder im alten Beruf), he photographed, among others, a jazz trumpeter, "Bardame (female nightclub entertainer)," teacher, and shoemaker; in the series "Returned to life—deported Jews return to Berlin" (*Dem Leben wiedergegeben*), he presented a mother walking through the rubble and then assigned with her children to a "still intact" apartment, and "two old friends from the concentration camp meet again in Berlin." In 1950, after the blockade, Gronefeld moved to Munich and continued

to publish his photos in German illustrated magazines, such as *Neue Berliner Illustrierte, Heute, Stern,* and *Quick* as well as in *Life,* ending his career as an animal photographer. Clearly, there is a story here still waiting to be written. For basic information, see Winfried Ranke, *Deutsche Geschichte kurz belichtet: Photoreportagen von Gerhard Gronefeld 1937–1965* (Berlin: Deutsches Historisches Museum, 1991), 146–151. Gronefeld's photo archive is in the Deutsches Historische Museum, Berlin.

103. See Pettiss, *After the Shooting Stopped,* 118, for a critical view of GIs' tendency to adopt (and then inevitably to abandon) orphaned DP boys as mascots.

104. Quarterly report, AJDC, March 1–June 1, 1946, 41 in YIVO LWS 294.1/516/MK488/R45, also in 446/R37.

105. Maginnis, *Military Government Journal,* January 7 and 4, 1946, 326.

106. Vincent Meyer, UNRRA chief in Berlin, advocated accepting Yiddish and Polish as official languages because it was "most important that these people should not be deprived of the comfort and morale building afforded by the opportunity for direct correspondence with their friends and relatives outside Germany." In Berlin Reports, 3 May 1946, UNRRAA 399.1.2.

107. Howley, *Berlin Command,* 88.

108. Lt. Col. Harold Mercer, chief of Displaced Persons and Welfare Section (OMG), February 5, 1946, LAB OMGUS 4/20–1/10.

109. See Nachama, "Nach der Befreiung," 272, and Angelika Königseder, "Durchgangsstation Berlin: Jüdische DPs 1945–1948," in *Überlebt und Unterwegs,* ed. Fritz Bauer Institut, 189–206. See also Maginnis, *Military Government Journal,* 323–329, for a detailed (and candid) discussion of the Polish-Jewish refugee crisis and the considerable problems it posed for the Allied Kommandatura and especially the American occupiers. On the Kielce pogrom and its context, see David Engel, "Patterns of Anti-Jewish Violence in Poland, 1944–1946," *Yad Vashem Studies* 26 (1998): 43–85; also Abraham J. Peck, "Jewish Survivors," 35. See also the important new book (which appeared after I had finished my manuscript) by Jan T. Gross, *Fear: Anti-Semitism in Poland after Auschwitz; An Essay in Historical Interpretation* (New York: Random House, 2006). On the *Bricha* network, which transported Jews into the American zone of Germany and Italy for eventual aliyah to Palestine, see especially Bauer, *Flight and Rescue.* On the organization of clandestine immigration more generally, see also Zertal, *From Catastrophe to Power.*

110. Maginnis, *Military Government Journal,* January 8 and January 7, 1946, 327, 326. In his winter 1945/46 entries, this American official is preoccupied with the "critical issue" and "unpleasant" discussions about the Polish-Jewish refugees. See entries from December 28, 1945, through January 11, 1946, 324–329. "Hands off" quote from Philip Skorneck, Report on Berlin to Joint, YIVO LWS 294.1/516/MK488/R45.

111. Magistrat meeting, December 23, 1945, LAB LAZ Film Nr. 40, 8500/32.

112. According to UNRRA statistics, there were 6,644 Jewish DPs in Berlin in May 1947. These numbers included over 1,000 Jewish infants and children. UNRRAA/399.1.2, Berlin Reports.

113. Maginnis, *Military Government Journal,* 299.

114. Berger, *Displaced Persons: Growing Up American*, 305, quoted from his mother's composition book.

115. See for example the memories of Mayer Abramowitz, "Dps, GIs and Cos: Working Undercover in Post-war Europe," *Moment* 7: 44–48. On the relationship of Jewish displaced persons, the *Bricha*, and Jewish relief agencies to the American occupiers in Berlin and throughout Germany, see among many sources, Maginnis, *Military Government Journal*, Hyman, *Undefeated*, and Grobman, ed., *In Defense of the Survivors: The Letters and Documents of Oscar A. Mintzer*.

116. *Transcript (not verified for accuracy) of oral history testimony during videotaped interview with Herbert Friedman on June 12, 1992, Washington, D.C., on behalf of USHMM. Bricha* officials, who actually shared with the U.S. military the goal of moving Jews out of Berlin as quickly as possible, smuggled Jewish refugees, disguised as nurses or aid workers, onto special trains evacuating children and the sick to the western zones.

117. Abramowitz, "Dps, GIs and Cos."

118. Report on Conditions in Poland, July 1, 1946, contains such notices, CJA 5A1/39, 1–3. These experiences are also detailed in (among many other reports) Skorneck, Report on Berlin, February 21, 1946, YIVO LWS 294.1/516/MK488/R45.

119. According to Skorneck, Report on Berlin, Howley told him "that he is a graduate of a 'Jewish University,' by which he means New York University, which has a large Jewish registration."

120. Berlin Reports, November 23, 1946. Weekly Report Nr. 33. UNRRA liaison officer to acting chief of Operations, Germany, UNRRAA 399.1.2.

121. AJDCA/446, Quarterly Report, Berlin Office, March 1–June 1, 1946, 12. Ironically, some German Jews living in the United States complained to the Joint about favoritism toward the East European DPs. Letter from American-Jewish K C Fraternity, February 21, 1946.

122. Hyman, *Undefeated*, 281. Photos document the good relations among Jewish, JDC, and U.S. officials. See for example the photo of a dinner party honoring General Joseph McNarney, at Schlachtensee DP camp, with Rabbi Philip Bernstein, Chaplain Herbert Friedman, Eli Rock (JDC director for Berlin), and Hans-Erich Fabian of the Gemeinde. Photo number W/S 15516, USHMM.

123. Nachama, "Nach der Befreiung," 272.

124. All these numbers are inexact. See also Königseder, "Durchgangsstation Berlin," 189–206. The Berlin Sector/Public Welfare Branch of the Office of Military Government estimated on June 20, 1947, that there were 8,000 German Jews in Berlin receiving aid from the American Joint Distribution Committee, plus 6,300 Polish Jews in two DP camps. Another memorandum, also on June 20, 1947, for the Jewish Agency for Palestine, counted 8,000 persons in Düppel and 4,000 in Wittenau camps. See also Gay, *Safe among the Germans*, 182–201.

125. See, for example, Hyman, *Undefeated*, 340.

126. Eli Rock, January 28, 1998, RG-50.030–0386, oral history testimony transcript from videotaped interview, Washington, D.C., USHMM.

127. Berger, *Displaced Persons: Growing Up American*, 306.

128. K.E., "Juden in Deutschland," *Der Tagesspiegel* 39 (December 5, 1945), 3.

129. Hans-Erich Fabian, "D.P.," *Der Weg* 2:7 (February 14, 1947), 2.

130. Habe, *Aftermath*, 124, 132. On the lack of interest in the return of Jewish academics or professionals, see Frank Stern, "Academia without Jews: The Universities in the Wake of *Entjudung*," in *Whitewashing*, 158–212. On the bitter disappointment of returnees, see also Anthony Heilbut, *Exiled in Paradise: German Refugee Artists and Intellectuals in America from the 1930's to the Present* (New York: Viking Press, 1983), 325–349. Even anti-Nazi political refugees planning a post-Nazi Germany had assumed that antisemitism would continue, that Jews would remain an "alien element," and warned against any substantial return. See David Bankier, "The Jews in Plans for Postwar Germany," *Jewish Political Studies Review* 14:3–4 (Fall 2002). From web of Jerusalem Center for Public Affairs, jcpa.org/phas/phas-bankier.

131. Ernst-Günter Fontheim, "Befreite Juden," *Der Weg* 1:28 (September 6, 1946), 5–6. The Gemeinde also collected the threatening letters it received complaining about German-Jewish attempts to repossess property and suggesting that the influx of East European Jews only provoked antisemitism. See CJA 5A1/39, 1–5. Other examples of threatening letters in 5A1/63, 9 (including an affidavit from film producer Artur Brauner about pogroms in Poland).

132. Appeals by friends to the western Allies for help proved fruitless, and Nelhans was convicted by a Soviet military tribunal on grounds of "anti-Soviet attitudes" and collaboration with Americans instigating anti-Soviet activites. He disappeared into the Gulag; all traces vanish after the 1950s, and he reportedly died in a Soviet labor camp in 1953. In 1997, two great-nephews managed to gain a formal reversal of the military tribunal verdict and a posthumous rehabilitation. Prenzlauer Berg Museum, http:/www.bmp.de/vorort/0101/a14.shtml. See also "Ein Zionist als Landesverräter," *Jungle World* Nr. 21 (2001), May 16, 2001 (from Internet). On concerns about abuse of Jewish identity cards both for black market trading and political purposes, see report of an angry meeting among Gemeinde officials, on December 7, 1945, in response to interrogations by Soviet authorities, CJA 5A1/63, 12–15. See also among many sources Offenberg, *Seid vorsichtig*, and Herf, *Divided Memory*.

133. *Der Weg* 1:39 (November 22, 1946), 2. See also commentary on "Lagerleben," *Der Weg* 1:27 (August 30, 1946), 1–2.

134. JDC Report on Berlin by David Resnick, October 11, 1946, AJDCA/446, Germany, Localities, Berlin, 1945–1946.

135. Report on Berlin by Philip Skorneck, Paris, February 21, 1946, in YIVO LWS 294.1/516/MK488/R45. According to Ulrike Offenberg, *Seid vorsichtig*, 24, Julius Meyer had been a *Kapo* (although it is entirely unclear what that might mean in this context) in Auschwitz, where his first wife and daughter were murdered. He survived the death marches back to Germany, returned to Berlin in July 1945, and then fled the antisemitic wave in the German Democratic Republic in 1953. He eventually settled in Brazil, where he died in 1979. For JDC comments on Berlin Gemeinde, see also notes 136 and 137.

136. Quarterly Report, Berlin Office: AJDC, March 1, 1946–May 31, 1946, 3. YIVO LWS 294.1/516/MK488/R45.

137. See Quarterly Report, Berlin office, March 1–May 31, 1946, 3–11. See also CJA 5A1/3, 256. Die Lage.

138. See *Der Weg* 2:15 (April 10, 1947).

139. Michal Bodemann argues that at a time when people moved relatively easily across the open borders between the Soviet and western zones, the Jewish and antifascist experiences were still closely linked, despite deep disagreements about the relative status of "resisters" and "victims" of fascism. See "Reconstructions of History: From Jewish Memory to Nationalized Commemoration of Kristallnacht in Germany," in *Jews, Germans, Memory*, ed. idem, 191–194. Berlin Jews disagreed on whether to join with other victims of fascism in the VVN (*Vereinigung der Verfolgten des Naziregimes*, Association of Victims of National Socialism), established on November 23, 1946, with 181 delegates representing 20,000 persecuted survivors, or to remain separate in exclusively Jewish associations. See also Nachama, "Nach der Befreiung," 279, and Herf, *Divided Memory*, esp. 69–105. On life in the SBZ shortly after the war, see also Victor Klemperer's postwar diary, *Und so ist alles schwankend: Tagebücher Juni bis Dezember 1945* (Berlin: Aufbau, 1995).

140. Amalie apparently died a year after her letter, in 1949. The Gemeinde received her Nachlass because presumably there was no one else interested in taking it. Nachlass Amalie Harnisch, CJA 5A1/367.

CHAPTER FOUR
The Saved and Saving Remnant: Jewish Displaced Persons in the American Zone

1. Letter from a teenage survivor to his only remaining relative in Berlin, December 21, 1945, Paris, Erich Nelhans papers, CJA 5A1/36, 127.

2. Marcus and Peck, eds., *Among the Survivors . . . Letters of Major Irving Heymont*, 38.

3. Bourke-White, *Fatherland*.

4. Joseph A. Berger, "Displaced Persons: A Human Tragedy of World War II," *Social Research* 14 (1947): 45–58, 45.

5. Quote from Albert A. Hutler papers, P-156, AJHSA. Hutler was chief of the Displaced Persons Office of Detachment F1E2, American Military Government, Mannheim.

6. Wyman, *DPs*, 17.

7. See among many other sources, W. Arnold-Forster, "U.N.R.R.A.'s Work for Displaced Persons in Germany," *International Affairs* 22 (1946), 1–13.

8. Berger, "Displaced Persons: A Human Tragedy," 46, 51. As always, the statistics are not precise. The wide range of figures cited depends on who is counting whom, when, and how DPs are defined. "Displaced Persons" (DPs) are also variously defined in various contemporary documents and later historical sources. A general definition drawn from UNRRA documents would include all those persons displaced and/or left stateless by the dislocations of the Second World War or all those UN nationals or nonenemy (or ex-enemy) nationals who were refugees in the Allied occupation zones, including (but not limited to) prisoners of war, forced or voluntary laborers, deportees, and camp prisoners. Other definitions

divide DPs into UN DPs and ex-enemy DPs (who were not eligible for aid and generally not included in the count). UNRRA, at least initially, considered all DPs to be in need of repatriation. Wahrhaftig, *Uprooted*, estimated that the Allied armies had to cope with over 7 million DPs in occupied territories, plus some 12 million ethnic German expellees. Robert G. Moeller, in *Protecting Motherhood: Women and the Family in the Politics of Postwar West Germany* (Berkeley: University of California Press, 1993), 21, refers to 10 million ethnic German expellees plus "another eight to ten million 'displaced persons'—foreigners forced to come to Germany as workers during the war and others removed from their homelands by the Nazis for racial, religious, or political reasons, including survivors of concentration camps." According to a recent German source, of the 5,856,000 foreigners in Germany at the end of the war, 1.2 million remained by 1946. Ulrich Müller, *Fremde in der Nachkriegszeit. Displaced Persons—zwangsverschleppte Personen in Stuttgart und Württemberg-Baden 1945–1951* (Stuttgart: Klett-Cotta, 1990), 18. Niewyk, ed. *Fresh Wounds*, 21, notes that in 1945 Jews were "less than one percent of the fourteen million refugees from Hitler's war, although by 1947, they made up a far larger proportion—perhaps as much as one third— of the approximately 700,000 unrepatriated displaced persons in Europe." It should be noted that, according to the Yalta agreement of February 1945, priority was given to the (sometimes forced) repatriation of Soviet citizens. By November 1945, some 2 million had been transported back, occasionally at gunpoint. For a fine overview of DPs in general, see Wyman, *DPs*, and Marrus, *The Unwanted*.

9. Padover, *Experiment*, 343. Many survivors recount their problems in convincing Soviet soldiers that they were Jews and not Germans; "Ivrey kaputt," they were frequently told.

10. For a brief discussion of the sources for this critical term, see Abraham J. Peck, "She'erit Hapletah: The Purpose of the Legacy," *Midstream* 37:3 (1990): 27–30, and Mankowitz, *Life between Memory and Hope*, 2–3. See also my introduction above, n. 31.

11. Statistical data are inexact and bewildering, largely because of change over time, inconsistencies in categorizations among those collecting data, and the difficulties of counting a highly mobile and sometimes illegal population. It is not always clear whether references are to all three western zones of Germany, only the American zone, or the American zones in Germany, Austria, and Italy. In November 1946, the JDC reported widely cited figures of 145,735 Jewish DPs officially registered in the American zone, including 101,614 in DP camps, 35,950 "free" livers in German towns and cities, 4,313 in children's homes, and 3,858 in *Hachscharot* (agricultural kibbutzim); see, for example Jacqueline Dewell Giere, "Wir sind Unterwegs, Aber Nicht in der Wüste: Erziehung und Kultur in den Jüdischen Displaced Persons—Lagern der amerikanischen Zone im Nachkriegsdeutschland, 1945–1949" (Ph.D. dissertation, Goethe Universität, Frankfurt/M, 1993), 102. Current estimates are considerably higher. Most sources now agree that by spring 1947 the Jewish DP population in Germany was approximately 200,000, but "Some 300,000 Jewish DPs and refugees are believed to have passed through Austria and/or Germany for longer or shorter periods of time." For the latter figure and a succinct summary of the estimates, see Lavsky, *New Beginnings*, 34, 27–36. Grodzinsky, *In the Shadow of the Holocaust*, 118 (revised English

translation of Hebrew text, *Human Material of Good Quality—Jews vs. Zionists in the DP camps, Germany, 1945–1951* [Tel Aviv: Hed Aertz, 1998]) has figures in a similar range (apparently covering Germany, Austria, and Italy): an estimated 70,000 in late summer 1945, 220,000–260,000 Jewish DPs altogether at the height of Jewish flight west in late 1946, and 245,000 in summer 1947. However, by looking at migration patterns to target countries (rather than trying to establish numbers in Europe), Grodzinsky, 117, comes to an even higher total of 330,000 Jewish DPs altogether "who passed through DP camps in Germany, Austria, and Italy" between 1945 and 1951. The higher figures for 1946 and 1947 include the influx into the American zone of mostly Polish Jews who had been repatriated to Poland from the Soviet Union, and a later wave in 1947 from Czechoslovakia, Hungary, and Romania. Given the conflicts with British authorities over immigration to Palestine and the American recognition of Jews as a special separate group, those "infiltrees" were steered, or themselves migrated, to the U.S. zone. In May 1947, the U.S. zone housed sixty assembly centers, fourteen children's centers, thirty-eight *Hachscharot*, seventeen hospitals, one convalescent home, three rest centers, three sanatoria, one transit camp, one staging area, and 139 recognized groups of "free-living" DPs in German communities. Additionally, there were two assembly centers in the American sector of Berlin and eighteen camps in the U.S. zone of Austria. By comparison, there were only two assembly centers and two children's centers in the British zone and one children's center in the French sector of Berlin. See Hyman, *Undefeated*, 146–147. There were also camps and *Hachscharot* in Italy. Jacobmeyer, "Jüdische Überlebende als 'Displaced Persons,'" counts sixteen small sites for Jewish DPs in the French zone and notes that German Jews were concentrated in communities in the north of the zone. There were also camps and *Hachscharot* in Italy. On Austria, see Thomas Albrich, *Exodus Durch Österreich: Die jüdischen Flüchtlinge* (Innsbruck: Haymon, 1987), and Helga Embacher, *Neubeginn ohne Illusion: Juden in Österreich nach 1945* (Vienna: Picus Verlag, 2000). At a minimum, a quarter million Jewish survivors lived in or passed through the American zone; fairly accurate probably is JDC official Theodore Comet's assessment (while reiterating that "exact figures are hard to come by") that "the total number of Jewish DPs was 300,000, mainly in occupied Germany, but also in Austria and Italy," in "Life Reborn in the Displaced Persons Camps (1945–51): An Untold Story of Courage," *Journal of Jewish Communal Service* (Summer 2000), 300. The same figure is used by Mankowitz, *Life between Memory and Hope*, 2.

12. On UNRRA planning and work, see the standard account by its chief historian, Woodbridge, *UNRRA*. For specific plans related to projected Jewish refugees, see Zorach Wahrhaftig, *Relief and Rehabilitation: Implications of the UNRRA Program for Jewish Needs* (New York: Institute of Jewish Affairs of the American Jewish Congress and World Jewish Congress, 1944).

13. For an excellent account of this hectic preparation and arrival, see the memoir by Pettiss, *After the Shooting Stopped.*

14. Wahrhaftig, *Relief and Rehabilitation*, 147, 162.

15. Arnold-Forster, "U.N.R.R.A.'s Work," 11.

16. Report on UNRRA Operations in the European Region, April/May, 1946, Committee of Council for Europe, UNRRAA/401.2.3.

17. Wahrhaftig, *Uprooted*, 38–39.

18. Ignatz Bubis (with Peter Sichrovsky), "*Damit bin ich noch längst nicht fertig": Die Autobiographie* (Frankfurt/M: Campus, 1996), 57.

19. Wahrhaftig, *Uprooted*, 75.

20. Report by Zorach Wahrhaftig, November 27, 1945, "Life in camps 6 months after liberation," in *Archives of the Holocaust*, vol. 9, ed. Abraham J. Peck, 130.

21. Brenner, "East European and German Jews in Postwar Germany, 1945–50," in *Jews, Germans, Memory*, ed. Bodemann, 50.

22. Wahrhaftig, *Uprooted*, 61, 63.

23. Kardorff, *Berliner Aufzeichnungen*, 291. She must have been referring to units of the British Army's Jewish Brigade from Palestine, which had entered Germany on June 20 from Italy via Austria.

24. Nadich, *Eisenhower and the Jews*, 97. See also the report by a German-Jewish GI, Pfc. Hans Lichtwitz, "Blau Weiss Marsch durch Deutschland," *Aufbau*, October 19, 1945, 32.

25. Schochet, *Feldafing*, 131.

26. Katie Louchheim, "DP Summer," *Virgina Quarterly Review* 61 (1985): 704.

27. By summer 1946, there were altogether nine large DP camps in the Munich region, five of them within the city limits. Only Feldafing, Föhrenwald, and Landsberg were reserved for Jewish DPs. See Holian, "Between National Socialism and Soviet Communism," 71–72, also 68–88 for a full discussion of "Munich as a DP city" for both Jews and non-Jews.

28. Klausner, *Letter to My Children*, 65–66. There are multiple versions of Grinberg's story and the Kaufering prisoners' liberation. See YIVO, LWS 294.1/(folder)535/MK(microfilm)488/R(eel)46; Schwarz, *Redeemers*, 3, 5–6, 155; Hyman, *Undefeated*, 80–83; Ernest Landau, "Men Versus Supermen," in Schwarz, *The Root and the Bough*, 127–132. See also Mankowitz, *Life between Memory and Hope*; Abraham J. Peck, "She'erit Hapletah: The Purpose of the Legacy," *Midstream* 37:3 (1990): 27–30; and, for a concise general summary, Bauer, "Initial Organization," esp. 143–155. It is important to keep in mind that many of the Zionist groups in the DP camps had arrived together via the *Bricha* and traced their origins back to the ghettos, partisan groups, and camps. In fact, much of the early DP leadership in Bavaria had already begun to organize in the Dachau Kaufering labor camp, which had received many Jews as they arrived on death marches from the East. See Bauer, "Initial Organization."

29. Smith quote in Louchheim, "DP Summer," 703. Numbers reported range from 1,000 to 3,000 in various sources.

30. See Haia Karni, "Life at the Feldafing Displaced Persons Camp, 1945–1952" (master's thesis, Baltimore Hebrew University, May 1997); also Schochet, *Feldafing*, for a survivor's account.

31. Nadich, *Eisenhower and the Jews*, 226.

32. Levin, *In Search*, 244. See also the report by welfare officer Ethel Ostry, to UNRRA, about 250 Polish-Jewish DPs at Schloss Langenzelle, July 1945, in Hutler Papers, AJHS.

33. Padover, *Experiment*, 359.

34. Louchheim, "DP Summer," 704.

35. Karni, "Life at the Feldafing Displaced Persons Camp." See Bauer, "Initial Organization," for discussion of this early politicization on Zionist terms.

36. This frequently used slogan derived from a partisan song composed by Hirsh Glik after the Warsaw Ghetto uprising. "[W]ritten not in pencil but in blood," it said, "Never say . . . that this is my final road and that the light of day is banished by the clouds / The hour we have waited for is near / Beneath our tread the earth shall tremble / We are here." See Peck, "Jewish Survivors," and Juliane Wetzel, "Mir szeinen doh: München und Umgebung als Zuflucht von Überlebenden des Holocaust 1945–1948," in *Von Stalingrad zur Währungsreform. Zur Sozialgeschichte des Umbruchs in Deutschland*, ed. Martin Broszat, Klaus-Dietmar Henke, and Hans Woller (Munich: R. Oldenbourg, 1988). See, in general, Shirli Gilbert, *Music in the Holocaust: Confronting Life in the Nazi Ghettos and Camps* (New York: Oxford University Press, 2005).

37. An irritated Judah Nadich called the Harrison Report an "exaggerated bombshell" in *Eisenhower and the Jews*, 63. For a similar view, see Hyman's recollections in *Undefeated*, 55, 63.

38. On Harrison see Senator Harris Wofford, "The Power of the Individual," Philadelphia Bar Association, 1992, listed on Schader Law Firm website, http://www.shsl.com/shs12.nsf. For an excellent analysis of the Harrison Report and the international politics of the DP issue, see Dan Diner, "Jewish DPs in Historical Context," paper for the workshop "Birth of a Refugee Nation: Displaced Persons in Postwar Europe 1945–1951," Remarque Institute, NYU (April 2001); Diner, "Elemente der Subjektwerdung," in *Überlebt und Unterwegs*, ed. Fritz Bauer Institut. See also the summary discussion in Holian, "Between National Socialism and Soviet Communism," 98–106. The full text of the report and Truman's response are available online at www.ushmm.org/dp/politic6 .htm. Quotes from report from Dinnerstein, *America and the Survivors*, appendix, 292–304. Despite the repeated emphasis on Harrison's most dramatic statements, most of his report is clearheaded and controlled. Its portrayal of the relative comfort of rural Germans compared to the miserable conditions of the Jewish survivors, as well as the understanding of U.S. military, UNRRA, and Jewish perceptions and intentions, is generally consistent with many other accounts.

39. Lewis F. Gittler, "Everyday Life in Germany Today," *American Mercury* 61 (October 1945), 406–407.

40. Union O.S.E. [Oeuvre de Secours des Enfants], *Report on the Situation of the Jews in Germany* (Geneva, 1946, based on reports from October/December 1945), 9–12, 18.

41. M.Sgt. Werner T. Angress to Dr. Curt Bondy, of Richmond, Va., article in *Richmond Times Dispatch*, June 4, 1945 (from Gross Breesen Letter 15, Richmond, Va.). On the experiences of Angress and fellow German Jews who served as interrogators in the U.S. Army, see the film *The Ritchie Boys*, directed by Christian Bauer, 2004, and Rebekka Goepfert and Christian Bauer, *Die Ritchie Boys: Deutsche Emigranten im amerikanischen Geheimdienst* (Munich: Hoffmann und Campe, 2005).

42. Letter from officer stationed near Dachau, September 17, 1945, AJDCA, AR 1945/1964, file 399A.

43. O.S.E., *Report*, 9–12, 18.

44. Dinnerstein, *America and the Survivors*, 292–304.

45. Dan Diner, "Elemente der Subjektwerdung," 230.

46. See survey of estimated numbers in n. 11 above.

47. The British immediately assumed that the American position was the result of Democratic Party pandering to the Jewish vote and "Zionist lobby" as midterm elections loomed. See Arieh J. Kochavi, "Anglo-American Discord: Jewish Refugees and United Nations Relief and Rehabilitation Administration Policy, 1945–1947," *Diplomatic History* 14 (1990): 529–551, esp. 540; also Lavsky, *New Beginnings*, 51–55; and Jo Reilly, David Cesarani, Tony Kushner, and Colin Richmond, eds., *Belsen in History and Memory* (London: Frank Cass, 1997).

48. For example, Hyman, *Undefeated*, 373.

49. Dinnerstein, *America and the Survivors*, 292–304.

50. Lt. Col. Mercer (U.S. Army), February 5, 1946, OMGUS 4/20–1/10, LAB. See also Wahrhaftig, *Uprooted*, 39.

51. Hutton and Rooney, *Conquerors' Peace*, 84. For sober critiques see Bendersky, *"Jewish Threat,"* and Dinnerstein, *America and the Survivors*. For a more tendentious report by one American soldier, see Robert L. Hilliard, *Surviving the Americans: The Continued Struggle of the Jews after Liberation* (New York: Seven Stories Press, 1997).

52. Levin, *In Search*, 232. For Heymont quote, see n. 2 above.

53. Hyman, *Undefeated*, 329. On Jewish chaplains in U.S.-occupied Europe and their manifold roles, see Grobman, *Rekindling the Flame*. For a different view, see also Andreas Brämer, "Rescue Aid as a Method of Repression—American Military Rabbis and the Problem of Jewish Displaced Persons in Postwar Germany," *Jewish Studies Quarterly* 2 (1995): 59–76; in general, see Lewis Barish, ed., *Rabbis in Uniform: The Story of the American Military Chaplain* (New York: J. David, 1962).

54. Marcus and Peck, eds., *Among the Survivors . . . Letters of Major Irving Heymont*, October 8, 1945, 25, and postscript, 109.

55. Letters from Sgt. Dave Katz, Frankfurt, June 19, 1945, June 21, 1945; letter by son of member of Sisterhood of the Yeshiva Talmud Torah of Crown Heights, September 19, 1945; all in AJDCA/AR 1945/1964/399A. Files 399 and 399A contain numerous such impassioned letters from American Jewish soldiers, generally passed on to Joint officials by relatives or congregation members who received them, as well as the official responses. These extraordinary primary documents deserve further study. On the general experience of Jewish soldiers in both World War II theaters, see Deborah Dash Moore, *GI Jews: How World War II Changed a Generation* (Cambridge, Mass.: Harvard University Press, 2004).

56. Letter from Chaplain Max B. Wall, with Ninth Infantry Division, August 19, 1945, AJDCA/399A.

57. Letter from Dave, Frankfurt, June 21, 1945, AJDCA/399A.

58. Letter from Chaplain Wall, August 19, 1945, AJDCA/399A.

59. Albert A. Hutler, Memories, Hutler Papers, AJHSA. "SNAFU" lingo appears in many sources; see, for example Dawidowicz, *From That Place and Time*, 290. For critiques of U.S. military, see especially Bendersky, *"Jewish Threat."*

60. Letter from Moe Leavitt, JDC, to Rabbi Leonard J. Mervis in Terre Haute, Ind., September 5, 1945, AJDCA/399A.

61. Klausner, *Letter to My Children*, 59.

62. The JDC had to invest a great deal of energy in responding to outraged letters from community leaders and relatives who, having received (and often enclosing) these passionate missives, inquired about what was happening to their donations. For responses, see AJDCA/399 and 399A.

63. Letter to Dr. Atlas, Hebrew Union College, from Abraham Klausner, Deutsches Museum Munich, August 28, 1945, on letterhead of Central Committee of Liberated Jews of Bavaria, AJDCA/399A.

64. Letter from Berlin, October 5, 1945, AJDCA/ 399A.

65. See Marcus and Peck, eds., *Among the Survivors . . . Letters of Major Irving Heymont*; comments at Munich DP conference, 1995.

66. Conversations with Shlomo Leser, Haifa, Israel, November 2005. I am grateful to Dr. Leser, who is working on his own manuscript about the experiences of Jewish DPs, for sharing his insights and memories.

67. Cable sent July 15, 1946, to JDC in Paris, AJDCA/390. Klausner returned to Kassel, Germany, in early 1947 but, disgusted with army regulations, left the service within months. He later became an iconoclastic Reform rabbi in the United States. See his memoir, *Letter to My Children*.

68. Letter from Morris to Sol, December 27, 1945, AJDCA/499/1.

69. The leaflet was included in letter from Sgt. Edward D. Mayer, Fifty-fifth Fighter Group, AJDCA/ 399A. Chaplain Klausner also presided over the first Passover seders in Munich, April 15–16, 1945; see the bitter rewriting of some of the traditional text in Saul Touster, ed., *A Survivors' Haggadah* (Philadelphia: Jewish Publication Society, 2005; originally printed by U.S. Army, 1946).

70. Letter from Jerry, AJDCA/399A.

71. Letter to his parents from Seymour after Rosh Hashanah services in Munich, September 9, 1945, AJDCA/399A.

72. Letter to Uncle Carol from Fred, September 9, 1945, AJDCA/399.

73. Letter from officer stationed near Dachau, September 17, 1945, AJDCA/399A.

74. Letter from Seymour, September 9, 1945, AJDCA/399A.

75. Ibid.

76. Quote from Biber, *Risen from the Ashes*, 14. See Zalman Grinberg, "We Are Living Corpses," in *Aufbau*, August 24, 1945. Phrases such as "human debris" or "living corpses" were ubiquitous in contemporary reports (indeed, there is a remarkably consistent and repetitive language in most documents describing Jewish DPs). For one example, see the accounts in Karen Gershon, *Postscript: A Collective Account of the Lives of Jews in West Germany since the Second World War* (London: Victor Gollancz, 1969). For a strong argument against the view of survivors as "living corpses" and for the agency, and what Abraham J. Peck in "Jewish Survivors" has called "the revolutionary ideology" of the *She'erit Hapletah*, see Ze'ev Mankowitz, "The Formation of *She'erit Hapleita*: November

1944–July 1945," *Yad Vashem Studies* 20 (1990): 337–370, and idem, "The Affirmation of Life in *She'erith Hapleita*," *Holocaust and Genocide Studies* 5:1 (1990): 13–21.

77. *Berlin Sector. A Report by Military Government From July 1, 1945 to September 1, 1949*, 113, LAB, Rep. 9.

78. Marcus and Peck, eds., *Among the Survivors . . . Letters of Major Irving Heymont*, letter to his wife, September 19, 1945.

79. For a smart critique, see Michael André Bernstein, "Homage to the Extreme: The Shoah and the Rhetoric of Catastrophe," *Times Literary Supplement*, March 6, 1998, 6–8.

80. Levin, *In Search*, 247.

81. Bartov, *Brigade*, 56, 148.

82. Zertal, *From Catastrophe to Power*, 8–9.

83. I. F. Stone, *Underground to Palestine and Reflections Thirty Years Later* (New York: Pantheon, 1978), 24.

84. Haas, *Aftermath*, 18.

85. Interviews with Helen (Zippi) Tichauer, New York, 2004/5. Patton quote from Dinnerstein, *America and the Survivors*, 16–17. See also Martin Blumenson, ed., *The Patton Papers: 1940–1945* (Boston: Houghton Mifflin, 1974), 751. Also cited in Constantin Goschler, "The Attitude towards Jews in Bavaria after the Second World War," *LBI Yearbook* 36 (1991): 447; reprinted in Moeller, ed., *West Germany under Construction*, 231–250; and Bendersky, *Jewish Threat*, 357. Soap story in Schochet, *Feldfing*, 37.

86. Quoted in Grobman, *Rekindling the Flame*, 57. See also Dinnerstein, *America and the Survivors*. For examples of such basically sympathetic but highly unsentimental and critical views of survivors, see the remarkable letters home to wives in the United States by two American-Jewish officials, one military and the other from the Joint: Marcus and Peck, eds., *Among the Survivors . . . Letters of Major Irving Heymont*, and Grobman, ed., *In Defense of the Survivors*.

87. Pettiss, *After the Shooting Stopped*, November 6, 1945, 126. Pettiss, who became a tireless advocate for the Jewish DPs, published these honest diary entries in 2004. See also the even more unblinkingly judgmental early description of "untidy and dirty" as well as "neurotic and unhappy" Jewish DPs in Feldafing and Föhrenwald by British UNRRA worker Francesca Wilson in *Aftermath*, 45, 117.

88. O.S.E., *Report*, 60.

89. Nadich, *Eisenhower and the Jews*, 66.

90. O.S.E., *Report*, 16–19.

91. Memoirs are filled with heartbreaking stories of comrades and relatives (or "camp sisters") who survived camps, death marches, and liberation together only to have one of them die afterward, or of survivors who cracked when they finally had to accept that even the one strong sibling that they had believed alive had not made it. For one example, among many, see Judith Sternberg Newman, *In the Hell of Auschwitz: The Wartime Memoirs of Judith Sternberg Newman* (New York: Exposition Press, 1963), 118, on the death of her sister.

92. Pettiss, *After the Shooting Stopped*, 127, 193.

93. Wilson, *Aftermath*, 138. Also quoted in Anton Gill, *The Journey Back from Hell: An Oral History, Conversations with Concentration Camp Survivors* (New York: William Morrow and Co., 1988), 138.

94. Report by Mrs. M. Warburg, February 12, 1946, AJDCA/398.

95. Hirschmann, *Embers Still Burn*, 161. See also Macardle, *Children of Europe*, 225, 250; also the thoughtful report by UNRRA worker Anton A. Pritchard, "The Social System of a Displaced Persons Camp," thesis in social relations, April 18, 1950, courtesy of Marion Pritchard (Vershire, Vermont). For a more recent brief discussion, see Nicholas Stargardt, *Witnesses of War: Children's Lives under the Nazis* (New York: Alfred A. Knopf, 2005), 348–377.

96. Letters from Arno Krakauer to Erich Nelhans, February 2, 1946, December 21, 1945, CJA 5A1/36, 126–127.

97. See William G. Niederland, *Folgen der Verfolgung: das Überlebenden-Syndrom, Seelenmord* (Frankfurt/M: Suhrkamp, 1980), based on his pioneering 1961 article in *Hillside Hospital Journal*. For a powerful relatively early study of the "psycho-sociological paradox" that a "remnant of a broken race, which began as a group of people shattered in body and soul, became an extremely active and militant faction," and for a sensitive analysis of "later pathological after-effects," see also Mark Dvorjetski, "Adjustment of Detainees to Camp and Ghetto Life and Their Subsequent Readjustment to Normal Society," *Yad Vashem Studies 5* (1963): 193–220. On trauma and trauma diagnoses of Jewish survivors, see, among many other more recent sources, Haas, *Aftermath*, and Israel W. Charny, *Holding on to Humanity: The Message of Holocaust Survivors; The Shamai Davidson Papers* (New York: New York University Press, 1992). Incredibly, it was not until 1965 that the German government physicians (*Vertrauensärzte*) who determined restitution eligibility recognized the validity of nonphysical complaints. See Martin S. Bergmann and Milton E. Jucovy, eds., *Generations of the Holocaust* (New York: Columbia University Press, 1982), 67–73.

98. "Report of Conference of AJDC Country Medical Directors, Paris, May 1947, 66–67, in YIVO LWS 294.1/271/MK488/R23. See also letter to Moe(ses) Leavitt, from Joseph Schwartz, JDC Paris, 9 November 1946, AJDCA/390. For observers' shocked impressions of the Feldafing survivors, with their "furtive look and gestures of hunted animals," and obsession with food, see Wilson, *Aftermath*, 41.

99. See Nadich, *Eisenhower and the Jews*, 77–78. Oscar Mintzer of the Judge Advocates Office counted 103 such cases in April 1946 alone. See Grobman, ed., *In Defense of the Survivors: The Letters and Documents of Oscar A. Mintzer*, 363. Mintzer reports repeated cases of violent and even deadly confrontations between Jews and Germans, including police. In fact, male DPs in particular were hauled into court with some frequency, usually on black marketeering or stolen property charges (sometimes after repossessing their own property). In most cases, the DPs were eventually released but not before having spent time in German jails, having their goods confiscated, and earning an arrest record that would compromise their chances for emigration to the United States.

100. Francesca Wilson expressed a common view that the DP camps benefited from the arrival of refugees from the East. Of Föhrenwald, she wrote, "The presence of so many Jews who had been fighting with the Partisans or hidden

by Aryan papers made our Jews more buoyant [*sic*] than groups from the concentration camps. They had kept hope and ideals, and they leavened the lump." *Aftermath*, 139.

101. To Leo Schwarz from Dr. Maurice Kaplan on meeting of Jewish Physicians Association at Berchtesgaden, January 13–14, 1947, YIVO LWS 294.1/272/ MK488/R23, 79–80.

102. Hyman, *Undefeated*, 257–258.

103. Dr. J. M. Shapiro, JDC Report, October 25–November 12, 1945, AJDCA/392.

104. Confidential report by Captain G. Weisz on field trip to U.S. zone, April 5, 1946, UNRRAA/ 399.1.1.

105. Frederic Morgan, unpublished diary, entries for March 23 and 26 and December 8, 1945; March 27 and March 23, 1946, Imperial War Museum Archives, London. I am grateful to Ben Shephard for giving me copies of these excerpts.

106. Figure is from Wyman, *DPs*, 129. According to Ronald Webster, "American Relief and Jews in Germany, 1945–1960," *LBI Yearbook* 38 (1993): 293–321, the Joint supported about 200,000 Jews in postwar Germany, with an initial budget of only $500,000; presumably the funding grew over time. See also Kurt R. Grossmann, *DP Problem*.

107. Interview, Sandor Muskal, Yonkers, N.Y., June 16, 2003, about Feldafing.

108. Klausner, *Letter to My Children*, 111, 114.

109. JDC cable, January 5, 1946 referring to UNRRA director Morgan's statements about DPs, quoting his claim from *Daily Telegraph and Morning Post*, January 3, 1946, AJDCA/446. This report has the quote as "pockets bulging with money." Cantor story from Vida, *Doom to Dawn*, 59. For a vivid account of UNRRA field workers' struggle to understand the nature of this postwar Jewish flight from Eastern Europe, see Pettiss, *After the Shooting Stopped*, 134–177. Bendersky, *"Jewish Threat,"* 362–363, notes that Fiorello LaGuardia finally removed Morgan on August 20, 1946, after he had supposedly described UNRRA as a "cover for Soviet espionage, black marketeers, and dope peddlers."

110. Captain G. Weisz, April 5, 1946 UNRRAA 399.1.1.

111. Louchheim, "D.P. Summer," 696. UNRRA fielded an extremely interesting group of mostly young women to work with the (not only Jewish) DPs. See, for example, the reports by Hulme, *Wild Place*; Pettiss, *After the Shooting Stopped*; Gitta Sereny, *The German Trauma: Experiences and Reflections, 1938–1999* (London: Allen Lane, 2000); Francesca Wilson in *Aftermath*; unpublished memoirs by Marion Pritchard (Vershire, Vermont).

112. Arnold-Forster, "U.N.R.R.A's Work" 12.

113. Pettiss, *After the Shooting Stopped*, 141, 151.

114. Nadich, *Eisenhower and the Jews*.

115. Morgan, unpublished diary, entry for March 27, 1946.

116. Dawidowicz, *From That Place and Time*, 279, 281–283, 286, 294–295.

117. Hyman, *Undefeated*, 282.

118. Mayer Abramowitz, "Dps, GIs and Cos: Working Undercover in Postwar Europe," *Moment* 7, 48.

119. Syrkin, *State of the Jews*, 34. First published in "My D.P. Students," *Jewish Frontier* (June 1965): 7–12.

120. Statement by Z. Grinberg in minutes of CK (Central Committee of Liberated Jews) and JDC Meeting, Munich, November 15, 1945, AJDCA/392.

121. O.S.E., *Report*, 51.

122. Hutton and Rooney, *Conquerors' Peace*, 83.

123. Grinberg, November 15, 1945, AJDCA/392.

124. Nadich, *Eisenhower and the Jews*, 86.

125. Ernst Landau, in his (rather condescending sounding) report "Purim auf Elmau," in *Aufbau*, collected in YIVO LWS 294.1/535/MK488/R46, 1060–1066. See also the similar report in Schwarz, *Redeemers*, 111–112.

126. See also Mankowitz, *Life between Memory and Hope*, 187.

127. See, for example YIVO DPG 249.2/(folder)167/MK(microfilm)483/R(eel)14, Cirkular Nr. 5, December 2, 1946, and May 6, 1947.

128. Hyman, *Undefeated*, 93.

129. "Up to Date Description of the Operation of J.A.F.P (Jewish Agency for Palestine) as at 15th June 1947," USHMM Archives.

130. Pinson, "Jewish Life," 113–114, 117. See also "Report of Conference of Country Medical Directors in Europe of the AJDC," Paris, May 1947, 66–70, in YIVO LWS 294.1/271/MK488/R23 as well as Grodzinsky, *In the Shadow of the Holocaust*, 49–51, 80–99. For detailed discussion of the youth movement and the kibbutzim among the DPs, see Patt, "Finding Home and Homeland." See also UNRRAA/401.7.5; 401.2.1 (Child Welfare Section); and 401.2.7 (Jewish Agency for Palestine).

131. Syrkin, *State of the Jews*, 27, different transliteration in "My D. P. Students."

132. Pettiss, *After the Shooting Stopped*, 146, diary entries for December 11 and 13, 1945. See 147–150 for a helpful analysis and population breakdown of the Jewish refugees pouring into Munich.

133. See the important report, written during the war, that calls the Soviet Union, "after France and Great Britain, the most important haven . . . for refugees." Arieh Tartakower and Kurt R. Grossmann, *The Jewish Refugee* (New York: Institute of Jewish Affairs of the American Jewish Congress and World Jewish Congress, 1944), 264, 266–267. There are no accurate numbers; 104,602 Polish Jews registered with Polish authorities, but since most refugees in the Soviet Union did not register, the actual number living there was certainly much higher. The majority, almost twice as many men as women, gathered in the South, in Soviet central Asia and southern Kazakhstan, with some in Siberia and European Russia. In 1943, the same institute still believed that "the only substantial group which survived the terror partially intact were the 1,800,000 Jews, mostly Polish and East European, who fled to Russia." Quoted from "Hitler's Ten-Year War on the Jews," Institute of Jewish Affairs, New York, 1943, 300, cited in Anton A. Pritchard, "The Social System of a Displaced Persons Camp." The Soviets even offered citizenship to the Polish Jews, although that would prove to be a very double edged sword after the war, and most Jews wisely resisted the offer. See Lucjan Dobroszycki, "Restoring Jewish Life in Post-war Poland," *Soviet Jewish Affairs* 3:2 (1973): 58–72. See also Keith Sword, "The Welfare of Polish-Jewish

Refugees in the USSR, 1941–43: Relief Supplies and Their Distribution," and Josef Litvak, "Polish-Jewish Refugees Repatriated from the Soviet Union to Poland at the End of the Second World War and Afterwards," in *Jews in Eastern Poland and the USSR, 1939–46*, ed. Norman Davies and Antony Polansky (New York: St. Martin's Press, 1991), 145–160 and 227–235. Some 500,000 Polish Jews sought refuge in the USSR, and over 200,000 were repatriated after the war. It is a sign of how awful the options for East European Jews were during the war that, despite the extremely difficult conditions endured by Polish Jews in the Soviet Union, a historian can conclude that the Soviets, themselves under tremendous pressure, "displayed greater generosity than any other country." Especially later in the war, a real Jewish cultural life was established, partly with aid from the Joint. See Josef Litvak, "Jewish Refugees from Poland in the USSR, 1939–1946," in *Bitter Legacy: Confronting the Holocaust in the USSR*, ed. Zvi Gittleman (Bloomington: Indiana University Press, 1997), 123–150, esp. 147. This crucial, complicated, and compelling story has not been adequately addressed by current historians. Although the postwar situation in Poland is well covered, there is to my knowledge remarkably little published material on the Soviet period, at least in English. For a very different view on the situation of Soviet Jews, see Amir Weiner, *Making Sense of War: The Second World War and the Fate of the Bolshevik Revolution* (Princeton: Princeton University Press, 2001).

134. Hautzig, *Endless Steppe*, 226. See also her brief recollections of life in Siberia in idem, *Remember Who You Are: Stories about Being Jewish* (New York: Crown, 1990), XI–XII. Berger, *Displaced Persons: Growing Up American*, conveys very well how murky this history still is; see especially the vivid segments from his mother Rachel Berger's account of her experiences in the Soviet Union, postwar Poland, and German DP camps, 276–312. A larger number of memoirs seem to have been produced by Jews deported to the Soviet Union from the Bukovina region and especially Czernowitz. See Rachelle Rosenzweig, *Russische Eisblumen. 35 Jahre in sowjetischer Unfreiheit* (Frankfurt/M: Haag + Herchen, 1993); Julius Wolfenhaut, *Nach Sibirien verbannt: As Jude von Czernowitz nach Stalinka 1941–1994* (Frankfurt/M: Fischer, 2005); and the fictionalized memoir by Dorothea Sella, *Der Ring des Prometheus. Denksteine im Herzen. Eine auf Wahrheit beruhende Romantrilogie* (Jerusalem: Rubin Mass Verlag, 1996).

135. Letter to Moe(ses) Leavitt, from Joseph Schwartz, JDC Paris, November 9, 1946, AJDCA/390. According to UNRRA statistics, of 14,689 Jewish DPs registered in Baden-Württemberg on December 7, 1946, only about 10% were KZ survivors; see Müller, *Fremde in der Nachkriegszeit*, 57.

136. Berger, *Displaced Persons: Growing Up American*, 307. On the "Asiatics," see Schwarz, *Redeemers*, 164. For brief references to Polish Jews in the Soviet Union, see also Königseder, *Flucht nach Berlin*, 33–43.

137. On the Kielce pogrom, in which a charge of ritual murder led to the massacre of at least 42 Jews who had tried to return to their hometown, and its general context, see David Engel, "Patterns of Anti-Jewish Violence in Poland, 1944–1956," *Yad Vashem Studies* 26 (1998): 43–85, and Peck, "Jewish Survivors," 35. See also Jan T. Gross, "A Tangled Web: Confronting Stereotypes Concerning Relations between Poles, Germans, Jews, and Communists," in *The Politics of Retribution in Europe: World War II and Its Aftermath*, ed. Istvan Deak, Jan T.

Gross, and Tony Judt (Princeton: Princeton University Press, 2000), 107–116, and, most recently, Gross, *Fear*. On the situation of surviving and returning Jews in postwar Poland, see also Litvak, "Polish-Jewish Refugees," 227–239; Dobroszycki, "Restoring Jewish Life"; and the Dr. Jerzy Glicksman collection at YIVO archives in New York. For a somewhat more (still) hopeful contemporary assessment, see section on Poland by Leon Shapiro, *American Jewish Yearbook* 49 (1947/48): 380–392.

138. Regina Kesler, MD, "A Pediatrician's Odyssey from Suwalki to Harvard," ed. Irving Letiner and Michael Kesler. In this case, the family avoided the DP camps, going via Sweden to the United States, where Rachel/Regina trained at Harvard Medical School and became a pediatrician in New Jersey. I am grateful to Ted Kesler for giving me a copy of his late mother's gripping, unpublished memoir. See also Berger, *Displaced Persons: Growing Up American*.

139. See for example Dietrich and Schulze-Wessel, *Zwischen Selbstorganisation und Stigmatisierung*, 47, 59.

140. Nadich, *Eisenhower and the Jews*, 129–130.

141. Schochet, *Feldafing*, 22–23, 131. German memories from interview, February 12, 2002, with Frau U. Jaschinski, former employee of Einwohnermeldeamt (resident registry), Gemeindeverwaltung, Feldafing. I am grateful to Frau Jaschinski for her openness and willingness to share her memories of the immediate postwar period in Feldafing. See also Angelika Heider, "Das Lager für jüdische 'Displaced Persons' Feldafing in der amerikanischen Besatzungszone 1945–1951" (master's thesis, Technische Universität Berlin, 1994).

142. Lewyn and Lewyn, *On the Run*, 314.

143. Wahrhaftig, "Life in camps 6 months after liberation," 133. Wahrhaftig was a representative of the Orthodox Jewish group Mizrachi.

144. Brenner, "East European and German Jews in Postwar Germany," 49–50. Angelika Eder, "Jüdische Displaced Persons im deutschen Alltag: Eine Regionalstudie 1945–1950," in *Überlebt und Unterwegs*, ed. Fritz Bauer Institut, 163–187 and Eder, *Flüchtige Heimat*, 1–22, esp. 5, has described the reaction of the some 11,000 German inhabitants of Landsberg when they were suddenly confronted with over 4,000 Jews. Approximately 23,000 DPs passed through the camp; before the war there had been only a few German Jews and not even a Jewish community or synagogue.

145. On DPs in Hesse, especially Zeilsheim camp near Frankfurt, see Hilton, "Prisoners of Peace," and Giere and Salamander, eds., *Ein Leben Aufs Neu: Das Robinson Album*.

146. Hulme, *Wild Place*, 211–12.

147. See for example Dietrich and Schultze-Wessel, *Zwischen Selbstorganisation und Stigmatisierung*, 47, 59. For an account more sympathetic to the "displaced" Germans, see Müller, *Fremde in der Nachkriegszeit*, who reports, 37, that by 1947 these confiscations had become so burdensome for German authorities also trying to integrate millions of ethnic German refugees that the Deutsche Städtetag protested the evictions as human rights violations and a violation of the 1907 Hague Agreement.

148. Gringauz, "Our New German Policy and the Dps," 510.

149. Wahrhaftig, "Life in camps 6 months after liberation," 133. For case studies of relations between Jewish DPs and a local German population in Landsberg, see Eder, "Jüdische Displaced Persons," and D. Kohlmannslehner, "Das Verhältnis von Deutschen und jüdischen Displaced Persons im Lager Lampertheim 1945–1949," unpublished paper, Fritz Bauer Institut archives, Frankfurt/Main.

150. Wahrhaftig, *Uprooted*, 39.

151. Berger, "Displaced Persons: A Human Tragedy," 50.

152. Quoted in documentary *The Long Way Home*, Simon Wiesenthal Center, Los Angeles, 1997.

153. Hyman, *Undefeated*, 251. See also YIVO DPG 294.2/175/MK483/R14, Abt[eilung] Public Relations.

154. See Nadich, *Eisenhower and the Jews*, 64.

155. For one of many such memories, see Kluger, *Still Alive*, 154. See also Suzanne Brown-Fleming, "'The Worst Enemies of a Better Germany': Postwar Antisemitism among Catholic Clergy and U.S. Occupation Forces," *Holocaust and Genocide Studies* 18:3 (Winter 2004): 379–401.

156. Such visits, however, could also backfire, as in the case of General Patton's disgusted reaction to his tour of Feldafing. See n. 84 above.

157. Hulme, *Wild Place*, 211–212.

158. Bendersky, *"Jewish Theat,"* quoting Clay, 369.

159. Hulme, *Wild Place*, 211–212.

160. Hyman, *Undefeated*, 153.

161. Text of AFN broadcast, Friday, August 30, 1946, Interview with ret. Brig. Gen. Vincent Meyer, deputy chief of operations, liaison, Berlin, and with Major R. N. Thompson, DP Division, Berlin District, Berlin Reports, UNRRAA/399.1.2.

162. Gringauz, "Our New German Policy and the Dps," 509, noted that "looking back," the period from autumn 1945 to summer 1947 "seems a kind of golden age."

163. See, for example, Wyman, *DPs*, 35–36, citing Hannah Arendt, "The Stateless People," *Contemporary Jewish Record* 8: (April 1945): 144. For differing views on this process, see Mankowitz, *Life between Memory and Hope*, and Diner, "Elemente der Subjektwerdung."

164. See Ronni Loewy, "These Are the People: Zu Abraham J. Klausners Film über das *Zentralkomitee der befreiten Juden in der amerikanschen Zone*," in *Überlebt und Unterwegs*, ed. Fritz Bauer Institut, 119–128.

165. Description from Hyman, intro to Kurt R. Grossmann, *DP Problem*, 7.

166. *These Are the People*, film produced by the Central Committee of Liberated Jews, 1946, Tape 2281, RG 60.3361, Steven Spielberg film and video archives, USHMM. Quotes from speeches are mine, translated from the video. For different, shorter versions taken from written summaries, see Mankowitz, *Life between Memory and Hope*, 118–120, and Kauders, *Democratization and the Jews* 79–84.

167. Landau, "The Jewish Future in Germany," YIVO LWS 294.1/535/MK488/R46. See the interview with Landau in Brenner, *After the Holocaust*, 79–86.

168. See Gay, *Safe among the Germans*.

169. Quarterly report, Berlin Office, AJDC, March 1–June 1, 1946, 18; see also YIVO LWS 294.1/516/MK488/R45.

170. Letter from son Elliot Goodman, who was serving with the JDC, December 5, 1945. Included with letter from his father L. L. Goodman, National Hosiery Mills, Indianapolis, December 19, 1945, to Mr. Edward M. Warburg, head of AJDC, AJDCA A/446.

171. Ernst Landau, "Wir Juden und die Umwelt. Ein Beitrag zum Problem der Kollektivschuld," response in *Unser Wort*, November 15, 1946, in YIVO LWS/294.1/535/MK488/R46. See also Landau's 1947 statement on the future of Jews in Germany, also in 294.1/535.

172. *Jüdische Rundschau* 2:16/17 (October 1947), 59. As a reminder of the "old" antisemitism, the cover showed the Levetzowstrasse Synagogue in Berlin as it looked after the attacks on "Kristallnacht."

173. See, among many sources, Zink, *United States in Germany*, 154. According to Zink, 163, German denazification tribunals "tried some 930,000 persons on various charges, though more than two million persons were reported as 'chargeable' after the amnesties had reduced the numbers. Of these only 1,549 were found guilty as major offenders and approximately 21,000 as offenders."

174. See Bendersky, *"Jewish Threat,"* 367.

175. See Hilton, "Prisoners of Peace," 215–217.

176. Mead, "Food and Feeding," 619–620.

177. See, for example UNRRAA/S-401, Box 7, File 1, Feeding.

178. Notes on hunger and work strike of all 3,441 Jews in Föhrenwald on November 15, 1945, YIVO DPG 294.2/584/MK483/R44, 36.

179. This widely publicized incident did lead to the banning of German police from Jewish DP camps, unless they were escorted by U.S. troops.

180. Conversations with Shlomo Leser, Haifa, Israel, November 2006.

181. Report of December 22, 1945, to Col. David Elliott from Dr. Joseph M. Shapiro, "Study of Health Conditions in Jewish Communities in Third Army Area," citing Dr. Henri Heitan's observations on Feldafing DP Camp, 15–23, YIVO LWS 294.1/272/MK488/R23.

182. Report of Conference of County Medical Directors in Europe of the AJDC, Paris, May 14–17, 1947, 67, YIVO LWS 294.1/271/MK488/R23. That these attitudes persisted long after the DP period was over is illustrated by an anecdote in Elizabeth Ehrlich's combination cookbook and family memoir, *Miriam's Kitchen: A Memoir* (New York: Viking, 1997), 305, in which Uncle Fred explains why he does not do buffets, "I was in a concentration camp for five years. . . . I don't stand in line for food."

183. See, for example, report to Col. David Elliott from Dr. Joseph M. Shapiro, "Study of Health Conditions in Jewish Communities in Third Army Area," December 22, 1945, 18–20, YIVO LWS 294.1/272/MK488/R23.

184. UNRRAA/S-401, Box 7, File 1. Feeding.

185. Syrkin, *State of the Jews*, 46.

186. Hulme, *Wild Place*, 71, 212–213.

187. Kieve Skiddel, unpublished letter, Ober Peissen, June 21, 1945. He was referring to young survivors at Kibbutz Buchenwald.

188. Macardle, *Children of Europe*, 250. See also "Captain G. Weisz," Berlin Reports, UNRRAA/399.1.2.

189. Hutton and Rooney, *Conquerors' Peace*, 86. For a nuanced discussion of Zionism, from 1945 to 1947, among the survivors, both in the DP camps and in international politics, see Mankowitz, *Life between Memory and Hope*, esp. 52–100.

190. On "catastrophic Zionism," see Anita Shapira, "The Holocaust and World War II as Elements of the Yishuv Psyche until 1948," in *Thinking about the Holocaust after Half a Century*, ed. Alvin Rosenfeld (Bloomington: Ind.: Indiana University Press, 1997), 61–82; on notion of "functional" Zionism, see Lavsky, *New Beginnings*.

191. See, for example Tom Segev, *The Seventh Million: The Israelis and the Holocaust*, trans. Haim Watzman (New York: Henry Holt, 2000); Zertal, *From Catastrophe to Power*; and Grodzinsky, *In the Shadow of the Holocaust*.

192. See Dalia Ofer, "Emigration and *Aliyah*: A Reassessment of Israeli and Jewish policies," in *Terms of Survival*, ed. Wistrich, 74. See also Pettiss, *After the Shooting Stopped*, 196

193. Figures collected in AJDCA/392.

194. Hyman, *Undefeated*, 370. See also Mankowitz, *Life between Memory and Hope*, 124–125, and Wyman, *DPs*, 139.

195. Even Yosef Grodzinsky, one of the fiercest Israeli critics of the "Zionist takeover"—on both the political organization and propaganda front—among the DPs, acknowledges the genuine passion behind the results, citing one response to a Jewish Agency emissary: "My traveling to America is my own private business, but the Jews need Palestine." See *In the Shadow of the Holocaust*, 139.

196. Pinson, "Jewish Life," 117.

197. Hyman, *Undefeated*, 378.

198. YIVO LWS 294.1/536/MK488/R46.

199. See, for example "Our Unfinished Job in Germany. A Report by David Rosenstein," October 13, 1953, AJDCA/398, Föhrenwald.

200. Wahrhaftig, "Life in camps 6 months after liberation," 130.

201. Lewyn and Lewyn, *On the Run*, 315, 337.

202. Term is Hagit Lavsky's in *New Beginnings*.

203. Jacob Biber, *Risen from the Ashes*, 14.

204. Wahrhaftig, *Uprooted*, 86. Edward A. Shils, in "Social and Psychological Aspects of Displacement and Repatriation," *The Journal of Social Issues* 2:3 (1946): 3–18, warned of the social effects of prolonged camp life but suggested, 18, that as long as the displaced have no other alternative, "the camps must be operated as experiments in group therapy." Bergmann and Jucovy, eds., *Generations of the Holocaust*, 287, refer to a "holding environment."

205. Magda Denes, *Castles Burning: A Child's Life in War* (New York: W. W. Norton, 1997), 304, 316. A letter to the editor of the American Jewish magazine *Moment*, June 1997, 21, recalled DP camp Föhrenwald as "a vibrant Jewish community . . . we needed this transition time after Nazi hell."

CHAPTER FIVE
Mir Zaynen Do: Sex, Work, and the DP Baby Boom

1. Hyman, *Undefeated*, 246. Same quote appears in Vida, *Doom to Dawn*, 76.

2. Haas, *Aftermath*, 102. See also the examples in the oral testimonies collected in 1946 by the American psychologist David P. Boder. See n. 74 below for discussion of Boder's project and the various forms in which it has been published, edited, and preserved.

3. Posener, *In Deutschland*, 144.

4. *Vital Statistics of the Jewish Population in the US Zone of Germany for the Year 1948*, issued by Medical Department AJDC-OSE-CC Munich, 7, in YIVO LWS 294.1/(folder)272/MK(Microfilm)488/R(eel)23, 216 (also in AJDCA/417). For same quote, see Kurt R. Grossmann, *DP Problem*, 19. See U. O. Schmelz, "The Demographic Impact of the Holocaust," in *Terms of Survival*, ed. Wistrich, 44. See, among numerous other sources, Peck, "Jewish Survivors," 38; Brenner, *After the Holocaust*, 23; and Margarete L. Myers, "Jewish Displaced Persons Reconstructing Individual and Community in the US Zone of Occupied Germany," *LBI Yearbook* 42 (1997): 306–308. Myers (now Myers Feinstein) and Judith Tydor Baumel, in "DPs, Mothers and Pioneers: Women in the *She'erit Hapletah*," *Jewish History* 11:2 (Fall 1997): 99–110, reprinted in Judith Tydor Baumel, ed., *Double Jeopardy: Gender and the Holocaust*, 234–247, were the first scholars to explore this marriage and baby boom from the perspective of gender history. See also the early article by Eva Kolinsky, "Experiences of Survival," *LBI Yearbook* 44 (1999): 245–270, esp. 255–258 on "New Beginnings."

5. Biber, *Risen from the Ashes*, 37, 49.

6. Edith Horowitz oral history in *Mothers, Sisters, Resisters: Oral Histories of Women Who Survived the Holocaust*, ed. Brana Gurewitsch (Tuscaloosa: University of Alabama Press, 1998), p. 73.

7. Edith Z interview in Niewyk, ed., *Fresh Wounds*, 171.

8. Letter to Stephen S. Wise, June 22, 1945, in Peck, ed., *Archives of the Holocaust*, vol. 9, *Papers of the World Jewish Congress*, 30. On the important role of U.S. military rabbis in dealing with Jewish DPs, see Grobman, *Rekindling the Flame*, and Louis Barish, *Rabbis in Uniform: The Story of the American Jewish Military Chaplain* (New York: J. David, 1962).

9. See photo W/S #37928 and accompanying story, USHMM photo archives.

10. Levin, *In Search*, 183–184, 245, 270. Precisely such a happy reunion scene (also similar to the story of Peter Dattel recounted above in chapter 3) appears in the American film *The Search* (1948, directed by Fred Zinnemann), in which Montgomery Clift plays a U.S. GI who picks up a lost and speechless child, clearly a victim of unspeakable brutality, wandering in the German ruins. At the movie's conclusion, the child is reunited with his concentration camp survivor mother, who has been searching for him in refugee assembly centers throughout war-torn Europe. She finally spies him walking past her in a row of children being prepared for aliyah for Palestine. "Karel," she calls out; "Mamischka," he cries and runs toward her, and the movie fades out. Only there is a twist familiar to Levin, who

later railed against the universalization and dejudaization of the Holocaust in *The Diary of Anne Frank*, and characteristic of the universalizing of Nazi victims in the postwar period: while the other orphans being prepared for emigration out of Europe are Jewish, little blond Karel is the child of anti-Nazi Czech intelligentsia parents. See Pettiss, *After the Shooting Stopped*, 202–203, for description of her tour in Germany in March 1947 with Zinnemann, his scriptwriter, and two photographers as they prepared the film.

11. For a fine analysis of this literature, see Isidor J. Kaminer, "'On razors edge'—Vom Weiterleben nach dem Überleben," in *Überlebt und Unterwegs*, ed. Fritz Bauer Institut, 146–147, 157. On notions of manic displacement, based on a Freudian understanding of trauma expressed by acting out, rather than remembering and working through, see, for example Ido de Haan, "Paths of Normalization after the Persecution of the Jews: The Netherlands, France and West Germany in the 1950s," in *Life after Death*, ed. Bessel and Schumann, 65–92. For Kaminer's argument that, in fact, "the quick marriages and family formations were an effort to once again join a human community which could even make mourning possible. It is a great misunderstanding—if not willfull ignorance—by psychoanalysis to interpret these actions as manic defenses" (*manische Abwehrversuche*), see his piece "Spätfolgen bei jüdischen KZ-Überlebenden," in *Geschichte als Trauma: Festschrift für Hans Keilson zu seinem 80 Geburtstag*, ed. Dirk Juelich (Frankfurt/M: Nexus, 1991), 28.

12. See also Wahrhaftig, *Uprooted*, 54.

13. Union O.S.E. [Oeuvre de Secours des Enfants], *Report on the Situation of the Jews in Germany, October/December 1945* (Geneva, 1946), 52. In her memoir, *Aftermath*, 57, British UNRRA worker Francesca Wilson also noted that many of the young women survivors she found in Feldafing "were dignified, reserved and hard-working, but some found too many temptations in their new freedom. Lonely and starved of affection, their defences were easily broken down." On hypersexuality and "delayed psychosexual development," see Paul Friedman, "The Road Back for the DP's: Healing the Psychological Scars of Nazism," *Commentary* 6:6 (1948): 502–510. For an uncritical rendering of the numerous reports and memoirs referring to the "sexual promiscuity" and ostensible "deviant" behavior of Jews in DP camps, see Thomas Albrich, *Exodus Durch Österreich: Die jüdischen Flüchtlinge* (Innsbruck: Haymon, 1987), 111.

14. Vida, *Doom to Dawn*, 81.

15. See AJDC US Zone Bulletin, Vol. 1, Nr. 1 (October 1, 1947), AJDCA/ 499 and *Rebuilding Jewish Lives and Jewish Life: The American Jewish Joint Distribution Committee in the Post-Holocaust* Years (pamphlet issued by AJDC, New York, n.d); also Judith Tydor Baumel, "DPs, Mothers and Pioneers," in *Double Jeopardy*, ed. idem, 103, and Myers, "Jewish Displaced Persons Reconstructing." It is worth noting how many "Holocaust memoirs" include (or conclude with) time in the DP camps and experiences of marriage, pregnancy, and childbearing. See, in general, Lenore Weitzman and Dalia Ofer, eds., *Women in the Holocaust* (New Haven: Yale University Press, 1998), and sources in Atina Grossmann, "Women and the Holocaust: Four Recent Titles," *Holocaust and Genocide Studies* 16:1 (Spring 2002): 94–108.

16. For some of these stories, see YIVO LWS 294.1/543/MK488/R48. See also Baumel, "DPs, Mothers and Pioneers," 103.

17. Derrick Sington, *Belsen Uncovered* (London: Duckworth, 1946), 161.

18. Kurt R. Grossmann, *DP Problem*, 19.

19. Hyman, *Undefeated*, 246, 270, 17.

20. Biber, *Risen from the Ashes*, 46.

21. In YIVO DPG 294.2/562/MK483/R42.

22. Berger, *Displaced Persons: Growing Up American*, 291.

23. Personal interview, Zippi (Helen) Tichauer, New York, October 14, November 1, 2004. On men's sexual insecurities, see also Haas, *Aftermath*, 98–99; in general, see also the sensitive discussion, 116–119.

24. See especially Nechama Tec's forthright treatment in *Resistance and Courage: Jewish Women During the Holocaust* (New Haven: Yale University Press, 2002). See also *Defiance: The Bielski Partisans; The Story of the Largest Armed Rescue of Jews by Jews during World War II* (New York: Oxford University Press, 1993), 126–170.

25. See for example Fanya Gottesfeld Heller's account of her relationship with the young Ukranian who helped hide her family in *Strange and Unexpected Love: A Teenage Girl's Holocaust Memoirs* (Hoboken, N.J.: KTAV, 1993), or Edith Hahn Beer's bizarre story in *The Nazi Officer's Wife: How One Jewish Woman Survived the Holocaust* (New York: Harper Collins, 1999). At the first conference on gender and the Holocaust in 1983, survivors Susan Cernyak-Spatz and Vladka Meed noted that, for women, sexuality presented not only a source of fear but "an intense affirmation of being alive, of being normal. Perhaps the relationships were more passionate, they were urgent." See Esther Katz and Joan M. Ringelheim, eds., *Proceedings of the Conference on Women Surviving the Holocaust* (New York: Institute for Research on Women, 1983). See also Christl Wickert, "Tabu Laberbordell: Vom Umgang mit der Zwangsprostitution nach 1945," in *Gedächtnis und Geschlecht: Deutungsmuster in Darstellungen des Nationalsozialistischen Genozids*, ed. Insa Eschebach, Sigrid Jacobeit, and Silke Wenk (Frankfurt/M: Campus, 2002), 41–58.

26. I am indebted to Michael Brenner for formulating this point about the particular experience of female survivors, based on his mother Henny Brenner's memoir, "*Das Lied ist aus.*" Fear of Red Army rapes comes up quite frequently in women's Holocaust memories. See Gurewitsch, ed., *Mothers, Sisters, Resisters*, quote from xviii. There is even less information on men's experiences of sexual violence and abuse. See Haas, *Aftermath*, 117.

27. Haas, *Aftermath*, 102.

28. According to JDC statistics, in January 1946 the U.S. zone housed only 120 children between one and five, 380 between six and nine, and 770 between ten and seventeen. By December 1946, the numbers had leaped to 4,431 between one and five, 4,355 between six and nine, and 8,859 between ten and seventeen. Cited in Hyman, *Undefeated*, 247. Figures for 1947 were similar. Of a total 130,350 DPs surveyed in the U.S. zone at the end of July 1947, of whom 28.5% were women of childbearing age (defined as eighteen to forty-five), 4,174 were pregnant and 7,960 nursing. For both sets of figures, also see YIVO DPG 294.2/432/MK483/R36, 3–4.

29. Statistics in YIVO DPG 294.2/437/MK483/R36, Religiöses Amt.

30. See comments in YIVO DPG 294.2/437/MK483/R36. D. Drutmann, "The Displaced Jews in the American Zone of Germany," *The Jewish Journal of Sociology* 4 (1961): 261–263, notes both a natural "trend towards increased fertility after a period of suppression" and that DPs came from "countries of relatively high fertility." Interestingly, the general surplus of men over women (Drutmann counts 808 women to 1,000 men) among survivors was not so apparent in the age group twenty to twenty-four, where "there was even a surplus of women over men expressed as a ratio of 1,125 women per 1,000 men." The blip is "explained by the fact that young unmarried women especially were taken for purposes of forced labor" and therefore had a chance for survival not available to slightly older women with children. The male surplus among the (mostly young) survivors was most pronounced in the twenty-five to sixty-four age group.

31. Grobman, ed., *In Defense of the Survivors: The Letters and Documents of Oscar A. Mintzer*, letter to his wife, February 17, 1946, 166. See also Friedman, "The Road Back," 506.

32. Biber, *Risen from the Ashes*, 1.

33. The theme from Hirsch Glik's partisan song appears in much of the literature by and about Jewish DPs. See n. 36 in chapter 4 above.

34. Hyman, *Undefeated*, 247, using JDC figures. In some cases, children who had been born in the Soviet Union were registered, for political or bureaucratic reasons, as having been born in Poland or in DP camps. As a German employee of the Feldafing registry office recalled dryly, "a lot of lies were told in those days." U. Jaschinksi interview, February 12, 2002. See Berger's story in *Displaced Persons: Growing Up American*, 276–281.

35. The poster for the United States Holocaust Memorial Museum exhibit "Life Reborn," as well as the covers of books by Gay, *Safe among the Germans*, Mankowitz, *Life between Memory and Hope*, and David Bankier, ed., *The Jews Are Coming Back: The Return of the Jews to Their Countries of Origin after WWII* (New York: Berghahn, 2005), all feature the same or very similar images of women pushing baby carriages at the forefront of Zionist demonstrations; none make gender or reproduction central to their analysis. See also the presentation in the American documentary film *The Long Journey Home* (Simon Wiesenthal Center, Los Angeles, 1997) and in *Ein Leben Aufs Neu: Das Robinson Album*, as well as the photographs in the 2001 calendar of the United States Holocaust Memorial Museum, culled from the exhibition "Life Reborn: Jewish Displaced Persons 1945–1951," and the accompanying volume, Menachem Z. Rosensaft, ed. *Life Reborn*.

36. U.O. Schmelz, "Demographic Impact of the Holocaust," 44, 50.

37. For detailed comparative statistics on population developments as well as birth, death, and marriage rates in Europe, see B. R. Mitchell, *International Historical Statistics: Europe, 1750–1988* (New York: Stockton, 1992), 3–4, 101–105. In peaceful Sweden, for example, the birthrate per thousand population was 15.4 in 1939 and 19.7 in 1946; in recovering France, where it had been 15.3 in 1939, it was 20.9 in 1946. Even Poland's relatively (and traditionally) high postwar birthrate of 26.2 in 1947 (compared to 24.3 in 1938) was much lower than the Jewish DP figures. For comparison to Germany, see n. 39 below.

38. *Vital Statistics . . . 1948*, 7–9, in YIVO LWS 294.1/272/MK488/R23, 216–218; also in AJDCA/417. See also Kurt R. Grossmann, *DP Problem*, 18–20, and Abraham Hyman, "Displaced Persons," *American Jewish Yearbook* 51 (1950): 317, which contrasts the Jewish rate of 50.2 per thousand for 1947 to a German rate of 7.6 per thousand. Also cited in Gay, *Safe Among the Germans*, 68. According to the somewhat less dramatic figures in Mitchell, *International Historical Statistics*, 102 (western) Germany's birthrate had dipped from a high 20.9 per thousand in 1939 on the eve of war to 16.1 in 1946 and 16.4 in 1947 (he gives no rates for eastern Germany). For 1946 figures in Bavaria (29/1,000 for Jews, only 7.35/1,000 for Germans) see Jacobmeyer, "Jüdische Überlebende als 'Displaced Persons,'" 437. According to *Vital Statistics*, 7–8 (216–217), by 1948, the Jewish birthrate of 31.9 per thousand population was significantly lower than it had been in 1946 and already "lower than the birthrate of the general DP population in the US zone in 1947/1948." For comparative purposes: the German birthrate in 1933 stood at 14.7 (9.9 in Berlin); in the aftermath of the First World War it had reached 25.9 in 1920. The JDC report, however, acknowledges, 7 (216), that "the abnormal composition of our population did not permit us to draw comparisons between our birthrate and that of other nations." Nonetheless, whatever the discrepancies in the exact figures or the inadequacies of comparative data, the point about the extremely and uniquely, albeit temporary, high Jewish DP birthrate stands.

39. YIVO LWS 294.1/278/MK488/R24, illustrations on 326–327.

40. *Yiddische Bilder*, February 1948 and August 1948. The journal solicited entries from Germany, Austria, and Italy, and required a hefty RM 50 fee for processing. I am grateful to Tamar Lewinsky for alerting me to this contest and showing me copies of the relevant pages.

41. Bartley C. Crum, *Behind the Silken Curtain: A Personal Account of Anglo-American Diplomacy in Palestine and the Middle East* (Jerusalem: Milah Press, 1996; orig. New York, 1947), 90.

42. Cited in Sara R. Horowitz, "Memory and Testimony of Women Survivors of Nazi Genocide," in *Women of the World: Jewish Women and Jewish Writing*, ed. Judith R. Baskin (Detroit: Wayne State University Press, 1994), 280, 279. On the issue of generational transmission of trauma, see, among many, Martin S. Bergmann and Milton E. Jucovy, eds., *Generations of the Holocaust* (New York: Columbia University Press, 1982).

43. O.S.E. *Report*, 65.

44. Leslie H. Hardman, told by and written by Cecily Goodman, *The Survivors: The Story of the Belsen Remnant* (London: Vallentine Mitchell, 1958), 64–65. For a similar view of this "craving for pleasure," see Sington, *Belsen Uncovered*, 160–161.

45. O.S.E. *Report*, 66–67, also presents arguments among physicians about abortion. For "superhuman" efforts, see Wahrhaftig, *Uprooted*, 118–119. On efforts "to encourage the birth of children and to combat any thought of abortion," see also YIVO LWS 294.1/286/MK488/R24, 2.

46. Report by the *Gesundheitsamt* of the Central Committee of Liberated Jews in the American Zone (*Um ein Erlaubnis für unsere Frauen Aborte zumachen ist*

eine Kommission von 5 Ärzten gegründet, welche diese Sache entscheidet), YIVO DPG 294.2/173/MK483/R14, 420.

47. *Vital Statistics . . . 1948*, 12, in YIVO LWS 294.1/272/MK488/R 23, 221, and AJDCA/417. An UNRRA report from 1946 does draw attention to a large number of abortions while conceding that not only was there no way to stop them; there was also no way of accurately measuring their incidence. UNRRAA 401.7.4, Medical.

48. On the eagerness for hormone treatments see YIVO LWS 294.1/277/ MK488/R24 and 294.1/286/MK488/R24. See also Nadich, *Eisenhower and the Jews*, 166, 213, and O.S.E. *Report*, 61.

49. Marcus and Peck, eds., *Among the Survivors . . . Letters of Major Irving Heymont*, 44.

50. O.S.E. *Report*, 67, 65.

51. Levin, *In Search*, 360, notes, "And the urge to arrive in time for the birth of the child in Eretz was real on every vessel that left for Palestine with its host of pregnant women, some of whom were smuggled onto the ships in their ninth month despite the Haganah regulation making the seventh month the limit." See also Wahrhaftig, *Uprooted*, 52–54.

52. Klein and Klein, *Hours After*, 71–72, 272–273.

53. Niewyk, *Fresh Wounds*, 94.

54. UNRRA spent much time and effort on locating, repatriating, placing, and adjudicating conflicting claims over abandoned, orphaned, stolen, and hidden children, both Jewish who had been hidden as "Aryans," and non-Jewish Eastern European children who had been kidnapped for "aryanization" under the Lebensborn program. See UNRRAA 401.2.1–2, Child Welfare Section. See Nicholas Stargardt, *Witnesses of War: Children's Lives under the Nazis* (New York: Alfred A. Knopf, 2006), 348–377; also Debórah Dwork on the contest over children in postwar Netherlands in *Lessons and Legacies: The Meaning of the Holocaust in a Changing World*, ed. Peter Hayes (Evanston: Northwestern University Press, 1998); paper by Marion P. Pritchard on Jewish DP children for "Lessons and Legacies: The Meaning of the Holocaust in a Changing World," Dartmouth College, 1994, revised 1997; and the revealing memoir by UNRRA child welfare worker Susan T. Pettiss, *After the Shooting Stopped*. In a fascinating article based on numerous memoirs by women survivors, legal scholar Fionnuala Ni Aolain has attempted to identify the specific gender-based harm caused to women by forcible separation from children as experiences that are "sex-based" even if they are not categorizable within what we generally understand as sexual violence. See Fionnuala Ní Aoláin, "Sex-Based Violence and the Holocaust—A Reevaluation of Harms and Rights in International Law," *Yale Journal of Law and Feminism* 12:1 (2000): 53.

55. In October 1946, UNRRA estimated that of some 20,000 "infiltree" children, 6,000 were "unaccompanied." See "Interzonal conference on child search and repatriation," October 16–18, 1946, and Joint conference with Austrian mission on unaccompanied children, Bad Wiessee, Germany, January 7–8, 1947, in UNRRAA/401.2.2; also 401.2.7, file on Jewish Agency for Palestine. In one case of three unaccompanied youngsters, distant relatives in England agreed to let two boys go to Palestine but insisted that the teenage girl who had no relatives in

Palestine should join them in England. Since she was sixteen or seventeen, UNRRA took the position that she was entitled to make her own decision and noted that in interviews the girl had been clear about wanting to travel to Palestine with "very close friends" from her DP camp. The files document much back and forth discussion between the UNRRA child welfare workers and the refugee committee in London, which represented the "extremely upset" relatives. UNRRA and Military Government were "of the opinion that any child of 16 could make his own decision on a matter of this kind." See in general UNRRAA/ 401.2.1–401.2.7.

56. Pettiss, *After the Shooting Stopped*, 196; see her thoughtful commentary, esp. 187–196.

57. The most insistent critic of any attempts to lend "meaning" to the Holocaust has been Lawrence L. Langer. See his *Admitting the Holocaust: Collected Essays* (New York: Oxford University Press, 1995). On this theme also, there is a huge literature, ranging from the theological to the psychoanalytic and political.

58. Ze'ev Mankowitz, "The Formation of *She'erit Hapleita*: November 1944– July 1945," *Yad Vashem Studies* 20 (1990): 351.

59. Nadich, *Eisenhower and the Jews*, 67.

60. LaCapra, *History and Memory after Auschwitz* (Ithaca: Cornell University Press, 1998), 204–205.

61. Borneman, "Reconciliation after Ethnic Cleansing," 281–304, here 282– 283, 285.

62. Bessel A. Van Der Kolk and Onno Van Der Hart, "The Intrusive Past: The Flexibility of Memory and the Engraving of Trauma," in *Trauma: Explorations in Memory*, ed. Cathy Caruth (Baltimore: Johns Hopkins University Press, 1995), 178. On the problem of destroyed trust, and the influence of psychiatric work done with Holocaust survivors on later treatment of refugee trauma, see the essays in E. Valentine Daniel and John Chr. Knudsen, eds., *Mistrusting Refugees* (Berkeley: University of California Press, 1995), esp. introduction, 4. On the relationship between survivors and their children, see among many studies, Bergmann and Jucovy, eds., *Generations of the Holocaust*.

63. Klein and Klein, *Hours After*, 274. She also admitted, 271, that in her eagerness to be "normal," she probably "overdid" the American-housewife-of-the-1950s routine. In an AP story about her life and rescue, Gerda was photographed in her Buffalo kitchen, with little boy Jim and her two girls Leslie and Vivian on a countertop; on the phone while stirring a pot, she looks the picture of the American suburban housewife. If she was "hopelessly inadequate" in her education and language skills, she could nonetheless make "Thanksgiving dinner with all the trimmings. . . . Cooking, baking and homemaking in general were skills I was able to manage. They connected me with the role model I wanted to emulate, my mother."

64. Mark Dvorjetski, "Adjustment of Detainees to Camp and Ghetto Life and Their Subsequent Readjustment to Normal Society," *Yad Vashem Studies* 5 (1963): 215, sees in the "miracle of the she'erit ha-pleyta" both "a spiritual" and a "biological miracle." I am grateful to Samuel Kassow, History Department, Trinity College, Hartford, Connecticut, for the reference to *Maschiachskinder*.

65. Quoted in *Rebuilding Jewish Lives and Jewish Life: The American Jewish Joint Distribution Committee in the Post-Holocaust Years* (New York: JDC, n.d.). The quote is accompanied by a photograph of a nurse presenting triplets to a young DP mother lying in a maternity ward.

66. Rhoda Ann Kanaaneh, *Birthing the Nation: Strategies of Palestinian Women in Israel* (Berkeley: University of California Press, 2002), 68.

67. Anthropologists have also reminded us that refugee camp settings encourage "construction and reconstruction of [their] history 'as a people'" and analyzed how "children are a crucial element in the representation of refugees." See Lisa Malkii, *Purity and Exile: Violence, Memory and National Cosmology among Hutu Refugees in Tanzania* (Chicago: University of Chicago Press, 1995), 3, 11. Conversely, Helen Fremont underscores her mother's denial of her Jewish past by citing her unwillingness to bear children in the DP camps: "'I didn't have a child on either hip in the DP camps, as all the other women did,' my mother says with obvious disdain for the procreative impulse." *After Long Silence: A Memoir* (New York: Random House Dell, 1999), 301–302.

68. On the historical commissions, see Laura Jockusch, "Jüdische Geschichtsforschung im Lande Amaleks. Jüdische historische Kommissionen in Deutschland 1945–1949," in *Zwischen Erinnerung und Neubeginn*, ed. Schönborn, 20–41. Interestingly, the commissions did not collect memoirs of life in the Soviet Union.

69. Hyman, *Undefeated*, 252. Hyman is especially eloquent about interpreting memorialization as a "step into the land of the living."

70. Pinson, "Jewish Life," 108–109. Similarly, the British were highly irritated by the insistence of Jewish DPs in their zone—a conscious maneuver by their leader Josef Rosensaft—on still calling their DP camp in Hohne, near the former concentration camp, Bergen Belsen. See Hyman, *Undefeated*, 78.

71. The DPs' proposed Day of Remembrance, on the date of liberation, the fourteenth day of the Hebrew month of Ijar, was never accepted either in the Diaspora or in Palestine. Israel declared *Yom HaShoah* for the twenty-seventh of Nissan because it fell right between the remembrance of the Warsaw Ghetto uprising and the establishment of the state, thus safely bracketing Holocaust remembrance between two markers of resistance and rebirth. For a fine analysis of the debates about remembering, see Nicholas Yantian, "Studien zum Selbstverständnis der jüdischen 'Displaced Persons' in Deutschland nach dem Zweiten Weltkrieg" (master's thesis, Berlin, 1994), 27–42.

72. On the relationship between our memory panic and memory boom, see Andreas Huyssen, *Twilight Memories: Marking Time in a Culture of Amnesia* (New York: Routledge, 1995); on the "fetishizing" of memory, see Marita Sturken, "The Remembering of Forgetting: Recovered Memory and the Question of Experience," *Social Text* 57 (Winter 1998): 102–125; for a critique of our fascination with (and confusion of) individual and collective trauma, see Pamela Ballinger, "The Culture of Survivors: Post-Traumatic Stress Disorder and Traumatic Memory," *History and Memory* 10:1 (Spring 1998): 99–132.

73. See Dori Laub, "Truth and Testimony: The Process and the Struggle," *American Imago* 48:1 (1991): 75–91.

74. David P. Boder, *I Did Not Interview the Dead* (Urbana: University of Illinois Press, 1949). David Pablo Boder, a Russian-Latvian-born psychology profes-

sor at the Illinois Institute of Technology, interviewed over 100 survivors in the summer of 1946. Jürgen Matthäus, who has critically examined the history of Boder's remarkable project in "Displaced Memory: The Transformation of an Interview" (unpublished paper, forthcoming in a volume edited by Matthäus and dedicated to Zippi [Helen] Tichauer), notes that Boder "recorded their stories— and also songs—on about 190 forty-to-fifty minute spools of carbon wire, thus amassing more than 120 hours of audio documentation." In five weeks in France he conducted 42 interviews in France; in Germany he did only 16 (including with Tichauer), all within one week. David P. Boder, *Topical Autobiographies of Displaced People* (Los Angeles: n.p., 1957), contained 70 interviews translated into English; his *I Did Not Interview the Dead* (Urbana: University of Illinois Press, 1949) included translations of 8 of his interviews. Niewyk, ed. *Fresh Wounds*, published in 1998, contains 34 revised and edited versions of the already edited *Topical Autobiographies*. All remaining original oral material and transcripts are now finally available in the USHMM archives, oral material also at the Performing Arts Reading Room of the Library of Congress. See also the website "Voices of the Holocaust," http://voices.iit.edu. I am grateful to Jürgen Matthäus, Alan Rosen, and Zippi Tichauer for their help in understanding these interviews.

75. Van de Kolk and van der Hart refer to "speechless terror" in "The Intrusive Past," in *Trauma*, ed. Caruth, 158–182, here 172. Some of the texts from *Fun letstn Churbn* and other memoirs were published in English in 1949 by Leo W. Schwarz in *The Root and the Bough*. On the *She'erit Hapletah*'s efforts to collect documentation and testimonials (including historical commissions and essay contests) and the debates about memorialization, see Mankowitz, *Life between Memory and Hope*, 192–225, and Jockusch, "Jüdische Geschichtsforschung."

76. Pinson, "Jewish Life," 109, also quoted in Hyman, *Undefeated*, 160.

77. See n. 11 above.

78. See Susan Brison, "Outliving Oneself: Trauma, Memory, and Personal Identity," in *Feminists Rethink the Self*, ed. Diana T. Meyers (Boulder, Co.: Westview Press, 1997), 12–39; also her book *Aftermath: Violence and the Remaking of a Self* (Princeton: Princeton University Press, 2002).

79. Ní Aoláin, "Sex-Based Violence and the Holocaust," 52. The article takes very seriously from the point of view of feminist and legal theory the "stubborn question[s]" about the centrality of motherhood in women's lives raised by Denise Riley, "Some Peculiarities of Social Policy concerning Women in Wartime and Postwar Britain," in *Behind the Lines: Gender and the Two World Wars*, ed. Margaret Higonnet, Jenson, Michel, and Weitz (New Haven: Yale University Press, 1987), 269. See also her *Am I That Name? Feminism and the Category of Women in History* (Minneapolis: University of Minnesota, 1989). On "the fantasy of maternal love" as a force in feminist theory and women's activism, see Joan W. Scott, "Fantasy Echo: History and the Construction of Identity," *Critical Inquiry* (Winter 2001): 284–304, esp. 303–304.

80. *Lang ist der Weg*, German/Polish coproduction (1947/48). Available as *Long Is the Road*, The National Center for Jewish Film, 1995, Brandeis University. For a critical analysis, see Cilly Kugelmann, "Lang ist der Weg: Eine jüdische-deutsche Film-Kooperation," in *Überlebt und Unterwegs*, ed. Fritz Bauer Institut, 353–370.

81. Syrkin, *State of the Jews*, 12. The term "nullification" is taken (with apologies for the crude appropriation) from a paper presented by Yotam Hotam, "Klages-Lessing-Klatzkin: Life Philosophy, Modern Gnosticims and Zionism," at the conference "Rethinking German and Jewish Cultural and Intellectual History," Schloss Elmau, July 12–14, 2004.

82. Schochet, *Feldafing*, 80.

83. Dieter E. Kesper, *Unsere Hoffnung. Die Zeitung Überlebender des Holocaust im Eschweger Lager 1946* (Eschwege, 1996). Newspaper of UNRRA camp in Eschwege, Nr. 1. June 4, 1946, Heimatarchiv Eschwege collected in Fritz Bauer Institut archives. The published German text is a translation of the original Yiddish.

84. Maj. John J. Maginnis referred to the DP influx in Berlin as a "red hot" political crisis in his *Military Government Journal*, January 7, 1946, 326. For the ubiquitous babies and baby carriages, see for example the extraordinary photo collection in *Ein Leben Aufs Neu: Das Robinson Album*. See also the propaganda films produced by the JDC, the Central Committee of Liberated Jews, and the U.S. Army Signal Corps. See esp. films 142a and b, 143, in Spielberg Film and Video Archives.

85. Quoted by Schwarz in *Redeemers*, 87.

86. On the image of women in the resistance and their valorization in Palestine and early Israeli society, as well as their simultaneously central and marginal roles in the DP camps, see Baumel, "Heroism" and "Post-war Life and Representation," in her *Double Jeopardy*, 143–247. Baumel speaks, 24, of a "biological deterrent towards female organizational activism." On women in the DP camps, and especially the drudgery of their makeshift housework, see also Margarete L. Myers, "Jewish Displaced Persons Reconstructing," and (as Margarete Myers Feinstein), "Jewish Women Survivors in the DP Camps in Postwar Germany: Transmitters of the Past, Caretakers of the Present, and Builders of the Future," *Shofar* 24:4 (Summer 2006): 67–89.

87. Baumel, *Double Jeopardy*. See also the pioneering article by Sybil Milton, "Women and the Holocaust: The Case of German and German-Jewish Women," in *When Biology Became Destiny: Women in Weimar and Nazi Germany*, ed. Renate Bridenthal, Atina Grossmann, and Marion Kaplan (New York: Monthly Review, 1984) 297–333.

88. Joan Ringelheim, " 'Women and the Holocaust: A Reconsideration of Research' (with Postscript)," in *Different Voices: Women and the Holocaust*, ed. Carol Rittner and John Roth (New York: Paragon House, 1993), 392.

89. Berger, *Displaced Persons: Growing Up American*, quoting his mother, 306.

90. Samuel Bak tells the story of a child born with a severe disease whose family was immediately provided with a visa for the United States so that specialists could study and treat the case. Interview by Fran Bartowski, spring 2002.

91. Claude Lefort, *The Political Forms of Modern Society: Bureaucracy, Democracy, Totalitarianism* (Cambridge: Cambridge University Press, 1986), 261–263, cited in Annette Timm, "The Politics of Fertility: Population Politics and Health Care in Berlin, 1919–1972" (Ph.D. dissertation, University of Chicago, 1999), 53. Avinoam Patt has noted the general importance of a rhetoric of respon-

sibility and obligation in DP life and politics. Presentation, DP Workshop, USHMM, July 2005.

92. See health reports in YIVO DPG 294.2/173/MK483/R14.

93. See reports from JDC field nurses, YIVO LWS 294.1/285/MK488/R24, and in 294.2/173/MK483/R14.

94. See records of Health Commission, YIVO DPG 294.2/402–410/MK483/R33–34. In October 1947, the Feldafing sanitation police issued 83 pretyped warnings threatening "strictest measures" and fines. See especially file 405.

95. Confidential report made by Captain G. Weisz on field trip to US zone, April 5, 1946, UNRRAA/399.1.1.

96. For discussion of the enormous significance of (often very rowdy) games and athletic competitions—especially soccer and boxing—as entertainment, outlet, and physical rehabilitation, see Philipp Grammes, "Sports in the DP Camps, 1945–1948," in *Emancipation through Muscles: Jews and Sports in Europe*, ed. Michael Brenner and Gideon Reuveni (Lincoln: University of Nebraska Press, 2006), 187–212. YIVO DPG 294.2/834/MK483/R61 contains announcements for numerous soccer, boxing, track and field, but also basketball, volleyball, tennis, and table tennis competitions, between DP teams and sometimes also with American military teams. The same folder deals with DP police. On sports, see also 294.2/845/MK483/R61.

97. See films in Steven Spielberg Film and Video Archive, USHMM, produced by the United Jewish Appeal (UJA), the JDC, the (American Jewish) Hebrew Immigrant Aid Society (HIAS), and the Central Committee of Liberated Jews itself. Most of these films incorporate (often the same) footage from U.S. Army Signal Corps films. The Central Committee produced two films, *These Are the People* with Chaplain Klausner and a ten-minute report on a January 1947 boxing match in Munich titled *Die Boksmeisterschft fun der Scherit Hapleta*. See Ronni Loewy, "These Are the People: Zu Abraham J. Klausners Film über das Zentralkomitee der befreiten Juden in der amerikanschen Zone," in *Überlebt und Unterwegs*, ed. Fritz Bauer Institut, 119–128. See the fund-raising films *The Persecuted* (RG-60-0092, tape 142B) and *The Future Can Be Theirs* (RG-6.2616, tape 2311) as well as the army films on tapes 142A, 142B and 143.

98. Schochet, *Feldafing*, 79–81. On the role of photography in the lives and memories of Holocaust survivors and their families, see Marianne Hirsch, *Family Frames: Photography, Narrative and Postmemory* (Cambridge, Mass.: Harvard University Press, 1997).

99. See Michael Berkowitz, *The Crime of My Very Existence: Nazism and the Myth of Jewish Criminality* (Berkeley: University of California Press, 2007), chapters 6 and 7 on DPs. For a fascinating discussion of the relationships that emerged in the 1950s in West German towns and villages among Germans, American occupiers (especially also African-American GIs), and remaining Polish-Jewish DP bar owners, see Höhn, *GIs and Fräuleins*.

100. At the height of the baby boom, Elisabeth Hospital in Feldafing had 1,200 beds, 28 German doctors and 71 German nurses; with time, more DP staff was added. Cited in Haia Karni, "Life at the Feldafing Displaced Persons Camp, 1945–1952," (master's thesis, Baltimore Hebrew University, May 1997), 49.

101. Levin, *In Search*, 398.

102. YIVO DPG 294.2/402/MK483/R33, 446. See further the medical affidavits and applications from Feldafing in YIVO DPG 294.2, files of Central Committee Health Department, MK483, reels 33 and 34, files 402, 403, 410, 413. File 402 contains about 150 such applications, for May, June, and July 1947, submitted by DP camp residents and local physicians requesting German aides for pregnant or postpartum (and in some cases postabortus) Jewish women.

103. YIVO DPG 294.2/402/MK483/R33, 427.

104. YIVO DPG 294.2/402/MK483/R33, 433. In an interesting continuity of Nazi and KZ language, the term used for "custodian" was *Blockverwalter*. Using similar terminology, a man requesting "a German" household helper (*eine Deutsche dinst cum oifroimen un helfen in der arbait*) notes (in Yiddish) that his wife has a young child and works as the *Blockelteste* of their barrack, 294.2/402/MK483/R33, 429.

105. YIVO DPG 294.2/410/MK483/R34, 439; the husband requests a *Gehilfsfrau* (female helper).

106. Baumel, *Double Jeopardy*, 31.

107. Request, May 13, 1947, YIVO 294.2/402/MK483/R33, 513.

108. For harrowing accounts, see, for example Rachelle Rosenzweig, *Russische Eisblumen. 35 Jahre in sowjetischer Unfreiheit* (Frankfurt/M: Haag + Herchen, 1993), and the fictional memoir Dorothea Sella, *Der Ring des Prometheus. Denksteine im Herzen. Eine auf Wahrheit beruhende Romantrilogie* (Jerusalem: Rubin Mass Verlag, 1996). The JDC also noted a relatively high incidence of venereal disease, certainly underreported because many sufferers preferred to seek more discreet treatment from German physicians outside the DP camps. See YIVO LWS 294.1/285/MK488/R24, for example, report of December 24, 1947.

109. "Catastrophic anxiety" diagnosis in Bergmann and Jucovy, eds., *Generations of the Holocaust*, 283.

110. One of the c. 150 applications (and notices of approval) collected in YIVO DPG 294.2/402/MK483/R33. Many, but not all, requests were officially approved. File 402 also contains rejections. This section is based on applications from DPs and the accompanying medical certificates in files 398, 400–403. I first read the original documents in unpaginated folders at YIVO; they are now available only on microfilm. I have now supplied the microfilm and reel numbers and, if appropriate, page numbers.

111. To Sanitätsamt, May 7, 1947, YIVO DPG 294.2/402/MK483/R33, 435.

112. Letter to Moe(ses) Leavitt, from Joseph Schwartz, JDC Paris, 9 November 1946, AJDCA/390.

113. Patton quote in Dinnerstein, *America and the Survivors*, 16–17. See also Martin Blumenson, ed., *The Patton Papers: 1940–1945* (Boston: Houghton Mifflin, 1974), 751. Also cited in Constantin Goschler, "The Attitude towards Jews in Bavaria after the Second World War," *LBI Yearbook* 36 (1991): 447. Interpretation of Patton's statement, Zippi Tichauer, personal interviews and phone conversations, New York, October and November 2004, and ongoing through June 2006.

114. YIVO DPG 294.2/400/MK483/R33, 341. Letter from Dr. Valentin Behr, Bad Kissingen, to Feldafing Lagerleitung, November 3, 1947.

115. UNRRAA/S-401 Box 7, File 1, Feeding. Karni, "Life at the Feldafing Displaced Persons Camp," notes, 40, that in Feldafing, German employees were generally paid in special Military Government currency, called "yellow dollars." Camp administration files for February 1947, for example, list (*Lohnliste*) monthly salaries for "German personnel" in reichsmarks (RM). Salaries were quite substantial, ranging from RM 510 for a (female) physician to RM 103 for a male menial laborer. Most women earned between RM 100 and 200 a month, including social insurance benefits. See YIVO DPG 294.2/398/MK483/33, 227.

116. Quotes from interview with Frau U. Jaschinski, former village clerk, Feldafing, February 12, 2002. She remembered her mother baking for a wealthy Munich Jew who had summered in Feldafing.

117. I found only one letter that seemed defensive about asking for a German baby nurse; a father wrote in Yiddish that "throughout her whole pregnancy my wife worked and managed without German help" (*mit kajn dajczkis*), but now, after the birth, his wife's health (*gezunt custand*) was such that they "must have a *Kinder Szwester.*" Letter, Feldafing, May 8, 1947, YIVO DPG 294.2/402/MK483/R33, 451.

118. Oral history interview with Elizabeth (Ita) Muskal, Yonkers, New York, June 16, 2003.

119. Reference to SS boots from friend's personal story.

120. UNRRAA/401.7.4, Memo, May 4, 1946, "Segregation of Jewish Dps in Hospitals without German Staff," to UNRRA Central HQ in Arolsen from Mr. C. H. Martini, acting director Relief Services. Especially given the dire shortage of DP physicians and apparent preference of German-Jewish physicians to practice on their own rather than in the camps, both UNRRA and JDC officials were inclined to see complaints about "a difficult psychological situation arising from the treatment of Jewish DPs in hospitals staffed by German doctors" as yet another manifestation of the DPs' well-known propensity (more understandable to some observers than others) never to feel properly or adequately cared for. Eventually, Bogenhausen Hospital in Munich, which had six Jewish and five German doctors on staff in April 1946 and a surgical chief who was a "well known and active Nazi," was turned over to the Central Committee of Liberated Jews. See also YIVO DPG/294.2/46/MK483/R4.

121. Letter from Geheimer Sanitätsrat Hofrat. Dr. Th. and Frau Struppler, Pr. Arzt, to Sanitätsamt Feldafing, April 13, 1947, YIVO 294.2 DPG/410/MK483/R34, 390–391.

122. Frau Jaschinski recalled that the past was "wrapped in deathly silence" (*völlig totgeschwiegen*). Interview, February 12, 2002.

123. The literature on trauma, memory, and the Holocaust is, by now, enormous. For one overview see Caruth, ed., *Trauma.* For a critique of our fascination with (and confusion of) individual and collective trauma, see Pamela Ballinger, "Culture of Survivors." Dietrich and Schulze-Wessel, *Zwischen Selbstorganisation und Stigmatisierung*, 105, surmise a certain "bitter satisfaction" (*Genugtuung*) but note that it still seems hard to understand why Jewish DPs would entrust their children to of all people Germans" (*erscheint dennoch schwer nachvollziehbar*). For brief, thoughtful reflections on the baby boom and the turn to German caregivers, see Hillel Klein, "Die Familien der Überlebenden Opfer und die

Gesellschaft," in "Was ist der Mensch Heute Wert? Orientierung im Schatten des Nationalsozialismus," Proceedings of conference, April 29–May 1, 1983, Evangelische Akademie, Bad Boll, 36–81.

124. Borneman, "Reconciliation after Ethnic Cleansing," 282–283.

125. *Vital Statistics . . . 1948*, 9 (218 in YIVO LWS 294.1/272/MK488/R23) lists the infant mortality rate at 26.1 per 1,000 live births, "last on the list" for other national populations. According to Kurt R. Grossmann, *DP Problem*, 20, by 1948 the Jewish DP infant mortality rate stood at a "phenomenal low" of 5.3 per 1,000 live births. On health and mortality, see also the numerous reports in AJDCA/418B, Germany Medical 1946–June 1949.

126. Michael Brenner, "East European and German Jews in Postwar Germany, 1945–50," in *Jews, Germans, Memory: Reconstructions of Jewish Life in Germany*, ed. Michal Bodemann (Ann Arbor: University of Michigan Press, 1996), 49–50. He adds, "Ironically, some places that the Nazis never had to make *judenrein* because Jews had never lived there were eventually populated by several hundreds, if not thousands, of Jews."

127. See "Hinweise zu den Ergebnissen der ersten Ausländererhebung des Bayer.Stat.Landesamtes vom 30. Juni 1948," in Bayerisches Hauptstaatsarchiv, Staatskanzlei Akte 14890. Interestingly this report was composed by Friedrich Burgdörfer, a *völkisch* nationalist population policy expert during the Weimar Republic who continued his work during and after the Third Reich. According to Gisela Bock, *Zwangssterilisation im Nationalsozialismus: Studien zur Rassenpolitik und Frauenpolitik* (Opladen: Westdeutscher Verlag, 1986), 143, Burgdörfer was temporily denazified and removed from his position at the Bavarian Statistical Bureau, but back at work in 1949. Apparently, he was already on active duty again in 1948. For high 1947 statistic, see Abraham S. Hyman, "Displaced Persons," *American Jewish Year Book* 1:51 (1950): 317, also cited in Gay, *Safe Among the Germans*, 68.

128. Jacobmeyer, "Jüdische Überlebende als 'Displaced Persons,' " 437. According to Central Committee health records (Bericht über ärztlichen Tätigkeit für die Sherith Hapletah in Deutschland, Munich, February 13, 1949), the overall Jewish mortality rate was 3.1% compared to 12% for Germans in Bavaria. See YIVO LWS 294.1/279/MK488/R24.

129. "Hinweise zu den Ergebnissen der ersten Ausländererhebung."

130. *Vital Statistics . . . 1948*, 9, in YIVO LWS 294.1/272/MK488/R23, 218.

131. Bernstein, *Seamstress*, 300–315. In another not unusual twist, she discovered shortly after she had married and become pregnant that the man she had loved before her deportation had survived and hoped for a reunion. She put the letter away and did not respond. The book features a photograph of Sara, her husband Meyer, and a young DP friend standing in front of the house with their Bavarian landlady, who is beaming and wearing a stitched blouse of local design. The three women are photographed close together; Meyer is off somewhat to the side gazing at the women.

132. Schochet, *Feldafing*, 160.

133. Borneman, "Reconciliation after Ethnic Cleansing," 281–304, 282. In an indication of the limits to the personal connection among these German and Jewish women, even in the relatively rare cases where German women also had ba-

bies, child care interactions did not extend to the use of wet nurses. Jewish women sought out Jewish *Milchschwestern* (nursing sisters) if they did not have enough milk, a relatively easy task since so many women were pregnant or had infants at the same time. Personal conversations, Cilly Kugelmann, Berlin, spring 2002.

134. Lewyn and Lewyn, *On the Run*, 315.

135. For a local perspective on, and memories of, Jewish-German relations in Feldafing, I am grateful to my interview partner, U. Jaschinski. See also Angelika Heider, "Das Lager für jüdische 'Displaced Persons' Feldafing in der amerikanischen Besatzungszone 1945–1951" (master's thesis, Technical University Berlin, 1994), 90. Officially, the Central Committee of Liberated Jews banned Jewish sports teams from engaging German players, trainers, and referees, but it is clear from the bitter disputes recorded about such matters that Germans (and DPs of other nationalities) were sometimes recruited for DP teams. Moreover, as Philipp Grammes points out in the most recent examination of the subject, "Sports in the DP Camps, 1945–1948," 207, "it was the associations that prohibited such competitions and imposed drastic sanctions for violations of the ban, while the 'simple' athletes did not seem to consider contact with the Germans to be such a bad thing."

136. Tamar Lewinsky, "Displaced Writers? Zum kulturellen Selbstverständnis jiddischer DP-Schriftsteller," in *Zwischen Erinnerung und Neubeginn*, ed. Schönborn, 210–211. The short stories by Hershl Vaynroykh, "di tfile in tsug" and "a voynung far a bafraytn" were published in *goles bayern* (Munich 1947). On DP press and literature, see also the *Guide for Jewish Displaced Persons Periodicals from the Collections of the YIVO Institute*, YIVO Archives.

137. See complaints that curfew is not being observed, YIVO DPG 294.2/40/MK483/R4. For discussion of Germans working in the DP camps and handling of permits, see especially 294.2/402/MK483/R33; for lists of German employees see also 294.2/398/MK483/R33, and 409/MK483/R34, 325–337, and 410/MK483/R34, 705–714.

138. Letter, September 13, 1947, YIVO DPG 294.2/413/MK483/R34, 896.

139. Letter, December 24, 1946, DPG 294.2/366/MK483/R31, 72.

140. See Kauders, *Democratization and the Jews*. When informed that a DP child born in Feldafing was chagrined that his U.S. passport had been stamped with his birthplace as Germany, my interview partner, who had registered those births, spontaneously exclaimed, "but he wasn't born in Germany, he was born in Bavaria." Interview, Jaschinski, February 2001. Boehling, *A Question of Priorities*, 106–107, notes that, ironically, Munich, the center of the Nazi movement, prided itself on its "self-liberation" by anti-Nazis who successfully averted severe last-minute bombing.

141. Anonymous. Virtually every friend of mine born to DPs in Germany whom I have queried on this issue has recalled German maids or nannies; many attest to the importance of devoted and affectionate German nannies in helping them cope with traumatized and overworked parents.

142. Phone conversation with Arnold Kerr, August 5, 2004. In January 1947, Ruth Kluger was exceptional in that she studied literature; see her memoir, *Still Alive*. Jeremy Varon and Bela Brodski are preparing a study on Jewish DP students in postwar Germany. The Jewish Student Union in Munich counted some 400

members in the late 1940s and early 1950s; 570 Jewish students were enrolled in German universities; and over a third were women. See Syrkin, *State of the Jews*, 31. Of a total of 449 in Munich, 408 were members of the Jewish Student Union. Frankfurt had 72 and Berlin 70 in 1947. See Königseder, *Flucht nach Berlin*, 155; also YIVO LWS 294.1/529/MK488/46.

143. Angelika Eder describes these encounters in nearby Landsberg: "Indeed trade relations were so good that when the DPs pulled out in 1948/49, local businessmen worried about losing business and sources of goods." See "Jüdische Displaced Persons im deutschen Alltag,"in *Überlebt und Unterwegs*, ed. Fritz Bauer Institut, 163–187. See also idem, *Flüchtige Heimat*, and D. Kohlmannslehner, "Das Verhältnis von Deutschen und jüdischen Displaced Persons in Lager Lampertheim 1945–1949," unpublished paper, Fritz Bauer Institut archives.

144. Patt, "Finding Home and Homeland."

145. Levin, *In Search*, 363.

146. See Schochet, *Feldafing*, 166, also 47–50 on DP "jargon."

147. Interview with Elizabeth (Ita) Muskal, Yonkers, New York, June 16, 2003.

148. In November 1945, Jews in Föhrenwald went on a hunger strike to protest the use of German cooks and kitchen personnel. YIVO DPG 294/2/44/MK584/R4, 36. Other sources mention early protests against German cooks in Feldafing as well. See Karni, "Life at the Feldafing Displaced Persons Camp," 51.

149. See the (uncomfortably sympathetic) discussion of German grievances in Ulrich Müller, *Fremde in der Nachkriegszeit. Displaced Persons—zwangsverschleppte Personen in Stuttgart und Württemberg—Baden 1945–1951* (Stuttgart: Klett-Cotta, 1990), 74–77.

150. Ruth Klüger, *Weiterleben: Eine Jugend* (Göttingen: Wallstein, 1992), 196. In the revised English version, Kluger, *Still Alive*, 154, "*Parasiten*" is changed to "protégés."

151. UNRRAA/399.1.2, Confidential report by Captain G. Weisz on field trip to US zone, 5 April 1946.

152. See Mintzer, "Report on Disturbances at Landsberg Camp," April 29, 1946, and "Report on Shooting at Foehrenwald Camp," July 27, 1946, in *In Defense of the Survivors*, ed. Grobman, 377–381 and 356–367. See also Hyman, *Undefeated*, 23–28.

153. Report of Oscar A. Mintzer, "The Legal Situation of Jewish DPs in the American Zone," Germany, September 23, 1946, in AJDCA/390. For a critical view, see Mankowitz, *Life between Memory and Hope*, 259–260; for an American Jewish view, see Hyman, *Undefeated*, and Mintzer in *Defense of the Survivors*, ed. Grobman. On the conflicts in Landsberg, see Angelika Eder's careful study, *Flüchtige Heimat*.

154. Report of Oscar A. Mintzer, "The Legal Situation of Jewish DPs."

155. Pinson, "Jewish Life," 111–112.

156. Vida, *Doom to Dawn*, 21, describes his satisfaction at ordering 12 gallons of herring to serve after fall 1945 High Holy Day services in the old Frankfurt synagogue in the Freiherr von Stein Strasse, after it had been cleaned up by a special detail of 23 former SS men. Theodor W. Adorno makes a point in his *Soziologische Schriften II* (Suhrkamp: Frankfurt/M, 1975), pp. 258–260, of dis-

cussing the *"Rachesucht"* (lust for revenge) Germans attributed to DPs and Jews.

157. See YIVO LWS 294.1/286/MK488/R24, esp. 802–803. See one description in Alicia Appleman-Jurman, *Alicia: My Story* (New York: Bantam, 1988), 390–391.

158. Landau, "Purim auf Elmau," in *Aufbau*, collected in YIVO LWS 294.1/535/MK488/R46, 1060–1066. See also the similar report in Schwarz, *Redeemers*, 111–112. On Purim celebrations in the DP camps, see Toby Blum Dobkin, "The Landsberg Carnival: Purim in a Displaced Persons' Center," in *Purim: The Face and the Mask*, ed. Shifra Epstein (New York: Yeshiva University Art Museum, 1979), 52–60, also YIVO 249.2 DPG/847/MK483/R61.

159. Avraham Fuchs, quoted in Gutman and Saf, eds., *She'erit Hapletah, 1944–1948*, 532–533.

160. Figure from Yantian, "Studien zum Selbstverständnis," 43. Königseder, *Flucht nach Berlin*, 145 (citing *Undser Lebn*, December 27, 1946, 34), describes the case of two DPs in Berlin accused of relations with German women. They had allegedly gotten drunk in local bars, dishonored their Jewish wives, and endangered the community through the possible transmission of venereal disease. Stated punishment ranged from a warning for a first offense to six months banishment from the DP camp, although it is unclear whether such sanctions were actually enforced.

161. Chaim Meir Gottlieb, "Kibbutz Buchenwald," reporting on June 21, 1945, meeting, in Schwarz, *The Root and the Bough*, 315–316. Also cited in Mankowitz, *Life between Memory and Hope*, 244. See also Judith Tydor Baumel, *Kibbutz Buchenwald: Survivors and Pioneers* (New Brunswick, N.J.: Rutgers University Press, 1997).

162. Quotes from *Unser Wort*, Nr. 15, November 15, 1946, in YIVO DPG 294.2/548/MK483/R41. The reference to liaisons between German men and Jewish women is surprising given the general (and surely correct) assumption that Jewish women were far less likely to engage in such relationships and that, moreover, there was a severe shortage of eligible German men.

163. The British chaplain at Belsen recalled his efforts to convince a woman doctor who had lost her husband and son in the camps that her responsibility to await in the DP camps a possible Jewish future in Palestine should outweigh the temptation to marry the British medical officer who had tended her and was now promising her a secure life in Britain. When last heard from she was struggling and alone in New York City, studying for her medical boards. See Hardman, *Survivors: . . . Belsen Remnant*, 66.

164. See, for example, Klein and Klein, *Hours After*, or the oral history interview projected on the screen at the conclusion of the main tour in the USHMM.

165. Macardle, *Children of Europe*, 266.

166. Elly Stern, "Joy Cometh in the Morning" in Schwarz, *The Root and the Bough*, 178.

167. Phone interview, AK, August 5, 2004.

168. Zippi Tichauer, personal and phone interviews, New York City, October 2004–June 2006.

169. Meyer Kron, "Through the Eye of a Needle," chapter 10, "Stopover in Germany," in memoir collection, Concordia University Chair in Jewish Studies, Montreal Institute for Genocide and Human Rights Studies, 2001, http://migs. Concordia.ca/survivor.html.

170. Tichauer interviews. See Fehrenbach, *Race after Hitler.*

171. Schochet, *Feldafing,* 161–162. For descriptions of such love affairs, see Jack Eisner, *Die Happy Boys: Eine jüdische Band in Deutschland 1945 bis 1949,* translated from his English text (Berlin: Aufbau, 2004), 118–120, 163–178. Ruth Kluger describes her complicated relationship with fellow student Christoph (a fictionalized version of German writer Martin Walser), *Still Alive,* 165–166.

172. Hyman, *Undefeated,* 35, 393.

173. See Mankowitz's excellent political study, *Life between Memory and Hope,* or Peck, "Jewish Survivors," 33–45. Hyman, *Undefeated,* referred to "sublimated forms of revenge," 346.

174. For example, Ira A. Hirschmann, LaGuardia's inspector general for the UNRRA, in his passionate book *The Embers Still Burn,* 149, 145. On these plans for (and limited actions of) revenge, see Jim G. Tobias and Peter Zinke, *Nakam: Jüdische Rache an NS-Tätern* (Berlin: Aufbau Taschenbuch, 2003); Rich Cohen, *The Avengers: A Jewish War Story* (New York: Alfred A. Knopf, 2000); and Michael Bar-Zohar, *The Avengers* (New York: Hawthorn Books, 1967), 20–52. See also the remarkable story about an American (German) Jewish officer's collaboration with DPs in Matthew Brzezinski, "The Secret: Giving Hitler Hell," *The Washington Post Magazine,* July 24, 2005, 8–17, esp. 26.

175. Susan Brison, *Aftermath,* 13. Lynn Rapaport, *Jews in Germany after the Holocaust: Memory, Identity, and Jewish-German Relations* (Cambridge: Cambridge University Press, 1997), 75, uses Mary Douglas's analysis of taboo and pollution to suggest that Jews and Germans employed silence and avoidance as strategies to cope with a "polluted social environment."

176. Lucille Eichengreen, with Harriet Hyman Chamberlain, *From Ashes to Life: My Memories of the Holocaust* (San Francisco: Mercury House, 1994), 155.

177. Mintzer, in *In Defense of the Survivors,* ed. Grobman, 301.

178. See, among many others, Abraham Hyman's description in *Undefeated,* 76.

179. Pfc. Hans Lichtwitz, "Die 'Dachaver' kommen zurück: Erlebnisse eines jüdischen Soldaten in Bayern und Oesterreich," *Aufbau,* August 10, 1945, 32.

180. Nadich, *Eisenhower and the Jews,* 193.

181. Dawidowicz, *From That Time and Place,* 283.

182. Lichtwitz, "Erlebnisse," 32.

183. Hyman, *Undefeated,* 75.

184. Letter from Klein and Klein, *Hours After,* 110. For the perspective of an UNRRA worker who also worked in the Deutsches Museum, see Pettiss, *After the Shooting Stopped.*

185. Levin, *In Search,* 363.

186. Hyman, *Undefeated,* 35, 139, 155, 393. See also Patt, "Finding Home and Homeland."

187. Cited in Hyman, *Undefeated,* 16–17.

188. Richard W. Sonnenfeldt, *Mehr als ein Leben: Vom jüdischen Flüchtlings-ungen zum Chefdolmestscher der Anklage bei den Nürnberger Prozessen*, translated from his English text (Bern: Scherz, 2003), 174.

189. "Fahrt durch Berlin. Aus einem Brief von Master Sgt Charles Gregor," posted from Berlin on July 14; in a favorite move, it was written on letterhead from the Führer's bunker. *Aufbau*, August 17, 1945, 32.

190. Dietrich and Schulze-Wessel, *Zwischen Selbstorganisation und Stigmatisierung*, 311. ˙

191. *Landsberger Lager Caijtung* (No. 16, p. 9, n.d.), and *Die Jüdische Rundschau*, quoted in Pinson, "Jewish Life," 114. Gringauz himself emigrated to the United States in September 1947. See also Mankowitz, *Life between Memory and Hope*, 190–191, and Wyman, *DPs*, 138.

192. Posener, *In Deutschland*, 144. Also cited in Brenner, *After the Holocaust*, 52.

193. Klein and Klein, *Hours After*, 191.

194. As Richard Bessel and Dirk Schumann point out in the introduction to their edited collection *Life after Death*, historians have invested a great deal of effort to understanding how the crises of the 1930s and 1940s developed and unfolded, but less to comprehending their aftermath. Studying the voices of the survivors and those who observed them in the early postwar years is one way of getting at questions such as, 13, "how did people emerge from these horrors?" and comprehending the return to a "normality" of "after" that was entirely shadowed by the extreme horror of what had come before.

CHAPTER SIX
Conclusion: The "Interregnum" Ends

1. Levin, *In Search*, 175.

2. Genêt, "Letter from Aschaffenburg, October 20," *The New Yorker*, October 30, 1948, 98–101.

3. Dr. B. Sagalowitz, report to World Jewish Congress on trip to Germany, April 1950, in *Archives of the Holocaust*, vol. 9, *Papers of the World Jewish Congress*, ed. Peck, 377.

4. On the complexities of the *Exodus* Affair, in which mostly young Zionist DPs battled British troops in the port of Haifa before being forced to return to Germany—a pyrrhic victory for the British, who clearly lost the propaganda battle to the Zionists—see Aviva Halamish, *The Exodus Affair: Holocaust Survivors and the Struggle for Palestine*, trans. Ora Cummings (Syracuse, N.Y.: Syracuse University Press, 1998); Kochavi, *Post-Holocaust Politics*; Lavsky, *New Beginnings*.

5. Gringauz, "Our New German Policy and the DPs," 508, 509; "golden age" comment on 509.

6. See Annan, *Changing Enemies*.

7. See Habe, *Love Affair*, 181, 51.

8. As Col. Frank Howley put it in *Berlin Command*, 257, "This sounds like an extraordinary statement to make about a conquered people and their conquer-

ors, but it was brought about by the German fear of a greater internal enemy, fostered by the Russians—communism. They felt that their only protection came from the Western occupying authorities."

9. Among many analyses, see Norbert Frei, *Adenauer's Germany and the Nazi Past: The Politics of Amnesty and Integration*, trans. Joel Gold (New York: Columbia University Press, 2002).

10. See the poignant letters from homesick children collected in LAB LAZ, Rep. 280, Film Nr. 16. Berlin newspapers and authorities publicized heartrending stories of malnourished but still spunky—with *Berliner Witz*—children being fattened up in the West. Delighted by the bright lights and abundance of cities in the western zone, they feared for their mothers who were sick and dying of tuberculosis behind the iron curtain.

11. Middleton, *Last July*, 168–169. It is interesting to note the multiple uses of the term "holocaust" in the immediate postwar years, in contexts having nothing to do with the genocide of European Jewry. Secretary of State James F. Byrnes referred in his 1947 account, *Speaking Frankly*, 306, to the danger of another world war: "If we are to prevent such a holocaust, not only must we halt acts of aggression, but we must seek to eradicate the causes of these acts."

12. Howley, *Berlin Command*, 258.

13. Airlift myths have now been rather thoroughly dismantled by many historians. See Paul Steege, *Black Market, Cold War: Everyday Life in Berlin, 1946–1949* (Cambridge: Cambridge University Press, 2007).

14. Joseph B. Phillips, "The Germans in Berlin," *Newsweek* 32:1 (July 5, 1948): 41.

15. Middleton, *Last July*, 168–169.

16. The September 9 rally was followed by an "antifascist" counterdemonstration of about 50,000 at the Lustgarten, with French and British but not American flags. See *Newsweek* 32:12 (September 20, 1948): 36–38.

17. For an early interview with Wolff , see Boehm, *We Survived*, 253–280.

18. Howley, *Berlin Command*, 87, 5.

19. See BAB Sapmo SED IV/2/17/86 ZK SED, Abt. Frauen, DFD.

20. Howley, *Berlin Command*, 196–197.

21. Middleton, *Last July*, 169.

22. For provocative reflections on German women's attitudes, see Tröger, "Between Rape and Prostitution."

23. *The Big Lift*, 1950, produced by William Perlberg, directed by George Seaton.

24. *Der Weg* 2:1 (January 3, 1947).

25. *Der Weg* 2:9 (February 28, 1947). See also Hans-Erich Fabian, "Unheimliches Deutschland," *Der Weg* 2:5 (January 31, 1947), 1.

26. *Der Weg* 2:11 (March 14, 1947).

27. Fabian, "Unheimliches Deutschland." On Schumacher, see also Geller, *Jews in Post-Holocaust Germany*, 124–132.

28. Heinrich Busse, letter, December 12, 1945.

29. Busse, letter, June 16, 1946.

30. Busse, letter from London, 1947 (n.d.).

31. Moskowitz, "The Germans and the Jews."

32. Stern, in *Whitewashing*, posits that antisemitism was in many ways more visible in Germany after the war than before. For one German-Jewish perspective on postwar Germans, see Hannah Arendt's much-quoted lament about Germans' "deep-rooted, stubborn, and at times vicious refusal to face and come to terms with what really happened," in "Aftermath of Nazi Rule," 342–343.

33. Moskowitz, "The Germans and the Jews," 13. The Gemeinde itself estimated in mid 1946 that about 45% of its members wished to leave Germany, about half to Palestine. That number increased with time, and would surely have been even larger were it not for the fact that so many of Berlin's Jews were elderly and ailing. See "Die Lage der jüdischen Gemeinde," in CJA 5A1/3, 251–252.

34. Busse, letter to Hermann Paul, 1947 (n.d.).

35. Busse, letter to Hohenwalds from London 1947 (n.d.). For original German of these letters, see Atina Grossmann, "Home and Displacement in a City of Bordercrossers: Jews in Berlin, 1945–1948," in *Unlikely History: The Changing German-Jewish Symbiosis, 1945–2000*, ed. Leslie Morris and Jack Zipes (New York: Palgrave, 2002), 98. All letters in Heinrich Busse collection, LBI Archives. Busse's words are echoed by Ralph Giordano's charge against Germans: "In all earnest, he equates his empty stomach, that is to say an immediate consequence of the policy of criminality which he, following 'higher orders' had defended until five minutes past twelve, with the monster crimes of Auschwitz, Lidice, Vercros and Maidanek." Quoted in Kolinsky, *After the Holocaust*, 200.

36. Information in Heinrich Busse's files in the Wiedergutmachungsamt and Entschädigungsamt (offices for restitution and reparations), Berlin, and in Oberfinanzpräsidium (OFP) files for Berlin Brandenburgisches Landeshauptarchiv, Potsdam.

37. Letter from Erich Nelhans, November 25, 1946, CJA 5A1/36, 161.

38. Siegmund Weltlinger papers, LAB, Rep. 200, Acc. 2334, letter to Mrs. Mally Corey, December 1, 1951. Weltlinger even argued—forty years in advance—that Berlin would become the logical destination for a future, inevitable exodus of Jews from the Soviet Union. See letter to Max, December 15, 1949.

39. Hans-Erich Fabian, "Liquidationsgemeinden?" *Der Weg* 2:18 (May 2, 1947).

40. Jacobmeyer, "Jüdische Überlebende als 'Displaced Persons,' " 432. For film footage of DPs, with babies and shabby valises, being loaded onto trucks for transport to the airport and then climbing ladders into waiting U.S. Army cargo planes, see Steven Spielberg Video and Film Archive, USHMM, tape 2273, RG 60–2441.

41. Geller, *Jews in Post-Holocaust Germany*, 105. On JDC, see Zweig, *German Reparations*, 133.

42. See Peck, ed., *Archives of the Holocaust*, vol. 9, 398ff. ("if Jews in small or larger groups choose to continue to live among the people who are responsible for the slaughter of six millions of their brothers, that is their affair").

43. Vorstandssitzung, September 6, 1949, CJA 5A1/6. In fact, the World Jewish Congress, under Nahum Goldmann, was (and not without enormous controversy) the only international Jewish organization that maintained a presence in Germany.

44. Syrkin, *State of the Jews*, 11–13.

45. On British policy, see Lavsky, *New Beginnings*, and Kochavi, *Post-Holocaust Politics*.

46. Term is taken from John Borneman and Jeffrey Peck, *Sojourners: The Return of German Jews and the Question of Identity* (Lincoln: University of Nebraska Press, 1995).

47. Hyman, *Undefeated*, 126. Hyman argued, 131, that "even in 1946," acceptance of the Anglo-American committee's recommendation would have "taken the edge off the pressure exercised by the Jewish DP camps on the United States and Britain." He was not alone in pondering whether such early opening of emigration possibilities might have led to a different and less embattled outcome in the Middle East.

48. Genêt, "Letter from Aschaffenburg," 98–101. On non-Jewish DPs see Hilton, "Prisoners of Peace."

49. Oral history interview with Elizabeth (Ita) Muskal, Yonkers, New York, June 16, 2003.

50. "Das Land im Kampf," CJA 5A1/44.

51. Yablonka, *Survivors of the Holocaust*, 142. On the controversial issue of whether the survivors were treated as, or felt like, "cannonfodder" in the Arab-Israeli conflict after the declaration of independence, see her sensitive (and heartbreaking) discussion, 131–142. For more contemporary observations and discussions, see Hyman, *Undefeated*, 365–366, who notes that the prohibition on immigration was never applied, and Schwarz, *Redeemers*, 278; also Yablonka, *Survivors of the Holocaust*, 82. Newer research by Emmanuel Sivan and corroborated by Yosef Grodzinsky clearly shows, however, that the DPs were not "cannonfodder." In part because of the timing of their arrival in Israel (relatively late in the war of independence), they did not die in disproportionate numbers; in fact their casualty rate was relatively low. In any case, the institution, enforcement, and consequences of this unprecedented draft on foreign soil for a new state are the subject of lively discussion among historians of Israel and Zionism. See Grodzinsky *In the Shadow of the Holocaust*, 176, 215, 212–213. For an excellent, judicious untangling of the many issues involved, including the motivation and agency of the young DPs, see Patt, "Finding Home and Homeland," esp. chapter 5, "Between Hope and Disappointment: Jewish DP Youth and *Aliyah*."

52. Interview, Elizabeth and Sam Muskal.

53. Lower numbers from Michael Brenner, entry on DPs, *Encyclopedia of the Holocaust*, ed. Israel Gutman (New York: Macmillan, 1990), 154; higher numbers from Wyman, *DPs*, 155, 178–204.

54. On the sanatorium, see Walter Fürnrohr and Felix Muschialik, *Überleben und Neubeginn. DP-Hospital Gauting ab 1945* (Munich: P. Kirchheim, 2005).

55. See Hyman, *Undefeated*, 376, and, Wyman, *DPs*, 194. In general on this phase, see Wyman, *DPs*, 155, 178–204; Dinnerstein, *America and the Survivors*, summary in Haia Karni, "Life at the Feldafing Displaced Persons Camp, 1945–1952" (master's thesis, Baltimore Hebrew University, 1997), 67–68. According to Kurt R. Grossmann, *DP Problem*, 28–29, as of July 11, 1951, 250,000 DPs had entered the United States, of whom 20%, 77,500, were Jews. Other significant DP (not only Jewish) destinations were South America, Australia, and Canada, which took in about 20,000 Jews. DPs also went to Belgium, France, Holland,

and Sweden as labor migrants. The statistics for the end of the DP period are almost as confusing and inconsistent as those for the beginning. Hyman, *Undefeated*, 376, says that of c. 250,000 Jewish DPs, 142,000 (56%) went to Palestine and Israel and 72,000 to the United States. He has Canada taking 16,000, Belgium 8,000, France 2,000, and 10,000 going to various other countries in South America and the British Commonwealth. Hyman also counts a relatively high 35,000 remaining in Germany in 1949. For further figures see also Ronald Sanders, *Shores of Refuge: A Hundred Years of Jewish Immigration* (New York: Henry Holt, 1988), 586–587, and Dalia Ofer, "Emigration and *Aliyah*: A Reassessment of Israeli and Jewish Policies," in *Terms of Survival*, ed. Wistrich, 82, n. 11. Grodzinsky, *In the Shadow of the Holocaust*, counts 140,000 (42%) emigrating to Israel and 120,000 (36%) to the United States out of a total 330,000. See his table of emigration destinations between 1945 and 1951, 223.

56. Brenner, entry on on DPs in *Encyclopedia of the Holocaust*, 154.

57. U. O. Schmelz, "The Demographic Impact of the Holocaust," in *Terms of Survival*, ed. Wistrich, 45. David Weinberg (paper, USHMM DP workshop, July 2005) counters assertions of a "void" in postwar Jewish life by pointing to significant reconstruction and renewal efforts, especially in France and Britain. In 1948 there were about 625,000 Jews left in Eastern Europe outside the Soviet Union. See Zweig, *German Reparations*, 44.

58. Boehling, *Question of Priorities*, 7. The State Department, which had been so chary of giving visas to desperate German Jews in the 1930s and had vigorously resisted Morgenthau's plans to fully deindustrialize a defeated Germany, was considered more hostile to Jews than the Military Government had been.

59. Report from William Haber, adviser on Jewish Affairs in American zone of Germany, to Meir Grossman, American Jewish Conference, N.Y., June 10, 1948, in Peck, ed., *Archives of the Holocaust*, vol. 9, 312; see also 319–321.

60. Hulme, *Wild Place*, 222.

61. In general see Zweig, *German Reparations*. On the end of denazification, see especially John H. Herz, "The Fiasco of Denazification," *Political Science Quarterly* 63:4 (1948): 569–594. Already in 1948, émigré political scientist John Herz had concluded, 590, "Nothing could be more revealing than the strange modification of meaning that the term 'denazification' itself has undergone. While at first signifying the elimination of Nazis from public life, it has now in German everyday language come to mean the removal of the Nazi stigma from the individual concerned; that is, the procedure by which he gets rid of certain inhibitions or restrictions." Also cited in Boehling, *Question of Priorities*, 239.

62. Unless otherwise noted, all quotes from "Conference on 'The Future of the Jews in Germany,'" Heidelberg, July 31, 1949. Minutes edited by Harry Greenstein, adviser on Jewish Affairs, U.S. Military Government in Germany, dated September 1, 1949. See esp. pp. 5–6, 10–14, 19–22, 24, 29, 41, 45–46, 52, LBI Archives. Greenstein had convened a smaller preliminary meeting in Heidelberg in March. See also Geller, *Jews in Post-Holocaust Germany*, 72–77, and Brenner, *After the Holocaust*, 74–77.

63. In Berlin, with 80% of the community German-Jewish, 34% were over fifty-five and only 11% under 17; in Frankfurt, where only 45% were German, 16% were fifty-five and over, 14% under seventeen. The communities were gener-

ally elderly, with very few children—the opposite demographic profile of the DP camps. See also Kolinsky, *After the Holocaust*, who claims, 215, that intermarriage rates in cities were up to 75%, with only 2 of 10 non-Jewish partners converting. On relations between DPs and German Jews in the Gemeinden, see, among others, Wetzel, *Jüdisches Leben in München* and Harry Maor, "Über den Wiederaufbau der jüdischen Gemeinden in Deutschland Seit 1945" (Ph.D. dissertation, Mainz, 1961). Maor's unfortunately still unpublished thesis remains the best and most comprehensive study of Jewish Gemeinden in early postwar Germany. Parts are available in English on the web, www.harrymaor.com.

64. In contrast to McCloy's remarks about the status of Jews as a test of West German "progress," Fehrenbach, *Race after Hitler*, 94, points out that many "liberal" Germans preferred to point to their treatment of "colored" Germans (*Mischlinge*), generally the offspring of German women and African-American soldiers, as the test of their "social maturity." Her book opens up many possible questions about comparisons between postwar West German reactions to Jews and the new racial others, especially African-Americans. Geller, *Jews in Post-Holocaust Germany* (which I read after I had completed my own research), 75, also notes McCloy's placing "onus" on Jews.

65. Ronald Webster, "American Relief and Jews in Germany, 1945–1960," *LBI Yearbook* 38 (1993): 304, referring to the Joint.

66. On this conflict, see Zweig, *German Reparations*, 57ff.

67. On the history of the Zentralrat, see Maor, "Über den Wiederaufbau"; Geller, *Jews in Post-Holocaust Germany*; idem, "Die Enstehung des Zentralrats der Juden in Deutschland," in *Zwischen Erinnerung und Neubeginn*, ed. Schönborn, 60–75; and Udi Chadasch, "Der Zentralrat der Juden in Deutschland von seiner Entstehung Bis Zum Ende der Adenauer-Ära" (master's thesis, Cologne, 1992), Zentral Archiv, Heidelberg.

68. Report by Dr. B. Sagalowitz, in *Archives of the Holocaust*, ed. Peck, vol. 9, 361–362, 368, 377–378. Hannah Arendt, in "Aftermath of Nazi Rule," 348, made the same observation in 1950: "Germans who confess their own guilt are in many cases altogether innocent in the ordinary, down-to-earth sense, whereas those who are guilty of something real have the calmest consciences in the world." For a later reflection by someone who had been deeply involved in both DP and restitution matters, see Kurt R. Grossmann, "The Problem of Forgetting: Thoughts on the Nazi War Crimes Trials," *Patterns of Prejudice* (Institute of Jewish Affairs) 2:6 (November–December 1968): 10–16. There is by now a vast literature on this "problem of forgetting." See, for example, Moeller, *War Stories*, and Frei, *Adenauer's Germany and the Nazi Past*.

69. Schwarz, *Redeemers*, 114, quoting Samuel Gringauz, "There are no Nazis in Germany."

70. Despite resentments and tensions, the much more numerous expellees were integrated into the German national community, in ways that Jewish DPs would and could never be. See for example Pertti Ahonen, *After the Expulsion: West Germany and Eastern Europe, 1945–60* (Oxford: Oxford University Press, 2003).

71. Report of Oscar A. Mintzer, "The Legal Situation of Jewish DPs in the American Zone," Germany, September 23, 1946, AJDCA/390.

72. Werner Bergmann, "'Der Antisemitismus in Deutschland brauch gar nicht übertreiben zu warden . . .' Die Jahre 1945–1953," in *Leben im Land der Täter*, ed. Schoeps, 205.

73. Quoted from *Neues Volksblatt*, July 13, 1950; see also *Fränkischer Tag*, July 8, 1950, filed in YIVO DPG 294.2/49/MK483/R5. The local refugee office (*Flüchtlingsausschuss*) protested housing "foreigners" together with expellees (*Heimatvertriebenen*) "because they are heavily involved in the black market and constitute a moral danger to the [German] refugee youth." Numerous such press accounts were collected and retyped by the DP organizations, to be used as evidence with both the West German and the American authorities. On later years, see Höhn, *GIs and Fräuleins*.

74. For further discussion of this self-imposed outsider status, see for example Michal Bodemann, "Mentalitäten des Verweilens. Der Neubeginn jüdischen Lebens in Deutschland," in *Leben im Land der Täter*, ed. Schoeps, 15–29. On philosemitism, see Stern, *Whitewashing*. On shifting the language of "race" from Jews to groups defined by skin color, especially African-Americans, see Fehrenbach, *Race after Hitler*.

75. August 31, 1949, report from Mr. Harry Greenstein, adviser on Jewish Affairs to U.S. Commander in Germany, on riot of August 10, 1949, in AJDCA/ 499. Here too, there are myriad somewhat different versions of the events. See, for example, Muhlen, *Return of Germany*, 163–165; Kauders, *Democratization and the Jews*, 139. A year earlier, on April 17, 1948, the *Süddeutsche Zeitung* had published an article in its "Debate" section titled "Antisemitismus-1948," which blamed the "asocial behavior" of the DPs for antisemitism and favorably contrasted the "unobtrusive" profile of remaining German Jews. See also Bergmann, "Der Antisemitismus," 195, and Juliane Wetzel, "Trauma und Tabu, Jüdisches Leben in Deutschland nach dem Holocaust," in *Ende des Dritten Reiches—Ende des Zweiten Weltkriegs*, ed. Hans-Erich Volkmann (Munich: Piper, 1995), 433–444 and 454, n. 30.

76. See reports in AJDCA/396 (Foehrenwald 1955–62), 397B (Foehrenwald 1954), and 398 (Foehrenwald). On venting, see Paul Friedman, "The Road Back for the DPs: Healing the Psychological Scars of Nazism," *Commentary* 6:6 (December 1948): 502–510.

77. The statistics are inconsistent and confusing. Webster, "American Relief and Jews in Germany," 309, says that in 1953 there were still 30,000 former DPs and their families in the Federal Republic. Brenner, entry on DPs in *Encyclopedia of the Holocaust*, 159, lists 30,000 in late 1948 and only 12,000 in 1952.

78. Angelika Heider, "Das Lager für jüdische 'Displaced Persons' Feldafing in der amerikanischen Besatzungszone 1945–1951" (master's thesis, Technische Universität Berlin, 1994), 124.

79. Hyman, *Undefeated*, 402.

80. Y. Michal Bodemann, in *A Jewish Family in Germany Today: An Intimate Portrait* (Durham, N.C.: Duke University Press, 2005), uses the sociological term "*Verweiler*," borrowed from Simmel, to categorize this long-term commitment to transience; see introduction, 1–35, also in *Leben im Land der Täter*, ed. Schoeps, 15–29. Zweig, *German Reparations*, refers to "sojourners, 58, and "itinerants,"

56. Jeffrey Peck and John Borneman titled their book about Jews in postwar Germany *Sojourners: The Return of German Jews and the Question of Identity.*

81. Report to Charles Jordan from Leonard Seidenman, October 6, 1952, AJDCA/398.

82. JDC Report, January 26, 1949, AJDCA/392, YIVO DPG 294.2/65/ MK483/R6, also 163–166. Also see YIVO DPG 294.2/580/MK483/R43 and AJDCA/398 on Föhrenwald "hard core."

83. Kauders, *Democratization and the Jews*, 61–62, n. 28, quoting JDC reports from 1954, 1952, and 1951. By 1950, there are also many reports—similar in language and intent to those dealing with the absent American GI fathers of illegitimate German children—about local welfare agencies' efforts to track down Jewish DP fathers in order to claim child support. As was the case with the Americans, the DPs had invariably decamped (or were said to have), for Israel or elsewhere, leaving responsibility (*Vormundschaft*) for German women's babies— who, if illegitimate, were automatically German citizens—with the West German state. See examples in YIVO DPG 294.2/559/MK483/R42. On the situation of American "occupation children," see Fehrenbach, *Race after Hitler*, 74ff.

84. Minutes of Administration Committee of Joint Distribution Committee, Edward Warburg presiding, November 3, 1953, marked "highly confidential," AJDCA/398. See also Zweig, *German Reparations*, 124.

85. Vida, *Doom to Dawn*, 85–87.

86. See, among many sources, Brenner, *After the Holocaust*; Schoeps, ed., *Leben im Land der Täter*; Kauders, *Democratization and the Jews.*

87. Memorandum from Oscar Karlbach to Robert S. Marcus, June 16, 1950, in Peck, ed., *Archives of the Holocaust*, vol. 9, 398–399.

88. Recorded in Schwarz, *Redeemers*, 198.

89. Elke Fröhlich, "Philipp Auerbach (1906–1952), 'Generalanwalt für Wiedergutmachung,' " in *Geschichte und Kultur der Juden in Bayern: Lebensläufe, Veröffentlichung zur Bayerischen Geschichte und Kultur* 18/88, ed. Manfred Treml and Wolf Weigand, 315–320, here p. 320. This complicated story has not yet been fully told or unraveled. For a judicious analysis, see Constantin Goschler, "The Attitude towards Jews in Bavaria after the Second World War," *LBI Yearbook* 36 (1991): 443–458; reprint in Moeller, ed., *West Germany under Construction*, 231–250; idem, "Der Fall Philipp Auerbach. Wiedergutmachung in Bayern," in *Wiedergutmachung in der Bundesrepublik Deutschland*, ed. Ludolf Herbst and Constantin Goschler (Munich: Oldenbourg, 1989), 77–98. See also, among other sources, Wolfgang Kraushaar, "Die Auerbach-Affäre," in *Leben im Land der Täter*, ed. Schoeps, 209–218. The tensions around restitution and conflicts with Auerbach were exacerbated by the Nazi past of his German counterpart, Theodor Oberländer, the Bavarian state secretary for refugee affairs. See Zweig, *German Reparations*, 124. Auerbach's papers are now open for researchers in the Bavarian State Archives; I am grateful to Gerhard Fürmetz for information on the Auerbach papers. The Munich *Landesrabbiner* Aron Ohrenstein, who had been charged along with Auerbach, had made himself particularly unpopular with Jewish organizations not only because he was perceived as corrupt but also because he was known for "his willingness to convert Christian women." See Kauders, *Democratization and the Jews*, 141–142, 61–62, n. 28. The accusation of a new Dreyfus

case in the Bavarian courts was not new but had been used in the Weimar Republic; see Douglas Morris, *Justice Imperiled: The Anti-Nazi Lawyer Max Hirschberg in the Weimar Republic* (Ann Arbor: University of Michigan Press, 2005).

90. Habe, *Love Affair*, 128. According to Schwarz, *Redeemers*, 208–211, citing a *New York Times* report of August 17, 1952, John J. McCloy rejected appeals by Auerbach and his friends to move the case from a German to an Allied court. For another tragic and mysterious trial story involving a man who worked for Auerbach and his State Commission for the Racially, Religiously, and Politically Persecuted in Bavaria, see Anita Kugler, *Schweritz: Der jüdische SS Offizier* (Cologne: Kiepenhauer and Witsch, 2004).

91. "Our Unfinished Job in Germany," October 13, 1953, Report by David Rosenstein, AJDCA/398. As Mary Palevsky, director of the Munich office, wrote to JDC official Charles Jordan on September 2, 1955, about the difficulties attending the closing of the Föhrenwald hospital, "So ends another chapter of Foehrenwald history. To paraphrase a famous sentence, never have so few people created so much work for so many, for so little." In AJDCA/396.

92. Report from December 31, 1952, AJDCA/ 398.

93. Letter to Dr. Arthur T. Jacobs, executive director, February 24, 1954, AJDCA/499. A memo from Charles H. Jordan of the JDC in Germany, November 1, 1953, referred to the Föhrenwalders as a "racketeering committee" trying to blackmail the Jewish Claims Conference into giving each person between $3,500 and $5,000 as an incentive to leave the DP camp.

94. Zweig, *German Reparations*, 124.

95. Eugen Steppan, *Waldram: "Anspruch auf Vergangenheit und Zukunft" Die Geschichte des Wolfratshauser Ortsteiles Waldram*, 1982, 67–68, in Zentral Archiv, Heidelberg, file 033.5 (433.6).

96. In 1956, 633 people remained in Föhrenwald; 12 turned the key in February 1957. See Webster, "American Relief and Jews in Germany," 292. According to Zweig, *German Reparations*, 125, most of those who emigrated went to Australia. These sensational descriptions, from both Germans and Jews, of Föhrenwald as a center of crime and asocial behavior contrast to the much more rosy memories of the young Jewish children who grew up and went to school there in the early 1950s, as expressed for example by Rahel Salamander and Sam Norich at the 1995 DP conference in Munich.

97. For a discussion of Harmsen's long career, see Atina Grossmann, *Reforming Sex: The German Movement for Birth Control and Abortion Reform 1920–1950* (New York: Oxford University Press, 1995), esp. 204–211.

98. For example, the historical commissions set up by survivors in Poland and the DP camps apparently did not collect testimonies about experiences in the Soviet Union. On the commissions, see Laura Jockusch, "Jüdische Geschichtsforschung im Lande Amaleks. Jüdische historische Kommissionen in Deutschland 1945–1949," in *Zwischen Erinnerung und Neubeginn*, ed. Schönborn, 20–41.

99. Johannes Menke, "Die soziale Integration jüdischer Flüchtlinge des ehemaligen Regierungslagers 'Föhrenwald' in den drei Westdeutschen Grossstädten Düsseldorf, Frankfurt und München, Nach im Sommer 1959 (vom 6.8.-25.9) durchgeführten sozialhygienischen Feldstudien über die ehemaligen Lagerinsassen," in vol. 2, *Sozialhygienische Forschungen*, ed. Hans Harmsen (Hamburg, 1960), esp.

3, 6, 27–29, 59–68. The study was based on 100 completed questionnaires as well as interviews and home visits. It is worth comparing the language and tone of this report to that of similar ones prepared on the integration of ethnic German refugees from the East and also on the "mixed breed" children of German women and African-American GIs. On the latter, especially the "liberal" postwar discourse on race, see Fehrenbach, *Race after Hitler*, 74–106.

100. Maor, "Über den Wiederaufbau," 19. According to Maor's 1961 study, in March 1949, Jewish communities in Germany, including the Soviet zone, had 21,645 members, of which 50.7% were German, 49.3% DP; without the East, which had admitted no DPs, the balance was 52% DP and 48% German-Jewish. Statistics are even less reliable for the Soviet occupation zone (SBZ) and the German Democratic Republic, since fewer Jews registered as official community members. In 1946 there were 3,480, in 1952 about 3,000 members. By the mid-1980s, there were only 400. See for example Robin Ostow, "Imperialist Agents, Anti-Fascist Monuments, Eastern Refugees, Property Claims: Jews as Incorporations of East German Social Trauma, 1945–94," in *Jews, Germans, Memory*, ed. Bodemann, 229, 227.

101. In 1950, 24,431 Jews registered as community members. In 1959, the official number stood at 23,070. See Bodemann, "'How can one stand to live there as a Jew . . .': Paradoxes of Jewish Existence in Germany," in *Jews, Germans, Memory*, ed. idem, 21.

102. Angelika Eder, "Jüdische Displaced Persons im deutschen Alltag," in *Überlebt und Unterwegs*, ed. Fritz Bauer Institut, and idem, *Flüchtige Heimat*. Germany currently has the fastest-growing Jewish community in Europe. On the remarkable expansion of Jewish life in contemporary Germany, see Jeffrey Peck, *Being Jewish in the New Germany* (New Brunswick, N.J.: Rutgers University Press, 2006).

Select Bibliography

Diaries, Memoirs, Published Letters and Oral Histories, and Fiction

Andreas-Friedrich, Ruth. *Schauplatz Berlin: Tagebuchaufzeichnungen 1945 bis 1948*. Frankfurt/Main: Suhrkamp, 1984.
———. *Berlin Underground, 1933–1945*, trans. Barrows Mussey. New York: Paragon House, 1989.
Annan, Noel. *Changing Enemies: The Defeat and Regeneration of Germany*. London: Harper Collins, 1995.
Anonymous. *A Woman in Berlin: Eight Weeks in the Conquered City*, trans. Philip Boehm, with foreword by Antony Beevor. New York: Metropolitan Books, 2005.
Bach, Julian, Jr. *America's Germany: An Account of the Occupation*. New York: Random House, 1946.
Bartov, Hanoch. *The Brigade*, trans. David S. Segal. New York: Holt, Rinehart and Winston, 1968.
Beck, Gad. *An Underground Life: The Memoirs of a Gay Jew in Nazi Germany*, trans. Allison Brown. Madison: University of Wisconsin Press, 1999.
Berger, Joseph. *Displaced Persons: Growing Up American after the Holocaust*. New York: Scribner, 2004.
Berger, Thomas. *Crazy in Berlin*. New York: Ballantine, 1958.
Bernstein, Sara Tuvel. *The Seamstress: A Memoir of Survival*. New York: Berkley Books, 1999.
Biber, Jacob. *Risen from the Ashes: A Story of the Jewish Displaced Persons in the Aftermath of World War II*. San Bernardino, Calif: Borgo Press, 1990.
Boehm, Eric H. *We Survived: Fourteen Histories of the Hidden and Hunted in Nazi Germany*. Boulder, Colo.: Westview, 2003; revised, orig. 1949.
Botting, Douglas. *In the Ruins of the Reich: Germany, 1945–1949*. London: Allen and Unwin, 1985.
Bourke-White, Margaret. *Dear Fatherland, Rest Quietly: A Report on the Collapse of Hitler's "Thousand Years."* New York: Simon and Schuster, 1946.
Boveri, Margaret. *Tage des Überlebens: Berlin 1945*. Munich: Piper, 1985, orig. 1968.
Brenner, Henny. *"Das Lied ist aus": Ein jüdisches Schicksal in Dresden*. Zurich: Pendo, 2001.
Brockway, Fenner. *German Diary*. London: V. Gollancz, 1947.
Burke, James Wakefied. *The Big Rape*. Frankfurt am Main: Friedrich Rudl Verleger Union, 1951.
Byrnes, James F. *Speaking Frankly*. New York: Harper and Brothers, 1947.

Chamberlin, Brewster S., ed. *Kultur auf Trümmern*. Stuttgart: Deutsche Verlags Anstalt, 1979.

Clark, Delbert. *Again the Goose Step: The Lost Fruits of Victory*. Indianapolis: Bobbs-Merrill, 1949.

Davidson, Eugene. *The Death and Life of Germany: An Account of the American Occupation*. New York: Alfred A. Knopf, 1959.

Dawidowicz, Lucy S. *From That Place and Time: A Memoir 1938–1947*. New York: Norton, 1989.

Deutscher, Issac. *Reportagen aus Nachkriegsdeutschland*, Mit einem Vorwort von Tamara Deutscher, trans. Harry Maor. Hamburg: Junius Verlag, 1980.

Deutschkron, Inge. *Ich trug den gelben Stern*. Munich: Deutscher Taschenbuch Verlag, 1987.

Dörr, Margarete. *"Wer die Zeit nicht miterlebt hat . . . " Frauenerfahrung im Zweiten Weltkrieg und in den Jahren danach*, vols. 1–3. Frankfurt: Campus Verlag, 1998.

Dos Passos, John. *Tour of Duty*. Boston: Houghton Mifflin, 1946.

Gollancz, Victor. *In Darkest Germany*, with an introduction by Robert M. Hutchins. Hinsdale, Ill.: Henry Regnery Company, 1947.

Grobman, Alex, ed. *In Defense of the Survivors: The Letters and Documents of Oscar A. Mintzer, AJDC Legal Advisor, Germany 1945–46*. Berkeley: Judah Magnes Museum, 1999.

Habe, Hans. *Aftermath*, trans. Richard F. Hansen. New York: Viking, 1947.

———. *Our Love Affair with Germany*. New York: G. P. Putnam's Sons, 1953.

Hautzig, Esther. *The Endless Steppe: Growing Up in Siberia*. New York: Harper Collins, 1968.

Hirschmann, Ira A. *The Embers Still Burn: An Eye-Witness View of the Postwar Ferment in Europe and the Middle East and Our Disastrous Get-Soft-With Germany Policy*. New York: Simon and Schuster, 1949.

Höcker, Karla. *Beschreibung eines Jahres: Berliner Notizen 1945*. Berlin: arani, 1984.

Howley, Frank. *Berlin Command*. New York: Putnam, 1950.

Hulme, Kathryn. *The Wild Place*. Boston: Beacon Press, 1953.

Hutton, Bud (Oram C.), and Andrew Rooney. *Conquerors' Peace: A Report to the American Stockholders*. Garden City, N.Y.: Doubleday, 1947.

Hyman, Abraham S. *The Undefeated*. Jerusalem/Hewlett, N.Y.: Gefen, 1993.

Kardorff, Ursula von. *Berliner Aufzeichnungen aus den Jahren 1942 bis 1945*, rev. ed. Munich: Bilderstein, 1962.

Klausner, Abraham J. *A Letter to My Children from the Edge of the Holocaust*. San Francisco: Holocaust Center of Northern California, 2002.

Klein, Gerda Weissmann, and Kurt Klein. *The Hours After: Letters of Love and Longing in War's Aftermath*. New York: St. Martins, 2000.

Kluger, Ruth. *Still Alive: A Holocaust Girlhood Remembered*. New York: Feminist Press, 2001.

Knef, Hildegard. *The Gift Horse: Report on a Life*. New York: McGraw-Hill, 1971.

Kopelev, Lew. *Aufbewahren für alle Zeit*, afterword by Heinrich Böll. Munich: DTV, 1979; Russian, 1975.

Leonhard, Wolfgang. *Child of the Revolution*, trans. C. M. Woodhouse. Chicago: H. Regnery Co., 1958.

Levin, Meyer. *In Search: An Autobiography.* New York: Horizon Press, 1950; Paris: Authors Press, 1950.

Lewyn, Bert, and Bev Saltzman Lewyn. *On the Run in Nazi Berlin, Holocaust Memoirs.* Self-published, Xlibris, 2001.

Maginnis, John J. *Military Government Journal: Normandy to Berlin*, ed. Robert A. Hart. Amherst: University of Massachusetts Press, 1971.

Marcus, Jacob Rader, and Abraham J. Peck, eds. *Among the Survivors of the Holocaust—1945. The Landsberg DP Camp Letters of Major Irving Heymont, United States Army.* Monographs of the American Jewish Archives, No. 10, Cincinnati: American Jewish Archives, 1982.

McGovern, James. *fräulein.* New York: Crown, 1956.

Middleton, Drew. *Where Has Last July Gone? Memoirs.* New York: Quadrangle, 1973.

Murphy, Robert. *Diplomat among Warriors.* Garden City, N.Y.: Doubleday, 1964.

Niewyk, Donald L., ed. *Fresh Wounds: Early Narratives of Holocaust Survival.* Chapel Hill, N.C.: University of North Carolina Press, 1998.

Orbach, Larry, and Vivien Orbach-Smith. *Soaring Underground: A Young Fugitive's Life in Nazi Berlin.* Washington D.C.: Compass Press, 1996.

Padover, Saul K. *Experiment in Germany: The Story of an American Intelligence Officer.* New York: Duell, Sloan, Pearce, 1946.

Pettiss, Susan T., with Lynne Taylor. *After the Shooting Stopped: The Story of an UNRRA Welfare Worker in Germany, 1945–1947.* Victoria, B.C.: Trafford Press, 2004.

Posener, Julius. *In Deutschland 1945 bis 1946*, ed. and with afterword by Alan Posener. Berlin: Siedler, 2001.

Reich-Ranicki, Marcel. *Mein Leben.* Stuttgart: Deutsche Verlags Anstalt, 1999.

Riess, Curt. *Berlin Berlin, 1945–1953.* Berlin: Non Stop Bücherei, 1953; reprint, Steffen Damm, ed., Berlin: Bostelmann & Siebenhaar, 2002.

Rosenthal, Hans. *Zwei Leben in Deutschland.* Bergisch Gladbach: Gustav Lübbe, 1980.

Schochet, Simon. *Feldafing.* Vancouver, B.C.: November House, 1983.

Schwarz, Leo W. *The Redeemers: A Saga of the Years 1945–1952*, with preface by Lucius Clay. New York: Farrar Strauss and Young, 1953.

———. *The Root and the Bough: The Epic of an Enduring People.* New York: Rinehart and Co, 1949.

Settel, Arthur, ed. *This Is Germany*, with an introduction by General Lucius D. Clay. New York: William Sloane Associates, 1950.

Shirer, William L. *End of a Berlin Diary.* New York: A. A. Knopf, 1947.

Smith, William Gardner. *Last of the Conquerors.* New York: Farrar, Straus Giroux, 1948.

Syrkin, Marie. *The State of the Jews.* New York: New Republic, 1980.

Thurnwald, Hilde. *Gegenwartsprobleme Berliner Familien: Eine soziologische Untersuchung an 489 Familien.* Berlin: Weidmann, 1948.

Vida, George. *From Doom to Dawn: A Jewish Chaplain's Story of Displaced Persons*. New York: Jonathan David, 1967.

Wilson, Francesca. *Aftermath: France, Germany, Austria, Yugoslavia, 1945 and 1946*. New York: Penguin, 1947.

Wolf, Markus. *Die Troika*. Düsseldorf: Claasen, 1989.

Zuckmayer, Carl. *Als wär's ein Stück von mir: Horen der Freundschaft*. Vienna: S. Fischer, 1996.

Books and Theses

Bauer, Yehudah. *Flight and Rescue: Bricha*. New York: Random House, 1970.

———. *Out of the Ashes*. New York: Pergamon Press, 1989.

Baumel, Judith Tydor. *Double Jeopardy: Gender and the Holocaust*, ed. idem. London: Valentine Mitchell, 1998.

Beevor, Antony. *The Fall of Berlin, 1945*. New York: Viking, 2002.

Bendersky, Joseph W. *The "Jewish Threat": Anti-Semitic Politics of the U.S. Army*. New York: Basic Books, 2000.

Bessel, Richard, and Dirk Schumann, eds. *Life after Death: Approaches to a Cultural and Social History of Europe During the 1940s and 1950s*. Cambridge: Cambridge University Press, 2003.

Bodemann, Y. Michal, ed. *Jews, Germans, Memory: Reconstructions of Jewish Life in Germany*. Ann Arbor: University of Michigan Press, 1996.

Boehling, Rebecca. *A Question of Priorities: Democratic Reform and Economic Recovery in Postwar Germany*. Providence: Berghahn, 1996.

Brenner, Michael. *After the Holocaust: Rebuilding Jewish Lives in Postwar Germany*. Princeton: Princeton University Press, 1997.

Davis, Franklin M. *Came as a Conqueror: The United States Army's Occupation of Germany 1945–1949*. New York: Macmillan, 1967.

Dietrich, Susanne, and Julia Schulze-Wessel. *Zwischen Selbstorganisation und Stigmatisierung: Die Lebenswirklichkeit jüdischer Displaced Persons und die neue Gestalt des Antisemitismus in der deutschen Nachkriegsgesellschaft*. Stuttgart: Klett-Cotta, 1998.

Dinnerstein, Leonard. *America and the Survivors of the Holocaust*. New York: Columbia University Press, 1982.

Eder, Angelika. *Flüchtige Heimat: Jüdische Displaced Persons in Landsberg am Lech. 1945 bis 1950*. Munich: UNI-Druck, 1998.

Fehrenbach, Heide. *Race After Hitler: Black Occupation Children in Postwar Germany and America*. Princeton: Princeton University Press, 2005.

Fritz Bauer Institut, ed. *Überlebt und Unterwegs: Jüdische Displaced Persons im Nachkriegsdeutschland, Jahrbuch 1997 zur Geschichte und Wirkung des Holocaust*. Frankfurt: Campus, 1997.

Gay, Ruth. *Safe Among the Germans: Liberated Jews after World War. II*. New Haven: Yale University Press, 2002.

Geller, Jay Howard. *Jews in Post-Holocaust Germany, 1945–1953*. Cambridge: Cambridge University Press, 2004.

Goedde, Petra. *GIs and Germans: Culture, Gender, and Foreign Relations 1945–1949*. New Haven: Yale University Press, 2003.

Grobman, Alex. *Rekindling the Flame: American Jewish Chaplains and the Survivors of European Jewry, 1944–1948*. Detroit: Wayne State University Press, 1993.

Grodzinsky, Yosef. *In the Shadow of the Holocaust: The Struggle between Jews and Zionists in the Aftermath of World War II*. Monroe, Maine: Common Courage Press, 2005.

Gross, Jan T. *Fear: Anti-Semitism in Poland after Auschwitz: An Essay in Historical Intepretation*. New York: Random House, 2006.

Grossmann, Kurt R. *The Jewish DP Problem: Its Origin, Scope, and Liquidation*, with introduction by Abraham S. Hyman. New York: Institute of Jewish Affairs, World Jewish Congress, 1951.

Haas, Aaron. *The Aftermath: Living with the Holocaust*. Cambridge: Cambridge University Press, 1995.

Heineman, Elizabeth D. *What Difference Does a Husband Make? Women and Marital Status in Nazi and Postwar Germany*. Berkeley: University of California Press, 1999.

Herf, Jeffrey. *Divided Memory: The Nazi Past in the Two Germanys*. Cambridge, Mass.: Harvard University Press, 1997.

Herzog, Dagmar, ed. *Sexuality and German Fascism*. New York: Berghahn, 2005).

———. *Sex after Fascism: Memory and Morality in Twentieth-Century Germany*. Princeton: Princeton University Press, 2005.

Hilton, Laura. "Prisoners of Peace: Rebuilding Community, Identity and Nationality in Displaced Persons Camps in Germany, 1945–52." Ph.D. dissertation, Ohio State University, 2001.

Höhn, Maria. *GIs and Fräuleins: The German-American Encounter in 1950s West Germany*. Chapel Hill: University of North Carolina Press, 2002.

Holian, Anna Marta. "Between National Socialism and Soviet Communism: The Politics of Self-representation among Displaced Persons in Munich, 1945–1951." Ph.D. dissertation, University of Chicago, 2005.

Jacobmeyer, Wolfgang. *Vom Zwangsarbeiter zum Heimatlosen Ausländer. Die Displaced Persons in Westdeutschland, 1945–51*. Göttingen: Vandenhoeck & Ruprecht, 1985.

Kaplan, Marion. *Between Dignity and Despair: Jewish Life in Nazi Germany*. New York: Oxford University Press, 1988.

Kauders, Anthony. *Democratization and the Jews: Munich 1945–1965*. Lincoln: University of Nebraska Press, 2004.

Kochavi, Arieh J. *Post-Holocaust Politics: Britain, the United States, and Jewish Refugees, 1945–1948*. Chapel Hill: University of North Carolina Press, 2001.

Kolinsky, Eva. *After the Holocaust: Jewish Survivors in Germany after 1945*. London: Pimlico, 2004.

Königseder, Angelika. *Flucht nach Berlin: Jüdische Displaced Persons 1945–1948*. Berlin: Metropol, 1998.

Königseder, Angelika, and Juliane Wetzel. *Waiting for Hope: Jewish Displaced Persons in Post-World War II Germany*, trans. John A. Broadwin. Evanston, Ill.: Northwestern University Press, 2001.

Krauss, Christine, and Daniel Küchenmeister, eds. *Das Jahr 1945: Brüche und Kontinuitäten*. Berlin: Dietz, 1995.

Lavsky, Hagit. *New Beginnings: Holocaust Survivors in Bergen-Belsen and the British Zone in Germany*. Detroit: Wayne State University Press, 2002.

Macardle, Dorothy. *Children of Europe: A Study of the Children of Liberated Countries; Their War-Time Experiences, Their Reactions and Their Needs, with a Note on Germany*. London: Gollancz, 1949.

Mankowitz, Zeev W. *Life between Memory and Hope: The Survivors of the Holocaust in Occupied Germany*. Cambridge: Cambridge University Press, 2002.

Marrus, Michael. *The Unwanted: European Studies in the Twentieth Century*. New York: Oxford University, 1985.

Moeller, Robert G. *War Stories: The Search for a Usable Past in the Federal Republic of Germany*. Berkeley: University of California Press, 2001.

Moeller, Robert G., ed. *West Germany under Construction: Politics, Society, and Culture in the Adenauer Era*. Ann Arbor: University of Michigan Press, 1997.

Muhlen, Norbert. *The Return of Germany: A Tale of Two Countries*. Chicago: Henry Regnery Company, 1953.

Nachama, Andreas. Julius H. Schoeps and Hermann Simon, eds. *Jews in Berlin*. Berlin: Henschel, 2002.

Nadich, Judah. *Eisenhower and the Jews*. New York: Twayne, 1953.

Naimark, Norman. *The Russians in Germany: A History of the Soviet Zone of Occupation, 1945–1949*. Cambridge, Mass.: Harvard University Press, 1995.

Patt, Avinoam. "Finding Home and Homeland: Jewish Youth Groups in the Aftermath of the Holocaust." Ph.D. dissertation, New York University, 2005.

Sander, Helke, and Barbara Johr, eds. *BeFreier und Befreite. Krieg, Vergewaltigungen, Kinder*. Munich: Antje Kunstmann, 1992.

Schissler, Hanna, ed. *The Miracle Years: A Cultural History of West Germany 1949–1968*. Princeton: Princeton University Press, 2001.

Schivelbusch, Wolfgang. *In a Cold Crater: Cultural and Intellectual Life in Berlin 1945–1948*. Berkeley: University of California Press, 1998.

Schoeps, Julius H., ed. *Leben im Land der Täter: Juden im Nachkriegsdeutschland. 1945–1952*. Berlin: Jüdische Verlagsanstalt, 2001.

Schönborn, Susanne, ed. *Zwischen Erinnerung und Neubeginn: Zur deutsch-jüdischen Geschichte nach 1945*, with foreword by Michael Brenner. Munich: Martin Meidenbauer, 2006.

Senat Berlin, ed. *Berlin: Kampf um Freiheit und Selbstverwaltung 1945–1946*. Berlin: Heinz Spitzing Verlag, 1961.

Stern, Frank. *The Whitewashing of the Yellow Badge: Antisemitism and Philosemitism in Postwar Germany*, trans. William Templar. Oxford: Pergamon Press, 1992.

Wahrhaftig, Zorach. *Uprooted: Jewish Refugees and Displaced Persons after Liberation. From War to Peace. No. 5*. New York: Institute of Jewish Affairs for the American Jewish Congress and World Jewish Congress, November 1946.

Weckel, Ulrike, and Edgar Wolfram, eds. *"Bestien" und "Befehlsempfänger"*: *Frauen und Männer in NS-Prozessen nach 1945*. Göttingen: Vandenhoeck and Ruprecht, 2003.

Wetzel, Juliane. *Jüdisches Leben in München, 1945–1951: Durchgangsstation oder Wiederaufbau?* Munich: UNI-Druck, 1987.

Wistrich, Robert S., ed. *Terms of Survival: The Jewish World since 1945*. New York: Routledge, 1995.

Woodbridge, George. *UNRRA: The History of the United Nations Relief and Rehabilitation Administration*. Prepared by a special staff under the direction of George Woodbridge, chief historian of UNRRA, in three volumes. Vol. 3. New York: Columbia University Press, 1950.

Wyman, Mark. *DPs: Europe's Displaced Persons, 1945–1951*. Ithaca: Cornell University Press, 1998.

Yablonka, Hanna. *Survivors of the Holocaust: Israel after the War*, trans. Ora Cummings. New York: New York University Press, 1999.

Zertal, Idith. *From Catastrophe to Power: Holocaust Survivors and the Emergence of Israel*. Berkeley: University of California Press, 1998.

Ziemke, Earl F. *The U.S. Army in the Occupation of Germany 1944–46*. Washington, D.C.: Army Historical Series, 1975.

Zink, Harold. *American Military Government in Germany*. New York: Macmillan, 1947.

———. *The United States in Germany, 1944–1955*. Princeton, N.J.: Van Nostrand, 1957.

Zweig, Ron. *German Reparations and the Jewish World: A History of the Claims Conference*, 2nd ed. London: Frank Cass, 1998.

ARTICLES

Arendt, Hannah. "The Aftermath of Nazi Rule: Report from Germany, " *Commentary* 10 (October 1950): 342–353.

Bauer, Yehudah. "The Initial Organization of the Holocaust Survivors in Bavaria." *Yad Vashem Studies* 8 (1970): 127–157.

Borneman, John. "Reconciliation after Ethnic Cleansing: Listening, Retribution, Affiliation." *Public Culture* 14:2 (Spring 2000): 281–304.

Diner, Dan. "Elemente der Subjektwerdung: Jüdische DPs in historischem Kontext." In *Überlebt und Unterwegs*, ed. Fritz Bauer Institut, 229–248.

Gringauz, Samuel. "Our New German Policy and the Dps: Why Immediate Resettlement Is Imperative." *Commentary* 5 (1948): 508–514.

Grossmann, Atina. "A Question of Silence: The Rape of German Women by Occupation Soldiers." *October* (Spring 1995): 43–63. Slightly revised in *West Germany under Construction*, ed. Robert G. Moeller, 33–52.

———. "Trauma, Memory, and Motherhood: Germans and Jewish Displaced Persons in Post-Nazi Germany, 1945–1949." In *Life after Death*, ed., Richard Bessel and Dirk Schumann, 93–127.

———. "Victims, Villains, and Survivors: Gendered Perceptions and Self-perceptions of Jewish Survivors in Postwar Germany." In *Sexuality and German Fascism*, ed. Dagmar Herzog, 291–318.

Heineman, Elizabeth. "The Hour of the Woman: Memories of Germany's 'Crisis Years' and West German National Identity." *American Historical Review* 101:2 (April 1996): 354–395.

Hughes, Michael L. " 'Through No Fault of Our Own': West Germans Remember Their War Losses," *German History* 18:2 (2000): 193–212.

Jacobmeyer, Wolfgang. "Jüdische Überlebende als 'Displaced Persons': Untersuchungen zur Besatzungspolitik in den deutschen Westzonen und zur Zuwanderung osteuropäischer Juden 1945–1946." *Geschichte und Gesellschaft* 9 (1983): 421–452.

Leonard Krieger, "The Inter-Regnum in Germany: March–August 1945, " *Political Science Quarterly* 64 (1949): 507–532.

Mead, Margaret. "Food and Feeding in Occupied Territory." *Public Opinion Quarterly* 7:4 (Winter 1943): 618–628.

Moskowitz, Moses. "The Germans and the Jews: Postwar Report; The Enigma of German Irresponsibility." *Commentary* 2 (July–December 1946): 7–14.

Peck, Abraham J. "Jewish Survivors of the Holocaust in Germany: Revolutionary Vanguard or Remnants of a Destroyed People?" *Tel Aviver Jahrbuch für deutsche Geschichte* 19 (1990): 33–45.

Pinson, Koppel S. "Jewish Life in Liberated Germany: A Study of the Jewish DPs." *Jewish Social Studies* 9:2 (January 1947): 101–126.

Stern, Frank. "Antagonistic Memories: The Post-war Survival and Alienation of Jews and Germans." In *Memory and Totalitarianism, Volume I, International Yearbook of Oral History and Life Stories*, ed. Luisa Passerini. New York: Oxford University Press, 1992, 21–43.

———. "The Historic Triangle: Occupiers, Germans, and Jews in Postwar Germany." *Tel Aviver Jahrbuch für deutsche Geschichte* 19 (1990): 47–76; republished in *West Germany under Construction*, ed. Robert G. Moeller, 199–229.

Tröger, Annemarie. "Between Rape and Prostitution: Survival Strategies and Chances of Emancipation for Berlin Women after World II." In *Women in Culture and Politics: A Century of Change*, ed. Judith Friedlander et al. Bloomington: University of Indiana Press, 1986, 97–117.

DOCUMENT COLLECTIONS, CONFERENCE PROCEEDINGS, AND CATALOGUES

Giere, Jacqueline, and Rachel Salamander, eds. *Ein Leben Aufs Neu: Das Robinson Album. DP-Lager: Juden auf deutschen Boden 1945–1948*. Vienna: Verlag Christian Brandstätter, 1995.

Gutman, Yisrael, and Avital Saf, eds. *She'erit Hapletah, 1944–1948: Rehabilitation and Political Struggle; Proceedings of the 6th Yad Vashem International Historical Conference*. Jerusalem: Yad Vashem, 1990.

Peck, Abraham J., ed. *Archives of the Holocaust*, vol. 9, containing *The Papers of the World Jewish Congress 1945–1950: Liberation and the Saving Remnant*, collected in American Jewish Archives, Cincinnati. New York: Garland, 1990.

Rosensaft, Menachem Z., ed. *Life Reborn: Jewish Displaced Persons, 1945–1951; Conference Proceedings*. Washington D.C.: United States Holocaust Memorial Museum, 2000.

NEWSPAPERS AND MAGAZINES

Aufbau—Reconstruction
Berliner Zeitung
Neue Berliner Illustrierte
Newsweek
The New Yorker
sie
Der Tagesspiegel
Time
Der Weg. Zeitschrift für Fragen des Judentums

ARCHIVES

American Jewish Historical Society, Center for Jewish History, New York.
American Jewish Joint Distribution Committee, New York.
Bundesarchiv Berlin, Stiftung Archiv Parteien und Massenorganisationen.
Deutsches Historisches Museum, Berlin, photo archive.
Fritz Bauer Institut Archives, Frankfurt/M.
Jewish Museum, Berlin.
Landesarchiv, Berlin.
Leo Baeck Institute, Center for Jewish History, New York.
Oberfinanzpräsidium Brandenburg, Staatsarchiv Brandenburg, Potsdam.
Stiftung "Neue Synagoge Berlin–Centrum Judaicum" Archive.
United Nations Relief and Rehabilitation Administration (UNRRA), New York.
United States Holocaust Memorial Museum, Washington, D.C.
      General, Oral History, Photo, Steven Spielberg Film and Video Archives.
Wiedergutmachungsamt and Entschädigungsamt, Berlin.
YIVO Institute for Jewish Research, Center for Jewish History, New York.
      Record Group 294.1, Leo W. Schwarz Collection.
      Record Group 294.2, Displaced Persons Camps and Centers in Germany, 1945–1952.
Zentral Archiv zur Erforschung der Geschichte der Juden in Deutschland, Heidelberg.

Acknowledgments

WRITING THESE acknowledgments is both rewarding and daunting. I am delighted to thank the many friends, colleagues, and institutions on whose help I relied, and also troubled by the inadequacies of such a listing, especially for a project that has taken a long time and challenged me in more ways than I can express here. I am grateful for indispensable institutional sustenance; research and writing was generously supported by grants from the National Endowment for the Humanities, the American Council of Learned Societies, and the German Marshall Fund, as well as residencies at the American Academy in Berlin and the Remarque Institute at New York University. President George Campbell, Dean John Harrington, and Acting Dean David Weir facilitated the leaves from Cooper Union that made it possible to take advantage of these fellowships.

I first began to conceptualize this book in 1997/98 during a precious year at the School of Social Science of the Institute for Advanced Study in Princeton. I am especially grateful to Joan W. Scott for her encouragement and to Susan Brison and Jodi Halpern for the questions we shared in our mini "trauma study group." A Spring 2000 workshop, "Birth of a Refugee Nation: Displaced Persons in Post-War Europe," co-organized with Daniel Cohen and funded by the Remarque Institute, provided my first real connection to the growing community of "DP scholars." I count myself very lucky to have maintained my affiliation with the Remarque; the Institute's biweekly lunch seminars, led by director Tony Judt and administrator Jair Kessler, are a highlight of New York intellectual life.

Buoyed by the prospect of a three-semester leave, I began serious research a few days before September 11, 2001. During the anxious and confusing weeks that followed, the reading room of the Center for Jewish History in New York—and perhaps ironically, YIVO's DP files—became a welcome refuge. From January to June 2002, the American Academy in Berlin offered a home for my children and myself, away from a New York that was deeply scarred (and now, five years later, it's surprisingly hard to remember) by the events of the fall. As I worked my way into and through this book, I have presented pieces at more lectures, conferences and seminars than I can list, in the United States, Germany, England, and Israel, and each time I benefited from comments and criticism. Two summer scholars' workshops at the United States Holocaust Memorial Museum Center for Advanced Holocaust Studies in Washington, D.C., crucially informed my research. I am indebted to the participants in the 2004 workshop on Gender and the Holocaust, Jane Caplan, Tim Cole, Jennifer Evans, Sara Horowitz, Irene Kacandes, Claudia Koonz, Björn Krondorfer, Christa Schikorra, and Nechama Tec, as well as Michael Berkowitz, Boaz Cohen, Laura Hilton, Laura Jockusch, Avi Patt, Tamar Lewinsky, and David Weinberg, members of the 2005 workshop on Jewish displaced persons.

Cilly Kugelmann, who knows more about the subject than just about anybody I know, first suggested that I should write about Jewish DPs in postwar Germany, and much to my pleasure our conversation has never stopped. Michael Muskal first introduced me to the very fact of Jewish DP camps in Germany; many years later he facilitated the interview with his parents that became part of this book. I am sorry that his mother Elizabeth passed away before I could present her with a (brief) printed version of her story. Zippi (Helen) Tichauer answered my questions about Feldafing and then pushed me to ask more. I am one of several historians who have benefited from her knowledge, honesty, and courage. Shlomo Leser graciously shared his memories for my book while trying to write his own. Nechama Tec flagged holes in my argument while offering unflagging encouragement. As always, I am grateful for the tough love offered by the German Women's History Group in New York; that we continue to meet every month to "show and tell," and to critique each other's work, is a testament to the strength of the feminist politics and scholarship that originally brought us together.

It is one of the happy peculiarities of academia that the categories of friend and colleague are so often meshed, and a (partial) listing of names cannot do justice to the comradeship and collaboration they represent. Marion Kaplan and Jan Lambertz read parts of the manuscript, corrected errors, and admonished me to try again. Molly Nolan worked her way through an entire early draft; Andy Rabinbach did the same with a later version. Geoff Eley's support has been unstinting. I am indebted as well to Bonnie Anderson, Dolores Augustine, Omer Bartov, Fran Bartowski, Rebeccca Boehling, Renate Bridenthal, Michal Bodemann, Michael Brenner, Daniel Cohen, Belinda Davis, Dan Diner, Irith Dublon-Knebel, Helen Epstein, Heide Fehrenbach, Amy Hackett, Marianne Hirsch, Maria Höhn, Anna Holian, Young Sun Hong, Jeff Herf, Gertrud Koch, Jürgen Matthäeus, Douglas Morris, Susan Ochshorn, Molly O'Donnell, Jeff Peck, Nancy Reagin, Carola Sachse, Ben Shephard, Carol Shookhoff, Frank Stern, Joan Ringelheim, Julie Sneeringer, Ann Snitow, Leo Spitzer, Maren Stange, Natan Sznaider, Yfaat Weiss, and Rakefet Zalashik. At critical points, the editorial skills of Lauren Osborne and Ghilia Lipman-Wulf helped create order out of chaos. Kierra Carro-Schneider and Mara

Heifetz came to my rescue with last-minute endnote checks when my eyes threatened to go on strike. Jennifer Suri invited me to test my ideas on the Intel Social Science Research Seminar at Stuyvesant High School. I am grateful to my students at Cooper for tolerating my distractions and fascinations; they often heard rather more about the Nazis, the Holocaust, and postwar displacements than they had signed up for. At the same time their commitment to art, architecture, and engineering has taught me about other ways of apprehending the world.

I thank also the archivists who make research possible. In Berlin: Hermann Simon and Barbara Welker, Centrum Judaicum; Monika Nakath, Brandenburgisches Staatsarchiv; Eckhard Kraef, Entschädigungsamt-Landesverwaltungsamt Berlin; Anna-Dorte Krause, photo archives of the Deutsches Historisches Museum; Aubrey Pomerance, Leo Baeck Archives in the Jewish Museum; Ruth Recknagel, (retired) director of the Wiedergutmachungsamt; and Jürgen Wetzel, (retired) director of the Landesarchiv. In New York: Fruma Mohrer of YIVO; Aurora Tangkeko, UN Archives; Sherry Hyman at the American Jewish Joint Distribution Committee; and Frank Mecklenburg of the Leo Baeck Institute. At the Holocaust Museum in Washington, Sharon Muller, Maren Read, Judy Cohen, and Bruce Levy guided me through the extraordinary photo and video collection; Michlean Amir connected me to colleagues and archives. Sharon Hartman (and Victor Pulupa of Dodge Color) cheerfully handled my ever-changing and last-minute requests for reproductions and permissions.

At Princeton University Press, Brigitta van Rheinberg's patience had just enough of an edge to keep me going; her enthusiasm for the project meant a great deal. Will Hively caught mistakes, tolerated my many copyediting queries, and kept me updated on the state of global warming in New Hampshire. Heath Renfroe, Clara Platter, and Jill Harris steered me through the production process with remarkable calm.

Earlier versions of this work have appeared as articles in journals and edited volumes, and I thank the editors and readers (as well as the two anonymous readers for Princeton) who questioned, corrected, and prodded me along: "Defeated Germans and Surviving Jews: Gendered Encounters in Everyday Life in Occupied Germany 1945–1949," in Neil Gregor, Nils Roemer, and Mark Roseman, eds., *German History from the Margins* (Bloomington: Indiana University Press, 2006), 204–225; " 'The survivors were few and the dead were many': Jewish Identity and Memory in Occupied Berlin," in Marion Kaplan and Beate Meyer, eds., *Jüdische Welten: Juden in Deutschland vom 18 Jahrhundert bis in die Gegenwart* (Göttingen: Wallstein Verlag, 2005), 317–335; "Victims, Villains, and Survivors: Gendered Perceptions and Self-Perceptions of Jewish Displaced Persons in Postwar Germany," *Journal of the History of Sexuality* 11:1–

2 (January–April 2002): 291–318 [reprinted in Dagmar Herzog, ed., *Sexuality and German Fascism* (New York: Berghahn Books, 2004); German version in Insa Eschebach and Silke Wenk, eds., *Gedächtnis und Geschlecht: Deutungsmuster in Darstellungen des Nationalsozialistischen Genozids* (Frankfurt: Campus, 2002), 297–326; Israeli edition in Tova Cohen, Shmuel Feiner, and Judith Baumel, eds., *Gender, Place and Memory in the Modern Jewish Experience* (London: Valentine Mitchell, 2003), 78–107]; "Versions of Home: German Jewish Refugee Papers Out of the Closet and Into the Archives," *New German Critique* 90 (Fall 2003): 95–122 [revised from "Heimatversionen: Deutsch-jüdische Flüchtlingspapiere aus dem Schrank in die Archive," in Frank Stern, ed., *Herausforderungen deutsch-jüdischer Kultur: Interdisziplinäre Perspektiven* (Berlin: Aufbau Verlag, 2002), 259–292]; and "Trauma, Memory, and Motherhood: Germans, Occupiers, and Jewish Displaced Persons in Post-Nazi Germany 1945–1949," in Richard Bessel and Dirk Schumann, eds., *Life After Death: Approaches to a Cultural and Social History of Europe During the 1940s and 1950s* (Cambridge: Cambridge University Press, 2003), 93–127 [revised from *Archiv für Sozialgeschichte* 38 (October 1998): 230–254]. All these articles, in one way or another, grew out of conferences, a reminder of how much we depend on the personal and intellectual exchanges established and renewed at our seemingly endless round of seminars and panels. I look forward to continuing research, discussion, and debate.

Finally—traditionally last but never least—comes my acknowledgment of those who have lived with me while I lived with this book. Thank you to Max Mecklenburg and Nelly Mecklenburg for asking all the right questions and for following me and my work with the bemused, critical, and loving eyes of teenagers. And to Frank Mecklenburg for helping me to answer questions and for always being there.

Index

Page numbers printed in italics refer to photographs in the text.